SUSTAINABLE DEVELOPMENT, INTERNATIONAL LAW, AND A TURN TO AFRICAN LEGAL COSMOLOGIES

This original book analyses and reimagines the concept of sustainable development in international law from a non-Western legal perspective. Built upon the intersection of law, politics, and history in the context of Africa, its peoples and their experiences, customary law and other legal cosmologies, this ground-breaking study applies a critical legal analysis to Africa's interaction with conceptualising and operationalising sustainable development. It proposes a turn to non-Western legal normativity as the foundational principle for reimagining sustainable development in international law. It highlights eco-legal philosophies and principles in remaking sustainable development where ecological integrity assumes a central focus in the reimagined conceptualisation and operationalisation of sustainable development. While this pioneering book highlights Africa as its analytical pivot, its arguments and proposals are useful beyond Africa. Connecting global discourses on nature, the environment, rights, and development, Godwin Eli Kwadzo Dzah illuminates our current thinking on sustainable development in international law.

GODWIN ELI KWADZO DZAH is an assistant professor at the Faculty of Law, University of Alberta. He was a postdoctoral fellow at Osgoode Hall Law School, York University; and previously a United Nations-Nippon Foundation Fellow at the Division for Ocean Affairs and the Law of the Sea, Office of Legal Affairs, United Nations Secretariat. His doctoral research was awarded the Allard Law Dissertation Prize by the University of British Columbia.

CAMBRIDGE STUDIES IN INTERNATIONAL AND COMPARATIVE LAW: 185

Established in 1946, this series produces high quality, reflective, and innovative scholarship in the field of public international law. It publishes works on international law that are of a theoretical, historical, cross-disciplinary, or doctrinal nature. The series also welcomes books providing insights from private international law, comparative law, and transnational studies which inform international legal thought and practice more generally.

The series seeks to publish views from diverse legal traditions and perspectives, and of any geographical origin. In this respect, it invites studies offering regional perspectives on core *problématiques* of international law and, in the same vein, it appreciates contrasts and debates between diverging approaches. Accordingly, books offering new or less orthodox perspectives are very much welcome. Works of a generalist character are greatly valued and the series is also open to studies on specific areas, institutions, or problems. Translations of the most outstanding works published in other languages are also considered.

After seventy years, Cambridge Studies in International and Comparative Law sets the standard for international legal scholarship and will continue to define the discipline as it evolves in the years to come.

A list of books in the series can be found at the end of this volume.

SUSTAINABLE DEVELOPMENT, INTERNATIONAL LAW, AND A TURN TO AFRICAN LEGAL COSMOLOGIES

GODWIN ELI KWADZO DZAH

University of Alberta

CAMBRIDGE
UNIVERSITY PRESS

CAMBRIDGE
UNIVERSITY PRESS

Shaftesbury Road, Cambridge CB2 8EA, United Kingdom

One Liberty Plaza, 20th Floor, New York, NY 10006, USA

477 Williamstown Road, Port Melbourne, VIC 3207, Australia

314–321, 3rd Floor, Plot 3, Splendor Forum, Jasola District Centre, New Delhi – 110025, India

103 Penang Road, #05-06/07, Visioncrest Commercial, Singapore 238467

Cambridge University Press is part of Cambridge University Press & Assessment,
a department of the University of Cambridge.

We share the University's mission to contribute to society through the pursuit of education, learning and research at the highest international levels of excellence.

www.cambridge.org
Information on this title: www.cambridge.org/9781009354042

DOI: 10.1017/9781009354059

First published 2024

A catalogue record for this publication is available from the British Library

Library of Congress Cataloging-in-Publication Data
Names: Dzah, Godwin Eli Kwadzo, author.
Title: Sustainable development, international law, and a turn to African legal cosmologies / Godwin Eli Kwadzo Dzah, Faculty of Law, University of Alberta.
Description: Cambridge, United Kingdom ; New York, NY : Cambridge University Press, 2024. | Series: Cambridge studies in international and comparative law ; 185 | Includes bibliographical references and index.
Identifiers: LCCN 2023039441 (print) | LCCN 2023039442 (ebook) | ISBN 9781009354042 (hardback) | ISBN 9781009354073 (paperback) | ISBN 9781009354059 (epub)
Subjects: LCSH: Sustainable development–Law and legislation–Africa. | International law–Africa. | Cosmology, African.
Classification: LCC KQC706 .D94 2024 (print) | LCC KQC706 (ebook) | DDC 343.07–dc23/eng/20231002
LC record available at https://lccn.loc.gov/2023039441
LC ebook record available at https://lccn.loc.gov/2023039442

ISBN 978-1-009-35404-2 Hardback

To my children
Eli, Senam, and Seli

CONTENTS

FOREWORD

Given the growing and inescapable magnitude of the climate crisis, it is surely the case that the term 'sustainable development' invokes a new and unprecedented urgency. Formulated originally with the broad idea of somehow managing the tensions between the imperatives of economic growth and environmental protection, the term has always been a subject of ongoing debate and interpretation from the time it officially appeared in the Brundtland Commission Report of 1987 and was later popularised in the Rio Declaration of 1992.

Dr Godwin Eli Kwadzo Dzah's outstanding book takes on the ambitious task of 'Reimagining Sustainable Development' and, even more ambitiously, he makes African customary law and Indigenous cosmologies the foundation of this project. It is this perspective, one that is inspired by Third World Approaches to International Law (TWAIL) scholarship, that sharply distinguishes his work and offers a new vantage point from which to examine the many issues raised by sustainable development since its articulation.

It is a great strength of this book that it operates at several levels even while it presents a clear and compelling line of argument. In exploring the history of the concept of sustainable development, Dr Dzah engages with some of the major theoretical debates of our discipline – on the writing of the history of international law, the concept of crisis, and issues of global governance. He is also acute in his analysis of the different neoliberal and Eurocentric dimensions of the more orthodox versions of sustainable development and how these impede a truly ecological vision of the concept. Dr Dzah is clearly an expert in the relevant literature, and he adroitly connects his themes with these debates, both to illuminate sustainable development and to enrich the debates themselves. This is especially evident in his subtle revisiting of the Bandung Conference, and his argument that Bandung must be seen as an ongoing project extending to the present and beyond. And his study of legal pluralism, legal anthropology, and transnational law is a rich jurisprudential inquiry into how law can be reconceptualised to accommodate and draw upon ethics and customary laws that have been so central to the lives of African peoples.

At a more general level, Dr Dzah outlines and explores a history that needs to be recovered, and that illuminates important themes and events in international (environmental) law, including the history of the African contribution to, and engagement with, sustainable development. He expertly analyses how sustainable development and the environment got featured in various instruments of African regional organisation, such as the African Charter on Human and Peoples' Rights, and its relevance to the African Commission on Human and Peoples' Rights and the African Court on Human and Peoples' Rights. In this respect, Dr Dzah demonstrates how colonial concepts continue to shape African jurisprudence, even today.

The book builds towards the conclusion, the foundations laid for a powerful examination of African cosmologies and how they can contribute to sustainable development, and how they might do so in a jurisprudentially coherent manner. This is reconstructive scholarship at its best, and a compelling account of how TWAIL scholarship, in all its many facets, can enable an urgent reimagining of international (environmental) law.

Antony Anghie
Professor, Faculty of Law, National University of Singapore and S. J. Quinney College of Law, University of Utah

PREFACE

This book began as a small idea on how to think differently about the concept of sustainable development. It became a PhD topic and blossomed into a doctoral dissertation which I completed at Peter A. Allard School of Law, University of British Columbia. From conceptualisation, through refinement and completion of this book, I spent the better part of almost a decade thinking and writing about international law and its relationship with sustainable development. During this time, I went in several directions, explored different approaches, and, in the process, I went down a few rabbit holes in my journey to understand the meaning of sustainable development as a concept in international law. This being a broad concept with increasing complexity for its deployment in international law and beyond, it was evident that I needed to narrow the scope of this work to allow for a much deeper inquiry. By restricting the scope of this book to interactions between sustainable development and international law through an Africa-oriented lens, I critically engaged with the law, politics, and the history of the concept in its global, less-than-global, and domestic manifestations.

By limiting the scope of this legal study to Africa, this book and its analyses recognise the hazards of over-generalisation in the applicability of the concept as demonstrated in the varied dimensions of sustainable development as a concept in international law. By restricting the scope and ensuing analyses, this book engages reflexively yet critically with the concept of sustainable development within its historical and political contexts, and how that interface informs and determines the legal aspects of the concept. Even so, the inquiry is sufficiently broad enough in its querying of central or supposedly universalist assumptions on the fundamental attributes of sustainable development including nature, environment, development, environmental rights, rights of nature, and how these ideas arise and operate in international (environmental) law.

My analysis also pursues a much deeper consideration of non-Western legal systems and related plural legal schemes in reimagining sustainable development. The purpose is to adapt the concept to geopolitical distinctions while retaining its relevance within the broader framework of international law. By challenging sustainable development's Eurocentrism, this monograph pushes at the boundaries of legal imagination through its engagement with ecological integrity as the organising principle of sustainable development.

I argue that ecological law and ecocosmologies are the new bases for reorienting the law on sustainable development. In this respect, I propose turning to non-Western legal normativity as a necessary starting point in advancing the pursuit of this alternative vision of human–nature interrelations as the normative core in reimagining the concept of sustainable development in international law. Accordingly, this book emphasises eco-legal philosophies in renewing sustainable development from an ecolegality perspective. Here, ecological integrity, acting through ecological law, assumes a central role in rehabilitating the flawed conceptualisation and operationalisation of sustainable development.

While this book highlights Africa as its analytical pivot, its arguments and propositions are useful beyond Africa as they illuminate the broader discussion on sustainable development in international law. Above all, this book contributes to the development of international and comparative law by demonstrating how international law and domestic law can enable or constrain each other's domain in the context of sustainable development. This is achieved by foregrounding customary law and relational ontologies as central to the project of remaking international law from the periphery.

ACKNOWLEDGEMENTS

Like the popular African maxim 'it takes a village to raise a child' goes, I am indebted to a host of hands and minds that helped me along the way as I wrote this book. My sincerest gratitude goes to Natasha Affolder, Dennis Pavlich, Asad Kiyani, Afshin Akhtar-Khavari, Margot Young, David Morton, Gordon Christie, Pitman Potter, Ljiljana Biukovic, Karin Mickelson, Jedidiah Kroncke, Stepan Wood, Michelle LeBaron, and Richard Frimpong Oppong. I also owe a debt of gratitude to the ever-growing network of Third World Approaches to International Law (TWAIL) scholars whose works have provided much-needed inspiration as I wrote this book. In this respect, I am extremely grateful to Antony Anghie, one of the world's leading international law scholars, for writing the foreword to this book.

This book's core is derived from my doctoral research, which I wrote at Peter A. Allard School of Law, University of British Columbia. It was supervised by Professor Natasha Affolder and was awarded the Allard Law Dissertation Prize for the best doctoral research. Natasha Affolder played a significant role in how I approached this complex subject of sustainable development in international law. She is a great scholar and an exceptional mentor. I appreciate her efforts in helping me complete this book and cannot thank her enough. I am also grateful to Dennis Pavlich and Asad Kiyani for being a part of my doctoral supervisory committee and for providing me valuable advice and helpful direction. Special thanks to Asad Kiyani for his kind introductions that led me to some wonderful people who have since supported my work. My external examiner, Afshin Akhtar-Khavari, equally provided me illuminating comments and suggestions that helped recast this book project for a broader audience. As a collective, these wonderful people provided a congenial atmosphere for lively scholarly engagement and pushed back several times so I could think more critically and write even more purposefully. I have been able to translate my ideas into this book because of the devotion of these kind people and many more who helped along the way.

My international law teachers including Moira Lynn McConnell, Kwadwo Appiagyei-Atua, and the late Emmanuel Yaw Benneh provided space for curiosity and critical reflection in the early days of my studies. David Dzidzornu also helped me think about different approaches to undertaking international law analysis. Richard Lazarus foregrounded my learning on environmental law during my LLM studies at Harvard Law School. His guidance has been valuable in my scholarship and practice concentration. I have since approached the interaction across environmental law and international law, other fields of law, and non-law disciplines by embracing a broader view on the multiple entry and exit points that are less evident at this confluence. These important contributions have shaped much of my work and this book.

I am grateful to the Faculty of Law, University of Alberta for providing me with the academic home and financial resources during the final stages of completing this book; and thank you to my colleagues and the staff at the law school and other faculty members across the university for supporting my research. I also acknowledge the support of Osgoode Hall Law School, York University during my time as a postdoctoral fellow and a visiting professor. I appreciate the teaching opportunities I benefitted from during my stint at Osgoode. It was at Osgoode that I had the pleasure of meeting and working with Obiora Chinedu Okafor, a leading TWAIL scholar. I also thank all my former colleagues at the Faculty of Law, Ghana Institute of Management and Public Administration for my time there.

I gratefully acknowledge Cambridge University Press and the wonderful series editors of the Cambridge Studies in International and Comparative Law: Larissa van den Herik and Jean d'Aspremont, for choosing my work to feature alongside prominent entries in this prestigious series. I am grateful to the past commissioning editor of the series, Tom Randall, for his industry and patience as he guided me through the initial processes leading to the book contract. I thank the current commissioning editor, Marianne Nield, and members of the editorial team, including Rachel Imrie and Biju Singh, for working with me over the past few years to get this book out and into the world. Balamuthukumaran Pasupathy also deserves special mention for his efforts in successfully managing the book production processes.

I thank the two anonymous readers who reviewed my manuscript and graciously offered their positive opinions, comments, and constructive suggestions. I especially acknowledge Gideon Gabor for providing excellent research assistance throughout the writing process and supporting me in other ways that contributed to the success of this book project.

I am also grateful to Alexander Farries for his research assistance and reformatting sections of this work.

Just as importantly, I am deeply indebted to my family and friends: my late dad, Christoph, who I wish was still here; my wife, Edem, for her invaluable support, and our three boys for enduring my long absences so I could finish this book. Many thanks to my mother, Justina, for all the care she provided so I could work on this project; my siblings, Fo Edem, Fo Senyo, Kwasi, and Kafui; and my good friends Selase Sabah and Kafui Tsekpo for their encouragement and editorial assistance. I hope to make it up to you all now that this book is published. Always remember, you are all part of this book's story.

Akpe na mi.

ABBREVIATIONS

AfCHPR	*African Court on Human and Peoples' Rights*
Afr Aff	*African Affairs*
Afr Dev	*Africa Development*
Afr Human Rights LJ	*African Human Rights Law Journal*
Afr Human Rights YB	*African Human Rights Yearbook*
Afr J Envt'l Science and Tech	*African Journal of Environmental Science and Technology*
Afr J Leg Studies	*African Journal of Legal Studies*
Afr J Soc Work	*African Journal of Social Work*
Afr J Sust Dev	*African Journal of Sustainable Development*
Afr Res Rev	*African Research Review*
Afr Studies Q	*African Studies Quarterly*
Afr Studies Rev	*African Studies Review*
Afr YB Int'l L	*African Yearbook of International Law*
Akron L Rev	*Akron Law Review*
Alta L Rev	*Alberta Law Review*
Alternative LJ	*Alternative Law Journal*
Am Bar Foundation Research J	*American Bar Foundation Research Journal*
Am J Comp L	*American Journal of Comparative Law*
Am J Juris	*American Journal of Jurisprudence*
Am JIL	*American Journal of International Law*
Am JIL Unbound	*American Journal of International Law Unbound*
Am SIL: Proc Annual Mtg	*American Society of International Law: Proceedings of the Annual Meeting*
Am U Int'l L Rev	*American University International Law Review*
Annual Rev Envt and Res	*Annual Review of Environment and Resources*
Annual Rev L and Soc Science	*Annual Review of Law and Social Science*
Annual Rev Pol Science	*Annual Review of Political Science*
Anthro Today	*Anthropology Today*
Appeal: Rev Current L and L Reform	*Appeal: Review of Current Law and Legal Reform*

Ariz J Int'l and Comp L	*Arizona Journal of International and Comparative Law*
Asian Pol and Pol'y	*Asian Politics and Policy*
Asian YB Int'l L	*Asian Yearbook of International Law*
AU	*African Union*
Australian J Int'l Aff	*Australian Journal of International Affairs*
Bandung: J Global South	*Bandung: Journal of the Global South*
BCSC	British Columbia Supreme Court
Beijing L Rev	*Beijing Law Review*
Boston College Envt'l Aff L Rev	*Boston College Environmental Affairs Law Review*
Boston College Third World LJ	*Boston College Third World Law Journal*
Brazilian Admin Rev	*Brazilian Administrative Review*
Brill Open L	*Brill Open Law*
Brit J Gen Practice	*British Journal of General Practice*
Brit YBIL	*British Yearbook of International Law*
Brown J World Aff	Brown Journal of World Affairs
Buff HRL Rev	*Buffalo Human Rights Law Review*
Buff L Rev	*Buffalo Law Review*
Cambridge Rev Int'l Aff	*Cambridge Review of International Affairs*
Can J Afr Studies	*Canadian Journal of African Studies*
Can J Comp and Contemp L	*Canadian Journal of Comparative and Contemporary Law*
Can JL and Jur	*Canadian Journal of Law and Jurisprudence*
Can JL and Soc'y	*Canadian Journal of Law and Society*
Case Western Reserve JIL	*Case Western Reserve Journal of International Law*
Chicago JIL	*Chicago Journal of International Law*
Chicago-Kent L Rev	*Chicago-Kent Law Review*
Chinese J Envt'l L	*Chinese Journal of Environmental Law*
Chinese JIL	*Chinese Journal of International Law*
Citizenship Soc and Econ Educ	*Citizenship, Social and Economic Education*
Cogent Soc Sciences	*Cogent Social Sciences*
Colo J Int'l Envt'l L and Pol'y	*Colorado International Environmental Law and Policy*
Colum J Envt'l L	*Columbia Journal of Environmental Law*
Colum J Transnat'l L	*Columbia Journal of Transnational Law*
Commonwealth L Bull	*Commonwealth Law Bulletin*
Comp and Int'l LJ S Afr	*Comparative and International Law Journal of Southern Africa*
Conservation and Soc'y	*Conservation and Society*

Consilience: J Sust Dev	*Consilience: Journal of Sustainable Development*
Crit Rev Int'l Soc and Pol Phil	*Critical Review of International Social and Political Philosophy*
Cumb L Rev	*Cumberland Law Review*
Current Leg Probs	*Current Legal Problems*
De Jure LJ	*De Jure Law Journal*
Dev	*Development*
Dev in Practice	*Development in Practice*
Dev Studies Research	*Development Studies Research*
Duke J Comp and Int'l L	*Duke Journal of Comparative Law and International Law*
Ecol Econ	*Ecological Economics*
Ecol LQ	*Ecological Law Quarterly*
Ecol and Soc'y	*Ecology and Society*
Econ and Pol Weekly	*Economic and Political Weekly*
Educ Phil and Theory	*Education, Philosophy and Theory*
Elec J Sust Dev	*Electronic Journal of Sustainable Development*
Emory Int'l L Rev	*Emory International Law Review*
Emory LJ	*Emory Law Journal*
Envt Dev and Sustainability	*Environment, Development and Sustainability*
Envt and Nat Res Research	*Environment and Natural Resources Research*
Envt and Plan C: Govt and Pol'y	*Environment and Planning C: Government and Policy*
Envt and Plan D: Soc'y and Space	*Environment and Planning D: Society and Space*
Envt and Plan E: Nature and Space	*Environment and Planning E: Nature and Space*
Envt'l Archaeo	*Environmental Archaeology*
Envt'l Educ Research	*Environmental Education Research*
Envt'l Ethics	*Environmental Ethics*
Envt'l History	*Environmental History*
Envt'l Imp Assess Rev	*Environmental Impact Assessment Review*
Envt'l L Rep News and Analysis	*Environmental Law Reporter News and Analysis*
Envt'l Pol	*Environmental Politics*
Envt'l Pol'y and Gov	*Environmental Policy and Governance*
Envt'l Pol'y and L	*Environmental Policy and Law*
Envt'l Sciences	*Environmental Sciences*
Envt'l Sociology	*Environmental Sociology*
Envt'l Val	*Environmental Values*
Erasmus L Rev	*Erasmus Law Review*
ESIL	*European Society of International Law*
Ethics and Envt	*Ethics and Environment*

Ethics and Int'l Aff	*Ethics and International Affairs*
European HRL Rev	*European Human Rights Law Review*
European J Cultural Studies	*European Journal of Cultural Studies*
European J Int'l Rel	*European Journal of International Relations*
European J Sociology	*European Journal of Sociology*
European JIL	*European Journal of International Law*
European LJ	*European Law Journal*
Florida A and M UL Rev	*Florida A and M University Law Review*
Fordham Envt'l LJ	*Fordham Environmental Law Journal*
Geographic J	*Geographic Journal*
Georgetown Envt'l L Rev	*Georgetown Environmental Law Review*
Georgetown Int'l Envt'l L Rev	*Georgetown International Environmental Law Review*
Georgetown JIL	*Georgetown Journal of International Law*
Georgia J Int'l and Comp L	*Georgia Journal of International and Comparative Law*
Global Envt'l Pol	*Global Environmental Politics*
Global Pol'y	*Global Policy*
Glocalism: J Cult Pol and Innov	*Glocalism: Journal of Culture, Politics and Innovation*
Golden Gate U Envt'l LJ	*Golden Gate University Environmental Law Journal*
Griffith L Rev	*Griffith Law Review*
Groningen JIL	*Groningen Journal of International Law*
Harvard Int'l LJ	*Harvard International Law Journal*
Harvard L Rev	*Harvard Law Review*
Hastings Int'l and Comp L Rev	*Hastings International and Comparative Law Review*
Hist J	*Historical Journal*
History and Anthro	*History and Anthropology*
How LJ	*Howard Law Journal*
Human Rights Q	*Human Rights Quarterly*
Hung YBIL and European L	*Hungarian Yearbook of International Law and European Law*
ICJ	*International Court of Justice*
ICLQ	*International and Comparative Law Quarterly*
ILM	*International Legal Materials*
ILSA J Int'l and Comp L	*ILSA Journal of International and Comparative Law*
Ind J Global Leg Studies	*Indiana Journal of Global Legal Studies*
Indian J Pol Science	*Indian Journal of Political Science*
Indian JIL	*Indian Journal of International Law*

Indigenous LJ	*Indigenous Law Journal*
Indonesian J Int'l and Comp L	*Indonesian Journal of International and Comparative Law*
Indonesian JIL	*Indonesian Journal of International Law*
Int'l Aff	*International Affairs*
Int'l Community L Rev	*International Community Law Review*
Int'l Envt'l Agrmts: Pol, L and Econ	*International Environmental Agreements: Politics, Law and Economics*
Int'l Human Rights L Rev	*International Human Rights Law Review*
Int'l J Afr Ren Studies	*International Journal of African Renaissance Studies*
Int'l J Con L	*International Journal of Constitutional Law*
Int'l J Hist Archaeo	*International Journal of Historical Archaeology*
Int'l J Innov Research and Dev	*International Journal of Innovative Research and Development*
Int'l J Peace Studies	*International Journal of Peace Studies*
Int'l J Transitional Just	*International Journal of Transitional Justice*
Int'l JHR	*International Journal of Human Rights*
Int'l Organisations L Rev	*International Organisations Law Review*
Int'l Phil Q	*International Philosophical Questions*
Int'l Pol Science Rev	*International Political Science Review*
Int'l Studies Q	*International Studies Quarterly*
Int'l Theory	*International Theory*
Int'l YB Leg Anthro	*International Yearbook of Legal Anthropology*
Iowa L Rev	*Iowa Law Review*
J Afr History	*Journal of African History*
J Afr and IL	*Journal of African and International Law*
J Afr L	*Journal of African Law*
J Agric and Envt'l Ethics	*Journal of Agricultural and Environmental Ethics*
J Animal Ethics	*Journal of Animal Ethics*
J Brit Studies	*Journal of British Studies*
J Current Southeast Asian Aff	*Journal of Current Southeast Asian Affairs*
J Energy and Nat Res L	*Journal of Energy and Natural Resources Law*
J Envt'l L	*Journal of Environmental Law*
J Envt'l Planning and Mgt	*Journal of Environmental Planning and Management*
J Forest History	*Journal of Forest History*
J Global Ethics	*Journal of Global Ethics*
J Global History	*Journal of Global History*
J Hist Soc'y Nigeria	*Journal of Historical Society of Nigeria*
J History Ideas	*Journal of the History of Ideas*
J History IL	*Journal of the History of International Law*

J Human Rights and Envt	*Journal of Human Rights and the Environment*
J Human Rights Practice	*Journal of Human Rights Practice*
J Imp and Commonwealth History	*Journal of Imperial and Commonwealth History*
J Indian L Institute	*Journal of Indian Law Institute*
J Integrative Envt'l Sciences	*Journal of Integrative Environmental Sciences*
J Int'l Aff	*Journal of International Affairs*
J Int'l Econ L	*Journal of International Economic Law*
J Int'l and Global Studies	*Journal of International and Global Studies*
J Int'l Wildlife L and Pol'y	*Journal of International Wildlife Law and Policy*
J Jur Sciences	*Journal of Juridical Sciences*
J L Med Ethics	*Journal of Law, Medicine and Ethics*
J Leg Anthro	*Journal of Legal Anthropology*
J Leg Pluralism	*Journal of Legal Pluralism*
J Leg Pluralism and Crit Soc Anal	*Journal of Legal Pluralism and Critical Social Analysis*
J Leg Pluralism and Unofficial L	*Journal of Legal Pluralism and Unofficial Law*
J Media and Comm Studies	*Journal of Media and Communication Studies*
J Nat and Soc Phil	Journal of Natural and Social Philosophy
J Nat Res and Envt'l L	*Journal of Natural Resources and Environmental Law*
J Pan Afr Studies	*Journal of Pan African Studies*
J Pol Ecol	*Journal of Political Ecology*
J Southeast Asia Studies	*Journal of Southeast Asia Studies*
J Sust Dev in Afr	*Journal of Sustainable Development in Africa*
J Sust Dev and Pol'y	*Journal of Sustainable Development and Policy*
J Val Inquiry	*Journal of Value Inquiry*
James Cook UL Rev	*James Cook University Law Review*
Japanese YBIL	*Japanese Yearbook of International Law*
JL and Soc'y	*Journal of Law and Society*
L and Anthro	*Law and Anthropology*
L & Bus Rev Americas	*Law and Business Review of the Americas*
L and Contemp Probs	*Law and Contemporary Problems*
L and Critique	*Law and Critique*
L Culture and Humanities	*Law, Culture and Humanities*
L and Dev	*Law and Development*
L Envt and Dev J	*Law, Environment and Development Journal*
L and Soc Inquiry	*Law and Social Inquiry*
L Soc'y Rev	*Law and Society Review*
Leiden JIL	*Leiden Journal of International Law*
Lewis and Clark L Rev	*Lewis and Clark Law Review*

Liberty U L Rev	*Liberty University Law Review*
Local Envt	*Local Environment*
London Rev IL	*London Review of International Law*
Loyola U Chicago Int'l L Rev	*Loyola University of Chicago International Law Review*
Mac Int'l	*Macalester International*
Macq J Int'l and Comp Envt'l L	*Macquarie Journal of International and Comparative Environmental Law*
Manchester J Int'l Econ L	*Manchester Journal of International Economic Law*
Marine Pol'y	*Marine Policy*
Max Planck YB UN L	*Max Planck Yearbook of United Nations Law*
McGill J Sust Dev L and Pol'y	*McGill Journal of Sustainable Development Law and Policy*
McGill LJ	*McGill Law Journal*
Md JIL	*Maryland Journal of International Law*
Melbourne UL Rev	*Melbourne University Law Review*
Mershon Int'l Studies Rev	*Mershon International Studies Review*
Mexican L Rev	*Mexican Law Review*
Michigan J Envt'l and Admin L	*Michigan J Environmental and Administrative Law*
Michigan JIL	*Michigan Journal of International Law*
Michigan State Int'l L Rev	*Michigan State International Law Review*
Millennium: J Int'l Studies	*Millennium: Journal of International Studies*
Nat Res Forum	*Natural Resources Forum*
Nat Res J	*Natural Resources Journal*
Nethl Int'l L Rev	*Netherlands International Law Review*
Nethl QHR	*Netherlands Quarterly of Human Rights*
Nethl YBIL	*Netherlands Yearbook of International Law*
New Pol Econ	*New Political Economy*
New Zealand J Envt'l L	*New Zealand Journal of Environmental Law*
New Zealand J Public and IL	*New Zealand Journal of Public and International Law*
Nnamdi Azikiwe U JIL and Juris	*Nnamdi Azikiwe University Journal of International Law and Jurisprudence*
No Foundations: Interdis JL and Just	*No Foundations: Interdisciplinary Journal of Law and Justice*
NYU JIL and Pol	*New York University Journal of International Law and Politics*
NZSC	*New Zealand Supreme Court*
OAU	*Organisation of African Unity*

OGIRISI: New J Afr Studies	*OGIRISI: New Journal of African Studies*
OIDA Int'l J Sust Dev	*OIDA International Journal of Sustainable Development*
Open J Phil	*Open Journal of Philosophy*
Oregon Rev IL	*Oregon Review of International Law*
Organisation and Dev	*Organisation and Development*
Organisation and Envt	*Organisation and Environment*
Osgoode Hall LJ	*Osgoode Hall Law Journal*
Oxford J Legal Studies	*Oxford Journal of Legal Studies*
Pac McGeorge Glob Bus and Dev LJ	*Pacific McGeorge Global Business and Development Law Journal*
Pace Envt'l L Rev	*Pace Environmental Law Review*
Penn State Int'l L Rev	*Penn State International Law Review*
Phil Papers	*Philosophical Papers*
Pol and Leg Anthro Rev	*Political and Legal Anthropology Review*
Potchefstroom Electronic LJ	*Potchefstroom Electronic Law Journal*
Proc Nat Acad Sciences	*Proceedings of the National Academy of Sciences*
Queen Mary LJ	*Queen Mary Law Journal*
RAIS J Soc Sciences	*RAIS Journal of Social Sciences*
RECIEL	*Review of European, Comparative and International Environmental Law*
Rev Int'l Studies	*Review of International Studies*
Revus: J Const Theory and Phil L	*Revus: Journal for Constitutional Theory and Philosophy of Law*
S Cal L Rev	*Southern California Law Review*
SADC LJ	*SADC Law Journal*
SAJHR	*South African Journal on Human Rights*
Santa Clara JIL	*Santa Clara Journal International Law*
SCA	*Supreme Court of Appeal (South Africa)*
Scand J History	*Scandinavian Journal of History*
Science Tech and Soc'y	*Science, Technology and Society*
Singapore YBIL	*Singapore Yearbook of International Law*
Soc and Leg Studies	*Social and Legal Studies*
Soc'y and Bus Rev	*Society and Business Review*
Stan JIL	*Stanford Journal of International Law*
Studies in Bus and Econ	*Studies in Business and Economics*
Sust Dev	*Sustainable Development*
Tech in Society	*Technology in Society*
Theor Inq L	*Theoretical Inquiries in Law*
Theory and Soc'y	*Theory and Society*
Third World Q	*Third World Quarterly*
Trade L and Dev	*Trade, Law and Development*

Trans Inst Brit Geographers	*Transactions of the Institute of British Geographers*
Transnat'l L and Contemp Probs	*Transnational Law and Contemporary Problems*
Transnat'l Envt'l L	*Transnational Environmental Law*
Transnat'l Leg Theory	*Transnational Legal Theory*
Tul European & Civ LF	*Tulane European and Civil Law Forum*
TWAIL	*Third World Approaches to International Law*
TWAILR	*Third World Approaches to International Law Review*
TWAILR: Reflections	*Third World Approaches to International Law Review: Reflections*
UC Davis L Rev	*UC Davis Law Review*
UN	*United Nations*
UNEP	*United Nations Environment Programme*
UNTS	*United Nations Treaty Series*
Utrecht L Rev	*Utrecht Law Review*
Va L Rev	*Virginia Law Review*
Vand J Transnat'l L	*Vanderbilt Journal of Transnational Law*
Wash L Rev	*Washington Law Review*
Wash U LQ	*Washington University Law Quarterly*
Water L	*Water Law*
Widener L Symp J	*Widener Law Symposium Journal*
William and Mary Envt'l L and Pol'y Rev	*William and Mary Environmental Law and Policy Review*
Windsor YB Access Just	*Windsor Yearbook of Access to Justice*
Wisconsin Int'l LJ	*Wisconsin International Law Journal*
World Dev	*World Development*
Yale Human Rights and Dev LJ	*Yale Human Rights and Development Journal*
Yale Int'l LJ	*Yale International Law Journal*
Yale JL and Hum	*Yale Journal of Law and Humanities*
Yale LJ	*Yale Law Journal*
YB of Disaster L	*Yearbook of Disaster Law*
YB Int'l Envt'l L	*Yearbook of International Law*
Zagreb Int'l Rev Econ and Bus	*Zagreb International Review of Economic and Business*

Introduction

> The ideas of the ruling class are in every epoch the ruling ideas, i.e. the class which is the ruling material force of society, is at the same time its ruling intellectual force. The class which has the means of material production at its disposal, consequently also controls the means of mental production, so that the ideas of those who lack the means of mental production are on the whole subject to it. The ruling ideas are nothing more than the ideal expression of the dominant material relations, the dominant material relations grasped as ideas; hence of the relations which make the one class the ruling one, therefore, the ideas of its dominance. The individuals composing the ruling class possess among other things consciousness, and therefore think. Insofar, therefore, as they rule as a class and determine the extent and compass of an historical epoch, it is self-evident that they do this in its whole range, hence among other things rule also as thinkers, as producers of ideas, and regulate the production and distribution of the ideas of their age: thus, their ideas are the ruling ideas of the epoch.*

I.1 Sustainable Development, International Law, and the (Im-)possibility of Progress

International law typifies the expression of knowledge and politics as power.[1] Conceptualised as the politics of (international) justice, international law is fundamental to how we organise international society.[2] Yet, international law so often disguises the character of international politics by universalising its partisan principles concealed as global (social)

* Karl Marx and Friedrich Engels, *The German Ideology* (Prometheus Books 1998) 67.

1 Martti Koskenniemi, 'International Law in Europe: Between Tradition and Renewal' (2005) 16:1 European JIL 113, 123; China Miéville, *Between Equal Rights: A Marxist Theory of International Law* (Brill 2005) 319; Samuel Moyn, 'Knowledge and Politics of International Law' (2016) 129:8 Harvard L Rev 2164.

2 Jan Klabbers, 'On Epistemic Universalism and the Melancholy of International Law' (2018) 29:4 European JIL 1057, 1068.

progress.[3] It also silences resistance to its principles through the (vacuous) promise of compromise.[4] Set against this equivocal backdrop, international law operates in its hidden and not-so-hidden forms as epistemic (in)justice by mimicking a universalist and seemingly objective outlook.[5] In this sense, international law functions as a 'pseudo-objective defence of ruling ideologies'.[6]

This veiled character of international law perpetuates historical injustices frequently disguised as international (rule of) law.[7] Injustice and exclusionary politics are deeply ingrained in its sub-disciplines, including international environmental law.[8] All the same, international law possesses an inherent transformative power to renew and remake itself if we

[3] Anibal Quijano, 'Coloniality of Power, Eurocentrism, and Latin America' (2000) 1:3 Nepantla: Views from South 533, 533. Quijano defines Eurocentrism as 'the social classification of the world's population around the idea of race, a mental construction that expresses the basic experience of colonial domination and pervades the more important dimensions of global power'; Kathleen Morrison, 'Provincialising the Anthropocene: Eurocentrism in the Earth System' in Gunnel Cederlöf and Mahesh Ragarajan (eds.), *At Nature's Edge: The Global Present and Long-Term History* (Oxford University Press 2018) 3. Morrison adopts a panoptic view of Eurocentrism in reference to epistemologies and practices that we '"build out" from Europe and the temperate zones, taking other regions as variants on this unmarked category'; Ntina Tzouvala, 'The Spectre of Eurocentrism in International Legal History' (2021) 13:2 Yale JL and Hum 413. Tzouvala recently argued Eurocentrism is 'an important empty signifier'. By this, Tzouvala suggests the term is a site for contestation and alternative constructions of what constitutes Eurocentrism). I draw on these meanings and similar ones as I use Eurocentrism in reference to the historical dominance of the Global North in relation to the influences of colonialism, imperialism, and neoliberalism in the Global South. These are not intended to be perfect descriptors but they do convey both historical and contemporary import for this book and its central arguments.

[4] Gerry Simpson, 'The Globalisation of International Law' in Tim Dunne and Christian Reus-Smit (eds.), *The Globalisation of International Society* (Oxford University Press 2017) 266.

[5] Miranda Fricker, *Epistemic Injustice: Power and Ethics of Knowing* (Oxford University Press 2007) 1.

[6] Jochen von Bernstorff, 'International Legal Scholarship as a Cooling Medium in International Law and Politics' (2014) 25:4 European JIL 977, 977–978.

[7] John Linarelli, Margot E. Salomon, and Muthucumaraswamy Sornarajah, *The Misery of International Law: Confrontations with Injustice in the Global Economy* (Oxford University Press 2018) 1–37.

[8] Mario Prost and Alejandra Torres Camprubí, 'Against Fairness? International Environmental Law, Disciplinary Bias, and Pareto Justice' (2012) 25:2 Leiden JIL 379; Carmen G. Gonzalez and Sumudu Atapattu, 'International Environmental Law, Environmental Justice, and the Global South' (2017) 26:2 Transnat'l L and Contemp Probs 229, 233.

are committed to reimagining the discipline and its fundamental characteristics, including the concept of sustainable development.

In this book, I explore the interaction of international law and the politics of exclusion and how this complex interaction is problematised and (can be) resolved within international law. Africa and the project of reimagining sustainable development provide a useful space for this analysis. While African knowledge and African influences on the evolution of international law are routinely peripheralised and obscured, a critical inquiry uncovers the transformative potential of African law and experiences in remaking international law. In this respect, it is crucial to turn to so-called non-Western legal impulses and how they can help make sustainable development better both in conceptualisation and practice. Thus, I undertake this task by focusing on the law, politics, and history of conceptualising, evolving, and operationalising sustainable development.[9]

In pursuing this objective, I call into play my own experiences in search of valuable lessons that these experiences teach about the history, the present state, and the future of sustainable development. Two significant developments impact my thinking on the law on sustainable development and have since shaped my thinking on the broader character of international law. First, in summer 2012, the world marked the fortieth anniversary of the 1972 United Nations Conference on the Human Environment (the 1972 Stockholm Conference). Often described as being the precursor of the discipline of international environmental law, the 1972 Stockholm Conference is distinguished as having midwifed sustainable development.[10] The main highlight of this commemoration was the United Nations Conference on Sustainable Development (the Rio +20 Conference). At this time, I was completing a United Nations fellowship on the protection of the marine environment at the Marine and

[9] Chukwumerije Okereke, *Global Justice and Neoliberal Environmental Governance: Ethics, Sustainable Development and International Co-operation* (Routledge 2008) 3; Fricker, Epistemic Injustice, 1.

[10] Philippe Sands and Jacqueline Peel, *Principles of International Environmental Law* (Cambridge University Press 2012) 3; Avi Brisman, 'Stockholm Conference, 1972' in Deen K. Chatterjee (ed.), *Encyclopedia of Global Justice* (Springer 2011) 1040; Carl Mitcham, 'Sustainable Development: Its Origins and Ambivalence' (1995) 17:3 Tech in Society 311. Mitcham credits the first formal recording of the term 'sustainable development' to the World Conservation Strategy in 1980. Of course, this kind of argument is typical of the ahistorical treatment of core ideas with a much more global presence.

Environmental Law Institute, Schulich School of Law at Dalhousie University.[11] The Rio+20 Conference, which was essentially a re-enactment of the United Nations Conference on Environment and Development, 1992 (Rio Earth Summit) two long decades later, seemed an opportune time for international law scholars and lawyers alike as well as other experts working in international environmental law circles to reconsider the value of sustainable development. Like them, I too keenly followed the frenzied reports on the many legal and political developments linked to these commemorative events.[12]

Some of the commentaries produced in the aftermath of the celebrations, which comprised faith, optimism, exasperation, and even downright dismay, fascinated many international law scholars.[13] However, long after the Rio+20 Conference had ended and the euphoria had eventually waned, I was baffled by the silence that greeted Africa's participation at the 1972 Stockholm Conference in these reports emanating from the Rio+20 Conference. Although the reports coming in from Rio de Janeiro in Brazil, where the events took place, emphasised the efforts of the Global South, primarily India's role at the two-decades old historic 1972 Stockholm Conference, there was very scant news on Africa's participation.[14]

[11] Marine and Environmental Law Institute, '2011–2012 Annual Report: Celebrating 30 Years of the United Nations Convention of the Law on the Sea' (Marine and Environmental Law Institute 2012) 48. I spent the first part of my fellowship at the Schulich School of Law at Dalhousie University in Halifax, Nova Scotia. From there, I moved to the Division of Ocean Affairs and Law of the Sea, Office of Legal Affairs at the United Nations (UN) Secretariat in New York. Since the commemoration was a year-long UN event, I had the opportunity to observe, during my time at the UN Secretariat, how very little attention was given to discussions about Africa's participation at the Rio Earth Summit.

[12] Richard Black, 'Rio Revisited: Glass Half-Full?', *BBC News* (London, 24 July 2012), available at: <www.bbc.com/news/science-environment-18967011> (last accessed 20 November 2022); Brian Clark Howard, 'Rio+20 Brings Hope and Solutions Despite Weak Talks', *National Geographic News* (Washington, 21 June 2012), available at: <www.nationalgeographic.com/science/article/120621-rio-20-hope-solutions-official-talk> (last accessed 20 November 2022); Connie Watson, 'Rio+20 Earth Summit Concludes with Few Commitments', *CBC News* (22 June 2012), available at: <www.cbc.ca/news/politics/rio-20-earth-summit-concludes-with-few-commitments-1.1270257> (last accessed 20 November 2022).

[13] Ann Powers, 'One Participant's Diary' (2012) 42:3 Envt'l Pol'y and L 140, 141; Ann Powers, 'The Rio+20 Process: Forward Movement for the Environment?' (2012) 1:2 Transnat'l Envt'l L 403, 410.

[14] Bimal N. Patel, *The State Practice of India and the Development of International Law* (Brill 2016) 198–240; Karin Mickelson, 'Taking Stock of TWAIL Histories' (2008) 10:4 Int'l Community L Rev 355, 356–357. Mickelson reminds us that, when appraising these developments in international law, it is important to be guided by the historical Eurocentric obstruction of international 'story-telling' that is not so obvious in international law.

Interestingly, not much has changed since, even on the occasion of the 50th anniversary of the 1972 Stockholm Conference which was recently commemorated at the Stockholm+50 meeting in June 2022.

Second, an edited volume was published on the relationship between international environmental law and the Global South in 2015.[15] Rich in its scholarly diversity, especially in its account on the role played by the Global South in the making of the discipline of international environmental law and sustainable development, this remarkable intellectual effort was also silent on Africa's role in conceptualising and operationalising sustainable development.[16] While one of the chapters in this exceptional body of scholarship attempted to map the contribution of the Global South to the evolution of sustainable development and ultimately link it to the 1972 Stockholm Conference, that chapter (and, to some extent, the other chapters in that edited volume) said very little about Africa's contribution at the 1972 Stockholm Conference and beyond.[17]

These examples that I have provided here paint a real-life portrait of the broader, yet frequently unanswered questions about the ahistoricism of international law.[18] These experiences are also key reflection points now more than ever for international law as the emergence of the coronavirus

[15] Shawkat Alam, Sumudu Atapattu, Carmen G. Gonzalez and Jona Razzaque (eds.), *International Environmental Law and the Global South* (Cambridge University Press 2015).

[16] Louis J. Kotzé and Caiphas B. Soyapi, 'African Courts and Principles of International Environmental Law: A Kenyan and South African Study' (2021) 33:2 J Envt'l L 257, 261–264. Kotzé and Soyapi have attempted to fill part of this gap with their recent work which briefly highlighted the preparatory meetings of African states in Senegal ahead of the conference in Stockholm, the active contribution of Kenya during the negotiation of the Stockholm Declaration, the Nairobi Declaration in 1982, and later post-Stockholm developments. Yet, these histories and their related normativity were barely spotlighted at the Rio+20 Conference. Thus, it is important to give some more focused attention to this issue.

[17] Karin Mickelson, 'The Stockholm Conference and the Creation of the South–North Divide in International Environmental Law and Policy' in Shawkat Alam, Sumudu Atapattu, Carmen G. Gonzalez and Jona Razzaque (eds.), *International Environmental Law and the Global South* (Cambridge University Press 2015) 109.

[18] Andrew Fitzmaurice, 'Context in the History of International Law' (2018) 20:1 J History IL 5, 30; Anne Orford, *International Law and the Politics of History* (Cambridge University Press 2021) 99–104. Orford revisits her longstanding position that the past is not merely history; but the past is law. In her view, international law scholars should be interested in consulting the past to understand the present state and future of law and accompanying developments.

pandemic has ushered the world into a new era, further nuancing the North–South divide.[19] On this subject of ahistoricism, there seems to be a rushed attempt to depoliticise the ecological context of this pandemic and efface its connection to the continuing relevance of the North–South divide.[20] For instance, there have been recent attempts at reinterpreting the pandemic as a catastrophic global health challenge, and in this process, obscuring (and severing) the ecological subtext across wildlife management, nature conservation, and the coronavirus pandemic.[21]

This reinterpretation of the possible origins of the pandemic sidesteps its sustainable development dimensions and its consequences for both the Global North and Global South in international law.[22] These discussions also fail to consider the historical links between the pandemic and other recent efforts aimed at rereading similar global events, including the avian flu epidemic in Asia and the Ebola epidemic in Africa. I reflect on these histories and draw lessons from the complicated relationships they spawn within international law. I also reflect on how the discipline of international law has failed to draw on experiences from the Global South to construct a more responsive system that might have anticipated a global disease outbreak such as the coronavirus pandemic.[23]

Predictably, the response to the coronavirus pandemic has forced an unprincipled reset of global interactions that impeded critical reflections on the causes of this pandemic. This is demonstrated in how the world

[19] Upendra Baxi, 'Disasters, Catastrophes and Oblivion: A TWAIL Perspective' (2021) 2:1 YB Disaster L 72.

[20] Francisco-José Quintana and Justina Uriburu, 'Modest International Law: COVID-19, International Legal Responses, and Depoliticisation' (2020) 114:4 Am JIL 687, 690.

[21] Jorge Viñuales, Suerie Moon, Ginevra Le Moli and Gian-Luca Burci, 'A Global Pandemic Treaty Should Aim for Deep Prevention' (2021) 397:10287 Lancet 1791; Jeffrey A. McNeely, 'Nature and COVID-19: The Pandemic, the Environment, and the Way Ahead' (2021) 50:4 Ambio 767, 770–771.

[22] Alexander Gilder, 'International Law and Human Security in a Kaleidoscopic World' (2020) 59:1–4 Indian JIL 111, 114; Ngozi Finette Unuigbe, *Traditional Ecological Knowledge and Global Pandemics: Biodiversity and Planetary Health Beyond COVID-19* (Routledge 2021) 17–18. I reflect on the pandemic through the lens provided by Unuigbe's work to understand the geopolitical implication of the COVID pandemic. During the pandemic, I observed the inequities and inefficiencies in the different responses in both the Global North and the Global South. I also saw the disparities in global responses and how international law was often rallied to obscure these inequities.

[23] David P. Fidler, 'To Fight a New Coronavirus: The COVID-19 Pandemic, Political Herd Immunity, and Global Health Jurisprudence' (2020) 19:2 Chinese JIL 207, 207–210; Alexandra Phelan and Matiangai Sirleaf, 'Decolonisation of Global Health Law: Lessons from International Environmental Law' (2023) 51:2 J L Med Ethics 450.

has been preoccupied with developing vaccines, finding a cure, or other ways of medically containing the spread of the coronavirus disease.[24] Similarly, international law has resisted a critical re-evaluation of the law, politics, and history of sustainable development and its practical legal implementation. This resistance is predicated upon the grounds that the concept is already widely acknowledged as a universal ideal, and all that is needed is to make it work; yet, without much direction as to how that ought be done.[25] It is in this respect that the recent Stockholm+50 meeting held in 2022 has failed to achieve comparable influence of predecessor international mega-conferences on the environment and sustainable development. Little wonder the 2022 meeting ended regrettably, with no significant programme of action nor major (aspirational or enforceable) outcomes.

I have pondered these questions but with no easy answers. However, I am not alone in this struggle. International (environmental) law scholars like Karin Mickelson have asked similar questions – with her most unrelenting query being: 'What might the history of international environmental law look like from the perspective of the South?'[26] Understandably, this question is inherently overly broad, and pursuing this question might lead us nowhere. With reference to the concept of sustainable development, I find good reason to narrow down further, since, as other legal scholars have cautioned regarding sustainable development, 'if poorly designed, a broad question may be a dead end'.[27]

On that account, the epistemological referent for this critical inquiry is Africa. My motivation is evident: that as an African, a lawyer, and legal scholar, it is important that this inquiry begins from – and returns – 'home'.[28] More importantly, there is a great deal of work being done

[24] Ghassan Hage 'The Haunting Figure of the Useless Academic: Critical Thinking in Coronavirus Time' (2020) 23:4 European J Cultural Studies 662, 664; Saptarishi Bandopadhyay, *All Is Well: Catastrophe and the Making of the Normal State* (Oxford University Press 2022).

[25] Antonio Cardesa-Salzmann and Endrius Cocciolo, 'Global Governance, Sustainability and the Earth System: Critical Reflections on the Role of Global Law' (2019) 8:3 Transnat'l Envt'l L 437, 442–443.

[26] Karin Mickelson, 'South, North, International Environmental Law, and International Environmental Lawyers' (2001) 11:1 YB Int'l Envt'l L 52, 55.

[27] Jorge E. Viñuales, 'The Rise and Fall of Sustainable Development' (2013) 22:1 RECIEL 3, 3.

[28] Daniel Marc Segesser and Mats Deland, 'The Lawyer as Actor in History and Society' in Mats Deland, Mark Klamberg, and Pål Wrange (eds.), *International Humanitarian Law and Justice: Historical and Sociological Perspectives* (Routledge 2019) 175. I use home in at least two senses: in the sense of an African perspective, and in the sense of a lawyer and

by other scholars on international law within Africa, on Africa by African legal scholars in Africa and those located outside the continent, and within African legal (and international) institutions which is hidden in plain sight, as African insights and efforts tend to be routinely ignored or nudged to the periphery.[29] This concern is now urgent, as critical inquiries into international law are increasingly gaining a foothold in parts of the Global South but less so in Africa.[30] This concern emphasises observations that the omission of geographical spatiality even happens in critical legal scholarship.[31] Thus, these anxieties necessitate considerable attention as contemporary developments such as China's role and its economic interests in Africa are expanding, with its Belt and Road Initiative likely to exacerbate Africa's complicated ecological challenges.[32]

However, while Africa is the site of myriad challenges, it is still able to inspire change.[33] In her recent commentary on turning to Third World

legal scholar. Like Segesser and Deland point out, lawyers must be attentive to the history underlying their training and the histories underpinning their work. In this sense, I add that legal scholars must also be sensitive to the histories that shaped and continue to shape their scholarship. These are two of the senses in which I use the term 'home'.

29 Tiyanjana Maluwa, 'Reassessing Aspects of the Contribution of African States to the Development of International Law through African Regional Multilateral Treaties' (2020) 41:2 Michigan JIL 327; Duncan French, 'Revisiting Missed Opportunities: A Self-Reflection on (Not Always) Writing Meaningfully' (2021) 33:3 J Envt'l L 513. French admonishes international (environmental) law scholars to increasingly write from a self-reflective point of view. This book is guided by French's insight as it is a useful way of inserting the agency of an author into their scholarship.

30 James Thuo Gathii, 'The Agenda of Third World Approaches to International Law (TWAIL)' in Jeffrey L. Dunoff and Mark Pollack (eds.), *International Legal Theory, Foundations and Frontiers* (Cambridge University Press 2022) 153. Gathii's point invites timely works such as the present book to address this gap.

31 James Thuo Gathii, 'The Promise of International Law: A Third World View' (2020) 114 Am SIL: Proc Annual Mtg 165, 167–185.

32 James Thuo Gathii, 'Beyond China's Human Rights Exceptionalism in Africa: Leveraging Science, Technology and Engineering for Long-Term Growth' (2013) 51:3 Colum J Transnat'l L 664; Johanna Coenen, Simon Bager, Patrick Meyfroidt, Jens Newig and Edward Challies, 'Environmental Governance of China's Belt and Road Initiative' (2021) 31:1 Env Pol'y and Gov 3, 9–11. Third World scholars, including Gathii, have raised concerns over the human rights dimensions of China's engagements with Africa; Carmen G. Gonzalez, 'China in Latin America: Law, Economics and Sustainable Development' (2010) 40:2 Envt'l L Rep News and Analysis 10171. Others like Gonzalez are equally concerned about China's relationship with Latin America in respect of its extraction of natural resources which has led to serious environmental problems in that region.

33 I need to state at the outset that this book does not seek to generalise and homogenise all of Africa. Rather, the similarities across histories, peoples, laws, aspirations, and efforts suggest it is methodologically feasible to think in such broad terms.

sources in reviving international law, Fleur Johns argues that the growing interest in looking to Africa, rather than to the 'usual centres' of international law, advances the radical proposition that '[t]here is another canon from which [we] may learn. There is another ground from which to begin'.[34] In pondering what we might learn from the Global South including Africa, it is necessary to retell the story of the concept of sustainable development to adequately reflect Africa's legal, political, and historical role in its conceptualisation, evolution, and implementation. But, beyond this attempt at re-historicising the concept, it is equally important to critically examine how a renewed international (environmental) law correspondingly reinvigorates sustainable development through incorporating customary law, Indigenous cosmologies including ethics and other non-Western systems of law into international law to enhance the effective legal (and practical) implementation of the concept of sustainable development.[35]

Before turning to this undertaking, it is important I highlight the significance of this book. First, this book is a primer on Africa's contribution to the law, politics, and history of the concept of sustainable development. It is a timely intervention as it fills a gap in African and international legal scholarship.[36] It offers the first book-length analysis on the subject and gives meaning and form to the task of realising the legal character of sustainable development in Africa. I do so through a Third World analysis of the concept's legal, political, and historical components. This intellectual interest in Africa invites an attentiveness to African legal theorising and practical implementation of sustainable development. Therefore, this legal inquiry analyses how sustainable development, as one of the principal concepts of international law, has evolved, is influenced by different ideas, and is being operationalised in a

[34] Fleur Johns, 'Disciplinary Privilege and the Promise of Decampment: A Response to James Thuo Gathii's "The Promise of International Law: A Third World View"' (2020) 114 Am SIL: Proc Annual Mtg 187, 189.

[35] David Wilson, 'European Colonisation, Law, and Indigenous Marine Dispossession: Historical Perspectives on the Construction and Entrenchment of Unequal Marine Governance' (2021) 20:4 Maritime Studies 387, 388. I use the term 'Indigenous' in much the same way as Wilson does. He describes it as 'an imperfect catch all to describe the diverse groups, populations, and authorities that inhabited dissimilar regions prior to European arrival and who experienced various different forms of colonisation'.

[36] Frans Viljoen, Humphrey Sipalla, and Foluso Adegalu (eds.), *Exploring African Approaches to International Law: Essays in Honour of Kéba Mbaye* (Pretoria University Law Press 2022). This edited volume attempts to fill this gap. However, it is a collection of essays focusing on discrete subjects with only one contribution specifically on Africa and international environmental law.

manner that conceals African legal influences and ignores African cosmologies on the law on sustainable development.

Still, this book is not merely soliciting acknowledgement of Africa's contributions to international law. But also, in accordance with its radical theoretical and methodological bases; that is, Third World Approaches to International Law (TWAIL), it invites a sustained scrutiny of the concept as used in international law. Thus, the word 'contribution' as used in this book is not advanced in the same sense as *contributionism*.[37] Rather, its use follows the path of critical reflection as a fundamental resistance to the routine peripheralisation of African legal influences in international law generally, and particularly in sustainable development. To borrow from James Thuo Gathii, his dichotomy between TWAIL's critical focus and contributionism notes that:

> Critical theorists, unlike contributionists, centre their analysis on the structural and economic underpinnings of the place of African states in the world as their point of departure. While contributionists identified the exclusion of Africa from contributing to international law, critical scholars of the immediate post Second World War era in Africa focused on questions of power and wealth imbalances between African countries and the rest of the world as reasons to be sceptical of the possibilities for reform within or through the use of international law. As their central project, critical scholars examined the imperial and colonial character of international law.[38]

[37] Babatunde Fagbayibo, 'A Critical Approach to International Legal Education in Africa: Some Pivotal Considerations' (2019) 12 TWAILR: Reflections 1. Fagbayibo adopts Gathii's classificatory framework by arguing, 'Gathii usefully classifies African scholars into contributionists who provided a historical perspective of precolonial Africa's contributions to internationality, and critical traditionalists who expose unequal structural relations in global realpolitik and call for an overhaul of the international system.'

[38] James Thuo Gathii, 'Mapping African International Law' (2011) 2:3 Transnat'l Leg Theory 429, 441. I find Gathii's dichotomy of contributionism and radical resistance within the TWAIL tradition useful for appreciating the historical progress of the Third World effort in international law. Nonetheless, I still think this classification ought to be attentive to the relevant history since the supposed contributionist efforts of the earlier period may well fit contemporary expressions of radical resistance ascribed to latter TWAIL scholars. My point is that it might be useful, at this time, to pause and reflect on how those early years of the TWAIL tradition were radical in and of themselves if we think about the historical circumstances of those scholars and practitioners who, often, were lone voices railing against a system designed to keep their voices out of international legal discourse. Their modest efforts in the face of violent exclusionary practices invite a deeper reflection on their scholarship and practice as the radical resistance of that time. Still, Gathii's differentiation is a useful way of thinking through this unique history.

Thus, in sharing in Gathii's description, my position on Africa's *contribution* is not one searching for validation of African legal influences from classical international law; rather, it seeks 'to actively resist knowledge production systems that silence them and their engagements with international law'.[39]

Accordingly, this book adopts a history-facing approach. This historicised view of sustainable development, which is a key constituent element of international law, proceeds on the premise that international law must be necessarily history-oriented even if this view is sometimes not readily acknowledged by some international law scholars.[40] However, critical international law scholars have long argued that a historicised approach assists in 'retrieving, reconstructing, and giving meaning to past texts, doctrines, concepts, and practices for the sake of the present'.[41]

Therefore, in reimagining sustainable development for its present and future juridical application, I adopt a critical focus which inspires a radical scholarly attitude to the significance of international law in drawing upon history and ideas from the Global South to enrich the discipline.[42] This critical angle to international law promises a radical approach to researching and doing international law.[43] A critical lens must deeply query central but flawed assumptions. Linked to Africa, a critical approach helps us to discover (and even uncover) the contributions of Africa, its peoples, and its rich cosmologies to international law. Importantly, this radical approach helps international law scholars (and practitioners) to assess the significance of African ontologies to international law.[44] Thus, regarding the deconstruction of the concept of sustainable development and making international environmental law more responsive to Third World knowledge, a necessary first step is

[39] Gathii, 'Promise of International Law'.

[40] Anne Orford, 'International Law and the Limits of History' in Wouter Werner, Marieke de Hoon, and Alexi Galán (eds.), *The Law of International Lawyers: Reading Martti Koskenniemi* (Cambridge University Press 2017) 297.

[41] Jean d'Aspremont, 'Critical Histories of International Law and the Repression of Disciplinary Imagination' (2019) 7:1 London Rev Int'l L 89, 89–90.

[42] Manuela Lavinas Picq, 'Situating the Amazon in World Politics' in Celine Tan and Julio Faundez (eds.), *Natural Resources and Sustainable Development: International Economic Law Perspectives* (Edward Elgar 2017) 165, 177.

[43] d'Aspremont, 'Critical Histories'. I share d'Aspremont's view that critical international legal scholarship must break away from the orthodoxy of conforming to the precepts of history writing by turning to radical approaches on what constitutes history and how the history of international law is written.

[44] Fagbayibo, 'Critical Approach', 2.

grasping the awareness that a historicised view of sustainable development can only emerge from a similarly situated history-sensitive appreciation of international law.

In this sense, it is important to reflect on how history connects back to the principal requirement to infuse international law scholarship with critical perspectives. On this subject, TWAIL scholars have reinterpreted the origins of sustainable development as signifying the import of history into the legal dimensions of the concept of sustainable development. To this end, I agree with scholars like Karin Mickelson, who have argued that:

> To a large extent, the early history of international environmental law is narrated as a series of agreements, strung along in chronological order, with perhaps a passing judgment as to their 'progressiveness' (or lack thereof) from an environmental or ecological standpoint. Little or no effort is made to portray the conditions to which these agreements were meant to respond or the broader political and economic backdrop against which they emerged. From there, a jump is usually made to the latter half of the twentieth century particularly to the 1960s, when the 'real story' of international environmental law is said to have begun with the emergence of ecological consciousness.[45]

The same observation holds true even today. Five decades since the 1972 Stockholm Conference, sustainable development is still unsuccessful at turning its promise of a better and healthier planet into a reality. This challenge reflects the imperialist (and continuing postcolonial) influences of the Eurocentric conditioning of the emergence of the concept in international law. As Kishan Khoday rightly observed, the 'current planetary crisis requires looking beyond the evolutionary pathways of the present normative frameworks with their conventional underpinnings in Western environmentalism and the systems that emerged from the Stockholm summit'.[46] This is an apt observation, and that is why it is necessary to look to places like Africa for intellectual and practical inspiration and as a correction of the injustice perpetrated by the Eurocentrism of international law.[47]

[45] Mickelson, 'South, North', 55.

[46] Kishan Khoday, 'Decolonising the Environment: Third World Approaches to the Planetary Crisis' (2022) 19:2 Indonesia JIL 189, 191.

[47] Arpitha Kodiveri, 'The Delicate Task of Including Different Voices in Environmental Law Making in India' (2022) 33:3 J Envt'l L 495, 496. Even at the national level, there have been some concerns regarding the exclusion and marginalisation of certain groups in environmental law as the field has become 'an important site of struggle for the inclusion of different voices and their histories of injustice'. This domestic experience mirrors similar trends of injustice at international law.

Importantly, it is against this truncated and fragmented history that Africa and its non-Western counterparts that were colonised during the European imperial project have been written out of the disciplinary history of international environmental law and sustainable development.[48] Where the histories of these oppressed classes were included in such narratives, their essence was conjoined to the convenient exploitation of their natural resources and environment for the intellectual and material pursuits of the imperial and colonising powers.[49] Viewed this way, the ahistoricism of sustainable development irradiates universalist principles from its Eurocentric core to the non-European periphery. In this sense, international law overrules globally different histories while freezing out the evolution of context-specific ideas and legal philosophies as the alternatives to existing Eurocentric knowledge.[50] As a result, the ahistoricism of sustainable development and its related legal Eurocentrism hinder appreciating and operationalising the legal

[48] B. S. Chimni, 'Is there an Asian Approach to International Law? Questions, Theses, and Reflections' (2008) 14 Asian YB Int'l L 247, 262.

[49] Albert Memmi, *The Coloniser and the Colonised*, translated by Howard Greenfeld (Earthscan 1990); Douglas de Castro, 'The Colonial Aspects of International Environmental Law: Treaties as Promoters of Continuous Structural Violence' (2017) 5:2 Groningen JIL 168, 169.

[50] Picq, 'Situating the Amazon in World Politics', 177–182; Jean d'Aspremont, 'International Law, Universality, and the Dream of Disrupting from the Centre' (2018) 7:7 ESIL Reflections 1, 6–7. d'Aspremont admonishes us not to restrict critiques of universality in international law to colonialism and neo-colonialism. I agree with this viewpoint. Undoubtedly, these critically important framings of the colonial (and postcolonial) character of the universality of international law are important to this book. However, the universality of international law must be observed more broadly as 'whenever international lawyers turn particular preferences, constructions, or ideals into a legal claim that is allegedly applicable and opposable to all'. In this sense, colonialism and neo-colonialism only then accentuate this so-called universal phenomenon and are not necessarily the only culprits responsible for its creation. For there may be cognate elements of universality that are not connected to the colonial (nor the postcolonial) yet central to its formation. So, borrowing once more from d'Aspremont, I argue that TWAIL's task is to disrupt such broad categories of universality. Again, d'Aspremont describes this position thus as, '[d]isruption means emptying some of our common claims about the universality of international law. Disruption means being suspicious when universality is invoked in international legal discourses. Disruption means shedding light on the ambiguity of resistance, reform, and contestation and revolution.' Accordingly, the challenge of universality in this book follows this line of suspicion: an idea that is intended to resist, reform, contest, and even revolt against the orthodoxy of international (environmental) law.

dimensions of sustainable development, with long-term consequences for the continuing utility of the concept in Africa and elsewhere.[51]

I.2 Structure of the Book

This book focuses on the intersection of international law and environmental law in the making of sustainable development. While the analysis in this book pivots around sustainable development as occurring within international law, it equally speaks broadly to the general character of law, legal normativity, Eurocentrism, and the juridical pertinence of so-called non-legal norms such as ethics or non-Western legal ideas and related legal systems. In this respect, the analysis is built around Africa's role; both invisible and ascertainable, in respect of the law, politics, and history of sustainable development.

In this sense, this book utilises TWAIL to excavate both latent and observable ideas and values at the law–environment nexus. TWAIL both anchors and critiques how foundational philosophies on Africa's legal contribution to sustainable development are overlooked in international law. In its overarching function, TWAIL embodies the juridical ethos guiding this book as the ensuing chapters identify, critique, accept, and reject (even where necessary) the ideas, principles, and concepts that are central to the socio-intellectual constitution on sustainable development. The reason for this approach is that, while this book is materially legal, it is equally sensitive to how law is politically bordered by its social outline – what has become known as 'law as politics'.[52] In view of this, this book critically invites a socio-historical, socio-ecological, and a contextualised legal reading of sustainable development. Accordingly, the ensuing chapters both challenge and push at the frontiers of legal orthodoxy broadly construed, legal Eurocentrism, and the socio-technical *milieu* that frame the law, power, politics, history, and policy of international law in respect to sustainable development.[53]

[51] B. S. Chimni, 'Capitalism, Imperialism, and International Law in the 21st Century' (2012) 14:1 Oregon Rev Int'l L 17, 22.

[52] Duncan Kennedy, 'Three Globalisations of Law and Legal Thought: 1850–2000' in David Trubek and Alvaro Santos (eds.), *The New Law and Development: A Critical Appraisal* (Cambridge University Press 2006) 19, 72; Julen Extabe,'Law as Politics: Four Relations' (2020) 16:1 L Culture and Humanities 24.

[53] Mohsen al Attar, 'TWAIL: A Paradox within a Paradox' (2020) 22:2 Int'l Community L Rev 163, 172.

This book comprises six chapters across three parts, excluding the present Introduction and the concluding Chapter 7. Part I consists of Chapters 1 and 2. Chapter 1 provides a historical framework, a theoretical and methodological outline, and a discussion of the general issues underlining a critical rereading of sustainable development. Chapter 2 provides a conceptual and genealogical tracing of the ideation of sustainable development that began as nature, was quickly transformed into the environment, much later became development, and finally arrived at its present destination of sustainable development. Each terminology presents a nuanced angle to the storied interrelations between humans and the natural world. The ensuing analysis has implications for international law considering the concepts and ideologies discussed here are embedded in the evolution and integration of the emergent sub-discipline of international (environmental) law. By entwining a TWAIL-oriented analysis into this inquiry, the colonial and (neo-)imperialist character of the subsequent evolution of sustainable development becomes self-evident. As a result, I challenge the Eurocentric foundations of these themes by analysing the objectification, commodification, and financialisation of nature or the environment as the central logic of sustainable development.[54]

Part II unites two sides of one discussion. First, Chapter 3 focuses on the concept of sustainable development as occurring in international law. It problematises the presumed universality of the concept by arguing sustainable development embodies the power and knowledge of the politics that has its heritage and pedigree in colonialism, imperialism, and Eurocentrism. The analysis challenges the perceived universalism of sustainable development as it tacitly overshadows the disciplinary progress of international environmental law itself through the uneasy interaction of historical and materialist conditions. Sustainable development thus emerges from this disciplinary distortion as compromise, as indeterminateness, and a well-crafted (but nonetheless tenuous) temperance on the evolutionary capacity of international law to reorient ecological awareness in the unfolding global ecological crisis.

Second, Chapter 4 expands on the debate on this totalising effect of sustainable development that I started in Chapter 3. It extends the analysis to the normative trajectory of the concept in Africa by exploring its evolution, internalisation, and operationalisation. This analysis maps Africa's contribution to the rise of this concept of sustainable development

[54] Walter D. Mignolo, 'Delinking: The Rhetoric of Modernity, the Logic of Coloniality, and the Grammar of De-Coloniality' (2007) 21:2–3 Cultural Studies 449.

which has gained much prominence, first in the form of the colonial conservation of nature. This historico-legal analysis unpacks Africa's exclusion from early imperially informed Africa-focused treaties on the environment. Following its entry onto the international scene and subsequent participation in international (environmental) law, Africa's (national and continental) endeavours at operationalising sustainable development have since become a very complex crusade. The international legal discourse on sustainable development was truncated and supplanted by a human rights-based framework. I explore this shifting disciplinary progression by mapping the continental-level interpretation and implementation of the concept as seen in either the quasi-judicial system under the African Commission on Human and Peoples' Rights or its judicialised equivalent under the African Court on Human and Peoples' Rights. In examining both quasi-judicial and judicialised approaches, this chapter highlights how and why African states are reluctant or unwilling to translate the judgments of the regional and continental courts and decisions of other adjudicative tribunals on sustainable development into meaningful, practical, or action-oriented juridical results at the national (both the state and sub-state) level.

Part III breaks away from the problematique core of Part II and focuses on the changes needed to address the problems identified with the concept of sustainable development. Chapter 5, which begins this line of inquiry argues that an alternative legal ontology derived from non-Eurocentric cosmologies is both possible and urgent for reimagining sustainable development. In this respect, I explore relational ontologies from the Global South including from across Africa. The chapter challenges and contributes to the global discourse on sustainable development by evolving a radical view on customary law and Indigenous legal cosmologies (including ethics as law). In addressing the fundamental relevance of customary law to renewing sustainable development, I am not seeking to replace one form of law with another, as this will amount to privileging one legal order over the other. Rather, in investigating the deficiencies of the concept of sustainable development, it is evident that part of its ineffectiveness derives from the inordinate focus of international law on its Euro-American origins and presecriptions. The discussion draws on legal pluralism, legal anthropology, and transnational law – as law, in and of themselves – to demonstrate that, while these three juridical forms are not strictly state-sanctioned law; they, nonetheless, evoke legal normativity. Drawing on this notion of legal normativity outside of state-sanctioned law, I focus on these examples to advance the case for the legal normativity of African customary law in renewing sustainable development through ethico-legal values and principles. I refer to this expansive undertaking on environmental ethics as Southern environmental ethics since these ethico-legal values and principles are endogenous across the Global South (and in Indigenous societies in the Global North). In this respect, I propose Southern environmental ethics as eco-legal philosophies that can inspire ecolegality aimed at untangling the Eurocentric grip over the concept of sustainable development.

Chapter 6 proposes a renewal and reimagining of sustainable development by inviting a radical shift – where ecolegality becomes the pivot around which the revitalisation of the legal content of sustainable development occurs. Using the imaginative capacity of law as myth, I discuss the significance of environmental ethics to African customary law and Indigenous cosmologies. This radical approach rejects the positivist limitations imposed on the constitution of law by embracing a broader meaning of law. This legal reconstruction is established on the central premise that law occurs in and is found in many different contexts; and that positivist constructions of international law are neither foundational nor neutral, as has been claimed. I argue our legal cosmos ought to embrace pluralist legal approaches and different sources of law like relational ontologies. This viewpoint invites a corresponding recognition of law as regulating our planetary existence, including human relationships with non-human domains, even if that view on law seems unintelligible to positivist (legal) attitudes. The idea of ecolegality enters the discourse by recharacterising the interrelations between law and ecology. It does this by restraining the overbearing rule of law and retrenching its disproportionate influence in human–nature relations. Therefore, ecolegality is significant in bringing new life to the concept of sustainable development as it introduces and foregrounds a necessary alternativeness by recalibrating the unsubstantiated self-imposed dominance of law which is an unhealthy, distorted, and unequal exertion of human will over nature.

The book concludes by returning to some central themes like the politics of sustainable development and TWAIL's influence over the progress and future of sustainable development in international law. I reflect on the potential, never-ending normative expansion of sustainable development by stressing its co-evolution with TWAIL, and TWAIL's own ever-evolving character within international law. I highlight some limits of (international) law and the false, uncritical claims of Eurocentric legal superiority in sustainable development discourse. I demonstrate how international law itself can benefit from promoting Indigenous and customary law changes that are rapidly transforming this discourse in both the Global North and the Global South. I conclude my analysis by reflecting on how sustainable development might be emancipated from epistemic injustice by inquiring into how dominant terminologies in international law could be repurposed in the hope of advancing TWAIL's reconstructionist objectives.[55]

[55] Jean d'Aspremont, 'Wording in International Law' (2012) 25:3 Leiden JIL 575, 577.

PART I

Mise en Scène

1

The Rise, Fall, and Rise Again of Sustainable Development

The concept of sustainable development, as gradually refined over the last three decades, intends to guide communities toward balanced social, economic, and environmental sustainability. Sadly, the outcome thus far has been a paying of lip service to the concept of sustainable development, while pursuing economic growth based on the exploitation of the poor and of nature.*

1.1 Introduction

More than half a century since its 'official' inauguration, the concept of sustainable development is still used in many different senses to mean or suggest many different things. Ironically, the strength of sustainable development derives from its ambivalent conceptualisation where it professes the protection of the environment; while in fact, and in many ways, the concept is responsible for its very opposite.[1] Sustainable development has thus been uncritically deployed within its conceptual ambivalence as 'a "diplomatic trick" uniting all stakeholders under a common banner'.[2]

Emerging from this muddle, sustainable development has avoided the difficult questions of what its intentions were and what its expectations will be. It quietly slipped into general discourse as an acceptable aspirational goal.[3] Nonetheless, as sustainable development quickly advanced from conceptualisation and evolution towards practical implementation,

* Usha Natarajan, 'Environmental Justice in the Global South' in Sumudu A. Atapattu, Carmen G. Gonzalez and Sara L. Seck (eds.), *The Cambridge Handbook of Environmental Justice and Sustainable Development* (Cambridge University Press 2021) 39, 49.

[1] Mitcham, 'Sustainable Development', 322.

[2] Viñuales, 'Rise and Fall', 4.

[3] Ibid.

its incoherence inevitably distorted much of its legal implementation.[4] The chief manifestation of the concept's fluctuation has been that states, in both the Global North and Global South, have engaged in the deliberate instrumentalisation of the concept's uncertainty to serve parochial and self-interested objectives, and not for the benefit of their peoples nor the environment. Thus, in terms of law, it is evidently paradoxical that sustainable development's defining power had also become its greatest flaw.[5]

This chapter thus reveals how the concept of sustainable development began its life as a promise of hope, slipped into the depths of despair, and how it is yet possible to revitalise the concept to inspire confidence. First, the discussion in this chapter reimagines the legal dimensions of sustainable development and how to endow sustainable development with legal normativity that promotes its performance and implementation. This task arises from the failure of the concept to deliver on its assurance to link the environment, society, and economy into a workable harmony. This misalignment is discernible as the implementation of sustainable development became more established in both national and international processes and as economic growth increasingly subordinated environmental concerns. But, while the concept is acknowledged as a product of international consensus and distinguished as a 'universal' concept, its legal observance is rather honoured in compromise.[6] Second, the analysis demonstrates how hegemonic influences and power, inspired by legal Eurocentrism and Western ideas, foreground sustainable development as a concept that emerged from Global North-led conferences and not as an idea that was intrinsic to all societies. Third, the discussion expands on the question of the noticeable absence of non-Western influences by emphasising Africa as a source of normativity in revitalising sustainable development. Fourth, this chapter highlights the theoretical and methodological prominence of Africa (and the broader Global South) through a Third World analysis. While highlighted in this chapter, this analytical framework underpins all chapters of this book and is central to its main arguments.

4 Jorge E. Viñuales, 'A Concise Research Agenda for Environmental Law' (2018) 1 Brill Open L 1, 2.

5 Viñuales, 'Rise and Fall', 4.

6 Ibid.

1.2 Diversity of Sustainable Development and Pursuit of Meaning and Performance

There are several entry points into an analysis on the myriad senses of the concept of sustainable development. However, based on the radical perspectives adopted in this book, I find that a history-informed critical angle is a more suitable choice. In this respect, it is important to contextualise the formal incidence of sustainable development within an emerging decolonial agenda. The emergence of the concept thus triggered creative Eurocentric techniques that fought back at an impending postcolonial aspiration for reversing the structural deficiencies that characterised the Global South as a hub of natural resources with attendant ecological despoliation.

Predictably, the irresolution of sustainable development veneered ecological anxieties by misrepresenting seeming consensus on its emergence as mutual global reassurance.[7] In this respect, if sustainable development has failed to make desired progress beyond its perceived universality, it is only appropriate that this failure is properly situated within the unbalanced character of international law and how that heritage continues to play an important role in the life of the discipline, even to this day.[8] The call to rally the concept for better and effective implementation thus requires reimagining the conceptual substance of sustainable development and retrenching its perceived universality.[9] This call is dictated by the current neoliberal conceptual constitution of sustainable development which has long impeded a rethinking of the concept for harmony between society and nature.[10]

On this subject, it is noteworthy that, despite its Eurocentric character, sustainable development exists outside the confines of legal formalism, and has long operated as an age-old concept that is integral to Indigenous systems of law.[11] Embedded in ethics and Indigenous or customary law, these legal ideas have always existed outside of positivist prescriptions

[7] Emmanuelle Jouannet, 'Universalism and Imperialism: The True–False Paradox of International Law' (2007) 18:3 European JIL 379, 385.

[8] Sumudu Atapattu, 'Comments on Environmental Justice, Human Rights, and the Global South by Carmen Gonzalez' (2015) 13:1 Santa Clara JIL 197, 198.

[9] Viñuales, 'Concise Research Agenda', 2.

[10] Sabrina Tremblay-Huet, 'Should Environmental Law Learn from Animal Law? Compassion as a Guiding Principle for International Environmental Law Instead of Sustainable Development' (2018) 31 Revue Québécoise de Droit International 125, 129.

[11] Usha Natarajan and Kishan Khoday, 'Locating Nature: Making and Unmaking International Law' (2014) 27:3 Leiden JIL 573, 593.

that have been elevated through major international events like the 1972 Stockholm Conference and similar summitry such as the 1992, 2012, and 2022 mega-conferences on the environment and sustainable development. These normative orders that are based on plural schemes of law, including African customary law, are manifested in the knowledge systems of the peoples of the Global South. If these juridical alternatives can enhance international law by provoking a better and more effective legal implementation of sustainable development, then their significance must be amplified through further clarification.[12] Thus, sustainable development must be revitalised for effective implementation by consulting non-Western sources of law. This effort requires remediating the politics of exclusion and focusing on how *new* sources like customary law and Indigenous cosmologies can augment the content of the concept through an illumination of its legal dimensions.[13]

The challenge of clarifying the conceptual foundations of sustainable development and adapting the concept for effective implementation through infusing it with alternative understandings must become a matter of interest for international law scholarship. An array of concerns is implicated and will thus inform subsequent discussions in this book. Nonetheless, it is useful to point out some immediate challenges. For instance, when international law scholars discuss the ecological crisis in terms of sustainable development, the inclination is to overlook the 'inequalities within humans' and their corresponding social groupings like states, regional or continent-level political or economic alliances that are formed based on similarly-situated ideologies.[14] Additionally, factors such as colonialism and imperialism and their impacts on socio-technical transformation across different levels of economic growth and resulting effects on human interactions with nature tend to be absent from this discussion. And, as multilateral international environmental law treaties are negotiated across both the North and the South, a false assumption of substantive equality begins to supplant formal inequality, thereby eliding difference across states.

[12] David V. Wright, 'Environmental Rule of Law: In Need of Coherence in Contested Terrain' (2020) 15:1 McGill J Sust Dev L and Pol'y 1, 6.

[13] David L. VanderZwaag, 'Edging Towards Principled Ocean Governance: Law of the Sea and Beyond' in International Ocean Institute–Canada (ed.), *The Future of Governance and Ocean Development: Essays in Honour of Elisabeth Mann Borgese (1918–2002)* (Brill 2018) 117, 121.

[14] Viñuales, 'Concise Research Agenda', 9.

This point might suggest the dynamic of difference is of little concern today.[15] Yet, these are still relevant themes for international law, including Third World Approaches to International Law (TWAIL), to take more seriously. Here, TWAIL is interested in the structural inequality embedded in the idea of the 'international' in international law.[16] This concern is observable in the North–South debate that is still very alive in international law and sustainable development discourse.[17] TWAIL's concern here emerges from the role international environmental law plays as a springboard for colonial and imperial technologies deployed to subjugate colonised peoples and deprive them of their laws, lands, and natural resources. In this sense, sustainable development continues an historical inequality through its muted promise of guaranteeing the development–environment balance.[18] The argument has been that, while sustainable development appears far from attaining its lofty objectives, it still has succeeded in nurturing interest and knowledge in the concept as a subject of critical inquiry.[19] Thus, critical scholars argue we cannot overlook the place of reform in advancing radical transformations in the discipline since sustainable development is particularly central to international environmental law and international law broadly.[20]

Perhaps it might seem a lot easier to simply discard sustainable development altogether. However, I do not think that would make the task any less difficult. My position, then, in remaining with sustainable development as a concept, is informed by the understanding that, while ambition is good, it is important to be grounded in the awareness that 'over-sophistication may hinder rather than help practical implementation'.[21] To simply abandon the term sustainable development completely and pursue a new one might not necessarily curtail the underlying challenges. It may well be a naïve attempt at resolving a very complicated problem. Then there is also the more practical challenge of rallying international actors to agree on a new vocabulary while bearing in mind the characteristic snail pace of international

[15] Wright, 'Environmental Rule of Law', 5–6.

[16] Anthea Roberts, *Is International Law International?* (Oxford University Press 2017) 1–3.

[17] Cait Storr, 'Islands and the South: Framing the Relationship between International Law and Environmental Crisis' (2016) 27:2 European JIL 519, 524.

[18] Chimni, 'Capitalism, Imperialism, and International Law', 22.

[19] Usha Natarajan and Julia Dehm, 'Where Is the Environment? Locating Nature in International Law' (2019) 3 TWAILR: Reflections 1, 2.

[20] Usha Natarajan, 'TWAIL and the Environment: The State of Nature, the Nature of State, and the Arab Spring' (2012) 14:1 Oregon Rev Int'l L 177, 178.

[21] Viñuales, 'Concise Research Agenda', 5.

negotiations. Even that might be difficult to achieve among states in the Global South who share similar concerns. A more useful, radical enterprise will rather be to reorient the normative content of the concept with a new foundation that prepares it for better and effective implementation since much of what is known about sustainable development happens within this conceptual configuration. My point follows what other international law scholars like Jorge Viñuales have rightly contended that the concept's 'use in international practice is pervasive, and it is still the most powerful tool for gathering stakeholders around the same table of negotiation'.[22] Therefore, it might be naïve or ill-advised to risk a bigger burden by assuming these concerns are trivial when reimagining sustainable development.

Perhaps an even more radical stance might be an immediate rejection of sustainable development as unworkable. Still, I think that too might fail. Although a concept may oppress a group or bring undesirable results, that awareness must not stop us from retrenching its negative characteristics while retaining its positive attributes. This task involves reimagining the concept and remaking it into a creative technology that can be adapted to serve the interest of marginalised peoples and nature.

This is the focus of TWAIL: to deconstruct and re-make international law.[23] In the deconstructionist sense, Michael Fakhri has argued that TWAIL 'provides a historical record of what not to do'.[24] As a reconstructionist technology, TWAIL adherents are of the view that critical scholarship can radically reform and rebuild international law to work for Third World interests and the marginalised peoples of the Global South.[25] In reconciling these seemingly diametrically-opposed aims of TWAIL, Luis Eslava and Sundhya Pahuja have observed that:

> Resistance and reform then come together in TWAIL to form a single process of the destabilisation and renewal of international law's history and operation. Rather than replacement, TWAIL scholarship is more interested in overcoming international law's problems while still remaining committed to the idea of an international normative regime.[26]

[22] Viñuales, 'Rise and Fall', 11.

[23] I delve further into this in Section 1.5.

[24] Michael Fakhri, 'Third World Sovereignty, Indigenous Sovereignty, and Food Sovereignty: Living with Sovereignty Despite the Map' (2018) 9:3–4 Transnat'l Leg Theory 218, 231.

[25] Obiora Chinedu Okafor, 'Newness, Imperialism, and International Legal Reform in Our Time: A TWAIL Perspective' (2005) 43:1–2 Osgoode Hall LJ 171, 176–177.

[26] Luis Eslava and Sundhya Pahuja, 'Beyond the (Post)Colonial: TWAIL and the Everyday Life of International Law' (2012) 45:2 Verfassung und Recht in Übersee 195, 204.

Nonetheless almost a decade after Eslava and Pahuja's remarks, it is time to push forward. A contemporary rendition of the co-constitution of TWAIL's deconstructionist and reconstructionist objectives must align with the view that 'the complex and proliferating challenges we face today, evidence the inadequacy of perpetual law reform and cyclical disciplinary re-invention, pointing to the need for systemic and foundational change'.[27]

In relating these insights to whether we should abandon sustainable development, it is important to recall that Third World scholarship has previously been enlisted to advance radical causes like permanent sovereignty over natural resources – a high point in Third World activism involving an adaptation of Westphalian sovereignty to the needs of the Global South.[28] The same is true for what is popularly known as solidarity rights which have a collectivist character – a marked departure from the individualistic, mainstream, and liberal conception of human rights, yet not departing wholly from the wider framework of rights.[29]

TWAIL endorses these deconstructionist and reconstructionist registers on retrenching the Eurocentric coordinates of international law. At the same time, it re-envisions the legal dimensions of sustainable development through alternative ideation. Thus, this realignment of the concept of sustainable development includes revitalising its legal content to reflect changes introduced through the observance of the normative value of environmental ethics and other Indigenous and local knowledge as law and a similarly conforming outlook on law as ecology and ecology as law.[30]

1.3 Denouncing Hegemony and Setting the Scene

There are different lenses through which to examine sustainable development. Even so, critical attitudes tend to be more helpful as they assist

[27] Usha Natarajan, Laura Betancur-Restrepo, Amar Bhatia, John Reynolds, Ntina Tzouvala and Sujith Xavier, 'Third World Approaches to International Law Review: A Journal for a Community' (2020) 1 TWAILR 7, 8.

[28] David P. Fidler, 'Revolt against or from within the West? TWAIL, the Developing World, and the Future Direction of International Law' (2003) 2:1 Chinese JIL 29, 41–42.

[29] Shawkat Alam and Abdullah al Faruque, 'From Sovereignty to Self-Determination: Emergence of Collective Rights of Indigenous Peoples in Natural Resources Movement' (2019) 32:1 Georgetown Envt'l L Rev 59.

[30] Andreas Philippopoulos-Mihalopoulos, 'Looking for the Space between Law and Ecology' in Andreas Philippopoulos-Mihalopoulos (ed.), *Law and Ecology: New Environmental Foundations* (Routledge 2011) 1, 4–5.

us to understand the (Eurocentric) cultural context of the concept. In this sense, cultural hegemony, operating as the subtext of this legal inquiry, clarifies the place of TWAIL in critiquing sustainable development. Emanating from a Marxist premise, cultural hegemony echoes the view that '[t]he ideas of the ruling class are in every epoch the ruling ideas, i.e. the class which is the ruling material force of society, is at the same time its ruling intellectual force'.[31] Still, cultural hegemony goes further in pushing at the boundaries of this Marxist insight by contending that class control and dominance are fostered through a cultural (ideological) apparatus, and that this interaction has a direct effect on the role law plays in social organisation.[32]

Cultural hegemony paints a conceptual portrait of a dominant worldview of the ruling class. It is a process that manifests through institutions, social attitudes, norms, concepts, and ideations, and how they present themselves as representing widespread social interests. Yet, this ideological (and institutional) infrastructure is purposely designed for the benefit of the ruling class. The acceptance of this dominance by the ruling class develops into a culturally-situated explanatory framework for how key ideas elicit universal consensus even though they are simply projecting the self-interested goals of a specific group – in this case, the Global North, the postcolonial elite in the Global South, and the adjacent comprador bourgeoisie.[33] Hegemonic deconstruction, therefore, explains the logic of the politics of exclusion and its dominance in determining the content of law even as law seeks to maintain a value-neutral outlook.[34]

When cultural hegemony is applied in international law, the contradictions within the historical habituation of law – including sustainable development – unravel and reveal the politics embedded in international environmental law.[35] In that context, sustainable development becomes the dominant vocabulary of its time, a concept that is key to 'maintaining capitalist hegemony by counteracting environmentalist

31 Marx and Engels, *German Ideology*, 67.

32 Martti Koskeniemmi, 'What Should International Lawyers Learn from Karl Marx?' (2004) 17:2 Leiden JIL 229; A. Claire Cutler, 'Gramsci, Law and the Culture of Global Capitalism' (2006) 8:4 Critical Rev Int'l Soc and Pol Phil 527, 528.

33 Ryan Gunderson, 'Ideology Critique for the Environmental Social Sciences: What Reproduces the Treadmill of Production?' (2017) 12:3 Nature and Culture 263, 269–270.

34 Sonja Buckel and Andreas Fischer-Lescano, 'Gramsci Reconsidered: Hegemony in Global Law' (2009) 22:3 Leiden JIL 437, 438.

35 Vito De Lucia, *The 'Ecosystem Approach' in International Environmental Law: Genealogy and Politics* (Routledge 2019) 143.

demands'.[36] This concern invites greater interest in uncovering the depoliticised character of the concept. For example, just when international environmentalism started taking root in the late 1960s, dominant state and corporate interests in the North began a seemingly pro-environmentalist discourse around this new phase of (international) engagement. These voices professed their sensitivity to the global transmission of sustainable development in the decades that followed while at the same time devising schemes aimed at taming the influence of sustainable development, including over economic growth.[37] Accordingly, in respect of sustainable development, it has been suggested that 'Gramscian notions of hegemonic rule are pertinent, as particular social, political, and cultural factors generate "historic blocs", where consensus over knowledge and practice reigns and a close alliance of actors maintains a particular position'.[38]

Drawing on this culture-informed Gramscian framework, the capacity to recognise difference helps critical scholars to avoid lumping together marginalised Southern peoples and their challenges under the totalising effects of globalisation.[39] It also helps to unpack the complicated connections between peoples, concepts, and issues. In this respect, TWAIL scholars share similar concerns over the constitution and meaning of sustainable development since the concept functions as a hegemonic device for disciplining development by (mis-)representing itself as an acceptable cultural aspiration.[40] This analysis thus immerses sustainable development in a TWAIL context by advancing the agenda for rewriting the histories of human interrelations with nature from a history-from-below perspective, while resisting dominant narratives that frequently represent, maintain, and consolidate the interests of the Global North or those of Southern elites.[41] As a result, it is important to acknowledge

[36] Thomas Wanner, 'The New Passive Revolution of the Green Economy and Growth Discourse: Maintaining the "Sustainable Development" of Neoliberal Capitalism' (2015) 20:1 New Pol Econ 21, 24.

[37] Leslie Sklair, 'The Corporate Capture of Sustainable Development and its Transformation into a "Good Anthropocene" Historical Bloc' (2019) 19:2 Civitas 296, 300.

[38] Ian Scoones, 'The Politics of Sustainability and Development' (2016) 41:1 Annual Rev Envt and Res 293, 305–306.

[39] Brian-Vincent Ikejiaku, 'International Law is Western Made Global Law: The Perception of Third-World Category' (2013) 6:2–3 Afr J Leg Studies 337, 339.

[40] Balakirshnan Rajagopal, 'Counter-Hegemonic International Law: Rethinking Human Rights and Development as a Third World Strategy' (2006) 27:5 Third World Q 767, 769.

[41] Usha Natarajan, 'Third World Approaches to International Law and the Environment' in Andreas Philippopoulos-Mihalopoulos and Victoria Brooks (eds.), *Research Methods in Environmental Law: A Handbook* (Edward Elgar 2017) 207, 222–223.

the existence of multiple histories as there is no master history from which all other histories derive their source.[42]

By denouncing the hegemony of international law over sustainable development and turning to an alternative, non-hegemonic history, it is possible to adapt the legal normativity of sustainable development into a pluralist norm.[43] In this respect, I confine my task to Africa's relationship with sustainable development. Still, my motivation travels beyond Africa to similar concerns in the wider Global South. While the intention is not to generalise outcomes, it is notable that the African context that piqued interest in the writing of this book is similar in many respects to the broader situation across the Global South.[44]

Hence, this study inspires related inquiries that focus on aspects of the Global South to improve the understanding of where the African experience is shared and where it is distinct, and to see how much there is to learn from both difference and commonality. Admittedly, a sea-change in perspective will not simply come from only one study of Africa that engages with one Eurocentric norm. It calls for a commitment to continually re-examine and rewrite the histories and concepts in a way that is attentive to the world beyond either Europe and America, or Africa. As a result, if the themes to be explored in this book and the ensuing analyses impel radical change within and outside Africa, then it aligns with my mission to revitalise the legal dimensions of the concept of sustainable development from a Global South perspective. This radical approach, in turn, will advance international law and enhance the subsequent internationalisation of the central proposition of ecolegality in this book as the outcome of that radical paradigm shift.

[42] Jeffrey James Byrne, 'Reflecting on the Global Turn in International History or: How I Learned to Stop Worrying and Love Being a Historian of Nowhere' (2018) 1 Rivista Italiana di Storia Internazionale 11; Vidya Kumar, 'Revolutionaries' in Jean d'Aspremont and Sahib Singh (eds.), *Concepts for International Law: Contributions to Disciplinary Thought* (Edward Elgar 2019) 773.

[43] De Lucia, *'Ecosystem Approach'*, 217. De Lucia highlights the dangers of counter-hegemonic approaches. He prefers non-hegemony as counter-hegemony is evocative of replacing one hegemonic form with another. It would be interesting to reconcile non-hegemony in this sense with Rajagopal's counter-hegemonic discourse.

[44] These sentiments are applicable to the 'South' in the Global North; that is, Indigenous societies in the Global North.

1.4 Africa and Sustainable Development Discourse

The legal materiality of Africa's place in the reading of the concept of sustainable development is a complex undertaking that requires an effort at defining what is implicated by the subject matter itself. Any amount of scholarly effort devoted to discussing Africa in this book must be seen as only a modest scratch on a canvas of different and rival ideas strung together. Faced with this dilemma, it is not surprising that some scholars on Africa argue any attempt at understanding Africa must be treated as 'a very short introduction to a very big topic'.[45]

Thus, to begin, the 'making' of Africa is an ahistoricised process.[46] Its construction influenced the process of international law-making and over time impacted how the colonial encounter produced marked changes to nature and Africa's environment through law.[47] As a unit of analysis, Africa lends itself to the charge of generalisation which in turn evokes critiques of Eurocentrism.[48] This is a complicated topic as the manoeuvrability of Africa since the advent of colonialism raises questions for its usage in the academic literature. This anxiety raises concerns over homogenising Africa which further provokes challenges for emancipating African customary norms from (mis-)description as non-law. Accordingly, as some postcolonial scholars have argued:

> In an attempt to represent subaltern cultures and peoples from around the world that have been systematically put under erasure for centuries, writers and scholars from various marginalised non-Western societies have been continually writing back to the metropoles and creating a countervailing balance to the hegemonic Western discourse, thereby opposing the homogenisation of their rich and diverse cultures and histories.[49]

[45] John Parker and Richard Rathbone, *African History: A Short Introduction* (Oxford University Press 2007) 1.

[46] V. Y. Mudimbe, *The Invention of Africa: Gnosis, Philosophy and the Order of Knowledge* (James Currey 1988); Edward Said, *Orientalism* (Pantheon Books 1978); Teshale Tibebu, *Hegel and the Third World: The Making of Eurocentrism in World History* (Syracuse University Press 2010).

[47] Nicole Graham, 'Dephysicalisation and Entitlement: Legal and Cultural Discourses of Place as Property' in Brad Jessup (ed.), *Environmental Discourses in Public and International Law* (Cambridge University Press 2014) 96, 105.

[48] Thomas Kwasi Tieku and Linnéa Gelot, 'An African Perspective on Global Governance' in Anna Triandafyllidou (ed.), *Global Governance from Regional Perspectives* (Oxford University Press 2017) 119, 119.

[49] Arun Kumar Pohkrel, 'Eurocentrism' in Deen K. Chatterjee (ed.), *Encyclopedia of Global Justice* (Springer 2011) 321, 325.

Despite this call to imprint Third World influences on global developments, the political class in the Global South has been unsuccessful in matching the corrective enthusiasm of its counterpart Southern critical scholarly cadre. For the most part, to model the postcolonial state after the European colonising power and to transplant Eurocentric ideologies into the postcolonial state meant that former colonies, including African states, had to resort to 'homogenisation policies in the face of multi-ethnic, multi-lingual, and multi-religious communities their states constitute'.[50] In this respect, critical international law scholars persistently urge a review of these Eurocentric epistemologies that are adopted by postcolonial states on the basis of the homogenising depiction of the Global South that assured managerialism over the socio-cultural and epistemological diversity of Southern peoples.[51]

Flowing from this awareness, the concerns regarding essentialising Africa will appear not to be without some basis. Critical scholars have frequently cautioned against the implications of homogenising Africa and its peoples. Homogenisation can lead to oversimplification, and generalisation undermines uniqueness due to an over-reliance on unsatisfactory descriptors.[52] It is thus unsurprising that some African legal scholars have been criticised as homogenising Africa owing to the manner in which these scholars generalise African themes in their scholarship.[53] In much the same way, critical legal anthropologists and legal historians are united in their conviction that a sanguine turn to homogenisation was the consequence of the colonial attempt at evolving non-Europeanised law in Africa through a warped Western 'standardisation'.[54]

[50] Berihun Adugna Gebeye, 'The Janus Face of Legal Pluralism for the Rule of Law Promotion in Sub-Saharan Africa' (2019) 53:2 Can J Afr Studies 337, 346.

[51] Gustavo Gozzi, *Rights and Civilisations: A History and Philosophy of International Law* (Cambridge University Press 2019) 293.

[52] Obiora Chinedu Okafor, '"Righting", Restructuring, and Rejuvenating the Postcolonial African State: The Case for the Establishment of an AU Special Commission on National Minorities' (2005) 13:1 Afr YBIL 43, 50.

[53] Carl Landauer, 'Taslim Olawale Elias: From British Colonial Law to Modern International Law' in Jochen von Bernstorff and Philipp Dann (eds.), *The Battle for International Law: South–North Perspectives on the Decolonisation Era* (Oxford University Press 2019) 318, 321–322. Landauer discusses the works of the celebrated Nigerian jurist T. O. Elias by highlighting parts of his scholarship that have been critiqued for their seeming generalisation of Africa.

[54] Sally Falk Moore, 'Treating Law as Knowledge: Telling Colonial Officers What to Say to Africans about Running "Their Own" Native Courts' (1992) 26:1 L and Soc'y Rev 11, 25.

Ironically, the colonising powers promoted an intentional but disorganised co-existence of both homogenisation and difference. This feature was somewhat discernible in the othering of non-European reality – in 'making distinctions at the colonial periphery, drawing boundaries between the coloniser and colonised, and classifying and categorising differences (religious, ethnic, tribal, regional) within the "native" population'.[55] Emerging from this confusion was the normative risk associated with essentialising these differences even within the knowledge that generalisation tends to disregard marked distinctions between the colonised and the coloniser.[56] Thus, while I am aware of the pitfalls of homogenisation, my preference for using Africa as an analytical framework only follows the understanding that 'essentialist forms of cultural identity may be important to transcending the assimilation effects of colonialism'.[57]

Flowing from this colonial attempt at standardising law, African customary law was regularly filtered through a Eurocentric legal prism – a test customary law was ordained to fail repeatedly – and to be finally consigned to the realms of non-legality.[58] Here, legal imperialism delegitimised customary law.[59] African customary law was thus contingent upon this exclusionary process which denied its pre-existence, normativity, agency, and self-determining evolution.[60]

[55] Jonathan Wyrtzen, 'Colonial Legitimisation–Legibility Linkages and the Politics of Identity in Algeria and Morocco' (2017) 58:2 European J Sociology 205, 207.

[56] Mai Taha, 'Self-Determination, Oil, and Islam in the Face of the League of Nations: The Mosul Dispute and the "Non-European" Legal Terrain' in Duncan French (ed.), *Statehood and Self-Determination: Reconciling Tradition and Modernity in International Law* (Cambridge University Press 2013) 324, 326.

[57] Stella M. Mkomo, 'A Postcolonial and Anti-Colonial Reading of "African" Leadership and Management in Organisation Studies: Tensions, Contradictions, and Possibilities' (2011) 18:3 Organisation 365, 369.

[58] Laurence Juma, 'From "Repugnancy" to "Bill of Rights": African Customary Law and Human Rights in Lesotho and South Africa' (2007) 21:1 Speculum Juris 88, 90. Juma provides an excellent analysis of the repugnancy test as used in British-administered colonies to assess the acceptability and subsequent application of customary law in the context of British common law. I deal extensively with the doctrine of repugnancy in Part III of this book.

[59] Basil Ugochukwu, 'From Reaction to Agency: A "Subaltern" Response to William Twining's Globalisation and Legal Scholarship' (2013) 4:4 Transnat'l Leg Theory 549, 554.

[60] Brian Z. Tamanaha, 'A Proposal for the Development of a System of Indigenous Jurisprudence in the Federated States of Micronesia' (1989) 31:1 Hastings Int'l and Comp L Rev 71, 100–101.

The return of customary law into contention as law was thus tied to an excavation and exploration of the history of the relationship between colonialism and the existence of legal orders which predated imperial rule.[61] This return is an outcome of the criticism that the ahistorical treatment of non-Western law by classical legal anthropologists accounted for the presumed non-legal status of customary law.[62] In pushing back on this corrupted history, these anthropologists seem to (mis-)appreciate the fact that, '[i]t is not simply that customary law has changed in both content and form during the colonial period. It is that the circumstances of its development made it a part of an idealisation of the past developed as an attempt to cope with social dislocation.'[63]

Flowing out of this (mis-)characterisation of customary or Indigenous law and local knowledge, much of what is known as customary law is defined as non-law.[64] It is unsurprising that a larger aspect of the legal discourse on Africa is then forced into a non-legal essence.[65] Yet, I also find it reassuring that this situation is increasingly being challenged on the basis that law must be studied through the lenses of broader normative systems including customary and Indigenous law. Here, the interplay of legal norms occurring within the context of legal pluralism must be understood as a diverse interaction within an equally multifarious legal pluriverse.[66]

In this respect, this book is not committed to a positivist, doctrinal position. It rejects the idea that ethical values and principles are not law and, in its place, proposes customary law and Indigenous cosmologies as sources of international law.[67] Understandably, for some legal scholars, the legal universe is limited to positivist law, and everything outside that narrow system is, to them, non-law.[68] This apprehension is equally true

[61] Sally Engle Merry, 'From Law and Colonialism to Law and Globalisation' (2003) 28:2 L and Soc Inquiry 569, 572.

[62] June Starr and Jane F. Collier, 'Introduction: Dialogues in Legal Anthropology' in June Starr and Jane F. Collier (eds.), *History and Power in the Study of Law: New Directions in Legal Anthropology* (Cornell University Press 1989) 1, 2.

[63] Martin Chanock, *Law, Custom and Social Order* (Cambridge University Press 1985) 4.

[64] Anthony Costa, 'The Myth of African Customary Law' (1998) 14:4 SAJHR 525, 526.

[65] Buluma Bwire, 'Integration of African Customary Legal Concepts: Restorative Justice: A Kenyan Example' (2019) 9:1 Societies 17.

[66] Paul Schiff Berman, 'The New Legal Pluralism' (2009) 5:1 Annual Rev L and Soc Science 225, 226.

[67] Peter D. Burdon, 'The Earth Community and Ecological Jurisprudence' (2013) 3:5 Oñati Socio-Legal Series 815, 818.

[68] Richard Collins, 'In Pursuit of Method in Pluralist Jurisprudence: What Exactly Is Wrong with "Non-Pluralist Jurisprudence"?' (2017) 8:4 Transnat'l Leg Theory 407, 408–409.

for international law as it demonstrates an inordinate pro-positivist proclivity in how international law obscures Third World knowledge.[69] Accordingly, a reconstructionist outlook must insist that non-Western forms of knowledge are not merely now acceptable and integrated into Eurocentric epistemologies. Rather, we must adopt a critical attitude towards law with the view to undoing the unwarranted limits imposed by homogenised knowledge frames through decentring mainstream positivist perspectives in international law.[70]

In keeping with this critique, this analysis denounces the characterisation of Indigenous and local knowledge, including African customary law and ethics as non-law. My concept of law is broader than those consigned to the constricted passageways of positivism.[71] My legal cosmos is broad enough to permit and accommodate these ideas of resistance and allow that which has been incorrectly labelled as non-law to find a way back home as law. To the extent that positivism denies the moral dimensions of law, which is a key feature of African legal theory, a singular view of law as deriving from the positivist stock is inapplicable to all legal traditions nor supportable.[72] To this end, I argue that, a strict distinction only leads to imprinting doctrinal formalism on law while excluding African legal influences. This distinction is founded on a contrived excision of law from its social context.[73] Thus, I engage with and analyse the concept of sustainable development in its visible and not-so visible forms, and within and outside popular constructions of law through an Africa-sensitive analytical framework.

1.5 Sustainable Development and Critical Third World Approaches

Sustainable development as presently theorised and practicalised emanates from a Eurocentric premise. However, as a branch of international

[69] Steven Ratner, 'Ethics and International Law: Integrating the Global Justice Project(s)' (2013) 5:1 Int'l Theory 1, 7.

[70] Picq, 'Situating the Amazon in World Politics', 178.

[71] Anne Orford, 'Positivism and the Power of International Law' (2000) 24:2 Melbourne UL Rev 502, 504.

[72] F. U. Okafor, 'Legal Positivism and the African Legal Tradition' (1984) 24:2 Int'l Phil Q 157; F. U. Okafor, 'A Philosophical Reflection on African Native Law' (1988) 22:1 J Val Inquiry 39, 49–50; Idowu William, 'Eurocentrism and the Separability–Inseperability Debate: Challenges from African Cultural Jurisprudence' (2009) 2:9 J Pan Afr Studies 123.

[73] Jiří Přibáň, 'A Sociology of Legal Distinctions: Introducing Contemporary Interpretations of Classic Socio-Legal Concepts' (2017) 44:1 JL and Soc'y 1, 3.

law, international environmental law evokes deep concerns for a marginalised transnational subclass of peoples and the environment relative to the concept of sustainable development. These critiques are spawned by critical scholarship including postcolonial theory and TWAIL. These theories and methods thus help in parsing the political and epistemological character of sustainable development.[74]

Considering that law and politics are in a never-ending cycle of normative interaction and reproduction, it is necessary to review social and economic progress on the one hand, and to reconceive the humanity–nature connection on the other hand as mutually constitutive and not separate paradigms. Based on this understanding, it is important to inculcate into this appreciation, the moral dimensions that should attend the law–ecology nexus but are often excluded by positivist law.[75] Thus, TWAIL scholars are upfront about TWAIL's intentions and value for international law – just as I argue here that sustainable development must be imbued with alternative legal conceptions derived from non-Western legal ontologies.[76]

TWAIL builds up on the theoretical base of other critical approaches including generations of Third World scholarship.[77] Its critical heritage aids Third World challenges to Eurocentrism.[78] I deploy TWAIL's open-textured radicalism as it undertakes both historical and postcolonial critiques of international law.[79] Here, a critical Third World analysis assesses how international law fosters the creation and maintenance of an unequal and inequitable international system that is veiled by an universalist aura. So, my interest in TWAIL becomes even more pronounced considering the evolution and practice of sustainable development are patterned along the classical divisions of the North and South in international relations.[80]

74 Peer Zumbansen, 'Transnational Law as Socio-Legal Theory and Critique: Prospects for "Law and Society" in a Divided World' (2019) 67:3 Buff L Rev 909, 949.

75 Alf Hornborg, 'Colonialism in the Anthropocene: The Political Ecology of the Money–Energy–Technology Complex' (2019) 10:1 J Human Rights and Envt 7, 15.

76 Joyeeta Gupta, 'Toward Sharing Our Ecospace' in Simon Nicholson and Sikina Jinnah (eds.), *New Earth Politics Essays from the Anthropocene* (MIT Press 2016) 271, 284–285.

77 Steven R. Ratner and Anne-Marie Slaughter, 'Appraising the Methods of International Law: A Prospectus for Readers' (1999) 93:2 Am JIL 291; Makau Mutua and Antony Anghie, 'What is TWAIL?' (2000) 94 Am SIL: Proc Annual Mtg 31, 38.

78 Fagbayibo, 'Critical Approach', 1.

79 Eslava and Pahuja, 'Beyond the Post(Colonial)', 196; Dipesh Chakrabarty, *Provincialising Europe: Postcolonial Thought and Historical Difference* (Princeton University Press 2000).

80 Carmen G. Gonzalez, 'Bridging the North–South Divide: International Environmental Law in the Anthropocene' (2015) 32:2 Pace Envt'l L Rev 407, 434.

A Third World perspective provides key insights into the doctrinal aspects of the core–periphery relations in international law by examining how those relations regularly constitute, re-constitute, and undermine the international legal order.[81] This collaborative effort between international law and social organisation is important in fostering an understanding of how social phenomena like poverty, development, ecological degradation, and disease are understood as possessing a global character; with each of them requiring a separate international legal regime.[82] Such nuancing of perspectives is important, mainly because international environmental law generally, and more particularly sustainable development, is at the intersection of the oppositional politics of the North–South within international law-making.[83] Hence, a Third World analysis must similarly approach international environmental law as a field in international law that was already a deeply flawed disciplinary form conceptualised to over-promise and under-deliver as a result of this North–South politics.[84]

To better understand TWAIL's utility, I briefly explore the history of the Third World in critical scholarship. As the French version of *tiers monde*, the Third World refers to the shared experiences of the peoples of the Global South who experienced the imperial domination and violence of European colonialism.[85] The expression mimicked the 'third estate' as used in pre-revolutionary France, but also described the countries that belonged neither to the First World (the United States and Western Europe) nor to the Second World (the Soviet Union). At the end of Cold War bipolarity, the term 'Third World' assumed a much lesser descriptive-analytical significance.[86] However, its continued use was based on the

[81] Anita M. Halvorssen, *Equality among Unequals in International Environmental Law: Differential Treatment for Developing Countries* (Westview Press 1999) 27–28.

[82] Antony Anghie, 'Domination' in Jean d'Aspremont and Sahib Singh (eds.), *Concepts for International Law: Contributions to Disciplinary Thought* (Edward Elgar 2019) 222, 231.

[83] Parvez Hassan, 'Role of the South in the Development of International Environmental Law' (2017) 1:2 Chinese J Envt'l L 133, 145.

[84] Natarajan and Khoday, 'Locating Nature' (2014), 577.

[85] Marcin Solarz, 'Third World': The 60th Anniversary of a Concept that Changed the World' (2012) 33:9 Third World Q 1561; Vera Chouinard, 'Living on the Global Peripheries of Law: Disability Human Rights Law in Principle and Practice in the Global South' (2018) 7:1 Laws 1, 2; Ida Nursoo, 'Indigenous Law, Colonial Injustice and the Jurisprudence of Hybridity' (2018) 50:1 J Leg Pluralism and Unofficial L 56.

[86] Vicky Randall, 'Using and Abusing the Concept of the Third World: Geopolitics and the Comparative Political Study of Development and Underdevelopment' (2004) 25:1 Third World Q 41, 43.

commonality of a geo-historical experience rather than uniformity.[87] Today, the expression is now more than just a group of states participating in international law. It incorporates marginalised and disenfranchised peoples across the globe by welcoming 'the project of subalternity, in which those who do not fit the frames of Eurocentrism and modernity can be heard and become full participants in their governance'.[88] As a consequence, since the post-Cold War period began, there has ceased to be a distinguishable coherence in reference to the Third World.[89]

While this historical trajectory suggests the expression, the Third World, emerges in the Global South, its counterhegemonic significance goes beyond the state in international law by invoking a unique identity that acknowledges a wider, yet oft-neglected, political geography within the international legal system.[90] States from the Global South and their peoples have since appropriated the term to advance a panoply of interests including claims to or opposing the international system.[91] And, while the emergence of TWAIL is fairly recent, its connection to the other more established fields of critical scholarship like postcolonial (legal) theory lends support to the central tenets of the Third World.[92] It is hardly surprising then that some TWAIL scholars have described it as 'an established postcolonial theory of law'.[93] Even so, TWAIL's identity is distinct in its commitment to connecting Third World intellectualism and activism to the marginalised peoples of the South.[94]

[87] Okafor, 'Newness, Imperialism, and International Legal Reform', 171.

[88] Mutua and Anghie, 'What is TWAIL?', 37.

[89] Andrea Bianchi, *International Law Theories: An Inquiry into Different Ways of Thinking*, 1st ed. (Oxford University Press 2017) 205.

[90] Mark T. Berger, 'The End of the 'Third World' (1994) 15:2 Third World Q 257, 270; Obiora Chinedu Okafor, 'Critical Third World Approaches to International Law (TWAIL): Theory, Methodology, or Both?' (2008) 10:4 Int'l Community L Rev 371.

[91] Bernard Green, 'Toward a Definition of the Term Third World' (1980) 1:1 Boston College Third World LJ 13, 15.

[92] Madhav Kholsa, 'The TWAIL Discourse: The Emergence of a New Phase' (2007) 9:3 Int'l Community L Rev 291. TWAIL as a legal tradition is quite recent, but its predecessor intellectual impulses are much older, dating to the period of decolonisation when the works of jurists including T. O. Elias, Mohammed Bedjaoui, and R. P. Anand pushed for significant reform in international law.

[93] Tracy-Lynn Humby, 'Evaluating the Value of TWAIL, Environmental Justice, and Decolonisation Discourses as Framing Lenses for Environmental Law' (2017) 26:2 Transnat'l L & Contemp Probs 318, 319.

[94] Natarajan, 'Third World Approaches', 221.

Accordingly, the Third World remains an appropriate intellectual self-description for reimagining the project of sustainable development.[95]

In like manner, the expression Global South is linked to the Third World. The historical description of the Third World was altered with the rise in 'globalised' social and economic changes and other geopolitical shifts secured during international negotiations.[96] Together with these geopolitically-informed changes, the process of globalisation further threatened to expose the hidden inequalities in human society.[97] These changes animated further exchanges on renewing non-Western inquiry.[98] In search of a better description of these advances, the term 'South' or the 'Global South' emerged alongside the 'Global North' or 'North' as a scholarly concern and a practitioner-oriented guidepost to describing advances occurring in different geographies and geopolitics that are linked to global inequities.[99] Thus, as Nour Dados and Raewyn Connell have both argued:

> the North–South terminology, then, like core–periphery, arose from an allegorical application of categories to name patterns of wealth, privilege, and development across broad regions. The term Global South functions more as a metaphor for underdevelopment. It references an entire history of colonialism, neo-colonialism, neo-imperialism, and differential economic change through which large inequalities in living standards, life expectancy, and access to resources are maintained.[100]

The term Global South has since seen increasing analytical usage with a growing body of literature especially in subaltern studies.[101] However, its use in this book is informed by the TWAIL tradition which considers the idea

[95] Obiora Chinedu Okafor, 'Globalism, Memory and 9/11: A Critical Third World Perspective' in Fleur Johns, Richard Joyce, and Sundhya Pahuja (eds.), *Events: The Force of International Law* (Routledge 2011) 234, 236; Antony Anghie, 'Rethinking International Law: A TWAIL Retrospective' (2023) 34:1 European JIL 7, 10.

[96] Martin W. Lewis, 'Is There a Third World?' (1999) 98:631 Current History 355.

[97] Marc Williams, 'The Third World and Global Environmental Negotiations: Interests, Institutions and Ideas' (2005) 5:3 Global Envt'l Pol 48.

[98] Edward W. Said, 'Representing the Colonised: Anthropology's Interlocutors' (1989) 15:2 Critical Inquiry 205; Andrew Hurrell, 'Narratives of Emergence: Rising Powers and the End of the Third World?' (2013) 33:2 Revista de Economia Politica 203, 207.

[99] T. Tu Huynh and Danson Sylvester Kahyana, 'A General Introduction' (2020) 19:1–2 Afr and Asian Studies 1, 2.

[100] Nour Dados and Raewyn Connell, 'The Global South' (2012) 11:1 Contexts 13.

[101] Arghyrios A. Fatouros, 'International Law and the Third World' (1964) 50:5 Va L Rev 783, 784–785.

of the Third World as both an intellectual force and a political project.[102] The intellectual impetus of the Third World category keeps alive the historical dynamic of difference that traces, beyond the formal emergence of the term, back into the imperialist decimation and suppression of knowledge in the Global South. This wider conception of what constitutes the Third World thus has its history dating back to more than half a century ago.[103] However, since the end of Cold War politics, it is difficult to ascertain a distinguishable distinction between the expressions, the Global South and Third World.

For some international law scholars, 'the very notion of the "Third World" is ill-conceived to begin with'.[104] Here, there has been concern over how some Third World scholars see China, which self-identifies as Third World, as mimicking some of the exploitative practices of the Global North while fiercely claiming a Global South identity.[105] Still, interestingly, China prefers to self-identify as a developing state. Presumably, this self-identification is meant to under-emphasise the contentious political significance of China being labelled as a Third World or Global South state.[106] Admittedly, this ambivalence can help or hurt Southern efforts or affect the framing of Third World resistance in international law. It is in this sense that some scholars argue the term Third World is less relevant today. In their view, the disproportionately wide-ranging economic resources and political power the world is now witnessing among some states that have always self-identified as part of the Third World including China, Brazil, Singapore, and India, obliterate the remaining significance of the application of the Third World category to these states and their peoples.[107]

102 Ibid.

103 Ibid.

104 Bianchi, *International Law Theories*, 205.

105 Sumudu Atapattu and Carmen Gonzalez, 'The North–South Divide in International Environmental Law: Framing the Issues' in Shawkat Alam, Sumudu Atapattu, Carmen G. Gonzalez and Jona Razzaque (eds.), *International Environmental Law and the Global South* (Cambridge University Press 2015) 1, 5.

106 Zhian Wang, 'The Functional Approach in le Droit International de Développement: A Theoretical Appraisal' in Shotaro Hamamoto, Hironobu Sakai, and Akiho Shibata (eds.), *"L'Être Situé", Effectiveness and Purposes of International Law: Essays in Honour of Professor Ryuichi Ida* (Brill 2015) 37, 37.

107 Okafor, 'Globalism, Memory and 9/11', 235; Robert B. Zoellick, 'The End of the Third World: Modernizing Multilateralism for a Multipolar World' (2010) 16:3 L & Bus Rev Americas 317; Robert H. Wade, 'Emerging World Order? From Multipolarity to Multilateralism in the G20, the World Bank and the IMF' (2011) 39:3 Pol and Soc'y 347.

Either way, the Third World is a political project and an intellectual concept that underpinned a re-conceptualisation of a less unequal and a more just world.[108]

The Third World is also praxis, since it recognises the 'inseparability of theory and practice'.[109] Praxis is central to TWAIL, requiring in essence, a transformation of the politics of scholarship to a politics of practice.[110] This scholarly choice does not seek to undermine the value of the Global South (or the South, Southern states, or similar iterations) which I adopt in describing geo-historical spaces of historically marginalised classes; a description which, where appropriate, suggests there can be a South in the North and *vice versa*.[111] Rather, TWAIL uncovers this South in the North phenomenon by demonstrating how, for instance, settler colonial states like Australia, Canada, New Zealand, and the United States also created a 'Southern' subclass in the Global North.[112] In this respect, the expression, Global South, has flourished within TWAIL and in its analytical relevance.[113] Therefore, as a 'historically aware methodology', TWAIL is a standard-bearer of the Third World confrontation with the Eurocentric character of international law.[114]

Accordingly, TWAIL highlights how non-European experiences are often relegated through legal instrumentalism. This is also seen in the oppression of non-European peoples through Eurocentric institutions,

[108] Sundhya Pahuja, *Decolonising International Law: Development, Economic Growth and the Politics of Universality* (Cambridge University Press 2011) 261–262.

[109] Obiora Chinedu Okafor, 'Enacting TWAILian Praxis in Non-Academic Habitats: Toward a Conceptual Framework' (2016) 110 Am JIL Unbound 20, 21.

[110] Natarajan et al., 'Third World Approaches', 1947; Obiora Chinedu Okafor, 'Praxis and the International (Human Rights) Law Scholar: Towards the Intensification of TWAILian Dramaturgy' (2016) 33:3 Windsor YB Access Just 1; Georges Abi-Saab, 'The Third World Intellectual in Praxis: Confrontation, Participation, or Operation behind Enemy Lines?' (2016) 37:11 Third World Q 1957, 1962.

[111] Annette Trefzer, Jeffrey T. Jackson, Kathryn McKee and Kirsten Dellinger, 'The Global South and/in the Global North: Interdisciplinary Investigations' (2014) 8:2 Global South 1. The South in the North refers to marginalised classes, including Indigenous communities, whose lives and experiences have been equally peripheralised in much the same way as most of the peoples of the Global South.

[112] Amar Bhatia, 'The South of the North: Building on Critical Approaches to International Law with Lessons from the Fourth World' (2012) 14:1 Oregon Rev Int'l L 131, 150. Bhatia uses TWAIL analysis to explain this 'South in the North' phenomenon by showing how settler colonial states created a 'Southern' class in the Global North.

[113] Fatouros, 'International Law and the Third World', 784–785.

[114] James Thuo Gathii, 'TWAIL: A Brief History, of Its Origins, Its Decentralised Network, and a Tentative Bibliography' (2011) 3:1 Trade L & Dev 26, 33–34.

practices, and attitudes.[115] TWAIL queries these hegemonic attributes of international law. The concern is that international law influences international relations through less visible strategies.[116] Since international law has the capacity to elide difference and incommensurability by glossing over inequity and inequality across both spatiality and temporality, a TWAIL analysis exposes these less obvious matters that are routinely ignored by international law scholars.[117] Accordingly, it is unsurprising that key vocabularies like 'development', 'sustainability', 'rights', and 'the environment', while commonly used in the literature, continually evoke multiple meanings; are poorly explained; are often presumed to mean the same thing to different interest groups; or are purposefully constructed to mask ecological harm.[118]

In this respect, TWAIL's purpose for deconstructing and reconstructing law is aimed at alleviating the conditions of Southern peoples. This viewpoint adopted by TWAIL endorses a rehabilitated vision of international law as less state-centred and more people-centric.[119] In mulling over the critical invitation to decamp from the idea of the state as the organising framework of international law and mooring to peoples, I am also mindful of how classist hierarchies among states can be transported into peoples based on this 'instrumentality of international law'.[120] Still, I agree it is important that legal scholarship highlights peoples, even individuals and their experiences and the lessons they teach us.[121] By imagining the peoples of the South beyond artificial (national)

[115] Mutua and Anghie, 'What Is TWAIL?', 32.

[116] B. S. Chimni, 'Third World Approaches to International Law: A Manifesto' (2006) 8:1 Int'l Community L Rev 3.

[117] Dianne Otto, 'Subalternity and International Law: The Problems of Global Community and Incommensurability of Difference' in Peter Fitzpatrick and Eve Darian-Smith (eds.), *Laws of the Postcolonial* (University of Michigan Press 1999) 145.

[118] Muthucumaraswamy Sornarajah, 'Power and Justice: Third World Resistance in International Law' (2006) 10 Singapore YBIL 19, 29. Sornarajah offers a vivid account of the continuum of capitalism dating back to the colonial enterprise, and how it manifests in the contemporary international legal context. He notes, thus, '[t]he linkages between the areas isolated for study must be stressed again. Multinational business, now conducted through multinational corporations, is crucial to the maintenance of economic power, as it was in the times of colonialism.'

[119] Kwadwo Appiagyei-Atua, 'Ethical Dimensions of Third-World Approaches to International Law (TWAIL): A Critical Review' (2015) 8:3–4 Afr J Leg Studies 209; Opeoluwa Adetoro Badaru, 'Examining the Utility of Third World Approaches in International Law for International Human Rights Law' (2008) 10:4 Int'l Community L Rev 379, 381.

[120] Muthucumaraswamy Sornarajah, 'On Fighting for Global Justice: The Role of a Third World International Lawyer' (2016) 37:11 Third World Q 1972, 1972.

[121] Natasha Affolder, 'Transnational Environmental Law's Missing People' (2019) 8:3 Transnat'l Envt'l L 463, 469.

frontiers, TWAIL fulfils its reformatory assertion to join Indigenous peoples in the Global North – the South of the North – to the peoples of the Global South.[122] This approach is a significant point as Indigenous peoples are twice marginalised: first, through their colonial experience; and, second, by the postcolonial state. In consequence, for international law scholars, a necessary first step is to understand the history behind the struggles of marginalised sub-classes before proceeding to engage with their present conditions else such scholarly endeavour would only further worsen the conditions of these peoples.[123]

Therefore, as a scholarly choice, I adopt TWAIL in unbundling global power structures as demonstrated through the geo-historical conditioning of contemporary phenomena.[124] My choice thus motivates a scrutiny of the dynamic of difference and the jurisdiction of non-Europeanised epistemological experience in international legal discourse as demonstrated in the 'ecology of knowledges'.[125] Even so, my inquiry travels beyond the historicity of the origins of international law to examine its current manifestations and how the discipline continues to irradiate colonial legacies of disempowerment and subjugation.[126] This interdependence between TWAIL and other critical theories, including postcolonial theory, broadly construed, is inspired by a common thread of resistance operating at different levels through the work of Third World scholars or in the ground-breaking decisions of judges from the Global South sitting on international courts and other tribunals.[127] For example,

122 Bhatia, 'South of the North', 156.

123 Mickelson, 'Taking Stock of TWAIL Histories', 360; Gerardo J. Munarriz, 'Rhetoric and Reality: The World Bank Development Policies, Mining Corporations, and Indigenous Communities in Latin America' (2008) 10:4 Int'l Community L Rev 431, 432.

124 Gathii, 'TWAIL: A Brief History', 40.

125 Boaventura de Sousa Santos, *Toward a New Legal Common Sense: Law, Globalisation, and Emancipation*, 3rd ed. (Cambridge University Press 2020) 470–471; Boaventura de Sousa Santos, *Epistemologies of the South: Justice against Epistemicide* (Routledge 2014) 189. I agree with Santos that the recognition of 'the principle of incompleteness of all knowledges is a pre-condition for epistemological dialogues and debates among different knowledges'. What this means is that one normative expression, like Eurocentrism, cannot hold a place of epistemological pre-eminence and privilege over others.

126 Srinivas Burra, 'TWAIL's Others: A Caste Critique of TWAILers and Their Field of Analysis' (2016) 33:3 Windsor YB Access Just 111, 113; Luis Eslava, 'Istanbul Vignettes: Observing the Everyday Operation of International Law' (2014) 2:1 London Rev IL 3.

127 Christopher Weeramantry and Nathaniel Berman, 'The Grotius Lectures Series' (1999) 14:6 Am U Int'l L Rev 1515, 1528–1529; Antony Anghie, 'C. G. Weeramantry at the International Court of Justice' (2001) 14:4 Leiden JIL 829, 844–848; Michelle L. Burgis, *Boundaries of Discourse on the International Court of Justice: Mapping Arguments in Arab Territorial Disputes* (Martinus Nijhoff 2009) 22–27.

the Somali jurist, Judge Abdulqawi Yusuf, who was President of the International Court of Justice (ICJ), is distinguished as 'a leading figure in the progressive wing of the Court, writing on African contributions to international law, bringing a strong African voice in international academic and adjudicative circles'.[128] The intermingling of ideas and their advocates as demonstrated in the works of the likes of Judge Yusuf ensures the durability of TWAIL not only in its ideational deployment, but also in its material manifestation in international law and practice.

Other scholars from the Global South, like the late Sri Lankan Judge Christopher Weeramantry, in prominent cases at the ICJ, affirmed the relevance of Third World approaches and Indigenous legal cosmologies to sustainable development.[129] Judge Weeramantry's enduring radical mark of Third World legal thought on ICJ jurisprudence is demonstrated in notable decisions on environment-related themes like 'the precautionary principle, the concept of sustainable development, the concept of duties *erga omnes*, principles of individual responsibility, of trusteeship of earth resources, of intergenerational equity, of planetary responsibility and so forth'.[130] Thus, Third World approaches are central to explaining why the transformative potential of sustainable development in international law currently seems impossible to attain as there is little effort at reorienting current paradigms of legal Eurocentrism.[131]

In thinking through TWAIL's reformatory force, history becomes that important missing piece of the puzzle. Taking this historical turn into account, critical scholars encourage analyses into international law for further evidence on TWAIL's anticolonial objective.[132] Here, while TWAIL scholars like Antony Anghie, B. S. Chimni, James Thuo Gathii,

[128] Abi-Saab, 'Third World Intellectual in Praxis', 1962–1963.

[129] Gathii, 'Promise of International Law'. As Gathii has argued, Third World judges have been leading innovative approaches to interpreting law at all levels, including at the International Court of Justice. For example, 'Third World jurists like Justice Christopher Weeramantry's powerful pro-environmental dissenting opinion in the ICJ's 1999 decision in Kasikili/Sedudu Island is particularly noteworthy.'

[130] Punsara Amarasinghe, 'In Praise of Kaleidoscopic Judge: A Different Reading of Judge C. G. Weeramantry's Jurisprudence before the Power Politics of the ICJ' (2020) 3 Przegląd Politologiczny 109, 112.

[131] Klaus Bosselmann, 'A Vulnerable Environment: Contextualising Law with Sustainability' (2011) 1:1 J Human Rights and Envt 45, 51.

[132] Mohsen al Attar and Vernon Tava, 'TWAIL Pedagogy: Legal Pedagogy for Emancipation' (2009) 15:1 Palestine YB Int'l L 7; Valentina Vadi, 'International Law and Its Histories: Methodological Risks and Opportunities' (2017) 58:2 Harvard Int'l LJ 311.

and an ever-increasing cadre of newer critical law scholars have demonstrated an unwavering commitment to uncovering and retrenching the *longue durée* of international law, a longstanding criticism is that TWAIL lacks serious commitment to history.[133]

On this subject, TWAIL scholars are criticised for doing very little with the historicity of international law.[134] However, this criticism is misconceived and misplaced. The commitment of TWAIL scholars to history has led to important insights into the presumed neutrality of key terminologies and concepts in international law that have rarely been subjected to any critical inquiry nor have had their contexts challenged with the intentionality to examine their origins and presumed universal acceptance absent their Eurocentric specificity.[135] It is in this sense that the ahistoricism of international environmental law becomes apparent as most accounts on the history of the discipline periodise its emergence along with the 1972 Stockholm Conference. This is done while paying little or no attention to the historical, imperially sanctioned ecological destruction and resulting awareness that predated that conference. Accordingly, I share in the views of TWAIL scholars like Karin Mickelson over the ahistoricism of international law as leading international environmental law texts and other source materials have routinely obscure relevant disciplinary histories or simply give them casual treatment.[136]

Recent observations support Mickelson's point. In this respect, it is observed that other general international law texts simply also fail to refer to or take seriously works 'associated with TWAIL or other non-European histories of international law'.[137] Nonetheless, ever since Mickelson's prodigious work challenged this aspect of the history

[133] Antony Anghie, 'Francisco de Vitoria and the Colonial Origins of International Law' (1996) 5:3 Soc and Leg Studies 321; Antony Anghie, 'Finding the Peripheries: Sovereignty and Colonialism in Nineteenth-Century Law' (1999) 40:1 Harvard Int'l LJ 1; B. S. Chimni, 'Customary International Law: A Third World Perspective' (2018) 112:1 Am JIL 1. Chimni provides an excellent Third World account on the connection between customary international law and the origins of capitalism in this article.

[134] John Harrington and Ambreena Manji, 'The Limits of Socio-Legal Radicalism: Social and Legal Studies and Third World Scholarship' (2017) 26:6 Soc and Leg Studies 700, 709.

[135] Gathii, 'Agenda of Third World Approaches', 167–172.

[136] Mickelson, 'South, North', 54–60.

[137] Henry Jones and Aoife O'Donoghue, 'History and Self-Reflection in the Teaching of International Law' (2022) 10:1 London Rev IL 71, 92–93.

of international law, newer members of TWAIL's growing network have slowly followed up and also cautioned against ahistoricising international law by recounting how it has fostered a certain (often Western) view of environmental consciousness, which is still alive today.[138] Thus, in seeking to move past these histories, TWAIL scholars caution against 'the willed forgetting of international law's imperial past'.[139]

So, in keeping with how the process of retooling histories leads to telling contrived stories, I adopt a 'radical historical critique' of sustainable development to unravel the usefulness of the turn to history.[140] This radical approach proceeds on the grounds that both classical historical accounts of international law and the critique of those accounts often rely on a similar set of vocabularies that tend to close off newer perspectives.[141] This approach might open itself to challenges on the basis of the absence of rigour occasioned by 'linguistic barriers'; 'social and cultural obstacles' which suggest new histories only seek to resist 'settled' histories; or at the 'risk of unintelligibility' which suggests critical historical reviews might not be understood within the orthodox systems of writing histories on international law.[142] Even so, I do not think these concerns over the place and use of history should operate to restrict a rereading of the multiple histories of international law. International law scholars should not be helplessly bound to disciplinary canons if meaningful alternatives are discoverable.[143] Neither do I think international law scholars should be unduly confined by the ever-present charge of anachronism levelled at them by historians.[144] My reasoning is quite

138 Natarajan and Dehm, 'Where Is the Environment?', 3.

139 Orford, 'International Law and the Limits of History', 298.

140 Jean d'Aspremont, 'Turntablism in the History of International Law' (2020) 22:2–3 J History IL 472, 490.

141 Liliana Obregón, 'Martti Koskenniemi's Critique of Eurocentrism in International Law' in Wouter Werner, Marieke de Hoon, and Alexi Galán (eds.), *The Law of International Lawyers: Reading Martti Koskenniemi* (Cambridge University Press 2017) 360.

142 d'Aspremont, 'Turntablism', 489–490.

143 David Armitage and Jennifer Pitts, '"This Modern Grotius": An Introduction to the Life and Thought of C. H. Alexandrowicz' in Charles H Alexandrowicz (ed.), *The Law of Nations in Global History* (Oxford University Press 2017) 1, 28–31. Armitage and Pitts have suggested Hugo Grotius, the supposed father of modern international law, drew upon the knowledge of Southeast Asia local maritime law and practice he gained through his work with the Dutch East India Company. This knowledge significantly contributed to the writing of his *Mare Liberum*; Johns, 'Disciplinary Privilege', 189.

144 Orford, *International Law and the Politics of History*, 105–177. Orford discussed anachronism in the study of the history of international law. For her current position

simple – a 'legal reading differs from a historical reading, in that it is not concerned with the past as history but with the past as law'.[145] So, despite pockets of resistance, we must remember that such claims of 'intelligibility of current histories should not be exaggerated, for many of the histories found in the international legal literature rest on impressions of intelligibility'.[146]

Thus, it is impossible to discount the ahistoricising effects of international environmental law in making sustainable development, since law, for TWAIL scholars, is a continuum, with the past, present, and future interlinked and interlocking with each other seamlessly.[147] The reading of this aspect of international law from a history-oriented point must thus engage with the emergence of sustainable development, its evolution, and normativity.[148] While I am conscious of the pitfalls of reductionist arguments, I think what 'matters is that these new markers, periodisation and causal sequencing displace the markers, periodisation and causal sequencing of common disciplinary histories'.[149] It is at this point that terminologies or expressions such as nature, the environment, sustainable development, and similar vocabularies of international law induce substantive anxieties for Third World aspirations.[150]

This commitment to look beyond a pristine reading of history re-echoes Simon Chesterman's reflection that, 'the international law academic – more, I would argue, than perhaps any other discipline – has the potential to affect the subject matter of the study. We are not scientists merely observing the phenomena around us.'[151] Drawing upon

on the issue, see chapter 4 (History's Lawyers) of Orford's new book on how she revisited the Cambridge (historical) school on international law and anachronism.

145 Anne Orford, 'On International Legal Method' (2013) 1:1 London Rev IL 166, 177.

146 d'Aspremont, 'Turntablism', 490.

147 George Forji Amin, 'A Marxist and TWAIL Reading of the Oxford Handbook of the Sources of International Law' (2020) 19:1 Chinese JIL 182; Gathii, 'Agenda of Third World Approaches', 163–168.

148 Matthew Craven, 'Theorising the Turn to History in International Law' in Anne Orford and Florian Hoffmann (eds.), *The Oxford Handbook of the Theory of International Law* (Oxford University Press 2016) 22, 33.

149 Jean d'Aspremont, *The Critical Attitude and the History of International Law* (Brill 2019), 45.

150 Antonius R. Hippolyte, 'Foreign Investment Law and Developing Countries' in Markus Krajewski and Rhea T. Hoffmann (eds.), *Research Handbook on Foreign Direct Investment* (Edward Elgar 2019) 72, 102–103.

151 Simon Chesterman, 'Herding Schrödinger's Cats: The Limits of the Social Science Approach to International Law' (2021) 22:1 Chicago JIL 49, 56.

this caution, I embark upon a legal reading of these histories with an awareness of the limits of this intellectual exercise. However, reading the past as law is necessary to discover law for the present and future, as well as its alternative frames. This point is also true for the study of the concept of sustainable development since I am not studying the concept merely for the sake of historiography.[152]

[152] Orford, 'International Law and the Limits of History', 297; Kate Purcell, 'On the Uses and Advantages of Genealogy for International Law' (2020) 33:1 Leiden JIL 13, 16.

2

The Logic of Sustainable Development

Law, Politics, and the History of an Idea

> Man is an animal whose politics places his existence as a living being in question.*

2.1 Introduction

This chapter undertakes a conceptual journey that moves through four different manifestations of the idea underpinning our human relations with the non-human world. It argues that the analytical framework for the concept of sustainable development tends to move through four phases of conceptual progression: beginning with 'nature', which morphed into 'the environment', became 'development', and finally transmuted into 'sustainable development'. These different moving parts are, however, interconnected, as it is principally the idea of human intervention that defines this conceptual fluidity. This chapter demonstrates that this periodisation is flawed as these different phases continue to influence each other even if not readily perceptible. The fundamental concern is that ecological integrity is at the periphery of all these stages and, until it assumes centre-stage, the attempts at realising sustainable development will remain elusive.

The conceptual mutability discussed in this chapter involves an interplay of history, law, politics, and ethics. The broad approach adopted here is crucial as sustainable development draws upon different sources and cognate theories to build up its content.[1] Even so, I am interested in these other theoretical motivations only to the extent that they illuminate the present analysis. Additionally, to arrive at the legal content of the concept of sustainable development, it is necessary to devote some effort

* Michel Foucault, *The History of Sexuality: An Introduction*, translated by Robert Hurley (Vintage Books 1990) 143.

1 Virginie Barral, 'Sustainable Development in International Law: Nature and Operation of an Evolutive Legal Norm' (2012) 23:2 European JIL 377.

to examining how these other cognate theories are reflected in the structural constitution of sustainable development.

Thus, a substantial part of the discussion in this chapter is informed by the far-reaching consequences of neoliberal ideologies and Eurocentric philosophies in constituting the interaction between law and nature (and its different iterations).[2] Here, the interaction between capitalism and neoliberal ideologies manifests in the evolution of the four-fold idea under consideration. While the issues and concerns described and analysed in this chapter and the critical perspectives they invoke are worthy of a longer treatment, the discussions are necessarily curtailed and exploratory as I am seeking only to foreground a conceptual framework for further analysis in the subsequent chapters in this book.

The analysis in this chapter spans other ideas that facilitated human efforts to subjugate nature and inaugurate a human-centred dominance. These ideas, which were mostly founded on modern European thought, were constructed around religion, capitalism, and international law.[3] It is no surprise then that some legal scholars suggest that this interplay of ideas came together to form a 'matrix of power' with Eurocentric interests at its centre.[4] These ideas blended to project a conceptual division between humanity and nature that would become more pronounced at the height of the European colonial project when nature was ushered into the next phase, this time called the environment. By creating the environment, Eurocentric legal thought embodied this natural phenomenon in a legal expression and technique of governance called environmental law. This marked the beginning of a field of legal specialisation and imperial control in the colonised world. Regrettably, it also marked the beginning of the peripheralisation of non-European views on the natural world.

The concerns raised in the conceptual evolution of the environment are equally true for development. The conceptualisation of development demonstrates the connection between an inherently Eurocentric idea and how it interconnects with the environment to weaken the progress

[2] Larry Lohmann, 'Neoliberalism, Law and Nature' in Philippe Cullet and Sujith Koonan (eds.), *Research Handbook on Law, Environment and the Global South* (Edward Elgar 2019) 32.

[3] Usha Natarajan and Julia Dehm, 'Introduction: Where Is the Environment?' in Usha Natarajan and Julia Dehm (eds.), *Locating Nature: Making and Unmaking International Law* (Cambridge University Press 2022) 1, 8.

[4] Elena Blanco and Anna Grear, 'Personhood, Jurisdiction and Injustice: Law, Colonialities and the Global Order' (2019) 10:1 J Human Rights and Envt 86, 91.

towards sustainable development and ecological temperance. This idea of development, which was externalised beyond its European centre, became an attraction for the Global South in the period immediately following decolonisation. The South was goaded on by the North to pursue development, which was deliberately styled as the path out of poverty and under-development, and much in the same way as development was conceptualised and practised in the Global North. Besides, insofar as the Global South sought to reorient development to align with its interests, this enthusiasm failed to translate into a realisable objective since the South's own legal prescriptions did not significantly peel away from the neoliberal milieu of the prevailing development ideologies informed by colonial legacies and capitalism. It is in this sense that the study of sustainable development, and more closely development, is a critical investigation into the 'burgeoning "world history" that realigns the relative importance of the "[N]orth and [S]outh in grand narratives of development"'.[5]

In conceptualising sustainable development, the discussion here is woven around the other three themes by connecting them to the emergence of the concept, its global diffusion, and the crystallisation of its legal essence. In charting this conceptual framework, my analysis draws attention to the Eurocentric character of international law but also reflects on the subsequent application of 'Afrosensitivity' – which is a responsiveness to Africa as a conceptual technology – in sustainable development discourse and as a necessary alternative route for imprinting African legal cosmologies on this (global) phenomenon.[6]

2.2 Conceptualising Nature

Nature defies easy description. The disputation over nature's meaning and scope poses challenges to what can be done with and within its etymology.[7] However, a systematic inquiry into its history suggests an earlier socioecological awareness that united the non-human planetary community with human society. While human society had continuously

[5] Sverker Sörlin and Paul Warde, 'The Problem of the Problem of Environmental History: A Re-reading of the Field' (2007) 12:1 Envt'l History 107, 112.

[6] Modestus Nnamdi Onyeaghalaji, 'Afrosensitivity in Eurocentric and Afrocentric Narratives for Sustainable Development in Africa' (2015) 17:4 J Sust Dev in Afr 86.

[7] Frédéric Ducarme, Fabrice Filpo, and Denis Couvet, 'How the Diversity of Human Concepts of Nature Affects Conservation of Biodiversity' (2021) 35:3 Conservation Biology 1019. The authors provide an excellent discussion on the etymological diversity and linguistic significance of the term 'nature' as used across the world.

relied on the non-human domain for survival and improvements in the human condition, that process did not lead to a significant alteration in this human–nature interaction until such a time that the 'Christianisation' of Europe introduced a significant linguistic change in what nature meant and in the process, it severed the interrelationship of human society and non-human domains. This process effectively placed humanity in a dominant position as regards nature.[8] Since then, nature has been in a never-ending evolution within human control, and firmly fixed to its later iterations.[9]

In this respect, an understanding of the place of nature in the history of international law is an antecedent that presages the project of reimagining sustainable development and the future of the discipline of international environmental law.[10] The conceptualisation of nature is thus imperative to this legal inquiry since nature is the subtext for the evolution of the latter concept of sustainable development. Its import to the concept is that the two are co-constitutive of each other. They both speak to an ongoing interaction between human and non-human domains. In that paradoxical sense, without this 'social connection' between nature and sustainable development, where human intervention emerges, nature cannot be studied outside of its social context.[11]

2.2.1 Humanity and Nature: A Forced Divergence

We often think about nature as an abstract thing when we study its place in law. Yet, nature is no abstract notion.[12] We are nature, and nature is us, and nature is all around us. But, frequently, discussions on nature imply a separation between the human and non-human spheres.[13] Most

[8] Frédéric Ducarme and Denis Couvet, 'What Does "Nature" Mean?' (2020) 6:1 Palgrave Communications 1.

[9] Raymond Williams, *Ideas of Nature: Problems of Materialism and Culture* (Verso Books 1980) 68.

[10] Anna Grear and Evadne Grant, 'Introduction: In Search of Better Future Histories' in Anna Grear and Evadne Grant (eds.), *Thought, Law, Rights, and Action in an Age of Environmental Crisis* (Edward Elgar 2015) 1, 9.

[11] Michael Redclift and Graham Woodgate, 'Sustainable Development and Nature: The Social and the Material' (2013) 21 Sust Dev 92, 93.

[12] Bettina Lange, 'How to Think about "Nature–Society" Interactions in Environmental Law "in Action"' in Andreas Philippopoulos-Mihalopoulos and Victoria Brooks (eds.), *Research Methods in Environmental Law: A Handbook* (Edward Elgar 2017) 29, 37.

[13] Cait Storr, 'Denaturalising the Concept of Territory in International Law' in Usha Natarajan and Julia Dehm (eds.), *Locating Nature: Making and Unmaking International Law* (Cambridge University Press 2022) 179, 194.

academic analyses on the subject thus proceed on the grounds that this separation between human and non-human domains is central to our thinking on what nature means. However, the construction of nature is chiefly the outcome of the history of human dominance.[14] Nature, then, is a product of human knowledge and 'like everything else, is a social construct, and thus its meaning changes across time and space. In this sense, one cannot consider (let alone defend) nature independent of human experience'.[15] Even if it was possible to create such a separation, that distinction was not impervious as human existence was intrinsically a blended engagement marked by a constant interaction between human society and its ecological contexts.[16] As a result, a review of humanity's present association with nature – one that gives rise to a radical shift in our thinking of nature as an abstract entity at society's disposal to an ontologically higher duty to nature – is more urgent than ever.[17]

Accordingly, in the quest to harness law in aid of conceptualising sustainable development, nature should have been the first port of call. Nature ought to be the primary ethical consideration that should determine the content of sustainable development.[18] Yet, quite evidently, the focus has hardly ever been about nature's integrity; rather, it has been about its resources and related uses.[19] To this end, nature was theorised and practicalised as separate from human society.[20] Even recent juridical attempts at reconstructing our relationship with non-human entities, while seemingly progressive, still retain the anthropocentric register.[21] Consequently, the conceptual severability of humanity and nature arises

[14] Williams, *Ideas of Nature*, 67.

[15] Paul Wapner, 'The Changing Nature of Nature: Environmental Politics in the Anthropocene' (2014) 14:4 Global Envt'l Pol 36, 37.

[16] Margaret Davies, *EcoLaw: Legality, Life, and the Normativity of Nature* (Routledge 2021) 22.

[17] Linda Sheehan, 'Implementing Rights of Nature through Sustainability Bill of Rights' (2015) 13:1 New Zealand J Public and IL 89, 98–99.

[18] Hans Christian Bugge, 'Twelve Fundamental Challenges in Environmental Law: An Introduction to the Rule of Law of Nature' in Christina Voigt (ed.), *Rule of Law for Nature: New Dimensions and Ideas in Environmental Law* (Cambridge University Press 2013) 3, 5.

[19] Klaus Bosselmann, 'Grounding the Rule of Law' in Christina Voigt (ed.), *Rule of Law for Nature: New Dimensions and Ideas in Environmental Law* (Cambridge University Press 2013) 75, 82.

[20] Jorge E. Viñuales, *The Organisation of the Anthropocene: In Our Hands?* (Brill 2018) 13.

[21] Maneesha Deckha, 'Initiating a Non-anthropocentric Jurisprudence: The Rule of Law and Animal Vulnerability under a Property Paradigm' (2013) 50:4 Alta L Rev 783, 786. Deckha argues that animal law is treated as more about humans, and less about animals.

from our (human) inability or deliberateness to appreciate 'the true dimension of man in nature'.[22]

This economy-driven character of nature was allied to the Eurocentric conception of property. The argument being that private property is acquired when one appropriates nature.[23] For example, Eurocentric legal theorists who were writing as the Americas were being colonised, and who were interested in providing a theoretical basis for extracting the natural resources of these colonies for Europe's imperial advantage, argued that '[t]he natural world remained opaque. Only when it could be imagined as serving to fulfil the needs of Europeans did the natural world become visible, and then only as property'.[24]

On this subject, Ileana Porras revisits this telling observation in her recent review by arguing that the transformation of nature into commoditised property was achieved through European instrumentation where 'they articulated it as a material thing subject to appropriation, reducible to property, and capable of entering the stream of commerce, conceptually transforming nature into what we today call a natural resource'.[25] This telling account of the Eurocentric philosophy of private property was galvanised through the consequent theme that a government's purpose was to secure the enabling conditions for the acquisition of private property. Accordingly, such a conception of property pivots around the idea of the state that is vested with expansive powers to determine the allocation or distribution of natural resources.[26]

The Lockian concept of property extended the chasm between society and nature, dispossessed colonised peoples of their lands and resources, and obliterated Indigenous conceptions of the unity between humans and nature.[27] Again, using the example of the colonisation of the Americas,

[22] Julián Santiago Vásques Roldán and Robert Henao Ng, 'Sustainable Development and Human Development: Evolution or Transition in the Scientific Conception of Sustainability?' (2017) 2:2 Producción + Limipia 103, 106.

[23] John Locke, *Two Treatises of Government*, edited by Peter Laslett (Cambridge University Press 1960).

[24] Ileana Porras, 'Appropriating Nature: Commerce, Property and the Commodification of Nature in the Law of Nations' (2014) 27:3 Leiden JIL 641, 647.

[25] Ileana Porras, 'Appropriating Nature: Commerce, Property and the Commodification of Nature in the Law of Nations' in Usha Natarajan and Julia Dehm (eds.), *Locating Nature: Making and Unmaking International Law* (Cambridge University Press 2022) 111, 112.

[26] Matt Huber, 'Resource Geographies I: Valuing Nature (or Not)' (2018) 42:1 Progress in Human Geography 148, 149.

[27] James (Sákéj) Youngblood Henderson, 'The Context of the State of Nature' in Marie Ann Battiste (ed.), *Reclaiming Indigenous Voice and Vision* (UBC Press 2000) 11, 18–21.

the notion of private property was reinforced by a warped Eurocentric analytic that distorted the Indigenous conception of common property to suggest that the European appropriation of nature and its resources in the colonies caused no harm to Indigenous peoples and their ways of living and knowing.[28] However, since nature was being converted into property through the power of law, these exchanges formed the foundations for new economic and social interactions and, along with that, the proliferation of new rights which enjoyed protection under law.[29]

The transformation of nature into property became one of the significant characteristics of European legal traditions which individualised human society and equally compartmentalised nature for consequent human control.[30] Emerging from this commoditised view, nature was the object of 'exploitation colonialism' in the Americas, Africa, and elsewhere.[31] So, the forced separation between humanity and nature only created fertile conditions for the exploitation of the latter.[32]

2.2.2 Religion Meets Nature

Religion has been a major influence in sustainable development discourse and has for a long time been integral to the conceptual distinction of society from nature. A deeper appreciation of this conceptual wedge

Henderson argues the Lockian theory of property was used to validate the dispossession of lands in Indigenous America; Paul Corcoran, 'John Locke on Native Right, Colonial Possession, and the Concept of Vacuum Domicilium' (2018) 23:3 European Legacy 225. Corcoran makes an interesting argument that the Lockian theory of private property recognised and protected Indigenous property rights. Strangely, Corcoran's view does not account for the concept of property in Indigenous societies which was communal (and not individual) ownership. It is important to highlight these kinds of historical revisionisms aimed at rehabilitating Eurocentric influences that have now come under sustained scrutiny.

[28] Ileana M. Porras, 'The Doctrine of the Providential Function of Commerce in International Law: Idealising Trade' in Martti Koskenniemi, Mónica García-Salmones Rovira, and Paolo Amorosa (eds.), *International Law and Religion: Historical and Contemporary Perspectives* (Oxford University Press 2017) 313, 321.

[29] James (Sákéj) Youngblood Henderson, 'Postcolonial Indigenous Legal Consciousness' (2002) 1 Indigenous LJ 1, 9.

[30] Leah M. Gibbs, '"A Beautiful Soaking Rain": Environmental Value and Water beyond Eurocentrism' (2010) 28:2 Envt and Plan D: Soc'y and Space 363, 364.

[31] Martti Koskenniemi, 'International Law and Religion: No Stable Ground' in Martti Koskenniemi, Mónica García-Salmones Rovira, and Paolo Amorosa (eds.), *International Law and Religion: Historical and Contemporary Perspectives* (Oxford University Press 2017) 3, 14.

[32] Laurence Tribe, 'Ways Not to Think about Plastic Trees: New Foundations for Environmental Law' (1974) 83:7 Yale LJ 1315, 1333.

between society and nature points in the direction of the grand part international law played in this separation.

Critical international law scholars have argued that Christian theologians, including Francisco de Vitoria and members of the famed Salamanca school, through their early work in international law, planted in the minds of a 'Christian readership' the idea of an endless nature. In the construction of these early (Christian) theorists, nature was infinite and seemingly without limits.[33] Their readership, comprising European imperialists, were goaded on in their plunder of the new colonies in the (mistaken) belief that they were exercising their God-given power over nature. In this most compelling manner, the Christian religion played a radical role in evolving the character of nature, a role which continues to this day.[34]

It is also little secret that Christian doctrines were enlisted as imperial technology for dispossessing and dislodging colonised peoples of their ways of life, governance, law, and lands.[35] As it turned out, the Christian religion laid the grand foundation for an imperially informed interference, including through colonial conservation policies that led to novel exchanges between society and nature, hitherto unknown to these colonised (Indigenous) peoples. Here, '[t]he result has been the creation of a dominant metaphor of nature, most closely associated with economic and scientific sources, and a competing ideology of nature more closely connected to religion'.[36] Thus, the ecological crisis can be partly traced to religion and especially to the tripartite consolidation of God, humanity, and nature as proffered by the Judeo-Christian tradition.[37]

[33] Porras, 'Appropriating Nature', Leiden JIL 650.

[34] Edith Brown Weiss, 'The Evolution of International Environmental Law' (2011) 54 Japanese YBIL 1, 2; Lucia A. Silecchia, '"Social Love" as a Vision of Environmental Law: Laudato Si' and the Rule of Law' (2016) 10:3 Liberty U L Rev 371.

[35] Robert J. Miller, 'The International Law of Colonialism: A Comparative Analysis' (2011) 15:4 Lewis and Clark L Rev 847, 854–863.

[36] Alex Geisinger, 'Sustainable Development and the Domination of Nature: Spreading the Seed of the Western Ideology of Nature' (1999) 27:1 Boston College Envt'l Aff L Rev 43, 64; Wapulumuka O. Mulwafu, 'The Interface of Christianity and Conservation in Colonial Malawi, c. 1850–1930' (2004) 34:3 J Religion in Afr 298, 305. I discuss the legal implications of colonial conservation policies on sustainable development in Africa in Chapter 4.

[37] Lynn White Jr, 'The Historic Roots of Our Ecologic Crisis' (1967) 155:3767 Science 1203, 1205.

The suggestion is not that ecological despoliation is solely the creation of Western epistemologies and their related religious precepts.[38] Rather, the point is that Christian theology's connection to imperialism formed it into a willing ally in the totalising mission of colonialism to dominate nature. The reliance of Europe's colonising powers on the divine existence of God as superior to nature and its related philosophy of human domination of nature resulted in a diminished view of nature, thereby giving rise to permissible destruction of nature styled as uses of natural resources.[39] As Porras rightly observed, 'the notion that nature in distant places could be understood as a thing available for appropriation, complemented the Judeo-Christian belief that God had given dominion over the created Earth to human beings, and reinforced the tendency to assume that the material world, wherever located, was there for human exploitation'.[40]

Nonetheless, this view on Christian doctrine has been resisted by some scholars, who argue that Christian theology did not entail an inauspicious relationship between humans and nature.[41] These scholars have contended that Christianity promoted the protection of nature, resulting in some instances where there have been positive outcomes for nature.[42] Even so, the connection between capitalism and transnationalism fostered by the Global North (mainly professing Christianity alongside these developments) over an extended period in its contact with non-European peoples, aided by colonialism and imperialism, reinforces the view that the Judeo-Christian faith played a significant role in producing the current ecological crisis.[43] Therefore, in accordance with recent calls for ecological restoration, the Christian religion has a major role to play

38 Geisinger, 'Sustainable Development and the Domination of Nature', 50.

39 White, 'Historic Roots of Our Ecologic Crisis', 1205.

40 Porras, 'Appropriating Nature', Leiden JIL, 660.

41 Robin Attfield, 'Christian Attitudes towards Nature' (1983) 44 J History Ideas 369; Jason Kawall, 'A History of Environmental Ethics' in Stephen M. Gardiner and Allen Thompson (eds.), *The Oxford Handbook of Environmental Ethics* (Oxford University Press 2017) 13.

42 Gregory E. Hitzhusen and Mary Evelyn Tucker, 'The Potential of Religion for Environmental Stewardship' (2013) 11:7 Frontiers in Ecology and Environment 370; Aimie L. B. Hope and Christopher R. Jones, 'The Impact of Religious Faith on Attitudes to Environmental Issues and Carbon Capture Storage (CCS) Technologies: A Mixed Method Study' (2014) 38 Tech in Soc'y 48, 49.

43 Wouter Hammink, 'Mother Nature and the Heavenly Father: Christianity and the Environment in a Globalised World' (2012) 30:1 Mac Int'l 63, 64–66.

in revitalising the concept of sustainable development and redressing the ills it partly sponsored.[44]

Legal commentaries on the role the Christian religion plays in remedying these ecological injustices symbolise attempts to rehabilitate the classical view that Christianity was human-centred, and disavowing the view that it adopted an exploitative outlook in regard to nature over a long period in human history.[45] The argument here is that Christianity is not necessarily the worst religion relative to nature. Rather, as a key aspect of the organising logic of European public life in the wake of European imperial expansion, it played a key role in enabling the despoliation of nature.[46] As Lois Ann Lorentzen aptly puts it, the main reason it stands out as guilt-ridden is that, '[u]nder particular material and historical conditions [Christianity] has served as a religious ideology that has encouraged violence against nature'.[47] In this regard, international law's origins and early developments have been linked to 'Eurocentric Christendom, and to Eurocentric trade, mercantilism, capitalism, corporate power and resource extraction, all of which were facilitated by law's calculative imperial design and philosophical underpinnings'.[48] Religion, then, is important to the organising ambition of humanity's control over nature. Consequently, some eco-theologians contend that, since religion is partly responsible for disrupting humanity–nature relations, religion must assume a greater role in addressing the ecological crisis.[49]

This view aligns with contemporary interest in religion as capable of incentivising international law's mission for a solution to the ecological predicament.[50] Even so, it is important not to overlook the different

[44] Gretel Van Wieren, *Restored to Earth: Christianity, Environmental Ethics, and Ecological Restoration* (Georgetown University Press 2013) 173.

[45] Massimiliano Montini and Francesca Volpe, 'The Need for an "Integral Ecology" in Connection with the UN Sustainable Development Goals' in Frank Pasquale (ed.), *Care for the World: Laudato Si' and Catholic Social Thought in an Era of Climate Crisis* (Cambridge University Press 2019) 56, 61.

[46] Rosemary Radford Ruether, 'Religious Eco-Feminism: Healing the Ecological Crisis' in Roger S. Gottlieb (ed.), *The Oxford Handbook of Religion and Ecology* (Oxford University Press 2006) 362, 362–363.

[47] Lois Ann Lorentzen, 'Religion and Violence against Nature' (2006) 19 Scripta Instituti Donneriani Aboensis 242, 252.

[48] Blanco and Grear, 'Personhood, Jurisdiction and Injustice', 93.

[49] Robert H. Nelson, 'Rethinking Church and the State: The Case of Environmental Religion' (2011) 29:1 Pace Envt'l L Rev 121, 123.

[50] Neil Walker, 'Christianity and the Rule of Global Law' in Rafael Domingo and John Witte Jr (eds.), *Christianity and Global Law* (Routledge 2020) 197, 210.

ways in which the Christian religion also provided both rationale and means for protecting nature.[51] Recent statements by prominent Christian leaders like Pope Francis, who announced in his seminal encyclical that, 'the actual focus of ecology is the fellowship of all living things and the responsibility of human beings towards this fellowship', provide a glimmer of hope.[52] This papal statement is a profound acknowledgement of ecological integrity as central to the mission to reimagine sustainable development in international law, and the role that religion can play in achieving this objective.

Accordingly, religion cannot be detached from the ever-present postcolonial logic of dominance. Religion is integral to the constitutive force of international law.[53] Here, the Christian doctrine, for the most part, flourished as subtext of international governance, including the governance of nature.[54] This embeddedness of religion in international law's relationship with nature is demonstrated in de Vitoria's argument that 'security and the good life are the final cause of political power, nature (and in the end God, as nature's author) is its efficient cause, and the community itself is the material cause of political power'.[55] In envisioning God as external to the Earth, the Christian faith, first, conceives 'God as an other-worldly entity – one standing apart from, and above, the world'.[56] Then, second, humanity is God's representative on Earth.[57] When we reflect on this idea of God removed from the Earth and standing in an ecclesiastical hierarchy to the planet; humanity, as God's earthly representative, is immediately elevated to the vaunted position of custodian-beneficiary of the Earth, while exerting dominion

[51] Mark Somos and Anne Peters, 'Christianity, Global Environmental Protection, and Animal Law' in Rafael Domingo and John Witte Jr (eds.), *Christianity and Global Law* (Routledge 2020) 365, 366.

[52] Wolfgang Sachs, 'The Sustainable Development Goals and *Laudato Si'*: Varieties of Post-Development?' (2017) 28:12 Third World Q 2573, 2582.

[53] Anghie, 'Francisco de Vitoria'; Miller, 'International Law of Colonialism', 849.

[54] Koskenniemi, 'International Law and Religion', 8.

[55] Andreas Wagner, 'Francisco de Vitoria and the Global Commonwealth' in Rafael Domingo and John Witte Jr (eds.), *Christianity and Global Law* (Routledge 2020) 72, 74.

[56] Tribe, 'Ways Not to Think about Plastic Trees', 1333.

[57] Ben Boer, 'Social Ecology and Environmental Law' in R. B. Singh and Suresh Misra (eds.), *Environmental Law in India: Issues and Responses* (Concept Publishing Company 1996) 35, 57.

over all other members of this planetary community.[58] It is at this point that humanity, as God's alternative self, is imbued with immanent power to dominate nature through several technologies including law.[59]

This imprint of God's earthly dominion through humans was carefully worked into the subtext of colonial laws on conquest, dispossession, and control over nature. As a result, as one of colonialism's crucial features, this Judeo-Christian philosophy which united the human and divine by means of anthropomorphism was bequeathed to the colonies and has since assumed permanence in most jurisdictions including the Global South, even to this day. Regrettably, this philosophy has weakened previously existing conciliatory customary law and Indigenous legal worldviews on the nexus between religion and nature.[60]

2.2.3 Beyond Religion and Nature: The Quiet Entry of International Law

Religion and international law thus intersect as religion is an element of international law-making.[61] An extension of the analysis beyond religion and nature, into international law, demonstrates the role of religion in Western intellectual advances in the evolution of sustainable development.[62] In relating this to international law, its role in governing nature emerges from two closely-related legacies.[63] First, and prior to the eighteenth century, there existed a Euro-Christian conception of nature as sacred and inviolable.[64] Much later, Europe experienced an intellectual

[58] Edith Brown Weiss, 'Intergenerational Equity' in Yann Aguila and Jorge E. Viñuales (eds.), *A Global Pact for the Environment: Legal Foundations* (C-EENRG 2019) 51, 55; Amaya Amell, *Francisco de Vitoria and the Evolution of International Law: Justifying Injustice* (Lexington Books 2021).

[59] Stephen Humphreys and Yoriko Otomo, 'Theorising International Environmental Law' in Anne Orford and Florian Hoffmann (eds.), *The Oxford Handbook of the Theory of International Law* (Oxford University Press 2016) 797, 802.

[60] Susan Power Bratton, 'Eco-Dimensionality as a Religious Foundation for Sustainability' (2018) 10 Sustainability 1021, 1022.

[61] Mashood Baderin, 'Religion and International Law: An Analytical Survey of the Relationship' in David Armstrong (ed.), *Routledge Handbook of International Law* (Routledge 2009) 165, 165.

[62] Carmen G. Gonzalez, 'Environmental Justice, Human Rights, and the Global South' (2015) 13:1 Santa Clara JIL 151, 164.

[63] Humphreys and Otomo, 'Theorising International Environmental Law', 799.

[64] S. Ravi Rajan, 'Classical Environmentalism and Environmental Human Rights: An Exploration of their Ontological Origins and Differences' (2011) 2:1 J Human Rights and Envt 106, 109–110. This refers to the period before the eighteenth century.

transformation, the Romantic period, which started in the late eighteenth century which also valorised nature; however, not from a religious standpoint.[65] Thinkers of the Romantic period advocated an inherent value for nature by initiating a public-oriented attitude towards the management of nature.[66] The descriptive language used by Romantic scholars in describing nature foreshadowed how the later Eurocentric scholarship constructed new forms of expressing nature.[67] This kind of language was subsequently adapted in the latter restatement of nature as the environment.[68]

The Romantic scholars were entangled in a struggle with two sources of resistance: first, the Age of Enlightenment. This started the process of decentring society from nature. Second, the flourishing of European imperial and colonially-commoditised interest in nature became firmly established in Europeanised thinking as the final stage in separating humanity from nature.[69] Here, the colonies became valuable resource hubs; and, even when conservation measures were undertaken, these interventions were only targeted at sustaining nature in satisfaction of this commercialised imperial objective.[70] It is this paradoxical circumstance of nature being celebrated for its unique, innate value on the one hand, and also distinguished as an object of colonial control and exploitation on the other hand, which places the relationship between international law and nature in a state of permanent irresolution.[71]

Accordingly, a fundamental conception of a divinely ordained dominance by humanity was further modified in the Age of Enlightenment. Nature became an object of scientific inquiry by birthing the never-ending construction of a deeply exploitative relationship between it and humanity.[72] At this time, the separation between humanity and nature had become quite distinct, as nature was rapidly being altered by human activity as witnessed by the fracturing of nature and its resources to

[65] Jedidiah Purdy, 'The Politics of Nature: Climate Change, Environmental Law, and Democracy' (2010) 119 Yale LJ 1122, 1137. This relates to the post-eighteenth-century period.

[66] Ibid., 1145–1149.

[67] Ibid., 1130.

[68] Humphreys and Otomo, 'Theorising International Environmental Law', 805.

[69] Ibid., 799.

[70] Antony Anghie, 'Towards a Postcolonial International Law' in Prabhakar Singh and Benoît Mayer (eds.), *Critical International Law: Postrealism, Postcolonialism, and Transnationalism* (Oxford University Press 2014) 123, 136.

[71] Humphreys and Otomo, 'Theorising International Environmental Law', 818–819.

[72] Ibid., 803.

facilitate efficient human control.[73] This change became more prominent in international law as human society assumed increased agency over nature, with nature consequently becoming observed through a passive lens as a pliable phenomenon for society's interminable materialistic desires.[74]

2.2.4 Taming Nature: An Imperialised Intervention

While religion played an important role in structuring our understanding of international law's engagement with nature, it is international law's colonial origins that offer an enduring account of this complex history between humanity and nature.[75] This narrative is borne out by the organising logic of European colonialism which was driven by resource access in the Global South.[76] Notably, Hugo Grotius, following in the footsteps of Francisco de Vitoria's forceful religious defence of Europe's imperial mission, supported his own (Grotian) secular assertions, this time grounded on 'the doctrine of the providential function of commerce'.[77] This Grotian theory rationalised the European imperialist commodification of nature as benevolent commerce.[78] Expectedly, wherever nature was under threat, colonialism responded by instituting a number of legal interventions styled as governance, ostensibly for nature's protection, yet this was only to secure nature and its resources for continued imperial interests and exploitation.[79]

Little wonder, then, that Africa, for example, was absorbed into the global capitalist system as a provider of natural resources, a process that was paradoxically aided by colonial laws and policies supposedly aimed

[73] Ibid.

[74] Ntina Tzouvala, *Capitalism as Civilisation: A History of International Law* (Cambridge University Press 2020) 7–43. Tzouvala's seminal work renews TWAIL's call to study the materialist dimensions of international law.

[75] Bhatia, 'South of the North', 151.

[76] Porras, 'Appropriating Nature', *Locating Nature*, 111; Humphreys and Otomo, 'Theorising International Environmental Law', 811–812.

[77] Ileana M. Porras, 'European Origins, the Doctrine of the Providential Function of Commerce, and International Law's Embrace of Economic Growth' (2013) 107 Am SIL: Proc Annual Mtg 374, 375.

[78] Martti Koskenniemi, 'Imagining the Rule of Law: Rereading the Grotian "Tradition"' (2019) 30:1 European JIL 17, 25; David M. Lantigua, *Infidels and Empires in the New World Order: Early Modern Spanish Contributions to Legal Thought* (Cambridge University Press 2020) 200.

[79] Humphreys and Otomo, 'Theorising International Environmental Law', 813–814.

at conserving nature.[80] Drawing upon the conspiratorial influence of colonialism, Europe's imperial and colonising powers began experimenting with the idea of nature conservation across their colonies in Asia, the Americas, and Africa. In Africa, these interventions were disguised as conservation policies. Yet, they functioned as colonial technologies for dominating nature: first, through establishing the botanical garden; and, second, by introducing international treaties on nature conservation.[81]

On this subject, Africa's experience was no different from that of the American colonies or colonies elsewhere. There too, nature was subordinated through self-imposed imperial guardianship which did little to protect nature beyond securing European vested interests in natural resources while disregarding and dislodging the interests of the colonised (Indigenous) peoples.[82] This understanding of nature conservation in Africa, and in other places, paints a different portrait away from the popular myth of colonial conservation being undertaken with altruistic fervour. It illuminates the stark reality of the application of colonial laws to 'serve the recreational and scientific interests of outsiders'.[83]

Relatedly, colonial science was employed to aid this vicious totalising trend of law that held sway over nature.[84] Here, colonial science epitomised both 'metaphor and means of legitimate colonial aspiration'.[85] If the doctrine of discovery was the legal basis for establishing colonial

[80] Elizabeth Garland, 'The Elephant in the Room: Confronting the Colonial Character of Wildlife Conservation in Africa' (2008) 51:3 Afr Studies Rev 51, 60.

[81] Humphreys and Otomo, 'Theorising International Environmental Law', 811–813. In respect of Africa, two significant examples of international (imperial) wildlife treaties are the 1900 International Convention of Wild Animals, Birds, and Fish in Africa and the 1933 Convention Relative to the Protection of Flora and Fauna in the Natural State.

[82] Manuel Jiménez Fonseca, 'The Colonisation of American Nature and the Early Development of International Law' (2010) 12:2 J History IL 189, 210; Chase Blair, 'Indigenous Sacred Sites and Lands: Pursuing Preservation through Colonial Constitutional Frameworks' (2020) 25 Appeal: Rev Current L and L Reform 73.

[83] Benjamin J. Richardson, 'Ties that Bind: Indigenous People and Environmental Governance' in Benjamin J. Richardson, Shin Imai, and Kent McNeil (eds.), *Indigenous Peoples and the Law: Comparative and Critical Perspectives* (Hart Publishing 2009) 337, 337–338.

[84] Richard Grove, 'The East India Company, the Raj and the El Niño: The Critical Role Played by Colonial Scientists in Establishing the Mechanisms of Global Climate Teleconnections 1770–1930' in Richard H. Grove, Vinita Damodaran, and Satpal Sangwan (eds.), *Nature and the Orient: The Environmental History of South and Southeast Asia* (Oxford University Press 1998) 301, 303.

[85] David Wade Chambers and Richard Gillespie, 'Locality in the History of Science: Colonial Science, Technoscience and Indigenous Knowledge' (2000) 15 Osiris 221, 226.

sovereignty, property ownership, and dominion, then 'scientific discovery' was a vital technology for aiding colonial domination and dispossession.[86] Whether it was the French, English, or German colonialists, human mediation was often styled as scientific advance; a process that permitted the exploitation of nature as a necessary objective of imperialism.[87] Although Indigenous and other local knowledge provided evidence that was incorporated into Euro-American scientific epistemologies, these Eurocentric records and accounts purposefully ignored how 'the periphery provided both initiative and innovation in extending human knowledge'.[88] For example, German improvements in water accessibility in colonial South-West Africa were developed on the back of Indigenous knowledge obtained from the Herero and Nama peoples, yet this history is written without acknowledging this fundamental relevance of Indigenous African knowledge systems to German colonial science.[89] Law was then only the resultant complement of the political character of colonial science masked as a noble advancement, as a civilisational tool and an inevitable correction of Indigenous environmental inexperience.[90] Accordingly, it is important to understand the symbiotic relationship between colonial science and law in aid of the despoliation of nature.[91]

From the foregoing analysis, the historical and theoretical precursors of international law are governed by a particular appreciation of the society–nature relationship. This connection is traceable to European imperialism and its related epistemologies which have systematically displaced non-Western worldviews, including the link between African

[86] Miller, 'International Law of Colonialism', 851–854; Rebecca Tsosie, 'Indigenous Peoples and Epistemic Injustice: Science, Ethics and Human Rights' (2012) 87:4 Wash L Rev 1133, 1136; M. Rafique Islam, 'History of the North–South Divide in International Law: Colonial Discourses, Sovereignty, and Self-Determination' in Shawkat Alam, Sumudu Atapattu, Carmen G. Gonzalez and Jona Razzaque (eds.), *International Environmental Law and the Global South* (Cambridge University Press 2015) 23, 24.

[87] Lys Kulamadayil, 'Placed in Between: The Natural Environment in International Law' (2022) 13:4 Transnat'l Leg Theory 466.

[88] Grove, 'East India Company', 319.

[89] Martin Kalb, *Environment Empire: Nature, Infrastructure, and the Making of German Southwest Africa* (Berghahn Books 2022) 141.

[90] Ravi Rajan, 'Imperial Environmentalism or Environmental Imperialism? European Forestry, Colonial Foresters and the Agendas of Forest Management in British India 1800–1900' in Richard Grove, Vinita Damodaran, and Satpal Sangwan (eds.), *Nature and the Orient* (Oxford University Press 1998) 324, 353.

[91] de Castro, 'Colonial Aspects of International Environmental Law', 169.

legal cosmologies and nature.[92] These intrusions, designed by and for colonial interests, have made their way into the prevailing discourse on international law. Here, it is least surprising that, while international law is presented as if it is concerned with the ecological crisis; it is, in fact, interested in the 'management and commodification of industrial externalities'.[93]

Consequently, the turn to ecological integrity as the core of sustainable development must 'aspire to build a "bio-centric" society where nature is at the centre of the concerns of citizens, who should be considered inseparable from the same (nature)'.[94] What is of concern, yet under-theorised, is how colonial techniques long adopted in subordinating nature now function as the 'de facto templates for "sustainable development", perhaps the foremost principle in international environmental law today'.[95] Given this challenge, critical scholars are suspicious that the concept is lacking transformative content. It is understandable why these scholars then quite anxious about the promise of sustainable development. Little wonder, some argue, that it is simply a new technology of neo-imperialism working under the guise of 'contemporary global environmental discourses'.[96]

To a much lesser concern but of comparable relevance, while human dominance over nature is often associated with the neoliberal (capitalist) order, the evidence also suggests socialism (or communism) equally reified humanity above nature. Human-centric technologies or management tools were thus integral to this prevailing duopoly and ideological polarities of Western society. Following the end of the Cold War bipolarity, and with the emergence of capitalism as having survived that

[92] Brian-Vincent Ikejiaku, 'International Law Is Western Made Global Law: The Perception of Third World Category' (2013) 6 Afr J Leg Studies 337, 349; Jacob Olupona, 'Religion and Ecology in African Culture and Society' in Roger S. Gottlieb (ed.), *The Oxford Handbook of Religion and Ecology* (Oxford University Press 2006) 259, 260–261.

[93] Olivier Barsalou and Michael Hennessy Picard, 'International Environmental Law in an Era of Globalised Waste' (2018) 17:3 Chinese JIL 887, 897.

[94] Antonio Luis-Hidalgo-Capitán and Ana Patricia Cubillo-Guevara, 'Deconstruction and Genealogy of Latin American Good Living (Buen Vivir): The Triune Good Living and its Diverse Intellectual Wellsprings' in Gilles Carbonnier, Humberto Campodónico, and Sergio Tezanos Vázquez (eds.), *Alternative Pathways to Sustainable Development: Lessons from Latin America* (Brill 2017) 23, 29.

[95] Humphreys and Otomo, 'Theorising International Environmental Law', 815.

[96] Subhabrata Bobby Banerjee, 'Who Sustains Whose Development? Sustainable Development and the Reinvention of Nature' (2003) 24:1 Organisational Studies 143, 146.

ideological conflict and triumphed over socialism; neoliberalism, a principal feature of capitalism, became the most visible torchbearer of human control over nature.[97] Soon, it took a foothold in international legal governance. As a result, an enduring critique of international law is that it birthed the concept of sustainable development as a Eurocentric technology to govern the post-Cold War relationships between postcolonial societies and former colonising powers regarding the uses of the environment.[98]

2.3 Constructing the Environment

International law de-historicises the humanity–nature nexus. It does this by severing the bond that held these domains together, thereby drawing a wedge between the two.[99] This conceptual excision revolves around how international law de-localises nature by transforming it into 'the environment' as was subsequently concretised under (international) environmental law.[100] This technique placed humans in a novel relationship with nature.[101]

The exercise of this unique political authority over nature was key to this new relationship and ubiquitous in international law where nature was only a desirable end in itself, and at the same time, nature was humanity's sustenance.[102] As Leo Marx has argued, 'in the 1970s, with the onset of the ecological "crisis", the refurbished, matter-of-fact word environment took over a large part of the niche in public discourse hitherto occupied by the word nature'.[103] These foundational changes immobilised nature's evolution by universalising new principles of international law including those on the environment, with the concomitant consequence of peripheralising related Indigenous or customary law in aid of ecological integrity.[104]

97 Alexander Gillespie, *International Environmental Law, Policy and Ethics* (Oxford University Press 2014) 10.

98 Humphreys and Otomo, 'Theorising International Environmental Law', 818.

99 Ibid., 804–805.

100 Ibid., 800.

101 João Aldeia and Fátima Alves, 'Against the Environment: Problems in Society/Nature Relations' (2019) 4 Frontiers in Sociology 1, 3.

102 Humphreys and Otomo, 'Theorising International Environmental Law', 811.

103 Leo Marx, 'The Idea of Nature in America' (2008) 137:2 Daedalus 8, 8.

104 Humphreys and Otomo, 'Theorising International Environmental Law', 802; Anna Grear, 'Questioning the Constructs: "The Environment" and "(Human) Rights"' (2016) 7:2 J Human Rights and Envt 165, 165; Enrique Leff, 'Power–Knowledge

2.3.1 The Environment: Foregrounding an Idea

The exploitation of the environment inspires inventive ways of thinking about the humanity–nature nexus. Colonial legacies continue to define the relationship between humanity and nature in a profound manner.[105] With human society distancing itself from nature in order to dominate it, it became necessary to conceptualise an explanatory framework to justify that separation; hence the creation of the environment – the *othering* of nature for its consequent subordination.[106] Since the introduction of this conceptual separation '[t]here had been a shift from a world where man was moulded by the environment to him being able to alter the nature of his world'.[107]

Thus, the environment was conceptualised as an invention at both ends of a broad spectrum: first, for its use; and second, for its protection. The premise of this dualised orientation was that nature was an abstract idea that needed legal embodiment. In Erin O'Donnell's view, this binarisation made the 'environment both visible and comprehensible (what I term as legible) to the law'.[108] As other scholars have also observed, when nature 'becomes the object of politics and planning, [nature] turns into "environment"'.[109] What, then, should be our concern when confronted with the question of how the environment came to be in law? In response, it is important to understand that the environment was constructed out of the history of human progress in subjugating nature to our human devices and by debasing its intrinsic value, and consequently setting up a devalued nature amenable to a corresponding set of social values that made nature this 'inferior' non-human realm visible to law and to society.[110]

Relations in the Field of Political Ecology' (2017) 20:3 Ambiente and Sociedade 225, 232–239.

105 Diane Wallman, E. Christian Wells, and Isabel C. Rivera-Collazo, 'The Environmental Legacies of Colonialism in the Northern Neotropics: Introduction to the Special Issue' (2018) 23:1 Envt'l Archaeo 1.

106 Vito de Lucia, 'Competing Narratives and Complex Genealogies: The Ecosystem Approach in International Environmental Law' (2015) 27:1 J Envt'l L 91, 114.

107 Paul Warde, Libby Sorlin, and Sverker Sörlin, *The Environment: A History of the Idea* (John Hopkins University Press 2018) 8.

108 Erin O'Donnell, *Legal Rights for Rivers: Competition, Collaboration and Water Governance* (Routledge, 2019) 3.

109 Wolfgang Sachs, 'Environment' in Wolfgang Sachs (ed.), *The Development Dictionary: A Guide to Knowledge and Power*, 2nd ed. (Zed Books 2010) 24, 33.

110 Erin O'Donnell, *Legal Rights for Rivers: Competition, Collaboration and Water Governance* (Routledge, 2019) 3–4.

As the environment became established in thought and action within the imperialist ambitions of Europe, it became a civilising technology for dominating non-Europeanised knowledge. It also helped with marginalising the peoples of the Global South as the natural resources in these places became increasingly important to the colonial enterprise.[111] In this respect, '[t]he traditional relationships between people and their environment in the peripheral parts were shattered as Europe extracted the potential of the land and its vegetation, commodifying nature for its use'.[112] Much more, as a basis for its consequent yet paradoxical protection, the environment 'had to be named, and in some measure invented, before it could be understood as endangered and available for saving'.[113] This new role assumed by the environment was an important part of the civilising ethos of Eurocentrism in the context of subduing nature. As a result, whether the protection of nature was for economic uses or aesthetical value, the underlining European imperial interests lingered on in both distinct and imperceptible forms.[114]

This fundamental tension in the social transformation of nature defines contemporary interpretations of the global ecological crisis.[115] As some scholars have argued, the environment is nature's embodiment.[116] In this light, colonialism and capitalism join together to convert nature into an exchangeable object now known as the environment.[117] Relatedly, the historical origins of the ecological crisis are visible through this kind of influence that colonialism has over nature.[118] Thus, terminologies such as *terra nullius* (unoccupied land), *aqua nullius* (unoccupied water), and *res communis* (the common heritage of mankind) were critically important to

[111] Ikejiaku, 'International Law is Western Made Global Law', 349; Olupona, 'Religion and Ecology in African Culture and Society', 349–350.

[112] Michael Williams, 'The Role of Deforestation in Earth and World-System Integration' in Alf Hornborg, J. R. McNeill, and Joan Martinez-Alier (eds.), *Rethinking Environmental History: World-System History and Global Environmental Change* (AltaMira Press 2007) 101, 109.

[113] Purdy, 'Politics of Nature', 1176.

[114] Hélène Maynard, 'From Classical Liberalism to Neoliberalism: Explaining the Contradictions in the International Environmental Law Project' (2020) 50:1 Revue Générale de Droit 57, 63.

[115] Brian M. Napoletano and Brett Clark, 'An Ecological–Marxist Response to the Half-Earth Project' (2020) 18:1 Conservation and Soc'y 37, 38.

[116] Sachs, 'Environment', 33.

[117] Stephen A. Mrozowski, 'Colonization and Commodification of Nature' (1999) 3:3 Int'l J Hist Archaeo 153, 155.

[118] Annie Patricia Kameri-Mbote and Philippe Cullet, 'Law, Colonialism and Environmental Management in Africa' (1997) 6:1 RECIEL 23.

making both normative and practical fields of colonial and imperial overrule in regard to nature.[119]

Within this movement from nature to environment, the colonial encounter curtailed existing Indigenous resource management practices in places like Africa.[120] The colonial apologists who transformed these precolonial conceptions of nature and commodified them showed little or no interest in treating the environment as anything other than the commodity that it had become.[121] This commodification of nature persists even today as the sub-disciplines of international law including international investment law, international trade law, and even international health law continue to privilege neo-imperial interests over critical efforts aimed at imbuing international law with an ecologically-attuned legal philosophy.[122]

Yet, what is truly remarkable in the complication of the ecological crisis confronting the planet, and especially the South and its peoples, was how neoliberal scholarship essentialises and de-politicises the ecological crisis by attaching the moniker *global* to the environment.[123] As the colonies had little involvement in institutionalised international law-making up until sometime after World War II, it was quite easy for Europe's colonising powers to fit in the *global* narrative of problematising the environment. This situation reflects an epistemological shift occurring at a time where the significance of framing nearly every significant phenomenon including the environment with the prefix *global* was on the rise.[124] For this reason, it is understandable that when contemporary international law emerged alongside decolonisation, it was relatively easy to relegitimise Eurocentrism through postcolonial

[119] Karin Mickelson, 'The Maps of International Law: Perceptions of Nature in the Classification of Territory' (2014) 27:3 Leiden JIL 621, 637.

[120] Kameri-Mbote and Cullet, 'Law, Colonialism', 23.

[121] Kate Miles, *The Origins of International Investment Law: Empire, Environment and the Safeguarding of Capital* (Cambridge University Press 2013) 24; Michael Mason, 'Transnational Environmental Obligations: Locating New Spaces of Accountability in a Post-Westphalian Global Order' (2001) 26:4 Trans Inst Brit Geographers 407, 408.

[122] Jessica Pearson-Patel, 'Promoting Health, Protecting Empire: Inter-Colonial Medical Cooperation in Post-War Africa' (2015) 7:1 Monde(s) 213, 222; Tomoko Akami, 'Imperial Polities, Intercolonialism, and the Shaping of Global Governing Norms: Public Health Experts in Asia and the League of Nations Health Organisation' (2017) 12:1 J Global History 4; Walter Rodney, *How Europe Underdeveloped Africa* (Bogle L'Ouverture 1972).

[123] Lorenzo Cotula, '(Dis)integration in Global Resource Governance: Extractivism, Human Rights, and Investment Treaties' (2020) 23:2 J Int'l Econ L 431, 445.

[124] Warde et al., *The Environment*, 125–126.

societies, as these states were quickly absorbed into the *global* village at independence.[125]

2.3.2 Environmental Rights: A Silent Neoliberal Turn

The progression of this idea – from nature to the environment – conditioned by neoliberalism was hurriedly transitioned into new thinking that connected the environment to human rights.[126] This neoliberal thought which emphasised human rights also distorted the progress of conceptualising the environment by conjoining the environment and human rights.[127] The insertion of human rights in this discourse assumed a defining role in 'juridifying the environmental problem'.[128] The introduction of rights into the environmental domain involved norm fusion – which is a blending of legal rules from at least two different domains; here, the environment and human rights – to create this novel sphere of human control that called for a different jurisprudential toolkit for parsing this new disciplinary province.[129]

Though this argument is infrequently advanced, the introduction of human rights into the language on the environment was one of the legacies of the 1972 Stockholm Conference.[130] This led to the connection between human rights and the concept of sustainable development.[131] To understand its place within sustainable development, environmental rights must thus be seen as an expanded neoliberal perspective on human rights.[132]

125 Humphreys and Otomo, 'Theorising International Environmental Law', 801.

126 Diana M. Liverman and Silvina Vilas, 'Neoliberalism and the Environment in Latin America' (2006) 31:1 Annual Rev Envt Res 325, 332.

127 Elia Apostolopoulou, *Nature Swapped and Nature Lost: Biodiversity Offsetting, Urbanisation, and Social Justice* (Palgrave MacMillan 2020) 31–32.

128 Dániel Deák, 'Innovation in the Intervention into Nature by Legal Means' in Luk Bouckart, Knut J. Ims, and Peter Rona (eds.), *Art, Spirituality and Economics: Liber Amicorum for Laszlo Zsolnai* (Springer 2018) 225, 228.

129 Defne Gönenç, 'Conceptualising Norm Fusion through Environmental Rights' (2021) 30:3 Envt'l Pol 442.

130 Melissa J. Durkee, 'International Environmental Law at Its Semicentennial: The Stockholm Legacy' (2022) 50:3 Georgia J Int'l and Comp L 748, 751.

131 Linda Hajjar Leib, *Human Rights and the Environment: Philosophical, Theoretical and Legal Perspectives* (Brill 2011) 108.

132 Mohsen al Attar and Rosalie Miller, 'Towards an Emancipatory International Law: The Bolivarian Reconstruction' (2010) 30:1 Third World Q 347, 355.

Environmental rights as part of the extended conceptualisation of human rights permits that language to be employed to 'civilise economic globalisation and allow for sustainable development'.[133] Additionally, a long-held view was that environmental rights would moderate the excesses of the corporatist dimensions of colonialism, which has since been styled as development.[134] Expectedly, even critical international law scholars who were also enthralled by the allure of the transformative power of environmental rights have lent their voices to this legal revolution. Some of these scholars argue that:

> Human rights has become one of the dominant discourses for the articulation and adjudication of environmental disputes. Because the environmental legal regime lacks the sophisticated institutional framework and redress mechanism of the human rights regime, victims of environmental abuse have increasingly resorted to the human rights framework to seek redress.[135]

The point is not an attempt to provide a history of environmental rights (not even a partial one). Rather, it is to locate the place of environmental rights discourse in the debate on the conceptual evolution of the relevance human rights to sustainable development.

Incidentally, other legal scholars have provided rich and detailed histories and analyses on environmental rights.[136] Rather than repeating these historical accounts, I analyse and critique how environmental rights arose as the outcome of judicial interpretation or explicit juridical recognition.[137] Environmental rights thus emerged from these histories as either a

[133] Jeremy Perelman, 'Human Rights, Investment and the Rights-fication of Development: The Practice of "Human Rights Impact Assessments" in Large Scale Foreign Investment in Natural Resources' in Katharine G. Young (ed.), *The Future of Economic and Social Rights* (Cambridge University Press 2019) 434, 434.

[134] Chimni, 'Capitalism, Imperialism, and International Law', 37.

[135] Gonzalez and Atapattu, 'International Environmental Law', 235–236.

[136] Dinah Shelton, 'Human Rights, Environmental Rights, and the Right to Environment' (1991) 28:1 Stan JIL 103; John G. Merrills, 'Environmental Rights' in Daniel Bodansky, Jutta Brunnée, and Ellen Hey (eds.), *The Oxford Handbook of International Environmental Law* (Oxford University Press, 2008) 663; Susan Glazebrook, 'Human Rights and the Environment' (2009) 40:1 VUWLR 293; Joshua Gellers, *The Global Emergence of Constitutional Environmental Rights* (Routledge 2018).

[137] Svitlana Kravchenko, 'Environmental Rights in International Law: Explicitly Recognised or Creatively Interpreted?' (2012) 7:2 Florida A and M UL Rev 163.

precondition or an outcome of the relationship between the environment and human rights, and now a central feature of sustainable development.[138]

However, other legal critics contend that, 'while human rights have been used to address many global justice concerns arising from colonisation, international law has consistently resisted providing a global right to a clean, healthy and safe environment'.[139] Even with the recent recognition of such a right by both the UN Human Rights Council and the General Assembly, this recognition is far from becoming a binding right at international law and, most likely when it does, it will become part of the global environmental regulatory governance architecture.[140] As a result, international law's abrupt transition from nature to the environment, and now with the silent turn to environmental rights, failed to deliver the protection that nature, now styled as the environment, desperately required in response to society's relentless exploitation.

Thus, notwithstanding the apparent progress made by conjoining human rights to the environment, this was not exactly the radical change needed to transform sustainable development.[141] The human-centric ontology of environmental rights was firmly preserved at the intersection of international environmental law and human rights law.[142] Although it seems both fields are juridical opposites, they conveniently unite to form environmental rights and, in doing so, retain the colonial register of Eurocentrism and neoliberalism which are intrinsic to both domains of law. In this regard, environmental rights extend the objectification of nature while preserving human

[138] Philippe Cullet, 'Definition of an Environmental Right in a Human Rights Context' (1995) 13:1 Nethl QHR 25, 25–26; Rebecca Bratspies, 'Do We Need a Human Right to a Healthy Environment?' (2015) 13:1 Santa Clara JIL 31, 53–54.

[139] Louis J. Kotzé, Louise de Toit, and Duncan French, 'Friend or Foe? International Environmental Law and its Structural Complicity in the Anthropocene's Climate Injustices' (2021) 11:1 Oñati Socio-Legal Series 180, 193.

[140] United Nations Human Rights Council, *The Human Right to a Safe, Clean, Healthy and Sustainable Environment* 48/L.23/Rev.1 (2021); United Nations General Assembly, *Promotion and Protection of Human Rights: Human Rights Questions, including Alternative Approaches for Improving the Effective Enjoyment of Human Rights and Fundamental Freedoms*, A/Res, 76/300 (2022).

[141] Dinah Shelton, 'The Benefits and Limitations of a Human Rights Approach to Environmental Protection' (2014) 2 Hung YBIL and European L 141, 143–154.

[142] Anna Grear, 'Human Rights and the Environment: A Tale of Ambivalence and Hope' in Douglas Fisher (ed.), *Research Handbook on Fundamental Concepts in Environmental Law* (Edward Elgar 2016) 146, 152.

control over the environment.[143] Frédéric Mégret reiterates this concern in his critique of the romanticisation of the place and language of rights in nearly every conceivable aspect of social progress including the area of the environment. The caution here is that, even if this approach yields substantive positive results, it still might not justify endowing every phenomena with the language of rights.[144] As a result, the pathway towards attaining sustainable development remains far from being realised as environmental rights focuses on human benefits as opposed to the condition of non-human entities.[145]

This telling description is often missed by many international law scholars who are fascinated by the appeal of human rights as a panacea for environmental challenges. Third World and critical international law scholars are equally culpable. They too see environmental rights as a remedy for curing sustainable development's problems. For instance, long before the recognition of the right to a clean, healthy, and sustainable environment at the UN, critical scholars like Sumudu Atapattu argued that, following the recognition of the human rights–environment nexus in international law, 'it is rather surprising that a distinct right to environment has not yet been recognised at the international level'.[146] However, both conventional and Third World scholars of international law alike have contended that, while treaty-based environmental rights have been described as progressive and capable of emphasising the significance of human rights to the environmental agenda, the incorporation of such rights into treaty language without qualification amounts to deepening the anthropocentric control over the environment, and further extending state-centred power over Indigenous peoples in the realisation of such rights.[147]

This situation accounts for why international law concepts such as sustainable development fail to mediate issues at the heart of the North–South

[143] Ngaire Naffine, 'Legal Personality and the Natural World: On the Persistence of the Human Measure of Value' (2012) 3 (Special Issue) J Human Rights and Envt 68, 83.

[144] Frédéric Mégret, 'Where Does the Critique of International Human Rights Stand? An Exploration of 18 Vignettes' in José María Beneyto and David Kennedy (eds.), *New Approaches to International Law: The European and American Experiences* (TMC Asser Press 2012) 3, 24–25.

[145] Helen Kopnina and Brett Cherniak, 'Neoliberalism and Justice in Education for Sustainable Development: A Call for Inclusive Pluralism' (2016) 22:6 Envt'l Educ Research 827, 831.

[146] Sumudu Atapattu, *Human Rights Approaches to Climate Change: Challenges and Opportunities* (Routledge 2015) 48.

[147] Marie-Catherine Petersmann, 'Narcissus' Reflection in the Lake: Untold Narratives in Environmental Law Beyond the Anthropocentric Frame' (2018) 30:2 J Envt'l L 235, 236.

divide.[148] For instance, although treaty-based environmental rights abound, some states are unwilling to translate these rights into enforceable domestic law, nor are they keen to embark upon national legal and policy measures to implement domestic translations of environmental rights.[149] The reason is not far-fetched considering at the height of the age of human rights, rights language became an important resource for evangelising the link between human autonomy, individual agency, and capitalism with little or no tangible connection to ecological temperance.[150] Thus, environmental rights were followed as part of a normative framework that produced destructive consequences for the environment.[151]

2.3.3 *Ecologising Rights: From Environmental Rights to Rights of Nature?*

There is presently a shift underway from environmental rights to rights of nature.[152] The legal and political salience of infusing nature with rights raises fundamental questions on the future of sustainable development law and practice. This shift is based on disillusionment and disappointment with how sustainable development has been overrun by neoliberal influences through the instrumentality of human rights which has left behind a trail of ecological wrongs.[153] Following calls on opening up a new frontier in both international and environmental law to address the insufficiency of environmental rights, the emergence of the rights of nature has moved in step with a contemporary appreciation and application of rights to the non-human domain of nature.[154] Since then, the idea of the rights of nature have catalysed an evolving inclination which

[148] Natarajan, 'TWAIL and the Environment', 187.

[149] Manisuli Ssenyongo, 'Responding to Human Rights Violations in Africa: Assessing the Role of the African Commission and Court on Human and Peoples' Rights (1987–2018)' (2018) 7:1 Int'l Human Rights L Rev 1, 29–30.

[150] Samuel Moyn, 'A Powerless Companion: Human Rights in the Age of Neoliberalism' (2014) 77:4 L and Contemp Probs 147, 148; Anna Spain Bradley, *Human Choice in International Law* (Cambridge University Press 2021) 19.

[151] Grear, 'Human Rights and the Environment', 158.

[152] Gwendolyn J. Gordon, 'Environment Personhood' (2018) 43:1 Colum J Envt'l L 49, 53.

[153] Louis J. Kotzé, 'The Anthropocene, Earth System Vulnerability and Socio-Ecological Injustice in the Age of Human Rights' (2019) 10:1 J Human Rights and Envt 62, 67.

[154] Mária Valeria Berros, 'Rights of Nature in the Anthropocene: Towards the Democratization of Environmental Law?' in Michelle Lim (ed.), *Charting Environmental Law Futures in the Anthropocene* (Springer 2019) 21; D. Paul Emond, 'Co-operation in Nature: A New Foundation for Environmental Law' (1984) 22:2 Osgoode Hall LJ 323, 325–332.

beckons return to customary law or Indigenous legal conceptions as inspiration for transforming sustainable development.[155]

To begin, the Eurocentric intellectual inspiration behind bestowing nature with rights dates back, perhaps, to Charles Darwin's work. According to Darwin's theory, morality's normative progress must be measured by how its scope can be amplified through the application of moral and social principles in non-human domains.[156] Drawing on this Darwinist inspiration, some scholars are sanguine about the prospects of rights of nature as capable of challenging the persistence of capitalist views on sustainable development.[157] For instance, in his revelatory statement on the importance of exploring the connection between rights and nature, Christopher Stone remarked that:

> The fact is, that each time there is a movement to confer rights onto some new 'entity', the proposal is bound to sound odd or frightening or laughable. This is partly because until the rightless thing receives its rights, we cannot see it as anything but a thing for the use of 'us' – those who are holding rights at the time.[158]

Unsurprisingly, the contemporary interest in the idea of the rights of nature in international law has attributed to Stone's revelatory insights.[159] And, in view of the precedential import of the language of rights, environmental law specialists, ethicists, scholars of environmental politics, and a host of other scholars of different disciplines have all embarked upon a radical mission to undo the Western-inspired conceptualisation of rights

155 Cristiano Gianolla, 'Human Rights and Nature: Intercultural Perspectives and International Aspirations' (2013) 4:1 J Human Rights and Envt 58, 78; Erin L. O'Donnell and Julia Talbot-James, 'Creating Legal Rights for Rivers: Lessons from Australia, New Zealand and India' (2018) 23:1 Ecol and Soc'y 7; Laura S. Lynes, 'The Right to Nature and the Duty to Consult in Canada' (2019) 37:3 J Energy and Nat Res L 353; Harriet Harden-Davies, Fran Humphries, Michelle Maloney, Glen Wright, Kristina Gjerde and Marjo Vierros, 'Rights of Nature: Perspectives for Global Ocean Stewardship' (2020) 122 Marine Pol'y 3.

156 Charles Darwin, *Descent of Man*, 2nd ed. (Merrill Baker 1874) 119; Christopher Stone, 'Should Trees Have Standing? Towards Legal Rights for Natural Objects' (1972) 45 S Cal L Rev 450, 450–451.

157 Craig M. Kauffman and Pamela L. Martin, 'Can Rights of Nature Make Development Sustainable? Why Some Ecuadorian Lawsuits Fail and Others Fail' (2017) 92 World Dev 130, 130.

158 Stone, 'Should Trees Have Standing?', 455.

159 Holly Doremus, 'Environmental Ethics and Environmental Law: Harmony, Dissonance, Cacophony, or Irrelevance?' (2003) 37:1 UC Davis L Rev 1, 3–5.

that privileged human interests above those of other members of the planetary community.[160] Believing in the promise of the new-fangled talk of rights of nature, even some TWAIL scholars welcomed the prospects of reform by arguing the present thinking on the human rights-based approach to sustainable development tended to endorse the inherency of rights of nature within Indigenous cosmologies.[161] Thus, this new wave of thinking on rights has been described as resisting the force of environmental rights.[162]

The revolutionary impetus of the rights of nature has not been restricted to academic analyses nor philosophical postulations. This historic moment has thus provoked a rise in international political and legal declarations of considerable significance, a host of constitutional–legal reforms, and a raft of judicial decisions that are quickly establishing this rights regime in legal jurisprudence.[163] As Cristina Espinosa rightly contends, what was previously thought of as, '[o]nce a strictly theoretical concept, the [r]ights of [n]ature (RoN) is now a meaningful reference in environmental politics'.[164]

Since then, it has been directly translated into national law and policy in some states in the Global South like Ecuador and Bolivia.[165] Africa has not been left out of this global development, with Uganda being the first African state to incorporate rights of nature in its National Environment Act.[166] Still, while these are early days in this conceptual evolution,

[160] Roderick Nash, *The Rights of Nature: A History of Environmental Ethics* (University of Wisconsin Press 1989) 16.

[161] Sara L. Seck, 'Transnational Labour Law and the Environment: Beyond the Bounded Autonomous Worker' (2018) 33:2 Can J L and Soc'y 137, 147.

[162] Susana Borràs, 'New Transitions from Human Rights to the Environment to Rights of Nature' (2016) 5:1 Transnat'l Envt'l L 113, 128.

[163] Louis J. Kotzé and Paola Villavicencio Caldazilla, 'Somewhere in between Rhetoric and Reality: Environmental Constitutionalism and the Rights of Nature in Ecuador' (2017) 6:3 Transnat'l Envt'l L 401; Lidia Cano Pecharromán, 'Rights of Nature: Rivers that Can Stand in Court' (2018) 7:1 Res 13, 15; Erin L. O'Donnell, 'At the Intersection of the Sacred and Legal: Rights for Nature in Uttarakhand' (2018) 30:1 J Envt'l L 135, 137.

[164] Cristina Espinosa, 'The Advocacy of the Previously Inconceivable: A Discourse Analysis of the Universal Declaration of the Rights of Mother Earth' (2014) 23:4 Envt and Dev 391, 392; United Nations, *International Mother Earth Day*, GA Res 63/278, UNGAOR, 63rd Session, UN Doc A/Res/278.

[165] Borràs, 'New Transitions from Human Rights', 134.

[166] Act 5 of 2019, sec 4; Kevin Bakulumpagi, 'Resolution of the African Commission on Human and Peoples' Rights on the Protection of Sacred Natural Sites and Territories: A Critical Overview' (2021) 5 Afr Human Rights YB 305, 318.

ecological concerns have succeeded in animating a discourse on rights of nature in the progress towards sustainable development.[167]

Also, while rights of nature seem to herald a promising turn in international law, critical international law scholars admonish a cautious approach.[168] Their warning emanates from the concern that the absorptive capacity of international law can capture and liquidate resistance. This includes neutralising resistance framed in terms of rights of nature and enmeshing these rights into corporatism. This anxiety is evidenced by how capitalism elides internal divisions across international law by continuously reconstituting and retaining an international governance that projects particular interests disguised as rights. To this end, critical international law scholars are anxious about capitalism in its function as the standard measure of progress where 'the non-European world was civilisationally inferior and that the influx of (Western) capital would remedy these shortcomings'.[169] Human rights discourse can, thus, eclipse the reform potential of rights of nature since these rights draw upon the conceptual tools of the broader language and category of (human) rights.[170]

In the end, the neoliberal stance on rights discourse raises major concerns for rights of nature too. The complicated ubiquity of sustainable development in international law finally seemed destined for rescue through an expanded dialogue on the scope and application of rights that promotes a healthy and harmonious human and non-human interaction.[171] Yet, emerging from this anxiety, the inability to effectively link the intricate strands of conceptual interaction across these apparently unconnected divisions in law obscures our understandings of how, for example, rights of nature, framed in the sense of public law and guaranteed in national constitutions as a public virtue, inadvertently protect dominant private economic interests.[172]

[167] Louis J. Kotzé and Duncan French, 'A Critique of the Global Pact for the Environment: A Stillborn Initiative or the Foundation for Lex Anthropocene?' (2018) 18:6 Int'l Envt'l Agreements: Pol L and Econ 811.

[168] Antony Anghie, *Imperialism, Sovereignty and the Making of International Law* (Cambridge University Press 2005) 21; Jérémie Gilbert, Elizabeth Macpherson, Emily Jones, and Julia Dehm, 'The Rights of Nature as a Legal Response to the Global Environmental Crisis? A Critical Review of International Law's "Greening" Agenda' (2021) 52 Nethl YBIL 47.

[169] Tzouvala, *Capitalism as Civilisation*, 1.

[170] Rajagopal, 'Counter-Hegemonic International Law', 772.

[171] Rafi Youatt, 'Interspecies Relations, International Relations: Rethinking Anthropocentric Politics' (2014) 43:1 Millennium: J Int'l Studies 207, 211.

[172] Alexandra Kemmerer, 'We Do Not Always Need to Look to Westphalia: A Conversation with Martti Koskenniemi and Anne Orford' (2015) 17:1 J History IL 1, 14.

The shortcomings in legal studies on rights of nature become more evident as the traditional lawyer's perspective and assumptions about nature as private property are difficult to overcome.[173] This is a matter of concern since progress in the rights of nature requires a willingness by lawyers and legal experts to embrace its critical value. In this respect, despite its positive attributes, the growing interest in rights of nature must not lead to a rushed assumption that it is a unitary concept, nor must its theorists and users slip down the path of optimism to assume it is a quick solution to the messy character of historical and present ecological challenges.[174] Arising from this situation, the reliance on rights of nature as legal revolution might do very little to improve the acceptability of the legal content of sustainable development even though there is now a train of cases (judicial precedents) showcasing the utility of rights of nature.[175] Regrettably, another serious concern is that, like sustainable development, and other terminologies or expressions, 'the idea of [r]ights of [n]ature could easily become just another catchphrase wielded by politicians, activists, NGOs, and the like to justify all sorts of decisions' that are considered symbolically important but no more.[176]

2.4 Theorising Development

The interaction between development and international law also tends to undermine sustainable development.[177] This is often the case as development functions as a complex ideology with multiple meanings owing to the varied interests embedded in its invention.[178] In this light, while development seems closely linked to the post–World War II era, its evolution dates back to an earlier history.[179] As an historical idea,

[173] Cormac Cullinan, 'The Rule of Nature's Law' in Christina Voigt (ed.), *Rule of Law for Nature: New Dimensions and Ideas in Environmental Law* (Cambridge University Press 2013) 94, 105.

[174] Alex Putzer, Tineke Lambooy, Ignace Breemer and Aafje Rietveld, 'The Rights of Nature as a Bridge between Land-Ownership Regimes: The Potential of Institutionalised Interplay in Post-Colonial Societies' (2022) 11:3 Transnat'l Envt'l L 501.

[175] Kotzé et al., 'Friend or Foe?', 192.

[176] Maria Valeria Berros, 'Defending Rivers: Vilcabamba in the South Ecuador' (2017) 6 RCC Perspectives 37, 43.

[177] Siobhán McInerney-Lankford, 'Human Rights and Development: A Comment on Challenges and Opportunities from a Legal Perspective' (2009) 1:1 J Human Rights Practice 51.

[178] Guy Fiti Sinclair, 'A "Civilising Task": The International Labour Organisation, Social Reform, and the Genealogy of Development' (2018) 20:2 J History IL 145, 147.

[179] Islam, 'History of the North—South Divide', 28.

development became prominent with the mainstreaming of the Lockian concept of private property into international governance.[180] Thus, international law and development have enjoyed a symbiotic relationship, particularly since the post–World War II period that led to the renewal of development ideologies which later frustrated the attainment of sustainable development.[181]

2.4.1 *A Short Introduction to a Long History*

A lot of ink has been spilt on development as an ideology. While an extended discussion is outside the scope of this book, I draw on aspects of development's history that inform the Global South's interaction with international law.[182] As a concept with deep Eurocentric roots, it spans an extensive historical timeline that stretches from the Graeco-Roman period to as recent as the eighteenth century.[183]

In its emergent intellectual period, development was described as human welfare.[184] Subsequently, development assumed greater significance as it was reinterpreted as progress in perpetuity which was intrinsic to European imperialism.[185] Following decolonisation, development was reinvented to accommodate the ongoing geopolitical transformations in newly independent (postcolonial) states, beginning in the late nineteenth century and running well into the twentieth century.[186]

180 Koskenniemi, 'International Law and Religion', 8.

181 Balakrishnan Rajagopal, *International Law from Below: Development, Social Movement and Third World Resistance* (Cambridge University Press 2003) 24; Helle Abelvik-Lawson, 'Sustainable Development for Whose Benefit? Brazil's Economic Power and Human Rights Violations in the Amazon and Mozambique' (2014) 18:7–8 Int'l JHR 795, 796.

182 Rajagopal, 'Counter-Hegemonic International Law', 776.

183 C. O. Olopade and N. Kara, 'Sustainable Development in Pre-Colonial, Colonial, and Post-Colonial Africa: Issues and Contexts' (2016) 6:1 Afr J Sust Dev 1; Jair Soares Jr and Rogério H. Quintella, 'Development: An Analysis of Concepts, Measurements and Indicators' (2008) 5:2 Brazilian Admin Rev 104, 105. Soares Jr and Quitella argue such discussions ignore or peripheralise non-Western ideas and practices of development that date back to the precolonial era.

184 Soares and Quintella, 'Development'.

185 Laëtitia Atlani-Dualt and Jean-Pierre Dozon, 'Colonisation, Development and Humanitarian Aid: Towards a Political Anthropology of International Aid' (2011) 41:3 Ethnologie Française 393, 396–397.

186 Frederick Cooper, 'Development, Modernisation, and the Social Sciences in the Era of Decolonisation: The Examples of British and French Africa' (2004) 10:1 Revue d'Histoire des Sciences Humaines 9, 11.

Despite this long history, recent attempts at theorising the connection between international law and development continue to situate development's origins within the 'post-war reconstruction of the international legal order'.[187] In keeping with this misconception, the orthodox starting point of the intellectual discourse on the subject of development links it to President Harry Truman's inaugural address and America's (global) capitalist mission to push back on the Soviet Union's proselytising mission on behalf of communism.[188]

Still, development was the mission statement of both capitalism and socialism. So, the triumph of capitalism over the latter was nothing more than the success of a unilateral vision of development and not necessarily the triumph of a better version of development.[189] It is at this time that the modern history of development was truncated and remade into a post–World War II miracle. This conceptual misalignment obscured development's history. It also masked its modern origin which is traceable to the civilising mission of international institutions to advance a globalised social reform agenda.[190] Therefore, a meaningful account of development's history must travel 'beyond the putative "age of development"'.[191]

At the heart of this civilising mission, development defined the content and object of treaties and other (investment) agreements in both colonial and postcolonial periods.[192] Acting as the subtext of international politics and its consequent instrumentalism of capitalism, development became a significant consideration in international governance as it endorsed underdevelopment and extended the North–South divide.[193]

187 Kerry Rittich, 'Theorising International Law and Development' in Anne Orford and Florian Hoffmann (eds.), *The Oxford Handbook of the Theory of International Law* (Oxford University Press 2016) 820, 820.

188 M. Shamsul Haque, 'The Fate of Sustainable Development under Neoliberal Regimes in Developing Countries' (1999) 20:2 Int'l Pol Science Rev 197, 202.

189 Yannick Mahrane, Marianna Fenzi, Céline Pessis and Christophe Bonneuil, 'From Nature to Biosphere: The Political Invention of the Global Environment, 1945–1972' (2012) 113:1 Vingtième Siècle: Revue d'Histoire 127, 131–132.

190 Sinclair, 'A "Civilising Task"', 152–153. Sinclair has described this idea of development as the mission of the International Labour Organisation since the 1920s.

191 Onur Ulas Ince, 'Development' in Jean d'Aspremont and Sahib Singh (eds.), *Concepts for International Law: Contributions to Disciplinary Thought* (Edward Elgar 2019) 179, 180.

192 George Forji Amin, 'International Law, the Civilising Mission, and the Ambivalence of Development in Africa: Conceptual Underpinnings' (2013) 6:1 J Afr and IL 191, 192; Viñuales, *Organisation of the Anthropocene*, 46.

193 Robert Knox, 'Civilising Interventions? Race, War and International Law' (2013) 26:1 Cambridge Rev Int'l Aff 111, 122; Onur Ulas Ince, *Colonial Capitalism and the Dilemmas of Liberalism* (Oxford University Press 2018) 22–28.

The false universalism of its ubiquity was heavily theorised by its specialists, routinely prescribed by North-led international development finance institutions, and implemented with religious fervour by the South as the path out of underdevelopment. This was done often with little care for the ecological ramifications of those decisions.[194] The choice between development and environment became the unseen arena for international development finance institutions to proselytise the redemptive power of development.[195] Hence, even where these institutions incorporated ecological considerations to guide development, those assurances often gave way to economic interests.[196]

2.4.2 *Parsing a Eurocentric Ideology*

Development thus emerged from its long history as international law's new rationality.[197] It became the reasonable aspiration for the South in overcoming poverty and underdevelopment.[198] As development was patently Eurocentric, its pursuit by the South only amounted to fulfilling

194 Jakob Vestergaard and Robert Wade. 'Protecting Power: How Western States Retain the Dominant Voice in the World Bank's Governance' (2013) 46 World Dev 153; Makane Moïse Mbengue and Stéphanie de Moerloose, 'Multilateral Development Banks and Sustainable Development: On Emulations, Fragmentation and a Common Law of Sustainable Development' (2017) 10:2 L and Dev Rev 389; Gonzalez, 'Bridging the North–South Divide', 431; Alberto Acosta, 'Post-Extractivism: From Discourse to Practice: Reflection for Action' in Gilles Carbonnier, Humberto Campodónico and Sergio Tezanos Vázquez (eds.), *Alternative Pathways to Sustainable Development: Lessons from Latin America* (Brill 2017) 77, 97.

195 Viñuales, *Organisation of the Anthropocene*, 46.

196 Ibrahim FI Shihata, 'The World Bank and the Environment: A Legal Perspective' (1992) 16:1 Md JIL 1, 3. Shihata was uniquely positioned to speak on this issue based on his role as a former Vice-President and General Counsel of the World Bank and a long-time development finance expert, but also as an African from Egypt. Dimitri van den Meerssche, *The World Bank's Lawyers: The Life of International Law as Institutional Practice* (Oxford University Press 2022) 48. However, van den Meerssche's analysis suggests Shihata was opposed to integrating human rights into the work of the World Bank as it risked the charge of politicisation. This point underscores the entrenchment of economic growth in the politics of international development finance institutions. Taking a leaf from this analysis, even though Shihata's tenure ended in 2000, and human rights and environmental considerations have since become key components of the work of the World Bank, his nuanced resistance provides insights into the World Bank's favourable posture towards economic growth. It also provides an insight into how international development finance institutions more generally treat the environment in decision-making.

197 Pahuja, *Decolonising International Law*, 38.

198 Arturo Escobar, *Encountering Development: Making and Unmaking the Third World* (Princeton University Press 2012) 23.

one of the central aspects of the civilising mission of international law.[199] Construed this way, it symbolised an 'evangelical ideology of salvation through industrialisation, modernisation, and integration into the global economy through free trade and the exploitation of natural resources'.[200] Nonetheless, while the South focused on development's allure of liberating society from underdevelopment and poverty; the North, on the contrary, found poverty a welcome, if circuitous conduit back to international law's neo-imperial mission, this time styled as development assistance.[201] So, it is hardly surprising that critical international law scholars see development as a contemporary site of control.[202]

In response, the Global South, including Africa, has sought to advance its version of development. These alternative (Southern) approaches have been driven by the urgency to retrench the colonial infrastructure of the North-led notion of development.[203] Designed around the collective postcolonial history of the South, the new international economic order (NIEO) became the radical platform for a Southern coalition to oppose the orthodoxy of international economic relations and law.[204] In keeping with the NIEO's extensive normative range, the South demanded fundamental changes to international law.[205] Notably, NIEO urged an expansion in the meaning and application of the coverage of the concept of permanent sovereignty over natural resources (PSNR).[206]

PSNR (and sustainable development, though not exactly articulated at this time) became the basis for newly-independent postcolonial, natural resource-rich states in the South to assume control over their national development planning.

199 Rajagopal, 'Counter-Hegemonic International Law', 27–28.

200 Sam Adelman, 'The Sustainable Development Goals, Anthropocentrism and Neoliberalism' in Duncan French and Louis J. Kotzé (eds.), *Sustainable Development Goals: Law, Theory and Implementation* (Edward Elgar 2017) 15, 18.

201 Rajagopal, 'Counter-Hegemonic International Law', 31.

202 José E. Alvarez, 'Legal Perspectives' in Thomas G. Weiss and Sam Daws (eds.), *The Oxford Handbook on the United Nations,* 2nd ed. (Oxford University Press 2018) 79, 93.

203 James Thuo Gathii, 'Africa and the Radical Origins of the Right to Development' (2020) 1 TWAILR 28, 39.

204 Kevin Gray and Barry K. Gills, 'South–South Cooperation and the Rise of the Global South' (2016) 37:4 Third World Q 557, 558.

205 Mohammed Bedjaoui, *Towards a New International Economic Order* (UNESCO 1979) 209.

206 B. S. Chimni, 'The Principle of Permanent Sovereignty over Natural Resources: Towards a Radical Interpretation' (1998) 38:2 Indian JIL 208, 214.

In this sense, the hope was that PSNR would make sustainable development visible as the South assumed control over its natural resources. PSNR, to some extent, thus reflected positively on sustainable development's conceptualisation as it emerged from the awareness that the South was opposed to conventional (Eurocentric) development.[207]

This Global South-led conceptualisation of PSNR was joined to other international interests like the Charter for Economic Rights and Duties of States.[208] The two – PSNR and the Charter – were recognised as marking 'the end of complete Northern hegemony and the emergence of a new interdependence of power and wealth'.[209] Equally important was the fact that PSNR and the concept of development joined with human rights to become a language of resistance that would later birth the right to development.[210]

The focus of this alternative vision, through the right to development, was 'self-reliance and self-sustaining development'.[211] Championed by African states and Southern scholars, the right to development translated into concrete support across the South.[212] This new vision fostered an approach that privileged law as the pathway to pursuing development.[213] Nonetheless, this paradigm shift rarely materialised as the South

[207] Antonius R. Hippolyte, 'Aspiring for a Constructive TWAIL Approach towards the International Investment Regime' in Stephan W. Schill, Christian Tams, and Rainer Hoffman (eds.), *International Investment Law and Development: Bridging the Gap* (Edward Elgar 2015) 180; Virginie Barral, 'National Sovereignty over Natural Resources: Environmental Challenges and Sustainable Development' in Elisa Morgera & Kati Kulovesi (eds.), *Research Handbook on International Law and Natural Resources* (Edward Elgar 2016) 3, 7.

[208] Nico Schrijver, *The Evolution of Sustainable Development in International Law: Inception, Meaning and Status* (Martinus Nijhoff 2008) 48–49; United Nations, *Charter for Economic Rights and Duties of States*, UNGAOR, 29th Sess., Supp. No. 31 (the Charter).

[209] Burns H. Weston, 'The Charter of Economic Rights and Duties of States and the Deprivation of Foreign-Owned Wealth' (1981) 75:3 Am JIL 437.

[210] Dorothée Cambou and Stefaan Smis, 'Permanent Sovereignty over Natural Resources from a Human Rights Perspective: Natural Resources Exploitation and Indigenous Peoples' Rights in the Arctic' (2013) 22:1 Michigan State Int'l L Rev 347, 357.

[211] Gathii, 'Africa and the Radical Origins', 40.

[212] Mohammed Bedjaoui, 'The Right to Development' in Mohammed Bedjaoui (ed.), *International Law: Achievements and Prospects* (UNESCO 1991) 1182; Nico Schrijver, 'A New Convention on the Human Right to Development: Putting the Cart before the Horse?' (2020) 38:2 Nethl QHR 84, 85.

[213] Michael Riegner, 'How Universal Are International Law and Development? Engaging with Postcolonial and Third World Scholarship from the Perspective of the Other' (2012) 45:2 Verfassung und Recht Übersee 232, 233.

continued to be trapped within the neoliberal setting that immobilised attempts at reorienting development along the lines envisioned by the South.[214] Thus for example, wherever Indigenous peoples found themselves, they were on the peripheries and in poverty despite relative progress in economic development.[215]

That development remains an illusion for the Global South is due to the prevailing North–South economic inequality and inequity. It is also linked to the South being enamoured by development in much the same way as the North was, despite the profound structural inefficiencies of development occurring in the South.[216] It was this attraction to development that trapped the South in the grips of these Euro-American prescriptions.[217] What becomes evident is that development produces poverty. Additionally, neo-imperial development assistance perpetuates the violence of underdevelopment through shrewd schemes that reroute development assistance back to the North or enrich the comprador bourgeoisie in the South.[218] Disappointingly, the plight of the peoples of the South is aggravated by the fact that development is seen as the ultimate neoliberal remedy for good governance as prescribed by North-controlled international development finance institutions.[219] Therefore, and at the urging of these institutions, sustainable development later became a central feature of Euro-American control through aid conditionality concealed as good governance.[220]

214 Umut Özsu, 'Neo-liberalism and the New International Economic Order: A History of "Contemporary Legal Thought"' in Justin Desautels-Stein and Christopher Tomlins (eds.), *In Search of Contemporary Legal Thought* (Cambridge University Press 2017) 330, 333.

215 Sergio Puig, *At the Margins of Globalisation: Indigenous Peoples and International Economic Law* (Cambridge University Press 2021).

216 Islam, 'History of the North—South Divide', 30.

217 Chimni, 'Third World Approaches to International Law', 18.

218 Ozay Mehmet, *Westernising the Third World: The Eurocentricity of Economic Development Theories*, 2nd ed. (Routledge 2002) 2; Umut Özsu, 'Determining New Selves: Mohammed Bedjaoui on Algeria, Western Sahara, and Post-Classical International Law' in Jochen von Bernstorff and Philipp Dann (eds.), *The Battle for International Law: South-North Perspectives on the Decolonisation Era* (Oxford University Press 2019) 341, 357.

219 Antony Anghie, 'Time Present and Time Past: Globalisation, International Financial Institutions, and the Third World' (2000) 32 NYU JIL and Pol 243, 251–252; Anghie, 'Towards a Postcolonial International Law', 138.

220 James Thuo Gathii, 'Good Governance as a Counter Insurgency Agenda to Oppositional and Transformative Social Projects in International Law' (1999) 5 Buff HRL Rev 107, 122; Penelope Simons, 'International Law's Invisible Hand and the Future of Corporate

Regrettably, the Global South has been unsuccessful at decoding the Eurocentricity of development.[221] The reason has been that development has been systematically depoliticised to ensure it remains attractive and appears to the South as an obvious choice. Its premise has been that the Global South 'could become *developed* through the transfer of capital and knowledge within a few decades'.[222] Here, the South's inability to unravel the role these development ideologies play in global inequity leads to institutionalising legal and policy reforms that continue to privilege economic (in-)efficiency over the environment and place the North's interests ahead of the South's progress.[223]

In a complicated way, the reproduction of the patterns of control and immobilisation of the South through development remains undetected considering development itself is not well-defined. The seeming inclusion of sustainability without clear objectives and the quiet reproduction of a Euro-American vision of development under the ever-vigilant tutelage of Global North-controlled international development finance institutions renders the effort of the Global South at producing a coherent vision of an alternative view on development impossible.[224] On this point, Alberto Acosta writes that, in our attempt '[t]o achieve progress, we are conditioned to believe that the only avenue is economic growth'.[225] It is little surprise then that development has markedly transformed the planet.[226] The changes in nature, this time styled as the environment, along with its associated ecological debt, are then traceable to development.[227] Trapped in this unattainable promise of development even in the postcolonial context, the South, including Africa, continues to pursue a Eurocentric vision of development in the

Accountability for Violation of Human Rights' (2012) 3:1 J Human Rights and Envt 5, 18.

221 Banerjee, 'Who Sustains Whose Development?', 146.

222 Aram Ziai, *Development Discourse and Global History: From Colonialism to the Sustainable Development Goals* (Routledge 2016) 103.

223 Rittich, 'Theorising International Law and Development', 835.

224 Rose Parfitt, *The Process of International Legal Reproduction: Inequality, Historiography, Resistance* (Cambridge University Press 2019) 400–403.

225 Acosta, 'Post-Extractivism', 77–78.

226 Donald Worster, *The Wealth of Nature: Environmental History and Ecological Imaginations* (Oxford University Press 1993) 7.

227 Karin Mickelson, 'Leading Towards a Level Playing Field, Repaying Ecological Debt, or Making Environmental Space: Three Stories about International Environmental Cooperation' (2005) 43:1–2 Osgoode Hall LJ 137, 156–157; J. Chidozie Chukwuokolo, 'Afrocentrism or Eurocentrism: The Dilemma of African Development' (2009) 6 OGIRISI: New J Afr Studies 24, 31.

hope that it will deliver desired progress.[228] On this matter, TWAIL scholars note that, '[d]evelopment has always been a hegemonic idea in that it has always been clear about who needs to be developed, who will do the "developing", how and in which direction'.[229]

Development has thus become a universalised global ideal, this time via the language of human rights – a right to development – yet with no real prospects of economic emancipation for the Global South and its peoples.[230] This rights framing constrains development's emancipatory potential, thwarting an alternative pursuit of its conceptualisation.[231] Owing to its neoliberal imprint, the restrictive character of development has curtailed the evolution of alternatives that are alert to the needs of marginalised classes in the Global South.[232] It is foreseeable, then, that the right to development will be evoked to continue disciplining the ecological aspirations of sustainable development.[233]

Given the injudicious transformation of nature by human society, if there should be a meaningful advance towards sustainable development, it would be imperative to rethink development.[234] The purpose for such significant change in course emerges from the concern that development plays an important role in the conceptualisation of other norms.[235] Nonetheless, these new concepts have not improved – and in their Eurocentric conceptualisation they were not intended to improve – conditions in the Global South. Like others, Jorge Viñuales emphasises this failure of development to answer to the needs of ecological integrity by noting that 'environmental protection has still to become part of the DNA of the law, including in those areas that organise production processes both domestically and internationally'.[236] Thus, the South's faith in the reformative potential of proposals that pivot

[228] Amin, 'International Law', 203.

[229] Rajagopal, 'Counter-Hegemonic International Law', 775.

[230] Antony Anghie, 'Legal Aspects of the New International Economic Order' (2015) 6:1 Humanity 145, 154.

[231] Ben Golder, 'Beyond Redemption? Problematising the Critique of Human Rights in Contemporary International Legal Thought' (2014) 2:1 London Rev Int'l L 77, 83.

[232] Acosta, 'Post-Extractivism', 80.

[233] Marc Limon, 'The Politics of Human Rights, the Environment, and Climate Change at the Human Rights Council' in John H. Knox and Ramin Pejan (eds.), *The Human Right to a Healthy Environment* (Cambridge University Press 2018) 189, 191.

[234] Jean-Charles Hourcade, 'The Geopolitical Stakes of Sustainable Development' (2008) 408:2 Études 175, 186.

[235] Ziai, *Development Discourse and Global History*, 90.

[236] Viñuales, *Organisation of the Anthropocene*, 44.

around development, whether of the sustainable variety or not, threatens to be a little misplaced.[237]

2.5 Conceptualising Sustainable Development

The concept of sustainable development has assumed great significance on the international plane. While it has generated an unrelenting crusade, sustainable development survives ill-definition yet occupies legal space where it has been transformed from a political objective to a semi-legal norm and, finally, to a legal concept. The ensuing discussion analyses the transformations of this concept over time.

2.5.1 From Historic Moment to Historic Movement

Sustainable development has different origin stories depending on whose account one reads. However, most accounts are Eurocentric narratives. For example, some scholars argue sustainable development did not begin with the 1972 Stockholm Conference, even though they do acknowledge 'the link between the environment protection and economic development was clearly established' at this time.[238] Other scholars have argued that sustainable development emerged in the report of the World Commission on Environment and Development.[239] Even some scholars have suggested that, sustainable development emerged long before the Brundtland Commission included it in its report; that the World Conservation Strategy had used the terminology back in 1980.[240] Still, others push further back into history by arguing that sustainable development was a concept that emerged in Europe in the eighteenth century as part of forest management policies.[241]

However, sustainable development predates its formalisation. As it has turned out, the exclusion of non-Western ideas and influences from

[237] Kotzé et al., 'Friend or Foe?', 197.

[238] Barral, 'Sustainable Development in International Law', 379.

[239] World Commission on Environment and Development, *Our Common Future* (Oxford University Press 1987).

[240] International Union for Conservation of Nature, *World Conservation Strategy: Living Resource Conservation for Sustainable Development* (IUCN 1980); Mitcham, 'Sustainable Development', 315–316.

[241] Peter H. Sand, 'Sustainable Development: Of Forests, Ships, and Law – Some Historical Annotations' (2007) 37:23 Envt'l Pol'y and L 201, 202.

these narratives reflect the Eurocentric othering of knowledge that is useful but not of the Euro-American epistemological stock. As Nico Schrijver has rightly argued, 'the concept of sustainable development has various roots from the period before it was introduced *expressis verbis* into international politics and international law'.[242] This view is echoed by Judge Christopher Weeramantry, a past Vice-President of the International Court of Justice (ICJ), who noted that sustainable development was 'one of the most ancient of ideas in the human heritage. Fortified by the rich insights that can be gained from millennia of human experience, it has an important part to play in the service of international law'.[243] Thus, as Schrijver points out, the concept of sustainable development comes 'from the practice of ancient civilisations and traditional legal systems in Asia, the Middle East, Africa, Europe, the Americas, the Pacific, and Australia'.[244]

Despite these discrepancies in its intellectual origins, sustainable development has progressed from a historic moment to a global historic movement. Given its ubiquitousness, the concept has been described as 'a navigation-principle and political and societal ideal of great importance in our 21st century global context'.[245] With the advent of industrialisation and its amplified utilisation of natural resources, a growing awareness of the ecological limits of these resources in supporting development, especially in the post–World War II era, marked the beginning of contemporary environment-related mindfulness. This consciousness inspired global interest in the concept of sustainable development.[246] Thus, even though the expression 'sustainable development' is a recent phenomenon, it easily assumed global prominence.[247]

However, if the 1972 Stockholm Conference birthed sustainable development, later international events were responsible for galvanising the

242 Schrijver, *Evolution of Sustainable Development*, 34.

243 *Gabçikovo-Nagymaros Project, Slovakia v Hungary*, (1997) ICJ Rep 7, 110–111.

244 Schrijver, *Evolution of Sustainable Development*, 34.

245 Annick Hedlund-de Witt, 'Rethinking Sustainable Development: Considering How Different Worldviews Envision "Development" and "Quality of Life"' (2014) 6 Sustainability 8310, 8311.

246 Jacobus Du Pisani, 'Sustainable Development: Historical Roots of the Concept' (2006) 3:2 Envt'l Sciences 83, 87.

247 Sarjerao A Salunkhe, 'The Concept of Sustainable Development: Roots, Connotations and Critical Evaluation' (2003) 33:1 Social Change 67; Jorge E. Viñuales, 'Sustainable Development in International Law' in Lavanya Rajamani and Jacqueline Peel (eds.), *The Oxford Handbook of International Environment Law*, 2nd ed. (Oxford University Press 2021) 1, 2.

concept's special place in international law.[248] The concept became more pronounced in the literature with the establishment of the Brundtland Commission in the aftermath of the 1972 Stockholm Conference.[249] Interestingly, the Brundtland Commission's true mission, which was to make development more acceptable, was concealed as an inherent tension in its official name. Here, the different objectives of development and environment, were downplayed by the preference for its informal designation as the Brundtland Commission.[250] This 'hidden agenda' becomes even more apparent as the Commission's name 'perpetuates the false antimony between ecology and capitalism, using it to achieve an equally false transcendence in which development can continue while being respectful of the environment'.[251] Since then, sustainable development has become a key concept in the pursuit of ecological consciousness alongside its unresolved challenges, and yet will continue to be relevant into the foreseeable future.[252]

2.5.2 Contemporary Manifestations of a Concept

Sustainable development has become a contemporary contagion as every imaginable subject or endeavour with some substantial intellectual or practical significance has attached to it one or another variation of the expression 'sustainable development'.[253] However, the concept's claim to modernity is called into question by historical accounts that demonstrate the term had been in use for a long time before its mainstream adoption and consequent application.[254]

[248] Karl-Werner Brand, 'Sustainable Development' in James D. Wright (ed.), *International Encyclopedia of the Social and Behavioural Sciences*, 2nd ed. (Elsevier 2015) 812, 812.

[249] United Nations, *Process of Preparation of the Environmental Perspective to the Year 2000 and Beyond*, GA Res 38/161 (19 December 1983); Weiss, 'Evolution of International Environmental Law', 10.

[250] Cheryl Lousley, 'Global Futures Past: Our Common Future, Postcolonial Times, and Worldly Ecologies' (2017) 4:2–3 Resilience 21.

[251] Laura A. Cisneros, 'Environmental Resistance: Defying Capitalism's Structure of False Rebellion' (2015) 8:4 Golden Gate U Envt'l LJ 5, 9.

[252] Benjamin J. Richardson, *Time and Environmental Law: Telling Nature's Time* (Cambridge University Press 2017) 49.

[253] Natasha Affolder, 'Contagious Environmental Law-Making' (2019) 31:2 J Envt'l L 187, 190–205. I borrow the metaphor from this article. As a contagion, I apply the metaphorical value of the global dispersal of Environmental Impact Assessment (EIA) to sustainable development.

[254] Philippe Sands, 'International Courts and the Application of the "Concept of Sustainable Development"' (1999) 3 Max Planck YB UN L 389, 395–396; Sumudu Atapattu,

However, some scholars acknowledge the Brundtland Commission report popularised the term as 'development that meets the needs of the present without compromising the ability of future generations to meet their own needs'.[255] This broad-based definition ensured the expression easily became part of regular linguistic use.[256] But, beyond the 1972 Stockholm Conference, the term's ahistoricism has been reiterated and dispersed through several international proceedings, including through the 1972 Stockholm Conference's outcome text, the Stockholm Declaration, and other similar historical documents. In this respect, a recent account observes that:

> [t]he international legal landscape changed in 1992 when the United Nations convened the Conference on Environment and Development in Rio de Janeiro. Instruments such as the Rio Declaration on Environment and Development, the Program of Action, Agenda 21, and the Conventions on Climate Change and on Biological Diversity emphasised sustainable development as a new objective or concern of the international community.[257]

With this contrived link between environment and development, sustainable development became a principal subject in international discourse.[258] In the process, the concept's evolution and manifestation have thus led to multiple dimensions which cast doubt over its legal dimensions.[259]

To begin, the literature characterises sustainable development in varied ways along its different meanings.[260] The ensuing analysis is restricted to three discrete expressions of the concept: vagueness (meaning everything to everyone), user-imposed ambiguity (meaning nothing

'Sustainable Development, Myth or Reality: A Survey of Sustainable Development under International Law and Sri Lankan Law' (2001) 14:2 Georgetown Int'l Envt'l L Rev 265, 283.

255 World Commission on Environment and Development, *Our Common Future*, 8.

256 Michael R. Redclift, 'Sustainable Development (1987–2005): An Oxymoron Comes of Age' (2006) 12:25 Horizontes Antropológicos 65, 66.

257 Makane Moïse Mbengue, 'On Sustainable Development: A Conversation with Judge Weeramantry' in Serena Forlati, Makane Moïse Mbengue, and Brian McGarry (eds.), *The Gabčíkovo-Nagymros Judgment and Its Contribution to the Development of International Law* (Brill 2020) 166, 180.

258 Joyeeta Gupta, 'Growth, the Environment, and Development in the Anthropocene' (2015) 114:775 Current History 311, 312.

259 Emelie Folkesson, 'Human Rights Court Interpreting Sustainable Development: Balancing Individual Rights and Collective Interest' (2013) 6:2 Erasmus L Rev 142, 144; Michael Hannis and Sian Sullivan, 'Relationality, Reciprocity, and Flourishing in an African Landscape' in Laura Hartman (ed.), *That All May Flourish: Comparative Religious Environmental Ethics* (Oxford University Press 2018) 279, 282–283.

260 Michael Redclift, 'The Multiple Dimensions of Sustainable Development' (1991) 76:1 Geography 36.

at all), and a moral imperative (invoking ethical factors or considerations). These manifestations of the concept demonstrate, through a panoramic view of its wide expanse, the confusion that defines the concept's legal character. As a result, it is only when we separate these distinct concerns to understand what each represents that we might inch closer to outlining the seemingly ever-elusive legal meaning of the concept.[261]

Before turning to the tussle over the concept's precise meaning in law, it is important to acknowledge that non-law fields too have contended with its definition.[262] The charge of vagueness does not only come from law. For instance, while sustainable development is understood in some fields as highlighting specific disciplinary aspirations, the concept is criticised for failing to specify what its respective disciplinary content is.[263] The result, for many, is a casual sidestepping or avoidance of definitional issues. To avoid these problems, these disciplines have rather turned their attention to giving meaning to what the concept does in practice.[264] For these scholars, definitional efforts are overly complicated, requiring multi-tiered considerations across ideological and special interest divides, and seldom yielding fruitful conclusions.[265]

2.5.2.1 Vagueness

The most common criticism of sustainable development is that it is vague.[266] Several decades since the expression came into existence, some

[261] Weiss, 'Evolution of International Environmental Law', 10.

[262] Marc A. Rosen, 'Issues, Concepts and Applications for Sustainability' (2018) 3 Glocalism: J Cult Pol and Innov 1, 12–13.

[263] Phil Jones and James Evans, *Urban Regeneration in the UK: Theory and Practice* (Sage 2013), 85; Stephen Polasky, Catherine L. Kling, Simon A. Levin, Stephen R. Carpenter, Gretchen C. Daily, Paul R. Ehrlich, Geoffrey M. Heal and Jane Lubchenco, 'Role of Economics in Analysing the Environment and Sustainable Development' (2019) 116:12 Proc Nat Acad Sciences 5233, 5235. In urban design and architecture, there 'has been a certain amount of ambiguity over what sustainable regeneration looks like in practice'; Trevor Thompson and Tim Ballard, 'Sustainable Medicine: Good for the Environment, Good for the People' (2011) 61:582 British J Gen Practice 3, 3. Sustainable development is defined in medicine as integrating medicine, the environment and people; John C. Dernbach and Federico Cheever, 'Sustainable Development and Its Discontents' (2015) 4:2 Transnat'l Envt'l L 247, 249. In the general sciences, the concept is described as a 'cliché' or '"too vague" and ill-defined to be useful'.

[264] Andrew Blowers, Jan Boersema, and Adrian Martin, 'Is Sustainable Development Sustainable?' (2012) 9:1 J Integrative Envt'l Sciences 1, 1.

[265] G. J. Paton, *Ecological Sustainability and Embeddedness* (Routledge, 2011) 15, 17.

[266] Ben Purvis, Yong Mao, and Darren Robinson, 'Three Pillars of Sustainability: In Search of Conceptual Origins' (2019) 14 Sustainability Science 681, 685.

scholars have contended with its vagueness.[267] The criticism of vagueness is linked to the technical operability of the concept as to what it does or can do in fact.[268] Indeed, some critics have quickly judged the concept to be 'so vague as to be operationally completely useless'.[269]

As a result, the concept's vague definition has given rise to questions about its meaning.[270] Vagueness allows it to slip down the path of conceptual overreach by extending into spaces that complicate attempts at gaining clearer insights into its meaning.[271] While both advocates and opponents of the concept struggle over its vagueness, they all agree that whatever else sustainable development is, the concept should support an enhanced society–nature interrelationship.[272] In their defence, I think that, if sustainable development is understood as an unfinished project and a work in progress, then it stands to reason that its vagueness is intrinsic and self-constitutive.[273]

2.5.2.2 User-Imposed Ambiguity

Sustainable development is ambiguous as various iterations of its conceptualisation have been instilled with 'sufficient ambiguity to be compatible with the conflicting ideals of sustainable development'.[274] Its definitional ambiguity emerges from the concept's characterisation as 'both an outcome of technique and a critique of technique' in how it

[267] Desta Mebratu, 'Sustainability and Sustainable Development: Historical and Conceptual Overview' (1998) 18:6 Envt'l Imp Assess Rev 493, 494; Carlos J. Castro, 'Sustainable Development: Mainstream and Critical Perspectives' (2004) 17:2 Organisation and Dev 195, 208. It is quite paradoxical that some scholars argue the concept's vagueness restricts a 'universal' definition. I find it difficult to reconcile their argument with the prevalence and ubiquity of sustainable development in nearly every discipline.

[268] Yosef Jabareen, 'A New Conceptual Framework for Sustainable Development' (2008) 10:2 Envt Dev and Sustainability 79, 79–80.

[269] Wilfred Beckerman, 'The Chimera of "Sustainable Development"' (2007) 1:1 Elec J Sust Dev 17, 24.

[270] Nancy Diana Panta, 'Clashing Perspectives on Sustainable Development' (2019) 14:1 Studies in Bus and Econ 181, 182.

[271] Wilfred Beckerman, 'Sustainable Development: Is It Still a Useful Concept?' (1994) 3:3 Envt'l Val 191, 193.

[272] Bruce Rich and Michael Hsu, 'Sustainable Development: A Broader Perspective' (1996) 3:2 Brown J World Aff 305, 316.

[273] Walter Alfredo Salas-Zapata and Sara Milena Ortiz-Muñoz, 'Analysis of Meanings of the Concept of Sustainability' (2019) 27:1 Sust Dev 153, 155.

[274] Alan Grainger, 'Introduction' in Martin Purvis and Alan Grainger (eds.), *Exploring Sustainable Development: Geographical Perspectives* (Earthscan, 2004) 1, 7.

rejects a particular understanding of the human–nature relationship while proposing another form that remains yet unknown.[275]

The architecture of sustainable development's definition suggests that it is purposefully ambiguous in order to be capacious, all-embracing, and thus capable of moderating rival economic, social, and environmental concerns.[276] In this sense, Frances Moore endorses the political history behind the concept's ambiguous definition that, 'this is precisely the point of constructive ambiguity – all parties, environmentalists included, can read their own meaning into the ambiguous term'.[277] Its user-imposed ambiguity thus evokes questions about the meanings that may be assigned to sustainable development.[278]

In keeping with this conceptual ambiguity, Sharachchandra Lélé's prescient observation contends that the concept functions as:

> a 'metafix' that will unite everybody from the profit-minded industrialist and risk-minimising subsistence farmer to the equity-seeking social worker, the pollution-concerned or wildlife-loving First Worlder, the growth-maximising policy maker, the goal-oriented bureaucrat, and therefore, the vote-buying politician.[279]

This observation leaves us wondering what the concept actually means as it is pliant.[280] Its user-imposed ambiguity assures environmental protection while guaranteeing economic growth.[281] Faced with uncertainty, this kind of ambiguity is regressive.[282] This challenge, thus, rises to become a concern at international law since sustainable development's disciplinary prominence emerged in the context of international

[275] Yvon Pesqueux, 'Sustainable Development: A Vague and Ambiguous "Theory"' (2009) 4:3 Soc'y and Bus Rev 231, 231.

[276] Tim O'Riordan and Heather Voisey, 'The Political Economy of Sustainable Development' (1997) 6:1 Envt'l Pol 1, 4.

[277] Frances C. Moore, 'Toppling the Tripod: Sustainable Development, Constructive Ambiguity, and the Environmental Challenge' (2011) 5 Consilience: J Sust Dev 141, 145.

[278] Teresa Kwiatkowska and Wojciech Szatzschneider, 'Sustainability, Uncertainty and Environmental Ethics' in Oliver Parodi, Ignacio Ayestaran, and Gerard Banse (eds.), *Sustainable Development: Relationships to Culture, Knowledge and Ethics* (KIT Scientific Publishing 2011) 201, 201.

[279] Sharachchandra M Lélé, 'Sustainable Development: A Critical Review' (1991) 19:6 World Dev 607, 613.

[280] Steve Connelly, 'Mapping Sustainable Development as a Contested Concept' (2007) 12:3 Local Envt 259, 260.

[281] Moore, 'Toppling the Tripod', 147.

[282] Volker Wenzel, 'Sustainable Development: Teleology and Ambiguity' in Hans-Joachim Schellnhuber and Volker Wenzel (eds.), *Earth System Analysis: Integrating Science for Sustainability* (Springer 1998) 210, 214.

environmental law.[283] It is also an international law concern because of the instrumentalised uncertainty that states that hide under this kind of ambiguity conveniently pursue for their self-interested objectives to the detriment of their peoples, especially those in the Global South.

Much more, this user-imposed ambiguity has an impact on scholars engaged in researching the subject. In agreeing with this dimension of the problem of definition, Frances Moore notes that:

> As a young environmentalist, part of a generation charged with solving the environmental problems of the twenty-first century, I fear repeating the failures of the last twenty years. I fear the illusory promise of sustainable development, which projects a mirage of consensus that evaporates when confronted with real problems that require real solutions. I fear that we too, like the founding generation before us, will fall into the trap of casually relying on superficial agreement without engaging with the very real trade-offs between consumption and conservation.[284]

Accordingly, due to challenges with its user-imposed ambiguity, some TWAIL scholars have criticised sustainable development as an empty concept.[285] Therefore, it is no surprise that the concept's indeterminateness continues to frustrate efforts aimed at achieving sustainable development.

2.5.2.3 Ethical Imperative

The concept of sustainable development's definition as a moral or ethical imperative lays emphasis on the significance of an alternative conceptualisation of the prevailing approaches to defining the concept.[286] This invitation to an alternative conceptualisation is to address the ethical dimensions of development and environment in a way that answers to the concept's original call to action.[287] On this subject, the Brundtland Commission report provides insights into the concept's ethical or moral significance as it observed that, 'human survival and well-being could depend on success in elevating sustainable development to a global ethics'.[288]

283 Storr, 'Islands and the South', 530.

284 Moore, 'Toppling the Tripod', 142.

285 Chimni, 'Third World Approaches to International Law', 25.

286 Peter Lawrence, 'Justice for Future Generations: Environment Discourses, International Law and Climate Change' in Brad Jessup and Kim Rubenstein (eds.), *Environmental Discourses in Public and International Law* (Cambridge University Press, 2012) 23, 45–46.

287 Kotzé et al., 'Friend or Foe?', 184.

288 World Commission on Environment and Development, *Our Common Future*, 306.

This ethical or moral dimension is now beginning to receive greater attention.[289] The premise for this ethical designation of sustainable development is that 'some practices may be sustainable but morally objectionable'.[290] The advocates of ethics argue the concept of sustainable development inheres with 'moral, legal and political obligations'.[291] These advocates go further in their calls for an ethical definition of sustainable development by arguing that, even if the Brundtland Commission report did not unambiguously emphasise the concept's 'philosophical foundation of moral duties and obligations', the factual embeddedness of its ethical core cannot be ignored or glossed over.[292] For them, the obligation to protect and preserve nature (or the environment) entails ethical considerations as a necessary outcome of sustainable development.[293] Thus, for these ethicists, the concept 'must be understood to raise ethical questions as well as scientific ones which ultimately must be addressed in law and public policy'.[294]

Hence, a contemporary moral conceptualisation of sustainable development must be defined by a society–nature interconnectedness that is informed by and grounded in ethico-legal values.[295] This line of reasoning is advanced by environmental ethicists who argue that the concept's 'moral imperative is implicit in other important themes in the definitions of sustainable development'.[296] In their view, sustainable

[289] Michael I. Jeffery, 'Environmental Ethics and Sustainable Development: Ethical and Human Rights Issues in Implementing Indigenous Rights' (2005) 2:1 Macq J Int'l and Comp Envt'l L 105, 105; Mohammed Reza Salamat, 'Ethics of Sustainable Development: The Moral Imperative for the Effective Implementation of the 2030 Agenda for Sustainable Development' (2016) 40:1–2 Nat Res Forum 3, 4.

[290] Shashi Motilal, 'Sustainable Development Goals and Human Moral Obligations: The Ends and Means Relation' (2015) 11:1 J Global Ethics 24, 25.

[291] Simon Meisch, 'Fair Distribution in the Anthropocene: Towards a Normative Conception of Sustainable Development' in Philipp Pattberg and Fariborz Zelli (eds.), *Environmental Politics and Governance in the Anthropocene: Institutions and Legitimacy in a Complex World* (Routledge 2016) 62, 66.

[292] Oluf Langhelle, 'Sustainable Development: Exploring the Ethics of Our Common Future' (1999) 20:2 Int'l Pol Science Rev 129, 139.

[293] M. Shamsul Haque, 'Environmental Discourse and Sustainable Development: Linkages and Limitations' (2000) 5:1 Ethics and Envt 3, 7.

[294] John Lemons and Donald A. Brown, 'The Role of Science in Sustainable Development and Environmental Protection Decision-Making' in John Lemons and Donald A. Brown (eds.), *Sustainable Development: Science, Ethics, and Public Policy* (Springer 1995) 11, 21.

[295] Martina Keitsch, 'Structuring Ethical Interpretations of the Sustainable Development Goals: Concepts, Implications and Progress' (2018) 10 Sustainability 829, 831.

[296] Kibaba Makokha, 'The Ethical Foundations of Environmental Conservation and Sustainable Development' (2013) 5:2 Thought and Practice 1, 10.

development 'must be used in its normative sense, which is to say, when a practice/policy cannot stand moral scrutiny in terms of globally accepted norms of morally correct practices or a global ethic, the practice cannot count as sustainable'.[297] However, it is also acknowledged that it is quite challenging to impel the concept's moral observance; rather, we 'ought to desire sustainability, not be policed into it'.[298] Nonetheless, while the turn to ethics affords us a unique pathway for defining sustainable development, I am not calling for more orthodoxy in international law. Instead, like other critical scholars, I call for a 'heterodox discourse ethics'.[299] Accordingly, the turn to ethics should not lead us down the path of universalising a particular, Eurocentric version of what ethics should mean in this definition.[300]

2.5.3 *Making Legal Sense of a Hydra-Headed Phenomenon*

With its integration into multilateral treaties, national constitutions, and other laws, the concept of sustainable development is now broadly recognised as a significant foundation of international law.[301] Yet, legal scholars contend over the meaning of the concept as its vagueness has turned the concept into an unwilling ally for what has been described as 'unsustainable development'.[302] The reason is that, despite its ubiquity in international law, the concept's normativity still receives mixed scholarly treatment because of its definitional challenges.[303] For example, legal scholars argue the concept is a political objective rather than a legal norm that possesses normative autonomy.[304] Other scholars see

297 Motilal, 'Sustainable Development Goals', 25.

298 Holmes Rolston III, 'Justifying Sustainable Development: A Continuing Ethical Search' (2002) 4:1 Global Dialogue 103, 113.

299 Felix Ekardt, *Sustainability: Transformation, Governance, Ethics, Law* (Springer 2020) 111.

300 I discuss the connections between ethics, law, and sustainable development in Chapter 5.

301 Barral, 'Sustainable Development in International Law', 384.

302 Schrijver, *Evolution of Sustainable Development*, 48–49.

303 David Hodas, 'The Role of Law in Defining Sustainable Development: NEPA Reconsidered' (1998) 3 Widener L Symp J 1, 15.

304 Jonathan Verschuuren, *Principles of Environmental Law: The Ideal of Sustainable Development and the Role of Principles of International, European, and National Environmental Law* (Nomos Verlag 2003) 144; Donald K. Anton, 'The 2012 United Nations Conference on Sustainable Development and the Future of International Environmental Protection' (2012) 7:1 Consilience: J Sust Dev 64.

sustainable development as an interstitial norm that is adaptable in judicial decision-making.[305]

However, an emerging strand of thought holds that the concept fits the mould of a legal norm.[306] The discussion here is constructed around a trajectory towards a legal norm as the concretisation of this conceptual journey. The directionality of this investigation confronts the problematique of the concept's meaning and operationalisation. The crux of this critique is that the concept's legal import is undermined without this conceptual clarification. This explanation is important to sustainable development's place in Africa and elsewhere since praxis is doomed to be unsuccessful where there is little understanding of the concept. Thus, the lingering doubt is, should its meaning in international law remain unascertained, its adaptability in national law will correspondingly suffer from the legacy of this definitional deficit.[307]

To address this issue, it is important to consider sustainable development's legal conceptualisation. This explanation is necessary as it sets the stage to scrutinise alternative (non-Eurocentric) legal ontologies relative to sustainable development.[308] It also foreshadows a discussion on the concept's supposed universality.[309] Additionally, it provides insights into the role customary law or Indigenous legal principles play in international law.[310]

This definitional challenge is articulated by international law scholars who argue such concepts must be explained before being applied effectively.[311] Here, a cultural turn towards embracing Indigenous law or customary law involves a return to non-Eurocentric knowledge as

[305] Vaughan Lowe, 'Sustainable Development and Unsustainable Arguments' in Alan Boyle and David Freestone (eds.), *International Law and Sustainable Development: Past Achievements and Future Challenges* (Oxford University Press 1999) 19, 26.

[306] Barral, 'Sustainable Development in International Law', 378.

[307] Andrea Ross, 'It's Time to Get Serious: Why Legislation Is Needed to Make Sustainable Development a Reality in the UK' (2010) 2 Sustainability 1101, 1116.

[308] Saskia Vermeylen, 'Special Issue: Environmental Justice and Epistemic Violence' (2019) 24:2 Local Envt 89, 91; Nick J. Fox and Pam Alldred, 'Sustainability, Feminist Posthumanism and the Unusual Capacities of (Post)humans' (2020) 6:2 Envt'l Sociology 121, 122.

[309] Chapter 3 focuses on this issue.

[310] Melissa L. Tatum, 'Customary Law of Indigenous Communities: Making Space on the Global Environmental Stage' (2020) 9 Michigan J Envt'l and Admin L 77, 105.

[311] Jürgen Kopfmüller, 'From the Cultural Dimension of Sustainable Development to the Culture of Sustainable Development' in Oliver Parodi, Ignacio Ayestaran, and Gerard Banse (eds.), *Sustainable Development: Relationships to Culture, Knowledge and Ethics* (KIT Scientific Publishing 2011) 93, 93.

inspiration for rethinking our current socioecological interactions.[312] The significance is that, '[i]n the attempt to move beyond the sustainability rhetoric and pursue a more meaningful agenda for sustainable development, a clear definition of this concept and an explanation of its key dimensions are needed'.[313] Therefore, the transformation of sustainable development into an effective practical force requires a reorientation of the present human link with the environment.

2.5.3.1 Political (Policy) or Philosophical Objective

Sustainable development is described as a political or philosophical objective. In this respect, the Stockholm Declaration, the outcome document of the 1972 Stockholm Conference, has been equally described as merely an aspirational goal as it was not intended to be binding on participating states nor envisioned to found new legal obligations between states and individuals.[314] Notably, Louis Sohn, who had participated in the preparatory work for the Stockholm Conference and later attended and observed its proceedings, wrote soon after it ended that participating states agreed the Stockholm Declaration would not be legally binding but serve as a set of guiding principles.[315]

This hortatory position attributed to the concept was informed by the processes leading up to the 1972 Stockholm Conference, and much later by the adoption of the Stockholm Declaration, which was marked by compromises.[316] As Greg Lynham also recounted, participating states at the conference agreed that, while the declaration would take the typical procedural form of UN resolutions, its substantive motivation firmly remained a set of common principles intended only to guide and inspire ecological awareness and action by states.[317] Thus, the legal

[312] José Edmilson De Souza Lima and Roberto José Covaia Kosop, 'Decolonial Turn and the Law: Beyond Colonial Restraints' (2019) 10:4 Revisto Direito e Práxis 2596, 2607–2612.

[313] Justice Mensah, 'Sustainable Development: Meaning, History, Principles, Pillars, and Implications for Human Action: Literature Review' (2019) 5:1 Cogent Soc Sciences 1, 2.

[314] *Report of the United Nations Conference on the Human Environment*, 1973, UN Doc A/CONF.48/14/Rev 1 (hereinafter called the Stockholm Declaration); Ludwik A. Teclaff, 'The Impact of Environmental Concern on the Development of International Law' (1973) 13:2 Nat Res J 357; Thomas Buergenthal, 'Louis B. Sohn (1914–2006)' (2006) 100:3 Am JIL 623, 625.

[315] Louis B. Sohn, 'The Stockholm Declaration on the Human Environment' (1973) 14:3 Harvard Int'l LJ 423, 426–427.

[316] Claire Brighton, 'Unlikely Bedfellows: The Evolution of the Relationship between Environmental Protection and Development' (2017) 66:1 ICLQ 209.

[317] Greg Lynham, 'The *Sic Utere* Principle as Customary International Law: A Case of Wishful Thinking?' (1995) 2 James Cook UL Rev 172, 177.

import of the Stockholm Declaration was discouragingly obscured at the time it was adopted, casting a long shadow that continues to loom over the concept to this day.[318]

Therefore, the concept's legal value is inherently restricted, as it is doubtful whether it truly assists in crafting relevant legal policy.[319] Construed differently, sustainable development is merely an ideal from which international environmental law principles derive 'good' impulses and no more.[320] Pushing further this line of inquiry, Virginie Barral argues that the concept:

> may be an important philosophical or political objective, but it is not a legal one. Its connection with the law is restricted to the fact that it may contribute to law formation. As a political objective, it will exert an impact on international negotiations, and as such may influence the content of the law while remaining separate from it.[321]

Accordingly, as a political (policy) or philosophical objective, the concept of sustainable development does not speak to the legal demands of its conceptual evolution.

2.5.3.2 Pseudo-Legal Norm

From an initial sceptical position, there seems to have been some progress in the direction of legal normativity.[322] The attempt to delineate the limits of the concept's legal character has tended to produce different results.[323] In this sense, the concerns relating to the indeterminacy of sustainable development yields place to its use, thus highlighting practical policy impact over a patchwork of conceptual clarification.[324] In line with this approach, the concept's imprecision paradoxically liberates it from local and international constraints. Meanwhile, its fluid alternation

318 Sohn, 'Stockholm Declaration', 435; Andrew Watson Samaan, 'Enforcement of International Environmental Treaties: An Analysis' (2011) 5:1 Fordham Envt'l LJ 261, 269.

319 Humphreys and Otomo, 'Theorising International Environmental Law', 820.

320 Verschuuren, *Principles of Environmental Law*, 144.

321 Barral, 'Sustainable Development in International Law', 378.

322 Christina Voigt, *Sustainable Development as a Principle of International Law: Resolving Conflicts between Climate Measures and WTO Law* (Martinus Nijhoff 2009) 167.

323 Viñuales, *Organisation of the Anthropocene*, 4.

324 Voigt, *Sustainable Development*, 163.

between both local and international spheres of influence assures its continuing legal significance.[325]

While the concept may not possess express, prescriptive legal import, it brings together different values and stimulates new norms by enduing sustainable development with legal content.[326] In conceptualising sustainable development as a pseudo-legal norm, Vaughan Lowe's argument is that the concept is 'a meta-principle, acting upon other legal rules and principles – a legal concept exercising a kind of interstitial normativity, pushing the boundaries of true primary norms when they threaten to overlap or conflict with each other'.[327]

As Lowe observed, to suggest that the concept of sustainable development is, by itself, a legal norm is quite indefensible because it lacks the capacity to impel state action.[328] Other legal scholars agree with Lowe's observation by arguing sustainable development is analogous to international environmental law principles which began their life as non-binding rules and subsequently transmuted into quasi-legal statuses.[329] Lowe's observation is that, while the concept might lack express legal definiteness, it still possesses some kind of normativity – the kind that impels other (legal) norms into action.[330] Regrettably, Lowe's state-centred view of law is typical of legal positivism. His analysis does not acknowledge pluralist sources of law like Indigenous and customary law which are outside positivist conceptions of law but are no less constitutive of law.[331]

The pseudo-legal character of sustainable development suggests its normative content is adaptable, and not that it lacks normative value.[332] In Lowe's account, the concept is 'like a convenient umbrella term to

325 Marie-Claire Cordonier Segger, 'Significant Developments in Sustainable Development Law and Governance: A Proposal' (2004) 28:1 Nat Res Forum 61, 62.

326 Marie-Claire Cordonnier Segger, 'Inspiration for Integration: Interpreting International Trade and Investment Accords for Sustainable Development' (2017) 3:1 Can J Comp and Contemp L 159, 185.

327 Lowe, 'Sustainable Development and Unsustainable Arguments', 31.

328 Ibid., 21–23. Perhaps, in Lowe's view, this flows from the supposed agreement at Stockholm that its principles would not be binding on states.

329 Michael G. Faure and Roy A. Partain, *Environmental Law and Economics: Theory and Practice* (Cambridge University Press 2019) 80.

330 Lowe, 'Sustainable Development and Unsustainable Arguments', 21.

331 I devote attention to this issue in Chapter 5 of this book even though it is a recurrent theme in this book.

332 Voigt, *Sustainable Development*, 161–163.

label a group of congruent norms'.[333] He suggests that there are different kinds of norms in the context of rules for governing conduct, and norms for judicial (interpretive) functions which are outside of the strict determinative appreciation of rules.[334] In this respect, sustainable development as a standalone norm is absent normative force, incapable of achieving legal compliance, or impelling change in conduct.[335] However, when joined to other rules, sustainable development comes to life and becomes a coalescing 'legal' rule that acts as a moderating normative force over competing rules. Viewed this way, the normative character of the concept lies in its applicability in judicial interpretation.[336] For instance, at the ICJ, Judge Weeramantry, in applying the concept of sustainable development as an interstitial norm noted, it demonstrates 'the potential impact of soft law general principles on the interpretation and application of treaties'.[337]

Pressed further, in the context of other sub-disciplines of international law like the law of the sea, sustainable development is still described as having no specific legal meaning.[338] Here, the concept is treated slightly differently. This time, it is not an aspirational goal that imitates law. Yet, its legal character is, again, only discernible through the co-application of more precise (legal) precepts.[339] The suggestion is that sustainable development is an umbrella concept that straddles sub-thematic areas in law spanning economic development, environmental protection, and human rights.[340]

What is apparent from this notion that sustainable development is an umbrella concept is the concept's coalescing hold over both legal and

[333] Lowe, 'Sustainable Development and Unsustainable Arguments', 26.

[334] Ibid., 31.

[335] Ibid.

[336] Ibid.

[337] *Gabçikovo-Nagymaros Project, Slovakia v Hungary*, 88, Weeramantry J. (Vice President), Separate Opinion; Alan Boyle, 'Further Development of the Law of the Sea Convention: Mechanism for Change' (2005) 54:3 ICLQ 563, 573.

[338] Niko Soininen and Daud Hassan, 'Marine Spatial Planning as an Instrument of Sustainable Ocean Governance' in Daud Hassan, Tuomas Kuokkanen, and Niko Soininen (eds.), *Transboundary Marine Spatial Planning and International Law* (Routledge 2015) 3, 7.

[339] Voigt, *Sustainable Development*, 161; Rosemary Rayfuse, 'The Challenge of Sustainable High Seas Fisheries' in Nico Schrijver and Friedl Weiss (eds.), *International Law and Sustainable Development: Principles and Practice* (Oxford University Press 2004) 467, 467.

[340] Philippe Sands, 'International Law in the Field of Sustainable Development' (1994) 65:1 Brit YBIL 303, 379.

policy principles.[341] This umbrella theory functions as an expansive interaction across the principles that inhere within sustainable development with an interpretive objective of impelling these principles toward a concentrating legal core.[342] While the concept may not possess qualities typically allied with law properly so-called, sustainable development is 'certainly not devoid of legal significance'.[343] If law then occurs outside regularly consulted sources, there should be very little reason why sustainable development's legal character must be constrained by those restrictive sources. Thus, this incomplete conceptualisation of sustainable development invites a further step towards the endowment of the concept with legal significance.

2.5.3.3 Towards a Legal Norm?

The debate over whether sustainable development possesses legal normativity is inching closer to the point where the concept is now recognised as multifaceted.[344] Relating this multidimensionality to sustainable development, a multifaceted concept evokes multiple normative expressions of which law is only one manifestation.[345] Here, the legal conceptualisation of sustainable development should not merely be for the sake of circumscribing a distinct sphere of normativity. Rather, it should lead to legal meaning that excavates the relevant manifestations of the concept.[346] In this sense, the concept's legal scope is derived from a broad range of normative impulses.[347] Here, the idea of legal scope implies a phenomenon that alters existing legal rules, or that, through its application or interpretive analysis, can transform previously existing legal rules.[348]

Drawing inspiration from this thinking, sustainable development was formed during the UN-led conferences and allied international processes. For example, the Rio Declaration provided direction on the concretisation

[341] Jaye Ellis, 'Sustainable Development as a Legal Principle: A Rhetorical Analysis' in Hélène Ruiz Fabri, Rüdiger Wolfrum, and Jana Gogolin (eds.), *Select Proceedings of the European Society of International Law* (Hart Publishing 2010) 642.

[342] Ibid.

[343] Lluís Paradell-Trius, 'Principles of International Environmental Law: An Overview' (2000) 9:2 RECIEL 93, 95.

[344] Schrijver, *Evolution of Sustainable Development*, 217.

[345] Gunther Handl, 'The Legal Mandate of Multilateral Development Banks as Agents of Change Toward Sustainable Development' (1998) 92:4 Am JIL 642, 644.

[346] Natasha Affolder, 'The Legal Concept of Sustainability' in Alan Ingleson (ed.), *Environment in the Courtroom* (University of Calgary Press 2019) 92, 100.

[347] Barral, 'Sustainable Development in International Law', 383.

[348] Ibid., 383.

of the concept at international law.[349] This position follows the argument that, while the Rio Declaration was very much like its predecessor, the Stockholm Declaration, it too was not conceived as legally binding, and was mostly intended to fix the conceptual deficit of the Stockholm Declaration.[350] Even so, since the concept fits the mould of legality, the conclusion ought to be that it possesses legal character.[351] As Peter Sand has noted in support, 'there is at least one area where the Rio Conference has already left its imprint on the evolution of sustainable development – by formally anointing the concept of "sustainable development" for legal use'.[352]

Nonetheless, an inordinate focus on the legal meaning of sustainable development might constrain its conceptual evolution. I recognise that the debate over legal meaning must respond to law's overarching rationale which is a normative creation emanating from its socioecological context.[353] This understanding immediately invites a resistance to attempt defining the concept in terms of its attendant politics.[354] In the attempt to invest sustainable development with legal force, I enlist alternate conceptions of law, including Indigenous law and customary law. Therefore, it is important to look to alternative conceptualisations of the concept's legal import considering that current Eurocentric notions are thoroughly deficient.[355]

2.6 Conclusion

In this chapter, I discussed the conceptual variability of an idea that began as nature, became the environment, soon transitioned to development, and finally arrived at sustainable development. Human control and dominance marked every stage of this conceptual journey. But importantly, each of the themes discussed under this chapter are connected to international law as they come together to define the concept of sustainable development.

349 Ibid.

350 Nabaat Tasnima Mahbub, 'Sustainable Development and its Evolution in the Realm of International Environmental Law' (2016) 7 Nnamdi Azikiwe U JIL and Juris 1, 2.

351 Barral, 'Sustainable Development in International Law', 383.

352 Sand, 'Sustainable Development', 201.

353 Mbengue, 'On Sustainable Development', 185.

354 Karl-Erik Sveiby, 'Aboriginal Principles for Sustainable Development as told in Traditional Law Stories' (2009) 17:6 Sust Dev 341, 342.

355 Gurdial Singh Nijar, 'Traditional Knowledge Systems, International Law and National Challenges: Marginalisation or Emancipation' (2013) 24:4 European JIL 1205, 1217.

While the concept is widely recognised as Eurocentric, it has proven itself to be both resilient and practically difficult to dislodge. Development, as the ultimate human aspiration ensured discussions revolving around human progress were contingent upon how society subordinated nature for economic interests.[356] Indeed, its conceptual foundations are firmly rooted in all aspects of modern socio-technical organisation. But it is in its evolution as the 'environment' that the impact of the idea of development is made most visible. Thus, the environment is a consequence of development ideologies.[357] In maintaining this onslaught on nature, Eurocentric epistemologies constructed the environment and joined it to development in a self-serving manner by constructing sustainable development as 'the [paradoxical] conceptual roof for both violating and healing the environment'.[358]

Thus, sustainable development emerges as the final stop in this journey and acts as a common thread running through the themes discussed in this chapter. Presently constituted, the concept reflects Western domination of Southern peoples through international law, albeit in an indirect and less visible form.[359] Viewed in this way, the postcolonial essence of international law, imagined as sustainable development, is transmuted from a vicious legal technology that was deployed in subjugating non-European peoples by universalising European ideals and values into a subtler hegemonic Eurocentrism.[360] This Eurocentric character of international law thus relegates Southern peoples and their concerns.[361] However, based on a supposed peer interaction among states based on formal sovereign equality, international law's false universalism is extended to sustainable development. It conceals the dynamic of difference by painting over the concerns of the subaltern and marginalised classes, especially in the Global South and the South in the North.[362] Accordingly, the next question is, why is such an elusive (legal) concept so universally relevant?[363] I address this question in the next chapter.

356 Sachs, 'Environment', 28.
357 Ibid., 25–27.
358 Ibid., 28.
359 Haque, 'Fate of Sustainable Development', 211.
360 Anne-Charlotte Martineau, 'Overcoming Eurocentrism? Global History and the Oxford Handbook of the History of International Law' (2014) 25:1 European JIL 329, 330.
361 Storr, 'Islands and the South', 532.
362 Bhatia, 'South of the North', 151.
363 Evgenia Pavlovskaia, 'Are We There Yet? A Legal Assessment and Review of the Concept of Sustainable Development under International Law' (2013) 2:1 J Sust Dev L and Pol'y 139, 151.

PART II

Universal, Pluriversal, and in Between

3

Sustainable Development and the Paradox of Legal Universalism

Universalism involves, as the etymology suggests, a 'turning' (versus) of the many into 'one' (uni-). This productive impulse ('turning') of universalism is critical to note, since a universal does not just begin with what exists ('nature') but defines and produces it.*

3.1 Introduction

International law's universalism advocates the ideal of internationalising society. This process requires eliding important differences.[1] Universalism subordinates non-Europeanised experiences while privileging Eurocentric law as a global standard.[2] In this respect, when international law scholars talk about universalism, the oft-unspoken point is that, the further afield international law's Eurocentrism extends, the more its disciplinary reach is viewed as progress.[3]

This paradox raises concerns for critical international law scholarship. Here, Third World Approaches to International Law (TWAIL) scholar Mohsen al Attar argues that 'we come to see that the articulation of global norms and principles is often little more than the expression of special interests, amplified through a bullhorn and superimposed on the world as a universal good'.[4] Yet, while critical international law scholars

* Alexander Laban Hinton, *The Justice Façade: Trials of Transitions in Cambodia* (Oxford University Press 2018) 15.

1 Jonathan I. Charney, 'Universal International Law' (1993) 87:4 Am JIL 529, 529. Charney argues that 'states that are not bound by international laws designed to combat universal environmental threats could become havens for the harmful activities concerned'.

2 Kenneth S. Carlston, 'Universality of International Law Today: Challenge and Response' (1962) 8:2 How LJ 79, 82.

3 Lauri Mälksoo, 'Civilisational Diversity as Challenge to the (False) Universality of International Law' (2019) 9:1 Asian JIL 155, 158.

4 Mohsen al Attar, 'Reframing the "Universality" of International Law in a Globalising World' (2013) 59:1 McGill LJ 95, 119.

have railed against the universality of the discipline, their classical counterparts have dismissed these critical reflections on international law's self-professed objectivity as exaggeration.[5] Thus, Sundhya Pahuja sums up this concern by noting that Eurocentric principles and concepts are 'not universal in fact, nor are they universal in origin'.[6]

The false universalism of international law has considerable implications. It fosters a dynamic of difference that subordinates alternative but helpful versions of an idea, a principle, or a concept that is being universalised.[7] Construed this way, international law is a pliant force bending its course to serve dominant interests.[8] Thus, it is unsurprising that international law extends its universality to its cognate components like sustainable development.[9]

In this chapter, I rely on an historical analysis to demonstrate the basis and scope of this universalism. This chapter partly continues the analysis on conceptualising sustainable development discussed in Chapter 2 while giving adequate independent treatment to sustainable development in international law and politics. The idea behind this analysis is to illuminate the concept as expressed in contemporary (domestic) manifestations as a never-ending struggle to place it within general legal (normative) registers. The analysis also demonstrates how sustainable development's ascent to become a universalist concept should interest critical international law scholarship in the way it mutes ecological violence and how that affects Southern peoples.[10] Considering sustainable development is an important aspect of international governance in how it regulates international environmentalism as a global project, it is important to understand its wider appeal as a worthy objective of international interest.[11]

[5] Bruno Simma, 'Universality of International Law from the Perspective of a Practitioner' (2009) 20:2 European JIL 265, 289.

[6] Pahuja, *Decolonising International Law*, 30.

[7] Humby, 'Evaluating the Value of TWAIL', 322.

[8] Yasuaki Onuma, *A Transcivilisational Perspective on International Law: Questioning Prevalent Cognitive Frameworks in the Emerging Multi-Polar and Multi-Civilisational World of the Twenty-First Century* (Brill 2010) 29; Yasuaki Onuma, *International Law in a Transcivilisational World* (Cambridge University Press 2017).

[9] Anna Aseeva, '(Un)Sustainable Development(s) in International Economic Law: A Quest for Sustainability' (2018) 10 Sustainability 4022, 4043.

[10] Sara L. Seck, 'Ecological Integrity and Third World Approaches to International Law' in Laura Westra, Klaus Bosselmann, and Colin Soskolne (eds.), *Globalisation and Ecological Integrity in Science and International Law* (Cambridge Scholars Publishing 2011) 165, 178.

[11] Paul Wapner, 'World Summit on Sustainable Development: Towards a Post-Jo'burg Environmentalism' (2003) 3:1 Global Envt'l Pol 1, 7.

Joined to this chapter's organising ambition, sustainable development also functions as a separate and distinct concern by establishing itself as a concept with universal presence. A historical inquiry into the concept's international *presence* illustrates this dimension, but more so in how this claim to universality impacts the North–South divide. Beginning with the concept's emergence within international law including events leading up to the 1972 Stockholm Conference, the post-1972 Stockholm Conference meetings, and other follow-up institutional arrangements, the discussion excavates the inherent tensions that were constitutive of the universality of sustainable development. Thus, this chapter problematises sustainable development's global diffusion and subsequent ubiquitous influence.

3.2 Knowledge, Power, and the Coloniality of Sustainable Development

The oft-repeated presumption of a unified world styled as the global village obscures the chasm of different perspectives including in international law.[12] Differences in epistemological outlooks between the Global North and Global South have direct consequences for our understanding of many issues including the evolution of the concept of sustainable development, its legal character, acceptability, and implementation.[13] Contestations over what sustainable development means have led to its characterisation as friend and foe alike.[14]

Understandably, sustainable development's presumed universality is an outcome of its internationalisation. This process of internationalisation is demonstrated in how 'economic growth has colonised international law, including international law in the field of sustainable development'.[15] Viewed this way, the formal emergence of this concept in international law became a universal goal worth pursuing since the 1970s.[16] Since then, it has become a catchphrase or buzzword, 'fit for

[12] Atapattu and Gonzalez, 'North-South Divide', 1.

[13] Karin Mickelson, 'Beyond A Politics of the Possible? South–North Relations and Climate Justice' (2009) 10:2 Melbourne JIL 411, 422.

[14] Viñuales, 'Sustainable Development in International Law', 4.

[15] Scott C. Fulton, Lalanath De Silva and Don Anton, 'Twenty Years after the Rio Summit: What Is the Agenda for the 2012 United Nations Conference on Sustainable Development?' (2012) 106 Am SIL: Proc Annual Mtg 91, 95.

[16] Jacobus Du Pisani, 'Sustainable Development: Historical Roots of the Concept' (2006) 3:2 Envt'l Sciences 83.

purpose' across nearly all human endeavours requiring temperance.[17] Therefore, the pervasiveness of sustainable development accounts for fundamental concerns about its origins and character that were quickly dismissed as unnecessary to permit its flourishing. Nonetheless, these concerns inform its contemporary normative ubiquitousness.[18]

3.2.1 TWAIL, Sustainable Development, and Universality

Critics of classical international law, including TWAIL scholars, resist the silencing of difference that universality is noted for. For TWAIL scholars, universality is imagined as excluding the Third World's intellectual contribution to the pursuit of a truly global intellectual order.[19] Richard Falk explains this concern by arguing that the label of *universal*, when applied to international legal phenomena, often disguises 'Western civilisational hegemony'.[20] Thus, critical international law scholars have often argued that universality acknowledges '*significant* difference as well as sameness in constituting a world order based on procedures and norms explicitly designed to ensure equitable participation'.[21]

In that context, TWAIL challenges the false universalism of international law. This false universalism goes back to the beginnings of the age of discovery when international law's civilising mission was basically to bring non-Western peoples into the Western civilisational circuit.[22] But beyond this historical reference, there is still a more modern history that provides the immediate foundation for this false universalism. In this case, the emergence of a global environmental consciousness is traceable to a particular version of environmentalism that begun in the United States soon after Rachel Carson published her book, *Silent Spring*,

17 Connelly, 'Mapping Sustainable Development', 261.

18 Herman E. Daly, 'On Wilfred Beckerman's Critique of Sustainable Development' (1995) 4:1 Envt'l Val 49, 50.

19 B. S. Chimni, 'The World of TWAIL: Introduction to the Special Issue' (2011) 3 Trade L and Dev 14, 18.

20 Richard Falk, 'False Universalism and the Geopolitics of Exclusion: The Case of Islam' (1997) 18:1 Third World Q 7, 8.

21 Ibid., 9.

22 Sujith Xavier, 'Learning from Below: Theorising Global Governance through Ethnographies and Critical Reflections from the Global South' (2016) 33:3 Windsor YB Access Just 229, 232; Antony Anghie, 'On Critique and Other' in Anne Orford (ed.), *International Law and Its Others* (Cambridge University Press 2006) 389, 394.

on the harmful effects of unregulated use of pesticides.[23] Carson's book, supposedly, set the Global North on a path of environmental reckoning.[24] Sweden, the host of the 1972 Stockholm Conference, was fascinated and anxious about the environmental awareness that had erupted in the aftermath of the publication of *Silent Spring* in the United States, and soon pushed for global action at the UN.[25] This global environmental awareness was tied to this popular narrative and along with it the rise of sustainable development.[26] Still, it is important to circumscribe the story of the *Silent Spring* and similar publications and their contingent neoliberal politics as only a small fraction of a global enterprise informed by an emergent environmental consciousness that was gradually taking hold in both the North and South.[27]

Emerging from this understanding, there has been an uncritical acceptance across both the North and South that sustainable development is linked to these stories and similar events.[28] In this sense, TWAIL's critique of this false universalism is a reaction to the fact that international law 'facilitated the drive to universalise Western notions of law and justice to the global space'.[29] This Third World concern over universality, thus, arises from the anxiety that an indeterminate concept with a particular history has been essentialised as universal. Therefore, sustainable development is deployed as a technology of control despite there being no agreement over the concept's meaning across space and time.[30]

[23] Rachel Carson, *Silent Spring* (Houghton Mifflin 1962).

[24] Philippe D. Tortell, 'Earth 2020: Science, Society, and Sustainability in the Anthropocene' (2020) 117:16 Proc Nat Acad Sciences 8683, 8684.

[25] Stephen J. Macekura, *Of Limits and Growth: The Rise of Global Sustainable Development in the Twentieth Century* (Cambridge University Press 2015) 91–93.

[26] Gayil Talshir, 'The Role of Environmentalism: From the Silent Spring to the Silent Revolution' in Yoram Levy and Marcel Wissenburg (eds.), *Liberal Democracy and Environmentalism: The End of Environmentalism?* (Routledge 2004) 10, 18–19; Habibul Haque Khondker, 'From the Silent Spring to the Globalisation of the Environmental Movement' (2015) 6:2 J Int'l and Global Studies 25, 26–28.

[27] Lynley Tulloch and David Neilson, 'The Neoliberalisation of Sustainability' (2014) 13:1 Citizenship Soc and Econ Educ 26, 32.

[28] Chris O. Ikporukpo, 'From Silent Spring to the Sustainable Development Goals: On the Development–Environment Nexus' (2017) 7:2 Afr J Sust Dev 25.

[29] Sujith Xavier, 'Top Heavy: Beyond the Global North and the Justification for Global Administrative Law' (2017) 57:3–4 Indian JIL 337, 340.

[30] Martti Koskenniemi, 'The Politics of International Law—20 Years Later' (2009) 20:1 European JIL 7, 10.

It is little surprise then that there has been no intentional effort towards imbuing sustainable development with legal normativity.[31] Yet, as the Global South continues to endure a disproportionate share of the ecological burden arising from the Global North's intemperate development, the endowment of sustainable development with legal normativity remains an important aspect of the South's struggles and of Third World knowledge-making. For example, as the 1972 Stockholm Conference provided the initial basis for the future evolution of international environmental law, it is important for scholars of the discipline, including those of the TWAIL strain, to frequently consult the intellectual record of that conference to derive insights on how linking the environment to development became a project of global dimensions.[32] Even more, it is important to extend our learning beyond the 1972 Stockholm Conference and related processes to fully appreciate how other (global, regional, and even local) events propelled the environment into global prominence as the focus of sustainable development, yet not supplying agreement on definitions of either the environment or sustainable development.[33]

This paradox of universalism fostered the outgrowth of new areas of practice and academic sub-disciplines in the context of a contemporary globalised society.[34] On this subject, while the universality of sustainable development continues to be contested, the internal constitution of international law backed by Eurocentrism nurtures the pervasive reach of this concept.[35] How the Global South and Third World scholarship reframe these basic elements of international law, including sustainable development, will go a long way in determining the extent to which the discipline may 'become an ever more strategic site from which Third World peoples, movements, scholars, and states can contest, negotiate, and resist international economic and development paradigms'.[36] Thus, Third World concerns on sustainable development invite scrutiny, considering how

[31] Chimni, 'Third World Approaches to International Law', 25.

[32] Malavika Rao, 'A TWAIL Perspective on Loss and Damage from Climate Change: Reflections from Indira Gandhi's Speech at Stockholm' (2022) 12:1 Asian JIL 63.

[33] Patricia Birnie, 'The Development of International Environmental Law' (1977) 3:2 Brit J Int'l Studies 169, 170–172; Mahrane et al., 'From Nature to Biosphere', 128.

[34] Jouannet, 'Universalism and Imperialism', 397.

[35] Michael Jacobs, 'Sustainable Development as a Contested Concept' in Andrew Dobson (ed.), *Fairness and Futurity: Essays on Environmental Sustainability and Social Justice* (Oxford University Press 1999) 22, 31.

[36] Natarajan, 'TWAIL and the Environment', 187.

sectional interests have captured the concept and turned it into a legal tool and an international mechanism for satisfying those interests.[37]

3.2.2 *Not Invisible, Yet Hidden*

While hidden in plain sight, sustainable development's evolution reflects a presumed objectivity and universality. Its political character is cloaked in the general language adopted in its various definitions.[38] The dilemma with the concept's mis-description is that international legal scholarship presents the view that there is such a thing as objective truth.[39] However, knowledge production is only partly an attempt at constructing a supposedly correct version or interpretation of an idea, value, or concept. This is done by articulating an inherently subjective viewpoint as objective truth. This point confirms the anxieties over how a small group of interests plays a gatekeeping role over knowledge production, organisation, and translation, and its subsequent application.[40]

I do not wish to exaggerate the import of knowledge to the construction and weaponisation of power.[41] Suffice to say knowledge is power and knowledge-making often serves powerful interests.[42] From this perspective, competing forms of knowledge are regularly othered, suppressed, or incorporated into a so-called functionalist coherence or formal systemisation of knowledge. From a Foucauldian viewpoint, a resistance of this contrived coherence helps in rediscovering the ruptured effects of the conflict and struggle that order this so-called functionalist assessment of knowledge which the systematisation of knowledge is designed to conceal.[43] In this respect, legal scholarship must excavate, analyse, and expose the claim that power 'is not only alongside

[37] Michel Daccache, 'Questioning Biodiversity Governance through Its Articulations' (2013) 18:1 Science Tech and Soc'y 51, 52.

[38] Andrew Jordan, 'The Governance of Sustainable Development: Taking Stock and Looking Forwards' (2008) 26:1 Envt and Plan C: Govt and Pol'y 17, 18.

[39] Bianchi, *International Law Theories*, 3.

[40] Michel Foucault, 'The Order of Discourse' in Robert Young (ed.), *Untying the Text: A Post-Structuralist Reader* (Routledge and Kegan Paul 1981) 48, 51–52.

[41] Michel Foucault, 'Two Lectures' and 'Truth and Power', translated by C. Gordon, *Power/Knowledge: Selected Interviews and Other Writings 1972–1977* (Pantheon Books 1980) 82.

[42] Moyn, 'Knowledge and Politics of International Law', 2165.

[43] Foucault, 'Two Lectures' and 'Truth and Power', 82.

knowledge, but dependent on it'.[44] This concern about the knowledge–power nexus is applicable to international law which has succeeded in maintaining a benign outlook in the face of persistent criticism.[45]

This point is equally true for sustainable development, as it maintains a carefully designed regime of knowledge production that constantly adapts itself to satisfy specific economic ends that may not necessarily be beneficial for ecological interests.[46] In linking sustainable development to the broad subject of development, development functions as discourse that is influenced by Eurocentric ideals. Within this manifestation, development dismisses non-Eurocentric and non-positivist parameters of this discursive method. Thus as, discourse, development aims 'at a total restructuring of the underdeveloped societies'.[47]

The serviceability of sustainable development for economic purposes ensures its language is easily transferrable as development itself aspires for universalism.[48] Barbara Stark points out this concern as she observed that sustainable development is a 'floating bottom line; that is, an unstable bottom line that may vary over time from place to place, reflecting shifting consensus and ongoing dialogue'.[49] This fluidity opens the concept up to multiple uses, a situation that must be seen as an opportunity to make the concept into what we want it to be. Thus, it is at this point that 'sustainable development discourses can be re-read as a new power/knowledge formation, aiming at accumulating power'.[50]

The adaptability of sustainable development in this analysis on economic growth leads critical scholars to argue its outward appearance, which suggests ecological considerations misalign with its internal, latent economistic structure. Emerging from this characterisation, some critical scholars argue

44 Paul R. Brass, 'Foucault Steals Political Science' (2000) 3:1 Annual Rev Pol Science 305, 306.

45 David Kennedy, *A World of Struggle: How Power, Law, and Expertise Shape Global Political Economy* (Princeton University Press 2016) 31–32.

46 Janaka Siyambalapitiya, Xu Zhang and Xiabing Liu, 'Is Governmentality the Missing Link for Greening the Economic Growth?' (2018) 10:11 Sustainability 4204, 4206–4207.

47 Marc Williams, 'Aid, Sustainable Development and the Environmental Crisis' (1998) 3:2 Int'l J Peace Studies 19, 21.

48 Yvonne Rydin, 'Can We Talk Ourselves into Sustainability? The Role of Discourse in the Environmental Policy Process' (1999) 8:4 Envt'l Val 467, 468–469.

49 Barbara Stark, 'Sustainable Development and Postmodern International Law: Greener Globalisation?' (2002–2003) 27:1 William and Mary Envt'l L and Pol'y Rev 137, 184.

50 Timothy W. Luke, 'Sustainable Development as a Power/Knowledge System: The Problem of "Governmentality"' in Frank Fischer and Michael Black (eds.), *Greening Environmental Policy: The Politics of a Sustainable Future* (Paul Chapman Publishing 1995) 21, 28.

sustainable development is an 'eco-capitalist ideology'.[51] For example, Hélène Maynard underlines this point by highlighting how international environmental law does not disavow the neoliberal character of international law; if anything at all, the discipline affirms this version of neoliberalism.[52]

This circular liaison of the co-constitutive character of knowledge and power pushes us in the direction of understanding the intermingling of politics and its association with law. It does so by recognising how and why certain labels, expressions, and terminologies attached to international phenomena contradict their legal character.[53] For instance, knowledge construction is doubly frustrated by the 'concept of coloniality', which ensures that the 'historical and cultural contexts' of Eurocentrism continue to constitute pathways for accepting and incorporating ideas about what knowledge is or not.[54]

On this subject, the process of constructing knowledge, which begins with theorising, is informed by a predetermined position and an ultimate purpose. This process also encompasses 'the politics of knowledge, that is, the origins of the knowledge within international law, or the foundations of international law'.[55] It follows that the idea of progress in respect of environmental consciousness, conceptualised as sustainable development, carries a Western imprint on international environmentalism.[56] Accordingly, it is least surprising that the contentious relation between the environment and development continues to underpin international law's endeavour to entrench the concept of sustainable development and embed it in international law.[57] Hence, even today, this environment–development nexus remains the focus of sustainable development.[58]

[51] Mark CJ Stoddart, 'The Gramsci-Foucault Nexus and Environmental Sociology' (2005) 21 Alternative Routes 40, 44.

[52] Hélène Maynard, 'From Classical Liberalism to Neoliberalism: Explaining the Contradictions in the International Environmental Law' in Usha Natarajan and Julia Dehm (eds.), *Locating Nature: Making and Unmaking International Law* (Cambridge University Press 2022) 45, 55.

[53] Tanja Aalberts and Ben Golder, 'On the Uses of Foucault for International Law' (2012) 25:3 Leiden JIL 603, 606.

[54] Johanna Bergström, 'Learning from Mayan Feminists' Interpretation of Buen Vivir' in Julie Cupples and Ramón Gosfoguel (eds.), *Unsettling Eurocentrism in the Westernised University* (Routledge 2019) 156, 158.

[55] Larissa Ramina, 'Third World Approaches to International Law and Human Rights: Some Considerations' (2018) 51 Revista de Investigações Constitucionais 261, 265.

[56] Banerjee, 'Who Sustains Whose Development?', 157.

[57] Petersmann, 'Narcissus' Reflection in the Lake', 242.

[58] Karin Mickelson, 'Rhetoric and Rage: Third World Voices in International Legal Discourse' (1998) 16:2 Wisconsin Int'l LJ 355, 388–390.

Accordingly, the presumed universality of the concept of sustainable development must be understood within the interaction between law and genealogies of knowledge. As Vito De Lucia has explained:

> [Genealogy] is a history that does not search for a single point of origin; it does not attempt to find the true essence, or original identity, of concepts and phenomena. Genealogy is rather aimed at the reconstruction of the contingencies and contestations constituting their complex history. And while every concept, understood genealogically, is the contingent result of an antagonistic 'play of forces', law is arguably a privileged point of emergence of such conflicts and contestations. All legal concepts can be then approached genealogically, and are arguably the result of an ensemble of competing forces each trying to assert hegemony.[59]

Moored to this genealogical exposition, international environmental law materialises as the expression of power that conditions our human relationship with nature. This takes the form of an initial control over resource access, which is later disguised as 'a series of positive interventions that aim at its care, at fostering and optimising its processes, and at the same time at the enhancement of its productive forces'.[60] Considering that sustainable development emerges from the idea of knowledge as power, ongoing efforts directed at reversing the concept's pervasiveness invite critical engagement with the power–knowledge nexus. Such engagements also reveal how the legal order and the international system come together to establish and disseminate sustainable development.[61] Thus, the project of reconstituting sustainable development requires revisiting the society–nature nexus as the foundation for excavating alternative ideations for a new version of the concept's legal focus; one that is responsive to the needs of ecological integrity.[62]

3.2.3 *Sustainable Development in a State of Flux*

Along with its seeming objectivity and its universality, the concept of sustainable development functions as a revolving door of knowledge production. Even more, international law's Eurocentric character

[59] De Lucia, 'Competing Narratives and Complex Genealogies', 93.

[60] Vito De Lucia, 'Bare Nature: The Biopolitical Logic of the International Regulation of Invasive and Alien Species' (2019) 31:1 J Envt'l L 108, 121.

[61] Leff, 'Power–Knowledge Relations', 225.

[62] Emmanuelle Jouannet, 'What Is the Use of International Law? International Law as a 21st Century Guardian of Welfare' (2007) 28:4 Michigan JIL 815, 822.

remains central to sustainable development's evolution and metastasis. The changing scenes of Western imperialist exploitation of nature viewed through international law's ever-present Eurocentric lens are translocated thus through different stages of which the most recent is christened sustainable development.[63]

Still, economic growth is central to this evolution.[64] Development, which incorporates sustainable development, is inherently Western-oriented. On this subject, seemingly 'externalised' efforts to rehabilitate the Western development model are only intended to disguise development's consequences and not to pull it back from pushing planetary integrity to the brink.[65] In this respect, the invitation to ignore compromises that inform sustainable development's claim to universality and objectivity must be treated with caution. Since sustainable development is aligned with the neoliberal, techno-managerial mission to contain development, sustainable development cannot claim to be a product of 'ecological sensitivities or environmental consciousness'.[66] In this light, I share in the caution that critical legal scholarship must be wary of sustainable development's ahistorical outlook. Accordingly, by accepting the concept without scrutiny would amount to overlooking the continuing legacies of international law's imperial past.[67]

The transdisciplinary disposition of the concept thus opens it up to mixed interpretation and application, leaving it in a state of flux.[68] Evidently, sustainable development's ambivalence is paradoxically its strength and weakness. As a result, the struggle to define sustainable development, in international and domestic law, has garnered support for its contrived use in both public and private decision-making.[69] Among various proposed definitions, the most widely cited, perhaps on account of its formal popularity, is that: 'Sustainable development is

63 Julien Vanhulst and Adrian E. Beling, 'Buen Vivir: Emergent Discourse or Beyond Sustainable Development?' (2014) 101 Ecol Econ 54, 58.
64 Adelman, 'Sustainable Development Goals', 18–19.
65 Ibid., 17.
66 Castro, 'Sustainable Development', 216.
67 Anghie, *Imperialism*, 315.
68 Keith Pezzoli, 'Sustainable Development: A Transdisciplinary Overview of the Literature' (1997) 40:5 J Envt'l Planning and Mgt 549.
69 Klaus Bosselmann, 'Losing the Forests for the Trees: Environmental Reductionism in Law' (2010) 2 Sustainability 2424, 2435.

development that meets the needs of the present generation without compromising the ability of future generations to meet their own needs'.[70] This definition suggests that socio-technical organisation (that is, development) takes precedence over ecological integrity since sustainable development is the product of a particular politics.[71] Thus, a retrospective analysis of the negotiation of sustainable development through international processes sharply calls into question the politics of 'superficial consensus', which makes the goal of ecological integrity elusive.[72]

While the instability of sustainable development limits its conceptual and practical effectiveness, this state of flux equally presents an escape route for the concept to re-establish itself without losing its evolutionary significance. But international law is evolving towards the integration of law and ecology, although with little attempt at outlining the content of sustainable development.[73] This process, manifesting either in domestic environmental law or international environmental law, is emerging from an initial diffidence as it rejects the 'legal illusion of control of the natural'.[74] In its more audacious outlook, sustainable development, as the interaction between law and ecology, proposes a reconceptualised view of law, which involves a 'possible meaning as *the disciplinary and ontological plane on which law finds itself*'.[75] Viewed this way, sustainable development escapes its present constraints and flux to set itself on a course of self-emancipation.

3.2.3.1 From Transition to Transilience: International Environmental Law as Sustainable Development

The challenges posed by sustainable development's universality are most profound in international environmental law.[76] This point requires a historical exploration. Notably, while the 1972 Stockholm Conference, and its

[70] World Commission on Environment and Development, *Our Common Future*, 44.
[71] Ibid., 9.
[72] Moore, 'Toppling the Tripod', 142–144.
[73] Bosselmann, 'Losing the Forests for the Trees', 2437.
[74] Andreas Philippopoulos-Mihalopoulos, 'Looking for the Space between Law and Ecology' in Andreas Philippopoulos-Mihalopoulos (ed.), *Law and Ecology: New Environmental Foundations* (Routledge 2011) 1, 1.
[75] Ibid., 2.
[76] Jutta Brunnée, 'The Stockholm Declaration and the Structure and Processes of International Environmental Law' in Aldo Chircop, Ted L. McDorman, and Susan J. Rolston (eds.), *The Future of Ocean Regime-Building: Essays in Tribute to Douglas M. Johnston* (Brill 2009) 41, 42; Cinnamon Carlane, 'Delinking International Environmental Law and Climate Change' (2014) 4:1 Michigan J Envt'l and Admin L 1.

outcome document, the Stockholm Declaration, outlined key principles for environmental protection from an international perspective, these environmental problems intensified, mainly in the context of the North–South debate.[77] Although international law scholarship recognised sustainable development as an emergent concept, its rise and intellectual adaptation across several fields caused a shift in attention from international environmental law's own disciplinary evolution to sustainable development's diffusion. Studies into proceedings from international conferences and diplomatic side meetings reveal sustainable development's increased growth in international circles and the commitment to forge a global bargain over its role and place in international affairs. In this sense, it becomes apparent the concept provides both subtext and content for disguising economic growth while shrewdly projecting a semblance of environmental consciousness. It is thus crucially important to contextualise the history of the normative processes underlying the formalisation of sustainable development in international law.[78]

To begin, what this history reveals is that, the 1972 Stockholm Conference was initially conceived by the North to address the growing incidence of transboundary pollution. The South's position was that environmental pollution was the outcome of the North's economic growth. That process meant that the 1972 Stockholm Conference was an opportunity to confront not only environmental concerns but also address complex development matters.[79]

Thus, at the conference and during the period immediately after, the South consistently argued the North was unwilling to commit the financial, logistical, and technological assistance needed in making sustainable development a realisable objective.[80] At the same time, the Global South was aware of the externalisation of environmental negativities by Global North-based transnational corporations. These corporations had been

A similar concept that overshadows international environmental law's (own) evolution is climate change, now sometimes called the climate emergency or climate crisis.

77 Chee Yoke Ling, *The Rio Declaration on Environment and Development: An Assessment* (Third World Network 2012) 1–2.

78 Marie-Claire Cordonnier Segger, 'International Law, Criminal Justice, and Sustainable Development' in Sébastien Jodoin and Marie-Claire Cordonnier Segger (eds.), *Sustainable Development, International Criminal Justice, and Treaty Implementation* (Cambridge University Press 2013) 17, 25.

79 Brunnée, 'Stockholm Declaration', 42.

80 R. R. Daniel, 'The North–South Divide and the Compulsions of the 21st Century' (1999) 77:6 Current Science 770, 773.

relocating to the Global South to avoid rigorous environmental regulation in their home states. Thus, the prospects of these corporations moving into the South complicated an already complex issue by provoking a nuanced appreciation of the relationship between development and environment.[81]

The UN organised yet another environmental mega-conference, the United Nations Conference on the Environment and Development, 1992 (Rio Earth Summit), two decades after the 1972 Stockholm Conference. This event was to assess efforts aimed at merging environmental and developmental imperatives.[82] It was this conference that revolutionised the understanding of the environment–development nexus. It was through this conference that the term 'sustainable development' became a lasting fixture in international legal discourse.[83] As Ulrich Beyerlin and Thilo Marauhn have noted, sustainable development was the primary focus of the Rio Earth Summit as the conference sought to perform the difficult assignment of formalising the relationship between the environment and development which had already begun at Stockholm.[84]

As was the case with the many compromises made at the 1972 Stockholm Conference over the environment–development nexus, the Rio Earth Summit saw a hurried transition in the evolution of international environmental law from a fledgling sub discipline of international law into 'a new (and yet to be defined) "law of sustainable development"'.[85] By this, the summit failed to reorganise the emerging sub-field of international environmental law. This happened as a result of the Rio Earth Summit's inability to endue international environmental law with the much-needed 'centralised authority for creation and enforcement of law'.[86] Rather, the conference ended up focusing on consolidating the language of sustainable development.

81 Ulrich Beyerlin, 'Bridging the North–South Divide in International Environmental Law' (2006) 66 ZaöRV 259, 260.

82 Adil Najam, 'Unraveling the Rio Bargain' (2002) 21:2 Pol and Life Sciences 46. Najam argues that based on the Global North's failure to fulfil the promises made at Stockholm, the Global South was quite reluctant in attending the Rio Earth Summit.

83 Rebecca M. Bratspies, 'Rethinking Decisionmaking in International Environmental Law: A Policy-Oriented Inquiry into Sustainable Development' (2007) 32:2 Yale Int'l LJ 363, 367.

84 Ulrich Beyerlin and Thilo Marauhn, *International Environmental Law* (Hart Publishing 2011) 8.

85 Peter H. Sand, 'International Environmental Law after Rio' (1993) 4:3 European JIL 377, 378.

86 Geoffrey Palmer, 'What Went Wrong at Rio?' (1992) 70:4 Wash ULQ 1005, 1009.

Interestingly, the proposal that would allegedly frustrate this advance at Rio reportedly came from the Global South. Peter Sand writes that:

> Meanwhile, there is at least one area where the Rio Conference has already left its imprint on the evolution of environmental law – by formally anointing the concept of 'sustainable development' for legal use. I still remember the malicious comment by a Brazilian delegate to the UNCED Preparatory Committee, my good friend Pedro Motta Pinto Coelho (Director of Environment in the Ministry of Foreign Affairs and political scientist by training), after he persuaded the Working Group III to change the term 'international environmental law' to read 'international law of sustainable development' throughout the text of Agenda 21. That will keep you lawyers busy well into the 21st century.[87]

Thus, it was at the Rio Earth Summit that sustainable development was firmly established as the alternate project to international environmental law without saying as much. In a circular manner, the concept became the embodiment of the disciplinary nerve of international environmental law while at the same time subverting its disciplinary evolution.[88]

However, this challenge of uniting the environment and development was not exactly the outcome of the Rio Earth Summit alone. Rather, it evokes the *longue durée* that international law scholars must commit to writing about.

On this subject, the development–environment characterisation has an extended history dating back to the period immediately before and during the 1972 Stockholm Conference and, more presently, to the United Nations Conference on Sustainable Development (the Rio+20 Conference). This long history 'represent[s] an important shift from environmental protection to sustainable development as a central global agenda'.[89] However, in parsing this historical progression since the 1972 Stockholm Conference, it is apparent the Rio Earth Summit had tried to expand on the previous work undertaken at the 1972 Stockholm Conference and much later by the World Commission on Environment

[87] Peter H. Sand, 'UNCED and the Development of International Environmental Law' (1992) 8:2 J Nat Res and Envt'l L 209, 228.

[88] Klaus Bosselmann, 'Sustainable Development and International Environmental Law' in Erika J. Techera (ed.), *Routledge Handbook of International Environmental Law* (Routledge 2012) 667, 667.

[89] Amado S. Tolentino Jr, 'Passage from Natural Resources Law to Environmental Law to Sustainable Development Law' in Rüdiger Wolfrum, Maja Seršic, and Trpimir M. Šošić (eds.), *Contemporary Developments in International Law: Essays in Honour of Budislav Vukas* (Brill 2016) 906, 910–911.

and Development (Brundtland Commission), to deliver on the promise of sustainable development.[90]

While five outcome documents were adopted at the Rio Earth Summit, my discussion is restricted to the Rio Declaration given its significance in setting out the structural dimensions of the concept.[91] The first four principles of the Rio Declaration are important here.[92] Principle 1 outlines the contradictory anthropocentric character of international efforts aimed at environmental protection while at the same time recognising that human society must live 'in harmony with nature'.[93] Principle 2 simply reproduces Principle 21 of the Stockholm Declaration as it reaffirms the right of states to resource sovereignty and a corresponding duty to prevent transboundary harm.[94] Principle 3 provides that states may undertake development as of right but must consider both developmental and environmental needs in this process.[95] However, this principle does very little to clarify the ambiguity in Principle 21 of the Stockholm Declaration as to whether development ranks above or that it was at par with the environment.[96] Finally, Principle 4 acknowledges environmental protection is fundamental to sustainable development.[97] Even so, this final principle has been criticised as failing to give clear direction on whether it imposes an obligation on states or that it is merely an aspirational goal.[98]

90 Peter H. Sand, 'International Law on the Agenda of the 1992 "Earth Summit"' (1992) 3:1 Colo J Int'l Envt'l L and Pol'y 343.

91 *Report of the United Nations on Environment and Development*, Rio de Janeiro, 3–14 June 1992, UN Doc A.CONF.151/267 Rev 1, vols I–II.

92 Tomislav Klarin, 'The Concept of Sustainable Development: From Its Beginning to the Contemporary Issues' (2018) 21:1 Zagreb Int'l Rev Econ and Bus 67, 75.

93 Principle 1 of the Rio Declaration: Human beings are at the centre of concern for sustainable development. They are entitled to a healthy and productive life in harmony with nature.

94 Principle 2 of the Rio Declaration. States have, in accordance with the UN Charter and the principles of international law, the sovereign right to exploit their own resources pursuant to their own environmental and developmental policies, and the responsibility to ensure that activities within their jurisdiction or control do not cause damage to the environment of other States or of areas beyond the limits of national jurisdiction.

95 Principle 3 of the Rio Declaration. The right to development must be fulfilled to equitably meet developmental and environmental needs of present and future generations.

96 Howard Mann, 'The Rio Declaration' (1992) 86 Am SIL: Proc Annual Mtg 405, 410.

97 Principle 4 of the Rio Declaration. In order to achieve sustainable development, environmental protection shall constitute an integral part of the development process and cannot be considered in isolation from it.

98 Ileana Porras, 'The Rio Declaration: A New Basis for International Cooperation' (1992) 1:3 RECIEL 245, 248.

Therefore, the Rio Earth Summit laid the foundations for a new global pact based on sustainable development.[99] To an extent, the principles emerging from the Rio Declaration contributed to an improved understanding and application of the concept.[100] Significantly, it was at Rio that the environment and development were conceptually coupled to inaugurate a new sphere of influence and control within international (environmental) regulation.[101] Paradoxically, these two domains, regardless of their interlinkages, continue to function discretely, leading to an ossification of differences in the pursuit of sustainable development even where there was supposed agreement that the concept moderates economic growth.[102]

The lack of normative clarity thus renders sustainable development ineffective in terms of its practical application since the balance between economic growth and environmental protection remains flexible.[103] This lack of clarity intensifies an already fractious relationship between the Global North and Global South. This challenge is exemplified in how the North's creative diplomacy has stalled attempts at getting it (the North) to commit financial and technical assistance to the South's development objectives where these objectives might conflict with the North's ever-increasing demands for greater environmental protection.

Even so, this is not exactly a situation where the North demonstrates noble intentions. This process of balancing competing interests date to the 1972 Stockholm Conference.[104] If anything at all, the North's seeming interest in the environment operated to close off any serious consideration of the ecological debt (and responsibility) owed the South due to the North's exploitative relationship with the environment. As B. S. Chimni explains what the North's motivation was, '[t]he general idea here is to displace the aspirations of Third World peoples and scale down development to more tolerable levels. This would help avoid the burden of sustainable development from falling on the North and help sustain its high consumption patterns'.[105]

99 Luis A. Aviles, 'Sustainable Development and Environmental Legal Protection' (2014) 6:2 Mexican L Rev 251, 256.

100 Ibid., 256.

101 Adil Najam and Cutler J. Cleveland, 'Energy and Sustainable Development at Global Environmental Summits: An Evolving Agenda' (2003) 5:1 Envt Dev and Sustainability 117, 118.

102 Aviles, 'Sustainable Development and Environmental Legal Protection', 257.

103 Ibid., 257–258.

104 Palmer, 'What Went Wrong at Rio?', 1021.

105 Chimni, 'Third World Approaches to International Law', 18.

So, these mega-conferences only veiled the already disagreeable relationship that the conferences eagerly strove to resolve. As Ileana Porras rightly noted, the 'Rio Declaration as adopted is a text of uneasy compromises, delicately balanced interests, and simply discernible contradictions, held together by the interpretative vagueness of classic UN-ese'.[106] Accordingly, despite sustainable development's many challenges, its global reach is firmly shielded and unaffected by its ambivalence. Its universality papers over the concept's fundamental tensions and is responsible for new outgrowths including the sustainable development goals (SDGs) that further obfuscate the concept's legal significance.[107]

3.3 Sustainable Development: Compromise as Universality

The formal emergence of the concept of sustainable development in the aftermath of the 1972 Stockholm Conference obscured the tensions that preceded this summit. However, not much scholarly attention has been devoted to this unique history of the concept's progress in international law.[108] In this context, a historical analysis brings together several strands of normative processes, emerging from historical events, that implicate the concept's evolution. This is not simply a call to a mere historical analysis or description; rather, it is an invitation to conduct and engage in a critical legal reading in which past proceedings are not understood simply as history but as an opportunity to think through past events as law-making.[109]

3.3.1 *Stockholm's Trade-Off: Meaning and Global Presence*

The 1972 Stockholm Conference has been labelled the 'first universalist conference on the questions of international environmental protection'.[110] This description evokes the emblematic narrative of a meeting of states in a large forum as synonymous with universal agreement. But

106 Porras, 'Rio Declaration', 247.

107 Rakhyun E. Kim and Klaus Bosselmann, 'Operationalising Sustainable Development: Ecological Integrity as a Grundnorm of International Law' (2015) 24:2 RECIEL 194, 206.

108 Mickelson, 'Stockholm Conference', 127.

109 Orford, 'On International Legal Method', 177.

110 Beyerlin and Marauhn, *International Environmental Law*, 7.

then, perhaps, what this description (like similar uses of the term 'universal') does, is simply to proselytise for a seemingly innocuous view of global consensus in a manner that is subsequently essentialised as legal normativity. This is a challenge with international law. As Anthea Roberts recently noted, international law extends the applicability of the terminology (universality) to international phenomena that influential actors choose to elevate to 'global' status.[111] This way, the distinction between the *local* and *international* is de-emphasised when powerful interests require a flattening of such difference.

When this understanding of universality is projected onto sustainable development, it immediately becomes a problematic concept. This concern emerges from the fact that the concept's grip over international environmental law suggests that, since its formal emergence, its ideal and manifestations reflect a universalist perspective that is globally representative.[112] Yet a closer reading of the processes leading up to the emergence of sustainable development in international law contradicts this popular narrative that seems to suggest common agreement. Rather, what is evident is that every recorded instance of the concept's progress and evolution has been marked by great compromise.[113] The essence of a universalist critique of sustainable development then is driven by the knowledge that universality does not guarantee a fair application of a concept even with the noblest of intentions.

Thus, to deconstruct how universality frames the normativity of sustainable development, it is important to return to the 1972 Stockholm Conference and the events leading up to that conference. The analysis reveals the Global North foresaw the possibility of a failed 1972 Stockholm Conference and forestalled it by proposing a preparatory meeting with the South. This meeting was held in Founex in Switzerland in 1971 (hence its name, Founex Meeting).[114] Twenty-seven development and environment experts from across the North and South were invited to attend

[111] Roberts, *Is International Law International?*, 19–20.

[112] Sudhir Anand and Amartya Sen, 'Human Development and Economic Sustainability' (2000) 28:12 World Dev 2029, 2030.

[113] Sakiko Fukuda-Parr and Desmond McNeill, 'Knowledge and Politics in Setting and Measuring the SDGs: Introduction to Special Issue' (2019) 10:S1 Global Pol'y 5, 12–14.

[114] Michael W. Manulak, 'Developing World Environmental Cooperation: The Founex Seminar and the Stockholm Conference' in Wolfram Kaiser and Jan-Henrik Meyer (eds.), *International Organisations and Environmental Protection: Conservation and Globalisation in the 21st Century* (Berghahn Books 2017) 103, 103–104.

the meeting.[115] This Founex Meeting attempted a preliminary reconciliation of the intractable positions of the North and the South over the environment's role vis-à-vis economic growth. This was a looming challenge the Global North anticipated might lead to non-attendance of leading states in the Global South, a situation capable of derailing the planned 1972 Stockholm Conference.[116]

A report was issued at the end of the meeting.[117] In his introductory remarks to this report, the Secretary-General of the 1972 Stockholm Conference, Maurice Strong, who coincidentally chaired the earlier Founex Meeting, noted that 'we have taken what I regard as a very significant step forward on the road to Stockholm'.[118] In these brief remarks, Strong achieved three things that continue to shape the future of sustainable development. First, Strong characterised the concern over the state of the environment as 'newly-perceived'.[119] This statement accounts for the perception of the 1972 Stockholm Conference as the origin story of sustainable development and, along with it, the subsequent ahistoricism that would follow international environmental law.[120] Second, he labelled the report as an 'outstanding contribution to a full understanding' of the environment–development debate.[121] Even though successive conferences challenged the durability of this supposed comprehensive understanding, still it operated as a strategic depoliticisation of the North–South divide in respect of sustainable development. Finally, Strong described the Founex Meeting as 'a historic turning point' in the 'development–environment' dialogue.[122] In its classic

115 Phillip Stalley, 'Norms from the Periphery: Tracing the Rise of the Common but Differentiated Principle in International Environmental Politics' (2018) 31:2 Cambridge Rev Int'l Aff 141, 146.

116 Scott MacLeod, *Financing Environmental Measures in Developing Countries: The Principle of Additionality*, No 6 (IUCN Environmental Policy and Law Paper 1974) 1, 48.

117 *Founex Report on Development and Environment Submitted by a Panel of Experts Convened by the Secretary-General of the United Nations Conference on the Human Environment*, 4–12 June 1971, Founex, Switzerland, (1972) International Conciliation 7, 10–11.

118 Maurice Strong, 'Introduction' in *Development and Environment: Report and Working Papers of a Panel of Experts Convened by the Secretary-General of the United Nations Conference on the Human Conference* (Mouton 1972) x.

119 Ibid.

120 Ibironke T Odumosu-Ayanu, 'Local Communities, Environment and Development: The Case of Oil and Gas Investment in Africa' in Kate Miles (ed.), *Research Handbook on Environment and Investment Law* (Edward Elgar 2019) 480, 492.

121 Strong, 'Introduction', x.

122 Ibid.

Eurocentric approach, Strong's statement quietly displaced a greater part of the historical evidence of environment-related issues that was to guide discussions much later at the 1972 Stockholm Conference. As a result, Strong's characterisation of the outcome of the Founex Meeting in such absolute terms, which contradicted the compromise that began at Founex, later found its way into the 1972 Stockholm Conference, and very well into successive environment-related mega-conferences.

Equally important, a key question leading to this preliminary meeting at Founex was the political character of the subject under consideration. As argued by some scholars, an analysis of the UN-related conferences on the environment and development demonstrated:

> This is a politically complex issue which again involves North–South concerns. Developing countries and their industries, starting from a lower base of environmental protection and more dependent upon resource-intensive industries, fear the impact of being forced by international standards to adopt the same level of environmental protection and costs as developed countries.[123]

The Founex report thus recounted the tensions between the North and the South by distinguishing their competing interests as the 'pollution of affluence' (the Global North's problem) and the 'pollution of poverty' (the Global South's concern).[124]

These tensions have become recurring concerns at subsequent conferences. The Global South was not only anxious about its historical situation as a site of extractivism with attendant environmental challenges. It was also concerned about the motivations and interests of intermediaries brokering agreements between the North and South. For example, during the Rio Earth Summit, Southern states and Non-Governmental Organisations (NGOs) were suspicious of the intimate link between corporate interests from the Global North and the former Secretary-General of the 1972 Stockholm Conference, Strong, who was still influential in diplomatic and negotiation circles.[125] This anxiety was not new to the Rio Earth Summit as it dates back to the Founex meeting where the

[123] Michael Grubb, Matthias Koch, Abby Munson, Francis Sullivan and Koy Thomson, *The 'Earth Summit' Agreements: A Guide and Assessments* (Earthscan Publications 1993) 39.

[124] Carl Marklund, 'Double Loyalties? Small-State Solidarity and the Debates on the New International Economic Order in Sweden during the Long 1970s' (2020) 45:3 Scand J History 384, 387.

[125] Jennifer Clapp and Peter Dauvergne, *Paths to a Green World: The Political Economy of the Global Environment*, 2nd ed. (MIT Press 2011) 67.

Global South was concerned about Strong's past corporate engagements and the possibility that, if Strong and these powerful corporations collaborated, they could significantly water down any outcome of the Rio Earth Summit.[126]

3.3.2 *Overcoming Resistance: Co-optation as Universality*

Despite all the suspicions, perhaps what is left out in many accounts on the success of the 1972 Stockholm Conference is how Strong skilfully co-opted Southern resistance and turned some Southern states into the Global North's allies.[127] When the UN voted to hold the 1972 Stockholm Conference, there was some scepticism in the Global South regarding the purpose of the conference.[128] Concerned about the effect of this scepticism on attendance and participation and how it might weaken the conference's legitimacy, the UN needed to make a difficult and compromising choice. Owing to the anxiety over balancing development and environment, and the corollary concern over the participation of the Global South, the UN sought after a conference chair who could broker compromises across diverse interests. Thus, it was little surprise when the UN Secretary-General, U Thant, appointed Strong to lead the conference.[129]

This appointment was a strategic choice. At the time, Strong, a wealthy business executive with extensive corporate experience, had transitioned to public service. Around the same time, he was the head of the Canadian International Development Agency (CIDA) and had prior experience working with Southern states.[130] Leveraging his past corporate liaison with these states, he was a politically desirable choice as it was evident the

[126] Michael W. Manulak, *Change in Global Environmental Politics: Temporal Focal Points and the Reform of International Institutions* (Cambridge University Press 2022) 98. Manulak notes that Strong shared close business relations with powerful interests who supported economic considerations over the environment. This information cannot be overlooked if we think more carefully about how sustainable development ended up been framed as a compromise.

[127] Marc Williams, 'Re-Articulating the Third World Coalition: The Role of the Environmental Agenda' (1993) 14:1 Third World Q 7, 17.

[128] David Satterthwaite, *Barbara Ward and the Origins of Sustainable Development* (International Institute for Environment and Development 2006) 11.

[129] Manulak, *Change in Global Environmental Politics*, 84–85. Strong was appointed to replace the Swiss national, Jean Mussard, who had held the position of director of studies of the conference secretariat.

[130] David R. Morrison, *Aid and Ebb Tide: A History of CIDA and Canadian Development Assistance* (Wilfrid Laurier University Press 1998) 57–98.

conference had outgrown its technical inspiration and had assumed a geopolitical character in dire need of corresponding political guidance. Strong took up this responsibility and succeeded in convincing governments and heads of state from Africa, Latin America, and Asia to attend the 1972 Stockholm Conference.[131] He did much of this by relying on his vast and invaluable business networks to co-opt development experts and leading Third World economists from the South who were also sceptical about attending the conference.[132]

Strong's mandate was to ensure that the 1972 Stockholm Conference was held, and that it was successful. That meant guaranteeing the attendance of the Global South; which, at the very least, was to satisfy the essential optics and performativity of representativeness.[133] He went about co-opting Southern economists and development experts to work in the conference secretariat ostensibly to create a 'healthy' public image for the conference and to reassure Southern states that their concerns would receive attention. Notably, Strong headhunted two renowned economists from Pakistan and Sri Lanka respectively: Mahbub ul Haq and Gamani Corea.[134] It is no surprise then that one of these two, Mahbub ul Haq, is credited with contributing to the success of the Founex Meeting and for writing its final report.[135]

In recent accounts, some scholars have reiterated the significance of the Founex Meeting which succeeded in averting a stalemate at the impending 1972 Stockholm Conference.[136] The Founex Meeting thus led to a major outcome considering it eased the suspicion and anxieties of the South that the impending 1972 Stockholm Conference was an ingenious process employed by the Global North to disguise its postcolonial management of the South by simultaneously contradicting and restricting the South's development agenda. For the Global South, their suspicion

[131] Satterthwaite, *Barbara Ward*, 11.

[132] Peter Willetts, 'From Stockholm to Rio and Beyond: The Impact of the Environmental Movement on the United Nations Consultative Arrangements for NGOs' (1996) 22:1 Rev Int'l Studies 57, 68.

[133] Donald W. Kaniaru, 'The Development of the Concept of Sustainable Development and the Birth of the UNEP' in Tuomas Kuokkanen, Ed Couzens, Tuula Honkonen and Melissa Lewis (eds.), *International Environmental Law-making and Diplomacy: Insights and Overviews* (Routledge 2017) 127, 129.

[134] Fulton et al., 'Twenty Years after the Rio Summit', 96.

[135] Ibid., 97.

[136] Edith Brown Weiss, 'Rule of Law for Nature in a Kaleidoscopic World' in Christina Voigt (ed.), *Rule of Law for Nature: New Dimensions and Ideas for Environmental Law* (Cambridge University Press 2013) 27, 29.

contemplated environmental protection while at the same time constraining the South's participation in the global economy.[137] The Founex Meeting was then a site for forging a so-called negotiated agreement to moderate the tensions at the heart of the contending concerns of economic development and environmental protection.[138] Going into the 1972 Stockholm Conference, these conflicts were central to the North–South divide and have remained a distinguishing feature of the North–South divide till date.[139]

Therefore, it is understandable that the urgency with which the Founex Meeting was organised reflected the growing apprehension of the South that a concerted global effort to protect the environment might result in imposing constraints on the South's development efforts.[140] As recounted in the Founex Meeting's report, Southern states had argued that the impending meeting at Stockholm must account for the fact that the development deficit of the South could only be resolved through more development.[141] Conceptualised differently, the South viewed development as the sure path to overcoming its internal environmental issues. This was some kind of paradox – that development could be attained only by joining the bandwagon of ecological damage as development envisaged here was of the Eurocentric stock. Thus, the South viewed the so-called invitation to dialogue over the global environmental crisis as a summons to a conversation over the effects of the North's development. Thus, the South had initially resolved that environmentalist objectives should not be pursued at the expense of its development programmes.[142]

If sustainable development is characterised as a compromise, then it is noteworthy to recall that the Founex Meeting and its inevitable outcome presaged this concession. In this context, the instrumentality of the Founex Meeting to the success of the 1972 Stockholm Conference must be revisited.[143] As Claire Brighton notes accurately, the historical success

[137] Chukwumekerije Okereke, 'Global Environmental Sustainability: Intragenerational Equity and Conceptions of Justice in Multilateral Environmental Regimes' (2006) 37:5 Geoforum 725, 726.

[138] Weiss, 'Evolution of International Environmental Law', 4.

[139] Björn-Ola Linnér and Merle Jacob, 'From Stockholm to Kyoto and Beyond: A Review of the Globalisation of Global Warming Policy and North South Relations' (2005) 2:3 Globalisations 403, 404.

[140] Weiss, 'Evolution of International Environmental Law', 4.

[141] Ibid.

[142] *Founex Report on Development and Environment*, International Conciliation 7, 10–11.

[143] Manulak, *Change in Global Environmental Politics*, 95.

of the conference was a direct consequence of the Founex Meeting which was to galvanise support among Southern states through a few concessions and compromises, and secure their attendance and commitment to its outcomes.[144] Preparing the way for an even grander compromise, the Founex Meeting concluded that 'economic development and environmental protection could and should proceed in tandem'.[145] Therefore, the Founex Meeting served as the little-known preparatory exercise for the establishment and acceptance of the future life of sustainable development.[146]

Then, it is not surprising that the Founex Meeting set the stage for the global acceptance of the concept of sustainable development.[147] While it sought to distinguish between the needs of the North and South, at the same time it was forging an unusual agreement across this divide. Oddly enough, the meeting acknowledged different kinds of environmental problems ostensibly to accommodate the North–South dichotomy. Yet, these problems were common enough to be interpreted as shared concerns.[148] Hence, in reaching back to the idea of knowledge as power, if the 1972 Stockholm Conference did not hold much promise for the Global North as a historic moment in establishing a new frontier of international regulation, the North would not have invested time and resources into ensuring its success.[149]

In this sense, the Founex Meeting's most significant contribution was the crucial compromise it struck between the North and South on the environment and development. Here, even though the Founex Meeting recognised the existence of various environmental issues, the meeting also concluded that these challenges were simply complementary sides of a common concern.[150] In one stroke, the Founex Meeting succeeded in imbuing international environmentalism with development as the South wanted to partake of global development as an ideal while it equally accommodated the North's prioritisation of the environment.

144 Brighton, 'Unlikely Bedfellows', 212.

145 Weiss, 'Evolution of International Environmental Law', 4.

146 Ibid., 4–5.

147 Ibid., 4.

148 Mickelson, 'Stockholm Conference', 113; *Development and Environment: Report and Working Papers of a Panel of Experts Convened by the Secretary-General of the United Nations Conference on the Human Conference* (Mouton 1972).

149 Emma A. Foster, 'Sustainable Development: Problematising Normative Constructions of Gender within Global Environmentality' (2011) 8:2 Globalisations 135, 137.

150 Brighton, 'Unlikely Bedfellows', 212.

It was in this context that 'the global politics of sustainable development' made its appearance.[151]

In retrospect, this compromise has since proved costly for the environment. While there has been some incremental change and progress in the environment–development connection since the consensus that ensured the South's attendance at the 1972 Stockholm Conference, this progress has been dogged by an incoherent approach to implementing sustainable development.[152] Nonetheless, it is evident that, without the moderating effect of the Founex Meeting, the 1972 Stockholm Conference would have been a Global North-only affair. Again, it would not have bridged the North–South divide in the context of the environment. It would also have failed in its ultimate mission to bring the Global South to the negotiation table and to validate the future regulatory force of sustainable development.[153] Since these were some of the pressing geopolitical and historical concerns at the time, it is little surprise that the underlying issues of the ecological crisis that led to the Founex Meeting and the 1972 Stockholm Conference 'still persist, but with greater ferocity'.[154] Thus, even though very little is known about the Founex Meeting's history it became the bedrock of the Stockholm success.[155]

3.3.3 *False Universalism and the Legacy of Compromise*

Whatever the outcome of the compromises secured at the Founex Meeting, the 1972 Stockholm Conference sought to enhance the modest achievements that the Global North had secured through its foundational work.[156] In this light, the Stockholm Declaration made little effort to resolve the North–South debate as it sought to place the environmental debates of the North side by side with the economic interests of the South.[157] Here, Brighton noted that there were several attempts by influence-peddling

[151] Adil Najam, 'Developing Countries and Global Environmental Governance: From Contestation to Participation to Engagement' (2005) 5:3 Int'l Envt'l Agrmts: Pol, L and Econ 303, 303.

[152] Brighton, 'Unlikely Bedfellows', 210.

[153] Ibid., 215.

[154] Santanu Rakshit, 'Revisiting Environmental Concern: The Role of the United Nations in Development Management' (2015) 22:1 J Pol Ecol 199, 208.

[155] Mickelson, 'Stockholm Conference', 115.

[156] Brighton, 'Unlikely Bedfellows', 212.

[157] Steven Bernstein, 'Ideas, Social Structure, and the Compromise of Liberal Environmentalism' (2000) 6:4 European J Int'l Rel 464, 469.

states from the Global North to restrict the items for negotiation at the 1972 Stockholm Conference and to reject the South's demands. Perhaps, what should be of greater interest is that Strong, the Secretary-General of the 1972 Stockholm Conference, and the host state, Sweden, were reportedly involved in side discussions which were alleged to be attempts to scuttle the efforts of the Global South at the conference.[158]

These events foreshadowed sustainable development's false start at its inception as they seemed to suggested that it was to be an empty *universal* rhetoric.[159] Seeing that, since the 1972 Stockholm Conference was an attempt to obtain the Global South's support, the emergence of sustainable development within these global events must be rightly understood as 'originally devised as a compromise between two contradictory aims' – the environment and development under international law.[160] What then became international environmentalism was an outcome of the growing concerns in the Global North regarding the negative environmental impacts of industrialisation and economic growth.[161] On the other hand, Southern states, most of which were only emerging from colonialism and had embraced the Western model of development, resisted this new wave of concern for the environment.[162] Subsequently, in the post-1972 Stockholm Conference period, the UN sought to extend this important compromise secured at the Founex Meeting and formalise its place in international law as a new field of engagement. Consequently, a most notable post-Stockholm action was the establishment of the United Nations Environment Programme (UNEP) which was, once again, headed by Strong who was the convener of the Founex Meeting and the former Secretary-General of the 1972 Stockholm Conference.[163]

As characteristic of the absorptive capacity of international law, recent scholarship has been keen on preserving these ideas on the universality of sustainable development. For example, the global targets set under the banner of the SDGs align with the 'universalist conception of

[158] Brighton, 'Unlikely Bedfellows', 216–218.
[159] Trent Brown, 'Sustainability as Empty Signifier: Its Rise, Fall, and Radical Potential' (2016) 48:1 Antipode 115, 116–122.
[160] Grainger, 'Introduction', 1.
[161] Bernstein, 'Ideas, Social Structure', 469.
[162] Brown, 'Sustainability as Empty Signifier', 121.
[163] Elizabeth DeSombre, *Global Environmental Institutions*, 2nd ed. (Routledge 2017) 14–15.

sustainable development'.[164] However, other scholars have challenged this claim.[165] These scholars insist sustainable development applies differently to different geographies.[166] It is this new understanding that is key to the construction of the normativity of the concept as its operationalisation necessarily anticipates specific geo-historical and geopolitical contexts.[167]

The false universalism of sustainable development thus follows international law's own false claims to universality. This supposed universal character of international law is the foundation of both its strengths and weaknesses.[168] The paradox of international law then lies in this dualised imperialist–universalist perspective which is shaped by both legal imperialism and universalism. In a simplified approach, international law's greatest capability is to 'combine a universalist façade with discriminatory and imperialistic practices'.[169] Drawing on this critical framework, a paradoxical link between international law and imperialistic hegemony emerges. This paradox gives international law its dominant Eurocentric character which localises international law as a product of European influences while seeking, at the same time it seeks to internationalise or universalise its canons.

Thus, this universalist outlook of international law has been a major strength that permits it to conceal its true essence by perpetuating a dominant legal culture that falsely appeals to universality.[170] This abstract character of international law explains the conflation of universality and generality.[171] In this sense, the paradox of universalism and imperialism in international law fosters an expansion of the discipline into new areas of practice and sub-disciplines in the context of a contemporary globalised society.[172] Accordingly, while the universality of sustainable development continues to be a contested space, international

164 Malcolm Langford, 'Lost in Transformation? The Politics of Sustainable Development Goals' (2016) 30:2 Ethics and Int'l Aff 167, 167.

165 Jan Vandemoortele, 'From Simple-Minded MDGs to Muddle-Headed SDGs' (2018) 5:1 Dev Studies Research 83, 86.

166 Ibid., 86.

167 Radha D'Souza, 'Imperial Agendas, Global Solidarity, and Third World Socio-Legal Studies: Methodological Reflections' (2012) 49:3 Osgoode Hall LJ 409, 412; Scoones, 'Politics of Sustainability and Development', 304.

168 Jouannet, 'Universalism and Imperialism', 382.

169 Ibid., 382.

170 Ibid., 381.

171 Ibid., 389.

172 Ibid., 397.

law's Eurocentrism continues the promotion of sustainable development's ubiquitousness.[173]

3.4 Sustainable Development: Deliberate Indeterminacy

Another layer of sustainable development's universalist outlook is that it is an indeterminate yet powerful go-to concept in international law. It has been described as a 'masker of failed consensus'.[174] Its indeterminacy arises from the collective failure of both North and South to reach an answer on how to redress the global ecological crisis. Its indeterminateness painted over the North–South divide and elided distinctions between the two geopolitical regions by extracting a compromise. Ostensibly, that contrived agreement was obtained to satisfy the necessity of concluding such mega-international meetings with some sort of substantial settlement.[175] However, this indeterminacy weakened the position of the Global South by blurring the North–South divide at a time when environmental consciousness became a critical geopolitical consideration.[176]

When sustainable development is observed through this lens of indeterminateness, the concept ceases to reflect the North–South divide. At this point, the concept's ambivalent character becomes decidedly deliberate.[177] However, one must not discount international law's infrastructure remains Eurocentric and imperialistic in form and content, and so are sustainable development's own bases. This awareness arouses the need to be cautious of so-called agreements between the Global South and the Global North as these negotiations and agreements have historically tended to favour the North.[178] For example, while the principle of common but differentiated responsibilities aims at addressing the North–South tension and has attained widespread appeal, the North has been unwilling to accept responsibility for its historical ecological debt.[179] While the general idea of

[173] Jacobs, 'Sustainable Development as a Contested Concept', 31.

[174] Christopher Stone, 'Deciphering Sustainable Development' (1994) 69:4 Chicago-Kent L Rev 977, 978.

[175] World Commission on Environment and Development, *Our Common Future*, 310.

[176] Jean-Phillipe Thérien, 'Beyond the North–South Divide: The Two Tales of World Poverty' (1999) 20:4 Third World Q 723, 726.

[177] Stone, 'Deciphering Sustainable Development', 979.

[178] Islam, 'History of the North–South Divide', 23.

[179] Mariama Williams and Manuel F. Montes, 'Common but Differentiated Responsibilities: Which Way Forward?' (2016) 59:1–2 Dev 114, 118. It is still questionable if the Global

environmental responsibility acknowledges the South's complicity in ecological damage, historical ecological debt reveals a causal connection between the Global North's unbridled wealth accumulation and the imperially-conditioned ecological devastation of the Global South for the North's material and intangible benefits.[180] This example of the North–South tension has lived on since the Rio Earth Summit as the South remains discontented over the North's reluctance to redress these historical ecological wrongs.[181]

Quite importantly, the outcome of this indeterminateness was that sustainable development is mired in immutable politics. Here, the concept is trapped within the contestation between the North and South over the ecological violence inflicted on the South as a result of the North's economic growth and wealth accumulation.[182] The politics of sustainable development thus conveniently invites a conceptual (re-)formulation that admits of a wide degree of normative motility.[183] What is less obvious though is the uncritical acceptance of the ubiquity of the concept which compels an equally 'universal' narrative that obscures the true mission of the politics of sustainable development which is 'anti-[S]outh, anti-poor, and thereby anti-ecological'.[184]

Furthermore, the indeterminate character of sustainable development is integral to international law. For instance, the Global North emerged from the 1972 Stockholm Conference determined to accelerate the hurried consensus obtained at that meeting into wider recognition as a new phase of global environmental governance.[185] The post-1972 Stockholm Conference period also witnessed the South's attempt to reinforce efforts at combining ecological remediation and economic growth, an agenda it (the South) had forcefully advanced at the Founex Meeting and at the 1972 Stockholm Conference.[186] On the other hand, the North pursued

North will accept prospective responsibility. Even if they do, a more difficult issue will be translating the acceptance of responsibility into financial and technical resolution.

180 Mickelson, 'Leading Towards a Level Playing Field, 166.

181 Duncan French, 'Developing States and International Environmental Law: The Importance of Differentiated Responsibilities' (2000) 49:1 ICLQ 35, 36.

182 Mohamed El-Kamel Bakari, *Sustainability in the Age of Globalisation: A Quest for a Paradigm of Development* (Lexington Books 2017) 133.

183 K. R. Nayar, 'Politics of "Sustainable Development"' (1994) 29:22 Econ and Pol Weekly 1327, 1328.

184 Ibid., 1328.

185 Ibid., 1327.

186 John Vogler, 'The International Politics of Sustainable Development' in Giles Atkinson, Simon Dietz, and Eric Neumayer (eds.), *Handbook of Sustainable Development* (Edward

a grander project, eventually culminating in the Brundtland Commission report, which has since attained the status of holy writ in international law.[187] With the Global North and Global South agreeing to the concept of sustainable development, albeit for different reasons, the concept suffers from indeterminacy as it 'opens the way to legitimising' either environmental protection or economic growth.[188] Thus, the Brundtland Commission report extended sustainable development from a relatively obscure discursive position to a well-established concept within international political and legal discourse without clearly delineating the practical contours of the concept.[189]

In mapping sustainable development's rise in international law, we encounter a concept that was intentionally imprecise from the outset.[190] Some legal scholars described it as 'artfully vague'.[191] As the outcome of a mega-conference that presumably focused on the environment, the Stockholm Declaration deliberately avoided the North–South friction by creating an ambivalent construct that was neither intended to deliver on the promise of a universal idea nor pursue an objective reorientation of the environment–development nexus.[192] This indeterminate character of sustainable development poses challenges to its evolution and practical use as its expansive and universal scope permits the concept to be adapted to varied interpretations.[193] As Eloise Scotford recently argued, 'the Brundtland formulation is ambiguous, due to its multi-faceted generational objectives, its "soundbite" nature, and the fact that value judgements are required in determining which needs should be accorded priority in achieving sustainable development'.[194] So, it is hardly

Elgar 2007) 430, 434. There was a lesser-known event, the Cocoyoc Meeting organised by the UN Conference on Trade and Development and the United Nations Environment Programme in 1974. The Cocoyoc Meeting was like the Founex Meeting but, this time, it was a follow-up to the 1972 Stockholm Conference.

[187] Nayar, 'Politics of "Sustainable Development"', 1327.

[188] Andrew Dobson, *Justice and the Environment: Conceptions of Environmental Sustainability and Theories of Distributive Justice* (Oxford University Press 1998) 242.

[189] Grainger, 'Introduction', 6.

[190] Eloise Scotford, *Environmental Principles and the Evolution of Environmental Law* (Hart Publishing 2017) 78.

[191] Christopher D. Stone, 'Ethics and International Environmental Law' in Daniel Bodansky, Jutta Brunnée and Ellen Hey (eds.), *The Oxford Handbook of International Environmental Law* (Oxford University Press 2007) 291, 308.

[192] Ibid., 309.

[193] Andrea Ross, 'Modern Interpretations of Sustainable Development' (2009) 36:1 JL and Soc'y 32, 34.

[194] Scotford, *Environmental Principles*, 78–79.

surprising that the post-1972 Stockholm Conference period mirrored this indefiniteness.[195]

Consequently, the North and South have since departed from following through on what they had agreed to and which was crystallised in the Stockholm Declaration.[196] As Steven Bernstein has suggested, the Stockholm Declaration did little about the environment–development connection.[197] As a matter of fact, the politics of negotiating the declaration led to a significant weakening of any attempt to include 'legal rights and obligations' with the exception of a few principles, notably in Principle 21.[198] Thus, it is least surprising that, when the Brundtland Commission presented its final report to the UN, long after the 1972 Stockholm Conference, its chairperson, Gro Harlem Brundtland, unsettled the fragile stability of the environment–development balance by describing sustainable development as 'a new concept for economic growth'.[199] Brundtland's statement has since been criticised as it placed greater emphasis on economic growth than on the environment.[200] The plausible conclusion here is that, even with contrived consensus and a supporting institutional framework, there has been no commitment to translate sustainable development into determinate legal observance.[201]

3.5 Sustainable Development: Integration as a Policy of Containment

There is yet another concern relating to operationalising the concept of sustainable development. This is characterised as the integration of the three pillars of sustainable development: economic growth, social

[195] Björn-Ola Linnér and Henrik Selin, 'The United Nations Conference on Sustainable Development: Forty Years in the Making' (2013) 31 Envt and Plan C: Govt and Pol'y 971, 978; Kailyn Ellison, 'Rio+20: How the Tension between Developing and Developed Countries Influenced Sustainable Development Efforts' (2014) 27:1 Pac McGeorge Glob Bus and Dev LJ 107, 118.

[196] Beyerlin and Marauhn, *International Environmental Law*, 10.

[197] Steven Bernstein, *The Compromise of Liberal Environmentalism* (Columbia University Press 2001) 43.

[198] Ibid., 43.

[199] Fulton et al., 'Twenty Years after the Rio Summit', 97.

[200] Oluf Langhelle, 'Sustainable Development: Exploring the Ethics of Our Common Future' (1999) 20:2 Int'l Political Science Rev 129, 130.

[201] Nicholas A. Robinson, 'Caring for the Earth: A Legal Blueprint for Sustainable Development' (1992) 22:1 Envt'l Pol'y and L 22, 24.

concerns, and environmental protection.[202] The unusual invitation to integrate these three dimensions of sustainable development is traceable to the Brundtland Commission report.[203] This evolving tripartite integration has been tied to the Rio Earth Summit and, recently, the Rio+20 Conference, along with their outcome documents.[204] However, 'in none of these documents is a clear framework or theoretical background made explicit'.[205] Therefore, it follows that these three pillars serve as conceptual prongs for thinking through and anchoring the origins and purpose of sustainable development and not as destinations in themselves.

Again, a historical exploration foregrounds an analysis around this three-tiered manifestation of the concept. This three-dimensional view of sustainable development had been Strong's idea. Bernstein contends that Strong had indicated at the time of his appointment that his objective as the Secretary-General of the 1972 Stockholm Conference was to integrate environment and development.[206] Much later, in his new role as the Executive Director of UNEP in the aftermath of the 1972 Stockholm Conference, Strong set about this integration plan. Like he did with the Founex Meeting, Strong's plan involved co-opting leading Global North-based environmental NGOs and other research organisations, including the International Union for Conservation of Nature (IUCN) and the International Institute for Environment and Development (IIED). The IIED was headed at the time by Barbara Ward, who had been one of Strong's protégé during the Stockholm process and who was later commissioned by Strong to author leading documents arising from the 1972 Stockholm Conference negotiations.[207]

Strong's influence remained immense and continued to grow even in the post-1972 Stockholm Conference period.[208] For instance, he was a member of the Brundtland Commission and extended his authority through the contributions of his protégé, Ward, and her work at the IIED.[209] At the same

[202] Hugh Wilkins, 'The Integration of the Pillars of Sustainable Development: A Work in Progress' (2008) 4:2 McGill J Sust Dev L and Pol'y 163, 166.

[203] World Commission on Environment and Development, *Our Common Future*, 62.

[204] Powers, 'Rio+20 Process', 407.

[205] Purvis et al., 'Three Pillars of Sustainability', 685.

[206] Bernstein, *Compromise of Liberal Environmentalism*, 42.

[207] Iris Borowy, *Defining Sustainable Development for Our Common Future: A History of the World Commission on Environment and Development (Brundtland Commission)* (Routledge 2013) 36; Manulak, *Change in Global Environmental Politics*, 92.

[208] James Radcliffe, *Green Politics: Dictatorship or Democracy?* (MacMillan 2000), 123–124.

[209] Stephen Macekura, 'Towards "Sustainable Development": The United Nations, INGOs, and the Crafting of the World Conservation Strategy' in Wolfram Kaiser and Jan-Henrik

time, he (Strong) and two members of the Brundtland Commission, Shidrath Ramphal and Jim MacNeill, were also board members of IIED; while two advisors to the IIED, Richard Sandbrook and Lloyd Timberlake reportly drafted chapters of the Brundtland Commission report.[210]

Again, at that time, some international environmental organisations were transitioning from their imperialist orientation. Sustainable development thus provided the ultimate opportunity for these institutions to exit that dark history. For example, the IUCN was enlisted in a partnership involving some UN agencies. Led again by Strong, this partnership, was called the Ecosystem Conservation Group.[211] In reviewing the developments at the time, the IUCN seemed less interested in internal reform and more inclined to disguise its interests in reinventing its public image. However, more recent studies demonstrate imperial control over natural resources in the Global South was re-enacted through Global North-led institutions like the IUCN which purported to support conservation yet were keenly advancing neo-imperial technologies of environmental managerialism.[212] Thus, the IUCN, which was caught in the politics of the decolonisation process, was eager to shed its pro-colonialist identity and found it expedient to embed itself in the growing decolonial influence of the UN system.[213]

Strong's influence was also noticeable not only in the negotiation processes but also in the outcome documents. In this sense, owing to his towering authority, the Brundtland Commission report was described as representing the views of many of its leading members including Strong.[214] If these three dimensions of sustainable development are traced to the Stockholm processes, the Brundtland Commission, or to the UN and allied organisations, it is easy to understand the absence of differences in opinion across these institutions since the leadership and membership were simply moving in and out of revolving doors. More significantly, the prominent voices in the design of sustainable development as the future language of international environmental regulation were, to a very large extent, the same voices from the Global North, North-influenced international development finance institutions, and

Meyer (eds.), *International Organizations and Environmental Protection: Conservation and Globalisation in the Twentieth Century* (Berghahn Books 2017) 241, 255.

210 Anne E. Egelston, *Sustainable Development: A History* (Springer 2013) 82.

211 Simone Schleper, *Planning for the Planet: Environmental Expertise and the International Union for the Conservation of Nature and Natural Resources* (Berghahn Books 2019) 48.

212 Kulamadayil, 'Placed in Between'.

213 Schleper, *Planning for the Planet*, 47.

214 Egelston, *Sustainable Development: A History*, 82.

corporate interests, all evidencing the neoliberal conditioning of this new frontier in international environmentalism.[215]

Since the Brundtland Commission recommended the reconciliation of economic development and environmental protection, sustainable development has advanced a three-dimensional integration: economic, environmental, and social prongs.[216] The Brundtland Commission proposal was informed by the recommendation of the Stockholm Declaration to integrate the environment and development.[217] The Rio Declaration later reiterated this connection between the environment and development that began at Stockholm and continued in Rio, but importantly it highlighted the social component as the third prong in this arrangement.[218]

However, this integration process is inherently indeterminate as there is no agreement over how to pursue integration.[219] The tussle over the functional variance of integration dominates sustainable development discourse. For example, in international trade, the integration of the environmental and social dimensions of sustainable development risks being opposed on grounds of domestic protectionism.[220] The concern over the meaning and role of integration leads to a dualist orientation in respect of sustainable development. First, integration defined as strong sustainability suggests no trade-offs among the economic, social, and environmental aspects of the concept.[221] Second, as weak sustainability, integration favours the presumption that economic growth yields returns that can be ploughed back into social and environmental protection.[222] This binarised approach towards sustainable development is informed by

215 Gabriela Kütting, 'Globalisation and the Environment: Moving Beyond Neo-Liberal Institutionalism' (2004) 9:1 Int'l J Peace Studies 29, 32.

216 Sumudu Atapattu, 'Climate Change, International Environmental Law Principles, and the North-South Divide' (2017) 26:2 Transnat'l L and Contemp Probs 247, 256.

217 Stockholm Declaration, Principle 13.

218 Rio Declaration, Principle 4; Brunnée, 'Stockholm Declaration', 48; Mensah, 'Sustainable Development', 16.

219 Wilkins, 'Pillars of Sustainable Development', 177.

220 Segger, 'Inspiration for Integration', 165.

221 Benjamin R. Richardson and Stepan Wood, 'Environmental Law for Sustainability' in Benjamin R. Richardson and Stepan Wood (eds.), *Environmental Law for Sustainability: A Reader* (Hart Publishing 2006) 1, 14; Begüm Özkaynak, Pat Devine, and Dan Rigby, 'Operationalising Strong Sustainability: Definitions, Methodologies, and Outcomes' (2004) 13:3 Envt'l Val 279.

222 Klaus Bosselmann, 'In Search of Global Law: The Significance of the Earth Charter' (2004) 8:1 Worldviews 62, 67; George Randal Davies, 'Appraising Weak and Strong Sustainability: Searching for a Middle Ground' (2013) 10:1 Consilience: J Sust Dev 111, 116.

anthropocentric and eco-centric considerations.[223] In the case of strong sustainability, the environmental pillar stands in equal competition with the other pillars; whereas, in regard to weak sustainability, the environment stands in an inferior relationship with the other aspects of the concept, especially economic growth.[224]

Yet, emerging out of this dualist sense of integration, neither characterisation as strong nor weak is adequate as both interpretations result in ambiguous integration.[225] What is lost between the two approaches is the centrality of ecological considerations. On this subject, placing the ecological dimension at the centre of integration ensures that other considerations take into account ecological integrity as a prerequisite for incorporating sustainable development's other dimensions.[226] Even so, other legal scholars contend the integrative core of environmental protection should be subordinated to economic growth to ensure 'environmental law will blend with other areas of law, thus strengthening respect for the rule of law and effectiveness of the law as a tool for the attainment of social justice'.[227]

In a recent scholarly revitalisation of these two ends of the integration debate – that is, strong and weak sustainability – it is argued that the environmental dimension is the 'fundament' while the economic and social dimensions should be construed as 'the two pillars'.[228] This view is shared by other legal scholars who argue that environmental protection should be the principal requirement for sustainable development.[229] Thus, as it relates to Southern interests, sustainable development's integration agenda is only likely to succeed when Southern concerns about the environment cease to be peripheral to concerns in international law.[230]

223 Paule Halley and Pierre-Olivier DesMarchais, 'Sustainable Development under Canadian Law' in Allan E. Ingelson (ed.), *Environment in the Courtroom* (University of Calgary Press 2019) 1, 9.

224 Ibid., 9.

225 Ibid.

226 Kim and Bosselmann, 'Operationalising Sustainable Development', 203–204.

227 Tolentino Jr, 'Passage', 913.

228 Virginie Barral, 'The Principle of Sustainable Development' in Michael Faure (ed.), *Elgar Encyclopedia of Environmental Law* (Edward Elgar 2018) 103, 110.

229 Halley and DesMarchais, 'Sustainable Development under Canadian Law', 11.

230 Mickelson, 'South, North', 54.

3.6 Conclusion

This chapter focused on the universality of sustainable development in a bid to understand its place within international law. The analysis, taking the path of a historical examination, accounted for a less-theorised view of sustainable development as the construction of knowledge as power. In this sense, the coloniality and the imperialistic interests underpinning sustainable development and the several meetings and conferences since the 1970s, from the Founex Meeting, to the 1972 Stockholm Conference and beyond, contradict the North's supposed commitment to the environment. Thus, this analysis demonstrated sustainable development was imagined as a neoliberal technology for making development more acceptable as a *universal* ideal.

Based on this understanding, sustainable development is discernibly a new frontier of international legal governance. Its grander purpose was to reinvent and reassert novel forms of control over the natural resources of the postcolonial states. It also provided a means, and a reason, for co-opting states in the Global South as well as disciplining the postcolonial elite into accepting the prevailing Western model of economic growth. These historical processes enabled an acceptance of the false universalism of sustainable development which was a compromise. Thus, the analysis resituated sustainable development's universality as a necessary tool to reproduce this compromise that was secured through several mega-conference events designed to assure a Global South buy-in for the evolving life of sustainable development.

The universality of sustainable development as compromise guaranteed the concept was discussed at these mega-conferences but only to be reimmersed in the prevailing international politics. Therefore, it is not surprising that every major international environmental law conference decidedly focused on this concept.[231] However, hiding in plain sight in the outcome documents of these conferences and meetings is the indeterminate language that is continuously relied upon to build consensus between the North and South. The diplomatic manoeuvres in these carefully negotiated documents reinforce the problematic indeterminacy that is entrenched through the universality of sustainable development. Even the popular integrative framework for implementing sustainable development has offered very little to clarify the universality of sustainable development. These uneasy tripartite dimensions of sustainable

[231] Egelston, *Sustainable Development: A History*, 13–18.

development have failed to make up for the lack of content. Widely identified by the conjoining of these three dimensions – economic, social, and environmental – sustainable development is in a perpetual stalemate over which of these three dimensions should take precedence. Thus, attempts at reconciling the three components have not succeeded in attaching primacy to ecological integrity which is the essence of the sustainable development turn.

To rethink its universality, sustainable development ought to be contemplated within a regulatory outlook.[232] This orientation must lead to ecological temperance. In that review, it would be crucial to retrace the concept's advance and universality, particularly as the Global South is embracing the concept. As Adil Najam has noted, despite its initial suspiciousness, the South has now become active in the sustainable development debate and has become a site of acceptance and contestation over the concept.[233] Even so, the challenges of universality, language obfuscation, and poor integration that plague sustainable development and that have dominated international legal contexts are becoming obvious even at regional environmental law, including in Africa.[234] Accordingly, in Chapter 4, I examined the normative journey of sustainable development in Africa.

[232] Luca Valera and Gonzalo Salazar, 'Challenging Sustainability: From Deconstruction to Reconstruction' (2020) 16:1 J Nat and Soc Phil 298, 311.
[233] Najam, 'Developing Countries and Global Environmental Governance', 317.
[234] Hennie Strydom, 'Introduction to Regional Environmental Law of the African Union' in Werner Scholtz and Jonathan Verschuuren (eds.), *Regional Environmental Law: Transregional Comparative Lessons in Pursuit of Sustainable Development* (Edward Elgar 2015) 21.

4

Problematising the Normative Trajectory of Sustainable Development in Africa

> The importance of searching for alternative approaches and solutions to Africa's development problems also calls for a critical examination of what 'sustainable development' means in the African context.*

4.1 Introduction

This chapter problematises the history, evolution, internalisation, and legal operationalisation of the concept of sustainable development in Africa. It also examines the coloniality of the sustainable development discourse. Here, the analysis explores how the concept which began as nature conservation in Africa came to exclude Africa as it evolved. It also examines how the politics of exclusion created fertile conditions for the long-term marginalisation of African influences in the emergence and progression of sustainable development.[1]

The concern is, essentially, how this discussion focuses on Africa as a subject; and not as an object, of the making of international law.[2] For example, Africa's influence in the development and adoption of the World Charter on Nature is an important aspect of retrenching the coloniality of Eurocentrism over international environmentalism. But, that history is suppressed in the writing of the history of international law.[3] Thus, this chapter focuses on the normative trajectory of sustainable development in Africa as a necessary starting point for this inquiry.

* George J. S. Dei, 'Sustainable Development in the African Context: Revisiting Some Theoretical and Methodological Issues' (1993) 18:2 Afr Dev 97.

1 Andrea M. Vásquez-Fernández and Cash Ahenekaw pii tai poo taa, 'Resurgence of Relationality: Reflections on Decolonising and Indigenising 'Sustainable Development'' (2020) 43 Current Opinion on Envt'l Sustainability 65.

2 Peter Jackson, 'A World Charter for Nature' (1983) 12:2 Ambio 133.

3 Harold W. Wood Jr, 'The United Nations World Charter for Nature: The Developing Nations' Initiative to Establish Protections for the Environment' (1985) 12:4 Ecol LQ 977.

As a secondary objective, this chapter traces the entry of Africa into international environmental governance. I explore how the commingling of Africa's standpoint on significant aspects of international environmental law and the viewpoints of its contemporaries in the Global South constitute parts of a broader, never-ending Third World international law-making project.[4] In this respect, the inquiry examines how supposedly unconnected matters, like sovereignty and Third World solidarity, combine to structure and condition the internalisation of sustainable development in Africa.[5] In this sense, my analysis contemplates how these meta-level conceptual aspects of the broader objective of sustainable development should concern us, not only as sub-disciplinary specialists but also as scholars and practitioners with a general interest in international law.[6] For example, a reformulation of sovereignty in the postcolonial struggle over natural resource access and use together with their associated socioecological consequences must be viewed as markedly different from its Westphalian interest; thus, the manifestation of this novel sovereignty must be studied from a different perspective.[7]

The third aim of this chapter is to analyse the legal operationalisation of sustainable development in Africa. This section of the analysis links up with the discussion of Africa's marginalisation in the early days of nature conservation, and later as Africa strove to establish sustainable development. Thus, the analysis here proceeds as a two-pronged discussion, featuring an inquiry into both quasi-judicial and non-judicial approaches to sustainable development. This dualised methodology has far-reaching consequences for international law. For example, using the legal instrumentality of the promotion and protection of rights, Africa's regional and sub-regional courts have been venturing into novel regional regulatory spheres including sustainable development. These adjudicative institutions have done this by attaching the language of rights to environmental

[4] N'Dri Therese Assie-Lumumba, 'Behind and Beyond Bandung: Historical and Forward-Looking Reflections on South–South Cooperation' (2015) 2:11 Bandung: J Global South 1, 4–8.

[5] Karin Mickelson and Usha Natarajan, 'Reflections on Rhetoric and Rage: Bandung and Environmental Injustice' in Luis Eslava, Michael Fakhri, and Vasuki Nesiah (eds.), *Bandung, Global History and International Law: Critical Pasts and Pending Futures* (Cambridge University Press 2017) 465, 467.

[6] Barral, 'Sustainable Development in International Law', 385–388.

[7] Ibironke T. Odumosu, 'The Law and Politics of Engaging Resistance in Investment Dispute Settlement' (2007) 26:2 Penn State Int'l L Rev 251, 259; Chimni, 'Permanent Sovereignty'.

protection which has gained prominence in contemporary rights jurisprudence.[8] However, my analysis critiques this pro-rights stance to expose the shortcomings of a rights-based approach to sustainable development. I conclude by noting that, in practice, these tribunals and their jurisprudence uncritically empower the state over non-state actors as they have failed to incorporate customary law and Indigenous legal governance into sustainable development.[9]

4.2 Locating Africa: Conservation as Internationalism

Early international environmental agreements frequently centred international conservation law as integral to international law.[10] Africa's historical connection to the development of international conservation law (sometimes called international wildlife law) opened new vistas for the pursuit of the concept of sustainable development.[11] In problematising this puzzling history, this analysis harkens back to the beginning of the twentieth century when nature conservation began receiving prominence as an international legal phenomenon and later served as the antecedent of sustainable development.[12] This analysis demonstrates the relationship between international wildlife law and sustainable development.[13] These similarities reflect how international wildlife law and policy like sustainable development are historically linked to colonial policies on nature conservation.[14]

[8] James T. Gathii, 'Saving the Serengeti: Africa's New International Judicial Environmentalism' (2016) 16:2 Chicago JIL 386.

[9] Conor Gearty, 'Do Human Rights Help or Hinder Environmental Protection?' (2010) 1:1 J Human Rights and Envt 7, 19; Louis J. Kotzé, 'Human Rights, the Environment and the Global South' in Shawkat Alam, Sumudu Atapattu, Carmen G. Gonzalez and Jona Razzaque (eds.), *International Environmental Law and the Global South* (Cambridge University Press 2015) 171, 190.

[10] Mario Prost and Yoriko Otomo, 'British Influences on International Environmental Law: The Case of Wildlife Conservation' in Robert McCorquodale and Jean-Pierre Gauci (eds.), *British Influences on International Law, 1915–2015* (Brill 2016) 192, 193.

[11] Werner Scholtz, 'Injecting Compassion into International Wildlife Law: From Conservation to Protection?' (2017) 6:3 Transnat'l Envt'l L 463, 482–483.

[12] Werner Scholtz, 'Trading Rhinoceros Horn for the Sake of Conservation: Dehorning the Dilemma through a Legal Analysis of the Emergence of Animal Welfare' in Werner Scholtz (ed.), *Animal Welfare and International Environmental Law* (Edward Elgar 2019) 235, 267.

[13] Scholtz, 'Injecting Compassion', 479.

[14] Guillaume Futhazar, 'Biodiversity, Species Protection, and Animal Welfare under International Law' in Anne Peters (ed.), *Studies in Global Animal Law* (Springer 2020) 95, 96.

Thus, the ensuing analysis deconstructs how Africa is dualised in the literature: first, Africa is an object, a point of reference in international conservation law and practice while not exactly being treated as the focus of a so-called global commitment to nature conservation; and, second, Africa emerges as a subject, a site for sustainable development norm-making in both international and regional law.[15] This analysis, thus, foreshadows the subsequent discussion as it maps the genealogy of sustainable development in Africa, 'moving from a non-rights-based approach to a rights-based approach'.[16]

4.2.1 Europe to Africa's Rescue: Systematising Exclusion via the London Intervention

At the turn of the twentieth century, the imperial powers of Europe, who had colonised much of Africa met in London to conclude a treaty to conserve wildlife in Africa.[17] This meeting was prompted by dwindling game for sport hunting.[18] To be precise, the treaty 'itself was largely negotiated by hunters'.[19] At this time, sport hunting was emblematic of colonial (and imperial) supremacy as it embodied a 'ritualised display of authority and a core component of the civilising mission'.[20] It was therefore not surprising that part of the preamble of this treaty; that is, the 1900 London Convention for the Protection of Wild Animals, Birds

[15] Amitav Acharya, '"Ideas-Shift": How Ideas from the Rest Are Reshaping Global Order' (2016) 37:7 Third World Q 1156, 1165–1166; Amtiva Acharya, *Constructing Global Order: Agency and Change in World Politics* (Cambridge University Press 2018); Charmaine Chua, 'Against Localisation: Rethinking Compliance and Antagonism in Norm Dynamics' in Charlotte Epstein (ed.), *Against International Relations Norms: Postcolonial Perspectives* (Routledge 2017) 87.

[16] Lilian Chenwi, 'The Right to a Satisfactory, Healthy, and Sustainable Environment in the African Human Rights System' in Robert Knox and Ramin Pejan (eds.), *The Human Right to a Healthy Environment* (Cambridge University Press 2018) 59, 61.

[17] Philippe Sands, *Principles of International Environmental Law*, 2nd ed. (Cambridge University Press 2003) 524.

[18] Angela Thompsell, *Hunting Africa: British Sport, African Knowledge and the Nature of Empire* (Palgrave MacMillan 2015) 12–13. Thompsell tells an interesting story of how the 'particular appeal of big game hunting in these decades was connected to the sport's capacity to symbolise Britain's imperial and manly prowess at a time when many were expressing grave doubts about both'. It would seem, at least from this description, that imperialism was also important in boosting European masculinity, and international law became a willing vehicle for this purpose.

[19] Humphreys and Otomo, 'Theorising International Environmental Law', 812.

[20] Prost and Otomo, 'British Influences', 195.

and Fish of Africa, which was negotiated and adopted by France, Italy, Britain, Spain, and Portugal, stated its aim as safeguarding 'the conservation of diverse wild animal species in their African possessions'.[21]

Yet, quite evidently, from the outset, this treaty had very little to do with conserving the wildlife of Africa.[22] Rather, colonial science and the notion of European intellectual pre-eminence were united in the objective of masking European domination of Africa's natural resources as a rational political choice through the instrumentality of conservation.[23] As I have previously noted, the treaty was negotiated by European trophy hunters with a focus on conserving prized game for sport hunting. In this sense, Africa was simply contemplated as a home to lions, giraffes, and zebras, and not people. The notion was that wildlife, which was viewed as constituting the essence of Africa's identity, was what was worth protecting for Europe's use. This was apparent in the treaty's adoption of 'a narrow approach to the notion of conservation and a substantially restrictive interpretation of the African ecosystem premised on the need to regulate and maintain the viability of commercial exploitation of the African flora and fauna'.[24] Therefore, the colonial laws and conservation practices that were passed only helped to preserve game for European settlers.[25] So, while the 1900 London Convention focused on Africa, there was very little in it that warranted the treaty being referred to as an African convention. It was, in all senses, a European arrangement for the ideational and material exploitation of Africa.

Without rigorous scrutiny, we are inclined to gloss over the fact that the insertion of *Africa* in this agreement concluded by European colonial powers typically obscures the absence of African peoples from the negotiations that established this influential treaty intended to regulate access

[21] *Convention Designed to Ensure the Conservation of Various Species of Wild Animals in Africa, which are Useful to Man or Inoffensive*, 19 May 1900, British Parliamentary Papers 1900, Cd 101, Vol 56, 825.

[22] Morne van der Linde, 'A Review of the African Convention on Nature and Natural Resources' (2002) 2:1 Afr Human Rights LJ 33, 35.

[23] Patrick Petitjean, 'Science and the "Civilising Mission": France and the Colonial Enterprise' in Benedikt Stuchtey (ed.), *Science across the European Empires 1800–1950* (Oxford University Press 2005) 107, 109.

[24] Bolanle T. Erinosho, 'The Revised African Convention on the Conservation of Nature and Natural Resources: Prospects for a Comprehensive Treaty for the Management of Africa's Natural Resources' (2013) 21:3 Afr J Int'l and Comp L 378, 378.

[25] Kasmira A. Cockerill and Shannon M. Hagerman, 'Historical Insights for Understanding the Emergence of Community-Based Conservation in Kenya: International Agendas, Colonial Legacies, and Contested Worldviews' (2020) 25:2 Ecol and Soc'y 15, 17–18.

to and the utilisation of Africa's natural resources. In this context, Africans were excluded from the defining moments of one of the fundamental aspects of international (environmental) law.[26] Thus, as Francis Situma has noted, '[i]t is axiomatic to state that for the most part of the development of international environmental law, Africa's contribution was indirect, the continent being an object, rather than a subject, of international law'.[27]

The 1900 London Convention did not enter into force because it was never ratified by all the parties.[28] Despite non-ratification, the European powers that negotiated the treaty text enacted colonial laws that, impliedly, gave effect to its treaty intent.[29] For example, the treaty's influence was predominant in parts of colonial Africa where the British administration had started incorporating its objectives into colonial game laws.[30] By the start of World War I, this treaty had fallen into desuetude as only two of its contracting parties, Britain and Germany, had ratified it.

The treaty's failure led to a second round of negotiations which resulted in the adoption of a revised treaty in 1933.[31] However, before this new treaty had entered into force, the older 1900 treaty had already begun shaping legal and policy developments elsewhere, even beyond Africa. For example, using the legal language distinguishing between useful and harmful animals in the 1900 treaty, the British colonial administration in India inspired 'Britons to vilify, hunt and shoot Indian wild animals'; a process that was patterned along these arbitrary categories.[32] Therefore, even though the 1900 treaty never became operational, its functional

[26] Mickelson, 'South, North', 58.

[27] Francis D. P. Situma, 'Africa's Potential Contribution to the Implementation of International Environmental Law' (2000) 10:2 Transnat'l L and Contemp Probs 385, 395.

[28] Peter H. Sand, 'Whither CITES? The Evolution of a Treaty Regime in the Borderland of Trade and Environment' (1997) 8:1 European JIL 28, 32.

[29] World Conservation Union, *An Introduction to the African Convention on Nature and Natural Resources,* 2nd ed. (IUCN 2006) 3; W. M. Adams, *Green Development: Environment and Sustainability in the Third World,* 2nd ed. (Routledge 2001) 32. Adams notes that the IUCN's role in Africa commands mixed reaction due to the organisation's 'Eurocentric and First World image'.

[30] Prost and Otomo, 'British Influences', 199; S. A. Jeanetta Selier, Rob Slotow, Andrew Blackmore and Arie Trouwborst, 'The Legal Challenges of Transboundary Wildlife Management at the Population Level: The Case of a Trilateral Elephant Population in Southern Africa' (2016) 19:2 J Int'l Wildlife L and Pol'y 101, 118.

[31] Sand, 'Whither CITES?', 32. The initial success of the 1933 London Convention encouraged the colonial powers to transplant these colonial laws to other parts of Asia as well.

[32] Vijaya Ramadas Mandala, 'The Raj and the Paradoxes of Wildlife Conservation: British Attitudes and Expediencies' (2015) 58:1 Hist J 75, 78.

relevance was a motivation for extensive imperially motivated ecological disruption in the Global South.

4.2.2 New Wine in Old Wineskin: Renewing the London Mandate

In the aftermath of World War I, European colonial powers met once again to negotiate a new treaty to replace the failed 1900 London Convention. This development culminated in the adoption of the 1933 Convention Relative to the Preservation of Fauna and Flora in their Natural State.[33] The dominant feature of this new treaty was the establishment of 'nature reserves and national parks' in the colonial territories of state parties.[34] Unlike its failed predecessor, this new agreement was applicable across large parts of the African colonies; and, this time, colonial game laws were expressly modelled on this imperialised treaty.[35]

While the treaty is recognised as an important intervention, environmental preservation measures undertaken within the remit of the 1933 London Convention disrupted the existing ecological balance between Indigenous communities and nature.[36] Quite apart from the marked shift from the central focus on conservation measures which evoked ideas of responsible natural resource utilisation earlier expressed under the 1900 London Convention, a new interest and emphasis on the preservation of fauna for long-term imperial exploitation emerged under the 1933 London Convention.[37]

But more importantly, the 1933 London treaty 'lacked a general policy for the protection of nature in Africa, which embraced the interests and expectation of the African people themselves'.[38] For example, the period following World War II witnessed a conservation boom in British colonial Africa.[39] This ushered in new approaches to nature conservation.

[33] 8 November 1933, 172 LNTS 241 [1933 London Convention].

[34] Joseph Diekola Ogundere, 'The Development of International Environmental Law and Policy in Africa' (1972) 12:2 Nat Res J 255, 256.

[35] Sand, 'Whither CITES?', 32.

[36] Jean-Frédéric Morin, 'Global Environmental Governance' in Mario Telò (ed.), *Globalisation, Multilateralism, Europe: Towards a Better Global Governance?* (Routledge 2014) 227, 242.

[37] John M. MacKenzie, *The Empire of Nature: Hunting, Conservation, and British Imperialism* (Manchester University Press 1988) 201. Even in the context of conservation, this has been described as the pursuit of 'game preservation for sport rather than true conservation'.

[38] Selier et al., 'Legal Challenges of Transboundary Wildlife Management', 119.

[39] Bernhard Gissibl, 'The Conservation of Luxury: Safari Hunting and the Consumption of Wildlife in Twentieth-Century East Africa' in Karin Hofmeester and Bernd-Stefan Grewe

Here, there are four theories relating to the 'content, implementation and enforcement of wildlife and national park laws' that were advanced in support of colonially-oriented nature conservation laws.[40] Roderick Neumann characterised them as follows:

> One was the initiation of the British colonial development and modernisation agenda for Africa. Second was the rising importance in Africa of the scientific expert in agriculture and natural resource management, particularly in wildlife conservation. Third was the establishment of international commercial air travel which encouraged, and made possible, mass tourism on a global scale. Fourth was the emergence and increasing importance of international conservation organisations in setting and implementing a national park and wildlife conservation program in Africa.[41]

Remarkably, none of these theories invoked Indigenous African perspectives as they were all aligned with the economic interests of the British colonial administration.

Therefore, it is surprising and even awkward that some African environmental law scholars have suggested that the bio-communitarian cosmology which is prevalent in African Indigenous and customary conceptions on the intersection of law, economy, and ecology can be traced to these early colonial and imperially imposed treaties and allied network of domestic laws. On this subject, Joseph Ogundere wrote that:

> Thus, the moral and material well-being of Africans, which would seem to embrace integration of their environment, and which were to be promoted by scientific institutions with the aim of bringing home to them the blessings of civilization, constitute the nucleus of environmental law and policy in Africa. The happy integration of man with and the maintenance of the ecological balance between man and his environment motivated the Conference held in London in 1933 on the African Environment which culminated in the conclusion of the 1933 London Convention.[42]

Ogundere's rather sanguine account of the 1933 London Convention is bewildering. Indeed, his narrative stands alone and contrasts with other accounts which depicted nature conservation under these treaties as a 'colonial undertaking' based on nature's 'usefulness and harmlessness',

(eds.), *Luxury in Global Perspective: Objects and Practices, 1600–2000* (Cambridge University Press 2016) 263, 265–266.

40 Roderick P. Neumann, 'The Post-War Conservation Boom in British Colonial Africa' (2002) 7:1 Envt'l History 22, 23.

41 Ibid., 23.

42 Ogundere, 'Development of International Environmental Law', 256.

which exhibited the colonial zeal to introduce Western-informed governmental (and legal) technologies to control Africa's natural resources for Europe's imperial and capitalist advantage.[43] Additionally, though the 1933 treaty is seen as an improvement over its 1900 predecessor owing to its perceived efforts aimed at introducing nature parks and natural reserves, both treaties were driven by an anthropocentric orientation. This anthropocentrism was pronounced in the post–World War II era when European colonial powers intensified the extraction of natural resources in their colonies (including in Africa) to augment their post-war reconstruction efforts in European metropoles.[44]

4.2.3 Twice-Told Tales: A Slightly International (Yet Not-So Environmentalist) Legacy

The significance and legacy of the 1900 and 1933 London treaties has received mixed scholarly treatment. While these two treaties are different, their respective foundations are not dissimilar as both sprung from the colonial commodification of nature.[45] Admittedly, the 1900 and 1933 London treaties broke new grounds on future efforts in developing an international approach to the protection of the environment at international law.[46] As a global first, the 1900 London treaty foregrounded a globalised attempt at nature conservation.[47] However, its contradictory pedigree cannot be glossed over. As the inaugural environment-specific treaty in Africa, this agreement was everything but international. In fact, it was simply the creation of a truly European (colonial) legal regime for natural resource management with no deliberate African participation.[48] In this context, nature conservation was defined by colonial domination and commodification of Africa's flora and fauna as an integral part

[43] J. Manyitabot Takang, 'From Algiers to Maputo: The Role of the African Convention on the Conservation of Nature and Natural Resources in the Harmonisation of Conservation Policy in Africa' (2014) 17:4 J Int'l Wildlife L and Pol'y 165, 169.

[44] Kees Bastmeijer, 'Introduction' in Kees Bastmeijer (ed.), *Wilderness Protection in Europe: The Role of International, European, and National Law* (Cambridge University Press 2016) 1, 16–20; Scott Kaufman, *The Environment and International History* (Bloomsbury 2018) 36–39.

[45] Bernhard Gissibl, *The Nature of German Imperialism: Conservation and the Politics of Wildlife in Colonial East Africa* (Berghahn Books 2016) 259.

[46] Sand, 'Whither CITES?', 36.

[47] Kaufman, *Environment and International History*, 1.

[48] Takang, 'Algiers to Maputo', 167.

of the European imperial mission's trinitarian objective of 'commerce, Christianity, and civilisation'.[49]

Another interesting feature was the absolute non-applicability of these treaties to 'the metropolitan areas of colonial powers'.[50] While the contracting parties were all European states, the 1900 treaty was inapplicable within their respective home states in Europe. This treaty was only relevant in Africa, and as between the imperial powers and their colonial possessions. This situation raises the question of why treaties that were supposedly considered timely and necessary interventions for Africa expressed convictions that were not applied within the respective geographies of the contracting European states that eagerly united to establish these conservation regimes. It is in this respect that I agree with Mario Prost and Yoriko Otomo that these imperial treaties were 'neither truly international nor genuinely conservationist' as this strange brand of 'internationalism was confined to the circle of "civilised" European imperial powers' where 'Africans were notably absent'.[51]

Aside from the apparent double standards, these treaties were paradoxical as their 'particular vision of conservation embodied in the treaties was problematic and illuminating'.[52] Specifically, the 1900 London Convention drew a distinction between fauna that were of use to humans and those that were not. This distinction became the propelling force behind whether some animal species were to be protected under the treaty or were to face possible extermination.[53] For example, animals listed on schedules 1 to 4 of the treaty were considered useful, and those listed on schedule 5 'were labelled as pests that could be killed at will'.[54] This kind of unfounded and uncritical distinction based on European scientific classifications among animals accounted for the unwarranted slaughter and consequent extinction of important wildlife in Africa. Construed differently, the 'most criticised aspect of the 1900 Convention was that it listed not only protected species, but also "noxious species" that were to be specifically targeted for eradication'.[55]

[49] Jonas Fossli Gjersø, 'The Scramble for East Africa: British Motives Reconsidered, 1884–95' (2015) 43:5 J Imp and Commonwealth History 831, 853.

[50] Nico Schrijver, *Development without Destruction: The UN and Global Resource Management* (Indiana University Press 2010) 27.

[51] Prost and Otomo, 'British Influences', 197.

[52] Mickelson, 'South, North', 58.

[53] Kameri-Mbote and Cullet, 'Law, Colonialism', 24.

[54] Kaufman, *Environment and International History*, 1. Animals listed in Schedule 5 included 'baboons, crocodiles, otters and poisonous snakes'.

[55] Mickelson, 'South, North', 58.

At the very least, the 1900 London Convention and its replacement, the 1933 Convention, seemed to take account of some environmental considerations judging from their recognition of the impact of the wanton killing of certain animals on the wildlife ecosystem.[56] To an extent, the two treaties acknowledged what was wrong with the indefensible mistreatment of wildlife.[57] This change in worldview was prominent in the 1933 London Convention. Quite significantly, the 1933 treaty did away with the disastrous distinction between useful and harmful animals in the 1900 London treaty which made it possible to extend the scope of protection that was denied animals on schedule 5 of the 1900 London Convention.[58]

Nonetheless, it is crucial to understand the context in which these initial interventions emerged. Taking a leaf from prior deconstructions of the importance and implications of such early environmental treaties, international law scholars are admonished to resist romanticising these agreements but to rather acknowledge their anthropocentric character.[59] In analysing the 1900 London Convention and its 1933 re-creation, legal scholars must seriously turn their attention to the fact that, when these early international environmental treaties were being negotiated, the contracting parties actively integrated economic considerations which 'emerged as a parallel driving force for environmental protection'.[60]

The most enduring lesson from this colonial conservation heritage and its devastating impact on Africans and their natural world lives on in the context of sustainable development. As Bernhard Gissibl has noted, the legacy of these early treaties 'was of even more tangible importance to Africans, for it actively drew the global colour line'.[61] In this sense, not only were economic considerations a primary motivation; the organising ambition of these treaty negotiations was inspired by racial considerations. Thus, environmental racism was equally a controlling aspect of the civilising mission of nature conservation even if it remains a less-explored theme.[62]

56 Andrew C. Blackmore, 'Public Trust Doctrine, Research and Responsible Wildlife Management in South Africa' (2017) 47:1 Bothalia 1.

57 Sand, 'Whither CITES?', 32.

58 Mickelson, 'South, North', 59.

59 Kaufman, *Environment and International History*, 2; Marie-Catherine Petersmann, *When Environmental Protection and Human Rights Collide: The Politics of Conflict Management by Regional Courts* (Cambridge University Press 2022) 17–28.

60 Petersmann, 'Narcissus' Reflection in the Lake', 239.

61 Gissibl, *Nature of German Imperialism*, 246.

62 Regis Musavengane and Llewellyn Leonard, 'When Race and Social Equity Matters in Nature Conservation in Post-Apartheid South Africa' (2019) 17:2 Conservation and Soc'y 135, 136.

In analysing the foundational importance of these early environmental treaties, I assert that these are more than historical artefacts pointing us in the direction of the initial efforts at environmental protection and sustainability at the international level.[63] These treaties were, to be more precise, a legal reaction to sustainability concerns occurring in a certain historical context. In this regard, I reject the unqualified reverence that is frequently extended to these treaties based on their racial motivations and exclusionary practices that froze Africa out of this initial effort.

If anything at all, these treaties worsened the ecological crisis. They seemed to provide solutions to the loss of flora and fauna while actively nuancing the ongoing ecological destruction, this time only through new forms of legal technologies. At this point, it is important to challenge Eurocentric scholarship that also valorised these early treaties. Consider, for example, Nico Schrijver's doubtful claim that the 1933 London Convention 'could be said to have started the modern approach to ecological issues'.[64] This is yet another unmerited generalisation of a specific European response to a Europe-made problem that is easily illustrated as a common global effort. This kind of analysis masks the devastation of Africa's natural resources by Europe. After all, these early treaties constituted a 'response to the threat to species that was posed by European expansion into the African continent'.[65]

Additionally, the scope of both the 1900 and 1933 London treaties was extensive. It imposed very harsh conditions on Africans who were neither responsible for the excesses that the treaties sought to address nor were Africans given the chance to participate in designing conservation and preservation schemes that were subsequently foisted on them under these treaties.[66] For example, these treaties weakened and adversely impacted African Indigenous approaches to sustainability as they paved the way for criminalising hunting by Africans through colonial legislation. These domestic laws were developed consequent to the treaties. These laws were aimed at restricting Indigenous hunting through the introduction of prohibitive and extortionate licence fees, banning local traps, and finally

63 Mickelson, 'South, North', 59; Michael Bowman, 'A Tale of Two CITES: Divergent Perspectives upon the Effectiveness of the Wildlife Trade Convention' (2013) 22:3 RECIEL 228, 234. States in the Americas adopted the 1940 Convention on Nature Protection and Wild Preservation in the Northern Hemisphere which was modelled along the 1933 London Convention.

64 Schrijver, *Development without Destruction*, 27.

65 Mickelson, 'South, North', 59.

66 Ibid.

outlawing the sale of guns to Africans, with the main goal of recharacterising 'subsistence hunting into poaching'.[67] As an exceptionally Eurocentric intervention, the 1933 London Convention was the applicable international law on nature conservation in Africa for well over three decades before it was replaced in 1968 with a new treaty that reflected Africa's nascent political independence and a seeming response to the continent's decolonising moment in respect of its natural resources.[68]

4.3 Bandung Revisited: Solidarising around the Environment

While the obvious logical step would be to proceed with an analysis of the 1968 treaty, a detour is necessary. This detour comprises a consolidation of the 1955 Asian-African Conference (Bandung Conference) as a historically significant conference for Third World scholarship and activism.[69] The Bandung Conference is 'given such importance in postcolonial histories of international law' due to its multiple implications across international trade and economic relations on natural resources, global social relations.[70] However, until recently, the legacy of the Bandung Conference appeared to be on its way out of mainstream accounts as it was on the verge of being consigned to the status of a dusty footnote in the history of international relations and of its law-making.[71] As Sally Percival Wood has contended, a fuller account of the successes, failures, contradictions, and controversies emerging from this historic moment is needed even today to provide necessary nuance, to impart much-needed 'balance and scope to understanding the East–West tensions at work' during this crucial period in global history, and to draw out the implications of key, subsequent post-Bandung Conference changes for Global South engagements in international law and politics.[72]

As a meeting organised and generally attended by Asian and African states (mostly under colonial rule), the Bandung Conference was

[67] Prost and Otomo, 'British Influences', 201–203.

[68] Michael Bowman, Peter Davies, and Catherine Redgwell, *Lyster's International Wildlife Law*, 2nd ed. (Cambridge University Press 2010) 264.

[69] Sally Percival Wood, 'Retrieving the Bandung Conference … Moment by Moment' (2012) 43:3 J Southeast Asia Studies 523, 530; Ahmad Rizky Mardhatillar Umar, 'Rethinking the Legacies of Bandung Conference: Global Decolonisation and the Making of the Modern International Order' (2019) 11:3 Asian Pol and Pol'y 461.

[70] Lys Kulamadayil, '"Petro-States" Shaping of International Law' (2022) 25:2 J History IL 161.

[71] Amitav Acharya, 'Studying the Bandung Conference from a Global IR Perspective' (2016) 70:4 Australian J Int'l Aff 342.

[72] Wood, 'Retrieving the Bandung Conference', 527.

fundamentally a dissent against Western imperialism and colonialism.[73] In Christopher Lee's apt description, the Bandung Conference 'helped to manifest what is taken as self-evident today: the idea of the Third World'.[74] Or, in Michael Fakhri's recent reflection, the Bandung Conference was the 'epitome of the Third World project'.[75]

These radical interpretations of the conference assist in reviewing the role Africa plays in international law-making. They demonstrate how that knowledge established Africa's contribution to the 'substantive rules of international law' beyond its political geography.[76] Considering a collectivist engagement was the preferred approach of the Global South in international relations, it is impractical to distinguish the African voice from those of its other Global South contemporaries. In this sense, the Bandung Conference bridged important aspects of Africa's influences on international environmental law in the period immediately preceding the decolonisation years and beyond.[77]

4.3.1 Bandung: (Re-)weaponising Sovereignty

The Bandung Conference heralded the beginning of new ideas in international relations and a sea-change of global interactions across political and economic dimensions.[78] In Antony Anghie and Makau wa Mutua's influential work on the origins of Third World Approaches to International Law (TWAIL), they underscore the criticality and embeddedness of Bandung in Third World scholarship and in how that conference provided a necessary and timely platform for Third World activism.[79] However, despite its

[73] Xu Jie, 'The Asian-African Legal Consultative Organisation and Its Relationship with the People's Republic of China' (2012) 1:1 AALCO JIL 15, 39.

[74] Christopher J. Lee, 'At the Rendezvous of Decolonisation: The Final Communiqué of the Asian-African Conference, Bandung, Indonesia, 18–24 April 1955' (2009) 11:1 Interventions 81, 87.

[75] Fakhri, 'Third World Sovereignty', 220.

[76] Tiyanjana Maluwa, 'The OAU/African Union and International Law: Mapping New Boundaries of Revising Old Terrain' (2004) 98 Am SIL: Proc Annual Mtg 232, 234.

[77] Ngonlardje Kabra Mbaidjol, *African Countries and the Global Scramble for China: A Contribution to Africa's Preparedness and Rehearsal* (Brill 2019), 136.

[78] Obiora Chinedu Okafor, 'The Bandung Ethic and International Human Rights Praxis: Yesterday, Today and Tomorrow' in Luis Eslava, Michael Fakhri, and Vasuki Nesiah (eds.), *Bandung, Global History and International Law: Critical Pasts and Pending Futures* (Cambridge University Press 2017) 515, 515.

[79] Mutua and Anghie, 'What Is TWAIL?', 32.

fundamentality to international law, the conference's connection to international environmental protection is not readily noticeable.[80]

TWAIL scholars argue the nexus between the Bandung Conference and the environment in Third World scholarship can only be discovered by first examining the conference's 'political, economic and legal significance'.[81] This view is accurate considering the term 'sustainable development' appeared much later in global discourse; while the environment is an older subject matter that has featured in global contestations over natural resources.[82] In this sense, a successful discussion weaves together the threads that unite the Bandung Conference to its several offshoots including the institutional and normative developments that created a unique interaction that was not expressly environmental yet connected to environmental issues.[83] It is in this sense that the Bandung Conference adapted Westphalian sovereignty into a Third World politico-legal construct to guide its 'particular idea of the nation-state'.[84]

As has been recounted in the literature, the Bandung Conference provided invaluable normative impetus for the Global South's international law-making adventures.[85] For example, the Asian African Legal Consultative Organisation (AALCO) was a Bandung outcome.[86] In line with its mandate to harmonise Asian and African positions on matters of international law, AALCO highlights international solidarity as central to the principle of good neighbourliness.[87] As part of its contributions, the environment and sustainable development featured prominently in AALCO's engagements on the codification and progressive

80 Mickelson and Natarajan, 'Reflections on Rhetoric and Rage', 465.

81 Ibid.

82 Lilian Aponte Miranda, 'The Role of International Law in Intrastate Natural Resource Allocation: Sovereignty, Human Rights, and People-Based Development' (2012) 45 Vand J Transnat'l L 785, 792–800.

83 Luis Eslava, Michael Fahkri, and Vasuki Nesiah, 'The Spirit of Bandung' in Luis Eslava, Michael Fakhri, and Vasuki Nesiah (eds.), *Bandung, Global History and International Law: Critical Pasts and Pending Futures* (Cambridge University Press 2017) 3, 13.

84 Antony Anghie, 'Bandung and the Origins of Third World Sovereignty' in Luis Eslava, Michael Fakhri, and Vasuki Nesiah (eds.), *Bandung, Global History, and International Law: Critical Pasts and Pending Futures* (Cambridge University Press 2017) 535, 535.

85 Amitav Acharya, 'Who Are the Norm Makers? The Asian-Africa Conference in Bandung and the Evolution of Norms' (2014) 20:3 Global Governance 405.

86 Jie, 'The Asian-African Legal Consultative Organisation', 17. This organisation was previously called the Asian-African Legal Consultative Committee.

87 Shikhar Ranjan, 'Asian-African Legal Consultative Organisation (AALCO)' in Petra Minnerop, Rüdiger Wolfrum, and Frauke Lanchemann (eds.), *International Development Law* (Oxford University Press 2019) 83, 83.

development of international law.[88] For instance, a key focal point of AALCO's work was the significant role it played in incorporating environmental considerations in the law-of-the-sea negotiations.[89]

Also, the establishment of the Non-Aligned Movement (NAM) was a Bandung outcome.[90] NAM and what it stood for was a much-needed intervention with its focus on the interests and concerns of the Global South, far removed from the bipolarity of the politics of the East–West divide. As Partha Chatterjee has noted, NAM 'created a new space of internationalism'.[91] In accordance with the principle of Third World solidarity agreed at Bandung, post-Bandung events later culminated in NAM's establishment amidst the Cold War's polarising security politics.[92] Nonetheless, NAM inspired sustainable development.[93] Working in concert with the negotiating community of states from the Global South, that is, the Group of 77 (G-77), NAM carved out room for environmental politics within international security engagements, by aligning itself with the G-77 position.[94]

As a foundation for consolidating an emerging South–South cooperation, the Bandung Conference was principally geared towards political freedom, sovereign equality, and economic emancipation of the Global South based on political self-autonomy and sovereignty.[95] In this respect, the Bandung Conference had questioned colonially-imposed international

88 Ibid., 88.

89 Edwin Egede, *Africa and the Deep Seabed Regime: Politics and International Law of the Common Heritage of Mankind* (Springer 2011) 83.

90 Francis Njenga, 'The Work and Role of the Asian-African Legal Consultative Committee and its Cooperation with the United Nations' in Najeeb Al-Nauimi and Richard Meese (eds.), *International Legal Issues Arising under the United Nations Decade of International Law* (Martinus Nijhoff 1995) 39, 40.

91 Partha Chatterjee, 'The Legacy of Bandung' in Luis Eslava, Michael Fakhri, and Vasuki Nesiah (eds.), *Bandung, Global History, and International Law: Critical Pasts and Pending Futures* (Cambridge University Press 2017) 657, 671.

92 Heloise Weber and Poppy Winanti, 'The "Bandung Spirit" and Solidarist Internationalism' (2016) 70:4 Australian J Int'l Aff 391, 392.

93 Mark T. Berger, 'After the Third World? History, Destiny and the Fate of Third Worldism' (2004) 25:1 Third World Q 9, 26; Devaki Jain and Shubha Chacko, 'Walking Together: The Journey of the Non-Aligned Movement and the Women's Movement' (2009) 19:7 Dev in Practice 895, 900.

94 Williams, 'Third World and Global Environmental Negotiations', 54; Carol Geldart and Peter Lyon, 'The Group of 77: A Perspective View' (1980–1981) 57:1 Int'l Aff 79, 80–84. While some scholarly accounts tend to single out Latin America and the former Yugoslavia's efforts in founding the G-77, the Bandung Conference and its Asian African coalition certainly played a significant role in its formation.

95 Mbaidjol, *African Countries and the Global Scramble for China*, 16.

hierarchies by arguing for a new international system based on substantive equality among states.[96] This radical post-Westphalian proposition (of Third World sovereignty) was inspired by the historical marginalisation of the South in international affairs, particularly in its visible absence at the founding of the UN in 1945.[97]

The South's pursuit of this new version of sovereignty was linked to another concept: the doctrine of non-interference in the internal affairs of another state.[98] On this subject, Ngonlardje Mbaidjol noted that, 'in the current realm of African international politics, Bandung 1955 is viewed as the genesis of the principle of non-interference'.[99] This view is also shared by TWAIL scholars who argue that the conference 'reinforced norms of non-intervention and non-interference'.[100] While these concepts were not exactly novel, having been long adopted as part of the Covenant of the League of Nations and much later under the UN Charter, African states and their other Southern counterparts took a hard-line position on these doctrines based on the real or perceived fear of the threat (or actual use) of force by these former colonial powers to destabilise their newly established postcolonial polities.[101] In this sense, it was understood that a reformulated doctrine of non-interference would limit the spectre of external aggression while at the same time, and quite paradoxically, permit Africa's unique formulation of a continental norm of internal intervention.[102] It is in this context, as Antony Anghie has suggested that the Southern states emerging from colonialism were apprehensive about reforming the structures of the colonial state that had been bequeathed to them by European imperial powers.[103]

Of course, these African states were equally invested in maintaining the existing state structures they had inherited at independence. While

96 Umar, 'Rethinking the Legacies of Bandung Conference', 463.

97 Anghie, 'Bandung and the Origins', 536.

98 Siba Grovogui, 'A Revolution Nonetheless: The Global South in International Relations' (2011) 5:1 Global South 175, 181.

99 Mbaidjol, *African Countries and the Global Scramble for China*, 17.

100 Anghie, 'Bandung and the Origins', 541.

101 Mbaidjol, *African Countries and the Global Scramble for China*, 17–22; Sylvia Wairimu Kang'ara, 'China and Africa: Development, Land, and the Colonial Legacy' in Luis Eslava, Michael Fakhri, and Vasuki Nesiah (eds.), *Bandung, Global History and International Law: Critical Pasts and Pending Futures* (Cambridge University Press 2017) 367, 377.

102 Amitav Acharya, 'Norm Subsidiarity and Regional Orders: Sovereignty, Regionalism, and Rule-Making in the Third World' (2011) 55:1 Int'l Studies Q 95, 115.

103 Anghie, 'Bandung and the Origins', 543–546. This point must not be understood as support for illegitimate or undemocratic rule in Africa. Rather, it only presents a nuanced approach to how African states approached state power in the post-independence period.

the Bandung Conference ushered the South into a new internationalism, the nationalist proclivities that became pronounced after the conference simultaneously functioned as an existential threat to citizens of the postcolonial state. A repurposed Third World nationalism that was founded on 'an anti-imperialist social mobilisation to modernise productive forces in order to create a more egalitarian and self-sufficient' postcolonial state rarely countenanced internal dissension.[104] This brand of nationalism emerged from Bandung aiming to reassert the 'right of a state to regain control over its natural colonial-based investment in natural resources and its affiliated system'.[105] However, while not expressly referenced at the conference, the manifestation of this natural resource nationalism was the introduction of the concept of permanent sovereignty over natural resources. This was the pivot around which Third World nationalism and sovereignty were redesigned, thus leading to expropriation *en masse* in the aftermath of independence.[106] Expectedly, nationalisation became a basis around which the Global South rallied its economic philosophy which it christened the new international economic order (NIEO).[107]

For African political elites and allies, anticolonial nationalism, a reconstituted sovereignty, and the doctrine of non-interference were tools to wage lawfare both abroad and home.[108] These renewed principles founded an anti-imperial impetus to supplant colonial overrule and not necessarily to bring about far-reaching or meaningful internal state reorganisation.[109]

[104] Joshua Barker, 'Beyond Bandung: Developmental Nationalism and (Multi)cultural Nationalism in Indonesia' (2008) 29:3 Third World Q 521, 523.

[105] M. Y. Aiyub Kadir and Alexander Murray, 'Resource Nationalism in the Law and Policies of Indonesia: A Contest of State, Foreign Investors, and Indigenous Peoples' (2019) 9:2 Asian JIL 298, 300.

[106] Anghie, 'Bandung and the Origins', 547–548; Kang'ara, 'China and Africa', 376–377.

[107] Bedjaoui, *Towards a New International Economic Order*, 209; Grégoire Mallard, *Gift Exchange: The Transnational History of a Political Idea* (Cambridge University Press 2019) 162–164; Gus Van Harten, 'TWAIL and the Dabhol Arbitration' (2011) 3:1 Trade L and Dev 211; Hippolyte, 'Foreign Investment Law and Developing Countries', 85. Hippolyte argued the Third World reinterpretation of sovereignty was partly influenced by the disappointment of the Global South that, when political independence was finally achieved, it was soon realised that it failed to deliver on the promises of economic development in the Global South.

[108] Sara Kendall, 'Cartographies of the Present: "Contingent Sovereignty" and Territorial Integrity' (2017) 47 Nethl YBIL 83, 91. I draw on the understanding of law fare as used in Kendall's work to argue states (and to an extent, some legal scholars) 'employ terms and principles from international law while disregarding the content of the law itself'.

[109] Julian Go and Jake Watson, 'Anticolonial Nationalism: From Imagined Communities to Colonial Conflict' (2019) 60:1 Archives Europeanopéennes de Sociologie 31, 45.

The pursuit of this brand of nationalism rarely permitted political solidarity (even from a regional standpoint) to translate into significant reform in the internal socio-political and economic life of these new African states.[110] As has emerged from some recent critiques on the subject, the rallying call of solidarity as the intrinsic quality of Bandung was decidedly equivocal and curated to serve as a platform to 'valorise competing development and state-building initiatives without binding states to concrete, genuinely revolutionary programs of action'.[111]

Commenting on the needs of the postcolonial (Global South) state to maintain internal political stability at all cost, Fakhri tellingly argues that:

> Postcolonial states often brutalise Indigenous peoples sometimes to the same degree as settler states. This way of concentrating power, organising it in bureaucratic hierarchy, or ruling over territory; the practice of disciplining people and excluding others; this preoccupation with economic development and market forces was and remains brutal not just in the Third World but as a universalised state practice in nearly all countries. It may be more accurate to describe our juridical global order today as Bandungian and not Westphalian.[112]

Emerging from this exposition, a key repressive canon of the Eurocentric character of international law that was used in subjugating Southern peoples was the doctrine of sovereignty.[113] Thus, it would be plainly naïve to assume that, given the chance, the postcolonial state would denounce Western sovereignty so easily considering its investment in safeguarding its new-found political autonomy.

It is no wonder these new states derived strength from retooling sovereignty for their own purposes. On this subject of the *nouveau* sovereignty problematique, not only were these postcolonial states very protective over their state sovereignty; they also masterfully reconstructed self-determination and the mission of development to reinforce this new kind of sovereignty. In the process, these states fine-tuned and enhanced

[110] Joseph Hongoh, 'The Asian-African Conference (Bandung) and Pan-Africanism: The Challenge of Reconciling Continental Solidarity with National Sovereignty' (2016) 70:4 Australian J Int'l Aff 374, 375.

[111] Umut Özsu, '"Let Us First All Have Unity Among Us": Bandung, International Law, and the Empty Politics of Solidarity' in Luis Eslava, Michael Fakhri, and Vasuki Nesiah (eds.), *Bandung, Global History and International Law: Critical Pasts and Pending Futures* (Cambridge University Press 2017) 293, 295.

[112] Fakhri, 'Third World Sovereignty', 227–228.

[113] Antony Anghie, 'The Evolution of International Law: Colonial and Postcolonial Realities' (2006) 27:5 Third World Q 738, 741.

sovereignty into 'a kind of sovereignty plus'.[114] Thus, by transforming sovereignty from a political construct to a resource management technology, postcolonial states in the Global South emerged from their colonial life with an enhanced organising motivation for state control with consequential effects on the making of international law.

Some scholars have linked the inspiration for these marked changes to South–South engagements including the Bandung Conference.[115] But, a retrospective analysis demonstrates this new approach went against the legal position at the Bandung Conference where it was rather affirmed that natural resources belong to the colonised peoples (not the artificial creation of the colonial nation-state) and that those formal, bureaucratic structures of the state were only to manifest the rights of its peoples and their aspirations if the exercise of sovereignty and political autonomy was to be legitimate.

Therefore, set against this dark portrait of a vicious ring-fencing of sovereignty by the postcolonial state, the Global South's credulous reception of the 'Western industrial development model' was made much easier in the absence of any credible domestic resistance. This was achieved by the assimilation of the 'Third World into the global economy', and with all the environmental challenges associated with that Western development model.[116] Despite its noble intentions, the Bandung Conference thus harnessed the colonial exploitation ethos to drive the decolonisation process in a direction that sometimes diverged from the aspirations of the peoples of the Global South.[117] It is in this context that the legacy of the Bandung Conference ought to be visualised as a broader discussion of the law and politics that sits at the intersection of development and the environment and its consequent weaponisation by the postcolonial state.[118]

4.3.2 The Bandung–Environment Nexus

Although there is an indication that a discernible discourse on the environment emerges from the 'Spirit of Bandung', the question that

[114] Robert H. Jackson, *Quasi-States: Sovereignty, International Relations and the Third World* (Cambridge University Press 1991) 40.

[115] Kulamadayil, '"Petro-States" Shaping of International Law',161.

[116] Mickelson and Natarajan, 'Reflections on Rhetoric and Rage', 466–467.

[117] Darina Petrova and Tomaso Ferrando, 'Three Enclosures of International Law: Commoning Premises, Processes and Aims' in Usha Natarajan and Julia Dehm (eds.), *Locating Nature: Making and Unmaking International Law* (Cambridge University Press, 2022) 255, 267.

[118] Mickelson and Natarajan, 'Reflections on Rhetoric and Rage', 469.

lingers is how exactly does the Bandung Conference's legacy illuminate sustainable development in international law?[119] In response, as I have already noted, the linkage between Bandung and the environment is not easily observable.[120] This not-so evident connection demonstrates how the progress of international law is routinely de-historicised, including some of its key themes like sustainable development.[121] Admittedly, it is no secret that the link between the Bandung Conference and the environment is missing in 'mainstream telling of environmental history because it precedes the creation of the specialised field of international environmental law'.[122] This point though is not exactly an accurate description. However, it readily demonstrates the ahistorical treatment of important connections within international law. Still, the ahistoricism of the Bandung Conference must be critically analysed to understand the *long durée* of sustainable development in international law and its connection to this unique historical trajectory.

Furthermore, in some more contemporary accounts on the Bandung moment and a detailed analysis of its processes, environmental protection emerges as one of the outcomes of the Bandung Conference.[123] Its connection to the environment as a Global South subject was, however, obscured with its absence caused by the ahistoricism of international environmental law, beginning in the early 1970s. Third World scholars have since contended that such accounts mis-periodise historical relevance and fail to address a much older history of the environment in international affairs which is linked to resource extraction, particularly during colonialism.[124] Therefore, to fully understand the relationship between the Spirit of Bandung and the environment, it is important to investigate the link between development and environment.[125] By encouraging a radical multipolar perspective on international engagements on economic development, the Bandung moment challenged several aspects of colonial legal orientation in both Asia and Africa and

[119] Luis Eslava, Michael Fakhri, and Vasuki Nesiah (eds.), *Bandung, Global History and International Law: Critical Pasts and Pending Futures* (Cambridge University Press 2017) 3, 9–10.

[120] Mickelson Usha Natarajan, 'Reflections on Rhetoric and Rage', 465.

[121] Mickelson, 'South, North', 54–60.

[122] Mickelson and Natarajan, 'Reflections on Rhetoric and Rage', 468.

[123] Susan Engel, 'South–South Cooperation in Southeast Asia: From Bandung and Solidarity to Norms and Rivalry' (2009) 38:2 J Current Southeast Asian Aff 281, 219.

[124] Eslava et al. (eds.), *Bandung, Global History and International Law*, 22–26.

[125] Mickelson and Natarajan, 'Reflections on Rhetoric and Rage', 469.

provoked a rethinking of the interaction between economic development and 'respect for the laws of ecology'.[126]

Thus, the Spirit of Bandung inspired a relentless quest for decolonisation and opened up opportunities and possibilities for the Global South to participate in international law and relations. However, this historic turn soon calcified any lingering prospects of substituting the prevailing degenerative international legal system with a substantially progressive international order.[127] With the gaze of the Global South fixed on (international) economic equality as the next phase of the decolonising mission, the Global South 'had uncritically accepted the Western industrial development model in either its capitalist or socialist forms'.[128]

In this context, the South was preoccupied with the decolonising moment while at the same seeking to match the pace of economic growth in the Global North. Here, the South's developmental-nationalist efforts decidedly mirrored the very patterns of imperialism which it hitherto railed against. As witnessed in many Southern states, having initially exercised sovereignty over natural resources to exclude Western interests and nationalised their economic activities, the postcolonial state paradoxically used that same logic of sovereignty to re-engage these Western (foreign) investors to return and again exploit natural resources in the South; this time, with a lax attitude towards environmental regulation and often as a partnership between the foreign investors from the Global North and the comprador bourgeoisie and political elite of the Global South.[129] Trapped within this intractable web, the Global South

126 Tukumbi Lumumba-Kasongo, 'Rethinking the Bandung Conference in an Era of "Unipolar Liberal Globalisation" and Movements Towards a "Multipolar Politics"' (2015) 2:9 Bandung: J Global South 1, 5.

127 Hongoh, 'Asian-African Conference'.

128 Mickelson and Natarajan, 'Reflections on Rhetoric and Rage', 466.

129 Kadir and Murray, 'Resource Nationalism in the Law', 332; Andreas Eckert, 'Radical Scholarship and Political Activism: Walter Rodney as Third World Intellectual and Historian of the Third World' in Gyan Prakash and Jeremy Adelman (eds.), *Inventing the Third World: In Search of Freedom for the Postwar Global South* (Bloomsbury Academic 2022) 117, 118. Eckert highlights that it was these kinds of schemes that Walter Rodney had warned against in his enduring work, *How Europe Underdeveloped Africa*. Eckert notes that Walter Rodney was concerned about the despoliation of Africa by the Global North even in the aftermath of political independence as these powerful interests instituted more creative arrangements to extract Africa's resources even more intensively but still avoiding ecological responsibility. It is this kind of attentiveness to the continuum of imperial exploitation that Third World scholars must remain conscious of (and alert to) even as neoliberal prescriptions are repeatedly foisted on the Global South by the Global North and their allied institutions.

intensified an already deteriorating ecological catastrophe as it failed 'to foresee further development along the same path will only deepen the current environmental crisis'.[130]

In response to this problem, a revitalised, people-centred approach to Third World natural resource engagement is gradually finding its way back into critical legal discourse. There have been recent calls urging the South to return to the solidarising principles of the Bandung Conference. This juridical renewal challenges and resists the orthodox position advanced by legal scholars such as Jorge Viñuales, that once the people delegate their legal authority over natural resources to the state, the way the state 'sells or transfers natural resources makes little difference from a strictly legal perspective'.[131]

These Third Worldist calls suggest a need to 'develop a legal basis for people-based resource nationalism' with the purpose of reversing the colonial approach to state control over natural resources, and encouraging extractivist regimes that promote the best interests of a state's peoples.[132] It is in this context that TWAIL scholars urge a rethinking of international economic structures and their structural implications. In sharing the radical advocacy of scholars like Karin Mickelson and Usha Natarajan, it is important to shift from state-dominated resource exploitation to a people-based resource management that is anchored on Indigenous self-reliance.[133] And, as Mbaidjol has rightly noted, 'from the environmental point of view, self-reliance has the advantage of placing the natural environment under the control of those who depend on it instead of mortgaging it to distant owners and abusers'.[134] This point underlines the criticality of a resource utilisation scheme that integrates customary approaches to ensuring resource extraction is balanced and respectful of the environment and beneficial to the interests of the peoples.

4.4 Sustainable Development in Africa: From Theory to Praxis

The Bandung Conference breathed new life into Global South engagements in international law.[135] Yet, if the value of this historic conference

130 Arif Dirlik, 'The Bandung Legacy and the People's Republic of China in the Perspective of Global Modernity' (2015) 16:4 Inter-Asia Cultural Studies 615, 626–627.

131 Jorge E. Viñuales, 'The Resource Curse: A Legal Perspective' (2011) 17:2 Global Governance 197, 207–208.

132 Kadir and Murray, 'Resource Nationalism in the Law', 322.

133 Mickelson and Natarajan, 'Reflections on Rhetoric and Rage', 471.

134 Mbaidjol, African Countries and the Global Scramble of China, 471.

135 Fakhri, 'Third World Sovereignty', 227.

was considered as just another international event, its legacy will be lost. Rather, it must be reimagined as the beginning of a project, and an idea that is yet to fully unravel. To imagine the Bandung Conference 'as a project is to approach its narration as a series of creative choices rather than an outcome of political contingencies'.[136] This point is a deeply reflective statement when contemplating such conferences and other international meetings as merely events spanning a few days without thinking about them as mighty seeds that are planted for us to nourish and grow into very great trees. In pursuing this idea, I examine Africa's post-Bandung interface with international environmental law as a Third World project. Thus, the Spirit of Bandung comes alive and becomes the normative tapestry that binds together the different moving parts of this unending project.

But even more than that, the recognition of the Bandung moment as a cord that binds Africa and Third World scholarship together helps foreground the foregoing analysis. On this subject, the Bandung Conference is recognised as 'the symbolic birthplace of TWAIL'.[137] To complete this analytical circle, I evaluate whether, in practice, Bandung's call to solidarity – as unity and respect for and within Southern peoples – travels beyond state alliances.[138] This analysis is also sensitive to Bandung's link to Pan-Africanism – a rather paradoxical connection underlining the primacy of Pan-African solidarity – which is an interaction that invites further critical contemplation.[139] Thus, I am interested in whether Africa carried forth Bandung's ethos in terms of the environment.

4.4.1 *Emerging from the Colonial: Reclaiming Nature/Environment in Africa*

Africa's decolonisation peaked as Bandung's aftershocks rallied the liberation struggle.[140] About the same time, matters of colonial preoccupation

[136] Vik Kanwar, 'Not a Place, But a Project: Bandung, TWAIL, and the Aesthetics of Thirdness' in Luis Eslava, Michael Fakhri and Vasuki Nesiah (eds.), *Bandung, Global History and International Law: Critical Pasts and Pending Futures* (Cambridge University Press 2017) 140, 142.

[137] Mutua and Anghie, 'What Is TWAIL?', 31.

[138] Issa G Shivji, 'Whither Africa in the Global South: Lessons of Bandung and Pan-Africanism' in Sam Moyo, Praveen Jha, and Paris Yeros (eds.), *Reclaiming Africa: Scramble and Resistance in the 21st Century* (Springer 2019) 257, 267.

[139] Hongoh, 'Asian-African Conference', 375.

[140] Assie-Lumumba, 'Behind and Beyond Bandung', 7; Michael Collins, 'Nation, State and Agency: Evolving Historiographies of African Decolonisation' in Andrew W. M. Smith

including nature conservation assumed greater interest for both Africans and European colonial powers.[141] At the heart of this new struggle was Africa's attempt to reclaim and reassert state sovereignty over natural resources while the European colonialists strongly desired to retain control over these resources well into Africa's post-independence future. This was the backdrop against which the new treaty that would replace the 1933 London Convention was negotiated. So, contrary to the popular narrative that at independence, Africa had regained full control over its natural resources in the immediate aftermath of decolonisation, it is necessary to reread the history of the successor treaty to the 1933 London Convention, that is the African Convention for the Conservation of Nature and Natural Resources, as the ultimate compromise between Africa and imperial Europe that it actually was.[142]

In rereading that history, it is important to resituate the adoption of the Algiers Convention in the politics of the times. To begin, the most notable post-independence act of African states, acting together, was the establishment of the regional political collective called the Organisation of African Unity (OAU).[143] Five years later, in 1968, the OAU negotiated and adopted the Algiers Convention to replace the imperial 1933 London Convention.[144] Thus, a major difference between this new treaty and the earlier 1900 and 1933 London agreements was the augmented scope of the Algiers Convention which went beyond protecting just a selection of fauna, nature reserves, and parks, by extending coverage to natural resources such as soil and water.[145]

The treaty's fundamental principle was its requirement that the state parties pursue the best interests of their peoples.[146] This objective was aligned with the broader goal of continental integration. Remarkably, the OAU itself was the outcome of the twinning of the Bandung moment and

and Chris Jeppessen (eds.), *Britain, France and the Decolonisation of Africa: Future Imperfect?* (UCL Press 2017) 17, 26–27.

141 Jeff Schauer, '"We Hold It in Trust": Global Wildlife Conservation, Africanisation, and the End of Empire' (2018) 57 J Brit Studies 516, 517.

142 1001 UNTS 4 (1976) [Algiers Convention]; R. M. Matheka, 'The International Dimension of the Politics of Wildlife Conservation in Kenya, 1958–1968' (2008) 2:1 J Eastern Afr Studies 112, 128.

143 *Charter of the Organisation of African Unity*, 479 UNTS 39 [OAU Charter]; T. O. Elias, 'The Charter of the Organisation of African Unity' (1965) 59:2 Am JIL 243.

144 1001 UNTS 4 (1976) [Algiers Convention].

145 Morne van der Linde, 'African Responses to Environmental Protection' (2002) 35:1 Comp and Int'l LJ S Afr 99.

146 1001 UNTS 4 (1976) [Algiers Convention], art II.

Pan-Africanism. The objective of linking these two significant ideas was the need to transform these Africa's newly independent states and their splinter political blocs into a single, integrated political union.[147] In the process, the Algiers Convention became Africa's continent-wide agreement on development and environment and an initial effort at balancing these two concerns. Nonetheless, the inherent tensions in political and economic integration meant environmental integration was challenged by economic growth – a situation that has continually dogged the course of sustainable development in Africa.[148]

Still, this Algiers Convention must not be misinterpreted as introducing environmental protection into Africa's normative and continental approaches. As Emeka Polycarp Amechi argues:

> It should be noted that while the adoption of the Convention by the then newly independent African nations constituted the first regional attempt to address environmental concerns in the region, it was not the start of environmental protection in Africa as the protection of the environment was an integral part of the religious, cultural and social life of Africans before their colonisation and subsequent independence.[149]

Therefore, despite these aspirational goals that were set out in the Algiers Convention, it was not surprising Africa engaged less with the environmental prescriptions of this treaty than it did with its resource exploitation regime. It marked a shifting away from ecological considerations to a time when economic growth was the mainstay of the postcolonial state. With hopes of a post-independence economic boom built around natural resource exploitation, the Algiers Convention became the 'most prominent expression of the newly independent African states' sovereignty over their natural resources'.[150]

Thus, these new African states did not necessarily commit to environmental protection under this treaty. Even if they did, it was merely based on the general principle to support the treaty's purpose. In this context, 'the Algiers Convention 1968 does not *per se* encourage a reversal of the colonial era's focus on exploitation in the use and management of natural

[147] Assie-Lumumba, 'Behind and Beyond Bandung', 9.

[148] David Dzidzornu, 'Economic Development and Environmental Protection in Africa: The Constitutional, Conventional and Institutional Contexts' in Francis Botchway (ed.), *Natural Resource Investment and Africa's Development* (Edward Elgar 2011) 462, 462.

[149] Emeka Polycarp Amechi, 'Linking Environmental Protection to Poverty Reduction in Africa: An Analysis of the Regional Legal Responses to Environmental Protection' (2010) 6:2 L Envt and Dev J 112, 115.

[150] Takang, 'Algiers to Maputo', 171.

resources and environment'.[151] As a result, the Algiers treaty was deficient in its enforcement objectives as it joined the environment to development in an ill-fitting manner.[152]

Even so, some African international law scholars have read sustainable development into the Algiers Convention. For example, Tiyanjana Maluwa has noted that, through this treaty, 'African states articulated the principles of sustainable development and respect for the environment as a common heritage or public good before they became more commonly acknowledged, even within the UN context'.[153] While Maluwa's statement sought to elevate the influence of Africa on the discourse on sustainable development, it is not entirely accurate as his hypothesis comes across as a far-fetched extrapolation of the ambitions of the Algiers treaty. As evidenced in the amendments to the Algiers Convention and other normative alterations to the Constitutive Act of the African Union (AU) which replaced the OAU Charter, sustainable development, as presently conceptualised, was a later addition to the constitutive (legal) rules on the subject of the environment in Africa.[154] Thus, with the Algiers Convention coming before the 1972 Stockholm Conference, the treaty's prescriptive domain seldom reflected the evolving sustainable development jurisprudence as the subject matter was substantially outside the treaty's immediate 'normative elasticity'.[155] This point cannot simply be glossed over.

4.4.2 The Sustainable Development Turn: A Band-Aid Solution?

As conceived since the historic 1972 Stockholm Conference, the concept of sustainable development has had about four discrete entry points into Africa's continental jurisprudence. Despite this seeming progress, the concept's juridical establishment remains a band-aid solution to a problem with a much more complex cause. These four dimensions of sustainable development in African regional environmental law manifest

[151] David M. Dzidzornu, 'Environment Protection in Africa: A Panorama of the Law and Practice' (2004) 22:2 J Energy and Nat Res L 148, 149.

[152] Dzidzornu, 'Economic Development and Environmental Protection in Africa', 462–463.

[153] Maluwa, 'OAU/African Union and International Law', 234.

[154] 1 July 2000, 2158 UNTS 37733; Corinne A. A. Packer and Donald Rukare, 'The New African Union and Its Constitutive Act' (2002) 96:2 Am JIL 365, 372.

[155] Dzidzornu, 'Economic Development and Environmental Protection in Africa', 463.

as enhanced nature conservation; as a political objective; as an economic development concern; and as a human rights aspiration.[156]

This four-dimension origin story further complicates sustainable development's utility as a continental objective. It is in this respect that sustainable development is referred to as 'largely a foreign concept' that made a late entry into Africa.[157] Sustainable development's 'failure to launch', so to speak, has been due to its poor formulation and ineffectual operationalisation which are reflected in the misperception (shared by even some African legal scholars) that the concept was alien to Africa.[158] Perhaps the problem with this perspective is the inability of these commentators to contemplate sustainable development beyond its Stockholm connections.[159] Hence, to understand the stunted legal performance of sustainable development in Africa, it is crucially important to unpack the internalisation of the concept in Africa to fully appreciate its evolutive disjointedness.[160]

4.4.2.1 Maputo Reboot: A Sequel to the Algiers Convention

The Algiers Convention's implementation mechanism, which was reliant on an OAU framework that was not keen on environmental protection, doomed it to failure.[161] Additionally, the evolving character of international environmental law, linked to the legacy of the 1972 Stockholm Conference, called into question the existing normative approaches to environmental

156 Zeray Yihdego, 'The African Union: Founding Principles, Frameworks and Prospects' (2011) 17:5 Eur LJ 568, 580.

157 Strydom, 'Introduction to Regional Environmental Law', 22. Considering the concerns raised in postcolonial critiques and the Eurocentric character of international law, it is quite unsettling that when environmental law (including African) scholars speak on the concept of sustainable development, they often leave no room for alternate conceptions that mirror Indigenous African thinking on the concept.

158 Jennifer Hadden and Lucia A. Seybert, 'What's in a Norm? Mapping the Norm Definition Process in the Debate on Sustainable Development' (2016) 22 Global Governance 249, 251.

159 Petersmann, *When Environmental Protection and Human Rights Collide*, 49. Petersmann links these regional developments to the post-1972 Stockholm Conference effect. In a sense, these kinds of connections at once deny regional agency as in Africa's case and at the same time lend legitimacy to these regional efforts as integral to a global push towards sustainable development.

160 Muthucumaraswamy Sornarajah, *Resistance and Change in the International Law on Foreign Investment* (Cambridge University Press 2015) 389. Sornarajah critiques the fragmented and *ad hoc* approaches to resolving international investment law disputes as 'band-aid solutions'. I adopt Sornarajah's imagery to convey, in a similar sense, the patchwork that sustainable development evokes in its formative journey in African continental jurisprudence.

161 Takang, 'Algiers to Maputo', 180–181.

protection. These challenges necessitated a review of the Algiers Convention by the OAU.[162] Yet the amendment process which began in 1981 and ended in 2002 did not completely disengage with the historical orientation of the treaty's state-centred politics as the negotiation of the amendments straddled both the defunct OAU and the newly-established AU.[163] This heritage compromised the outcome of the amendment process which has been described as the 'revision of the 1968 Algiers Convention rather than a completely new instrument'.[164]

The Revised African Convention for Nature and Natural Resources (Maputo Convention) which replaced the Algiers Convention was outstanding for a variety of reasons.[165] First, this new treaty is replete with references to sustainable development.[166] In this respect, some African legal scholars claim the Maputo Convention provides for 'sustainable development both as an overarching goal and also as procedural obligations'.[167] Second, as an obligation, the treaty requires state parties to actualise Indigenous legal conceptions on environmental protection in treaty domestication and implementation.[168] This express treaty injunction emphasises the importance of Indigenous governance and customary law to sustainable development.[169] Third, the treaty does not only focus on flora and fauna as it provides for sustainable utilisation of both renewable and non-renewable natural resources.[170]

Despite these positive attributes, the treaty has its own drawbacks. The Maputo Convention has an unusual history as the product of two eras: the OAU's state-centred orientation to environmental protection was carried over into the establishment of the AU. This treaty contains a defect that restricts sustainable development's broader utility.[171] This more significant issue limits the treaty's effectiveness as it is only

[162] World Conservation Union, *An Introduction to the African Convention on Nature and Natural Resources*, 5.

[163] Takang, 'Algiers to Maputo', 182. The AU replaced the OAU in 2002.

[164] Bowman et al., *Lyster's International Wildlife Law*, 266.

[165] *Revised African Convention on Conservation of Nature and Natural Resources*, 11 July 2003 (revised) [Maputo Convention].

[166] Ibid., Preamble, para 14.

[167] Erinosho, 'Revised African Convention', 388.

[168] *Revised African Convention on Conservation of Nature and Natural Resources*, art IV.

[169] Anel A. du Plessis and C. Rautenbach, 'Legal Perspectives on the Role of Culture in Sustainable Development' (2010) 13:1 Potchefstroom Electronic LJ 27, 37–46.

[170] Bowman et al., *Lyster's International Wildlife Law*, 268.

[171] *Revised African Convention on Conservation of Nature and Natural Resources*; Takang, 'Algiers to Maputo', 182.

enforceable within a state party's jurisdiction.[172] Here, the treaty applies to African states that are parties to it, whereas, in disputes between its contracting parties and other African states that are non-parties to the Maputo Convention but are rather parties to the Algiers Convention, it is the Algiers Convention that still applies.[173]

This flaw in the Maputo Convention reflects the classical understanding of treaty obligations (*pacta sunt servanda*) between contracting parties under international law. It leaves one wondering why the Algiers Convention is still subsisting if the intention was to establish a new basis for Africa's regional environmental law. This defect in the Maputo treaty disincentivises states from incorporating sustainable development and bringing it 'into state practice and subsequent internal action'.[174] Thus, some African environmental law scholars conclude that, as long as this provision remains unchanged in the Maputo Convention, 'the interaction among African states on sustainable development will continue to be administered under the constrictive scope of Article XXXIV of this treaty [Maputo Convention]'.[175] Despite this obvious problem, there seems to be no commitment to amend this restriction on effective continental environmental governance under the Maputo treaty.

4.4.2.2 Sustainable Development: All Things Good Governance

After more than two decades since its founding, the OAU had almost achieved its central mission of decolonisation as most African states became politically independent by the 1980s.[176] Just about the same time, Africa was undergoing a radical political transformation, with external and internal demands for the observance of good governance, democracy, and human rights.[177] Some accounts relating to external pressure

[172] Abba Kolo, 'Dispute Settlement and Sustainable Development of Natural Resources in Africa' in Francis Botchway (ed.), *Natural Resource Investment and Africa's Development* (Edward Elgar 2011) 49, 52.

[173] *Revised African Convention on Conservation of Nature and Natural Resources*, art XXXIV.

[174] Dzidzornu, 'Economic Development and Environmental Protection in Africa', 463.

[175] Takang, 'Algiers to Maputo', 182.

[176] Rahila Timothy Dantong, 'African Union and the Prospect of Sustainable Development in the Twenty First Century' (2015) 8:1 OIDA Int'l J Sust Dev 39, 40–43. However, there were notable exceptions, like South Africa, which was under the Apartheid regime until well into the 1990s.

[177] Stephen Sevidzem Kingah, 'The African Union's Capacity in Promoting Good Governance' (2006) 3:2 Int'l Organisations L Rev 317, 323.

for political and governance reforms indicate these calls were patterned along the lines of civilisational supremacy that are often encountered in the literature on the civilising mission of European imperialism.[178] This time, these external pressures reappeared in the context of the post-Washington consensus when international development finance institutions were seeking to excuse their complicity in the collapse of the economies of postcolonial states that had turned to these very institutions for development assistance.[179] It is unsurprising, then, that the World Bank always insists on good governance, by holding that, 'political legitimacy is a *sine qua non* for sustainable development'.[180]

However, the OAU is equally blameable; at least partly, for this situation. It is no secret that the OAU was not exactly suited for this new political reality – that is, the global wave of democracy – as the OAU's foremost organising principle, since its establishment was the political emancipation of Africa from colonial rule.[181] As Zeray Yihdego notes:

> The principles enshrined in the OAU Charter understandably, or perhaps unfortunately, emphasised state sovereignty and independence and not democratic governance, development and human rights values; understandably because that was the demand of most African states, and unfortunately because democratic principles were missing from this founding document.[182]

This was, in part, the legacy or heritage of the Bandung Conference where the adherence to state sovereignty and territorial integrity trumped nearly every other major concern.[183] Thus, the AU Constitutive Act which was adopted in 2001 established the AU as the OAU's replacement institution to usher Africa into a new, democracy-focused reality.[184]

[178] Dimitri Van Den Meerssche, 'Performing the Rule of Law in International Organisations: Ibrahim Shihata and the World Bank's Turn to Governance Reform' (2019) 32:1 Leiden JIL 47, 56–58.

[179] David Williams, 'Managing Sovereignty: The World Bank and Development in Sub-Saharan Africa' (2003) 123:3 Mondes en Développement 5, 13–20.

[180] Mashupye Herbert Maserumule and Shadrack B. O. Gutto, 'Critical Understanding of Good Governance and Leadership Concepts Written in the Context of New Partnership for Africa's Development (NEPAD) and the Challenges to the Contextual Discourses on Africa's Development Paradigms' (2008) 3:2 Int'l J Afr Ren Studies 63, 67.

[181] William Gumede, 'The Democracy Deficit of Africa's Liberation Movements Turned Governments' (2017) 44:1 Politikon 27.

[182] Yihdego, 'African Union', 573.

[183] Adekeye Adebajo, 'The Revolt against the West: Intervention and Sovereignty' (2016) 37:7 Third World Q 1187, 1191–1193.

[184] 1 July 2000, 2158 UNTS 37733, art 4(m).

The AU came into existence in 2002 with the promotion of democracy and good governance among its core objectives.[185] Under this renewed political framework, environmental protection assumed greater prominence as it was incorporated in the AU's regional law.[186] As a positive start, the AU Constitutive Act provides for sustainable development as a core (continental) objective.[187] As a principle of good governance within Africa's regional constitutional architecture, the concept of sustainable development indicates, at a minimum, the AU's willingness to bind itself and its member states to this objective as an essential constitutional element of the continental commitment to democracy and good governance.[188]

But sustainable development is only one of the many aims and purposes in a competing scheme of other continental objectives. On this subject, Yihdego remarked, once more, that:

> the political and policy-orientated nature of these (scattered) commitments, the widespread disregard of them in national jurisdictions and the fact that these are fundamentally intergovernmental undertakings (as opposed to domestic forces and actors) constitute a systemic weakness.[189]

In this sense, sustainable development manifests as a good governance principle. It embeds itself into the rule of law as it is often invoked to undertake policy synchronisation. Even so, it permits the AU to sidestep 'ideological arguments about political systems that are fundamental to a proper understanding of the rule of law'.[190] Thus, as sustainable development is ensconced in a motley group of so-called good governance principles, its uniqueness is either overshadowed or left competing with other non-ecologically inclined considerations.

185 Ibid., art 3; Strydom, 'Introduction to Regional Environmental Law', 22.

186 Oliver C. Ruppel, 'Environmental Law in the African Union' in Oliver C. Ruppel and Emmanuel D. Kam Yogo (eds.), *Environmental Law and Policy in Cameroon: Towards Making Africa the Tree of Life* (Nomos Verlag 2018) 119, 119.

187 1 July 2000, 2158 UNTS 37733, art 3(j) reads: 'The Objectives of the Union shall be to: . . . (j) promote sustainable development at the economic, social and levels as well as the integration of African economies'.

188 Dantong, 'African Union', 46.

189 Yihdego, 'African Union', 583.

190 Irene Khan, 'How Can the Rule of Law Advance Sustainable Development in a Troubled and Turbulent World?' (2017) 13:2 McGill J Sust Dev L and Pol'y 211, 217.

4.4.2.3 Sustaining Economic Integration: Treading the Path of Illusion

Sustainable development yet again emerges as a central feature in Africa's continental integration. This time, it is economic integration, as evidenced in Africa's flagship economic development platform, the New Partnership for Africa's Development (NEPAD).[191] When one considers the fact that NEPAD was adopted only a year before the Maputo Convention came into force, it is understandable why some scholars conclude NEPAD is the first instrument on sustainable development in African continental jurisprudence.[192] Accordingly, sustainable development only became an African preoccupation following NEPAD's establishment.[193]

Beginning as a separate entity, NEPAD did not 'create binding legal obligations'; however, it has now been integrated into the AU's governance architecture.[194] However, sustainable development's NEPAD origins raise challenges for the concept owing to NEPAD's patent economic development orientation. In view of its pandering to the Global North and the international development finance institutions allied to the North, NEPAD is labelled as 'a philosophy of development which appears to have a lot in common with the neoliberal approach to development'.[195] This neoliberal outlook has also been queried from an Afro-Asian perspective as Asian states have expressed some concern over whether this new development initiative under NEPAD signifies African states have reneged on Bandung's commitment to resist development theories and practices which have 'a North-driven neoliberal foundation'.[196] As a result, some legal experts have offered even less charitable assessments of NEPAD, as Adebayo Adedeji, for example, describes it as a 'feudo-imperial partnership'.[197]

191 Strydom, 'Introduction to Regional Environmental Law', 25–30.

192 Amechi, 'Linking Environmental Protection', 126–129.

193 Strydom, 'Introduction to Regional Environmental Law', 23.

194 Frans Viljoen, *International Human Rights Law in Africa*, 2nd ed. (Oxford University Press 2012) 168.

195 Osita Agbu, 'NEPAD: Origin, Challenges and Prospects' (2003) 64:1/2 Indian J Pol Science 97, 98.

196 Annette Skovsted Hansen, 'Africa–Asia Regional Partnerships and South–South Development Cooperation' in Pedro Amakasu Rapaso, David Arase, and Scarlet Cornelissen (eds.), *Routledge Handbook of Africa–Asia Relations* (Routledge 2017) 335, 346.

197 Adebayo Adedeji, 'From the Lagos Plan of Action to the New Partnership for Africa's Development and from the Final Act of Lagos to the Constitutive Act: Whither Africa?' (Keynote Address delivered at the African Forum for Envisioning Africa held in Nairobi, Kenya, 26–29 April 2002) 1, 12.

This critique of NEPAD as a neoliberal arrangement is extended to the entire AU constitutional framework.[198] If the debate over the meaning of sustainable development is far from being settled, and the concept is seen as calculatedly malleable, then its incorporation in a neoliberal development context must be understood as the shrewd embedding of a Eurocentric technology to maintain the balance in favour of economistic choices that ultimately benefit the interests of the Global North.[199] What emerges from this difficult, complex situation is that, in the AU's attempt to establish a 'development agreement' between Africa and the Global North, NEPAD became a pliant conduit for Western interventionist policy disguised as development assistance.[200]

In its classic double-mindedness, development assistance exacerbates the scourge of Africa's weak political leadership by reinforcing the problem of aid dependency.[201] NEPAD's pliability made the AU's legal, policy, and political framework susceptible to ill-intentioned development conditionalities that compromise and threaten Africa's operationalisation of sustainable development.[202] Regrettably, even the entry into force of the African Continental Free Trade Area Agreement in 2019 does not necessarily herald new prospects for sustainable development despite its ambitious outlook.[203] Thus, concerning this point, some African legal scholars have argued economic reforms must contemplate and integrate ecological considerations including sustainable development.[204]

198 Shivji, 'Whither Africa in the Global South', 262.

199 Ziai, *Development Discourse and Global History*, 66–67.

200 Viljoen, *International Human Rights Law in Africa*, 168–170.

201 Williams, 'Managing Sovereignty', 19.

202 Jong-Dae Park, *Reinventing Africa's Development: Linking Africa to the Korean Development Model* (Palgrave MacMillan 2019) 52.

203 Olabisi D. Akinkugbe, Ohio Omiunu, Amaka Vanni, Regis Y. Simo and Luwam Dirar, 'Africa's Participation in International Economic Law in the 21st Century: An Introduction' (2020) 17:1 Manchester J Int'l Econ L 1; Katrin Kuhlmann and Lisa Akinyi Agutu, 'The African Continental Free Trade Area: Toward a New Legal Model for Trade and Development' (2020) 51:4 Georgetown JIL 753.

204 Olabisi D Akinkugbe, 'Africanisation and the Reform of International Investment Law' (2021) 53:1 Case Western Reserve JIL 7, 32. This is on the assumption that sustainable development is not an economic consideration. But, as I have argued thus far; regrettably, the conceptualisation and practical implementation of sustainable development proceeds along economic lines.

4.4.2.4 On Terra Firma: Towards a Right to Sustainable Development?

The final instalment of sustainable development's African origin story deals with the construction of a 'right' to sustainable development.[205] In the other dimensions of the origin story, the concept is expressly provided for in institutional texts. However, the emergence of a right to sustainable development derives from the interpretation of the African Charter on Human and Peoples' Rights.[206] Article 24 of the African Charter provides that 'all peoples shall have the right to a general satisfactory environment favourable to their development'.[207] As has been advocated by some African legal scholars, Article 24 of the African Charter transforms into a right to sustainable development through interpretative analysis, and springs to life when it is read together with Article 3(j) of the AU Constitutive Act.[208]

The African Charter is the first human rights treaty to have incorporated an environmental right into an amalgam of individual and solidarity rights.[209] It provides for the classical collection of individual rights that are present across a host of international human rights instruments predating the adoption. But these are individual rights complemented by the inclusion of solidarity rights in the African Charter. The incorporation of individual and collective rights distinguishes the African philosophy of human rights law from 'the East and the West in their conception of the ideological function of human rights'.[210] In keeping with solidarity as its ideological pivot, the African Charter goes further to provide not only for environmental rights as part of solidarity rights, but also for a right to development.[211] Through human rights instrumentalism, the

205 1 July 2000, 2158 UNTS 37733, art 3 reads: 'The Objectives of the Union shall be to: ... (h) promote and protect human and peoples' rights in accordance with the African Charter on Human and Peoples' Rights and other relevant human rights instruments'.

206 1982, 21 ILM 58 (entered into force 21 October 1986) [African Charter] art 24.

207 Ibid., art 24.

208 Louis J. Kotzé and Anél du Plessis, 'The African Charter on Human and Peoples' Rights and Environmental Rights Standards' in Stephen J. Turner, Dinah L. Shelton, Jona Razzaque, Owen McIntyre and James R. May (eds.), *Environmental Rights: The Development of Standards* (Cambridge University Press 2019) 93, 99.

209 1982, 21 ILM 58 (entered into force 21 October 1986) [African Charter] art 24.

210 B. Obinna Okere, 'The Protection of Human Rights in Africa and the African Charter on Human and Peoples' Rights: A Comparative Analysis with European and American Systems' (1984) 6:2 Human Rights Q 141, 145.

211 1982, 21 ILM 58 (entered into force 21 October 1986) [African Charter] art 22(1): 'All peoples shall have the right to their economic, social and cultural development with due

African Charter expressly integrated environmental protection within human rights.[212] This human rights revolution which was founded on solidarising around environmental causes is credited to the Spirit of Bandung which catalysed 'a more inclusive vision of environmental protection and sustainability that encompasses concerns about social justice and human rights as well as ecological integrity'.[213]

However, the African Charter limits its ecological aspirations despite the elevation of environmental protection into a right under Article 24 of the African Charter. The problem arises from joining environmental protection to development under Article 24. When one analyses the inclusion of development in Article 24, it becomes apparent that this link (joining development to environment) downgrades the ecological side of the relationship because the enjoyment of a 'satisfactory environment' is contingent upon 'development'. This link also consigns the environment to a lower status than development by subordinating environmental protection to the idea of *favourable* development (whatever that means). Thus, as Louis Kotzé and Anel du Plessis rightly observed:

> This would not only mean that the core genesis of the environmental right is entirely anthropocentric, but also that any standards set out by the environmental right must be such that it ensures the 'favourable development' of people, including to ensure their right to development under article 22. The one right is thus conditional on the other; a notion which is affirmed by the ACHPR [the African Charter] in its preamble.[214]

This rights-based aspect of sustainable development provides the concept; at least outwardly, with a more stable constitution than do the other three conceptual dimensions. In this sense, the concept's connection to human rights makes it is easily relatable as evidencing legal reality.[215]

Conceived as a legal right, sustainable development evokes sentiments concerning the rule of law. Here, the rule of law is quickly elevated to a principle of justice.[216] This is quite encouraging for anyone interested in cloaking the concept of sustainable development with legal corporeality.

regard to their freedom and identity and in the equal enjoyment of the common heritage of mankind'; Benjamin Elias Winks, 'A Covenant of Compassion: African Humanism and the Rights of Solidarity in the African Charter on Human and Peoples' Rights' (2011) 11:2 Afr Human Rights LJ 447, 450.

212 Ruppel, 'Environmental Law in the African Union', 122.

213 Mickelson and Natarajan, 'Reflections on Rhetoric and Rage', 475.

214 Kotzé and du Plessis, 'African Charter', 100–101.

215 Karin Arts, 'Inclusive Sustainable Development: A Human Rights Perspective' (2017) 24 Current Opinion on Envt'l Sustainability 58.

216 Khan, 'Rule of Law', 217.

However, it is through this fascination with the language of rights that several undefined concepts and principles have slipped into Eurocentrism's 'universal teleology'.[217] Thus, expressions like sustainable development endow those undefined phenomena with legal character, including in the realm of international law; yet without, necessarily doing so with a clear sense of legal purpose.

Thus, the turn to national constitutions to secure environmental rights and sustainable development has now become global legal fashion.[218] The endowment of sustainable development with the language of rights frames its rather abstract essence in legal normativity and in the process, it rigidifies the never-ending North–South debate over the boundaries of sustainable development.[219] But, even before this issue is resolved, the flexible character of rights discourse presents a further challenge for Africa where the emergence of environmental rights could be likened to neoliberal development theory functioning through international development finance institutions which:

> possess a degree of power which they are prepared to use in order to shape what they see as advantageous constitutional and legal developments. This can manifest as pressure exerted during a pending constitutional drafting process to ensure that democratic norms are adhered to, or alternatively, may encourage entrenched regimes to initiate a process of constitutional reform.[220]

Hence, while environmental rights have become a popular choice and a domestic staple of Africa's legal operationalisation of sustainable development, notably as constitutionally-embedded rights, these rights are yet to translate into the legal subsidiaries of the continental–environmental right they ought to be.[221] This might be the result of two issues: first, the underlying principle and controlling force of Article 24 of the African Charter tilts more towards economic growth and not ecological integrity; and, second, human rights are frequently (mis-)construed as restrictions

217 Martti Koskenniemi, 'Histories of International Law: Dealing with Eurocentrism' (2011) 19 Rechtsgeschicte 152, 156.

218 Luis E Rodrígues-Rivera, 'The Human Right to Environment in the 21st Century: A Case for Its Recognition and Comments on the Systemic Barriers It Encounters' (2018) 34:1 Am U Int'l L Rev 143, 158–162.

219 Okereke, *Global Justice and Neoliberal Environmental Governance*, 149.

220 Roderic O'Gorman, 'Environmental Constitutionalism: A Comparative Study' (2017) 6:3 Transnat'l Envt'l L 435, 445.

221 Brian Y. K. Sang, 'Tending Towards Greater Eco-Protection in Kenya: Public Interest Environmental Litigation and Its Prospects within the New Constitutional Order' (2013) 57:1 J Afr L 29, 29–30.

on state sovereignty, a cardinal doctrine of statehood that African states are historically reluctant to relax their grip on.[222]

4.5 Environment, Development, and Rights in Practice: A Discordant Medley

The evolution of sustainable development in Africa has thus been derailed and supplanted by a right-based framework. Today, we are in a situation where the language of sustainable development is now filtered through the concept of human rights. This is what sustainable development practice looks like presently. This language of rights has now become a vital technology and a contemporary fixation. But how did we get here?

To answer this question, it is important to first understand that the four different formative strands of sustainable development's origin story in Africa unite to manifest as an inharmonious three-way interaction across human rights, the environment, and development.[223] First, the AU upholds the significance of human rights, and asserts, as one of its core objectives, compliance with the rights provided for under the African Charter.[224] Second, Africa's juridical joining of the environment and human rights immobilises the conceptual divide between human rights and the environment.[225] Overcoming this challenge requires a discussion encompassing Article 3(j) of the AU Constitutive Act on sustainable development and its complement in Article 24 of the African Charter on the right to a satisfactory environment.[226] Third, this rights turn is reinforced by the Maputo Convention and the African Charter; the latter providing the right to development and the right to a satisfactory environment should direct its implementation.[227] Despite that, environmental rights are not particularly novel. Little surprise some legal scholars have criticised its incorporation

[222] Rodrígues-Rivera, 'Human Right to Environment', 153.

[223] Werner Scholtz, 'Human Rights and the Environment in the African Union Context' in Werner Scholtz and Jonathan Verschuuren (eds.), *Regional Environmental Law: Transregional Comparative Lessons in Pursuit of Sustainable Development* (Edward Elgar 2015) 102, 102–104.

[224] Ibid., 103; 1982, 21 ILM 58 (entered into force 21 October 1986) [African Charter], art 3 (h).

[225] Alan Boyle, 'Human Rights and the Environment: Where Next?' (2012) 23:3 European JIL 613, 614.

[226] Scholtz, 'Human Rights and the Environment', 103.

[227] *Revised African Convention on Conservation of Nature and Natural Resources*, art III; World Conservation Union, *An Introduction to the African Convention on Nature and Natural Resources*, 6–7.

as only representing 'a "greening" of existing human rights law rather than the addition of new rights to existing treaties'.[228]

When development becomes a right, as demonstrated by Article 22 of the African Charter, it is conceptualised as a people's right to self-determination. But when it is analysed, we soon discover self-determination is intrinsically a sovereign endeavour of the state.[229] The embeddedness of this sovereign power across these three interconnected phenomena provokes a dilemma over environmental protection, development, and human rights, bearing in mind the state's unyielding dominance within each of these modalities of contested power.[230] This conundrum has consequences for the environment. Accordingly, to borrow a leaf from Karen Litfin, state sovereignty 'in its many guises appears to be both a friend and foe to nature'.[231]

This sovereignty matrix of development, environment, and human rights expressed within the concept of sustainable development raises implementation possibilities: either under a quasi-judicial approach or a directly judicial approach. The quasi-judicial perspective focuses on the work of the African Commission on Human and Peoples' Rights (the African Commission), while the judicial procedure focuses on the African Court on Human and Peoples' Rights (the African Court). Quite understandably, the two are bound together by legal scholars into a messy potpourri of legal operationalisation with very little effort to parse their jurisprudence and understand their differences.

Even so, both approaches ought to be construed as complementary in character.[232] Broadly conceived, complementarity embraces sub-regional

[228] Boyle, 'Human Rights and the Environment', 614; Ariel Rawson and Becky Mansfield, 'Producing Juridical Knowledge: "Rights of Nature" or the Naturalisation of Rights?' (2018) 1:1–2 Envt and Plan E: Nature and Space 99, 103. Rawson and Mansfield argue that the emergence of the rights of nature seems to make a strong case against environmental rights by tagging them anthropocentric and Eurocentric. However, as the authors also argue, by turning to 'rights of nature' as the basis for a new environmentalism we risk reinscribing 'the colonial history of legal personhood' in Indigenous legal cosmologies.

[229] Nicolaas Schrijver, 'Self-Determination of Peoples and Sovereignty over Natural Resources' in United Nations Office of the High Commissioner for Human Rights (ed.), *Realising the Right to Development: Essays in Commemoration of 25 Years of the United Nations Declaration on the Right to Development* (United Nations 2013) 95, 101.

[230] Williams, 'Managing Sovereignty', 13–15.

[231] Karen T. Litfin, 'Sovereignty in World Ecopolitics' (1997) 41:2 Mershon Int'l Studies Rev 167, 169.

[232] Solomon T. Ebobrah, 'Towards a Positive Application of Complementarity in the African Human Rights System: Issues of Functions and Relations' (2011) 22:3 European JIL 663, 665.

human rights courts as well. As such, the ensuing analysis is alive to the dynamics of these relevant sub-regional institutional and normative perspectives.[233] Thus, the organising logic of the following discussion is dictated by how human rights courts and other adjudicative tribunals in Africa judicialise sustainable development.[234]

4.5.1 Quasi-Judicial Operationalisation

The African Commission is the primary African regional human rights system's implementation mechanism.[235] It was established soon after the African Charter entered into force in 1986 and is tasked with interpreting and enforcing the rights provided in the Africa Charter.[236] Yet, despite its significance, the African Commission is doubtfully a judicial authority due to its constitution. As Frans Viljoen and Lirette Louw have noted:

> It is arguable that the nature and activity of the Commission does not support the conclusion that its decisions may place legal obligations on states responsible for violations. The Commission is not a judicial body and its finding on the merits of a case is not a judgment imposing an obligation on parties to observe and implement a remedy.[237]

Still, despite its non-binding character, the Commission's jurisprudence provides useful guidance on and insights into how to weld together the environment, human rights, and development in respect of sustainable development.[238]

The African Commission's jurisprudence offers insights into the rich diversity of how the concepts of the environment, development, and human rights interact within African regional law. Beginning with the environment–rights nexus, the African Commission recognises the interaction between human rights and the environment.[239] In this sense, the Commission's jurisprudence recognises the link between development

233 Ibid., 664.

234 Emelie Folkesson, 'Human Rights Courts Interpreting Sustainable Development: Balancing Individual Rights and the Collective Interest' (2013) 6:2 Erasmus L Rev 142.

235 1982, 21 ILM 58 (entered into force 21 October 1986) [African Charter], art 30.

236 Ibid., art 45; Chenwi, 'Right to a Satisfactory, Healthy, and Sustainable Environment', 62.

237 Frans Viljoen and Lirette Louw, 'The Status of the Findings of the African Commission: From Moral Persuasion to Legal Obligation' (2004) 48:1 J Afr L 1, 13.

238 Boyle, 'Human Rights and the Environment', 630–631.

239 Scholtz, 'Human Rights and the Environment', 102.

and human rights as symbolised by the right to development.[240] Having begun its journey as a theoretical construct, development is now clothed in rights language, and has since found its way into Article 22 of the African Charter.[241] Also, Africa's regional juridical perspectives on the environment as a right is equally immersed in a development orientation as the right to the environment is *qualified* by development under Article 24 of the African Charter.[242] This debate has been elevated into a human rights concern, not only with the inclusion of Articles 22 and 24 in the African Charter but also through the jurisprudence of the African Commission; thus, provoking an argument on the the existence of 'a binding human rights-based approach to environmental protection, linking the right to environment to the right to development'.[243] Thus, the environment–development debate should not be understood as novel – but rather, it ought to be understood as 'an ancient task in policy making'.[244]

As previously described, Africa's continental approach to sustainable development's operationalisation is undergirded by Article 24 jurisprudence. On this subject, the African Commission's decision in the *Social and Economic Research Centre (SERAC) and Centre for Economic and Social Rights* v *Federal Republic of Nigeria* is seen as the appropriate test in environmental rights adjudication.[245] The SERAC Decision stressed the broad character of Article 24 as it reinforced 'the principle of interdependency of rights,

240 Serges Alain Djoyou Kamga and Charles Manga Fombad, 'A Critical Review of the Jurisprudence of the African Commission on Human and Peoples' Rights' (2013) 57:2 J Afr L 196, 207.

241 Elisabeth Bürgi Bonanomi, *Sustainable Development in International Law Making and Trade: International Food Governance and Trade in Agriculture* (Edward Elgar 2015) 18; Daniel J. Whelan, '"Under the Aegis of Man": The Right to Development and the Origins of the New International Economic Order' (2015) 6:1 Humanity 93, 206. Bonanomi purports to correct the misconception that the right to development was first suggested by the Senegalese jurist Keba M'Baye. For most scholars, Keba M'Baye was the originator of the right to development. But, in Whelan's account, the first person who mooted this idea of the right to development was the former Senegalese former minister, Doudou Thiam at the United Nations in New York in 1966, six years before M'Baye wrote about the subject. Nonetheless, both M'Baye and Thiam were from Senegal.

242 Scholtz, 'Human Rights and the Environment', 110.

243 Ruppel, 'Environmental Law in the African Union', 132.

244 Bonanomi, *Sustainable Development*, 107.

245 *Social and Economic Research Centre (SERAC) and Centre for Economic and Social Rights v Federal Republic of Nigeria*, African Commission on Human and Peoples' Rights Communication 155/96 [SERAC Decision]; Justice C. Nwobike, 'The African Commission on Human and Peoples' Rights and the Demystification of Second and Third Generation Rights under the African Charter: Social and Economic Rights Action Centre and Centre for Economic and Social Rights v Nigeria' (2005) 2:1 African J Leg Studies 129.

which is a key principle in the Charter'.[246] The interconnectedness of development and environment was prominent in this case as the African Commission analysed both development and the environment, along with using sustainable development to resolve the inherent tension between the two domains.[247] Thus, according to Werner Scholtz, Article 24 of the African Charter 'is the most explicit normative statement of an environmental right in any binding human rights instrument'.[248]

In the SERAC Decision, the African Commission illuminated the legal philosophy underlying Article 24's interpretation.[249] In this case, it was alleged that Nigeria had violated several human rights provisions under the African Charter including Article 16 (on the right to health), Article 21 (on the peoples' right to freely dispose of their natural resources), and Article 24 (on the right to a satisfactory environment). These violations arose out of Nigeria's alleged failure to protect the Ogoni people from oil pollution linked to petroleum operations in the Niger Delta which had been caused by Shell PLC and the Nigerian National Petroleum Company. Indeed, as alleged in the case, the Nigerian government had deployed its military to brutalise the Ogoni people of the Niger Delta who protested these violations.[250]

In its analysis of Article 24 of the African Charter, the African Commission found Nigeria culpable of the allegations. It recommended Nigeria should take all 'reasonable steps and other measures to prevent pollution and ecological degradation, to promote conservation, and to secure an ecologically sustainable development and use of its natural resources'.[251] The Commission also found Articles 16 and 24 of the African Charter require a state party to take into account scientific and technical reports, environmental, social and health impact assessments in line with participatory environmental democracy.[252] In this respect, the state was enjoined to prevent conduct that threatened the health and ecological well-being of its peoples.[253] Therefore, in examining

[246] Chenwi, 'Right to a Satisfactory, Healthy, and Sustainable Environment', 66.

[247] Ibid.

[248] Scholtz, 'Human Rights and the Environment', 107.

[249] Chenwi, 'Right to a Satisfactory, Healthy, and Sustainable Environment', 74.

[250] Sigrun I. Skogly, 'Complexities in Human Resource Protection: Actors and Rights Involved in the Ogoni Conflict in Nigeria' (1997) 15:1 Nethl QHR 47.

[251] *Social and Economic Research Centre (SERAC) and Centre for Economic and Social Rights v Federal Republic of Nigeria*, para 52.

[252] Ibid., para 53; Scholtz, 'Human Rights and the Environment', 109.

[253] Fons Coomans, 'The Ogoni Case before the African Commission on Human and Peoples' Rights' (2003) 52:3 ICLQ 749, 753–754.

the conduct of Nigeria vis-à-vis these treaty obligations, the African Commission found that Nigeria had violated Article 24 of the Charter.[254]

The African Commission also addressed other matters including the definition of peoples.[255] Yet, it has failed to define peoples in the context of Article 24 jurisprudence. The absence of such definitions in the SERAC Decision confirms a longstanding resolution of the African Commission to avoid attaching a specific meaning or definition to 'peoples'.[256] As Werner Scholtz rightly observed, 'the Commission missed the opportunity to clarify the concept of "peoples". The Commission's finding merely refers, for instance, to "Ogonis", to the "Ogoni Community" and to the "Ogoni society", and does not dissect the conceptual or definitional elements of the term "peoples".'[257]

However, the African Commission gave some consideration to peoples in contexts other than those related to Article 24 of the African Charter. For example, it has given peoples a 'state-centred interpretation' by linking peoples to a state.[258] Other times, the African Commission has interpreted peoples 'as either a majority or minority in a particular state'.[259] But recently, the African Commission has offered a definition of peoples in the context of Indigenous peoples, their rights and governance systems.[260] Perhaps the only plausible explanation is that this definitional ambiguity reflects the deliberate decision of the OAU (now AU) and its constituent agencies to omit 'a definition of peoples to allow a more expansive interpretation' of peoples whenever the occasion demands.[261] This definitional challenge regarding peoples traces back to the political history of this reference, which 'was understood to refer either to the state, in those states led by liberation leaders, or to Indigenous peoples represented by liberation

[254] *Social and Economic Research Centre (SERAC) and Centre for Economic and Social Rights v Federal Republic of Nigeria*, para 69.

[255] Richard N. Kiwanuka, 'The Meaning of "People" in the African Charter on Human and Peoples' Rights' (1988) 82:1 Am JIL 80.

[256] Serges Alain Djoyou Kamga, 'The Right to Development in the African Human Rights System: The Endorois Case' (2011) 44:2 De Jure 381, 387.

[257] Scholtz, 'Human Rights and the Environment', 109.

[258] *Democratic Republic of Congo v Burundi, Rwanda and Uganda*, Communication No 227/99, para 87; Scholtz, 'Human Rights and the Environment', 110.

[259] *Sudan Human Rights Organisation v Sudan*, Communications No 297/03, para 220; Scholtz, 'Human Rights and the Environment', 110.

[260] *Centre for Minority Rights Development and Minority Rights Group International (on behalf of the Endorois Welfare Council) v Republic of Kenya*, Communication No 276/2003, 150 [Endorois Decision]; Kamga, 'Right to Development, 389.

[261] Godwin E. K. Dzah, 'Theorising the Right to Environment: An Africological Typology' (2019) 27:1 Afr J Int'l and Comp L 25, 48.

movements, in those states under colonial or white minority rule'.[262] Then, it stands to reason that, at the time of conceptualisation, 'peoples' as used historically excluded *peoples* in post-independence African states. Thus, the decolonisation currents at the time could well have intended the idea of peoples to be synonymous to the postcolonial state.

However, the expression of Article 24 of the African Charter as a peoples' right permits groups or individuals to bring communications before the African Commission for adjudication.[263] Accordingly, the African Commission's jurisprudence on the right to a healthy and satisfactory environment does not fully explain the content of Article 24 of the African Charter.[264] To resolve this ambiguity, the commission tasked its Working Group on Extractive Industries, Human Rights and the Environment to clarify the relationship between development and the environment.[265] However, the report of the Working Group again narrowly focused on development; failing to explain the intrinsic value of the environment as a stand-alone phenomenon.[266] Even so, much of the blame still lies with the African Commission as it forewent the opportunity to make an authoritative statement on the place of customary environmental protection which was 'both a time-honoured customary value and communal obligation across Africa'.[267] In clarifying the substance of Article 24 of the African Charter, the African Commission missed the opportunity to deeply consider traditional African cosmologies on the environment.[268] As Africa's premier continental institution for developing the substantive content of the rights provided under the African Charter; the African Commission must seize future opportunities to re-examine

262 Alexander Huneeus and Mikael Rask Madsen, 'Between Universalism and Regional Law and Politics: A Comparative History of the American, European, and African Human Rights Systems' (2018) 16:1 Int'l J Con L 136, 150.

263 Evadne Grant, 'International Courts and Environmental Human Rights: Re-imagining Adjudicative Paradigms' in Anna Grear and Louis J. Kotzé (eds.), *Research Handbook on Human Rights and the Environment* (Edward Elgar 2015) 379, 390.

264 Scholtz, 'Human Rights and the Environment', 109.

265 African Commission on Human and Peoples' Rights, *Rules of Procedure of the African Commission on Human and Peoples' Rights*, 2010, r 23(1); African Commission on Human and Peoples' Rights, *State Reporting Guidelines and Principles on Articles 21 and 24 of the African Charter Relating to Extractive Industries, Human Rights and the Environment*, 2018, 19–40.

266 Chenwi, 'Right to a Satisfactory, Healthy, and Sustainable Environment', 84.

267 Obiora C. Okafor and Godwin E. K. Dzah, 'The African Human Rights System as "Norm Leader": Three Case Studies' (2021) 21:2 Afr Human Rights LJ 669, 691.

268 Rachel Murray, *The African Charter on Human and Peoples' Rights: A Commentary* (Oxford University Press 2019) 548.

Article 24 of the African Charter, placing broader emphasis on African customary law and Indigenous law and relevant cosmologies.[269]

From the foregoing analysis, it is evident that a nonbinding regime for enforcing rights leaves room for selective compliance.[270] It is rather strange that, when Africa adopted a regional human rights treaty, it chose a non-binding mechanism to enforce and implement the treaty. However, we ought to understand that this approach was a deliberate decision by the OAU (now AU) based on claims that this preference was in consonance with a supposedly pacific African outlook on dispute resolution.

Yet, one cannot equally discount the suspicion of African states regarding the erosion of state sovereignty through human rights mechanisms which led to adopting non-binding adjudicative mechanisms.[271] This explanation is quite revelatory as it unravels the history behind the puzzling situation that led to the selection of a nonbinding mode of treaty realisation. If examined from this perspective, it immediately becomes clear that the African Commission's continuing failure to elevate environmental protection is linked to the predominance of state sovereignty and its related supremacy over other continental aims embedded in Africa's regional jurisprudence, including the right to development in Article 22 of the African Charter. Thus, the ineffectiveness of the African Commission's jurisprudence in respect of sustainable development must be properly contextualised. It cannot be understood merely as the result of a mistake in the making of African regional law. It must be seen as a self-imposed price paid by Africa's postcolonial states to ring-fence their sovereignty rather than to be truly accountable to their peoples or sensitive about ecological objectives. Even so, it is still possible to examine non-compliance with the decisions of the African Commission as violations of the African human rights system which can be remedied under the AU Constitutive Act or through a judicial remedy at the African Court.[272] However, this point is a tacit admission of the inherent weaknesses of this non-judicialised approach.

4.5.2 Remedying Weak Practice through Judicialisation

The OAU corrected the ineffectiveness and non-binding character of the findings and recommendations of the African Commission by enhancing

269 Ibid.

270 Chairman Okoloise, 'Circumventing Obstacles to the Implementation of Recommendations of the African Commission on Human and Peoples' Rights' (2018) 18:1 Afr Human Rights LJ 27, 29.

271 Gina Bekker, 'The African Court on Human and Peoples' Rights: Safeguarding the Interests of African States' (2007) 51:1 J Afr L 151, 153–154.

272 Okoloise, 'Circumventing Obstacles', 56.

human rights adjudication; this time by establishing a complementary, binding mechanism; that is, the African Court.[273] This new regional court was the OAU's response to the normative weakness and institutional deficiencies of the African Commission.[274] This court was established by the OAU in 1998 following the adoption of the Protocol to the African Charter.[275] Following its establishment, the African Court joined the global roll-call of regional human rights courts. As a regional institution clothed with binding authority, the African Court interprets and applies the African Charter and other relevant human rights instruments in Africa.[276] This special power of the court to interpret and apply both African and non-African human rights treaties positions the Court as possessing substantially expansive jurisdiction as compared with other regional or international human rights tribunals.[277]

In the performance of its adjudicative functions, the African Court has been endowed with two broad functions: rendering binding judgments in contentious cases and providing advisory opinions.[278] Under its first mandate, the courts renders judgments and state parties are required to comply with these decisions.[279] In carrying out its second mandate, a state party, an organ of the AU, or an 'African organisation' may request an advisory opinion from the court on the interpretation of the African Charter or another human rights treaty.[280] Additionally, a device in the

[273] African Commission on Human and Peoples' Rights, *Rules of Procedure of the African Commission on Human and Peoples' Rights*, 2010, r 114.

[274] Nsongurua J. Udombana, 'Towards the African Court on Human and Peoples' Rights: Better Late Than Never' (2000) 3:1 Yale Human Rights and Dev LJ 45, 110.

[275] *Protocol to the African Charter on Human and Peoples' Rights on the Establishment of an African Court on Human and Peoples' Rights*, 10 July 1998, OAU Doc OAU/LEG/EXP/AFCHPR/PROT III (entered into force 25 January 2004) [Protocol to the African Charter].

[276] Ibid., art 3.

[277] Adamantia Rachovista, 'The African Court on Human and Peoples' Rights: A Uniquely Equipped Testbed for (the Limits of) Human Rights Integration' in Emmanuelle Birbosa and Isabelle Rorive (eds.), *Human Rights Tectonics: Global Dynamics of Integration and Fragmentation* (Intersentia 2019) 69, 70.

[278] *Protocol to the African Charter on Human and Peoples' Rights on the Establishment of an African Court on Human and Peoples' Rights*, arts 3 and 4.

[279] Ibid., art 30.

[280] Ibid., art 4; Ssenyonjo, 'Responding to Human Rights Violations in Africa', 32; *Femi Falana v The African Union*, Judgment of the African Court on Human and Peoples' Rights, Application No 001/2011. Non-state parties and individuals may bring an action against a state party before the court if that state has undertaken to permit such an action by making a declaration to that effect under Article 34(6) of the Protocol to the African Charter. This procedure is a significant restraint on individuals who are seeking to bring

court's toolkit is the power to issue provisional measures.[281] This aspect of the African Court's authority is particularly significant considering ecological damage is often irremediable, thus requiring the court to be proactive in halting impending harm.

In this respect, the African Court recently issued provisional measures in the first environmental case brought before it pending the final outcome of the case of the *African Commission on Human and Peoples' Rights v Republic of Kenya.*[282] This Ogiek Decision is significant in many respects as it implicates a host of articles under the African Charter. It also revitalises African regional jurisprudence on many themes including the links across the environment, indigeneity, and the definition of peoples in the African Charter.[283] This case also unravels the coloniality of international conservation law and the postcoloniality of the heritage of conservation which stripped many African societies of the power to regulate the use of their own natural environment.[284]

In the Ogiek Decision, the Kenyan Forestry Service in 2009 had served an eviction notice on the Ogiek people and other minority communities living in the Mau Forest, asking them to vacate the forest within thirty days. In response, the Ogiek people protested and lodged a complaint against Kenya at the African Commission.[285] The applicants had argued that, as a minority group who have lived in and survived on the resources of the Mau Forest since time immemorial, the Ogiek people were bonded to the land and its resources. As a result, any attempt to remove them

an action before the African Court where their respective states have not permitted the institution of such legal proceedings under the Protocol to the African Charter.

281 African Commission on Human and Peoples' Rights, *Rules of Procedure of the African Commission on Human and Peoples' Rights*, 2010, r 98.

282 *African Commission on Human and Peoples' Rights v Republic of Kenya*, African Court of Human and Peoples' Rights, Application No 006/2012 [Ogiek Decision]; Manisuli Ssenyonjo, 'The African Commission and Court on Human and Peoples' Rights' in Gerd Oberleitner (ed.), *International Human Rights Institutions, Tribunals, and Courts* (Springer 2018) 479, 503; Chenwi, 'Right to a Satisfactory, Healthy, and Sustainable Environment', 77–78.

283 Lucy Claridge, 'The Approach to UNDRIP within the African Human Rights System' (2019) 23:1–2 Int'l JHR 267, 268.

284 Abra Lyman and Darren Kew, 'An African Dilemma: Resolving Indigenous Conflicts in Kenya' (2010) Georgetown J Int'l Aff 37, 38; Lucy Claridge, 'Litigation as a Tool for Community Empowerment: The Case of Kenya's Ogiek' (2018) 11:1 Erasmus L Rev 57, 64; Federica Cittadino, *Incorporating Indigenous Rights in the International Regime on Biodiversity Protection: Access, Benefit-Sharing, and Conservation in Indigenous Lands* (Brill 2019) 265.

285 *Centre for Minority Rights Development and Minority Group Rights (on behalf of the Ogiek People in the Mau Forest) v The Republic of Kenya*, African Commission on Human and Peoples' Rights, Communication 381/09.

from the forest would require a consultative process since the Kenyan government's decision threatened the livelihood, culture, and heritage of the Ogiek peoples as well as the future of the forests.[286] Upon receiving the application, the African Commission issued provisional measures to prevent irremediable damage to the Mau Forest pending the final outcome of its determination.[287] However, Kenya failed to comply with the provisional measures, necessitating a referral by the African Commission to the African Court in 2012 for a binding solution.[288]

The African Court repeated the provisional measures issued by the African Commission.[289] The court's provisional measures were highly significant as it was the first time this mechanism was deployed to protect and defend Indigenous peoples and ecological interests.[290] Substantively, the rights in the African Charter alleged to have been violated included the right to culture (under Article 17), the right to development (under Article 22), and the right to dispose of natural resources (under Article 21).[291] However, the pivot around which this case revolved was the meaning of 'Indigenous peoples' and 'whether the Kenyan government's alleged environmental concerns can justify non-compliance with its obligations toward these groups or its interference with their rights provided for under the African Charter'.[292]

In response to the first part of this legal inquiry, the African Court held the Ogiek community were an Indigenous people as they had an inseparable relationship with the Mau Forest.[293] The court reinforced the claims by the Ogiek peoples that the 'most salient feature of most Indigenous

286 Claridge, 'Approach to UNDRIP', 269.

287 *The Matter of African Commission on Human and Peoples' Rights v Republic of Kenya*, Application 006/2012, Order for Provisional Measures (15 March 2013); Ssenyonjo, 'African Commission and Court', 503.

288 African Commission on Human and Peoples' Rights, *Rules of Procedure of the African Commission on Human and Peoples' Rights*, 2010, r 118(2); Magnus Killander and Bright Nkrumah, 'Human Rights Development in the African Union during 2012 and 2013' (2014) 14:1 Afr Human Rights LJ 275, 284.

289 *The Matter of African Commission on Human and Peoples' Rights v Republic of Kenya*, Application 006/2012, Order for Provisional Measures (15 March 2013) para 25; Claridge, 'Approach to UNDRIP', 58.

290 Chenwi, 'Right to a Satisfactory, Healthy, and Sustainable Environment', 78.

291 The other alleged violations in this application include the right to life under Article 4 and the right to culture under Article 17 of the African Charter. These are inapplicable to my analysis of the case.

292 Chenwi, 'Right to a Satisfactory, Healthy, and Sustainable Environment', 78.

293 *African Commission on Human and Peoples' Rights v Republic of Kenya*, African Court of Human and Peoples' Rights, Application No 006/2012 [Ogiek Decision] para 112.

populations is their strong attachment with nature, particularly land and the natural environment'.[294] The Ogiek people as a distinct community were, thus, entitled to enjoy their right under Article 22 of the African Charter; particularly the right to development.[295] In that respect, the court further held that Kenya's failure to consult the Ogiek people before attempting to remove them from their ancestral land amounted to a violation of their right under Article 22 of the African Charter.[296]

In respect of the second part of the legal inquiry, the African Court held that the Ogiek people were not responsible for the alleged environmental crisis in the Mau Forest since the Kenyan government failed to establish, through evidence, that the continuing presence of the Ogiek people was the reason for the ecological destruction in the forest.[297] The court also held that Indigenous peoples had an intrinsic relationship with the environment relative to their religious practices, and a denial of access to the Mau Forest would therefore unfairly restrict the religio-cultural rights of the Ogiek peoples.[298]

In June 2022, the African Court delivered its final decision in this case and ordered the Kenyan government to pay reparations to the Ogiek people for disrupting their ways of living and for denying them the cultural and religious benefits of their ancestral home.[299] In this sense, the Ogiek Decision will be remembered as the first case before the African Court focusing on indigeneity and endorsing customary law.[300] Nonetheless, I consider the case a missed opportunity for the African Court to have made a unique, far-reaching and binding pronouncement on the environment and sustainable development in a manner that benefits African customary law jurisprudence. As Lucy Claridge has argued, the court 'considered that it had received significant evidence to affirm the Ogiek's assertion that the Mau Forest is their ancestral home, recognising the link between Indigenous populations and nature,

[294] Ibid., para 109.

[295] Ibid., para 209. Development here refers to Indigenous cosmologies, ways of living and knowing.

[296] Ibid., para 201.

[297] Ibid., para 130; Chenwi, 'Right to a Satisfactory, Healthy, and Sustainable Environment', 81.

[298] Chenwi, 'Right to a Satisfactory, Healthy, and Sustainable Environment', 80.

[299] *The Matter of the African Commission on Human and Peoples' Rights v Republic of Kenya*, Application No. 006/2012, Judgement (Reparations), 23 June 2022.

[300] Ibid.

their land and the natural environment'.[301] That was a missed opportunity for the court to demonstrate a more rigorous focus on Indigenous cosmologies and shine light on the greater role of customary law. Nonetheless, this case demonstrates development cannot be deployed to subordinate other (including ecological) concerns nor should Indigenous peoples and their practices (including their ways of living and knowing) be unjustifiably separated from efforts aimed at 'conserving and protecting land, natural resources and the environment'.[302]

Thus, the case presented the court with a unique opportunity to review the historical connection between colonial laws on conservation (and their contemporary continuation) and sustainable development.[303] In this case, it is surprising that neither party nor the African Court itself found it necessary to expressly reference the right under Article 24 of the African Charter. Steeped in what comes across as a pro-development orientation, the African Court did not take the route of express environmental protection even though the environment was the contextual framing for the issues before the African Commission, and later at the African Court. Thus, in reviewing the court's jurisprudence, it is somewhat difficult to grasp its conceptualisation of either the environment or sustainable development.

Nonetheless, the Ogiek Decision goes to the heart of the operationalisation of sustainable development even though the court did not make an explicit reference to the right to a satisfactory environment under Article 24 of the African Charter. As Lilian Chenwi noted, the case raises the profile of the African Charter and its transformative 'potential for ensuring accountability for violation of the right to a satisfactory, healthy, and sustainable environment through prosecution at the African regional level'.[304] Yet, it is not clear whether Kenya would comply with the orders of the African Court relative to the Ogiek Decision.[305] This uncertain situation demonstrates that it is not enough to place inordinate faith

301 Claridge, 'Approach to UNDRIP', 273.

302 Chenwi, 'Right to a Satisfactory, Healthy, and Sustainable Environment', 82.

303 Scholtz, 'Injecting Compassion', 479.

304 Ibid.

305 Adebayo Majekolagbe and Olabisi D. Akinkugbe, 'The African Court of Human and Peoples' Rights Decision in the Ogiek Case: An Appraisal' in Amissi Melchiade Manirabona and Yenny Vega Cárdenas (eds.), *Extractive Industries and Human Rights in an Era of Global Justice: New Ways of Resolving and Preventing Conflicts* (LexisNexis 2019) 163.

in compliance with law alone without a corresponding radical paradigm shift in equally important matters beyond the traditional enforcement mechanisms. The African Court must also demonstrate a sensitivity towards the normative value of customary norms and ethico-legal principles in its adjudication. Without this, we risk overlooking the constitutive interaction between law and politics and how that interaction impacts sustainable development praxis even at the African Court.[306]

4.6 Conclusion

In this chapter, I mapped sustainable development's normative trajectory and its internalisation in Africa. Trapped in the continent's colonial history, sustainable development's normative life cycle has had a close relationship with nature conservation to date. While some critics view contemporary critiques of Western imperialism as misplaced or that the discussion of colonialism is over as the spectre of colonialism is dead and gone, the coloniality of conservation and its contemporary iterations like sustainable development are compelling leitmotifs for undertaking Europe's continuing civilising mission of environmental colonialism.[307]

Paradoxically, the case for colonialism is seeing a revival in the form of historical revisionisms that are writing away colonialism's

[306] Robert Home and Faith Kabata, 'Turning Fish Soup Back into Fish: The Wicked Problem of African Community Law Rights' (2018) 9:12 J Sust Dev and Pol'y 1, 11–16; *Socio-Economic Rights and Accountability Project v Nigeria*, Case No ECW/CCJ/APP/08/08 (compliance with the decisions of sub-regional courts has not been any better than that of the African Court); Karen J. Alter, Laurence R. Helfer, and Jacqueline R. McAllister, 'A New International Human Rights Court for West Africa: The ECOWAS Community Court of Justice' (2013) 107:4 Am JIL 737, 767; *Ligue Ivoirienne des Droits de L'homme (LIDHO) and Others v Republic of Côte d'Ivoire*, Application No. 041/2016 (Judgement) [2023] AfCHPR 21, para. 186. In its latest decision implicating environmental protection, which was released on 5 September 2023, the court held, among many orders that, the Ivory Coast violated Article 24 of the Charter in respect of the dumping of toxic waste in that country. However, the court once more missed the opportunity to invoke or demonstrate how this violation also triggers customary law principles in aid of its interpretation.

[307] Tukumbi Lumumba-Kasongo, 'Land Reforms in the Democratic Republic of Congo (DRC): A Study of the Political Economy of Underdevelopment and Nation-State Building' in Tukumbi Lumumba-Kasongo (ed.), *Land Reforms and Natural Resource Conflicts in Africa: New Paradigms in the Era of Globalisation* (Routledge 2015) 150, 166.

centuries-old sins. Consider, for example, the recent work by Bruce Gilley, who has written in support of a return to colonialism by affirming the values of its civilising mission.[308] The resurgence of this kind of rhetoric which celebrates the perceived benefits of neo-colonialism is no different from the past rhetoric that sought to condition the reception of colonialism in Africa. Yet, a critical examination of the self-interestedness of the coloniality of international law, particularly its universality, requires a constant critique of its self-professed objectivity.[309] At least this is observed in international conservation law as seen through both the 1900 and 1933 London treaties. While these treaties assumed an altruistic outlook, they were in fact European legal technologies for controlling Africa's nature and resources.[310] Alongside such well-crafted regimes of resource control, Africans were dispossessed of their lands through colonial laws on preservation which subjected dislodged peoples to further colonial control including an erosion of customary legal systems that protected the environment.[311]

Africa's sustainable development praxis is also fraught with internal challenges and contradictions. Principally, its environmental (normative) framework including a rights-based approach to the concept of sustainable development and its related network (including regional courts and other quasi-judicial tribunals) are ill-designed to achieve effective legal implementation. Part of this problem occurs at the continental level as many African states are unwilling to activate Article 34(6) of the Protocol to the African Charter to permit non-state entities and individuals to challenge sovereign acts of state at the African Court, including challenging states on the steps taken in respect of operationalising sustainable development.[312] Similar

308 Bruce Gilley, 'The Case for Colonialism' (2018) 31 Academic Questions 167, 168.

309 Sundhya Pahuja, 'The Postcoloniality of International Law' (2005) 46:2 Harvard Int'l LJ 459, 461; Amardo Rodriguez, 'A Case against Colonialism' (2018) 21:2 Postcolonial Studies 254, 256. Rodriguez's critique of Gilley's article reads in part that, 'Gilley's article should have been entitled "The Case for Western/European Colonialism"'.

310 Bowman et al., *Lyster's International Wildlife Law*, 262.

311 Simon Batterbury and Frankline Ndi, 'Land-Grabbing in Africa' in Tony Binns, Kenneth Lynch, and Etienne Nel (eds.), *Routledge Handbook of African Development* (Routledge 2018) 573, 574.

312 Matiangai Sirleaf, 'The African Justice Cascade and the Malabo Protocol' (2017) 11:1 Int'l J Transitional Just 71, 76–78; Rachel Murray, 'The Human Rights Jurisdiction of the African Court of Justice and Human and Peoples' Rights' in Charles C. Jalloh, Kamari M. Clarke, and Vincent O. Nmehielle (eds.), *The African Court of Justice and Human*

advances have occurred in Africa's sub-regional courts where, in order to constrain the jurisdiction of these courts in environment-related suits, some states treat the human rights jurisdiction of these regional courts as a 'subversion of their sovereignty'.[313] As a result, some African states tend to restrict the human rights jurisdiction of sub-regional courts by actively limiting the capacity of private persons to initiate and sustain suits before these courts.[314]

On this subject, TWAIL scholars have urged a deeper sensitivity to Africa's peoples and not the African state since states (including those in the Global South) sometimes act against the interests of their peoples.[315] As B. S. Chimni admonishes, our understanding of the Third World must be transformed from an uncritical classical rendering as the underprivileged postcolonial Southern state to a vision of a transnational, marginalised, and exploited sub-class.[316] Other TWAIL scholars on environmental law like Usha Natarajan have lent their voice to this call.[317] Accordingly, a durable appreciation of sustainable development requires a fundamental reconceptualisation.

However, beyond that, it is important to embrace alternate histories and conceptions of the concept within international law that radically allow for contemplating context-appropriate implementation.[318] This call invites a serious consideration of alternative thinking and different notions of sustainable development as capable of informing and reforming international law. And, in giving voice and body to African

and Peoples' Rights in Context: Development and Challenges (Cambridge University Press 2019) 965, 967.

313 James T. Gathii, 'Mission Creep or a Search for Relevance: The East African Court of Justice's Human Rights Strategy' (2013) 24:2 Duke J Comp and Int'l L 249, 251.

314 Obonye Jonas, 'Neutering the SADC Tribunal by Blocking Individuals' Access to the Tribunal' (2013) 2:2 Int'l Human Rights L Rev 294, 295; Karen J. Alter, James T. Gathii, and Laurence R. Helfer, 'Backlash against International Courts in West, East and Southern Africa: Causes and Consequences' (2016) 27:2 European JIL 293.

315 John Reynolds, *Emergency, Colonialism, and Third World Approaches to International Law* (Cambridge University Press 2017) 28; Antony Anghie and B. S. Chimni, 'Third World Approaches to International Law and Individual Responsibility in Internal Conflicts' (2003) 2:1 Chinese JIL 77, 78.

316 B. S. Chimni, 'Anti-Imperialism: Then and Now' in Luis Eslava, Michael Fakhri, and Vasuki Nesiah (eds.), *Bandung, Global History and International Law: Critical Pasts and Pending Futures* (Cambridge University Press 2017) 35, 38–39.

317 Natarajan, 'TWAIL and the Environment', 179.

318 Natarajan and Dehm, 'Where Is the Environment?', 6–8.

customary law and Indigenous legal principles and their interface with sustainable development in domestic, regional and international law, we must be guided by the wise counsel that we do not have to 'flatten' or 'depeople' non-Western or Indigenous cosmologies just as state-centric law has historically done.[319]

[319] Natasha Affolder, 'Transnational Environmental Law's Missing People' (2019) 8:3 Transnat'l Envt'l L 463, 480–481.

PART III

Thinking Alternatives

5

Sustainable Development and the Turn to African Legal Ontologies

I am not asking for pointless African exceptionalism.*

5.1 Introduction

This chapter demonstrates that an alternative ontological infrastructure is both possible and urgent for renewing sustainable development. This new (legal) ontology must emerge from non-Western hegemonic influences over international law. It must be adapted to the task of making sustainable development relevant, achievable, and meaningfully translatable. In the context of this legal study, I argue that this legal ontology must derive from African ecocosmologies. While uniquely African, this legal ontology should be representative of the Global South and significant in redefining the law on sustainable development beyond Africa. Thus, in pursuing this environmental legal ontology, I am not making the case for African exceptionalism, neither am I reifying African legal ontologies; I am only interested in what is legally practicable.

The discussion here focuses on how Africa is a source of normativity even if that reality is repudiated by legal Eurocentrism.[1] It analyses how customary law was systematically supplanted by European law,

* Raymond A. Atuguba, 'An African Redefinition of Popular Democracy and Development Nomenclature' (2016) 5:10 Int'l J Innov Research and Dev 58, 61.

[1] Sa'kéj Henderson, 'Trans-Systemic Constitutionalism in Indigenous Law and Knowledge' in Smaro Kamboureli and Christl Verduyn (eds.), *Critical Collections: Indigeneity, Diaspora, and Ecology in Canadian Literary Studies* (Wilfrid Laurier University Press 2014) 49, 64; Jan Wilkens, 'Constructivism' in Anthony F. Lang Jr. and Antje Wiener (eds.), *Handbook on Global Constitutionalism* (Edward Elgar 2017) 117, 123–125. These views are echoed in other places, including in Indigenous scholarship in Canada and elsewhere.

including a Western form of environmentalism.[2] The analysis further highlights the normative similarities between African customary law and other informal sources of law. This discussion is not simply a comparison. Rather, the analysis demonstrates customary law, outside dominant legal domains, is law. In this respect, I draw on three manifestations of law outside the orthodox state-centric sphere – legal pluralism, legal anthropology, and transnational law – to showcase how customary law is in fact law, just as these modes of legal expressions are.[3]

5.2 Excavating the Path Back to Customary Law

There is now a new turning to Indigenous or customary sources of law to illuminate the concept of sustainable development.[4] This non-Western law turn recalls the historical moments that ushered in the introduction of imperially-driven conceptions of environmentalism that aided the almost boundless extractivist policies of the colonial project.[5] Even then, when colonial environmental laws were enacted, they functioned largely in an opaque manner as they were calculatedly intended to only secure natural resources in the colonies for Europe's industrialisation under the guise of caring for the colonies.[6]

In response, environmental destruction was a principal motivation that drove the decolonising process. Although there were glimpses of an inclination to doing environmental law differently in the immediate postcolonial period, that hope soon waned as self-determination, independence, and the resulting sovereign status of new states were built on

[2] Anthony C. Diala and Bethsheba Kangwa, 'Rethinking the Interface between Customary Law and Constitutionalism in Sub-Saharan Africa' (2019) 52:1 De Jure LJ 189, 191. Diala and Kangwa argue that '[w]hile Indigenous laws are remnants of the precolonial norms which people observe in their ancient forms, customary laws are adaptations of Indigenous norms'. In this sense, I use customary law, Indigenous law, and local legal orders flexibly and interchangeably.

[3] The discussion in this section is extended to cover what accounts for a broad topic with several wide-ranging parts: legal pluralism, legal anthropology, and transnational law, all wrapped around customary/Indigenous law in the context of international law.

[4] Peter Ørebech, 'The Place of Customary Law in Democratic Societies' in Peter Ørebech, Fred Bosselman, Jes Bjarup, David Callies, Martin Chanock and Hanne Petersen (eds.), *The Role of Customary Law in Sustainable Development* (Cambridge University Press 2006) 282, 290.

[5] Yasuhide Kawashima and Ruth Tone, 'Environmental Policy in Early America: A Survey of Colonial Statutes' (1983) 27:4 J Forest History 168.

[6] Humphreys and Otomo, 'Theorising International Environmental Law', 811–813.

the hopes of economic liberation.[7] On this subject, Third World Approaches to International Law (TWAIL) scholars invite us to critically engage with history by demonstrating a commitment to radical scholarship. As John Haskell has admonished, it is time for Third World (including critical African law) scholars to:

> return the discipline back to the 'scene of the crime' when European hegemony was first asserted over Indigenous populations and resuscitate these 'pre-colonial' identities – the 'African garden' – in their original forms and take account of their mutating practices of resistance and survival under the history of colonial domination.[8]

Haskell's caution is important considering how contemporary principles of international law have failed to incorporate Indigenous law. To bring Indigenous and customary law into international law's centre begins with revitalising peripheralised sites of knowledge that are law in and of themselves, but nonetheless command scant legal normativity in reorienting how law shapes and influences society.[9] This endeavour to excavate and recover neglected sources of law is critical to the exercise of uncovering new 'possibilities of sustainable development' at the nexus of international law and peripheralised sites of knowledge by validating 'ancient practices embodied in customary law'.[10] Thus, the discussion does not claim to discover a discrete body of environmental law but rather argues that these ethical principles possess legal normativity that can renovate the law on sustainable development.

Legal normativity occurs at 'multiple sites'.[11] There are different sources of laws operating at levels other than the classical, Western, formalist sources. Law in non-Western legal systems, that are typically categorised as customary or Indigenous law, are equally law.[12] In reflecting on law

[7] Natarajan and Dehm, 'Where Is the Environment?', 3.

[8] John D. Haskell, 'TRAIL-ing TWAIL: Arguments and Blind Spots in Third World Approaches to International Law' (2014) 27:4 Can JL and Jur 383, 404.

[9] Antonio Tavares, 'Common Features and Trends of Fisheries Legislation in Africa' in Beatrice Chaytor and Kevin R. Gray (eds.), *International Environmental Law and Policy in Africa* (Springer 2003) 181, 191.

[10] Nijar, 'Traditional Knowledge Systems', 1207.

[11] Maksymilian Del Mar, 'Beyond the State in and of Legal Theory' in Séan Patrick Donlan and Lukas Heckendorn Urscheler (eds.), *Concepts of Law: Comparative, Jurisprudential and Social Science Perspectives* (Ashgate 2014) 19, 33.

[12] Robyn Bartel, 'Place-Thinking: The Hidden Geography of Environmental Law' in Andreas Philippopoulos-Mihalopoulos and Victoria Brooks (eds.), *Research Handbook of Environmental Law: A Handbook* (Edward Elgar 2019) 159, 181.

across different sources, I am inspired by Eve Darian-Smith who argues that, it is important to 'appreciate the complex legal plurality of epistemologies within, between, and across, nations, localities, and regions that inform a diversity of legal conceptions, consciousness, and meaning'.[13] It is in this respect that international law stands to 'benefit from taking a multiple ontological stance'.[14] Consequently, this epistemological redirection follows the consideration that there are different senses and understandings of what sustainable development is and where it derives its law.

These different senses are also embedded in customary law that international law scholars must engage with to ensure sustainable development is made locally effective.[15] Yet, the challenge is that the positivist acculturation of law makes little room for legal phenomena that fall outside the positivist domain. As Saskia Vermeylen has argued:

> legal accounts tend to adopt the stories of those who are privileged and expel the stories and experiences of people of colour, the poor, women and those who cannot describe their experience in the positivistic language of the law. Those whose stories are rejected before the law become outsiders because they are judged to have a different history, a different set of background experiences and a different set of understandings.[16]

Still, it is important to remind ourselves that the turn to customary law is not entirely novel. This is evident in international law's recognition of the role of customary law as capable of moving us closer to sustainable development.[17] Thus, while the analysis comes across as non-law when juxtaposed with Western law, the customary legal norms that are unearthed in this legal excavation are analogous to any other system of law.

Following long episodes of global environmental crises, chiefly in the Global South, critical scholars have argued it is time to reform Eurocentric legal formulations that have delivered very little to bring about

[13] Eve Darian-Smith, *Laws and Societies in Global Contexts: Contemporary Approaches* (Cambridge University Press 2013) 97.

[14] Bartel, 'Place-Thinking', 181.

[15] Ifeoma Laura Owosuyi, 'The Pursuit of Sustainable Development through Cultural Law and Governance Frameworks: A South African Perspective' (2015) 18:5 Potchefstroom Electronic LJ 2012.

[16] Saskia Vermeylen, 'The Nagoya Protocol and Customary Law: The Paradox of Narratives in Law' (2013) 9:2 L Env and Dev J 185, 191.

[17] Donna Craig and Elisabeth Gachenga, 'The Recognition of Indigenous Customary Law in Water Resource Management' (2010) 20:5–6 Water L 278, 278.

much-needed ecological solutions. These scholars are searching for new inspiration, including in the direction of the transformative potential of environmental ethics.[18] This is a refreshing call as the metamorphic influence of African customary law can engender a renewed vision of sustainable development within international law. For Africa, this process must emphasise a *differently* legal impulse for sustainable development – that is, an African environmental legal ontology.[19]

This interest in customary law is connected to the significance of the growing turn to Indigenous conceptions of law. Customary law can facilitate changes in international law; and, in this instance, the operationalisation of sustainable development.[20] The introduction of these ethico-legal principles embedded in Indigenous or customary law can positively transform sustainable development into an effective international legal concept.[21] While this task seems a rather daunting one, it is made possible through a successful forging of a mutually beneficial alliance between TWAIL and customary law where TWAIL transforms its international focus to domestic relevance. In this respect, this partnership must be guided by an awareness that Indigenous law and international law are complementary systems of law that successfully integrate each other.[22]

As a necessary starting point, it is important to highlight how the call to new legal ontologies became prevalent in Third World analysis. At the dawn of decolonisation, the Bandung Conference of 1955 provided the platform for stringing together a new approach to postcolonial law-making.[23]

[18] Natarajan, 'Third World Approaches', 232.

[19] Sian Sullivan, 'What's Ontology Got to Do with It? On the Knowledge of Nature and the Nature of Knowledge in Environmental Anthropology' in Helen Kopnina and Eleanor Shoreman-Ouimet (eds.), *Routledge Handbook of Environmental Anthropology* (Routledge 2017) 155, 156.

[20] Emmanuella Doussis, 'Does International Environmental Law Matter in Sustainable Development?' (2017) 28:1 YB Int'l Envt'l L 3, 13.

[21] Jeffery, 'Environmental Ethics and Sustainable Development, 107; Brendan Tobin, *Indigenous Peoples, Customary Law and Human Rights: Why Living Law Matters* (Routledge 2014) 9. Some Indigenous scholars argues that 'while too narrow to cover all aspects of every variation of legal regime adopted by Indigenous peoples, the term "customary law" is broad enough to encompass a wide range of law, traditions and customs generated by Indigenous peoples in accordance with their own decisions-making practices'.

[22] Shaun McVeigh, 'Critical Approaches to Jurisdiction and International Law' in Stephen Allen, Daniel Costelloe, Malgosia Fitzmaurice, Paul Gragl and Edward Guntrip (eds.), *The Oxford Handbook of Jurisdiction in International Law* (Oxford University Press 2019) 182, 203.

[23] Mickelson and Natarajan, 'Reflections on Rhetoric and Rage', 470–475.

Africa emerged from the Bandung Conference with a seeming commitment to the nationalist ideals and principles that were central to this radical congregation of Southern states. Regrettably, since then, Africa like much of the Global South, slipped far away from the commitment to the ideology and philosophies of the Bandung Spirit, and consequentially lost much-needed momentum when it transitioned into the neoliberal moment.[24] Stuck in conditions similar to what had obtained under colonialism and from which it fought to disentangle itself, Africa adopted neoliberal prescriptions like state environmental agencies and environmental impact assessments that copycatted Euro-American models.[25]

While assimilating these ideas and principles seemed like progress, they were based upon Eurocentric impulses.[26] The significance of Bandung which foreshadowed Third World-nationalist identity, however, was focused on the tasks of decolonisation – that is, government formation, sovereignty, and territorial integrity – that it deliberately disempowered or inadvertently overlooked local peoples and their knowledge.[27] In addressing the prior failure of the South to engage with the environment, the new postcolonial commitment to the environment relies upon the idea of representing Third World intellectualism, knowledge, and ontology on its own terms and not as the creation of Eurocentric epistemologies.[28]

Emerging from this analysis, the objective is to draw on guidance from these ideas – customary law, environmental law, and international law – to outline an agenda for the law on sustainable development that takes customary law prescriptions more seriously, and that can reorientate the

24 Mickelson, 'Stockholm Conference', 113–114.

25 Tseming Yang, 'The Emergence of Global Environmental Law' (2009) 36 Ecol LQ 615, 640; Toby S. Goldbach, 'Why Legal Transplants?' (2019) 15:1 Annual Rev L and Social Science 583; Affolder, 'Contagious Environmental Law-Making', 190.

26 Chika Ezeanya-Esiobu, *Indigenous Knowledge and Education in Africa* (Springer 2019), 60–61.

27 Erica J. Techera, 'Legal Pluralism, Indigenous People, and Small Island Developing States: Achieving Good Environmental Governance in the South Pacific' (2010) 42:61 J Legal Pluralism and Unofficial L 171, 173. This peculiar development is akin to how TWAIL too began its life considering what is famously known as its first generation, with eminent scholars such as Ram P. Anand and Taslim O. Elias focusing on the constitution of the Southern state. The second generation of TWAIL scholars, including Antony Anghie, B. S. Chimni, James Thuo Gathii, and Karin Mickelson, have tended to focus their scholarship on directing us to the complicated inquiry of 'emancipating' the peoples of the Global South and their ways of living and knowing.

28 Arturo Escobar, 'Thinking-Feeling with the Earth: Territorial Struggles and the Ontological Dimension of the Epistemologies of the South' (2016) 11:1 Revista de Antropología Iberoamericana 11.

present outlook by offering newer perspectives. As a result, the necessary starting point should begin with revisiting why and how customary law was excluded from the (Eurocentric) legal space.[29]

5.3 Customary Law, Repugnancy, and Eurocentrism

Law, by itself, is quite meaningless without an interpretive paradigm and an implementation approach.[30] For colonised societies, the displacement of customary law went in tandem with the introduction of Europeanised law including Africa. This process was aided by judicial decision-making processes.[31] Thus, it is through interpretive analyses that law's underlying political impetus is invigorated to achieve its intended political force.[32]

It was within this grand design that colonial administrations introduced the standards by which customary law's acceptability was tested, received (or rejected), validated, and incorporated into colonial law. The British called this standard the doctrine of repugnancy.[33] The doctrine established a three-sided analytical framework through which a customary norm was evaluated: that the norm should not sin against equity, good conscience, or natural justice.[34] Thus, the assessment of customary norms and local legal orders was grounded in a pseudo-judicial process that was not Indigenous, not representative of the colonised peoples, nor sensitive to their cosmologies.

29 Taslim Olawale Elias, *The Nature of African Customary Law* (Manchester University Press 1956) 37–38.

30 Luc B. Tremblay, *The Rule of Law, Justice, and Interpretation* (McGill-Queen's University Press 1997) 46; Remigius Nwabueze, 'The Dynamics and Genius of Nigeria's Indigenous Legal Order' (2002) 1:1 Indigenous LJ 153, 157; Sonja Varbelow, 'Curriculum Theory and Ecology of Learning: Understanding Identity and Place' in Bryant Griffith and Douglas J. Loveless (eds.), *The Interdependence of Teaching and Learning* (Information Age Publishing 2013) 67, 74.

31 A. N. Allott, 'The Judicial Ascertainment of Customary Law in British Africa' (1957) 20:3 Modern L Rev 244; Kwame Opoku, 'Traditional Law under French Colonial Rule' (1974) 7:2 Verfassung und Recht Übersee 139, 182; A. N. Allott, 'What Is to Be Done with African Customary Law? The Experience of Problems and Reforms in Anglophone Africa from 1950' (1984) 28:1–2 J Afr L 56. Allott argues customary law in Francophone Africa, like in Anglophone Africa, did not enjoy a privileged status. This is not surprising since the intention behind colonial law-making and interpretation, as he described it, was to 'eliminate the Indigenous law from the areas of public law'.

32 Ronald Dworkin, 'Law as Interpretation' (1982) 9:1 Critical Inquiry 179.

33 Mikano E. Kiye, 'The Repugnancy and Incompatibility Tests and Anglophone Cameroon' (2015) 15:2 Afr Studies Q 85.

34 Nonso Okafo, *Reconstructing Law and Justice in a Postcolony* (Ashgate 2009) 63.

By establishing these courts to decide the validity of customary law, the British colonial administration institutionalised a long-lasting dualistic conception of law that subordinated customary law to colonially introduced (European) law.[35] Customary law was thus subject to judicial proof or judicial notice. With this introduction, the British colonial courts ingeniously tended to reinforce a particular version of customary law which was quite different from what was practised in the communities.[36] If the customary norm did not pass the judicial muster of the repugnancy test, it failed to be law, and the colonial administration ceased to accord that custom its legal validity.[37] This doctrine of repugnancy was replicated across all British colonies in Africa and elsewhere; with the doctrine persisting into the postcolonial era.[38]

The British and French colonial approaches to customary law were not entirely different as both imperial powers operated under similar conditions.[39] Law was central to the colonial project in Africa and elsewhere in Francophone colonies.[40] The French colonialists resorted to the infamous *indigenát*, a legal code that defined the laws applicable to African peoples within French colonies. *Indigenát* provided a framework for the French civil code to exclude Indigenous law.[41] Despite its applicability to African indigenes, the etymology of *indigenát* was misleading as it led to the belief that it derives from African customary law. Rather, it was a French administrative (legal) apparatus embedded in its civil code and intended for exclusion and social control.[42]

The story was no different in German-administered (colonial) Africa. In this case, while initial colonial administrative arrangements were based

[35] Paul Kuruk, *Traditional Knowledge, Genetic Resources, Customary Law, and Intellectual Property: A Global Primer* (Edward Elgar 2020) 350–352.

[36] *Angu v Attah* [1916] UKPC 53; Derek Asiedu-Akrofi, 'Judicial Recognition and Adoption of Customary Law in Nigeria' (1989) 37:3 Am J Comp L 571, 574; Tobin, *Indigenous Peoples*, 87–88.

[37] Bonny Ibhawoh, *Imperial Justice: Africans in Empire's Court* (Oxford University Press 2013) 60.

[38] Melissa Demian, 'On the Repugnance of Customary Law' (2014) 56:2 Comp Studies in History and Soc'y 508.

[39] B. Olatunji Oloruntimehin, 'Theories and Realities in the Administration of Colonial West Africa from 1890 to the First World War' (1972) 6:3 J Hist Soc'y Nigeria 289, 294.

[40] W. A. E. Skurnik, 'France and Fragmentation in West Africa' (1967) 8:2 J African History 317, 318.

[41] Xavier Blanc-Jouvan, 'The Encounter between Traditional Law and Modern Law in French-Speaking Africa: A Personal Reflection' (2010) 25 Tul & Civ LF 197, 200.

[42] Gregory Mann, 'What Was the "*Indigenát*"? The "Empire of Law" in French West Africa' (2009) 50:3 J Afr History 331, 335.

on a set of agreements between Germany and the colonised local communities, subsequent events unravelled the true intentions of the colonial administration. In this respect, disputes arising in the colonies were to be resolved under customary law, ostensibly guided by the belief that the local communities were playing host to the German colonial administration. Yet, very quickly, the German colonial administration supplanted customary law with the German civil code. As Jakob Zollmann observed:

> [p]ursuant to the 'Protectorate Agreements' between the German Reich and the individual 'tribes' and, as it may be, their 'chiefs' (as in the source language), conflicts between Africans were to be regulated according to their traditional law. In this capacity, the German colonial state acted similarly to its European counterparts when it unilaterally displaced the authority of the protectorate agreements, applying the German legal code to override Indigenous law as the administration deemed necessary for law and order.[43]

The explanation thus far demonstrates the Eurocentric defenestration of African customary law. The effectiveness of the repugnancy test in British colonial Africa, or similar exclusionary tests in La Francophonie, Lusophone Africa, or German-controlled Africa was informed by ingenious interpretive schemes employed by colonial legal officers and judges. As a matter of political expediency and institutional self-preservation, customary law was always going to be subordinated to colonial law.

Still, some customary law survived and was reshaped or co-opted in the colonial encounter. And, as regards the British colonial experience, judicial interpretation of customary law in the colonies had to accord with British legal concepts and expectations.[44] Judicial intervention in this instance thus led to massive reform in African social life as African customary laws were brought into the orbit of colonial law by incorporating them into criminal and civil offences and in the process making customary law comprehensible to British jurists.[45]

Large aspects of customary law adjudicated upon in the colonial courts failed the repugnancy doctrine. The reason was that the test was informed by European legalism without much consideration for local circumstances

[43] Jakob Zollmann, 'German Colonial Law and Comparative Law, 1884–1919' in Thomas Duve (eds.), *Entanglements in Legal History: Conceptual Approaches* (Max Planck Institute for European Legal History 2014) 253, 272.

[44] Moore, 'Treating Law as Knowledge', 12.

[45] Justice Modibo Ocran, 'The Clash of Legal Cultures: The Treatment of Indigenous Law in Colonial and Post-Colonial Africa' (2006) 39:2 Akron L Rev 465, 474–475.

and prevailing customary notions of law.[46] While the repugnancy doctrine is a legal assessment of non-Western rules, its broader implication is observed in the extension of European knowledge beyond Europe.[47] While the doctrine was a notable expression of colonial legal overrule, the different methodologies of colonisation and legal imperialism represented a common Eurocentric stance.[48] It was a politico-legal technology creatively designed to advance imperialist interests.[49] In this sense, the doctrine remains relevant to Africa-related legal studies that contend with the juridical applicability of African customary law.[50]

The repugnancy test is now part of the contemporary legal cosmos of postcolonial states. Today, the dangers of these colonially imposed juridical tests are being highlighted and evaluated across the world. In its rejection of the repugnancy test as a standard for assessing the legal normativity of Māori customary law (tikanga), Justice Susan Glazebrook of the Supreme Court of New Zealand held that:

> the requirements for a custom to be reasonable and not repugnant to justice and morality were based on colonial attitudes that are artefacts of a different time. They import notions of 'judging' tikanga and operate on the assumption of the superiority of Western values and a view that the common law inherited from the United Kingdom should be presumptively dominant. I therefore do not consider these requirements for the recognition of custom have any place in the contemporary common law of Aotearoa/New Zealand.[51]

The rejection of this antiquated practice in settler-colonial jurisdictions like New Zealand ought to provide much-needed inspiration for courts in other jurisdictions like Africa to begin a thorough process of reforming judicial attitudes towards customary law.

Even so, the doctrine's entrenchment in African law is so pervasive that discussing it in light of its colonial origins is almost uninspiring. The

[46] Bonny Ibhawoh, *Imperialism and Human Rights: Colonial Discourse of Rights and Liberties in African History* (State University of New York Press 2007) 58.

[47] Veronica Corcodel, *Modern Law and Otherness: The Dynamics of Inclusion and Exclusion in Comparative Legal Thought* (Edward Elgar 2019) 15.

[48] John R. Schmidhauser, 'Legal Imperialism: Its Enduring Impact on Colonial and Post-Colonial Judicial Systems' (1992) 13:3 Int'l Pol Science Rev 321.

[49] Ibhawoh, *Imperialism and Human Rights*, 58.

[50] Amos Enabulele and Bright Bazuaye, 'Validity and Enforceability of Customary Law in Nigeria: Towards a Correct Delimitation of the Province of the Courts' (2019) 63:1 J Afr L 79, 88.

[51] *Peter Hugh McGregor Ellis v The King* [2022] NZSC [114], para 115.

reason is that, its ahistoricism conceals its continuing significance to the future of African customary law.[52] This is equally true for customary law in respect of environmental protection.[53] Drawing on the doctrine's juridical framework, the concept of sustainable development has applied similar general rules of exclusion to customary norms relating to the environment.[54] Customary notions of environmental protection were constantly contesting for space and applicability with Eurocentric rules while seeking to regulate new forms of ecological violence hitherto unknown.[55] On this subject, legal scholars who are motivated by the content and consequence of customary law frequently return to the repugnancy doctrine and to its place in law-making in Africa due to the marked changes it effected on relational ontologies.[56]

As a result, it is not surprising that African legal scholars are divided over the doctrine's significance. Some scholars argue it removes customary law's negative and disobliging features.[57] Others insist customary law has been subordinated and obliterated by the doctrine to the point that the 'tripartite standard used in the determination of repugnancy namely, that the said custom is not repugnant to equity, good conscience and natural justice, is implicitly built on conceptions of justice derived from the common law and its legal narratives'.[58] Yet, in spite of the contentions of both schools of thought, one thing that is clear is that, broad and vague concepts at play like the repugnancy doctrine are capable of being filled with notions that suit colonial interests. Drawing on these criticisms, it is understandable how and why colonial powers deployed these

[52] Kiye, 'Repugnancy and Incompatibility Tests, 87.

[53] Uzuazo Etemire and Nelson Uwoh Sobere, 'Improving Public Compliance with Modern Environmental Laws in Nigeria: Looking to Traditional Norms and Practices' (2020) 38:2 J Energy and Nat Res L 1, 8.

[54] Oliver Njuh Fuo and Sama Memuna, 'Cameroon's Environmental Framework Law and the Balancing of Interests in Socio-Economic Development' in Michael Faure and Willemien du Plessis (eds.), *The Balancing of Environmental Interests in Africa* (Pretoria University Law Press 2012) 75, 79.

[55] Donna Craig and Michael I. Jeffery, 'The Recognition and Enforcement of Indigenous Customary Law in Natural Resource Management' in Lee Paddock, Du Qun, Louis J. Kotzé, David L. Markell, Kenneth J. Markowitz and Durwood Zaelke (eds.), *Compliance and Enforcement in Environmental Law* (Edward Elgar 2011) 535.

[56] David J. Bederman, 'Public Law and Custom' (2012) 61 Emory LJ 949, 957.

[57] Elijah A. Taiwo, 'Repugnancy Clause and Its Impact on Customary Law: Comparing the South African and Nigerian Positions: Some Lessons for Nigeria' (2009) 34:1 J Jur Science 89.

[58] Ernest Kofi Abotsi, 'Customary Law and the Rule of Law: Evolving Tensions and Re-Engineering' (2020) 37:2 Ariz J Int'l and Comp L 137, 152.

ambiguous standards to dispossess Indigenous peoples of their lands and values by substantially altering landholding rights and obligations and attendant environmental regulatory framework at customary law.[59]

As a result, while there is no discernible assembly of customary law that neatly fits categorisation as environmental law, colonial approaches to interpretation of customary law demonstrate a conceptual imposition on an existing customary law framework that does not self-articulate in terms of its interpretation. Thus, flowing from this understanding of the contention surrounding the repugnancy doctrine, I am interested in how this legal technology designed to guide colonial legality continues to define 'the relationship between subaltern and metropolitan laws and institutions' even today.[60]

The repugnancy doctrine, as a vestige of Roman law, has since travelled the world and flourished as a concept Europeans resorted to in their transactions with non-Europeans.[61] By the nineteenth century when Europe's imperial forces had firmly established their presence in so-called newly discovered territories they had conquered, the doctrine metamorphosed and assumed the character of English law; and, with that, its contemporary manifestation was patently English law.[62] Nonetheless, its variants can be seen in the civil codes of the French and German colonial administrations too. In contemplating the imperialist objective of othering non-European legal reality, the colonisers recalibrated African customary law by redesignating customary law as a problematic question left to judicial clarification. This was nothing more than empowering colonial courts to creatively exclude or discard these Indigenous laws under the pretext of failing to measure up to Eurocentric standards of justice.[63] Therefore,

[59] Chilenye Nwapi, 'Land Grab, Property Rights and Gender Equality in Pluralistic Legal Orders: A Nigerian Perspective' (2016) 9:2 Afr J Leg Studies 124, 133.

[60] Mark Toufayan, 'When British Justice (in African Colonies) Points Two Ways: On Dualism, Hybridity, and the Genealogy of Juridical Negritude in Taslim Olawale Elias' (2008) 21:2 Leiden JIL 377, 386.

[61] Bethel Chuks Uweru, 'Repugnancy Doctrine and Customary Law in Nigeria: A Positive Aspect of British Colonialism' (2008) 2:2 Afr Res Rev 286, 289–290.

[62] J. N. Matson, 'The Common Law Abroad: English and Indigenous Laws in the British Commonwealth' (1993) 42:4 ICLQ 753, 761.

[63] Ibhawoh, *Imperial Justice*, 54; William G. A. Ormsby-Gore, 'Some Contrasts in Nigeria' (1927) 69:6 Geographical J 497, 509. Notwithstanding the pervasive character of the doctrine, Europe's imperial powers were quite aware that reinventing law in the colonies, comprising a fundamental transformation in the character of customary law was an ill-advised approach to governance. As Ormsby-Gore pointed out, '[n]othing tends more to undermine native traditions, society, and organisation than the substitution of European for native legal forms'.

African customary law, if accepted at all, was only seen as subordinate to colonial law or it was adjudged as not law at all. In the end, colonial courts were programmed to finally displace existing traditional adjudicative systems and overrule the prevailing local legal orders.[64]

5.4 Suppressing African Customary Law into Legal Insignificance

Thus far, I have demonstrated that African customary law was dislodged from the African society with the ensuing colonial overrun.[65] Customary law's degeneration emanates from the overstated significance of judicial refinement imposed by colonial law.[66] This systematic discriminatory process of recognising one custom as law and another as not law repurposed (and consequently integrated) customary law as a by-product of European colonialism.[67] This was the same for environmental customs too.[68] Consequently, customary law was replaced with a distorted colonialist version of pre-existing law which was integrated into the official law of the colonies.[69]

Also, in the postcolonial period, customary law's inclusion in national constitutions did little to elevate its status. Its validity had long been diminished, and remained categorised as secondary within the postcolonial legal architecture.[70] As a result, some legal scholars pejoratively called it a 'constitutionally ordained "other" system of law'.[71] Nonetheless, in many jurisdictions, customary law is part of the legal corpus.[72] In such situations, customary law becomes a subset of officially recognised law. However, the reliance on case-law methodology and judicial precedents,

64 Moore, 'Treating Law as Knowledge', 11–17.

65 Sanele Sibanda, 'When Is the Past Not the Past? Reflections on Customary Law under South Africa's Constitutional Dispensation' (2010) 17:3 Human Rights Brief 31.

66 Eric C. Djamson, *The Dynamics of Euro-African Cooperation: Being an Analysis and Exposition of Institutional, Legal and Socio-Economic Aspects of Association/Cooperation with the European Economic Community* (Brill 1976) 210.

67 Kwame Akuffo, 'Equity in Colonial West Africa: A Paradigm of Juridical Dislocation' (2006) 50:2 J Afr L 132, 138.

68 Martin S. Shanguhyia, 'Colonialism and the African Environment' in Martin S. Shanguhyia and Toyin Falola (eds.), *The Palgrave Handbook of African Colonial and Postcolonial History* (Palgrave MacMillan 2018) 43.

69 Mark Fathi Massoud, *Law's Fragile State: Colonial, Authoritarian, and Humanitarian Legacies in Sudan* (Cambridge University Press 2013) 44–45.

70 Diala and Kangwa, 'Rethinking the Interface', 191.

71 Sibanda, 'When Is the Past Not the Past?', 32.

72 Nelson Tebbe, 'Inheritance and Disinheritance: African Customary Law and Constitutional Rights' (2008) 88:4 J Religion 466, 466.

together with the non-documentation of customary law, pushed customary law further down this artificially-constructed hierarchy of norms.[73] Still, it is important to understand that most of these national constitutions are Eurocentric (colonial) bequests that, in principle, were crafted to continue the colonial legacy in the postcolony by subjugating customary law through an artificially-constructed hierarchy of norms that placed customary law on the lower rungs of the normative ladder.[74] Most significantly, what is glossed over by many, including environmental law scholars, is that national constitutions are the bedrock for anthropocentric uses of nature and that the inclusion of customary law in these national constitutions does not necessarily assure its effectiveness. Fortunately, this awareness is gradually informing how postcolonial states are approaching the reformulation of their national laws away from 'constitutional law's Eurocentric logos'.[75]

Additionally, the former colonial powers found still more imaginative ways to carry on shaping laws in the postcolonial reality of many African states.[76] Through external legislative intrusions, these Western powers continue to supplant legislation and even customary law in the postcolonial states. They did this by reinventing Eurocentric legal transplants as part of the gamut of development aid they offered post-independence states, which was nothing more than a device to redefine the content of law in former colonies.[77] So, while it seems the postcolonial state is making informed choices in respect of its development needs, the continuing force of the juridical aspects of the colonial project persists and pervades these financial and technical interventions in less visible ways.[78] Accordingly, a nuanced reading and critical review of environmental law concepts such as sustainable development, which are so often

[73] Graham Hassall and Cheryl Sanders, *Asia-Pacific Constitutional Systems* (Cambridge University Press 2006) 29.

[74] Mikano Emmanuel Kiye, 'Conflict between Customary Law and Human Rights in Cameroon: The Role of the Courts in Fostering an Equitable Society' (2015) 36:2 Afr Study Monographs 75, 78–79.

[75] Michele Carducci, '"Cross-Constitutionalism" and Sustainable Comparison' in Alberto Febbrajo and Giancarlo Corsi (eds.), *Sociology of Constitutions: A Paradoxical Perspective* (Routledge 2016) 137, 144.

[76] Casper Njuguna, *African Customary Law: Assessing Its Status and Effects Today* (Lexington Books 2009) 19.

[77] Gordon R. Woodman, 'British Legislation as a Source of Ghanaian Law: From Colonialism to Technical Aid' (1974) 7:1 Verfassung und Recht Übersee 19, 29.

[78] Gordon Christie, *Canadian Law and Indigenous Self-Determination: A Naturalist Analysis* (University of Toronto Press 2019) 384–387.

de-historicised and then globally disseminated as constitutional guarantees or statutory obligations through 'colonial imposition, international financial institution-mediated mandate, and misguided legal "transplantation"' is plainly necessary.[79] The resolution of these questions on the utility of customary law have a direct impact on how sustainable development is revitalised in Africa on grounds of relational cosmologies.

5.5 Retrenching Eurocentrism and the Turn (Back) to Customary Law

Despite these normative challenges, the resilience of customary law assures its contemporary relevance even today.[80] Although colonial legal superimposition rendered customary law indiscernible, its relevance nonetheless persists.[81] A discussion of the future of customary law thus evokes questions about 'the concepts of official customary law and living customary law'.[82] David Bederman recalls this tension as he points out that 'it was understood that the act of codification transmuted a body of living custom into an "official" code'.[83] The hidden danger with this binarisation of official customary law and living customary law arises when the former is wrongly acknowledged within state-centred law as the standard and binding, and at the same time living customary law enjoys legal observance in applicable societies.[84] This distinction is significant – with conceptual and practical implications – considering reference to official customary law presupposes customary law that is validated in court judgments and other written texts and which emanate from colonial influence, as opposed to living customary law which is alert to social (re-)production and is adaptable to changing social circumstances.[85]

[79] Affolder, 'Contagious Environmental Law-Making', 203–204.

[80] Oche Onazi, 'Introduction' in Oche Onazi (ed.), *African Legal Theory and Contemporary Problems: Critical Essays* (Springer 2014) 1, 1.

[81] Abotsi, 'Customary Law and the Rule of Law', 138.

[82] Chuma Himonga, 'The Future of Living Customary Law in African Legal Systems in the Twenty First Century and Beyond, with Special Reference to South Africa' in Jeanmarie Fenrich, Paolo Galizzi, and Tracy E. Higgins (eds.), *The Future of African Customary Law* (Cambridge University Press 2011) 31, 32.

[83] Bederman, 'Public Law and Custom', 957–958.

[84] Rebecca Emiene Badejogbin, 'Judicial Discretion: Problematising the Ascertainment and Application of Customary Law by Formal Courts and Relevant Theories (Nigeria and South Africa)' (2022) 54:2–3 J Legal Pluralism and Crit Soc Anal 1, 5.

[85] Anthony C. Diala, 'The Concept of Living Customary Law: A Critique' (2017) 49:2 J Legal Pluralism and Unofficial L 143, 146–159; Gordon R. Woodman, 'Customary Land Laws

This notion of two competing versions of customary law is, however, problematic. But it is not unique to the Global North or the Global South. This anomalous situation can be seen in jurisdictions like Canada where the courts sometimes conflate Indigenous law with (the related but distinct) Aboriginal law.[86] In this process, the inappropriate classification of customary law has enduring and conflicting judicial (and juridical) consequences for the independent legal character of Indigenous cosmologies. While it is difficult to demarcate a fine line between official customary law and living customary law, I share in the view that, if customary law constitutes an integral part of the social and legal aspects of a people's reality, it is important to explore the opportunity this situation presents for integrating customary law into the received (colonial) law, 'with the tools for further evolution'.[87] Even so, official customary law is not free from equivocation; thus raising the importance of looking towards living customary law which is a constantly-evolving process.[88] In this respect, living customary law interacts with the concept of sustainable development in a manner that assures a co-evolution of both realms is neither truncated nor needlessly officialised by a yearning to embody sustainable development into a universal ideal.[89]

A reassessment of the significance of some of the historical tools that were deployed to constrain customary law is thus necessary to liberate customary law from its Eurocentric trappings.[90] To do this effectively, it

within Legal Pluralism over the Generations' (2014–2015) 1 SADC LJ 189. Woodman clarifies recognition of customary law by the state; while the latter, what he calls 'deep legal pluralism' is based on harmony between state-mandated laws and customary law as existing in and observed by respective (Indigenous) communities. Woodman's point is that, whichever way, there is bound to be some level of interaction between state-sanctioned law and customary law. And, when that happens, a modification of either realm arises. I agree with Woodman's view to the extent that the changes that occur within this interaction are not one-dimensional but alternating – where living customary law is modified to become official customary law, but that state-sanctioned law should also be open to modification subject to the influences of the living customary law.

86 Christie, *Canadian Law and Indigenous Self-Determination*, 4.

87 Lloyd Fallers, 'Customary Law in the New African States' (1962) 27:4 L and Contemp Probs 605, 606.

88 Fatima Osman, 'The Ascertainment of Living Customary Law: An Analysis of the South African Constitutional Court's Jurisprudence' (2019) 51:1 J Legal Pluralism and Unofficial L 98, 101; Ntebo L. Morudu and Charles Mailema, 'The Indigenisation of Customary Law: Creating an Indigenous Pluralism within the South African Dispensation: Possible or Not?' (2021) 54:1 De Jure LJ 54, 55.

89 Craig and Gachenga, 'Recognition of Indigenous Customary Law, 281.

90 James Thuo Gathii, 'International Law and Eurocentricity' (1998) 9:1 European JIL 184, 198.

is important to understand the burden imposed on customary law by European legal transformations as well as the potential of African customary law to influence international law.[91] On this subject, the repugnancy doctrine is illustrative of Eurocentric technologies deployed during colonialism for remaking African communities.[92] Therefore, the long-term import of the repugnancy doctrine was jettisoning major aspects of the corpus of customary conceptions of environmental law rules.[93]

This social transformation was manifest in how colonial policies were tilted towards dispossessing Indigenous knowledge, power, and control over the environment. This resulted in the financialisation of nature as colonial laws on environmental protection were designed to preserve and secure natural resources of imperial interest[94] Still, there is a considerable amount of customary law that exists and inheres in African societies that we must study in their historical context with a view as to how their reformatory potential can assist in readjusting the understanding of the current paradigm of sustainable development that have proved ineffective despite the promulgation of a plethora of environment-related laws.[95]

Perhaps, some will even argue customary law is already part of the body of laws and therefore needs no special attention. This may be true. However, my reaction is that, even where customary law is supposedly integrated into state-centred law, African states have wilfully ignored or severely distorted its 'traditional cosmological aspects'.[96] To be certain, customary law, viewed through a Eurocentric prism is 'in principle still applicable to environmental matters, but with major limitations – only if they are not considered to be repugnant to natural justice, equity, and

[91] Liz Lewis, 'Exploring the "Ecology" of Laws at the Interface between International Human Rights Law and Subnational Customary Law' (2011) 24:1 Afr J Int'l and Comp L 105; Obregón, 'Martti Koskenniemi's Critique of Eurocentrism', 368.

[92] Ibhawoh, *Imperial Justice*, 60.

[93] Brett M. Bennett, 'Decolonisation, Environmentalism, and Nationalism in Australia and South Africa' (2017) 41:1 Itinerario 27; Lara Domínguez and Colin Luoma, 'Decolonising Conservation Policy: How Colonial Land and Conservation Ideologies Persist and Perpetuate Indigenous Injustices at the Expense of the Environment' (2020) 9:3 Land 65, 71.

[94] Kameri-Mbote and Cullet, 'Law, Colonialism', 26; Velayutham Saravanan, *Colonialism, Environment and Tribals in South India, 1792–1947* (Routledge 2017) 100–101.

[95] Richardson et al., 'Environmental Law in Postcolonial Societies', 421.

[96] Melesse Damtie, 'Anthropocentric and Ecocentric Versions of the Ethiopian Legal Regime' in Peter Burdon (ed.), *Exploring Wild Law: The Philosophy of Earth Jurisprudence* (Wakefield Press 2011) 159, 165.

good conscience; contrary to public policy; or incompatible, directly or indirectly, with any existing (statute or case) law'.[97] When contrasted with customary environmental law, sustainable development backed by statutory law continues to prove ineffectual despite the promulgation of a raft of environmental laws across Africa.[98] Here, the turn to customary law for illumination is a well-timed intervention considering the ethico-legal foundations of African customary law which regard humans as 'mere co-occupants of nature with other species' is noticeably missing from the prevailing orientations of sustainable development which privilege human uses of the environment.[99] However, in the effort to consult customary law in order to reorient sustainable development, the outstanding question is whether customary law is actually law, and if it can aid sustainable development.

5.6 A (Critical) Restatement of Normativity: Taking Customary Law (More) Seriously

Whether customary law is law emerges from the question of what the nature of law is in the context of African customary law. In responding to this question, it is impossible to clearly define what law is without going beyond the hackneyed Eurocentric formulation of social control and order.[100] An evaluation of this proposition evokes the awareness that law does not emanate from a single worldview nor does it manifest in a singular normative outlook.[101] Its constitutive force derives from its social circumstances which are equally sources of law.[102] Thus, African customary law establishes social cohesion and order so there is no justification for denying 'the existence of law in [African] societies

97 Etemire and Sobere, 'Improving Public Compliance', 8.

98 Uchenna Jerome Orji, 'Enhancing Sustainable Development in Nigeria: A Discourse on the Legal Basis and Proposals to Strengthen Legal and Policy Strategies for Its Implementation' (2013) 39:1 Commonwealth L Bull 163, 179.

99 Mbih Jerome Tosam, 'African Environmental Ethics and Sustainable Development' (2019) 9:1 Open J Phil 172, 174.

100 John Griffiths, 'What Is Sociology of Law? (On Law, Rules, Social Control and Sociology)' (2017) 49:2 J Leg Pluralism and Unofficial L 93, 95.

101 Michael Davis, 'Law, Anthropology, and the Recognition of Indigenous Legal Systems' (2001) 11 Int'l YB Leg Anthro 298, 303.

102 Richard Abel, 'What Else Is Sociology of Law? Reflections on John Griffith's What Is Sociology of Law?' (2017) 49:3 J Leg Pluralism and Unofficial L 373, 374.

merely because the Western Austinian or neo-Austinian criteria of law fail to apply'.[103]

Despite these foundational views on the legal normativity of customary law, the challenge remains whether it is law, and what its role is in reimagining sustainable development in international law. To trace customary law and its potential to (re-)make international law, I explore three manifestations of non-state sanctioned law as law. For example, the triangular relationship across legal pluralism, anthropology, and customary law has received special mention for its capacity to remedy positivist deficiencies by 'developing a richer understanding of law as a normative system'.[104] In galvanising the argument that these customary conceptions are law, I elicit the assistance of legal pluralism, legal anthropology, and transnational law, all of which emphasise the theme that law is found outside state-centric prescriptions. To legal pluralists and legal anthropologists, law is not a concept endorsed only by the state nor is law the sole outcome of statist approaches to law-making. Rather, law is found in many different places outside the strictures of state power. These scholars argue that law found outside of the positivist realm of the state is law inasmuch as it evokes legal bindingness as regards the performance of obligations.[105] Therefore, if a person of a legal-positivist persuasion is unable to, neglects to, or otherwise fails to see local conceptions of the legal (that is, customary law) as law, that does not change the fact that these conceptions are law.[106]

Customary law is equally important as it affirms Africa's law-making capacity to create norms comparable to those established by positive law and also take account of 'arenas of international law on the African continent that lay outside the orbit of European domination'.[107] In this case, there is little doubt that colonialism's visible imprint is observed

[103] C. M. N. White, 'African Customary Law: The Problem of Concept and Definition' (1965) 9:2 J Afr L 86, 86.

[104] Paul Martin and Donna Craig, 'Accelerating the Evolution of Environmental Law through Continuous Learning from Applied Experience' in Paul Martin and Amanda Kennedy (eds.), *Implementing Environmental Law* (Edward Elgar 2015) 27, 35.

[105] John Borrows, 'Indigenous Legal Traditions in Canada' (2005) 19 Wash U JL and Pol'y 167, 180.

[106] Frederick Schauer, 'Pitfalls in the Interpretation of Customary Law' in Amanda Perreau-Sausine and James B. Murphy (eds.), *The Nature of Customary Law: Legal, Historical and Philosophical Perspectives* (Cambridge University Press 2007) 13, 17–20.

[107] Jakob Zollmann, 'African International Legal Histories–International Law in Africa: Perspectives and Possibilities' (2018) 31:4 Leiden JIL 897, 899–901.

through the Eurocentric displacement of Indigenous legal orders.[108] As observed in postcolonial states, the scars of the violent overthrow of Indigenous legal norms by European legal conceptions are pervasive.[109] State law – the imposed European law – was a central feature of colonial legal reality.[110] Accordingly, critical analysis on state-centric law strongly notes that it is a Eurocentric ideal.[111] Since Indigenous societies were not organised around the logic of European law, European colonising powers referred to non-European polities as non-state entities in the European sense – that is, they were not politico-legal orders with discrete bureaucracies – and their laws were diminished and circumscribed as mere history, and not law.[112] Through this process, customary law experienced a great deal of colonial alteration to make it graspable by the colonialists.[113] Thus, it is important to refocus on the broader marginalisation of African influences in international law, including in the realm of customary law.[114]

5.7 Sustainable Development as Legal Pluriversality

Legal pluralism is constituted around the notion that law can be found outside the state.[115] But until recently, legal pluralism was seldom considered an

[108] Russell Smandych, 'Colonialism, Settler Colonialism, and Law: Settler Revolutions and the Dispossession of Indigenous Peoples through Law in the Long Nineteenth Century' (2013) 3:1 Settler Colonial Studies 82.

[109] Brian Slattery, 'Aboriginal Sovereignty and Imperial Claims' (1991) 29:4 Osgoode Hall LJ 681, 691; Val Napoleon and Hadley Friedland, 'An Inside Job: Engaging with Indigenous Legal Traditions through Stories' (2016) 61:4 McGill LJ 725, 728.

[110] Diala, 'Concept of Living Customary Law', 145.

[111] Erika J. Techera, 'Legal Foundations for the Recognition of Customary Law in the Post-Colonial South Pacific' in Michael Freeman and David Napier (eds.), *Law and Anthropology* (Oxford University Press 2009) 218, 218.

[112] John Borrows, *Canada's Indigenous Constitution* (University of Toronto Press 2010) 65.

[113] T. W. Bennett, 'Comparative Law and African Customary Law' in Mathias Reimann and Reinhard Zimmermann (eds.), *Oxford Handbook of Comparative Law*, 2nd ed. (Oxford University Press 2019) 652, 656; Dermot Smith and Miya Isherwood, 'Protecting Sea Country: Indigenous Peoples and Marine Protected Areas in Australia' in James Fitzmons and Geoff Westcott (eds.), *Big, Bold & Blue: Lessons from Australia's Marine Protected Areas* (CSIRO 2016) 307, 309. This is true for Australia as well where the British imposed a revamped Roman idea of marine governance by opening the seas to individualistic uses as opposed to the customary law notions of communitarian guardianship and shared responsibility.

[114] Foluke Ifejola Ipinyomi, 'The Impact of African Philosophy on the Realisation of the International Community and the Observance of International Law' (2016) 18:1 Int'l Community L Rev 3, 15.

[115] Richard Nobles and David Schiff, 'Using Systems Theory to Study Legal Pluralism: What Could Be Gained?' (2012) 46:2 Law and Soc'y Rev 265, 265.

integral part of the legal architecture.[116] The exclusion of legal pluralism emerges from the influence of legal centralism: that is, the influence of state-centred law which was, itself, premised on legal positivism.[117] Yet, it is incongruous to suggest the normativity of law is a derivative of law itself. Rather, its normativity comes from society because law's essence derives from an amalgam of politics, economics, and culture.[118] Thus, 'the normative force of law is itself the creation of the moral aspirations and sense of responsibility of its subjects as members of a community'.[119]

For classical legal scholars, legal positivism is constitutive of 'the monopoly of the state in making and administering law'.[120] Of course, this is a long-held assumption that has survived throughout the history of legal positivism, notwithstanding some variations.[121] John Austin's classical positivism dominates this aspect of legal philosophy with its insistence that law is the command of a sovereign authority; an idea that became a premise of the Westphalian conception of the modern state.[122] However, despite their internal differences, legal positivists 'tie law's normativity and coerciveness to the state'.[123] Two distinguished legal scholars, H. L. A. Hart and Hans Kelsen, are prominent here. First, Hart's scholarship is one of the authoritative statements on legal positivism.[124] His theory is predicated on his conceptualisation of law (and, for that matter, of a legal system) as an aggregate of primary rules and secondary rules.[125] Primary

116 Keebet von Benda-Beckmann and Bertram Turner, 'Legal Pluralism, Social Theory, and the State' (2018) 50:3 J Leg Pluralism and Unofficial L 255, 258.

117 Gad Barzilai, 'Beyond Relativism: Where Is Political Power in Legal Pluralism?" (2008) 9:2 Theor Inq L 395, 396.

118 Hanisah Binte Abdullah Sani, 'State Law and Legal Pluralism: An Appraisal' (2020) 52:1 J Leg Pluralism and Unofficial L 82, 82.

119 William Twining, 'Normative and Legal Pluralism: A Global Perspective' (2010) 20:3 Duke J Comp and Int'l L 473, 484.

120 Ralf Michaels, 'Global Legal Pluralism' (2009) 5 Annual Rev L and Social Science 243, 245.

121 Stephen R. Perry, 'The Varieties of Legal Pluralism' (1996) 9 Can JL and Jur 361; David Dyzenhaus, 'The Genealogy of Legal Positivism' (2004) 24:1 Oxford J Leg Studies 39.

122 John Austin, *Lectures on Jurisprudence or the Philosophy of Positive Law*, 4th ed. (John Murray 1873) 231.

123 Berihun Adugna Gebeye, 'Legal Theory in Africa: Between Legal Centralism and Legal Pluralism' (2017) Queen Mary LJ 37, 40.

124 Robert S. Gerstein, 'Hart's Positivism' (1985) 10:3 Am Bar Foundation Research J 629, 630; Brian Z. Tamanaha, 'Socio-Legal Positivism and a General Jurisprudence' (2001) 21:1 Oxford J Leg Studies 1.

125 H. L. A. Hart, *The Concept of Law*, 2nd ed. (Oxford University Press 1994), 78–100; H. L. A. Hart, 'Positivism and the Separation of Law and Morals' (1958) 71:4 Harvard L Rev 593.

rules comprise what Hart describes as obligations, claims, or rights and duties, while secondary rules compositely represent rules of recognition which endorse these primary rules by validating the legal system.[126] Robert Gerstein explains Hart's two-tiered view of legal jurisprudence by arguing that 'in a legal system, the primary rules are created, administered, and enforced through the manipulation of a set of secondary rules'.[127]

Second, Kelsen's version of legal positivism complements Hart's concept of law. In his view, the concept of law is separate from morality.[128] He sees law and the legal system functioning jointly as a hierarchical order in which lower norms give rise to higher norms until we reach an apex; that is, the constitution, which itself is derived from a fictional or hypothetical basic norm (*grundnorm*).[129] Together with other legal scholars, Hart and Kelsen firmly established the field of legal positivism.[130] Consequently, legal positivism was built around the notion of what its proponents often call the separation of law from morals, and a corresponding advocacy to keep the two domains distinct.[131] Flowing from this point, the distinguishing assertion of legal positivism is that law, and to a large extent the legal system, as distinguished from morals originates in and from the Eurocentric idea of the state.[132]

In practice, this positivist view of law is not limited to municipal law although its genealogy is embedded in domestic law. Understandably, the positivist position was deftly translated onto the international plane in the nineteenth and twentieth centuries where the argument that positivism advanced was in support of the state as the only source of international law.[133] In response, scholars of legal pluralism like Brian Tamanaha reject this notion of the state-centredness of law, arguing that '[c]ustomary law and international law, for example, are no longer seen

[126] David Howarth and Shona Wilson Stark, 'H.L.A. Hart's Secondary Rules: What Do "Officials" Think?' (2018) 14:1 Int'l JL in Context 61, 62.

[127] Gerstein, 'Hart's Positivism', 630.

[128] Hans Kelsen, *Pure Legal Theory*, translated by Max Knight (The Lawbook Exchange 2005) 253.

[129] Reut Yael Paz, 'Kelsen's *Pure Theory of Law* as a "Hole in Time"' (2015) 7 Monde(s) 75, 82.

[130] Diala, 'Concept of Living Customary Law', 149; Joseph Raz, *The Authority of Law: Essays on Law and Morality* (Clarendon Press 1979) 37–52.

[131] Kelsen, *Pure Legal Theory*, 66–69.

[132] Dan Priel, 'Toward Classical Legal Positivism' (2015) 101:4 Va L Rev 987, 1007.

[133] Richard Collins, 'Classical Legal Positivism in International Law Revisited' in Jörg Kammerhofer and Jean d'Aspremont (eds.), *International Legal Positivism in a Post-Modern World* (Cambridge University Press 2014) 23, 28–29.

as pre-legal or as imperfect examples of state law'.[134] Other legal scholars like John Gardner echo this point by stating that '[i]n any legal system, whether a given norm is legally valid, and hence whether it forms part of the law of that system, depends on its sources, not its merits'.[135] In this sense, the concept of a pure theory of law fails on account of the inability of legal positivism to successfully advance its case since the value-laden ideals of morality are embedded in, and intrinsic to, law.[136]

Yet, these values cannot be easily separated from the prescriptive ethos of positive law. Nonetheless, the positivist view that the validity of law emanates from its source has been deployed to disaffirm customary law's normativity.[137] In defending the absence of a legal system in so-called *primitive* societies (which is an obscure reference to non-Western societies), legal positivists draw on Hart's conception of law to argue that while primary rules are present in such (non-Western) societies, they lack secondary rules; therefore, they equally lack a legal system.[138]

On this subject, Hart's argument on the distinction between primary rules and secondary rules and how modern societies privilege formalised legislative institutions that establish these secondary rules for the effective functioning of primary rules demands critical review.[139] This dichotomy emphasises secondary rules of recognition as derivative of the normative force of primary rules.[140] Nonetheless, Hart's division between primary rules and secondary rules (of recognition) must be rejected on grounds that secondary rules of recognition are just social facts born of social practice and not products of special legal rules that are absent in so-called *primitive* societies as Hart (mis-)conceptualises in his analysis.[141]

Importantly, non-Eurocentric law should not be assessed using Western canons and standards of legalism that do not engage with the political

[134] Tamanaha, 'Socio-Legal Positivism', 2.

[135] John Gardner, 'Legal Positivism: 5½ Myths' (2001) 46:1 Am J Juris 199, 199.

[136] Julius Cohen, 'The Political Element in Legal Theory: A Look at Kelsen's Pure Legal Theory' (1978) 88:1 Yale LJ 1, 2.

[137] Berihun A. Gebeye, 'Decoding Legal Pluralism in Africa' (2017) 49:2 J Leg Pluralism and Unofficial L 228, 232.

[138] Hart, *Concept of Law*, 91.

[139] K.-K. Lee, 'Hart's Primary and Secondary Rules' (1968) 77:308 Mind 561, 562.

[140] Luka Burazin, 'The Rule of Recognition and the Emergence of a Legal System' (2015) 27 Revus: J Const Theory and Phil L 116, 116–117.

[141] Grant Lamond, 'Legal Sources, the Rule of Recognition, and Customary Law' (2014) 59:1 Am J Juris 25, 39–43.

and cultural contexts underpinning non-Western legal systems.[142] This critique dovetails into the 'pre-eminence of Eurocentrism in international law by maintaining that only entities with centralised, hierarchical forms of governance, and control over territory, could be regarded as states'.[143] What legal positivists like Hart refer to as primitive societies, legal pluralists would call non-state legal orders.[144] Thus, customary law must not become the product and outcome of a legal methodology that is no more superior to it yet capable of subordinating and denying its autonomy; or much more, artificially conferring legal normativity on customary law.

Today, legal pluralism's growth is evidenced by the 'conspicuous crisis of traditional politics and the expansion of non-state rule-governed frameworks'.[145] However, it is not accurate to say that legal pluralism is particularly novel, because, as a normative phenomenon, every society has embedded in it some amount of pluralist legal jurisprudence.[146] Here, as Sally Engle Merry has noted, and most scholars of legal pluralism concede that, while Eurocentric law introduced a variety of juridical systems which were impliedly plural, European legalism equally obscured the pluriverse of Indigenous or customary law.[147] These non-Western systems of law often emanated from (or were linked to) religion and other cultural aspects of African social life, further evidencing the inherently plural character of law everywhere.[148]

Thus, the global escalation of legal pluralism as a 'hollowing-out of the state' and the rise of the political as law must lead us to a renewed legal philosophy that contemplates peripheralised notions of law. This position has been affirmed by courts even in the Global North confronted with similar questions. For example, the Supreme Court of New Zealand has upheld Māori customary law's normativity based on its ethical values by rejecting Eurocentric legalism that law emerges from a supposed rule-based system, and affirming the importance of mutual interaction

[142] Badejogbin, 'Judicial Discretion', 11.

[143] Islam, 'History of the North–South Divide', 25.

[144] Ralf Michaels, 'What Is Non-State Law?' in Michael A. Helfand (ed.), *Negotiating State and Non-State Law: The Challenge of Global and Local Pluralism* (Cambridge University Press 2015) 41, 46–47.

[145] Emmanuel Melissaris and Mariano Croce, 'A Pluralism of Legal Pluralisms', *Oxford Handbook Topics in Law*, online ed. (Oxford Academic 2017).

[146] John Griffiths, 'Legal Pluralism' in James D. Wright (ed.), *International Encyclopedia of Social and Behavioral Sciences*, 2nd ed. (Elsevier 2015) 757, 757.

[147] Sally Engle Merry, 'Legal Pluralism' (1988) 22:5 Law and Soc'y Rev 869, 869.

[148] Geoffrey Swenson, 'Legal Pluralism in Theory and Practice' (2018) 20:3 Int'l Studies Rev 438, 439.

between traditional and (received) colonial legal systems.[149] In this respect, our best efforts must be directed at harnessing the appropriate means and methods to moderate the interactions across and within this multilevel of exchanges in the legal pluriverse.[150]

Thus, the growing interest in the normative relevance of legal pluralism is demonstrated in the correspondingly increasing character of our global interconnectedness.[151] This turn to legal pluralism is a welcome development and a timely intervention in restraining the unidirectional movement of received European law. Gad Barzilai captures this point as he notes that:

> Legal pluralism has been one of the most salient and influential academic trends in law and society scholarship since the 1970s. It primarily articulates detachment from legal centralism revolving around state law, criticism of the exclusiveness of state law, decentralisation of court-centred judicial studies, exploration of non-state legal orders, unveiling of informal socio-legal practices, and an understanding of law as a multi-centred field that deals with the convergence of norms, localities, states, global sites, and practices. Scholarship of legal pluralism has underscored the ways in which various identities and traditions have decentralised state law and offered non-state legal orders.[152]

Arising from this treatment of pluralism, the classical conception of law, then, is a narrow default that fails to account for the normative and social forces that combine to make up law's constitutive force.[153] Law then is the product of social forces and surrounded by its social circumstances, which includes customary (legal) norms. Thus, scholars of legal pluralism contend the dichotomous relationship between positive law and non-positive law, state law and non-state law, cannot be a rigid one, as 'the distinction between customs and state law loses its convincing force'.[154] It is this positivist law–morality differentiation that is resisted in African customary law since African traditional legal philoso-

[149] *Peter Hugh McGregor Ellis v The King* [2022] NZSC [114], para 114.

[150] Michael W. Dowdle, 'Do We Really Need a 'Pluralist Jurisprudence'?' (2017) 8:4 Transnat'l Leg Theory 381, 387.

[151] Twining, 'Normative and Legal Pluralism', 484.

[152] Barzilai, 'Beyond Relativism', 396.

[153] Gerald J. Postema, 'Legal Positivism: Early Foundations' in Andrei Marnor (ed.), *The Routledge Companion to Philosophy of Law* (Routledge 2012) 31, 36.

[154] Klaus Günther, 'Legal Pluralism or Uniform Concept of Law? Globalisation as a Problem of Legal Theory' (2008) 5 No Foundations: Interdisc JL and Just 5, 13.

phy denounces a difference between law and morality.[155] It is in this sense that critical scholars admonish a recognition of how non-state legal domains are overshadowed by the more prominent state-centric law. In this respect, they forcefully urge a reconsideration of the uncritical acceptance of these experiences and a reappreciation of how these demoted legal orders are overlaid by state-centric law in the context of environmental protection and sustainable development.[156]

Consequently, the significance of legal pluralism emanates from the growing awareness that what is often called law is nothing but an avenue for politics to 'express power with technical precision' while seemingly performing a corresponding function as intrinsically obliging compliance.[157] Cognisant of this co-evolution of law and politics, legal pluralism offers a chance to re-engage with the concept of law in a manner that challenges the primacy of state-centred law as it is evident that legal centralism is state-sanctioned politics veiled as law. Thus, in this process of emancipating law, we can bring to the centre previously peripheralised legal orders such as customary law.[158]

Yet the task does not stop at merely acknowledging a plurality of legal orders. As has been argued elsewhere, it is insufficient to 'merely recognise that legal pluralism exists; scholars and policymakers must understand how legal pluralism actually functions'.[159] At this point, it is crucial to acknowledge that legal pluralism is merely functionally descriptive, and the ordinary identification of different complex normative orders does nothing to alter extant power relations articulated by a state's legal apparatus. Its power to transform must be demonstrated as well.

An analysis of power is implied in legal pluralist reviews, but it has to be made explicit as part of retrenching the (neo-)coloniality of modern law.[160] This point echoes the views of scholars of legal pluralism that 'virtually every society is legally plural, whether or not it has a colonial

[155] Clever Mapaure, 'Reinvigorating African Values for SADC: The Relevance of Traditional African Philosophy of Law in a Globalising World of Competing Perspectives' (2011) 1 SADC LJ 149, 151.

[156] Daniel F. Robinson and Nicole Graham, 'Legal Pluralisms, Justice and Spatial Conflicts: New Directions in Legal Geography' (2018) 184:1 Geographic J 3, 5.

[157] Nobles and Schiff, 'Using Systems Theory', 282.

[158] Baudouin Dupret, 'What Is Plural in the Law? A Praxiological Answer' (2005) 1 Égypte/Monde Arabe 1, 3.

[159] Swenson, 'Legal Pluralism in Theory and Practice', 440.

[160] Raza Saeed, 'Law and Coloniality of Empire: Colonial Encounter and Normative Orderings in the Indian Sub-Continent' (2018) 19:1 YB Islamic and Middle Eastern L 103.

past'.[161] However, to clarify the character of legal pluralism, it is insufficient to simply identify pluralism since its mere existence rarely disrupts power relations or powerful interests. Rather, the issue is to turn this knowledge into a practical, transformative force that counters customary law's suppression and defends its legal normativity. This point is significant in adapting African customary law to the task of remaking sustainable development within legal pluralism.[162]

In considering the normativity of non-state legal orders – in this case, African customary law – it is vital to expand the field of inquiry away from the limits of legal positivism to the methodologically redemptive capacity of legal pluralism.[163] Legal pluralism sees a plurality of norms as binding. To its scholars, the inability to see the normative essence of these non-state legal orders does not mean they cease to be law.[164] In line with this position, some legal scholars argue that 'normative communities articulate norms without formal state power behind them'.[165] Accordingly, in African jurisprudence, 'Indigenous or customary norms qualify as legal norms'.[166]

A pluralist conception of law echoes TWAIL's correspondingly pluralist outlook that re-envisions law as a multivarious legal space for co-existence and mutual (not hierarchical) interaction.[167] It also addresses, in a more wholesome way, this important fact that ongoing intellectual revivalism on the plurality of law is an important aspect of the re-creation of the conception and meaning of law. Viewed this way, the reference to the Global South and its law too ceases to be a monolithic construction as its 'qualifiers "Africa", "Chinese", or Islamic point to their distinctive features [rather] than their "otherness"'.[168]

Accordingly, for legal pluralists, the pressing question is why customary law should remain on the fringes of legal normativity and be denied

161 Merry, 'Legal Pluralism', 869.

162 Andreas Kahler, 'The Significance of Customary Law for Environmental Conservation in Cameroon' in Oliver C. Ruppel and Emmanuel D. Kam Yogo (eds.), *Environmental Law and Policy in Cameroon: Towards Making Africa the Tree of Life* (Nomos 2018) 913, 923–924.

163 Gebeye, 'Decoding Legal Pluralism in Africa', 244.

164 Michaels, 'What Is Non-State Law?', 47.

165 Paul Schiff Berman, 'Global Legal Pluralism' (2007) 80 S Cal L Rev 1155, 1157.

166 Gebeye, 'Legal Theory in Africa', 41.

167 Lucas Lixinski, 'Narratives of the International Legal Order and Why They Matter' (2013) 6:2 Erasmus L Rev 1, 3.

168 Dial Dayana Ndima, 'Reconceiving African Jurisprudence in a Post-Imperial Society: The Role of Ubuntu in Constitutional Adjudication' (2015) 48:3 Comp and Int'l LJ S Afr 359, 361.

legal validity.[169] The answer, perhaps, lies in the history of the making of the postcolonial state. In Africa's case, European imperial powers, based on the Westphalian concept of the state, divided Africa and forged its fragments into colonial states with artificial boundaries that were drawn up at the infamous Berlin Conference of 1855.[170] The creation of these new, artificial national frontiers failed to account for significant community similarities and distinctions and legal idiosyncrasies, neither did the colonial administrations take seriously the normative standards embedded in the social structures of these colonised societies. The received European colonial law was thus deployed to aid colonial natural resource extraction and the consequent alteration of social organisation including the violent overthrow of customary law.[171]

Predictably, European colonialists imposed their law on the colonised peoples, most of whom had, and still retain to this day, their own customary governance and multiple legal orders (even if those laws have undergone some transformation).[172] Regardless of whether these communities are, in the Eurocentric sense, societies with law and legal orders, or whether they qualify as states according to European definitions, the peoples in these societies still consider themselves bound by their legal orders; hence, what those customary legal orders have to say about the environment, for example, ought to carry considerable legal significance in the conceptualisation and practice of sustainable development.[173]

For legal pluralists, customary law is, therefore, law.[174] This point is supported by the history on the contestation between colonial law and customary law and each legal domain's attempt to assert its normative force over the other.[175] Customary law is law because it binds persons who share in a normative community. The proponents of legal pluralism uphold its significance for relational ontologies in terms of how we

[169] Martha-Marie Kleinhans and Roderick A. MacDonald, 'What Is a *Critical* Legal Pluralism?' (1997) 26:2 Can J L and Soc'y 25, 30–32.

[170] Gebeye, 'Decoding Legal Pluralism in Africa', 234.

[171] Francis G. Snyder, 'Colonialism and Legal Form: The Creation of "Customary Law" in Senegal' (1981) 13:19 J Legal Pluralism 49, 60.

[172] Diala, 'Concept of Living Customary Law', 144–145.

[173] Miriam Seemann, *Water Security, Justice and the Politics of Water Rights of Peru and Bolivia* (Palgrave MacMillan 2016) 26–48.

[174] Raymond A Atuguba, 'Legal Pluralism in Africa: Three Levels and Seven Types of Law' in Muna Ndulo and Cosmas Emeziem (eds.), *Routledge Handbook of African Law* (Routledge 2022) 17, 35–38.

[175] Harlan Grant Cohen, 'Finding International Law, Part II: Our Fragmenting Legal Community' (2012) 44:4 NYU JIL and Pol 1049, 1064.

rethink our present approach to the complex relationship between nature and society.[176] In regard to sustainable development, the future of international law involves a recognition of customary law and Indigenous conceptions of law, and also an enabling of these non-Western systems of law as integral to pluralism.[177] Consequently, this view invites an 'embracing of the plurality of global values that remain at the periphery of the dominant discourse'.[178]

Even so, the observation on the role legal pluralism plays in facilitating a renewed sustainable development leaves behind lingering doubt as to whether it signals facilitation as a descriptive or as a power-disruptive project. My preference is for the latter since it unties the presumed neutrality of sustainable development by inviting a radical reconstitution that is conscious of, and integrative of, non-European legal influences. Or, as has been suggested recently; legal syncretism may be a better approach to legal pluralism. On this subject, Berihun Adugna Gebeye notes that legal syncretism is the 'process and result of adoption, rejection, invention, and transformation of diverse and seemingly opposite legal rules principles, and practices into a constitutional state with imperial or colonial legacies'.[179] This view might be the path less trodden since the notion that legal pluralism has an applied component remains contested, although some legal scholars interested in legal pluralism have determined that it has some prescriptive content.[180] In this respect, I find that there is normative value in thinking through the lens of legal pluralism as it aids a critical evaluation of pluralist registers of law, an approach that may well serve as a catalyst for rethinking sustainable development in international law.[181]

176 Deborah Curran, 'Indigenous Processes of Consent: Repoliticising Water Governance through Legal Pluralism' (2019) 11:3 Water 571, 572.

177 Michelle Lim, 'Pathways to Equitable Sustainability in the Anthropocene: An Agenda for Legal Research' in Michelle Lim (ed.), *Charting Environmental Law Futures in the Anthropocene* (Springer 2019) 225.

178 Khoday, 'Decolonising the Environment', 202.

179 Berihun Adugna Gebeye, *A Theory of African Constitutionalism* (Oxford University Press 2021) 10.

180 Lando Kirchmair, 'Descriptive vs. Prescriptive Global Legal Pluralism: A Gentle Reminder of David Hume's Is–Ought Divide' (2019) 51:1 J Leg Pluralism and Unofficial L 48, 59.

181 James G. Stewart and Asad Kiyani, 'The Ahistoricism of Legal Pluralism in International Criminal Law' (2017) 65:2 Am J Comp L 393, 397.

5.8 Anthropologising Sustainable Development

Legal anthropology provides insights into how spheres of international regulation like sustainable development are designed by querying the 'anthropological sensitivities' of law.[182] Such inquiries provide valuable lessons for integrating Indigenous legal concepts into the evolution of sustainable development in international law. For example, sustainable development has engaged the attention of anthropologists who are working in an interdisciplinary context (including in law) to understand how Indigenous systems can provide alternative approaches to the knowledge and practice of sustainable development.[183] However, an analysis on legal anthropology attracts criticism because much of what is called legal anthropology may be subsumed under legal pluralism.[184]

Conversely, some scholars have argued legal pluralism is 'a guiding principle for the sub-disciplinary field of legal anthropology'.[185] On this question, the work of Keebet von Benda-Beckmann and Bertram Turner has described the connection between legal anthropology and legal pluralism and argued legal pluralism 'endorses anthropological findings indicating that, in their social and economic interactions, people resort to customary, religious law or unnamed new law, often mixed with parts of state law'.[186] In this respect, legal anthropologists 'invite us to abandon references to the concept of legal pluralism, not only in order to emerge definitively from the ethnocentric hierarchies with which it has been weighed down, but also to shine light on the very existence of a plurality of legal pluralisms'.[187]

Legal anthropology also overlaps with transnational law as ethnographic work sometimes involves the study of transnational legal orders

[182] Christopher Eberhard and David Napier, 'Law and Policy in a "Glocal" World: The Challenge of Dialogue' in Michael Freman and David Napier (eds.), *Law and Anthropological Review: Legal Issues Volume 12* (Oxford University Press 2009) 67, 70.

[183] Viacheslav Rudnev, 'Indigenous Knowledge: Searching for a Model of Sustainable Development for Humankind' (2015) 26:2 Global Ethics 46.

[184] Chris Fuller, 'Legal Anthropology, Legal Pluralism and Legal Thought' (1994) 10:3 Anthro Today 9, 10.

[185] Jonas Bens and Larissa Vetters, 'Ethnographic Legal Studies: Reconnecting Anthropological and Sociological Traditions' (2018) 50:3 J Leg Pluralism and Unofficial L 239, 241.

[186] von Benda-Beckmann and Turner, 'Legal Pluralism', 264.

[187] Véronique Champeil-Desplats, 'Law, the Plurality of Modes of Normativity and Their Interactions' (2019) 16 La Revue des Droits de L'Homme 1, 5.

and their related processes.[188] While this intersection evokes an image of law as interconnected across normative spaces, it is important to distinguish them and show how legal anthropology functions as law by itself. In this respect, some legal anthropologists have argued that, by 'examining law through its broader social and normative contexts, anthropologists have focused on the legal complexity produced by intersections among plural legal orders rooted in the community, the state, and international institutions and agents'.[189] It is, in this sense, that environmental anthropologists recommend a reconsideration of the Eurocentric foundations of sustainability by proposing non-Western impulses for rethinking the foundations of sustainable development.[190]

The study of legal anthropology in rethinking sustainable development follows the point that the relationship between human society and non-human entities must be reviewed 'through a historical–anthropological perspective, by paying attention to the different contexts in which the legal categories have been deployed, and by extending the inquiry beyond Western institutions'.[191] This critical point raises questions for sustainable development with every stratum of social relations that is peeled off.[192]

Here, two contending positions arise in the anthropology of law which impact the understanding of legal anthropology's guidance for sustainable development. In the first approach, legal anthropology may be described as a three-part endeavour. Bronislaw Malinowski argued that, first, it requires day-to-day engagement with a particular group of people in a particular society to better appreciate their culture, traditions, and institutions; second, an extended period of immersion in that particular society

[188] Sally Engle Merry, 'New Realism and the Ethnography of Transnational Law' (2006) 31:4 Law and Soc Inquiry 975; Elizabeth Mertz and Mark Goodale, 'Comparative Anthropology of Law' in David S. Clark (ed.), *Comparative Law and Society* (Edward Elgar 2012) 77, 78; Miia Halme-Tuomisaari, 'Toward a Lasting Anthropology of International Law/ Governance' (2016) 27:1 European JIL 235.

[189] Sally E. Merry and Michael C. Canfield, 'Law: Anthropological Aspects' in James D. Wright (ed.), *International Encyclopedia of the Social and Behavioural Sciences* (Elsevier 2015) 535, 535.

[190] Marc Brightman and Jerome Lewis, 'Introduction' in Marc Brightman and Jerome Lewis (eds.), *The Anthropology of Sustainability: Beyond Development and Progress* (Palgrave Macmillan 2017) 1.

[191] Alain Pottage, 'Introduction: The Fabrication of Persons and Things' in Alain Pottage and Martha Mundy (eds.), *Law, Anthropology, and the Constitution of the Social: Making Persons and Things* (Cambridge University Press 2004) 1, 5.

[192] Lon L. Fuller 'Human Interaction and the Law' (1969) 14:1 Am J Juris 1, 15l; Eli Elinoff, 'Sufficient Citizens: Moderation and the Politics of Sustainable Development in Thailand' (2014) 37:1 Pol and Leg Anthro Rev 89.

under study; and third, proficiency in that society's language to help one to understand the nuances of that society's culture.[193] This approach posits that law is embedded in every society, and in 'everyday life, rather than the state or other institutions'.[194]

Conversely, legal anthropologists like Alfred Radcliffe-Brown proffer a different view by defining law as a feature of state institutions; that is, 'social control through the systematic application of the force of politically organised society'.[195] This version, which advanced the viewpoint that law was absent from (non-Western) societies, has been criticised as deriving from a Eurocentric perspective, and particularly, as 'closely reflect[ing] the predominantly imperative and positivist orientation of Anglo-American legal theory'.[196] In transcending these national frontiers, if positivist law is 'the dominant approach to international law, it is because its historical pre-eminence has meant that scholars and state officials, including from weak nations, come to be socialised in its understanding of the workings of international law and institutions'.[197]

Away from these internally-contrasting positions on the constitution of legal anthropology, the discipline's evolving contemporary convergence rises from the perception that law is intrinsically part of social practice and a discourse of power.[198] Alongside this notion of law as a social process, a legal system within which law operates is demonstrative of its 'fundamental values and its normative order'.[199] Flowing from law's power as a social norm, law as a linguistic process of a particular society is acknowledged by some legal anthropologists as 'the social character of legal language'.[200] This linguistic character of law appeals to legal anthropologists as they examine how the language of law emerges from different cultural settings within different societies, and how this language either reinforces preconceived notions of law, resists such notions,

193 Bronislaw Malinoswki, *Crime and Custom in Savage Society* (Routledge 1926).

194 Merry and Canfield, 'Law: Anthropological Aspects', 535.

195 Alfred Radcliffe-Brown, 'Primitive Law' in Edwin Robert Anderson Seligman and Alvin Saunders Johnson (eds.), *Encyclopedia of the Social Sciences* (MacMillan 1933) 202, 202.

196 John L. Comaroff and Simon Roberts, *Rules and Processes: The Cultural Logic of Dispute in the African Context* (University of Chicago Press 1981) 6.

197 B. S. Chimni, *International Law and World Order: A Critique of Contemporary Approaches*, 2nd ed. (Cambridge University Press 2017) 12.

198 Sally Humphreys, 'Law as Discourse' (1985) 1:2 History and Anthro 241, 242.

199 Merry and Canfield, 'Law: Anthropological Aspects', 536.

200 Elizabeth Mertz, 'Language, Law, and Social Meanings: Linguistic/Anthropological Contributions to the Study of Law' (1992) 26:2 L and Soc'y Rev 413, 414.

or assists in discovering new forms of legal expressions which take up the form of law.[201] Accordingly, the value of legal anthropology to sustainable development requires attentiveness to the language used in describing and enduing the concept with content.[202]

As a field of inquiry, the methodological impetus of legal anthropology is particularly useful in how to approach anthropology's intimate connection to customary law-making.[203] Owing to the rejection of the idea of Eurocentric law built around the colonial (and now the postcolonial) state, and the acknowledgement of law's intrinsic character and embeddedness across different societies, there is a renewed interest in unearthing customary law as evolving separately from state-centred law.[204] It is its capacity to bring about the 'disruption of certainty' and, in this sense, the certainty of state-centric law that makes a legal anthropological analysis particularly useful.[205] Anne Griffiths rightly points out that this new anthropological curiosity in customary law has ushered scholars in the field into a historic moment of re-encountering customary law.[206] Nonetheless, it was the understanding that legal anthropology's quest to rediscover a pristine customary law was condemned to be an almost impossible task considering the far-reaching ramifications of colonial law on customary law.[207] This is the foundation of the critique that is levelled against 'the anthropologists' propensity to "edit out" the state, its law and administrative institutions from the analysis of "their" society'.[208] Thus, the suggestion is that, 'rather than arguing about the purity of customary law in terms of its historical pedigree, it is more important to take

201 Merry and Canfield, 'Law: Anthropological Aspects', 537.

202 Alf Hornborg, 'Ecology as Semiotics: Outlines of a Contextualist Paradigm for Human Ecology' in Philippe Descola and Gílsi Pálsson (eds.), *Nature and Society: Anthropological Perspectives* (Routledge 1996) 48, 54.

203 Mertz and Goodale, 'Comparative Anthropology of Law', 81.

204 Anne Griffiths, 'Broadening the Legal Academy, the Study of Customary Law: The Case for Social-Scientific and Anthropological Perspectives' (2017) 20:2 Potchefstroom Electronic LJ 1, 13.

205 Sally Engle Merry, 'Does Law Matter to Anthropology? A Comment' (2018) 2:2 J Leg Anthro 86, 87.

206 Griffiths, 'Broadening the Legal Academy', 13.

207 von Benda-Beckmann and Turner, 'Legal Pluralism', 258.

208 Franz Benda-Beckmann and Keebet von Benda-Beckmann, 'Legal Pluralism and Legal Anthropology: Experiences from Indonesia' in Gary F. Bell (eds.), *Pluralism, Transnationalism and Culture in Asian Law: A Book in Honour of M. B. Hooker* (ISEAS-Yusof Ishak Institute 2017) 70, 71.

account of the sources that give rise to it and the ways in which it is operating as the moment'.[209]

Therefore, the dual role of legal anthropology operates as the investigative (law-making) process within law. Here, as law-in-context or law as a social process, legal anthropology functions as a methodological tool that uncovers law, even if that law is seemingly indiscernible. This understanding is based on the idea that law is integral to the mechanics of social progress.[210] This processual framework aids the assimilation of customary law into other frameworks of law. In linking this insight to Africa's treatment in respect of legal anthropology, while customary law-making was key to local legal orders, the social mechanisms driving the procedures seemed to command little interest with colonial administrators.[211]

In using customary law to explain law-making processes, the normativity of law becomes visible through this anthropological lens, with law working principally as a function of politics embedded in the constant reconstruction of social phenomena.[212] In this respect, legal anthropology extends its sphere of inquiry and influence beyond querying formal systems of law to engaging within the interstices of the legal orders of the formal, non-formal and less formal legal domains.[213] Accordingly, by drawing on the explanatory framework of legal anthropology, the current understanding of sustainable development is exposed as:

> a (Western) cultural and ideological illusion that conceals a global environmental 'zero-sum game', in which the economic and technological expansion of the capitalist core nations necessarily occur at the expense of the peripheral areas of the world system.[214]

However, in consulting legal anthropology as a pathway for eliciting the alternativeness of customary law in charting a new course for pursuing sustainable development, we are reminded that an improper use of legal anthropology may lead to detrimental results. This caution is based on

[209] Griffiths, 'Broadening the Legal Academy', 13.

[210] Miia Halme-Tuomisaari, 'Toward a Lasting Anthropology of International Law/Governance' (2016) 27:1 European JIL 235; Merry and Canfield, 'Law: Anthropological Aspects', 536.

[211] Moore, 'Treating Law as Knowledge', 22–23.

[212] Joan Vincent, *Anthropology and Politics: Visions, Traditions, and Trends* (University of Arizona Press 1990) 29.

[213] Merry and Canfield, 'Law: Anthropological Aspects', 535.

[214] Cardesa-Salzmann and Cocciolo, 'Global Governance', 445.

the Eurocentric origins of anthropology.[215] Here, it is understood that the decolonisation process did not fully reorient anthropological studies.[216] In this respect, one cannot gloss over how the field of anthropology, of which legal anthropology is merely a sub-field, has been pivotal to the othering of non-Western worldviews.[217] For example, scholars of legal anthropology may fall into the temptation of treating custom as a rigid infrastructure whereas custom is ever-evolving and dynamic.[218] However, legal anthropology scholars like Benda-Beckmann resist such inflexibility, arguing on the contrary that, Indigenous law is not fixed in time but is evolving much in the same way as society is.[219]

The guiding principle in understanding this new role for legal anthropology is that, law emerges from custom.[220] Accordingly, the doctrinaire attitude that accepts anthropological statements as unassailable is a concern for TWAIL and other critical scholars who draw comparisons between the progress of international law and its co-evolution with legal anthropology as has been defined by Eurocentric interests.[221] For example, anthropologists intentionally curated customary law as a legal genre and, in the process, tainted customary law with Eurocentric mistrust.[222] Other legal scholars have been less charitable as they condemn 'the Eurocentrism of anthropological knowledge in the service of colonial administrations'.[223] To redress this problem of (mis-)characterising customary law as welded to notions of precolonial legal orders (erroneously)

215 Arturo Escobar, 'Sustaining the Pluriverse: The Political Ontology of the Territorial Struggles in Latin America' in Marc Brightman and Jerome Lewis (eds.), *The Anthropology of Sustainability: Beyond Development and Progress* (Palgrave MacMillan 2017) 237, 242.

216 Liliana Lizarazo-Rodriguez, 'Mapping Law and Development' (2017) 4:4 Indonesian J Int'l and Comp L 761, 802.

217 Ndima, 'Reconceiving African Jurisprudence', 361.

218 Leon Sheleff, *The Future of Tradition: Customary Law, Common Law, and Legal Pluralism* (Frank Cass 1999) 85.

219 Keebet von Benda-Beckmann, 'Environmental Protection and Human Rights of Indigenous Peoples: A Tricky Alliance' (1997) 9 L and Anthro 302. The oft-held view that Indigenous peoples live in harmony with nature ought not to be (mis)construed as a permanent interrelationship since Indigenous societies too sometimes engage in environmentally unsustainable conduct.

220 David J. Bederman, *Custom as a Source of Law* (Cambridge University Press 2010) 3.

221 Heejin Kim, *Regime Accommodation in International Law: Human Rights in International Economic Law and Policy* (Brill 2016) 93.

222 Mikhaïl Xifaras, 'The Global Turn in Legal Theory' (2016) 29:1 Canadian JL and Jur 215, 217.

223 Corcodel, *Modern Law and Otherness*, 171.

fixed in time, some legal scholars have urged the use of the idea of living customary law which entails a recurring social 'normative interaction'.[224]

This iterative engagement with customary law within sustainable development is a compelling approach to rethinking sustainable development and its relevant alternativeness that is guided by a sensitivity towards culture, relational ontologies, and related cosmologies.[225] It follows what Kishan Khoday argues that, it is possible to create 'global norms not from central nodes of power and knowledge, but instead reflect and engage with the plurality of subaltern ecocosmologies that have more holistic and accurate understandings of agency and relationality between people, planet and cosmos'.[226] Thus, customary law must be reread within the historical and contemporary expressions of sustainable development in order to reflect the juris-generative power and capacity of customary law to respond adequately to existing and new ecological challenges.[227]

5.9 Transnational Law, Normativity, and Sustainable Development

Transnational law focuses on law that occurs outside of the state's law-making process.[228] Its reach continues to spread and evolve as it has made significant inroads into environmental law research.[229] Since the Trail Smelter Case entered international law, the transnationalisation and cross-border movement of the international law on the environment

[224] Diala, 'Concept of Living Customary Law', 148.

[225] Kishan Khoday and Usha Natarajan, 'Fairness and International Environmental Law from Below: Social Movements and Legal Transformation in India' (2012) 25:2 Leiden JIL 415.

[226] Kishan Khoday, 'The Mythic Environment: Ecocosmology and Narrative Remakings of Environmental Consciousness' in Usha Natarajan and Julia Dehm (eds.), *Locating Nature: Making and Unmaking International Law* (Cambridge University Press 2022) 284, 306.

[227] Gregory H. Bigler, 'Traditional Jurisprudence and Protection of Our Society: A Jurisgenerative Tail' (2018) 43:1 Am Indian L Rev 1, 28–29; Peter Ørebech and Fred Bosselman, 'The Linkage between Sustainable Development and Customary Law' in Peter Ørebech, Fred Bosselman, Jes Bjarup, David Callies, Martin Chanock and Hanne Petersen (eds.), *The Role of Customary Law in Sustainable Development* (Cambridge University Press 2006) 12, 21.

[228] Veerle Heyvaert and Thijs Etty, 'Introducing Transnational Environmental Law' (2012) 1:1 Transnat'l Envt'l L 1, 3.

[229] Emily Webster and Laura Mai, 'Transnational Environmental Law in the Anthropocene' (2020) 11:1–2 Transnat'l Leg Theory 1, 15.

has been on a steady rise.[230] Transnational law provides insights into the movement of environmental consciousness across national borders. Yet, even long before the Trail Smelter Case, the complex interaction between imperial powers, imperially-chartered corporations, and powerful local interests in colonised states had already set in motion a process for the formation of a transnational law on the environment.[231]

However, this history is rarely discussed in the literature. In this respect, a critical review of transnational law explains the North–South divide regarding the interaction between international law and environmental law across borders is transformed over time into 'a recasting of the environmental concerns of the Global South as the substance of other disciplines, such as development law, natural resources law or sustainable development law'.[232]

The turn to transnational law supports the viewpoint that this type of *soft* international law is, in fact, law.[233] In Philip Jessup's frequently-cited definition, transnational law 'includes all law which regulates actions or events that transcend national frontiers, both public and private international law are included, *as are other rules which do not wholly fit into such categories*'.[234] This popular definition presumes a normative space that is neither solely within the remit of public international law nor fully occupied by private international law; thus, urging another set of legal rules that complements these two fields. Importantly, transnational law manifests as 'a *methodological* lens through which we can study the particular transformation of legal institutions in the context of an evolving complex society'.[235] In this respect, Jessup's prodigious work was a timely response to the growing disenchantment with the failure of international law to regulate aspects of the post-World War II reality and the complicated and intractable challenges posed to the law-and-

[230] International Arbitration, Trail Smelter Case (United States, Canada), Award of 16 April 1938 and 11 March 1941, RIAA, Vol III.

[231] Kulamadayil, 'Placed in Between', 466.

[232] Natasha Affolder, 'An Unknown Past, An Unequal Present, and an Uncertain Future: Transnational Environmental Law through Three Research Challenges' in Veerle Heyvaert and Leslie-Anne Duvic-Paoli (eds.), *Research Handbook on Transnational Environmental Law* (Edward Elgar 2020) 32, 40.

[233] Gregory Shaffer, 'Theorising Transnational Legal Ordering' (2016) 12 Annual Rev Soc Sciences 231, 233.

[234] Philip C. Jessup, *Transnational Law* (Yale University Press 1956) 2 (Italicised for emphasis).

[235] Peer Zumbansen, 'Defining the Stress of Transnational Law: Legal Theory, Global Governance and Legal Pluralism' in Günther Handl (ed.), *Beyond Territoriality: Transnational Legal Authority in an Age of Globalisation* (Brill, 2012) 53, 55.

society context within international law in a post-Cold War world, at both national and international levels.[236]

Despite suspicion over its normative importance, transnational law has been invoked as means and method for engaging with the link between law and society in the sense that it assists us in pursuing sociological and socio-legal inquiries into how different interactions arising from these disciplinary explorations assume legal significance.[237] Drawing on its transformative and normative capacity to illuminate transnational law, legal pluralism has been described as 'a powerful pathway towards a transnational legal methodology which traces the emergence of legal regulatory institutions in the context of an evolving society – at "national" and "international" level'.[238] Peer Zumbansen pushes this line of inquiry further by arguing that, since transnational law is decentred from the classical statist law-making structure, it is important to understand how this kind of law maintains 'its [present] status as *law* – a set of binding rules, created by a legitimate authority'.[239]

When examined closely, the difficulty encountered in recognising transnational law as law inheres within Jessup's mutable definition as a sharply contrasting phenomenon sitting at the intersection of public international law and private international law. Nonetheless, at the same time, transnational law qualifies as resting totally outside of these two fields.[240] Even more, owing to its ambulatory character, it 'is neither purely domestic nor purely international, but rather, a hybrid of the two'.[241] Codes of corporate conduct, for instance, which straddle both domestic and international law, have assumed prominence as sources of law.[242] In this respect, Natasha Affolder argues, for example that, contractual governance

[236] Gregory Shaffer and Carlos Coye, 'From International Law to Jessup's Transnational Law, from Transnational Law to Transnational Legal Ordering' in Peer Zumbansen (ed.), *The Many Lives of Transnational Law: Critical Engagements with Jessup's Bold Proposal* (Cambridge University Press 2020) 126, 126.

[237] Roger Cotterell, 'What Is Transnational Law?' (2012) 37:2 L and Soc Inquiry 500, 503.

[238] Zumbansen, 'Defining the Stress of Transnational Law', 56.

[239] Peer Zumbansen, 'Can Transnational Law Be Critical? Reflections on a Contested Idea, Field and Method' in Emilios Christodoulidis, Ruth Dukes, and Marco Goldoni (eds.), *Research Handbook on Critical Legal Theory* (Edward Elgar 2019) 473, 474.

[240] Armin von Bogdandy, Matthias Goldmann and Ingo Venzke, 'From Public International Law to International Public Law: Translating World Public Opinion into International Public Authority' (2017) 28:1 European JIL 115, 118–121.

[241] Harold Hongju Koh, 'Why Transnational Law Matters' (2006) 24:4 Penn State Int'l L Rev 745, 745.

[242] Wolfgang Fikentscher, 'United Nations Code of Conduct: New Paths in International Law' (1982) 30:4 Am J Comp L 577; Peer Zumbansen, 'Neither 'Public' nor 'Private',

can transform seemingly private influence into a set of calcified public legal rules that are binding on states and non-state actors alike.[243] Little wonder, transnational law's dual character has survived till now as it is often described as 'legal hybridisation' outside the false distinction between international and domestic law.[244]

Recently, some legal scholars have argued for a shift from transnational law to transnational legal ordering. Prominently, Gregory Shaffer and Carlos Coye argue this paradigm shift is vital to grasping the subtle distinctions of transnational law's 'political, social and legal implications'.[245] Following this call for a nuanced take on transnational law, transnational law scholarship seems to exhibits a lack of inclusivity and diversity. Here, Gregory Shaffer observes transnational law is deficient in its Third World focus and as its scholarly ambit is restricted to the Global North.[246] Shaffer's concern echoes the anxieties expressed by Third World scholars like Prabhakar Singh that transnational law is a reformulation of international legal rules during decolonisation with the objective of continuing colonial interests in the postcolonial period.[247]

TWAIL scholars agree with refocusing on the more expressive idea of transnational legal ordering. In Michael Fakhri's critical and methodological retooling of Jessup's old definition, he points out that:

> The irony is not lost on me that Philip Jessup developed his notion of transnational law at [a] time that coincided with and in effect disrupted rising claims of Third World sovereignty through international law. Jessup develops the concept to complicate distinctions between public and private, domestic and international. I [Fakhri] instead use transnational law in a narrower way to recognise and describe the legal tools that shape the direction and conditions of the movement of people and capital through borders.[248]

'National' or 'International': Transnational Corporate Governance from a Legal Pluralist Perspective' (2011) 38:1 JL and Soc'y 50.

243 Natasha Affolder, 'Transnational Carbon Contracting: Why Law's Invisibility Matters' in A. Claire Cutler and Thomas Dietz (eds.), *The Politics of Private Transnational Governance by Contract* (Routledge 2017) 215, 217.

244 Kaarlo Tuori, 'Transnational Law: On Legal Hybrids and Perspectivism' in Miguel Maduro, Kaarlo Tuori, and Tuvi Sankari (eds.), *Transnational Law: Rethinking European Law and Legal Thinking* (Cambridge University Press 2014) 17.

245 Shaffer and Coye, 'From International Law', 127.

246 Shaffer, 'Theorising Transnational Legal Ordering', 233.

247 Prabhakar Singh, 'The Private Life of Transnational Law: Reading Jessup from the Post-Colony' in Peer Zumbansen (ed.), *The Many Lives of Transnational Law: Critical Engagements with Jessup's Bold Proposal* (Cambridge University Press 2020) 419.

248 Fakhri, 'Third World Sovereignty', 221.

Fakhri's provocative reimagination of transnational law in the context of marginalised peoples and Singh's recharacterisation as reformation of international law in the postcolonial era challenge the traditional view of transnational law as state-like law. Here, TWAIL and other critical law scholars like Sara Seck, writing on transnational environmental regulation, have argued that, in filling this normative gap, TWAIL scholarship must empower the marginalised transnational subclass in the Global South to assume a fundamental obligation to make informed decisions as applicable to their relationship with the environment.[249]

Thus, despite the broader significance of transnational law, I am more interested in how its import is translatable in assisting to erect a firmer foundation for other non-classical formulations of law, such as customary law in the realisation of sustainable development. In this respect, I think of Affolder's description of transnational law as a journey in discovering an unseen law as fittingly capturing the essence of this legal inquiry.[250] Using the imagery of unseen law, Affolder argues transnational law is law even if its normative essence is often overlooked in the literature.[251] This point echoes Roger Cotterell's observation that transnational law queries legal standards and other rules that often peripheralise law and legal systems.[252] Accordingly, the interrogation of the 'relative silence surrounding the place of Indigenous law in accounts of global environmental law processes' brings into sharp focus the possibility of drawing on the capacity of transnational law to push us further into new sites of knowledge, and in excavating the normative force of what may be referred to as 'unseen law' including customary law.[253]

Nonetheless, in looking toward transnational law, I am wary that a significant aspect of this normative order is state-oriented law. For instance, the connection between transnational law and environmental harm raises concerns over the state-centric character of the observance of international human rights law. These norms and standards that have been developed through transnational legal processes are uncompromising in their application to the rights of marginalised peoples in cases of

[249] B. S. Chimni, 'Prolegomena to a Class Approach to International Law' (2010) 21:1 European JIL 57; Seck, 'Ecological Integrity and Third World Approaches', 172.

[250] Natasha Affolder, 'Transnational Law as Unseen Law' in Peer Zumbansen (eds.), *The Many Lives of Transnational Law: Critical Engagements with Jessup's Bold Proposal* (Cambridge University Press 2020) 364, 366.

[251] Ibid., 364–365.

[252] Cotterell, 'What Is Transnational Law?', 519.

[253] Affolder, 'Transnational Law as Unseen Law', 374.

transboundary environmental damage.[254] Thus, eco-legal philosophies have simply not influenced state-centric law that much.[255]

Another challenge is the relationship between foreign interests and the local comprador class. The two share common objectives in law-making spaces coupled with the fact that powerful non-local groups and their interests are asymmetrical to those of Southern marginalised peoples.[256] On this subject, TWAIL scholars have argued that transnational legal ordering produces a normative advance and a corresponding 'transnational elite' across the Global South who do not represent the interests of the transnational marginalised class.[257] Accordingly, TWAIL scholars like Fakhri again caution against depending excessively on Jessup's definition of transnational law as it fails to project or highlight the marginalised voices of 'rising claims of Third World sovereignty through international law', including peripheralised Indigenous law.[258]

To conclude, the grounding of new ideas on the similarities between transnational law as law and the legal pluriverse remains an important subject. This task reflects 'the socio-legal triangle of legal sociology, legal anthropology and "law in context"'.[259] Here, new grounds too must be attentive to interdisciplinary impulses. On this point, Peer Zumbansen notes that:

> [A]s we relativise contentions of society being the 'other' side of the state, which are running deep within continental legal imagination, we begin to recognise the necessity of 'defining' society as such rather than merely assuming it as a given background, against which we may freely theorise about the 'future of law'.[260]

On this subject, international law scholars are becoming increasingly aware that; ultimately, law is not only sanctioned by the state as is often argued from the Eurocentric perspective. It is also found in different places outside the state as the 'legal world is now awash with multiple and rival sets of institutions, law-identification and law-application practices,

[254] Tilmann Altwicker, 'Transnationalising Rights: International Human Rights Law in Cross-Border Contexts' (2018) 29:2 European JIL 581, 599.

[255] Margaret Davies, *EcoLaw: Legality, Life, and the Normativity of Nature* (Routledge 2021) 18.

[256] Paul Schiff Berman, 'From International Law to Globalisation' (2005) 43:2 Colum J Transnat'l L 485, 489; Sornarajah, 'Power and Justice', 23.

[257] Chimni, 'Third World Approaches to International Law', 6.

[258] Fakhri, 'Third World Sovereignty', 221.

[259] Zumbansen, 'Can Transnational Law Be Critical?', 475.

[260] Zumbansen, 'Defining the Stress of Transnational Law', 55.

each simultaneously mounting different and potentially conflicting authority claims'.[261] Likewise, TWAIL scholarship is re-examining the methodological significance of transnational law in helping locate law, considering that 'analytical legal philosophy has remained largely ignorant or non-cognisant of non-state forms of law'.[262] It is within this multi-layered context that African customary law emerges as capable of transcending both national and international borders, affecting international lawmaking, while still remaining grounded yet receptive of external normative influences.[263] Equally profound are the ways in which transnational law can nudge international (environmental) law in the direction of alternative ideas, while looking beyond classical fixations within the discipline.[264]

5.10 Conclusion

Customary law as international (environmental) law's alterity and, more narrowly, of sustainable development, derives from the need to constrain the idea that 'law is and should be the law of the state, uniform for all persons, exclusive of all other law, and administered by a single set of state institutions'.[265] As legal comparativists argue, law is a social and cultural creation present in all societies; yet legal positivist influences continue to peripheralise law that does not fit the positivist tradition.[266] In denouncing law's statist identity, it is also important to reflect on the principal understanding that international law is the 'manifestation of a form of law different from the law of the state'.[267] However, while the Eurocentric othering of customary law subconsciously conditions legal scholars to search for law through a binarised (state versus non-state)

[261] Julie Dickson, 'Who's Afraid of Transnational Legal Theory? Dangers and Desiderata' (2015) 6:3–4 Transnat'l Leg Theory 565, 570.

[262] Patrick Capps and Richard Collins, 'Doing Law beyond the State: Methodological Questions in International and Transnational Legal Theory' (2015) 6:3–4 Transnat'l Leg Theory 561, 563.

[263] Lauren Fielder, 'African Courts and African Values: Harmonising International Human Rights and Customary Law' in Kyriaki Topidi and Lauren Fielder (eds.), *Transnational Legal Processes and Human Rights* (Routledge 2013) 177, 179–182.

[264] Gilbert et al., 'Rights of Nature', 62–67.

[265] John Griffiths, 'What Is Legal Pluralism?' (1986) 18:24 J Leg Pluralism 1, 3.

[266] Jorge Esquirol, *Ruling the Law: Legitimacy and Failure in Latin American Legal Systems* (Cambridge University Press 2019). Chapter 1 of Esquirol's book, titled 'The Fiction of Legal Europeanness', provides an excellent account on this subject.

[267] Sébastien Jodoin, 'International Law and Alterity: The State and the Other' (2008) 21:1 Leiden JIL 1, 24.

approach, it is necessary to understand that this influence travels beyond a dualised view on law to a deeper and more systematic 'exclusionary construction of the non-West by reference to the West'.[268]

Even so, I am not arguing to replace one form of law with another. Legal scholarship directed this way is circular, as it is designed to address the very otherness it seeks to reform and will fall short of the 'plurality-focused analyses of law' I have advanced thus far.[269] This is the essence of the alternativeness of customary law in remaking sustainable development. It is a yearning for a deeper recognition of the transformative potential of plural legal ontologies in reimagining sustainable development.[270] Thus, it is important to think about every conceivable alternative source, including customary law and other Indigenous cosmologies, that enlarges the legal cosmos and enriches the disciplinary toolkit for realising sustainable development.[271]

In discussing customary law as an African ontological alterity, I do not wish to be (mis-)interpreted as privileging one epistemological form over another. Arguably, a discussion of a different version of legal reality risks attracting the very disapproval of otherness that TWAIL so often rails against in critiques of Eurocentric epistemologies.[272] Rather, drawing on the guidance derived from other non-dominant legal domains including legal pluralism, legal anthropology, and transnational law, this process should be seen as justifying customary law's normativity in the pursuit of sustainable development – one that brings customary law to the centre of legal epistemologies and out of the shadows of historically peripheralised influences on international law.[273] In this respect, customary law's link to sustainable development significantly relies on culture to transport these marginalised legal principles that illumine the discipline.[274] Still, culture, religion and other foundations within this customary law matrix, must be approached cautiously only with the objective of eliciting its positive

[268] Corcodel, *Modern Law and Otherness*, 48.

[269] Werner F. Menski, *Comparative Law in a Global Context: The Legal Systems of Asia and Africa*, 2nd ed. (Cambridge University Press, 2006), 83.

[270] Helen Dancer, 'Harmony with Nature: Towards a New Deep Legal Pluralism' (2021) 53:1 J of Leg Pluralism and Unofficial L 21.

[271] Corcodel, *Modern Law and Otherness*, 49.

[272] S. G. Sreejith, 'An Auto-Critique of TWAIL's Historical Fallacy: Sketching an Alternative Manifesto' (2017) 38:7 Third World Q 1511, 1515–1516.

[273] James Thuo Gathii, 'Africa' in Bardo Fassbender and Anne Peters (eds.), *Oxford Handbook of International Law* (Oxford University Press 2012) 407, 411.

[274] Ørebech and Bosselman, 'Linkage', 12.

attributes for the benefit of sustainable development while denouncing its negative characteristics.[275]

Reflecting on the criticality of revitalising international law broadly, Sébastien Jodoin helpfully remarks that:

> There is a need to work towards reconceptualising the discipline itself, a need to redefine both the modes and sites of what counts as law within the system: bringing new voices and discourses into the form, as well as imagining new ways and places in which we can be international lawyers. Indeed, to think in terms that are otherwise than the state is to acknowledge the multiplicity of orders, actors, and sources within and beyond conventional international law.[276]

This admonition underlies my proposal to reread the discourse on sustainable development for a deeper appreciation of the normative value in opening the concept up to different ways of knowing and doing law. This is a call to welcome and embrace plural legal ontologies and how this legal kaleidoscope can be adapted in renewing sustainable development.

[275] Gillespie, *International Environmental Law, Policy and Ethics*, 94. Gillespie reminds us that some aspects of culture are overly anthropocentric and damaging to the environment.

[276] Jodoin, 'International Law and Alterity', 24.

6

Ecocosmologies, Ecolegality, and African Environmentalisms as Ecological Law

> In my own field – environmental law and legal theory – many of my colleagues seem to be content with the world as it is. Or why is it that most books and articles are still written as if the 'the law' is a given that cannot be fundamentally changed, only gradually improved?*

6.1 Introduction

This chapter focuses on the legal value of African relational ontologies in reimagining sustainable development. The analysis focuses on the transformative facility of African environmental ethics as normative impulse for this legal reimagination. The central position advanced in this chapter is that the turn to marginalised sources of law and peripheralised knowledges in transforming international law can lead to a more effective system of operationalising sustainable development. This involves turning to Indigenous ways of knowing and living and the invaluable troves of knowledge they possess on planetary ecological integrity.

The analysis rejects the supposed supremacy of Western law. It welcomes African customary law as a valid normative order capable of reorienting sustainable development. I argue that sources of law are varied and derive from 'historical, sociological, economic, psychological, religious, ethical, political or logical' foundations.[1] My analysis appeals to sources within and outside law in search of an alternative paradigm for thinking about and doing sustainable development. This examination of multiple sources of law aligns with the urgent call by critical environmental and international law scholars that future studies must embrace a

* Klaus Bosselmann, 'Governing the Commons: Can States Be Trustees?' in Laura Westra, Janice Gray, and Antonio D'Aloia (eds.), *The Common Good and Ecological Integrity: Human Rights and the Support of Life* (Routledge 2016) 267, 269.

[1] Helen Silving, '"Customary Law": Continuity in Municipal and International Law' (1946) 31:4 Iowa L Rev 614, 614.

much wider theoretical and methodological framework that accommodates the different experiences that define law and the concept of sustainable development.[2]

However, my analysis is not limited to only African customary law. It draws on customary law and Indigenous legal cosmologies from both the Global North and Global South. For, after all, if the present challenges are increasingly global yet still very much localised, and if we are inclined to chip away at these present challenges even from a restricted geographical perspective, it is necessary to consult these sources of alternativeness for normative guidance that shine legal light on this less trodden path to an ecologically-attuned legal philosophy on sustainable development.[3] The discussion threads together seemingly discrete yarns of 'alternative ontologies, epistemologies, and methodologies' for a new vision of the interaction between law and nature.[4] This new vision, informed by eco-legal philosophies, is important in renewing sustainable development since African relational ontology spans norms including environmental ethics, norm pluralism, and anthropological approaches to law.[5]

6.2 African Environmentalisms: From Mythological Foundations to Legality

The concept of law across most societies is established upon a mythological foundation.[6] These mythological underpinnings equally extend to legal positivism.[7] With respect to this subject, Peter Fitzpatrick has argued that, H. L. A. Hart's concept of law is emblematic of the foundations of legal positivism erected upon a mythological basis as Hart's descriptive amalgam of primary and secondary rules was imaginary and thus simply an attempt to create legal positivism's own myth so as to clothe law within that fictional embodiment.[8]

[2] Lim, 'Pathways to Equitable Sustainability', 224.
[3] Carla Sbert, *The Lens of Ecological Law: A Look at Mining* (Edward Elgar 2020) 57.
[4] Bartel, 'Place-Thinking', 172.
[5] Chizoba Chinweze, Chukwuemeka Jideani, and Gwen Z. Abiola-Oloke, 'Traditional Norms and Environmental Law: The Sub-Saharan Africa' in Christina Voigt (ed.), *Rule of Law for Nature: New Dimensions and Ideas in Environmental Law* (Cambridge University Press 2013) 191.
[6] Lola Romanucci-Ross and Taurence Tancredi, *When Law and Medicine Meet: A Cultural View* (Springer 2008) 21.
[7] Gardner, 'Legal Positivism: 5½ Myths'.
[8] Peter Fitzpatrick, *The Mythology of Modern Law* (Routledge 1992) 193.

This mythological foundation of legal positivism was soon externalised from its origins in domestic law to international law. It also denounces ethical considerations in international law.[9] This mythological contextualisation exposes the artificial superiority of central legal Eurocentric concepts like sovereignty that are premised on myths, and how those myths underpin the history of the making of international law.[10] Thus, quite contrarily, legal positivism has a paradoxical link with the moral domain as positivists are unable to decouple law from moral considerations even if they do not openly acknowledge it.[11] On this score, legal positivists have failed to advance this so-called pure law argument since 'in the attempt at developing a "pure" conception of law, the legal technology distilled remains tributary of certain ontological conceptions'.[12]

African conceptions of environmentalisms are equally derived from a mythologised essence of law. This mythological infrastructure is integral to how Indigenous environmentalism interacts with law.[13] This is also true for international law as it is caught up in this mythological matrix, one that readily assures an uncritical (or unquestioned version of) international law.[14] And, through the instrumentality of the myth of law, other modes of power are equally sustained on the strength of their own myths.[15] For instance, the introduction of Eurocentric international law in the colonies was made possible because of the mythologised vehicles of the civilising mission and justification of empire which converged on the magisterial myth that non-Europeans had no law or, even if they did, such law was inferior to the law of Europe.[16]

9 Devika Hovell, 'The Elements of International Legal Positivism' (2022) 75:1 Current Leg Probs 71.

10 Pahuja, Decolonising International Law, 111; Yoriko Otomo, 'Her Proper Name: A Revisionist Account of International Law' (2014) 2:1 London Rev IL 149, 149; Simone Zurbuchen, 'Introduction' in Simone Zurbuchen (ed.), *The Law of Nations and Natural Law 1625 to 1800* (Brill 2019) 1. Zurbuchen calls this, 'the "myth" of Westphalia'.

11 Robert M. Cover, 'Foreword: Nomos and Narrative' (1983–1984) 97 Harvard L Rev 4, 23. Cover argues legal ideas, postulates, and rules are contingent upon normative constructions; and it is through these ideas, postulates, and rules that these normative worlds come to life. In a sense, a normative universe, *nomos*, is constituted by these ideas, postulates, and rules, and *vice versa*.

12 Viñuales, Organisation of the Anthropocene, 15–16.

13 Kirsten Manley-Casimir, 'Incommensurable Legal Cultures: Indigenous Legal Traditions and the Colonial Narrative' (2012) 30:2 Windsor YB Access Just 137, 138.

14 Carlo Focarelli, *International Law as a Social Construct: The Struggle for Global Justice* (Oxford University Press 2012) 50.

15 Azzedine Haddour, *History and Narrative* (Manchester University Press 2000).

16 Irene Watson, *Aboriginal Peoples, Colonialism and International Law: Raw Law* (Routledge 2015) 5–6; Abdulqawi A. Yusuf, *Pan-Africanism and International Law* (Brill 2014) 53.

On this subject, Eurocentrism diminishes Indigenous knowledge by peripheralising. Indigenous (non-Western) societies as being 'driven by irrational myths and remaining in a primitive "state of nature", in contrast with the modern nation-state as constructed by European culture'.[17] Contemporarily, international law also consolidated geological timescales and human histories in the myth of the Anthropocene, a concept that is interested in international law's progress and attention to human interference with planetary integrity.[18] Yet, when law's mythological knot is undone, myths from other disciplines, joined to law's own myth quickly unravel. This is true considering the Eurocentric view on nature is also a Western myth that is 'not independent of social action, politics or imagining'.[19] Consequently, it is important to be alive to how mythmaking in law is disingenuously welded to false narratives to justify questionable sources, foundations, and the supposed universality of law.[20]

Emerging from this mythological conditioning is the consciousness that the myth of law functions in a cyclical and contradictory manner. This challenging double-sidedness of law arises from its myth as the basis for either making or rejecting its very foundations.[21] For example, in thinking about the contemporary character of law, it seems law quickly drifts away from its mythological basis in search of more stable ground. At the same time, law conceals its frequent return to this mythological foundation for sustenance. To illustrate, international law's unspoken denial of its myth guarantees its contemporary stability, consistency, and legal validity.[22]

This understanding of law results in an overlooking or a deliberate glossing over its myth which is a constitutive technology for establishing law's contemporary influence. The intentional separation of law from its

Yusuf refers to this as the imposition of the '*ius publicum Europeaeum*' or the public law of Europe on Africa.

17 Khoday and Natarajan, 'Fairness and International Environmental Law', 425.

18 Justine Rose, Margaretha Wewerinke-Singh, and Jessica Miranda, 'Primal Scene to Anthropocene: Narrative and Myth in International Law' (2019) 66 Nethl Int'l L Rev 441, 444.

19 Linda H. Connor and Jonathan Paul Marshall, 'Ecologies, Ontologies and Mythologies of Possible Futures' in Linda H. Connor and Jonathan Paul Marshall (eds.), *Environmental Change and the World's Futures: Ecologies, Ontologies and Mythologies of Possible Futures* (Routledge 2016) 1, 5.

20 Fitzpatrick, *Mythology of Modern Law*, 193.

21 Costa, 'Myth of African Customary Law', 537–538.

22 David J. Bederman, *International Law in Antiquity* (Cambridge University Press 2001) 49.

myth is what assures legal normativity of its contrived consistency. This point is confirmed by Shane Chalmers that:

> The denial is what makes 'modernity' coherent: to identify modernity with mythology as a positive aspect of it, would be to contradict modernity's very being (as the ultimate overcoming of the mythological); and so, to secure modernity's coherence, any contradictory sign of myth within it is obliviated. In this way, by denying mythology any constitutive role, the identity of modernity as being opposed to mythology can remain intact.[23]

If law's own constitution is not inseparable from its social background, and if this social context is law's mythological origin; then law is, ultimately, myth. For instance, legal Eurocentrism uses convenient periodisations to demarcate and label different epochs for effective control.[24] Yet, periodisation can hide this mythological foundation. On these grounds, TWAIL and other critical approaches demand we strive to apprehend how the mythmaking underlying legal Eurocentrism deliberately eliminated Indigenous cosmologies and the distinctive normativity of customary law. These radical approaches invite us to query the reification of legal Eurocentrism's myths as superior legal impulse as seen in how it aligns itself with an outlook of scientific inquiry.[25] Through this complicated and paradoxical approach to lawmaking as myth, Indigenous cosmologies including ethics and customary law were effectively rejected for their presumed lack of (Eurocentric) scientificity. In this sense, they became part of the received (colonial) law only if these non-Western laws were rendered intelligible according to Eurocentric standards.

The denunciation of the mythological basis of one form of legal normativity (non-Western law) as illogical, then conveniently grounds the 'myth of rationality' for legal standardisation in accordance with Eurocentric law.[26] However, the myth of rationality was, itself, a contrived European technology that was exported beyond Europe to galvanise the political stability of the colonial project (through law).[27] Beyond the older historical interests in law's mythmaking, contemporary examples of mythmaking are seen in international law responses as

[23] Shane Chalmers, 'The Mythology of International Rule-of-Law Promotion' (2019) 44:4 L and Soc Inquiry 957, 961–962.

[24] Tatiana Cardoso Squeff, 'Overcoming the "Coloniality of Doing" in International Law: Soft Law as a Decolonial Tool' (2021) 17:2 Revista Direito GV 1, 3.

[25] Khoday and Natarajan, 'Fairness and International Environmental Law', 207.

[26] Focarelli, *International Law as a Social Construct*, 50.

[27] Alison Fischer, 'Colonialism, Context and Critical Thinking: First Steps towards Decolonising the Dutch Legal Curriculum' (2022) 18:1 Utrecht L Rev 18.

observed in the aftermath of the September 2001 terrorist attacks on the United States and similar actions were predicated on the 'myth of newness' that these *novel* situations require international action.[28]

A critical examination of the *longue durée* of mythmaking in law helpfully points in the direction of why customary law has been ineffective in its juridical application. It also confirms why the idea of ethics as law is also relentlessly interrogated by positivist apologists who consistently call for its normative exclusion.[29] Drawing on this awareness of the myth of law, it is important to welcome the opportunity to reread the mythological power of law as inherently plural where there is more than just one myth of law. This is necessary in order to remake the concept of law and deploy it in new situations.

This renewed sense of the myth of law, therefore, accords with the vision and aspirations of the Global South to infuse ethics and other non-Western legal cosmologies into the law on sustainable development. This renewing of environmental governance through the infusion of environmental ethics is being acknowledged across different jurisdictions.[30] Still, the mythologising effect of law is a captivating force and critical scholars might risk being pushed into reconceptualising laws relating to nature and the environment only to fit similar restrictive Eurocentric legal categories that subordinated nature.[31] After all, mythmaking is integral to the making of international environmental law based on the presumption that human progress was measured by the ideological and physical distancing between humans and nature.

In this respect, TWAIL scholars like Kishan Khoday have argued that international law is a product of mythmaking; and, as such, the myths underlying international law can be challenged by myths from other (including non-Western) legal systems in reimagining sustainable development from a pluriversal perspective.[32] Even so, in using myth as means

[28] Okafor, 'Newness, Imperialism, and International Legal Reform', 183.

[29] Jedidiah Purdy, 'Our Place in the World: A New Relationship for Environmental Ethics and Law' (2013) 62:4 Duke LJ 857, 861–862.

[30] Chunlin Li and Jianqing Chen, 'The Ethical Turn of the Rule of Law in the Global Environment under the Influence of the Concept of a Community of Shared Future for Mankind' (2019) 10:1 Beijing L Rev 98.

[31] Khoday and Natarajan, 'Fairness and International Environmental Law'.

[32] Khoday, 'Mythic Environment', 293–294; Roger S. Gottlieb, *A Greener Faith: Religious Environmentalism and Our Planet's Future* (Oxford University Press 2006) 123; Mónica García-Salmones Rovira, *The Project of Positivism in International Law* (Cambridge University Press 2013). Rovira's excellent account of the idea of mythmaking in law

and method for rethinking the making of law, I am fortified in this position that the sources of law are varied – emanating from 'historical, sociological, economic, psychological, religious, ethical, political or logical' foundations – and the normativity of law cannot simply be joined to a unique set of (Eurocentric) facts or a particular (Eurocentric) legal imaginary.[33]

6.3 In Search of a Higher Norm: African Environmental Ethics as Law

This ethical turn as law in respect of the concept of sustainable development must reflect an expansive continuum of the expression of law.[34] This ethics-as-myth proposition resonates with the view that the mythology of law facilitates the assurance of rationality amidst conflicting domains and systems of law.[35] Law's claim to internal coherence thus emerges from the intersection of its meaning and its operationalisation.[36]

It is in search of this internal coherence that, even in Indigenous societies, law's underlying myth is traceable to a higher order, founded on ethical principles and beliefs.[37] In this case, the mythological premise of African legal conceptions is founded on religio-cultural beliefs and precepts.[38] Religion and culture are the principal normative orders and organising principles for social relations in most Indigenous societies.[39]

demonstrates how economic considerations were both disguised and advanced in international law through the instrumentality of international legal positivism.

33 Silving, '"Customary Law"', 614; Anna Grear, 'Legal Imaginaries and the Anthropocene: "Of" and "For"' (2020) 31:3 L and Critique 1.

34 Massimiliano Montini and Francesca Volpe, 'Sustainable Development: Renaissance or Sunset Boulevard?' in Laura Westra, Janice Gray, and Franz-Theo Gottwald (eds.), *The Role of Integrity in the Governance of the Commons: Governance, Ecology, Law, Ethics* (Springer 2017) 169. Montini and Volpe argue sustainable development's 'inherent ethical dimension' has been relatively underexplored in the literature. This point is key to the central arguments in this book.

35 Fitzpatrick, *Mythology of Modern Law*, 2.

36 Manley-Casimir, 'Incommensurable Legal Cultures', 147.

37 Ocran, 'Clash of Legal Cultures', 466–468.

38 Fatou K. Camara, 'From Contemporary African Customary Laws to Indigenous African Law: Identifying African Human Rights and Good Governance Sensitive Principles as a Tool to Promote Meaningful Socio-Legal Reforms' in Jeanmarie Fenrich, Paolo Galizzi, and Tracy E. Higgins (eds.), *The Future of African Customary Law* (Cambridge University Press 2011) 494, 507.

39 M. Stuart Madden, 'Myth, Folklore, and Ancient Ethics' (2006) 37:1 Cumb L Rev 43, 45. This is not an attempt at an extensive discussion of the role of religion in the making of

In many African societies, religious beliefs govern the society–nature interface through the imposition of taboos and other sociocultural proscriptions as a collectivised restriction on the exercise of individual will.[40] It is from these religious and cultural principles that ethico-legal precepts arise and are derived for Indigenous legal cosmologies. In this respect, African environmental ethics are constructed around 'cultural belief systems via norms, myths, taboos, totems and closed seasons'.[41] Correlatively, legal meaning then emerges from the conscious commitment to mainstream these ethico-legal precepts into law. The search for meaning is then tied to a norm's capacity to tell a story that situates that norm in its social narrative.[42] As Kirsten Manley-Casimir puts it, law's normative justification is discoverable from its historicity.[43] Accordingly, the purpose and mission of law emerges from its mythological quintessence, the *raison d'être* behind its binding character.[44]

Law's religious base also transcends national frontiers, extending even into the international arena as religion is integral to international law.[45] David Bederman, speaking about the connection between religion and international law, argues this nexus reaches back into time as he describes the contemporary conceptual separation of law from its religious impulse as an imaginative design to centre law as 'distinctively rational'.[46] On this subject, religion assumes a central role as a constitutive force in international law-making, including in the environmental sphere.[47] Since

(international) law. My interest is simply to demonstrate the extent to which the normative power and interests of religion are manifest through the myth of law-making.

40 LoriKim Alexander, Andrews Agyekumhene, and Phil Allman, 'The Role of Taboos in the Protection of and Recovery of Sea Turtles' (2017) 4 Frontiers in Marine Science 1, 2.

41 Maryam Bayero-Jimoh, 'Traditional Beliefs and Legal Frameworks on Environmental Protection in Accessing Clean Water in Nigeria' in M. Christian Green and Muhammed Haron (eds.), *Law, Religion and the Environment in Africa* (African Sun Media 2020) 81, 93.

42 Cover, 'Supreme Court Term', 4–5.

43 Manley-Casimir, 'Incommensurable Legal Cultures', 147.

44 Focarelli, *International Law as a Social Construct*, 50.

45 Oscar Schachter, 'The Emergence of International Environmental Law' (1991) 44:2 J Int'l Aff 457, 466.

46 Bederman, *International Law in Antiquity*, 49.

47 Gillespie, *International Environmental Law, Policy and Ethics*, 51–67. Gillespie admonishes legal scholars to be wary of religion as it serves both good and bad ends. Nisbert Taringa, 'How Environmental Is African Traditional Religion?' (2006) 39:2 Exchange 191, 192. Taringa makes the point even more forcefully by noting that romanticising the role of religion in environmental consciousness is to erroneously assume 'an eco-golden age existed at some point in the past'.

international law is underpinned by ethical and religious interests that retain significance in international law's constitution, ethico-legal principles can be mainstreamed into international law for the benefit of sustainable development.[48]

These moral considerations play an active role in reshaping prevailing perspectives on the interrelations between humans and non-human entities through 'a non-dualistic paradigm'.[49] In this respect, African traditional religious beliefs proceed on the understanding that humans and non-human domains are conceptually bound together.[50] Viewed this way, African Indigenous jurisprudence perceived environmental destruction as an abomination of a high order, with serious personal and community repercussions.[51] Several examples abound across Africa. For instance, the Maasai of Kenya hold religious beliefs that operated as customary legal prescriptions which were central to human–nature harmony with the overriding objective of protecting and conserving the environment.[52] The Indigenous religious beliefs of the Shona peoples of Southern Africa were based on similar ideas of relational obligations between society and nature where human duties toward the environment were guided by sacred values.[53] In Nigeria, the 'religious and metaphysical orientation' of the Yoruba people placed nature at the heart of social relations and imposed significant obligations on communities to protect and conserve nature not only for humans, but for the non-human world, and for harmonious co-existence with deities.[54]

In this respect, environmental destruction in African legal thought was not simply an individuated customary violation. It was an 'abomination

[48] Mashood A Baderin, 'Religion and International Law: Friends or Foes?' (2009) 5 European HRL Rev 637, 647.

[49] Prue Taylor, *An Ecological Approach to International Law: Responding to the Challenges of Climate Change* (Routledge 2008) 34.

[50] Taringa, 'How Environmental Is African Traditional Religion?', 191.

[51] C. V. O. Eneji, 'Traditional African Religion in Natural Resources in Conservation and Management in Cross River State, Nigeria' (2012) 2:4 Envt and Nat Res Research 45, 47.

[52] G. Nasieku Tarayia, 'The Legal Perspectives of the Maasai Culture, Customs, and Traditions' (2004) 21:1 Ariz J Int'l and Comp L 183, 188.

[53] Vincent Mabvurira, George Alex Muchinako, and Elisabeth Ivy Smit, 'Shona Traditional Religion and Sustainable Environmental Management: An Afrocentric Perspective' (2021) 11:3 Afr J Soc Work 111.

[54] Ademola Kazeem Fayemi, 'African Environmental Ethics and the Poverty of Eco-Activism in Nigeria: A Hermeneutico-Reconstructionist Appraisal' (2016) 48 Matatu 363, 376.

or a breaking of a cosmic law (not mere social law)'.[55] Emerging from this awareness, African relational ontologies joined together both 'physical and spiritual worlds' for the wellbeing of the environment.[56] The ethical foundation of this African Indigenous environmental legality rests on the synthesis of human, non-human, and metaphysical domains variously described as African holism,[57] relational interdependence,[58] relationality,[59] eco-communitarianism,[60] or bio-eco-communitarianism.[61] In practical terms, these systems ensure a more comprehensive outlook of the interaction between the environment and Indigenous cosmologies, and along with it, the view that the environment 'should not be limited to the non-human natural environment, but should be defined broadly to specifically include the interrelationships between humans and the natural environment'.[62]

This ethics turn in environmental law therefore arises from the consciousness that contemporary reality requires a paradigm shift in the present approach to sustainable development.[63] Admittedly, revitalising African environmental ethics as law requires addressing historical challenges. Notably, Eurocentric environmental stewardship has historically challenged African Indigenous knowledge systems as lacking 'environmental

[55] Esi Sutherland-Addy, 'The Metaphysics and Politics of Gender in the Arts of Africa' in Helen Lauer and Kofi Anyidoho (eds.), *Reclaiming the Human Sciences and Humanities through African Perspectives* (Sub-Saharan Publishers 2012) 1311, 1314.

[56] Bednicho Nyoni, *Abundant Life and Basic Needs: African Religions as a Resource for Sustainable Development, with Special Reference to Shona Religion* (University of Bamberg Press 2017) 141.

[57] Kevin Behrens, 'Exploring African Holism in Respect of the Environment' (2010) 19:4 Envt'l Val 465.

[58] Kevin Behrens, 'African Relational Environmentalism and Considerability' (2014) 36:1 Envt'l Ethics 63.

[59] Hannis and Sullivan, 'Relationality, Reciprocity, and Flourishing', 289.

[60] Godfred B. Tangwa, 'Some African Reflections on Biomedical and Environmental Ethics' in Kwasi Wiredu (ed.), *A Companion to African Philosophy* (Blackwell 2004) 387, 389; Marilyn Matevia, 'Justice for All: Revisiting the Prospects for a Biocommunitarian Theory of Interspecies Justice' (2016) 19:3 J Int'l Wildlife L and Pol'y 189, 195.

[61] Ike Valentine Iyioke, 'Bioethics via Africology' in Shahul Hameed, Siham El-Kafafi, and Rawiri Waretini-Karena (eds.), *Handbook on Indigenous Knowledge and Bi-Culturalism in a Global Context* (IGI Global 2019) 21, 30.

[62] Loretta Feris, 'Protecting Traditional Knowledge in Africa: Considering African Approaches' (2004) 4 Afr Human Rights LJ 242, 254.

[63] P. A. Ojomo, 'Environmental Ethics: An African Understanding' (2011) 5:8 Afr J Envt'l Science and Tech 572, 578.

dimensions'.[64] In this light, the effort to transform international law's relationship with sustainable development must address this false narrative. But, my interest in African environmental ethics as law is not unusual as other scholars too are turning to ethics to illuminate international environmental law.[65] This understanding of the place of ethics is important to the future of international law as it highlights 'moral obligations' to posterity in respect of valuing nature for humans and non-human entities alike.[66]

In search of, and in respect of the application of environmental ethics to sustainable development, the intention is not to homogenise Africa as I am cognisant of the different religio-cultural divisions and other social distinctions across the continent.[67] Nonetheless, a common thread of environmental legal philosophy unites these multiple dimensions of African environmental ethics into a harmonised whole. This is made possible by drawing on the commonalities underlying these different cosmovisions by resisting the Eurocentrism of environmentalism and embracing a relational cosmology on the interrelations of the human and non-human.[68] Accordingly, I find Workineh Kelbessa's prodigious assertion to be a useful compass for navigating possible accusations of essentialising Africa and eliding differences in African worldviews. As he forcefully puts it:

> I [Kelbessa] do not claim that all Africans have one homogenous environmental ethics. There is no single African worldview because Africa has diverse societies that have different cultural values. However, there are common values and themes shared by African societies. So, by 'African environmental ethics' I [Kelbessa] am referring to the underlying common or shared environmental value of African societies.[69]

Kelbessa's harmonised African environmental philosophy resonates with the argument of TWAIL scholar Obiora Okafor that Third World thought

[64] Workineh Kelbessa, 'African Environmental Ethics, Indigenous Knowledge, and Environmental Challenges' (2015) 37:4 Envt'l Ethics 387, 387.

[65] Kevin Behrens, 'Moral Obligations towards Future Generations in African Thought' (2012) 8:2–3 J Global Ethics 179, 179; Elsabé Boshoff, 'Rethinking the Premises Underlying the Right to Development in African Human Rights Jurisprudence' (2022) 31:1 RECIEL 27.

[66] Jonathan O. Chimakonam, 'Introduction' in Jonathan O. Chimakonam (ed.), *African Philosophy and Environmental Conservation* (Routledge 2017) 1, 2.

[67] Tieku and Gelot, 'African Perspective on Global Governance', 119–120.

[68] Workineh Kelbessa, 'Environmental Philosophy in African Traditions of Thought' (2018) 40:4 Envt'l Ethics 309, 323.

[69] Kelbessa, 'African Environmental Ethics', 389.

and praxis are based on the commonality of experience rather than uniformity.[70] What is remarkable in thinking on African environmental ethics as commonality of experience is that it pushes for the establishment of an 'African metaphysico-religious and moral outlook regarding nature' built upon an Afrocentric consciousness.[71]

In this sense, a turn to African environmental ethics must not be conceived as novelty but seen as a turn to a relational ontology that was interrupted through the legal violence of the colonial intervention.[72] In this respect, I recognise that, environmental ethics is both ancient and contemporary as it is rooted in African Indigenous societies although known by different designations.[73] Its origin lies in its antiquity while remaining relevant for contemporary action. Its distinctions must therefore pose no challenges to its deployment. Still, it is necessary to situate its African distinctiveness within a pluriversal Indigenous context of multiple iterations of this legal normativity that elaborates on the ontological turn.

These cosmovisions reflect 'a deeply relational understanding of life' among peoples of the Global South and Indigenous peoples in the Global North.[74] But then, considering African environmental ethics are not standardised across the continent, it is necessary to approach ethics as 'a diversified discourse with competing different ideas and perspectives'.[75] Accordingly, while I am interested in African environmental ethics to the extent that it aspires to, and concomitantly advocates a shared African environmental-ethical commitment, I am not encouraging a single (or a unified) African worldview.[76] Rather, I find that the transformative power of environmental ethics for environmental law and international law is useful in reimagining sustainable development

[70] Okafor, 'Newness, Imperialism, and International Legal Reform', 175–176.

[71] Tosam, 'African Environmental Ethics', 173.

[72] Kameri-Mbote and Cullet, 'Law, Colonialism', 24; Domínguez and Luoma, 'Decolonising Conservation Policy', 73.

[73] Workineh Kelbessa, 'Indigenous Environmental Philosophy' in Jay L. Garfield and William Edelglass (eds.), *Oxford Handbook of World Philosophy* (Oxford University Press 2010) 574, 578. Kelbessa argues that, in Oromia (present-day Ethiopia), it is called *saffuu*, which translates to mean an ethical value that governs the interrelations between 'creator and the created, generations, families, human beings and nonhuman beings, and so on. *Saffuu* governs natural resources.'

[74] Escobar, 'Thinking–Feeling with the Earth', 22–23.

[75] Ojomo, 'Environmental Ethics', 573.

[76] Behrens, 'African Relational Environmentalism and Considerability', 90.

considering environmental ethics is present across and central to African societies.[77]

The case for environmental ethics as law is then grounded on eco-legal philosophies.[78] Eco-legal philosophies are also present and relevant in other parts of the world beyond Africa. It is called *buen vivir* in Latin America with different iterations (across several Indigenous tribes) which translates to mean living a good life of harmony between society and nature.[79] The central logic of this Andean ontology of *buen vivir* is the search for alternatives to the Eurocentric vision of sustainable development.[80]

There are ontological equivalents to *buen vivir*'s in African eco-legal philosophies. A notable expression is the Indigenous value system across Southern Africa called *ubuntu. Ubuntu* is erected upon a 'multifaceted philosophical system that involves logic, metaphysics, epistemology and ethics'.[81] *Ubuntu*'s predominant theme, 'I am because you are', therefore, distinguishes its communitarian ethos which subordinates the human will and preeminence of the individual to their membership in society.[82]

77 Zoe Makoul, 'Environmental Ethics and Environmental Law: A Virtuous Circle' (2022) 47:1 Colum J of Envt'l L 68.

78 Aïda C. Terblanché-Greeff, 'Ubuntu and Environmental Ethics: What the West Can Learn from Africa When Faced with Climate Change' in Munamato Chemhuru (ed.), *African Environmental Ethics: A Critical Reader* (Springer 2019) 91, 95.

79 Cara Victoria Sawyer, 'The Indigenous Alternative: TEK, IEL and Solutions for the Unsolvable' (2022) 18:1 Loyola U Chicago Int'l L Rev 113, 129.

80 Natasha Chassagne, *Buen Vivir as an Alternative to Sustainable Development: Lessons from Ecuador* (Routledge 2021).

81 Munyaradzi Mawere, *Environmental Conservation through Ubuntu and Other Emerging Perspectives* (Langaa Research & Publishing CIG 2014) 83. Mawere argues *ubuntu* takes its root from the Bantu language; but it is also used by Xhosa and Zulu people as well. Overall, its general appeal across African scholarship emanates from its relatability and relational ontological cosmologies.

82 Uchenna Okeja, 'Justification of Moral Norms in African Philosophy' in Eugene Etieyibo (ed.), *Method, Substance and the Future of African Philosophy* (Palgrave MacMillan 2018) 209, 217. Okeja argues *ubuntu* means 'the community is a site of human existence and is hence ontologically prior to the individual'; Robin Attfield, *The Ethics of the Global Environment*, 2nd ed. (Edinburgh University Press 2015) 29–30. Attfield makes a significant point about how we ought to go about engaging with the idea of communitarianism. His caution is that we must not assume; naively, that communitarianism, by itself, is a panacea since communitarianism may overshadow the place of individual will. He contends, therefore, that, 'communitarianism begins with a creditable belief in the value of community, and with the defensible premise that moralities mostly arise from, and are learned within, communities. Sometimes it simply comprises "a form of social criticism that is aimed at the disappearance of community in modern society". But it usually proceeds to the dubious conclusions that all moral rights and obligations depend on relationships, and that where

While *ubuntu* is analogous to Western humanism, the two are different; the former underscores relational interconnectedness while the latter emphasises individualism.[83] Based on this relationality, *ubuntu* crystallises as 'cultural commons and ecological intelligence' and advocates harmony between humans and the non-human world.[84] More importantly, it encompasses 'the relationship between humanity and the natural environment' where this version of eco-legal philosophies critiques the foundations of the Western model of development and its resulting impacts on Africa's environment.[85]

An ontological viewpoint similar to *ubuntu* is *ukama*.[86] But, there is a distinction between these two cosmovisions as *ubuntu* seems to emerge from an anthropocentric stance of humanness while *ukama* is premised on a direct relationality amongst humans, non-human entities, animals, deities, and the environment.[87] The dividing line between these two views is that, unlike *ubuntu*, which focuses on human connectedness, *ukama* contends personhood is not realisable only through human connectedness, but also through nature.[88] *Ubuntu* suffers from this comparison as it refracts an embedded anthropocentric value system that is not readily discoverable and may lead to invalid generalisations as well as a misreading of the incidence of *ubuntu* as generally applicable across Africa.[89] This critique reveals how some scholars on Africa as a

there are no ties of community there are no moral obligations, nor moral motivations either. Sometimes it is held, partly for these reasons, that whatever is locally accepted is right, and should be recognised as such.' Nonetheless, communitarianism is an important social ideal that unites both human and non-human into a composite whole.

83 Symphorien Ntibagirira, 'Ubuntu as a Metaphysical Concept' (2018) 52:1 J Val Inquiry 113, 124.

84 Overson Shumba, 'Commons Thinking, Ecological Intelligence and the Ethical and Moral Framework of *Ubuntu*: An Imperative for Sustainable Development' (2011) 3:3 J Media and Comm Studies 84, 85.

85 Kelbessa, 'Indigenous Environmental Philosophy', 578; Boshoff, 'Rethinking the Premises', 35.

86 Kundai V. Chirindo, 'Bantu Sociolinguistics in Wangari Maathai's Peacebuilding Rhetoric' in Eddah M. Mutua, Alberto González, and Anke Wolbert (eds.), *The Rhetorical Legacy of Wangari Maathai* (Lexington 2018) 1, 18–20.

87 Kai Horsthemke, 'Animals and African Ethics' (2017) 7:2 J Animal Ethics 119, 120.

88 Kai Horsthemke, 'Animal Rights and Environmental Ethics in Africa: From Anthropocentrism to Non-speciesism?' in Munamato Chemhuru (ed.), *African Environmental Ethics: A Critical Reader* (Springer 2019) 239, 243.

89 Ephraim Taurai Gwaravanda, 'Ubuntu Environmental Ethics: Conceptions and Misconceptions' in Munamato Chemhuru (ed.), *African Environmental Ethics: A Critical Reader* (Springer 2019) 79, 81.

knowledge phenomenon, in their quest to challenge the ethical foundations of Western environmentalism, might uncritically essentialising African environmental ethics that may impede inadvertently ecological aspirations.[90] In this respect, the inherent danger is placing African environmental ethics under a single rubric, and in the process risking reinscribing the coloniality of 'language hegemony and imperialism' in the realm of ethics.[91]

Nonetheless, the ethical core of eco-legal philosophies like *ubuntu* and *ukama* is present across Africa as they speak broadly to the commonality of experience and similar issues.[92] Even where differences arise across these strands of African environmental ethics, these differences and their ethical foundations are no more remarkable than their convergence on the shared theme of African eco-communitarianism.[93] Here, eco-communitarianism is reflected upon as 'holistic and synergistic in its ontological orientation'.[94] Here, African eco-communitarianism reconciles the human to non-human in a mutual relatedness that denounces human dominance over the non-human domain.[95] It also confronts the misalignment between society and nature which threatens ecological integrity; the challenge that must be overcome for sustainable development to achieve its objective.[96] Therefore, reference to *ubuntu* is only used *broadly* to signify the collective African ethos on the eco-legal philosophy that should direct the renewal of sustainable development.

[90] Okafor, '"Righting," Restructuring, and Rejuvenating', 50; James Thuo Gathii, 'A Critical Appraisal of the International Legal Tradition of Taslim Olawale Elias' (2008) 21:2 Leiden JIL 317, 325.

[91] Gwaravanda, 'Ubuntu Environmental Ethics', 84.

[92] Kelbessa, 'Indigenous Environmental Philosophy', 577.

[93] Munamato Chemhuru, 'Interpreting Ecofeminist Environmentalism in African Communitarian Philosophy and *Ubuntu*: An Alternative to Anthropocentrism' (2019) 48:2 Phil Papers 241, 257–258.

[94] Bruce Jennings, 'Governing Ecological Governance in the Anthropocene: A New Covenant of Eco-Communitarianism' in Peter Burdon, Klaus Bosselmann, and Kirsten Engel (eds.), *The Crisis in Global Ethics and the Future of Global Governance: Fulfilling the Promise of the Earth Charter* (Edward Elgar 2019) 126, 138.

[95] Ngozi Finette Unuigbe, 'African Eco-Philosophy and Its Implications for Ecological Integrity in Africa' in Laura Westra, Klaus Bosselmann, and Matteo Fermeglia (eds.), *Ecological Integrity in Science and Law* (Springer 2020) 99, 108.

[96] Patrick Giddy, 'Environmental Ethics in the Context of African Traditional Thought: Beyond the Impasse' in Munamato Chemhuru (ed.), *African Environmental Ethics: A Critical Reader* (Springer 2019) 47, 47.

The promise held by the ethics turn is thus grounded in the moral idea that rational choice is informed by considerations other than law.[97] In this context, the broad conception of environmental ethics as environmental law's myth unites the complementary (yet varied) aspects of this legal pluriverse into a consistent and adaptable normativity by realigning 'law's contradictory existences into a patterned coherence'.[98] As a normative principle and emerging from 'a deontological point of view, African communal ethics considers nature or the environment, human and harmonious communal relationships as part of the holistic community as ends in themselves which should be respected for its own sake'.[99] This epistemological excavation of the community of interests between human and non-human worlds unearths a latent moral concern with legal significance that can impel a turn to an African eco-legal philosophy.[100] The ethics-as-law turn thus delegitimises human flourishing as the foremost objective of our planetary existence and refocuses instead on our human obligations to the rest of the world as a necessary alternative to ensuring ecological integrity becomes the organising ambition of the law on sustainable development.[101]

6.4 African Environmental Ethics: What about It Is International?

This turn to environmental ethics merges into the wider use of African legal theory as a framework for analysing international legal phenomena. Since the dawn of decolonisation, Africa has played a key role in influencing international law. Operating under the banner of Pan-Africanism, African states have long challenged and resisted oppressive international legal principles, reforming and proposing new principles in this process.[102] The principal concern had been that international law hardly ever took Africa seriously or barely gave serious consideration to African

[97] Joseph Nkang Ogar and Samuel Akpan Bassey, 'African Environmental Ethics' (2019) 3:1 RAIS J Soc Sciences 71, 75.

[98] Fitzpatrick, *Mythology of Modern Law*, 2.

[99] Polycarp Ikuenobe, 'African Communal Ethics' in Nimi Wariboko and Toyin Falola (eds.), *Palgrave Handbook of African Social Ethics* (Palgrave MacMillan 2020) 129, 142.

[100] Frans Kruger, Adré le Roux and Kevin Teise, 'Ecojustice Education and Communitarianism: Exploring the Possibility for Eco-communitarianism' (2020) 52:2 Educ Phil and Theory 206, 214.

[101] Jennings, 'Governing Ecological Governance', 128.

[102] Yusuf, *Pan-Africanism and International Law*, 125.

legal principles.[103] As Babatunde Fagbayibo recently pointed out, 'Africa as both an idea and reality is centred in this engagement, and thus provides the prism through which the different aspects of international law are contested, reappraised and realigned'.[104]

Ethics can play a significant role in this process including the reappraisal of sustainable development. It plays a major role in customary law, and as customary law is acknowledged across several jurisdictions, environmental ethics within customary law is equally applicable in international law.[105] In this respect, recourse to African legal thought is useful in resisting the uncritical dimensions of international law, but it is also important in grounding African perspectives that advance the discipline.[106] Therefore, the revivalist effort in reimagining sustainable development through the lens of the eco-communitarian ontology of African environmental ethics is globally relevant since it reflects a collectivist concern for the planetary crisis.[107]

In extending the boundaries of environmental ethics in international law, it is important to highlight the Afrocentric (mythological) orientation that law is embedded with. Here, ethico-legal obligations must take centre-stage.[108] It is in this sense that the current over-reliance on state-centred law is misconceived; thus, must be cut back. In doing so, it is important to advance the point that it is possible for international law and ethical principles to form a mutually beneficial alliance to advance sustainable development.[109]

In relating the value of ethics to this analysis, recent developments across Africa cite *ubuntu* as representing a bundle of ethical values and principles that promote harmonious living between society and nature.

[103] Ibrahim J. Gassama, 'International Law, Colonialism, and the African' in Martin S. Shanguhyia and Toyin Falola (eds.), *The Palgrave Handbook of African Colonial and Postcolonial History* (Palgrave MacMillan 2018) 551.

[104] Babatunde Fagbayibo, 'Some Thoughts on Centring Pan-African Epistemic in the Teaching of Public International Law in African Universities' (2019) 21:2 Int'l Community L Rev 170, 185.

[105] Rhett B. Larson, 'Water, Worship, and Wisdom: Indigenous Traditional Ecological Knowledge and the Human Right to Water' (2012) 19:1 ILSA J Int'l and Comp L 43, 65.

[106] Onazi, 'Introduction', 2.

[107] Edwin Etieyibo, 'Ubuntu and the Environment' in Adeshina Afolayan and Toyin Falola (eds.), *The Palgrave Handbook of African Philosophy* (Palgrave MacMillan 2017) 633, 637.

[108] Dan Kuwali, 'Decoding Afrocentrism: Decolonising Legal Theory' in Oche Onazi (ed.), *African Legal Theory and Contemporary Problems: Critical Essays* (Springer 2014) 71, 73.

[109] Charlotte E. Blattner, *Protecting Animals within and across Borders: Extraterritorial Jurisdiction and the Challenges of Globalisation* (Oxford University Press 2019) 403–404.

Ubuntu demonstrates an awareness of the transformative potential of relational ontologies being mainstreamed into the legal interpretive framework and judicially-enforced network of constitutionally guaranteed environmental rights in a way that makes international law domestically relevant.[110]

On this subject, African states are exploring a return to the interconnection across ethics, law, and the environment. We see this happening in jurisdictions like Ghana where its Environmental Protection Agency has established an administrative platform for 'elder conservationists, artisanal salt producers and local fishermen to merge their customary observances with formal regulations, to modernise district-level policy'.[111] Similar efforts are underway in Nigeria where its national environmental policy requires an integration of customary environmental norms into so-called scientific (Western) approaches.[112] Another example is Benin, where it passed the national Sacred Forest Law, Interministerial Order of 2012 (No. 121) which has conferred legal subjecthood on sacred forests and empowered traditional priests and chiefs to govern these forests.[113] Again, Uganda's national law provides for customary environmental laws to interact with statutory law in a manner similar to Ghana's approach whereby 'pluri-legal systems comprising state and customary law can be implemented at district level'.[114]

[110] Louis J. Kotzé, 'Human Rights, the Environment, and the Global South' in Shawkat Alam, Sumudu Atapattu, Carmen G. Gonzalez and Jona Razzaque (eds.), *International Environmental Law and the Global South* (Cambridge University Press 2015) 171, 181; Louis J. Kotzé and Sam Adelman, 'Environmental Law and the Unsustainability of Sustainable Development: A Tale of Disenchantment and Hope' (2023) 34:2 L and Critique 227.

[111] Helen Lauer, 'Beyond the Labour Market: Reinforcing the Epistemic Advantage of African Universities in the Global Knowledge Society' in Helen Yitah and Helen Lauer (eds.), *Philosophical Foundations of the African Humanities through Postcolonial Perspectives* (Brill, 2019) 45, 63–64.

[112] Ngozi Finette Unuigbe, 'The Significance of the Stewardship Ethic of the Indigenous Peoples of Nigeria's Niger Delta Region on Biodiversity Conservation' in Cameron La Follette and Chris Maser (eds.), *Sustainability and the Rights of Nature in Practice* (CRC Press 2020) 167, 181.

[113] Dancer, 'Harmony with Nature', 33–34. This law retains its anthropocentric outlook despite being hailed as a major jurisprudential change in its integration of the 'cosmovisions of the forest peoples'. This concern suggests that the turn to customary law might not be enough in and of itself. Rather, a turn to customary law only marks the beginning of a long process in reordering and reorganising human inter-relations with nature, towards the ultimate objective of centring ecological integrity as law's normative impulse.

[114] Bakulumpagi, 'Resolution of the African Commission', 319.

These radical changes are at a nascent stage. Nevertheless, they demonstrate rethinking of sustainable development and its interaction with international law lies in reformulations and reinterpretations of environmental law that are broad enough to bring back these neglected ways of knowing and living. Even more, while these pluralist normative interactions occur within the restricted spaces of national jurisdictions, it is possible to externalise this interface. With growing calls for global action on the environment and a corollary interest in recognising Indigenous systems of law and governance, it is time to recentre eco-legal philosophies in international law.

Perhaps international law might learn from transnational environmental law on how to mainstream eco-legal philosophies into sustainable development. Transnational environmental law scholarship has been actively engaging with Indigenous legal ontologies in current efforts aimed at remaking environmental law and sustainability.[115] Kaarlo Tuori confirms the significance of transnational law within plural legal ontologies by noting that 'the most advanced type of legal pluralism – pluralism of legal systems – is intimately linked with the rise of transnational law'.[116] This invitation to borrow across legal domains to effect legal transplants remains a cautious one to be undertaken solely for the purpose of contributing to 'interdisciplinary governance'.[117] However, owing to the non-linear character of environmental problems, (international) environmental law offers a unique platform for regulation beyond the narrow focus of state-centric law.[118] Here, some intrepid legal scholars contend that international law is already endowed with the capacity to adapt to a new 'ethic based on respect and care

[115] Erin O'Donnell, Anne Poelina, Alessandro Pelizzon and Cristy Clark, 'Stop Burying the Lede: The Essential Role of Indigenous Law(s) in Creating Rights of Nature' (2020) 9:3 Transnat'l Envt'l L 403.

[116] Tuori, 'Transnational Law', 26.

[117] Merry, 'Legal Pluralism', 882; Peer Zumbansen, '*Lochner* Disembedded: The Anxieties of Law in a Global Context' (2013) 20:1 Ind J Global Leg Studies 29, 58; Yugank Goyal, '"Death of a Discipline": Locating Heterodoxy in Law' (2014) 56:4 J Indian L Institute 493, 512. Goyal cautions TWAIL's network of scholars to resist the tendency to use the 'same frames it criticises'. Building on this insight, I am wary of using the expression 'legal transplant' and instead employ 'legal borrowing' since the idea of legal transplant connotes a sense of compulsion. As Goyal reminds us, 'Western literature has a fascination for everything non-European as sources of institutional transplant and renewal'.

[118] Veerle Heyvaert, 'The Transnationalisation of Law: Rethinking Law through Environmental Regulation' (2017) 6:2 Transnat'l Envt'l L 205, 206.

for one another and the Earth'.[119] This intermingling of international law and Indigenous law is now prevalent in natural resource agreements of transnational character.[120] Thus, linking this transformation in the private arena to the broader interest of elevating customary law norms in international law supports the reversal of 'the silence surrounding the place of Indigenous law in accounts of global environmental law processes'.[121]

Accordingly, the relevance of environmental ethics to international law pivots around the idea that the planetary commons is one giant ecological universe consisting of variously connected (human and non-human) components.[122] Conceptualised this way, international law highlights the value of ethical reflection on common (global) environmental problems.[123] This conceptualisation of the planet as a network of ecological communities marks a significant improvement over the limited classical orientation of sustainable development as involving only 'responsibilities among groups of human beings: developed versus developing and present versus future'.[124] This broad approach permits pluralist conceptions of law, including ethical values, to confront sustainable development's deficiencies from multiple angles.

In this respect, international law scholars searching for that single 'ethical theory – a single philosophical touchstone – by which to answer all the problems at hand' must realise such an objective is elusive, as it is impossible (and antithetical) to standardise a universal principle of environmental ethics.[125] What matters is knowing sustainable development is the goal – the referent – while environmental ethics is a vehicle for realising this conceptual objective and operationalising its law.[126] Thus, to overcome the trappings of a single internationalised version of environmental ethics, both scholars and practitioners of sustainable

[119] Klaus Bosselmann, 'A Normative Approach to Environmental Governance: Sustainability at the Apex of Environmental Law' in Douglas Fisher (ed.), *Research Handbook on Fundamental Concepts of Environmental Law* (Edward Elgar 2016) 22, 29.

[120] Natasha Affolder, 'Looking for Law in Unusual Places: Cross-Border Diffusion of Environmental Norms' (2018) 7:3 Transnat'l Envt'l L 425, 426.

[121] Affolder, 'Transnational Law as Unseen Law', 374.

[122] Burns H. Weston and David Bollier, *Green Governance: Ecological Survival, Human Rights, and the Law of the Commons* (Cambridge University Press 2013) 123.

[123] Gillespie, *International Environmental Law, Policy and Ethics*, 2.

[124] Jonathan Verschurren, 'Sustainable Development and the Nature of Environmental Legal Principles' (2006) 9:1 Potchefstroom Electronic LJ 1, 36.

[125] Gillespie, *International Environmental Law, Policy and Ethics*, 3.

[126] L. Hens and C. Susanne, 'Environmental Ethics' (1998) 11:1–4 Global Bioethics 97, 111.

development alike must appreciate the benefit of a multifaceted view of environmental ethics within international environmental law and policy.[127]

In inquiring into African environmental ethics, this analysis presents a unique pathway to thinking about and doing sustainable development. An African Indigenous environmentalism installs 'an organic conception of nature that promotes ecological interdependencies among human, plant, and animal life'.[128] This ethico-legal foundation is fundamental to states and peoples alike who retain a significant part of their Indigenous legal systems or are committed to seeking replacements to failed approaches. It is equally useful to scholars and practitioners alike who are seeking alternative modes of engaging with sustainable development as law. Hence, while it is important to ring-fence the specificity of African environmental ethics, I think it is only fitting, in a TWAIL-inspired context, to emancipate these ethical principles by bringing them into international legal prominence broadly construed as Southern environmental ethics.[129]

Nonetheless, this proposal does not aim to flatten different experiences or approaches. To be clear, I do not claim the existence of a commonality of ethics across the Global South. I am also not equating Africa to the Global South since doing so threatens to dilute the strength of this framing referred to here as Southern environmental ethics. Neither am I advocating universality across the South. Even so, I share in the perspective advanced by Karin Mickelson that we should envision the Global South 'not as a bloc, but as a distinctive voice, or, more accurately, as a chorus of voices that blend, though not always harmoniously, in attempting to make heard a common set of concerns'.[130]

The moral force of this notion of Southern environmental ethics is expected to inaugurate the basis of a new 'political morality for a new ecological governance'.[131] This new environmental morality aligns with the revitalisation of sustainable development in a manner that intentionally integrates peripheralised knowledge into the core of international

127 Gillespie, *International Environmental Law, Policy and Ethics*, 3.

128 Kelbessa, 'Indigenous Environmental Philosophy', 578.

129 Nompumelelo Zinhle Manzini, 'African Environmental Ethics as Southern Environmental Ethics' in Munamato Chemhuru (ed.), *African Environmental Ethics: A Critical Reader* (Springer 2019) 111.

130 Mickelson, 'Rhetoric and Rage', 360.

131 Jennings, 'Governing Ecological Governance', 128.

environmental law.[132] Conceived in a more elaborate explanation on the legal normativity of ethics, African environmental ethics is transformed into a translatable concept of eclectic applicability that reaches beyond the confines of environmental law-making to become the capstone in renewing the legal dimensions of the concept of sustainable development. This is the place of a Southern environmental ethics within the vision for a new ecological governance. This new moral dynamism; that is environmental ethics, unlocks new vistas for visualising sustainable development and in the making of international environmental law and policy.[133]

However, a Southern (or Third World) view on the myth of environmental ethics is only a call to bring about much-needed transformation from an ontological abstraction to a place of practical legal operationalisation. It resists an ontology that promotes a cosmological outlook that disables law interacting successfully with ethical principles.[134] For instance, environmental ethics responds to the gendered character of sustainable development by infusing it with feminist philosophies.[135] This feminist orientation of sustainable development accords with African cosmologies that endow nature with a feminist composition.[136] Accordingly, theorising sustainable development through a Southern environmental ethics offers new theoretical insights and viable alternatives for the realisation of the concept's objectives. It speaks to an ecologically-inspired law and governance that translate into 'bringing

132 Bagele Chilisa, 'Decolonising Transdisciplinary Research Approaches: An African Perspective for Enhancing Knowledge Integration in Sustainability Science' (2017) 12 Sustainability Science 813, 820–821.

133 Donald Brown, 'Achieving Traction for Ethics in Environmental Policy-Making' in Laura Westra, Klaus Bosselmann, Janice Gray and Kathryn Gwiazdon (eds.), *Ecological Integrity, Law and Governance* (Routledge 2018) 149, 158.

134 Purdy, 'Our Place in the World', 862.

135 Karin Mickelson, 'Critical Approaches' in Daniel Bodansky, Jutta Brunnée, and Ellen Hey (eds.), *The Oxford Handbook of International Environmental Law* (Oxford University Press 2008) 262, 264.

136 Kyle Powys Whyte and Chris J. Cuomo, 'Ethics of Caring in Environmental Ethics: Indigenous and Feminist Philosophies' in Stephen Mark Gardiner and Allen Thompson (eds.), *The Oxford Handbook of Environmental Ethics* (Oxford University Press 2017) 234, 241–243; Manzini, 'African Environmental Ethics', 122; Peter Osuji, 'Laudato Si' and Traditional African Environmental Ethics' in Gerard Magill and Jordan Potter (eds.), *Integral Ecology: Protecting Our Common Home* (Cambridge Scholars Publishing 2018) 184, 199–200. Osuji argues the planet is called Mother Earth in many Indigenous societies, including across Africa, in consideration of its life-giving character in African and other Southern cosmologies.

philosophy down to earth' in reimagining sustainable development in international law.[137]

6.5 Sustainable Development as Ecological Law

Thus far, the Eurocentric origins of international law invites a rethink of the current approach to sustainable development praxis.[138] The growing dissatisfaction and increasing tension over the inability of international law to respond effectively to complex global environmental problems suggests international law as presently constituted lacks the transformative capacity and ethos to put the concept of sustainable development into practice. The concept is trapped in its Eurocentric heritage.[139] In this respect, the persistent resort to international law for answers might be epistemic evidence of a failure to contemplate the extent to which the current state of international law is itself part of the ecological crisis.[140]

Even critical approaches like TWAIL suffer from this circular logic. Kishan Khoday and Usha Natarajan describe this phenomenon as a three-step evolutionary process: first, TWAIL's early days were marked by its scholars seeking shelter under international law's classical treatment of the environment first as a natural resource to be exploited at will by states; second, TWAIL's engagement with international law reflected a situation where its scholars seldom addressed the environment as an independent subject but considered it only in the context of a broader discussion on natural resources and treated environmental protection as contingent upon economic growth in the Global South; and, third, it was only recently that the environment began to attract closer and deeper engagement from TWAIL scholars.[141] Since then, TWAIL has assumed a

[137] Laura Westra, 'The Ethics of Integrity and the Law in Global Governance' (2003) 37:1 UC Davis L Rev 127, 128.

[138] Dire Tladi, *Sustainable Development in International Law: Analysis of Key Enviro-Economic Instruments* (Pretoria University Law Press 2007) 14; Islam, 'History of the North-South Divide', 26.

[139] Geoffrey Garver, 'Moving from Environmental Law to Ecological Law: Frameworks, Priorities and Strategies' in Laura Westra, Klaus Bosselmann, Janice Gray and Kathryn Gwiazdon (eds.), *Ecological Integrity, Law and Governance* (Routledge 2018) 141, 146.

[140] Martti Koskeniemmi, *From Apology to Utopia: The Structure of International Legal Argument* (Cambridge University Press 2006) 9.

[141] Khoday and Natarajan, 'Fairness and International Environmental Law', 212–229.

more significant role at the epistemological intersection of the environment, the Global South, and its peoples.[142]

Nonetheless, while international law is acknowledged as inherently Eurocentric, TWAIL has not turned away from this inherency. Rather, it embraces the transformative potential of international law to remake the discipline. Here, TWAIL invests in studying how Eurocentrism recurrently defines and structures the evolution of 'new environmentalities'.[143] This new approach – defined by ecolegality – is endorsed by environmental lawyers and scholars alike who seek different approaches to international (environmental) governance.[144] For example, animal law experts urge a reframing of animal welfare in terms of rights, since that label unwittingly imprints the Western individualistic characterisation of human rights on phenomena that are more-than-human; communitarian rather than individualistic, and ideas in different cosmovisions which result in the separation between humans and nature.[145] African legal scholars who advocate ecological law as a turning point have also highlighted how the observance of Euro-American processes like environmental impact assessments in Africa persistently fail to stem the tide of ecological destruction.[146] Thus, a disciplinary overhaul is urgently needed to dislodge the existing state of affairs and allow ecolegality – that is founded upon ecological law – to substantially transform the sustainable development to become more ecologically sensitive to the planetary crisis.[147]

The progress towards ecological law is storied and has provoked multiple dimensions on rethinking sustainable development. Yet, what remains common to the different dimensions of this narrative is that reorienting international law for this purpose requires a return to a harmonious relationship between society and nature.[148] In this respect, critical environmental law scholars have advanced a compelling case for

142 Usha Natarajan, John Reynolds, Amar Bhatia and Sujith Xavier, 'Introduction: TWAIL: On Praxis and the Intellectual' (2016) 37:11 Third World Q 1946, 1947.

143 Khoday and Natarajan, 'Fairness and International Environmental Law'.

144 Geoffrey Garver, 'The Rule of Ecological Law: The Legal Complement to Degrowth Economics' (2013) 5 Sustainability 316.

145 Brian Favre, 'Is There a Need for a New, an Ecological, Understanding of Legal Animal Rights?' (2020) 11:2 J Human Rights and Envt 297.

146 Unuigbe, 'Significance of the Stewardship Ethic', 172.

147 Sbert, *Lens of Ecological Law*, 72.

148 Afshin Akhtar-Khatari, 'Restoration and Cooperation for Flourishing Socio-Ecological Landscapes' (2020) 11:1–2 Transnat'l Leg Theory 62, 68–71.

reimagining sustainable development by arguing such a rethink is needed to excavate and establish the ecological fundamentality of sustainable development.[149] This renewed vision of the conceptual core of sustainable development as ecological law proceeds on the understanding that economic growth has limits, and so does the planet.[150]

There have been recent developments on this subject. The Environmental Law and Governance Association (ELGA), a specialist body within the International Union for Conservation of Nature (IUCN), illuminates this ongoing investigation of the potency of ecological law in its pronouncement on the subject. It stated that:

> To overcome the flaws of environmental law, mere reform is not enough. We do not need more laws but different laws from which no area of the legal system is exempted. The ecological approach to law is based on ecocentrism, holism, and intra/intergenerational and interspecies justice. From this perspective, or worldview, the law will recognise ecological interdependencies and no longer favour humans over nature and individual rights over collective responsibilities. Essentially, ecological law internalises the natural living conditions of human existence and makes them the basis of all law, including constitutions, human rights, property rights, corporate rights and state sovereignty.[151]

This proposal fundamentally challenges current thinking around sustainable development and international law. It is at this point of a radical reconceptualising of sustainable development that the turn to ecological law becomes significant. Here, ecological integrity illuminates ecological law while clarifying other relevant ecology-based principles of international law.[152] Ecological law, therefore, represents a marked change

[149] Klaus Bosselmann, *The Principle of Sustainability: Transforming Law and Governance* (Ashgate 2008) 23.

[150] Sbert, *Lens of Ecological Law*, 32.

[151] Environmental Law and Governance Association, 'From Environmental Law to Ecological Law: A Call for Re-Framing Law and Governance' (2016), online (pdf): <www.elga.world/oslo-manifesto>, para 6 (last accessed 10 October 2023).

[152] Geoffrey Garver, 'Ecological Integrity in the Anthropocene: Lessons for Law from Ecological Restoration and Beyond' in Laura Westra, Janice Gray, and Franz-Theo Gottwald (eds.), *The Role of Integrity in the Governance of the Commons: Governance, Ecology, Law, Ethics* (Springer 2017) 191, 194; Afshin Akhtar-Khavari and Benjamin R Richardson, 'Ecological Restoration and Law: Recovering Nature's Past for the Future' (2017) 26:2 Griffith L Rev 147. Akhtar-Khavari and Richardson argue ecological integrity is inspiring a whole new sub-discipline called ecological restoration law. The same authors have produced an edited volume as a testament to this sub-discipline's staying power in Afshin Akhtar-Khavari and Benjamin R. Richardson (eds.), *Ecological Restoration Law: Concepts and Case Studies* (Routledge 2019).

and departure in thinking on environmental and international law.[153] This renewed approach, which draws on ethics, has been a long-awaited response to the frustration and increasing complexity of the inability of international law to respond to the failing role of sustainable development in the global environmental crisis.[154]

Ecological law thus reflects a body of critical scholarship that highlights eco-legal philosophies.[155] It is characterised by its commitment to reorient the important link between law and the environment, by focusing on disrupting human domination of nature while proposing relational accountability.[156] Additionally, it realigns human interests with the purpose of law in revitalising sustainable development. In this process of rethinking sustainable development as ecological law, law is assimilated as a subset of a wider normative organisation, where law is embedded and at the same time derivative of nature.[157] Law becomes an extension of ecology by being displaced from the apex of the mythologised hierarchy of norms and denied a self-assumed claim to normative superiority. This way, ecological law restricts the ahistorical significance of law to sustainable development by consigning it to being merely a constituent element of the planet's normative organisation.

However, I am not suggesting law ceases to function as an important aspect of planetary life. It does. Rather, it is the value of environmental ethics to law that is being highlighted in the discussion. Environmental ethics then assists in rethinking international law by revitalising planetary integrity as the principal referent for a renewed approach to sustainable

[153] An Cliquet, 'Ecological Restoration as a Legal Duty in the Anthropocene' in Michelle Lim (ed.), *Charting Environmental Law Futures in the Anthropocene* (Springer 2019) 59, 67.

[154] Environmental Law and Governance Association, 'From Environmental Law to Ecological Law', paras 10–11.

[155] Vito De Lucia, 'Ocean Commons, Law of the Sea, and Rights of the Sea' (2019) 32:1 Can JL and Jur 45, 53; Nathalie Rühs and Aled Jones, 'The Implementation of Earth Jurisprudence through Substantive Constitutional Rights to Nature' (2016) 8 Sustainability 174 (Earth Jurisprudence); Anna Wienhues, 'Sharing the Earth: A Biocentric Account of Ecological Justice' (2017) 30:3 J Agric and Envt'l Ethics 367 (Ecological Justice); Louis J. Kotzé and Rakhyun E. Kim, 'Earth System Law: The Juridical Dimensions of Earth System Governance' (2019) 1 Earth System Governance 1 (Earth System Law); Peter Burdon, 'Wild Law: The Philosophy of Earth Jurisprudence' (2010) 35:2 Alternative LJ 62 (Wild Law).

[156] Cliquet, 'Ecological Restoration as a Legal Duty', 67.

[157] Peter D. Burdon, 'Ecological Law in the Anthropocene' (2020) 11:1–2 Transnat'l Leg Theory 33; Thomas Berry, *The Great Work: Our Way into the Future* (Three Press 1999) 84.

development.[158] This transformed character of law is thus alive to the undesirable proclivities of sustainable development and mediates these inclinations by channelling ethical values and principles into legal discourse on the environment.[159] Put differently, international law requires a new approach to doing sustainable development – informed by eco-legal philosophies – that encourages a legal excavation of customary ways of knowing that establish nature itself as a source of legal normativity.[160]

The turn to ecolegality thus heeds the call of TWAIL scholars who contend that international environmental law is the 'disciplinary language of the future'.[161] However, it is important to understand the discipline shares in international law's own dark history of colonial and imperialist aspirations. This history of international environmental law reinforces sustainable development's ambivalence and absorptive capacity to distort helpful transformation. In this sense, Maxine Burkett criticises international environmental law as 'myopic in scope and constrained in reach'.[162] Khoday and Natarajan have equally argued the discipline has failed 'to deliver on its promise to stem ecological harm'.[163] Burkett re-echoes Khoday and Natarajan's view that international environmental law's inability to live 'up to the task is a painful understatement'.[164]

So, turning to ecological law promises a radical and progressive turn. However, a scrutiny of ELGA's inaugural statement, the Oslo Manifesto, regrettably contradicts the novelty of its proposal. The statement discloses reaffirmations of ideas of considerable antiquity repackaged as new ideas. Its reference to themes like holism, ecocentrism, and relationality evokes Indigenous cosmologies that have long existed and are central to

158 Klaus Bosselmann, 'The Ever-Increasing Importance of Ecological Integrity in International and National Law' in Laura Westra, Klaus Bosselmann, Janice Gray and Kathryn Gwiazdon (eds.), *Ecological Integrity, Law and Governance* (Routledge 2018) 225, 226.

159 Lim, 'Pathways to Equitable Sustainability', 232.

160 Fabiano de Andrade Correa and Marina Demaria Venâncio, 'International Environmental Law in the Anthropocene: Addressing the Gaps towards "Sustainable Development Law"' in Michelle Lim (ed.), *Charting Environmental Law Futures in the Anthropocene* (Springer 2019) 45, 56.

161 Khoday and Natarajan, 'Fairness and International Environmental Law'.

162 Maxine Burkett, 'Root and Branch: Climate Catastrophe, Racial Crises, and the History and Future of Climate Justice' (2021) 134 Harvard L Rev 326, 330.

163 Natarajan and Khoday, 'Locating Nature', 575.

164 Burkett, 'Root and Branch', 337.

Indigenous (including African) eco-legal philosophies.[165] In this sense, ecological law is not exactly new in its connection to relational ontologies, ethical values, and harmony between society and nature. Its more significant value is that its principles accord with Indigenous legal traditions and perspectives on the environment.[166] Like Louis Kotzé and Rakhyun Kim argued, international law requires a revivalism predicated upon a 'common shared *Grundnorm* (a fundamental norm underlying all other norms), such as planetary integrity in international environmental law that embodies its ultimate objective'.[167] Accordingly, the Oslo Manifesto ought to be understood as only amplifying existing eco-legal philosophies and its importance reinterpreted in the prominence it brings to Indigenous legal cosmologies within the attempt to find answers to the failure of international law.

Nonetheless, the Oslo Manifesto advances an important point that planetary (ecological) integrity is a 'precondition for human aspirations and a fundamental principle of law'.[168] The Oslo Manifesto thus rightly confirms other ecological approaches to law that are gaining prominence.[169] All the same, this declaration and its proposals are not without some challenges. For example, considering ecological integrity is linked to ethical reflections that transcend human-to-human interlinkages, ecological integrity as the normative force of ecological law proceeds in terms of moral significance.[170] But, since moral considerability derives from natural law analysis, natural law too is inadequate to counter the dominant positivist character of international law. The challenge here is that, contemporary explanations of natural law doctrine are also typical

165 Behrens, 'African Relational Environmentalism and Considerability', 65; Isabel Altamirano-Jimenez, *Indigenous Encounters with Neoliberalism: Place, Women, and the Environment in Canada and Mexico* (UBC Press 2013) 90–91.

166 Sbert, *Lens of Ecological Law*, 53.

167 Louis J. Kotzé and Rakhyun E. Kim, 'Towards Planetary Nexus Governance in the Anthropocene: An Earth System Perspective' (2022) 13:S3 Global Pol'y 86, 88.

168 Environmental Law and Governance Association, 'From Environmental Law to Ecological Law', para 6.

169 Lynda Collins, 'Environmental Resistance in the Anthropocene' (2020) 10:6 Oñati Socio-Legal Series 1317, 1329–1330.

170 J. Baird Callicott, 'Elements of an Environmental Ethic: Moral Considerability and the Biotic Community' (1979) 1:1 Envt'l Ethics 71. Callicott argues moral considerability attaches moral value to non-human entities; Seck, 'Ecological Integrity and Third World Approaches', 169–172; Konrad Ott, 'A Modest Proposal of How to Proceed in Order to Solve the Problem of Inherent Moral Value in Nature' in Laura Westra, Klaus Bosselmann, and Richard Westra (eds.), *Reconciling Human Existence with Ecological Integrity: Science, Ethics, Economics and Law* (Earthscan 2008) 39, 43.

of legal Eurocentrism.[171] Therefore, the Oslo Manifesto should be seen only as the humble beginnings of a long journey to reorient international environmental law.

As a result, it would simply be naïve to privilege the Oslo Manifesto's reference to natural law. Natural law, in the Eurocentric mould, is not the redeeming grace for recovering displaced and peripheralised knowledge. Such an approach would amount to glossing over natural law's own complicity in stabilising imperial control and its contemporary influence in aiding the ideational and substantive attacks on Indigeneity.[172] For example, the European subjugation and domination of the Americas were premised on a disingenuous adaptation of Francisco de Vitoria's natural law theory which at once endowed the Indigenous peoples with autonomy but at the same time treated them as not fully sovereign, a process that accelerated colonial dispossession in the Americas.[173]

Still, natural law theories continue to be re-purposed to serve the imperialist inclinations of international law.[174] To remedy this problem, natural law (in Eurocentric legalism) must be replaced with an advanced and cohesive ethical core.[175] Margaret Davies provides helpful direction on this matter where she argues that humans share a normative world with non-humans; she calls this the *nomos* – which 'refers to the idea that "nature" – animals, plants, the Earth, and so forth – produces its own values and norms, and that human norms are part of this natural nomos'.[176] This alternative impulse can be gleaned from TWAIL's reformative potential to retrench negative elements of natural (and positivist) international law. It does so by refracting international law through the prism of the needs and aspirations of the marginalised subclasses of the Global South.[177]

In rethinking sustainable development, it is imperative for legal scholarship to critically examine current approaches to international

[171] Bruce Buchan, 'The Empire of Political Thought: Civilisation, Savagery and Perceptions of Indigenous Government' (2005) 18:2 History Human Sciences 1.

[172] Geoff Gordon, 'Natural Law in International Legal Theory: Linear and Dialectical Presentations' in Anne Orford and Florian Hoffmann (eds.), *Oxford Handbook of International Legal Theory* (Oxford University Press 2016) 279, 298.

[173] Mattias Åhrén, *Indigenous Peoples' Status in the International Legal System* (Oxford University Press 2016) 7–38.

[174] Gathii, 'Agenda of Third World Approaches', 163.

[175] Seck, 'Ecological Integrity and Third World Approaches', 171.

[176] Davies, *EcoLaw*, 1.

[177] Rashwet Shrinkhal, 'Evolution of Indigenous Rights under International Law: A TWAIL Perspective' (2019) 19:1 Oriental Anthropologist 7, 8–9.

environmental law. It is also important to query their restrictive preoccupations with state-sanctioned law which overshadow the ethical principles in non-Western systems of law and sources like African customary law.[178] This concern evokes questions on the assimilation of the multiple manifestations of environmental ethics.[179] These observations are critically informed by the ecological integrity turn whose advocates see the methodological rejuvenation of international environmental law as putting Indigenous forms of knowledge in jeopardy by obscuring significant differences through generalisations and elision. Even so, incorporating Indigenous perspectives in international law affords rare insights and an invaluable opportunity to give voice to peripheralised knowledge; and unite, in a rather unique way, diverse strands of the notions of ecological integrity across artificial national frontiers.[180]

To approach this question more effectively, it is imperative to understand ecological integrity as a 'multi-disciplinary, foundational concept' defined by its own quest for 'wholeness, coherence and cohesion'.[181] For this reason, I do not attempt painting over the important differences that permeate environmental ethics; rather, I am advocating the excavation, study, and application of the invaluable reservoirs of wisdom and legal principles that have long been neglected in these peripheralised troves of knowledge.[182] Accordingly, the revitalisation of sustainable development as ecological law must be viewed as a timely opportunity to be guided by a new understanding of the union between humans and nature, one which is steered 'more intelligently and ethically'.[183] This reimagined concept of sustainable development would give meaning to the inter-

[178] Obijiofor Aginam, 'Saving the Tortoise, the Turtle, and the Terrapin: The Hegemony of Global Environmentalism and the Marginalisation of the Third World Approaches to Sustainable Development' in Obiora Chinedu Okafor and Obijiofor Aginam (eds.), *Humanising Our Global Order: Essays in Honour of Ivan Head* (University of Toronto Press 2003) 12, 14.

[179] Clare Palmer, Katie Shane, and Ronald Sandler, 'Environmental Ethics' (2014) 39:1 Annual Rev Envt and Res 419, 430.

[180] Affolder, 'Contagious Environmental Law-Making', 197; Affolder, 'Transnational Environmental Law's Missing People', 480–481.

[181] Bosselmann, 'Ever-Increasing Importance of Ecological Integrity', 225.

[182] Santos, *Epistemologies of the South*, 119; Sbert, *Lens of Ecological Law*, 60. Sbert advocates the need to evaluate and adopt environmentally helpful aspects of Indigenous law since not all of its dimensions are 'inherently sustainable'.

[183] Jennings, 'Governing Ecological Governance', 127.

connectedness between human society and nature as long conceptualised and practised in Africa.[184]

6.6 Conclusion

The revival of customary law and its controlling force, environmental ethics, are crucial insofar as they apply to the project of revitalising the concept of sustainable development. This attempt to seek out the helpful aspects of customary law is not to *primitivise* international law nor to return to the past where nature was pristine. Such an exercise would be illogical and a pointless effort because it is impossible to return to 'an untainted pre-colonial home'.[185]

The focus was rather a critique of international legal norms, how they come into existence through myths, and how these norms shape legal orders, including Indigenous legal governance.[186] This was not simply a call for the inclusion of Third World voices for the sake of universal inclusiveness.[187] Admittedly, this analysis is sure to attract some criticism as it seeks to elevate customary norms to become the co-equivalent of international norms. On this subject, some scholars suggest there is no need to excavate nor recover customary norms since the contemporary globalised character of the world means the international path is seemingly the obvious one to take. What I understand these scholars to mean is that the route of legal Eurocentrism is unavoidable. I see and hear the attachment of these scholars to the comfort of disciplinary dogma; but, as I argued in this chapter, customary law sources are equally substantive sources of law to which international law scholars ought to devote considerable attention.[188]

An important distinction to draw from my work as opposed to what others have done or are doing is that I acknowledge the risks of a single

[184] Ngozi Finette Unuigbe, 'African Eco-Philosophy on Forests: A Path Worth Exploring for the Implementation of Earth Jurisprudence' in Kirsten Anker, Peter D. Burdon, Geoffrey Garver, Michelle Maloney and Carla Sbert (eds.), *From Environmental to Ecological Law* (Abingdon 2021) 164.

[185] Amr Shalakany, 'Sanhuri and the Historical Origins of Comparative Law in the Arab World (or How Sometimes Losing Your Asalah Can Be Good for You)' in Annelise Riles (ed.), *Rethinking Masters of Comparative Law* (Hart Publishing 2001) 152, 154.

[186] Joshua Kleinfeld, 'The Double Life of International Law: Indigenous Peoples and Extractive Industries' (2016) 129 Harvard L Rev 1755.

[187] Mickelson, 'Rhetoric and Rage', 353.

[188] Khoday and Natarajan, 'Fairness and International Environmental Law'.

narrative of international law. Like Margaret Davies, I recognise that, '[t]he vision of a singular world in which there can be only one reality, one model human being, one law, one world, and one truth may work for a few, but not for most, humans, and not at all for the objectified world'.[189] On the strength of this admonition, I sought to excavate alternative sources of law by examining why international law must renounce its provincialising character and embrace transformation through 'ecocosmology'.[190] The analysis thus extends the boundaries of customary law as capable of altering present understandings of sustainable development from a linear, unidimensional vision to this richly diverse and multifaceted site for international law-making informed by Indigenous cosmovisions.[191]

Thus, this chapter proposed a radical shift away from the position that sustainable development should be taken for granted as a general principle of international law.[192] My argument is that universality has its place as there are some matters that easily lend themselves to general treatment.[193] Nonetheless, what I have argued here is that there are a lot of different spaces, senses, and understandings of what sustainable development is, and these distinctions are embedded in non-dominant systems of law.[194] Here, sustainable development must be reimagined in both its international and local senses to account for different legal needs wherever they emerge in reorganising human–non-human interrelations.[195] Evidently, the effectiveness of sustainable development cannot be assessed only at international levels; its utility must be necessarily local too. At this point, sustainable development must be operationalised on the principle of a locally-diverse legal ubiquity. Therefore, I agree with Yasuaki Onuma that, since legal Eurocentrism was advanced as a civilising technology, it is important that its antithesis disrupts that

189 Davies, *EcoLaw*, 100.

190 Khoday, 'Mythic Environment'.

191 Fagbayibo, 'Critical Approach'.

192 Scoones, 'Politics of Sustainability and Development', 303. Scoones similarly suggests that '[d]angers can emerge in monolithic social movements that assert unified globalism, a fixed view of technical solutions, and singular pathways of change'.

193 Andrew Sunter, 'TWAIL as Naturalized Epistemological Inquiry' (2007) 20:2 Canadian JL and Jur 475, 479.

194 Carina Wyborn, Amber Datta, Jasper Montana, Melanie Ryan, Peat Leith, Brian Chaffin, Clark Miller and Lorrae van Kerkhoff, 'Co-Producing Sustainability: Re-ordering the Governance of Science, Policy, and Practice' (2019) 44:1 Annual Rev Envt and Res 319, 320.

195 Lim, 'Pathways to Equitable Sustainability', 225.

unilaterality and focuses on promoting plural legal schemes and approaches as counterpoints to the orthodoxy of international law.[196]

To conclude, I am not promoting an unquestioned turn to customary norms. However, an uncritical denial of these customary laws will be deeply problematic. In this context, my interest in environmental ethics follows the notion that ethics is a moral compass for law, and for an informed choice from among plurilegal options on pursuing sustainable development.[197] Nonetheless, despite its normative value, the promise of ecological law must not take up the old form and structure of sustainable development which was eagerly embraced yet failed to yield much-needed results.[198] It is hoped that ecological integrity which comprises human–nature interconnectedness and ecocosmologies at the core of ecological law, which, like the all-embracing framework of sustainable development – environment, society, and development – does not lead the world down the path of further ineffective conceptualisation and poor operationalisation of the concept.[199]

[196] Yasuaki Onuma, 'When Was the Law of the International Society Born: An Inquiry of the History of International Law from an Intercivilisational Perspective' (2000) 2:1 J History IL 1, 6.

[197] Stone, 'Ethics and International Environmental Law', 291; Arturo Escobar, *Pluriversal Politics: The Real and the Possible* (Duke University Press 2020) 9. Escobar refers to these legal pluralist conceptions as the pluriverse, which is 'a world where many worlds fit'. I adopt this capacious view of legal normativity as it is essential to engendering and promoting imaginative ways to think about law without fixating on a particular notion of law (especially Eurocentric versions of law).

[198] Juan Auz, 'The Political Ecology of Earth System Law: Outlining a Lex Capitalocenae' (2023) 40:2 Wisconsin Int'l LJ 216, 235. Auz argues that Earth System Law and similar theoretical approaches to reforming environmental law can benefit from TWAIL's radical arguments that challenge racial and other discriminatory aspects of international (environmental) law.

[199] Laura Westra and Klaus Bosselmann, 'Introduction: The Development of the Global Ecological Integrity Group's Research and Its Future Aims' in Laura Westra, Klaus Bosselmann, Janice Gray and Kathryn Gwiazdon (eds.), *Ecological Integrity, Law and Governance* (Routledge 2018) 1, 1.

7

Conclusion

The Paradoxical Future of Sustainable Development in International Law

> If there is one clear lesson to take from Stockholm for the next 50 years, it is that we cannot solve environmental problems using the same logic that created the problems in the first place.*

7.1 TWAIL-*ing* Sustainable Development

This book undertook a Third World Approaches to International Law (TWAIL) inspired study into Africa's contribution to the law, politics, and history of the concept of sustainable development. Comprising analytical, descriptive, and conceptual discussions, this legal study offered insights into and proposed fundamental changes to current understandings of the concept and a rethink of our bio-cultural history. It also examined the legal operationalisation of sustainable development. In this respect, this book critically engaged with normative aspects of the intellectual and practical constitution of sustainable development. It equally critiqued the legal Eurocentrism of sustainable development, its neoliberal foundations, and the perception of universality. In place of Eurocentric legal epistemologies, I proposed an alternative future for sustainable development informed by a new approach that retrenched the centrality of the current thinking on sustainable development.[1] This approach advanced ecological

* Rebecca Bratspies, 'In Countless Ways and On an Unprecedented Scale: Reflections on the Stockholm Declaration at 50' (2022) 50:3 Georgia J of Int'l and Comp L 755, 768.

[1] B. S. Chimni, 'The Past, Present, and Future of International Law: A Critical Third World Approach' (2007) 8:2 Melbourne JIL 499; Basil Ugochukwu, 'When the T(W)AIL Wags Global Environmental Governance' in Frans Viljoen, Humphrey Sipalla, and Foluso Adegalu (eds.), *Exploring African Approaches to International Law: Essays in Honour of Kéba Mbaye* (Pretoria University Law Press 2022) 239, 241. Ugochukwu's suggestion aligns with calls to provide concrete proposals for reform that go beyond mere critique.

integrity as the normative core and operative significance of sustainable development. Accordingly, I argued that an ecological law perspective, informed by eco-legal philosophies, can profoundly modify and renew the law on sustainable development.

As a TWAIL-inspired inquiry, this book has steered away from grand narratives of international law, choosing to focus very closely on sustainable development as it occurs within international (environmental) law. However, where related general themes including state equality, sovereignty, and self-determination were implicated in the analysis, the critique was extended to reflect these thematic interactions within general international law. Here, my analysis drew upon politics and legal history (including environmental history, the history of ideas, and world history) while using the critical lens of TWAIL. I relied upon these insights only to the extent that they illuminated the focus of this book. To this end, the discussion in the chapters focused on different aspects of the relationship between law and sustainable development. While each chapter was developed and evolved around a unique theme, the theoretical and methodological impulses linked together its different sections through a TWAIL-inspired approach to tell the story of Africa's contribution to the conceptualisation, evolution, and implementation of the concept of sustainable development in international law.

Significantly, the Bandung Conference and the histories of its unique events illuminated the analysis in this book. First, the Bandung moment should be reconceptualised as an unending project. This radical approach to rethinking the multi-layered histories of that conference translated into an ongoing revelatory process as the conference and related (as well as subsequent) events continue to provide much-needed inspiration for contemporary Third World scholarship. Here, the Spirit of Bandung, as a treasure trove, supplied a useful guide for conducting a deeper analysis. This analytical impetus helped to situate this book within the more radical context of the contemporary significance of that historic moment by recentring Bandung as the 'epitome of the Third World project'.[2]

Furthermore, the history of the Bandung Conference as retold by Third World scholars retrieved radical proposals and recommendations that find contemporary purchase in current South–South alliances. In the context of reimagining sustainable development, there is some South–South collaboration for environmental causes, even at the level of the

[2] Fakhri, 'Third World Sovereignty' (2018), 220.

UN. There, Southern states are increasingly moving from aspirational objectives to collaborative efforts.[3] This practical application of the Spirit of Bandung shone legal light on my own intellectual struggle to piece together Africa's international law-making contributions in the global arena and the resulting internal operationalisation of Africa's interpretation of these internationally negotiated legal rules.

Emerging from this historical immersion occasioned by the exploration of the Spirit of Bandung, the connections that I sought to draw between TWAIL and sustainable development ceased to be a siloed project. The connection between TWAIL and sustainable development, as well as Third World knowledge production and activism, becomes more prominent as it manifests the reformatory promise of the Bandung moment which Third World scholars frequently return to for intellectual renewal. In this context, I argued the Bandung moment continues to inform every aspect of Third World intellectual endeavour, as it was the Bandung Conference that 'projected for the first time the consciousness of Third Worldism'.[4]

Third, the Bandung Conference also supplied the organising logic and rallying call for Third World activism.[5] Speaking directly to the contemporary application of the historical significance of the Spirit of Bandung to international environmental law broadly and sustainable development specifically, this book invites TWAIL (environmental law) scholars to undertake new inquiries into how to utilise the transformative potential of the Bandung Conference to pursue alternative thinking and action on themes such as sustainable development.[6] Therefore, the call to turn to ecological law and eco-legal philosophies only echoes the hallowed and historic force of the Spirit of Bandung for nature and the environment.[7]

Consequently, by denouncing the hegemonic allure of sustainable development and turning to an alternative, non-hegemonic outlook, this book argued for a pluralist normativity in conceptualising and operationalising sustainable development.[8] In this respect, this book was confined

[3] Assie-Lumumba, 'Behind and Beyond Bandung', 8.

[4] Tukumbi Lumumba-Kasongo, *Japan–Africa Relations* (Palgrave MacMillan 2010) 76.

[5] Weber and Winanti, 'The "Bandung Spirit"', 404.

[6] Mickelson and Natarajan, 'Reflections on Rhetoric and Rage', 471.

[7] Eslava et al., 'The Spirit of Bandung', 13; Darwis Khudori, 'Bandung Conference and its Constellation: An Introduction' in Darwis Khudori (ed.), *Bandung Legacy and Global Future: New Insights and Emerging Forces* (AAKAR Books 2018) 1, 13–19.

[8] Rajagopal, 'Counter-Hegemonic International Law'; De Lucia, '*Ecosystem Approach*', 217. De Lucia highlights the dangers of counter-hegemonic approaches, preferring the term 'non-hegemony'. For him, counter-hegemony is evocative of replacing one hegemonic

to the task of making a context-specific proposal for Africa's relationship with sustainable development. However, the book, rightly, spreads its tentacles to similar concerns over sustainable development across the Global South. While it did not seek to universalise its findings and propositions, it is noteworthy that the African context that provoked interest in its writing is similar in many respects to the broader context of the Global South.[9]

Thus, it is my hope that this legal study inspires similar inquiries on other areas of interest to the Global South. This approach will help improve our understanding of where the African experience is shared and where it is distinct, and to see how much there is to learn from these different canons and shared aims. Undoubtedly, a total transformation is unlikely to emerge from a single study of Africa that involves one legal norm. It will demand a consistent effort at examining the life of Eurocentric legal concepts both within and beyond their centres of production. This assessment must thus give rise to alternative perspectives including ecological law and eco-legal philosophies to inspire a new approach to the concept of sustainable development.

7.2 The Political and Legal Duplexity of Sustainable Development

This book demonstrated the double-sidedness of the concept of sustainable development. Contrary to popular narrative that sustainable development was inaugurated in the late-twentieth century, I have urged that its formal emergence should be reinterpreted as an ahistorical contrivance intended to address the global ecological crisis while still functioning, albeit quietly, in the interest of economic considerations. This Eurocentric posture of sustainable development easily shook off criticisms on its muted content. It achieved this by masking the inability to deliver on its promise through a constant reinvention of itself through new slogans and buzzwords like the green economy, green development, or sustainable development goals.[10]

form with another. I agree with De Lucia's approach to the extent that his admonition points us away from the trappings of hegemonies. However, it would be interesting to see how we reconcile De Lucia's non-hegemony, in this sense, with counter-hegemonic discourse as has been used by TWAIL scholars like Rajagopal.

9 The same is true for Indigenous societies in the Global North who are called the 'South in the North'.

10 Mickelson, 'South, North', 54–60; B. S. Chimni, 'Capitalism, Imperialism, and International Law', 22; Joyeeta Gupta and Nadia Sanchez, 'Global Green Governance: Embedding the

However, there is a whole world that lies outside this classical conception of of sustainable development.[11] This alternative vista of sustainable development, founded upon eco-legal ontologies, had long predated this Eurocentric contrivance which has existed since the second half of the twentieth century and has been closely linked to major developments within the UN's history. This other, alternative approach thus relates to an appreciation of sustainability as the ancient nature–society nexus that was fostered by the understanding that the primary foundation of that interrelationship is understanding law only as an ecological force.

The legal content of this revivalist vision of sustainable development is thus premised on ecological temperance. This alternative conceptualising of sustainable development revealed a structural need for marked changes in how we study and do international law. It also challenged the disciplinary building blocks of international (environmental) law that span law, the role of the state, and the primacy of peoples. Additionally, it invoked a return to nature as integral to our socio-ecological constitution and not simply as a natural resource for exploitation. In taking this alternative path, a reimagined sustainable development re-establishes the interconnectedness between nature and humans by making legal normativity one, and not the one and only, consideration in the socio-ecological constitution of our planetary existence.[12]

The manifestation of this dualised politics of sustainable development, and its embeddedness in international law is the basis for the division between society and nature. This division between nature and society is the ultimate source of the deteriorating interrelations between the two realms. In this respect, this 'epistemological error' unravels anxieties about how Eurocentric law and knowledge have othered non-European phenomena through peripheralising non-Europeanised legal cosmologies on sustainable development.[13] This epistemological misstep and its demonstration in contemporary attitudes to sustainable development hinders

Green Economy in a Global Green and Equitable Rule of Law Polity' (2012) 21:1 RECIEL 12, 16–18.

11 Mohsen al Attar, 'The Peculiar Double-Consciousness of TWAIL' (2022) 19:2 Indonesian JIL 239. Al Attar calls on TWAIL scholars to embrace the supposed inconsistency of staying within the discipline and pushing for reform at the same time to fashion a more radical and durable response to the problems that TWAIL scholarship identifies.

12 Natarajan, 'Third World Approaches', 236.

13 Erkka Laininen, 'Transforming Our Worldview towards a Sustainable Future' in Justin W. Cook (ed.), *Sustainability, Human Well-Being, and the Future of Education* (Palgrave MacMillan 2019) 161, 170.

progressist responses to the ecological crisis.[14] The way out of this complication is to move away from current approaches and turn to ecological integrity as the revitalised foundation of sustainable development. Accordingly, this point involves affirming law as not external to and imposed upon ecology, but rather that, it intersects with and is internally constitutive of ecology.[15]

7.3 Enduring Challenges with TWAIL in International (Environmental) Law

Despite TWAIL's far-reaching significance for reorienting international law, its methodological framework has prompted scepticism, suspicion, and even rejection from classical international law scholarship.[16] Despite these challenges, TWAIL's innovativeness can be seen in how new and old scholars alike flourish within its radical scope.[17] This deployment of TWAIL and associated tools of postcolonial theory and legal history, in the context of a sociological approach, has proved to be intellectually beneficial in its interests in renouncing state-centric analysis for a people-centred inquiry. Without concentrating on emancipating the peoples of the Global South, TWAIL theorising or praxis is meaningless.

In this respect, TWAIL must transform the politics of (international) law and governance to function effectively in the interest of all peoples. Here, the problem with a state-centric focus is that Southern states too often retain the oppressive and exploitative canons of the erstwhile colonising powers. Characteristically, the local elite and comprador bourgeoisie in the Global South were complicit in the neoliberal establishment (in the Global North) that worked against Third World interests. If TWAIL would address the questions raised by international (environmental) law, then TWAIL-related studies on the subject must undertake to protect nature and the interests of the peoples of the Global

14 Mohamed El-Kamel Bakari, "Mapping the Anthropocentric-Ecocentric' Dualism in the History of American Presidency: The Good, the Bad, and the Ambivalent' (2017) 17:1 Consilience: J Sust Dev 1, 21–22.

15 Kim and Bosselmann, 'Operationalising Sustainable Development', 207.

16 Kholsa, 'TWAIL Discourse', 293.

17 Fozia Nazir Lone, 'The 'One Country, Two Systems' Model and Political Reform in Hong Kong: A TWAIL Approach' (2018) 21:1 Max Planck YB UN L 404; Fozia Nazir Lone, 'Cross-Fertilisation of Westphalian Approaches to International Law: Third World Studies and a New Era of International Law Scholarship' (2020) 34:4 Emory Int'l L Rev 946. Lone is interested in how TWAIL influences Asian scholars and political leaders in the application of TWAIL ideas, methodologies, and tools to law and policy matters.

South who have long being marginalised and treated as an underclass. This posture requires challenging domestic actors in the Global South who act with similar enthusiasm as the external (Global North) does from outside.

Going forward, we must bring together Third World experiences to revive the 'epistemologies of the South'.[18] Epistemologies of the South are built around the idea that Western knowledge is not universal, and the world is inherently plural as are its peoples and its sources of knowledge. The uncritical reliance on Western schemes, knowledge, and their stock generalisations tend to freeze out legal plurality and a diversity of the sources of knowledge which are the bases of a much-needed epistemological alterity. This complex situation is the reason for the struggle within an epistemological space that silenced alternative thinking by reinforcing a restrictive intellectual register. Undoubtedly, this point explains why the redemption of sustainable development currently seems unpromising and elusive, yet we are reluctant to turn to other knowledge sources for inspiration.

Therefore, when I talked about alterity, I did not mean that diverse knowledge is inassimilable. Rather, this is a call to acknowledge the transformative power of 'alternative thinking of alternatives'.[19] In this context, we must understand that it is possible to be trapped in discourses that were once counter-hegemonic but have, over time, long been flattened by orthodox intellectual endeavours. By investing in the power of alternative imagination, critical discourse breaks free from the limits of orthodox argumentation. This is what ideas like ecological law invites us to do. By displacing the hegemonic power of positivist law, ecological law proposes a new understanding of sustainable development through the lens of ecolegality and related ontologies. This revitalisation of sustainable development holds emancipatory potential by recognising the ethicality of customary law and Indigenous cosmologies as possessing juridical substance of a different, non-Eurocentric character. Still, I am not suggesting ecological law instantly waves away the challenges of regulating the economic interests that threatens the human–nature balance. Rather, my argument is that this approach opens up alternative ways to reconceive of a new sustainable development founded on a TWAIL-inspired alterity.

[18] Boaventura de Sousa Santos, 'Public Sphere and Epistemologies of the South' (2012) 37:1 Afr Dev 43, 51.

[19] Ibid., 52.

7.4 Sustainable Development and the Limits of (International) Law

This book focused on reimagining the concept of sustainable development through retooling legal epistemologies in a wider effort to infuse non-Eurocentric cosmologies into international law. In this light, it challenged the exclusionary politics of international law. This analysis on the politics of exclusion involved insights from plural legal schemes. On this subject, Judge Christopher Weeramantry of the International Court of Justice (ICJ) has noted that:

> In the context of environmental wisdom generally, there is much to be derived from ancient civilisations and traditional legal systems in Asia, the Middle East, Africa, Europe, the Americas, the Pacific, and Australia – in fact, the whole world. This is a rich source which modern environmental law has left largely untapped.[20]

However, the incorporation of plural legal ontologies raises concerns on the limits of (international) law. While international law melds different legal traditions and perspectives into a juridical amalgam and further bolsters the assumption that learning from an international perspective is the reasonable choice, sometimes it might be necessary to go against this conventional thinking. This challenge is intensified at the intersection of domestic and international law where, without comparable domestic law that is willing to accept and apply non-Eurocentric legal ideas and impulses from international law, their domestic effectiveness will remain a distant possibility. This issue reflects the longstanding problem that, for a while, guidance in sustainable development or sustainability discourse was seen as either coming from international law itself, or a specific set of legal technologies from Euro-American states or centres of influence.

However, recent developments in both the Global South and Global North demonstrate legal borrowings are happening in the reverse, with customary law and Indigenous perspectives on sustainable development emerging from domestic law, engaging with and influencing international law too. I demonstrate this with three examples. First, the British Columbia Supreme Court in Canada recently held that the UN Declaration on the Rights of Indigenous Peoples (UNDRIP) is a source of 'robust interpretation' and implementation of law.[21] With the incorporation of UNDRIP into Canadian federal law and provincial law, at least in the province of British Columbia, there is a likelihood that reference to and application of Indigenous

[20] *Gabçikovo-Nagymaros Project, Slovakia v Hungary* (1997) ICJ Rep 7, para [98].

[21] *Thomas and Saik'uz First Nation v Rio Tinto Alcan Inc* [2022] BCSC 15.

law by the Canadian courts will increase.[22] The potential of increased use of Indigenous law thus opens up the prospects for ecocosmologies to be elevated in the relevant jurisprudence.

Second, following its recognition of *tikanga* Māori or 'Māori customary values and practices' as law, the New Zealand Supreme Court highlighted the cosmological (legal) relevance of environmental ethics in a recent case by noting that:

> the decision-maker would look at the tikanga itself and consider what it might say about the rights or interests of customary 'owners' or of the resources itself. To give just one illustration, the iwi [tribal] parties in this case emphasise the mauri [life force] of the area. Considering the proposed activity in terms of tikanga may indicate that material harm extends beyond the physical effects of a discharge, or that pollution can be spiritual as well as physical.[23]

This reference by the Supreme Court to ecological damage as having a spiritual dimension emphasises ethico-legal values and principles in judicial action. The statement by the court underscores its recognition of, and the increasing role of Māori customary law, together with its ethical principles, as law in and of itself.[24] This view has been endorsed in another important decision by the New Zealand Supreme Court which effectively renounced the Eurocentric ascertainment of customary law involving the repugnancy test, as having no more relevance in contemporary juridical analysis.[25] In affirming the legal normativity of ethical values and principles, the court held that, where a person is required to decide a legal matter or make an administrative decision in respect of

[22] *Gitxaala v British Columbia* (Chief Gold Commissioner) [2023] BCSC 1680. Regrettably, this recent case suggests that despite the adoption of UNDRIP into the provincial law of British Columbia, it "does not implement UNDRIP into the domestic law of British Columbia" nor does the provincial law create enforceable rights based on UNDRIP. The court stated that the adoption of UNDRIP under the relevant provincial law requires further steps including an action plan to bring UNDRIP into domestic law. As the court stated, the provincial law adopting UNDRIP can only serve as an "interpretive aid." Thus, this case only continues the earlier jurisprudence of the British Columbia courts on UNDRIP in *Thomas and Saik'uz First Nation v Rio Tinto Alcan Inc* [2022] BCSC 15 that UNDRIP is only an interpretive tool. Thus, we await the first instance of UNDRIP's substantive application and possible implementation in Canada.

[23] *Trans-Tasman Resources Limited v Taranaki-Whanganui Conservation Board and Others* [2021] NZSC 127, para 172.

[24] Elizabeth Macpherson, Jill Banwell, Robert Makgill and Adrienne Paul, '*Trans-Tasman Resources Limited v Taranaki-Whanganui Conservation Board and Others* [2021] NZSC 127; A New High Mark for Seabed Mining' (2021) 25 New Zealand J Envt'l L 277, 286.

[25] *Peter Hugh McGregor Ellis v The King* [2022] NZSC 114, para 115.

natural resources, and the decision-maker is confronted with a question on Māori customary law in environmental matters, the decision-making process must be guided by the fact that:

> tikanga Māori [customary law] has the same meaning as in s 2(1) of the RMA [Resource Management Act], that is, 'Māori customary values and practices'. That definition is not to be read as excluding tikanga as law, still less as suggesting that tikanga is not law. Rather, tikanga is a body of Māori customs and practices, part of which is properly described as custom law. Thus, tikanga as law is a subset of the customary values and practices referred to in the Act.[26]

The South African example provides an even more direct reference to the applicability of customary law to sustainable development. The South African Supreme Court of Appeal recently held in a marine conservation case that 'the customary law of the Dwesa Cwebe communities provides for sustainable conservation and utilisation of resources, [and that] the high court's finding that, by concluding the restoration agreement, the communities had accepted "that they would access the sea in accordance with the dictates of the law giving expression to the concept of sustainable development", is insupportable'.[27] In this case, the South African courts affirmed the validity of customary law as it held that the communities were bound by their customary law position on sustainable use of marine resources and not statutory prescriptions on conservation. The relevance of customary law and ecological law-making in this South African case highlights the rising significance of domestic legal developments embrace the substantive import of UNDRIP and its relationship with African Charter on domestic (African) law.[28] Thus, we need to look to the possibility of positive domestic law influences that can be externalised and embraced in the international domain.[29]

These very recent cases demonstrate greater promise for ecocosmologies to make their way into mainstream legal discourse. They demonstrate, even if belatedly, a supposed coming of age for customary law and, with it, a placing of customary law on equal pedestal as the received (colonial) law or

26 *Trans-Tasman Resources Limited v Taranaki-Whanganui Conservation Board and Others* [2021] NZSC 127, para 169.

27 *Gongqose v Minister of Agriculture, Forestry and Fisheries* [2018] 5 SA 104 (SCA), para 56.

28 *Gongqose v Minister of Agriculture, Forestry and Fisheries* [2018] 5 SA 104 (SCA), para 58.

29 Alexander Paterson, 'The Interface between Customary Rights and Environmental Legislation: Lessons from *Gongqose & Others vs Minister of Agriculture, Forestry and Fisheries and Others* (SCA) 2018' (2020) 26:1 South Afr J Envt'l L and Pol'y 134.

its contemporary (postcolonial) iterations.[30] These cases demonstrate that legal innovations are coming from all kinds of places, and that international law itself may best serve as a vehicle for blending and promoting these customary and Indigenous law developments emanating from domestic jurisprudence. These cases also highlight the interaction between international law and domestic law as most national constitutions either refer to or incorporate international law into domestic jurisprudence.

From the South African example, it is evident that African states are adjudicating domestic cases using international legal principles with increasing complexity. This ongoing development emphasises 'domestic environmental law does not stand alone in a state of local isolation but is embedded in the broader global context of' international law.[31] In observing this interface of domestic law and international law, the limits of (international) law become visible as states are likely to adopt an inverse approach where international law borrows in reverse fashion from these domestic legislative and judicial developments. Perhaps, it is time for African courts and other adjudicative tribunals, whether at the national, regional, or continental level, including the African Commission on Human and Peoples' Rights and the African Court on Human and Peoples' Rights, sub-regional courts, and domestic tribunals to do more by embracing and mainstreaming customary law jurisprudence. This process will inspire a healthy interface across all levels of judicial decision-making and impel political, legal, and social change across Africa. However, I acknowledge that this approach involves a deep commitment to reorienting the present modes and methods of teaching and learning international law in the Global South, including in Africa.[32]

7.5 Despair, Hope, and the Legal Futurities of Sustainable Development

I have outlined in this book a radical approach to reconceptualising and practicalising the concept of sustainable development. By focusing on

[30] Lesetja Monyamane and Mpho P. Bapela, '*Gongqose v Minister of Agriculture, Forestry & Fisheries* – A Tale of Customary Law Rituals and Practices in Marine Protected Areas' (2019) 22:1 Potchefstroom Electronic LJ 1, 14.

[31] Kotzé and Soyapi, 'African Courts', 279.

[32] Mohsen al Attar and Shaimaa Abdelkarim, 'Decolonising the Curriculum in International Law: Entrapments in Praxis and Critical Thought' (2023) 34:1 L and Critique 41; Mohsen al Attar, 'Must International Law Pedagogy Remain Eurocentric?' (2021) 11:1 Asian YBIL 176.

Africa's contribution to the law, politics, and history of sustainable development, the book answered the question I posed at the beginning of this legal study; that is how international (environmental) law might look from a Global South perspective. This standpoint is supported by recent claims that the future of international law is necessarily 'geographic and not historic'.[33] Nonetheless, this legal inquiry was focused on Africa – in keeping with the ever-present reminder that TWAIL scholarship must avoid slipping into grand narratives on international law.[34]

Even so, I am hopeful that the findings and outcomes of this analysis will illuminate the law on sustainable development even beyond the Global South.[35] It is in this sense that this book is not only a legal study but also an invitation to a radical (international) political project. Still, when I speak about radicalism, I do not mean political extremism which might suggest a fundamentalist kind of politics. Radicalism as I use it here is simply going to the root of things to bring about much-needed fundamental change. This perspective on radicalism links up with the reconstructionist admonition of TWAIL to international law scholars to disengage themselves from being preoccupied with rehabilitating international law but rather turn to an alternative focus. This radical view urges a turn in the direction of the promising and hopeful pursuit of 'the need for systemic and foundational change'.[36] That is what I mean by radicalism from a TWAIL-inspired perspective.

TWAIL and its adherents must, therefore, remain hopeful with this call to foundational change. Of course, TWAIL's relationship with hope is not new as hope has always been central to its mission. Third World scholars from the early days of TWAIL, through its transitional voices, and to its recent advocates all echo hopeful sentiments as grounds for fundamental change in international law.[37] Even so, I advocate a separation of hope from faith or optimism. Karin Mickelson signposts these

[33] Johns, 'Disciplinary Privilege'.

[34] Luis Eslava and Sundhya Pahuja, 'Between Resistance and Reform: TWAIL and the Universality of International Law' (2011) 3:1 Trade L and Dev 103, 105.

[35] Gathii, 'Promise of International Law', 170–174. Gathii argues that it is about time international law scholarship focused purposefully on Africa's contributions, including, in international environmental law, its scholars, experts, and institutions. Hopefully, this book makes a modest contribution to the call by Gathii and others like him.

[36] Natarajan et al., 'Third World Approaches', 8.

[37] Bedjaoui, *Towards a New International Economic Order*, 209; Christopher G. Weeramantry, 'International Law and the Developing World: A Millennial Analysis' (2000) 41:2 Harvard Int'l LJ 277; Obiora Okafor, 'Cascading toward "De-Solidarity"? The Unfolding of Global Refugee Protection' (2019) 2 TWAILR: Reflections 1, 7.

differences of hope in TWAIL wherein she points out that optimism is the expectation that 'things will turn out well', while faith is the conviction that 'a particular entity, process, or structure will help us achieve that outcome'.[38] Hope as defined here is simply the sense that things could become better. However, this idea does not mean we must simply sit and wait; nor does it mean we assume that by simply channelling our efforts into the present Eurocentric structure of international law, we will bring about the transformation we yearn to see. Rather, hope is somewhere in the middle between faith and optimism where it demonstrates a devotion and commitment to work for 'a desired outcome'.[39] In a sense, this kind of hope, that is 'angry or radical hope', might be defined slightly differently as a sense that things must get better, and that the current situation is intolerable.[40] At this point, TWAIL ceases to be merely an academic endeavour. It radically invites a transformation of thought and conviction into political action if the politics of exclusion that defines international law is to be pushed into a place of change.[41]

As a political undertaking, TWAIL helpfully shifts our gaze from a singular focus on academic writings and similar scholarly engagements to the *realpolitik* of our circumstances. Many examples abound, but I will stick with international (environmental) law. Let us take, for example, the prodigious work of Judge Christopher Weeramantry who was a former Vice President of the ICJ and whose work demonstrated he was committed to this hopeful agenda of TWAIL beyond academic writings and decisions as a judge of an international tribunal. He was quite invested in translating his critical reflections and writings into the politics of international adjudication including the interpretation of the concept of sustainable development in international law.[42] TWAIL scholars must embrace and consciously seek out these kinds of spaces for scholarly and practical action. These are the kinds of sites and interests for new legal impulses already hiding in plain sight. Accordingly, I find comfort in the view that '[i]nternational law's future may be already here – just not in the places and ways we tend to look for it'.[43]

[38] Antony Anghie, 'TWAIL: Past and Future' (2008) 10:4 Int'l Community L Rev 479; Karin Mickelson, 'Hope in a TWAIL Register' (2020) 1 TWAILR 14, 16–17.
[39] Ibid., 17.
[40] Ibid., 26.
[41] Johns, 'Disciplinary Privilege'.
[42] Anghie, 'C. G. Weeramantry of the International Court of Justice', 830; Tim Stephens, 'International Courts and Sustainable Development: Using Old Tools to Shape a New Discourse' in Brad Jessup and Kim Rubenstein (eds.), *Environmental Discourses in Public and International Law* (Cambridge University Press 2012) 195, 207–216.
[43] Johns, 'Disciplinary Privilege', 188.

Understandably, the political dimensions of Third World legal thought are open to critique. The concerns that have emerged, for instance, regarding international adjudication often relate to the issue of a judge's 'neutrality, bias, or activism'.[44] Whether these criticisms have merit or not, it is important that we constantly engage with the historical and structural deficiencies of the civilisational agenda of international law. This process should lead us to learn why Third World scholars and activists are suspicious of international law and are committed to reconstructing international law from the perspective of the Global South, its needs, and its marginalised peoples.

On this subject, the work of international tribunals and adjudicative tribunals become important for emancipating international law. Here, there is empirical evidence that suggests judges of international tribunals frequently vote in favour of states that share their economic, political, and cultural values.[45] If this assessment is accurate, then judges from the Global South who tend to be sympathetic to Third World issues should be looked upon as doing no worse than their counterparts from the Global North.

Returning to the example of Judge Weeramantry, while I understand that judges are called upon to be neutral and non-partisan, we must recognise that 'judicial representativeness' of Third World resistance in respect of 'classical interpretations of international law' is needed as a sign of hope.[46] In this context, through his work on sustainable development at the ICJ, Judge Weeramantry was able to humanise international law and bring hope to our understanding of sustainable development in his interpretive analyses which centred on customary law and Indigenous legal cosmologies through alternative readings at even the highest level of international adjudication.[47] From this perspective, it is still possible that for international law scholars who are interested in the redeeming power

[44] Liliana Obrégon, 'The Third World Judges: Neutrality, Bias or Activism at the Permanent Court of International Justice and the International Court of Justice' in William A. Schabas and Shannonbrooke Murphy (eds.), *Research Handbook on International Courts and Tribunals* (Edward Elgar 2017) 181.

[45] Eric A. Posner and Miguel F. P. de Figuieredo, 'Is the International Court of Justice Biased?' (2005) 32:2 J Leg Studies 625; Amarasinghe, 'In Praise of Kaleidoscopic Judge'. By discussing some of the key decisions of the ICJ involving Judge Weeramantry, Amarasinghe showcases the importance of reading in other factors, including the role of power and politics, language, relationality and culture, that might not readily be characterised as (international) law, yet often have a significant bearing on (international) judicial outcomes.

[46] Obrégon, 'Third World Judges', 182.

[47] Kalana Senaratne, 'Judge C. G. Weeramantry: An Alternative Reading' (2016) 56:3–4 Indian JIL 325, 330–331.

of the discipline for the Global South, it must be understood that achieving a desired outcome hinges on the awareness that 'hope for the future can exist even in an age characterised by eroding faith in mainstream institutions, including law'.[48]

In relating the theme of hope to the future of my own work, I am interested in expanding beyond the immediate task of reimagining sustainable development. Yet, I am still cautious of grand narratives. So, I prefer investigating one international law theme, one concept, or one idea at a time. Perhaps, for some legal scholars, it would seem unexciting to revisit foundational concepts. However, I am fortified in the knowledge that other international law scholars share similar views that it is necessary to recommit ourselves to the '(i) clarification of the architecture and inner structure of environmental legal systems; (ii) clarification of the principles of (international) environmental law; and (iii) clarification of the embeddedness of (international) environmental law within (international) law'.[49] On this subject, I am interested in rereading the occurrence of crises as everyday concerns in international law and not simply as episodic incidents. My interest lies in how the transformative power of crisis as an everyday occurrence can be reinterpreted as a significant element in the future of international (environmental) law-making, and in how we take international (environmental) law more seriously.

This future research scheme thus travels far beyond academic dimensions. It is radical in the sense that it responds to contemporary concerns including the current climate emergency that must be thoroughly reimagined as an everyday issue and not simply thought of as a global (historical) catastrophe. When disasters are theorised as everyday occurrences, their causes can be needfully repoliticised, making them visible and relatable. This approach can assist in crafting more viable political and legal responses. This is a distinct, yet hopeful technique for re-engaging the commitment of TWAIL to reversing the de-politicisation of international law that its orthodox scholarly core tend to push. Accordingly, by connecting TWAIL to the politics of contemporary (but historical) ecological problems like the climate emergency, my future scholarly interests join with the focus of this timely and pioneering book to invoke a praxis of hope that helpfully transforms ideas and concepts like sustainable development from legal theory into legal practice.

[48] Mickelson, 'Hope in a TWAIL Register', 17.
[49] Viñuales, 'Concise Research Agenda', 3.

BIBLIOGRAPHY

International Materials

African Charter on Human and Peoples' Rights, 1982, 21 ILM 58 (entered into force 21 October 1986).

African Commission on Human and Peoples' Rights. *Rules of Procedure of the African Commission on Human and Peoples' Rights*, 2010 (first adopted in February 1988, revised in 1995).

African Commission on Human and Peoples' Rights. *State Reporting Guidelines and Principles on Articles 21 and 24 of the African Charter Relating to Extractive Industries, Human Rights and the Environment* (adopted 30 October 2021).

African Convention for the Conservation of Nature and Natural Resources, 1976, 1001 UNTS 4.

Charter of the Organisation of African Unity, 25 May 1963, 479 UNTS 39.

Constitutive Act of the African Union, 1 July 2000, 2158 UNTS 37733.

Convention Designed to Ensure the Conservation of Various Species of Wild Animals in Africa, Which Are Useful to Man or Inoffensive, 19 May 1900, British Parliamentary Papers 1900, Cd 101, Vol 56, 825.

Convention Relative to the Preservation of Fauna and Flora in Their Natural State, 8 November 1933, 172 LNTS 241.

Protocol to the African Charter on Human and Peoples' Rights on the Establishment of an African Court on Human and Peoples' Rights, 10 July 1998, OAU Doc OAU/LEG/EXP/AFCHPR/PROT III (entered into force 25 January 2004).

Report of the United Nations Conference on the Human Environment, Stockholm, 5–16 June 1972, UN Doc A/CONF.48/14/Rev 1 (1973).

Report of the United Nations on Environment and Development, Rio de Janeiro, 3–14 June 1992, UN Doc A.CONF.15I/267 Rev 1 (1993).

Revised African Convention on Conservation of Nature and Natural Resources, 11 July 2003.

United Nations. *International Mother Earth Day*, 22 April 2009, GA Res 63/278, UNGAOR, 63rd Sess, UN Doc A/Res/278.

United Nations. *Process of Preparation of the Environmental Perspective to the Year 2000 and Beyond*, GA Res 38/161 (19 December 1983).

United Nations General Assembly. *Promotion and Protection of Human Rights: Human Rights Questions, Including Alternative Approaches for Improving the Effective Enjoyment of Human Rights and Fundamental Freedoms*, GA Res, 76/300 (28 July 2022).

United Nations Human Rights Council. *The Human Right to a Clean, Healthy and Sustainable Environment*, HRC 48/L.23/Rev.1 (8 October 2021).

Legislation

National Environment Act of Uganda (No. 5 of 2019).

Sacred Forest Law of Benin, Interministerial Order of 2012 (No. 121).

Jurisprudence

African Commission on Human and Peoples' Rights v Kenya, Application 006/2012, African Court on Human and Peoples' Rights, Order for Provisional Measures (15 March 2013).

African Commission on Human and Peoples' Rights v Peoples Republic of Kenya, Application No. 006/2012, Judgment (Reparations) (23 June 2022).

African Commission on Human and Peoples' Rights v Republic of Kenya, Judgment of the African Court of Human and Peoples' Rights, Application No 006/2012 (26 May 2017).

Angu v Attah, [1916] UKPC 53.

Centre for Minority Rights Development & Minority Group Rights (on behalf of the Ogiek People in the Mau Forest) v The Republic of Kenya, African Commission on Human and Peoples' Rights Communication 381/09 (5 August 2010).

Centre for Minority Rights Development and Minority Rights Group International (on behalf of the Endorois Welfare Council) v Republic of Kenya, African Commission on Human and Peoples' Rights Communication No 276/2003 (4 February 2010).

Democratic Republic of Congo v Burundi, Rwanda and Uganda, African Commission on Human and Peoples' Rights Communication No 227/99 (29 May 2003).

Femi Falana v The African Union, Judgment of the African Court on Human and Peoples' Rights, Application No 001/2011 (26 June 2012).

Gabçikovo-Nagymaros Project, Slovakia v Hungary, (1997) ICJ Rep 7.

Gitxaala v British Columbia (Chief Gold Commissioner) [2023] BCSC 1680.

Gongqose v Minister of Agriculture, Forestry and Fisheries, [2018] 5 SA 104 (SCA).

Ligue Ivoirienne des Droits de L'homme (LIDHO) and Others v Republic of Côte d'Ivoire, Application No. 041/2016 (Judgement) [2023] AfCHPR 21.

Peter Hugh McGregor Ellis v The King, [2022] NZSC 114.

Social and Economic Research Centre (SERAC) and Centre for Economic and Social Rights v Federal Republic of Nigeria, African Commission on Human and Peoples' Rights Communication 155/96 (27 May 2002).

Socio-Economic Rights and Accountability Project v Nigeria, ECOWAS Community Court of Justice, Case No ECW/CCJ/APP/08/08, Judgment ECW/CCJ/JUD/18/12 (14 December 2012).

Sudan Human Rights Organisation v Sudan, African Commission on Human and Peoples' Rights Communications No 297/03 (27 May 2009).

Thomas and Saik'uz First Nation v Rio Tinto Alcan Inc, [2022] BCSC 15.

Trans-Tasman Resources Limited v Taranaki-Whanganui Conservation Board and Others, [2021] NZSC 127.

Secondary Materials

Books

Acharya, Amitav. *Constructing Global Order: Agency and Change in World Politics* (Cambridge University Press 2018).

Adams, W. M. *Green Development: Environment and Sustainability in the Third World*, 2nd ed. (Routledge 2001).

Åhrén, Mattias. *Indigenous Peoples' Status in the International Legal System* (Oxford University Press 2016).

Akhtar-Khavari, Afshin and Benjamin R. Richardson (eds.), *Ecological Restoration Law: Concepts and Case Studies* (Routledge 2019).

Alam, Shawkat, Sumudu Atapattu, Carmen G. Gonzalez and Jona Razzaque (eds.). *International Environmental Law and the Global South* (Cambridge University Press 2015).

Altamirano-Jimenez, Isabel. *Indigenous Encounters with Neoliberalism: Place, Women, and the Environment in Canada and Mexico* (UBC Press 2013).

Amell, Amaya. *Francisco de Vitoria and the Evolution of International Law: Justifying Injustice* (Lexington Books 2021).

Anghie, Antony. *Imperialism, Sovereignty and the Making of International Law* (Cambridge University Press 2005).

Apostolopoulou, Elia. *Nature Swapped and Nature Lost: Biodiversity Offsetting, Urbanisation, and Social Justice* (Palgrave Macmillan 2020).

Atapattu, Sumudu. *Human Rights Approaches to Climate Change: Challenges and Opportunities* (Routledge 2015).

Attfield, Robin. *The Ethics of the Global Environment*, 2nd ed. (Edinburgh University Press 2015).

Austin, John. *Lectures on Jurisprudence or the Philosophy of Positive Law*, 4th ed. (John Murray 1873).

Bakari, Mohamed El-Kamel. *Sustainability in the Age of Globalisation: A Quest for a Paradigm of Development* (Lexington Books 2017).

Bandopadhyay, Saptarishi, *All Is Well: Catastrophe and the Making of the Normal State* (Oxford University Press 2022).

Bederman, David J. *Custom as a Source of Law* (Cambridge University Press 2010).

International Law in Antiquity (Cambridge University Press 2001).

Bedjaoui, Mohammed. *Towards a New International Economic Order* (UNESCO 1979).

Bernstein, Steven. *The Compromise of Liberal Environmentalism* (Columbia University Press 2001).

Berry, Thomas. *The Great Work: Our Way into the Future* (Three Press 1999).

Beyerlin, Ulrich and Thilo Marauhn. *International Environmental Law* (Hart 2011).

Bianchi, Andrea. *International Law Theories: An Inquiry into Different Ways of Thinking*, 1st ed. (Oxford University Press 2017).

Blattner, Charlotte E. *Protecting Animals within and across Borders: Extraterritorial Jurisdiction and the Challenges of Globalisation* (Oxford University Press 2019).

Bonanomi, Elisabeth Bürgi. *Sustainable Development in International Law Making and Trade: International Food and Governance and Trade in Agriculture* (Edward Elgar 2015).

Borowy, Iris. *Defining Sustainable Development for Our Common Future: A History of the World Commission on Environment and Development (Brundtland Commission)* (Routledge 2013).

Borrows, John. *Canada's Indigenous Constitution* (University of Toronto Press 2010).

Bosselmann, Klaus. *The Principle of Sustainability: Transforming Law and Governance* (Ashgate 2008).

Bowman, Michael, Peter Davies and Catherine Redgwell, *Lyster's International Wildlife Law*, 2nd ed. (Cambridge University Press 2010).

Bradley, Anna Spain. *Human Choice in International Law* (Cambridge University Press 2021).

Burgis, Michelle L. *Boundaries of Discourse on the International Court of Justice: Mapping Arguments in Arab Territorial Disputes* (Martinus Nijhoff 2009).

Carson, Rachel. *Silent Spring* (Houghton Mifflin 1962).

Chakrabarty, Dipesh. *Provincialising Europe: Postcolonial Thought and Historical Difference* (Princeton University Press 2000).

Chanock, Martin. *Law, Custom and Social Order* (Cambridge: Cambridge University Press, 1985).

Chassagne, Natasha. *Buen Vivir as an Alternative to Sustainable Development: Lessons from Ecuador* (Routledge 2021).

Chimini, B. S. *International Law and World Order: A Critique of Contemporary Approaches*, 2nd ed. (Cambridge University Press 2017).

Christie, Gordon. *Canadian Law and Indigenous Self-Determination: A Naturalist Analysis* (University of Toronto Press 2019).

Cittadino, Federica. *Incorporating Indigenous Rights in the International Regime on Biodiversity Protection: Access, Benefit-Sharing, and Conservation in Indigenous Lands* (Brill 2019).

Clapp, Jennifer and Peter Dauvergne. *Paths to a Green World: The Political Economy of the Global Environment*, 2nd ed. (MIT Press, 2011).

Comaroff, John L. and Simon Roberts. *Rules and Processes: The Cultural Logic of Dispute in the African Context* (University of Chicago Press 1981).

Corcodel, Veronica. *Modern Law and Otherness: The Dynamics of Inclusion and Exclusion in Comparative Legal Thought* (Edward Elgar 2019).

Darian-Smith, Eve. *Laws and Societies in Global Contexts: Contemporary Approaches* (Cambridge University Press 2013).

Darwin, Charles. *Descent of Man*, 2nd ed. (Merrill Baker 1874).

Davies, Margaret. *EcoLaw: Legality, Life, and the Normativity of Nature* (Routledge 2021).

d'Aspremont, Jean. *The Critical Attitude and the History of International Law* (Brill 2019).

De Lucia, Vito. *The 'Ecosystem Approach' in International Environmental Law: Genealogy and Politics* (Routledge 2019).

DeSombre, Elizabeth. *Global Environmental Institutions*, 2nd ed. (Routledge 2017).

Development and Environment: Report and Working Papers of a Panel of Experts Convened by the Secretary-General of the United Nations Conference on the Human Conference (Mouton 1972).

Djamson, Eric C. *The Dynamics of Euro-African Cooperation: Being an Analysis and Exposition of Institutional, Legal and Socio-Economic Aspects of Association/Cooperation with the European Economic Community* (Brill 1976).

Dobson, Andrew. *Justice and the Environment: Conceptions of Environmental Sustainability and Theories of Distributive Justice* (Oxford University Press 1998).

Ekardt, Felix. *Sustainability: Transformation, Governance, Ethics, Law* (Springer, 2020).

Egede, Edwin. *Africa and the Deep Seabed Regime: Politics and International Law of the Common Heritage of Mankind* (Springer 2011).

Egelston, Anne E. *Sustainable Development: A History* (Springer 2013).

Elias, Taslim Olawale. *The Nature of African Customary Law* (Manchester University Press 1956).

Escobar, Arturo. *Encountering Development: Making and Unmaking the Third World* (Princeton University Press 2012).

Pluriversal Politics: The Real and the Possible (Duke University Press 2020).

Esquirol, Jorge. *Ruling the Law: Legitimacy and Failure in Latin American Legal Systems* (Cambridge University Press 2019).

Ezeanya-Esiobu, Chika. *Indigenous Knowledge and Education in Africa* (Springer 2019).

Faure, Michael G. and Roy A. Partain. *Environmental Law and Economics: Theory and Practice* (Cambridge University Press 2019).

Fitzpatrick, Peter. *The Mythology of Modern Law* (Routledge 1992).

Focarelli, Carlo. *International Law as a Social Construct: The Struggle for Global Justice* (Oxford University Press 2012).

Foucault, Michel. *The History of Sexuality: An Introduction*, translated by Robert Hurley (Vintage Books 1990).

Founex Report on Development and Environment Submitted by a Panel of Experts Convened by the Secretary-General of the United Nations Conference on the Human Environment, June 4–12, 1971, Founex, Switzerland, 1972.

Fricker, Miranda. *Epistemic Injustice: Power and Ethics of Knowing* (Oxford University Press 2007).

Gebeye, Berihun Adugna. *A Theory of African Constitutionalism* (Oxford University Press 2021).

Gellers, Joshua. *The Global Emergence of Constitutional Environmental Rights* (Routledge 2018).

Gillespie, Alexander. *International Environmental Law, Policy and Ethics* (Oxford University Press 2014).

Gissibl, Bernhard. *The Nature of German Imperialism: Conservation and the Politics of Wildlife in Colonial East Africa* (Berghahn Books 2016).

Gottlieb, Roger S. *A Greener Faith: Religious Environmentalism and Our Planet's Future* (Oxford University Press 2006).

Gozzi, Gustavo. *Rights and Civilisations: A History and Philosophy of International Law* (Cambridge University Press 2019).

Grubb, Michael, Matthias Koch, Abby Munson, Francis Sullivan and Koy Thomson. *The 'Earth Summit' Agreements: A Guide and Assessments* (Earthscan Publications 1993).

Haddour, Azzedine. *History and Narrative* (Manchester University Press 2000).

Halvorssen, Anita M. *Equality among Unequals in International Environmental Law: Differential Treatment for Developing Countries* (Westview Press 1999).

Hart, H. L. A. *The Concept of Law*, 2nd ed. (Oxford University Press 1994).

Hassall, Graham and Cheryl Sanders. *Asia-Pacific Constitutional Systems* (Cambridge University Press 2006).

Hinton, Alexander Laban. *The Justice Façade: Trials of Transitions in Cambodia* (Oxford University Press 2018).

Ibhawoh, Bonny. *Imperial Justice: Africans in Empire's Court* (Oxford University Press 2013).

Imperialism and Human Rights: Colonial Discourse of Rights and Liberties in African History (State University of New York Press 2007).

Ince, Onur Ulas. *Colonial Capitalism and the Dilemmas of Liberalism* (Oxford University Press 2018).

International Union for Conservation of Nature, *World Conservation Strategy: Living Resource Conservation for Sustainable Development* (IUCN 1980).

Jackson, Robert H. *Quasi-States: Sovereignty, International Relations and the Third World* (Cambridge University Press 1991).

Jessup, Philip C. *Transnational Law* (Yale University Press 1956).

Jones, Phil and James Evans. *Urban Regeneration in the UK: Theory and Practice* (SAGE Publications 2013).

Kalb, Martin. *Environment Empire: Nature, Infrastructure, and the Making of German Southwest Africa* (Berghahn Books 2022).

Kaufman, Scott. *The Environment and International History* (Bloomsbury 2018).

Kelsen, Hans. *Pure Legal Theory*, translated by Max Knight (The Lawbook Exchange 2005).

Kennedy, David. *A World of Struggle: How Power, Law, and Expertise Shape Global Political Economy* (Princeton University Press 2016).

Kim, Heejin. *Regime Accommodation in International Law: Human Rights in International Economic Law and Policy* (Brill 2016).

Koskeniemmi, Martti. *From Apology to Utopia: The Structure of International Legal Argument* (Cambridge University Press 2006).

Kuruk, Paul. *Traditional Knowledge, Genetic Resources, Customary Law, and Intellectual Property: A Global Primer* (Edward Elgar 2020).

Lantigua, David M. *Infidels and Empires in the New World Order: Early Moderns Spanish Contributions to Legal Thought* (Cambridge University Press 2020).

Leib, Linda Hajjar. *Human Rights and the Environment: Philosophical, Theoretical and Legal Perspectives* (Brill 2011).

Linarelli, John, Margot E. Salomon and Muthucumaraswamy Sornarajah. *The Misery of International Law: Confrontations with Injustice in the Global Economy* (Oxford University Press 2018).

Ling, Chee Yoke. *The Rio Declaration on Environment and Development: An Assessment* (Third World Network 2012).

Locke, John. *Two Treatises of Government*, ed. by Peter Laslett (Cambridge University Press 1960).

Lumumba-Kasongo, Tukumbi. *Japan–Africa Relations* (Palgrave MacMillan, 2010).

Macekura, Stephen J. *Of Limits and Growth: The Rise of Global Sustainable Development in the Twentieth Century* (Cambridge University Press 2015).

MacKenzie, John M. *The Empire of Nature: Hunting, Conservation, and British Imperialism* (Manchester University Press 1988).

MacLeod, Scott. *Financing Environmental Measures in Developing Countries: The Principle of Additionality*, No 6 (IUCN Environmental Policy & Law Paper 1974).

Malinoswki, Bronislaw. *Crime and Custom in Savage Society* (Routledge 1926).

Mallard, Grégoire. *Gift Exchange: The Transnational History of a Political Idea* (Cambridge University Press 2019).

Manulak, Michael W. *Change in Global Environmental Politics: Temporal Focal Points and the Reform of International Institutions* (Cambridge University Press 2022).

Marine and Environmental Law Institute, *2011–2012 Annual Report: Celebrating 30 Years of the United Nations Convention of the Law on the Sea* (Marine & Environmental Law Institute 2012).

Marx, Karl and Friedrich Engels. *The German Ideology* (Prometheus Books 1998).

Massoud, Mark Fathi. *Law's Fragile State: Colonial, Authoritarian, and Humanitarian Legacies in Sudan* (Cambridge University Press 2013).

Mawere, Munyaradzi. *Environmental Conservation through Ubuntu and Other Emerging Perspectives* (Langaa Research & Publishing CIG 2014).

Mbaidjol, Ngonlardje Kabra. *African Countries and the Global Scramble for China: A Contribution to Africa's Preparedness and Rehearsal* (Brill 2019).

Mehmet, Ozay. *Westernising the Third World: The Eurocentricity of Economic Development Theories*, 2nd ed. (Routledge 2002).

Memmi, Albert. *The Coloniser and the Colonised*, translated by Howard Greenfeld (Earthscan 1990).

Menski, Werner F. *Comparative Law in a Global Context: The Legal Systems of Asia and Africa*, 2nd ed. (Cambridge University Press 2006).

Miéville, China. *Between Equal Rights: A Marxist Theory of International Law* (Brill 2005).

Miles, Kate. *The Origins of International Investment Law: Empire, Environment and the Safeguarding of Capital* (Cambridge University Press 2013).

Morrison, David R. *Aid and Ebb Tide: A History of CIDA and Canadian Development Assistance* (Wilfrid Laurier University Press 1998).

Mudimbe, V. Y. *The Invention of Africa: Gnosis, Philosophy and the Order of Knowledge* (James Currey 1988).

Murray, Rachel. *The African Charter on Human and Peoples' Rights: A Commentary* (Oxford University Press 2019).

Nash, Roderick. *The Rights of Nature: A History of Environmental Ethics* (University of Wisconsin Press 1989).

Njuguna, Casper. *African Customary Law: Assessing Its Status and Effects Today* (Lexington Books 2009).

Nyoni, Bednicho. *Abundant Life and Basic Needs: African Religions as a Resource for Sustainable Development, with Special Reference to Shona Religion* (University of Bamberg Press 2017).

O'Donnell, Erin. *Legal Rights for Rivers: Competition, Collaboration and Water Governance* (Routledge 2019).

Okafo, Nonso. *Reconstructing Law and Justice in a Postcolony* (Ashgate 2009).

Okereke, Chukwumerije. *Global Justice and Neoliberal Environmental Governance: Ethics, Sustainable Development and International Co-operation* (Routledge 2008).

Onuma, Yasuaki. *A Transcivilisational Perspective on International Law: Questioning Prevalent Cognitive Frameworks in the Emerging Multi-Polar and Multi-Civilisational World of the Twenty-First Century* (Brill 2010).

International Law in a Transcivilisational World (Cambridge University Press 2017).

Orford, Anne. *International Law and the Politics of History* (Cambridge University Press 2021).

Pahuja, Sundhya. *Decolonising International Law: Development, Economic Growth and the Politics of Universality* (Cambridge University Press 2011).

Parfitt, Rose. *The Process of International Legal Reproduction: Inequality, Historiography, Resistance* (Cambridge University Press 2019).

Park, Jong-Dae. *Reinventing Africa's Development: Linking Africa to the Korean Development Model* (Palgrave MacMillan 2019).

Parker, John and Richard Rathbone. *African History: A Short Introduction* (Oxford University Press 2007).

Patel, Bimal N. *The State Practice of India and the Development of International Law* (Brill 2016).

Paton, G. J. *Ecological Sustainability and Embeddedness* (Routledge 2011).

Petersmann, Marie-Catherine. *When Environmental Protection and Human Rights Collide: The Politics of Conflict Management by Regional Courts* (Cambridge University Press 2022).

Puig, Sergio. *At the Margins of Globalisation: Indigenous Peoples and International Economic Law* (Cambridge University Press 2021).

Radcliffe, James. *Green Politics: Dictatorship or Democracy?* (MacMillan 2000).

Rajagopal, Balakrishnan. *International Law from Below: Development, Social Movement and Third World Resistance* (Cambridge University Press 2003).

Raz, Joseph. *The Authority of Law: Essays on Law and Morality* (Clarendon Press 1979).

Reynolds, John. *Emergency, Colonialism, and Third World Approaches to International Law* (Cambridge University Press 2017).

Richardson, Benjamin J. *Time and Environmental Law: Telling Nature's Time* (Cambridge University Press 2017).

Roberts, Anthea. *Is International Law International?* (Oxford University Press 2017).

Rodney, Walter. *How Europe Underdeveloped Africa* (Bogle L'Ouverture 1972).

Romanucci-Ross, Lola and Taurence Tancredi. *When Law and Medicine Meet: A Cultural View* (Springer 2008).

Rovira, Mónica García-Salmones. *The Project of Positivism in International Law* (Cambridge University Press 2013).

Said, Edward. *Orientalism* (Pantheon Books 1978).

Sands, Philippe. *Principles of International Environmental Law*, 2nd ed. (Cambridge University Press 2003).

Sands, Philippe and Jacqueline Peel. *Principles of International Environmental Law* (Cambridge University Press 2012).

Saravanan, Velayutham. *Colonialism, Environment and Tribals in South India, 1792–1947* (Routledge 2017).

Satterthwaite, David. *Barbara Ward and the Origins of Sustainable Development* (International Institute for Environment and Development 2006).

Sbert, Carla. *The Lens of Ecological Law: A Look at Mining* (Edward Elgar 2020).

Schrijver, Nico. *Development without Destruction: The UN and Global Resource Management* (Indiana University Press 2010).

The Evolution of Sustainable Development in International Law: Inception, Meaning and Status (Martinus Nijhoff 2008).

Schleper, Simone. *Planning for the Planet: Environmental Expertise and the International Union for the Conservation of Nature and Natural Resources* (Berghahn Books 2019).

Scotford, Eloise. *Environmental Principles and the Evolution of Environmental Law* (Oxford: Hart Publishing 2017).

Seemann, Miriam. *Water Security, Justice and the Politics of Water Rights of Peru and Bolivia* (Palgrave MacMillan 2016).

Sheleff, Leon. *The Future of Tradition: Customary Law, Common Law, and Legal Pluralism* (Frank Cass 1999).

Sornarajah, Muthucumaraswamy. *Resistance and Change in the International Law on Foreign Investment* (Cambridge University Press 2015).

de Sousa Santos, Boaventura. *Epistemologies of the South: Justice against Epistemicide* (Routledge 2014).

Toward a New Legal Common Sense: Law, Globalisation, and Emancipation, 3rd ed. (Cambridge University Press 2020).

Taylor, Prue. *An Ecological Approach to International Law: Responding to the Challenges of Climate Change* (Routledge 2008).

Thompsell, Angela. *Hunting Africa: British Sport, African Knowledge and the Nature of Empire* (Palgrave MacMillan 2015).

Tibebu, Teshale. *Hegel and the Third World: The Making of Eurocentrism in World History* (Syracuse University Press 2010).

Tladi, Dire. *Sustainable Development in International Law: Analysis of Key Enviro-Economic Instruments* (Pretoria University Law Press 2007).

Tobin, Brendan. *Indigenous Peoples, Customary Law and Human Rights—Why Living Law Matters* (Routledge 2014).

Tremblay, Luc B. *The Rule of Law, Justice, and Interpretation* (McGill-Queen's University Press 1997).

Tzouvala, Ntina. *Capitalism as Civilisation: A History of International Law* (Cambridge University Press 2020).

Unuigbe, Ngozi Finette. *Traditional Ecological Knowledge and Global Pandemics: Biodiversity and Planetary Health Beyond COVID-19* (Routledge 2021).

Van den Meerssche, Dimitri. *The World Bank's Lawyers: The Life of International Law as Institutional Practice* (Oxford University Press 2022).

Verschuuren, Jonathan. *Principles of Environmental Law: The Ideal of Sustainable Development and the Role of Principles of International, European, and National Environmental Law* (Nomos Verlag 2003).

Viljoen, Frans. *International Human Rights Law in Africa*, 2nd ed. (Oxford University Press 2012).

Viljoen, Frans, Humphrey Sipalla and Foluso Adegalu (eds.) *Exploring African Approaches to International Law: Essays in Honour of Kéba Mbaye* (Pretoria University Law Press 2022).

Vincent, Joan. *Anthropology and Politics: Visions, Traditions, and Trends* (University of Arizona Press 1990).

Viñuales, Jorge E. *The Organisation of the Anthropocene: In Our Hands?* (Brill 2018).

Voigt, Christina. *Sustainable Development as a Principle of International Law: Resolving Conflicts between Climate Measures and WTO Law* (Martinus Nijhoff 2009).

Warde, Paul, Libby Sorlin and Sverker Sörlin, *The Environment: A History of the Idea* (John Hopkins University Press 2018).

Watson, Irene. *Aboriginal Peoples, Colonialism and International Law: Raw Law* (Routledge 2015).

Weston, Burns H. and David Bollier. *Green Governance: Ecological Survival, Human Rights, and the Law of the Commons* (Cambridge University Press 2013).

van Wieren, Gretel. *Restored to Earth: Christianity, Environmental Ethics, and Ecological Restoration* (Georgetown University Press 2013).

Williams, Raymond. *Ideas of Nature: Problems of Materialism and Culture* (Verso Books 1980).

World Commission on Environment and Development. *Our Common Future* (Oxford University Press 1987).

World Conservation Union. *An Introduction to the African Convention on Nature and Natural Resources*, 2nd ed. (IUCN 2006).

Worster, Donald. *The Wealth of Nature: Environmental History and Ecological Imaginations* (Oxford University Press 1993).

Yusuf, Abdulqawi A. *Pan-Africanism and International Law* (Brill 2014).

Ziai, Aram. *Development Discourse and Global History: From Colonialism to the Sustainable Development Goals* (Routledge 2016).

Book Chapters

Acosta, Alberto. 'Post-Extractivism: From Discourse to Practice: Reflection for Action' in Gilles Carbonnier, Humberto Campodónico and Sergio Tezanos Vázquez (eds.), *Alternative Pathways to Sustainable Development: Lessons from Latin America* (Brill, 2017) 77.

Adelman, Sam. 'The Sustainable Development Goals, Anthropocentrism and Neoliberalism' in Duncan French and Louis J. Kotzé (eds.), *Sustainable Development Goals: Law, Theory and Implementation* (Edward Elgar 2017) 15.

Affolder, Natasha. 'The Legal Concept of Sustainability' in Alan Ingleson (ed.), *Environment in the Courtroom* (University of Calgary Press 2019) 92.

'Transnational Carbon Contracting: Why Law's Invisibility Matters' in A. Claire Cutler and Thomas Dietz (eds.), *The Politics of Private Transnational Governance by Contract* (Routledge 2017) 215.

'Transnational Law as Unseen Law' in Peer Zumbansen (ed.), *The Many Lives of Transnational Law: Critical Engagements with Jessup's Bold Proposal* (Cambridge University Press, 2020) 364.

'An Unknown Past, An Unequal Present, and an Uncertain Future: Transnational Environmental Law through Three Research Challenges' in Veerle Heyvaert and Leslie-Anne Duvic-Paoli (eds.), *Research Handbook on Transnational Environmental Law* (Edward Elgar 2020) 32.

Aginam, Obijiofor. 'Saving the Tortoise, the Turtle, and the Terrapin: The Hegemony of Global Environmentalism and the Marginalisation of the Third World Approaches to Sustainable Development' in Obiora Chinedu Okafor and Obijiofor Aginam (eds.), *Humanising Our Global Order: Essays in Honour of Ivan Head* (University of Toronto Press 2003) 12.

Alvarez, José E. 'Legal Perspectives' in Thomas G. Weiss and Sam Daws (eds.), *The Oxford Handbook on the United Nations*, 2nd ed. (Oxford University Press 2018) 79.

Anghie, Antony. 'Bandung and the Origins of Third World Sovereignty' in Luis Eslava, Michael Fakhri and Vasuki Nesiah (eds.), *Bandung, Global History, and International Law: Critical Pasts and Pending Futures* (Cambridge University Press 2017) 535.

'Domination' in Jean d'Aspremont and Sahib Singh (eds.), *Concepts for International Law: Contributions to Disciplinary Thought* (Edward Elgar 2019) 222.

'On Critique and Other' in Anne Orford (ed.), *International Law and Its Others* (Cambridge University Press 2006) 389.

'Towards a Postcolonial International Law' in Prabhakar Singh and Benoît Mayer (eds.), *Critical International Law: Postrealism, Postcolonialism, and Transnationalism* (Oxford University Press 2014) 123.

Armitage, David and Jennifer Pitts. '"This Modern Grotius": An Introduction to the Life and Thought of C. H. Alexandrowicz' in Charles H. Alexandrowicz (ed.), *The Law of Nations in Global History* (Oxford University Press 2017) 1.

Atapattu, Sumudu and Carmen Gonzalez. 'The North–South Divide in International Environmental Law: Framing the Issues' in Shawkat Alam, Sumudu Atapattu, Carmen G. Gonzalez and Jona Razzaque (eds.), *International Environmental Law and the Global South* (Cambridge University Press 2015) 1.

Atuguba, Raymond A. 'Legal Pluralism in Africa: Three Levels and Seven Types of Law' in Muna Ndulo and Cosmas Emeziem (eds.), *Routledge Handbook of African Law* (Routledge 2022) 17.

Baderin, Mashood. 'Religion and International Law: An Analytical Survey of the Relationship' in David Armstrong (ed.), *Routledge Handbook of International Law* (Routledge 2009) 165.

Barral, Virginie. 'National Sovereignty over Natural Resources: Environmental Challenges and Sustainable Development' in Elisa Morgera and Kati Kulovesi (eds.), *Research Handbook on International Law and Natural Resources* (Edward Elgar 2016) 3.

'The Principle of Sustainable Development' in Michael Faure (ed.), *Elgar Encyclopedia of Environmental Law* (Edward Elgar 2018) 103.

Bartel, Robyn. 'Place-Thinking: The Hidden Geography of Environmental Law' in Andreas Philippopoulos-Mihalopoulos and Victoria Brooks (eds.), *Research Handbook of Environmental Law: A Handbook* (Edward Elgar 2019) 159.

Bastmeijer, Kees. 'Introduction' in Kees Bastmeijer (ed.), *Wilderness Protection in Europe: The Role of International, European, and National Law* (Cambridge University Press 2016) 1.

Batterbury, Simon and Frankline Ndi. 'Land-Grabbing in Africa' in Tony Binns, Kenneth Lynch and Etienne Nel (eds.), *Routledge Handbook of African Development* (Routledge 2018) 573.

Bayero-Jimoh, Maryam. 'Traditional Beliefs and Legal Frameworks on Environmental Protection in Accessing Clean Water in Nigeria' in M. Christian Green and Muhammed Haron (eds.), *Law, Religion and the Environment in Africa* (African Sun Media 2020) 81.

Bedjaoui, Mohammed. 'The Right to Development' in Mohammed Bedjaoui (ed.), *International Law: Achievements and Prospects* (UNESCO 1991) 1182.

Benda-Beckmann, Franz and Keebet von Benda-Beckmann. 'Legal Pluralism and Legal Anthropology: Experiences from Indonesia' in Gary F. Bell (ed.), *Pluralism, Transnationalism and Culture in Asian Law: A Book in Honour of M. B. Hooker* (ISEAS-Yusof Ishak Institute 2017) 70.

Bennett, T. W. 'Comparative Law and African Customary Law' in Mathias Reimann and Reinhard Zimmermann (eds.), *Oxford Handbook of Comparative Law*, 2nd ed. (Oxford University Press 2019) 652.

Bergström, Johanna. 'Learning from Mayan Feminists' Interpretation of Buen Vivir' in Julie Cupples and Ramón Gosfoguel (eds.), *Unsettling Eurocentrism in the Westernised University* (Routledge 2019) 156.

Berros, Mária Valeria. 'Rights of Nature in the Anthropocene: Towards the Democratization of Environmental Law?' in Michelle Lim (ed.), *Charting Environmental Law Futures in the Anthropocene* (Springer 2019) 21.

Boer, Ben. 'Social Ecology and Environmental Law' in R. B. Singh and Suresh Misra (eds.), *Environmental Law in India: Issues and Responses* (Concept Publishing Company 1996) 35.

Bosselmann, Klaus. 'The Ever-Increasing Importance of Ecological Integrity in International and National Law' in Laura Westra, Klaus Bosselmann, Janice Gray and Kathryn Gwiazdon (eds.), *Ecological Integrity, Law and Governance* (Routledge 2018) 225.

'Governing the Commons: Can States Be Trustees?' in Laura Westra, Janice Gray and Antonio D'Aloia (eds.), *The Common Good and Ecological Integrity: Human Rights and the Support of Life* (Routledge 2016) 267.

'Grounding the Rule of Law' in Christina Voigt (ed.), *Rule of Law for Nature: New Dimensions and Ideas in Environmental Law* (Cambridge University Press 2013) 75.

'A Normative Approach to Environmental Governance: Sustainability at the Apex of Environmental Law' in Douglas Fisher (ed.), *Research Handbook on Fundamental Concepts of Environmental Law* (Edward Elgar 2016) 22.

'Sustainable Development and International Environmental Law' in Erika J. Techera (ed.), *Routledge Handbook of International Environmental Law* (Routledge 2012) 667.

Brand, Karl-Werner. 'Sustainable Development' in James D. Wright (ed.), *International Encyclopedia of the Social & Behavioural Sciences*, 2nd ed. (Elsevier 2015) 812.

Brightman, Marc and Jerome Lewis. 'Introduction' in Marc Brightman and Jerome Lewis (eds.), *The Anthropology of Sustainability: Beyond Development and Progress* (Palgrave Macmillan 2017) 1.

Brisman, Avi. 'Stockholm Conference, 1972' in Deen K. Chatterjee (ed.), *Encyclopedia of Global Justice* (Springer 2011) 1039.

Brown, Donald. 'Achieving Traction for Ethics in Environmental Policy-Making' in Laura Westra, Klaus Bosselmann, Janice Gray and Kathryn Gwiazdon (eds.), *Ecological Integrity, Law and Governance* (Routledge 2018) 149.

Brunnée, Jutta. 'The Stockholm Declaration and the Structure and Processes of International Environmental Law' in Aldo Chircop, Ted L. McDorman and Susan J. Rolston (eds.), *The Future of Ocean Regime-Building: Essays in Tribute to Douglas M. Johnston* (Brill 2009) 41.

Bugge, Hans Christian. 'Twelve Fundamental Challenges in Environmental Law: An Introduction to the Rule of Law of Nature' in Christina Voigt (ed.), *Rule of Law for Nature: New Dimensions and Ideas in Environmental Law* (Cambridge University Press 2013) 3.

Camara, Fatou K. 'From Contemporary African Customary Laws to Indigenous African Law: Identifying African Human Rights and Good Governance Sensitive Principles as a Tool to Promote Meaningful Socio-Legal Reforms' in Jeanmarie Fenrich, Paolo Galizzi and Tracy E. Higgins (eds.), *The Future of African Customary Law* (Cambridge University Press 2011) 494.

Carducci, Michele. '"Cross-Constitutionalism" and Sustainable Comparison' in Alberto Febbrajo and Giancarlo Corsi (eds.), *Sociology of Constitutions: A Paradoxical Perspective* (Routledge 2016) 137.

Chatterjee, Partha. 'The Legacy of Bandung' in Luis Eslava, Michael Fakhri and Vasuki Nesiah (eds.), *Bandung, Global History, and International Law: Critical Pasts and Pending Futures* (Cambridge University Press 2017) 657.

Chenwi, Lilian. 'The Right to a Satisfactory, Healthy, and Sustainable Environment in the African Human Rights System' in Robert Knox and Ramin Pejan (eds.), *The Human Right to a Healthy Environment* (Cambridge University Press 2018) 59.

Chimakonam, Jonathan O. 'Introduction' in Jonathan O. Chimakonam (ed.), *African Philosophy and Environmental Conservation* (Routledge 2017) 1.

Chimni, B. S. 'Anti-Imperialism: Then and Now' in Luis Eslava, Michael Fakhri and Vasuki Nesiah (eds.), *Bandung, Global History and International Law: Critical Pasts and Pending Futures* (Cambridge University Press 2017) 35.

Chinweze, Chizoba, Chukwuemeka Jideani and Gwen Z. Abiola-Oloke. 'Traditional Norms and Environmental Law: The Sub-Saharan Africa' in Christina Voigt (ed.), *Rule of Law for Nature: New Dimensions and Ideas in Environmental Law* (Cambridge University Press 2013) 191.

Chirindo, Kundai V. 'Bantu Sociolinguistics in Wangari Maathai's Peacebuilding Rhetoric' in Eddah M. Mutua, Alberto González and Anke Wolbert (eds.), *The Rhetorical Legacy of Wangari Maathai* (Lexington 2018) 1.

Chua, Charmaine. 'Against Localisation: Rethinking Compliance and Antagonism in Norm Dynamics' in Charlotte Epstein (ed.), *Against International Relations Norms: Postcolonial Perspectives* (Routledge 2017) 87.

Cliquet, An. 'Ecological Restoration as a Legal Duty in the Anthropocene' in Michelle Lim (ed.), *Charting Environmental Law Futures in the Anthropocene* (Springer 2019) 59.

Collins, Michael. 'Nation, State and Agency: Evolving Historiographies of African Decolonisation' in Andrew W. M. Smith and Chris Jeppessen (eds.), *Britain, France and the Decolonisation of Africa: Future Imperfect?* (UCL Press 2017) 17.

Collins, Richard. 'Classical Legal Positivism in International Law Revisited' in Jörg Kammerhofer and Jean d'Aspremont (eds.), *International Legal Positivism in a Post-Modern World* (Cambridge University Press 2014) 23.

Connor, Linda H. and Jonathan Paul Marshall, 'Ecologies, Ontologies and Mythologies of Possible Futures' in Linda H. Connor and Jonathan Paul Marshall (eds.), *Environmental Change and the World's Futures: Ecologies, Ontologies and Mythologies of Possible Futures* (Routledge 2016) 1.

Correa, Fabiano de Andrade and Marina Demaria Venâncio. 'International Environmental Law in the Anthropocene: Addressing the Gaps towards "Sustainable Development Law"' in Michelle Lim (ed.), *Charting Environmental Law Futures in the Anthropocene* (Springer 2019) 45.

Craig, Donna and Michael I. Jeffery. 'The Recognition and Enforcement of Indigenous Customary Law in Natural Resource Management' in Lee Paddock, Du Qun, Louis J. Kotzé, David L. Markell, Kenneth J. Markowitz and Durwood Zaelke (eds.), *Compliance and Enforcement in Environmental Law* (Edward Elgar 2011) 535.

Craven, Matthew. 'Theorising the Turn to History in International Law' in Anne Orford and Florian Hoffmann (eds.), *The Oxford Handbook of the Theory of International Law* (Oxford University Press 2016) 22.

Cullinan, Cormac. 'The Rule of Nature's Law' in Christina Voigt (ed.), *Rule of Law for Nature: New Dimensions and Ideas in Environmental Law* (Cambridge University Press 2013) 94.

Damtie, Melesse. 'Anthropocentric and Ecocentric Versions of the Ethiopian Legal Regime' in Peter Burdon (ed.), *Exploring Wild Law: The Philosophy of Earth Jurisprudence* (Wakefield Press 2011) 159.

Deák, Dániel. 'Innovation in the Intervention into Nature by Legal Means' in Luk Bouckaert, Knut J. Ims and Peter Rona (eds.), *Art, Spirituality and Economics: Liber Amicorum for Laszlo Zsolnai* (Springer 2018) 225.

Dzidzornu, David. 'Economic Development and Environmental Protection in Africa: The Constitutional, Conventional and Institutional Contexts' in Francis Botchway (ed.), *Natural Resource Investment and Africa's Development* (Edward Elgar 2011) 462.

Eberhard, Christopher and David Napier. 'Law and Policy in a "Glocal" World: The Challenge of Dialogue' in Michael Freman and David Napier (eds.), *Law and Anthropological Review: Legal Issues, Volume 12* (Oxford University Press 2009) 67.

Eckert, Andreas. 'Radical Scholarship and Political Activism: Walter Rodney as Third World Intellectual and Historian of the Third World' in Gyan Prakash and Jeremy Adelman (eds.), *Inventing the Third World: In Search of Freedom for the Postwar Global South* (Bloomsbury Academic 2022) 117.

Ellis, Jaye. 'Sustainable Development as a Legal Principle: A Rhetorical Analysis' in Hélène Ruiz Fabri, Rüdiger Wolfrum and Jana Gogolin (eds.), *Select Proceedings of the European Society of International Law* (Hart Publishing 2010).

Escobar, Arturo. 'Sustaining the Pluriverse: The Political Ontology of the Territorial Struggles in Latin America' in Marc Brightman and Jerome Lewis (eds.), *The Anthropology of Sustainability: Beyond Development and Progress* (Palgrave MacMillan 2017) 237.

Eslava, Luis, Michael Fahkri and Vasuki Nesiah. 'The Spirit of Bandung' in Luis Eslava, Michael Fakhri and Vasuki Nesiah (eds.), *Bandung, Global History and International Law: Critical Pasts and Pending Futures* (Cambridge University Press 2017) 3.

Etieyibo, Edwin. 'Ubuntu and the Environment' in Adeshina Afolayan and Toyin Falola (eds.), *The Palgrave Handbook of African Philosophy* (Palgrave MacMillan 2017) 633.

Fielder, Lauren. 'African Courts and African Values: Harmonising International Human Rights and Customary Law' in Kyriaki Topidi and Lauren Fielder (eds.), *Transnational Legal Processes and Human Rights* (Routledge 2013) 177.

Foucault, Michel. 'The Order of Discourse' in Robert Young (ed.), *Untying the Text: A Post-Structuralist Reader* (Routledge & Kegan Paul 1981) 48.

'Two Lectures' & 'Truth and Power', translated by C. Gordon, in *Power/ Knowledge: Selected Interviews and Other Writings 1972–1977* (Pantheon Books 1980).

Fuo, Oliver Njuh and Sama Memuna. "Cameroon's Environmental Framework Law and the Balancing of Interests in Socio-Economic Development' in Michael Faure and Willemien du Plessis (eds.), *The Balancing of Environmental Interests in Africa* (Pretoria University Law Press 2012) 75.

Futhazar, Guillaume. 'Biodiversity, Species Protection, and Animal Welfare under International Law' in Anne Peters (ed.), *Studies in Global Animal Law* (Springer 2020) 95.

Garver, Geoffrey. 'Ecological Integrity in the Anthropocene: Lessons for Law from Ecological Restoration and Beyond' in Laura Westra, Janice Gray and Franz-Theo Gottwald (eds.), *The Role of Integrity in the Governance of the Commons: Governance, Ecology, Law, Ethics* (Springer 2017) 191.

'Moving from Environmental Law to Ecological Law: Frameworks, Priorities and Strategies' in Laura Westra, Klaus Bosselmann, Janice Gray and Kathryn Gwiazdon (eds.), *Ecological Integrity, Law and Governance* (Routledge 2018) 141.

Gassama, Ibrahim J. 'International Law, Colonialism, and the African' in Martin S. Shanguhyia and Toyin Falola (eds.), *The Palgrave Handbook of African Colonial and Postcolonial History* (Palgrave MacMillan 2018) 551.

Gathii, James Thuo. 'Africa' in Bardo Fassbender and Anne Peters (eds.), *Oxford Handbook of International Law* (Oxford University Press 2012) 407.

'The Agenda of Third World Approaches to International Law (TWAIL)' in Jeffrey L. Dunoff and Mark Pollack (eds.), *International Legal Theory, Foundations and Frontiers* (Cambridge University Press 2022) 173.

Giddy, Patrick. 'Environmental Ethics in the Context of African Traditional Thought: Beyond the Impasse' in Munamato Chemhuru (ed.), *African Environmental Ethics: A Critical Reader* (Springer 2019) 47.

Gissibl, Bernhard. 'The Conservation of Luxury: Safari Hunting and the Consumption of Wildlife in Twentieth-Century East Africa' in Karin Hofmeester and Bernd-Stefan Grewe (eds.), *Luxury in Global Perspective: Objects and Practices, 1600–2000* (Cambridge University Press 2016) 263.

Gordon, Geoff. 'Natural Law in International Legal Theory: Linear and Dialectical Presentations' in Anne Orford and Florian Hoffmann (eds.), *Oxford Handbook of International Legal Theory* (Oxford University Press 2016) 279.

Grainger, Alan. 'Introduction' in Martin Purvis and Alan Grainger (eds.), *Exploring Sustainable Development: Geographical Perspectives* (Earthscan 2004) 1.

Graham, Nicole. 'Dephysicalisation and Entitlement: Legal and Cultural Discourses of Place as Property' in Brad Jessup (ed.), *Environmental Discourses in Public and International Law* (Cambridge University Press 2014) 96.

Grant, Evadne. 'International Courts and Environmental Human Rights: Re-imagining Adjudicative Paradigms' in Anna Grear and Louis J. Kotzé (eds.), *Research Handbook on Human Rights and the Environment* (Edward Elgar 2015) 379.

Grear, Anna. 'Human Rights and the Environment: A Tale of Ambivalence and Hope' in Douglas Fisher (ed.), *Research Handbook on Fundamental Concepts in Environmental Law* (Edward Elgar 2016) 146.

Grear, Anna and Evadne Grant, 'Introduction: In Search of Better Future Histories' in Anna Grear and Evadne Grant (eds.), *Thought, Law, Rights, and Action in an Age of Environmental Crisis* (Edward Elgar 2015) 1.

Griffiths, John. 'Legal Pluralism' in James D. Wright (ed.), *International Encyclopedia of Social & Behavioral Sciences*, 2nd ed. (Elsevier 2015) 757.

Grove, Richard. 'The East India Company, the Raj and the El Niño: The Critical Role Played by Colonial Scientists in Establishing the Mechanisms of Global Climate Teleconnections 1770–1930' in Richard H. Grove, Vinita Damodaran and Satpal Sangwan (eds.), *Nature and the Orient: The Environmental History of South and Southeast Asia* (Oxford University Press 1998) 301.

Gupta, Joyeeta. 'Toward Sharing Our Ecospace' in Simon Nicholson and Sikina Jinnah (eds.), *New Earth Politics Essays from the Anthropocene* (MIT Press 2016) 271.

Gwaravanda, Ephraim Taurai. 'Ubuntu Environmental Ethics: Conceptions and Misconceptions' in Munamato Chemhuru (ed.), *African Environmental Ethics: A Critical Reader* (Springer 2019) 79.

Halley, Paule and Pierre-Olivier DesMarchais. 'Sustainable Development under Canadian Law' in Allan E. Ingelson (ed.), *Environment in the Courtroom* (University of Calgary Press 2019) 1.

Hannis, Michael and Sian Sullivan. 'Relationality, Reciprocity, and Flourishing in an African Landscape' in Laura Hartman (ed.), *That All May Flourish: Comparative Religious Environmental Ethics* (Oxford University Press 2018) 279.

Hansen, Annette Skovsted. 'Africa–Asia Regional Partnerships and South–South Development Cooperation' in Pedro Amakasu Rapaso, David Arase and Scarlet Cornelissen (eds.), *Routledge Handbook of Africa–Asia Relations* (Routledge 2017) 335.

Henderson, James (Sákéj) Youngblood. 'The Context of the State of Nature' in Marie Ann Battiste (ed.), *Reclaiming Indigenous Voice and Vision* (UBC Press 2000) 11.

'Trans-Systemic Constitutionalism in Indigenous Law and Knowledge' in Smaro Kamboureli and Christl Verduyn (eds.), *Critical Collections: Indigeneity, Diaspora, and Ecology in Canadian Literary Studies* (Wilfrid Laurier University Press 2014) 49.

Himonga, Chuma. 'The Future of Living Customary Law in African Legal Systems in the Twenty First Century and Beyond, with Special Reference to South Africa' in Jeanmarie Fenrich, Paolo Galizzi and Tracy E. Higgins (eds.), *The Future of African Customary Law* (Cambridge University Press 2011) 31.

Hippolyte, Antonius R. 'Aspiring for a Constructive TWAIL Approach towards the International Investment Regime' in Stephan W. Schill, Christian Tams and Rainer Hoffman (eds.), *International Investment Law and Development: Bridging the Gap* (Edward Elgar 2015) 180.

'Foreign Investment Law and Developing Countries' in Markus Krajewski and Rhea T. Hoffmann (eds.), *Research Handbook on Foreign Direct Investment* (Edward Elgar 2019) 72.

Hornborg, Alf. 'Ecology as Semiotics: Outlines of a Contextualist Paradigm for Human Ecology' in Philippe Descola and Gílsi Pálsson (eds.), *Nature and Society: Anthropological Perspectives* (Routledge 1996) 48.

Horsthemke, Kai. 'Animal Rights and Environmental Ethics in Africa: From Anthropocentrism to Non-speciesism?' in Munamato Chemhuru (ed.), *African Environmental Ethics: A Critical Reader* (Springer 2019) 239.

Humphreys, Stephen and Yoriko Otomo. 'Theorising International Environmental Law' in Anne Orford and Florian Hoffmann (eds.), *Oxford Handbook of the Theory of International Law* (Oxford University Press 2016) 797.

Ikuenobe, Polycarp. 'African Communal Ethics' in Nimi Wariboko and Toyin Falola (eds.), *Palgrave Handbook of African Social Ethics* (Palgrave MacMillan 2020) 129.

Ince, Onur Ulas. 'Development' in Jean d'Aspremont and Sahib Singh (eds.), *Concepts for International Law: Contributions to Disciplinary Thought* (Edward Elgar 2019) 179.

Islam, M. Rafique. 'History of the North–South Divide in International Law: Colonial Discourses, Sovereignty, and Self-Determination' in Shawkat Alam, Sumudu Atapattu, Carmen G. Gonzalez and Jona Razzaque (eds.), *International Environmental Law and the Global South* (Cambridge University Press 2015) 23.

Iyioke, Ike Valentine. 'Bioethics via Africology' in Shahul Hameed, Siham El-Kafafi and Rawiri Waretini-Karena (eds.), *Handbook on Indigenous Knowledge and Bi-Culturalism in a Global Context* (IGI Global 2019) 21.

Jacobs, Michael. 'Sustainable Development as a Contested Concept' in Andrew Dobson (ed.), *Fairness and Futurity: Essays on Environmental Sustainability and Social Justice* (Oxford University Press 1999) 22.

Jennings, Bruce. 'Governing Ecological Governance in the Anthropocene: A New Covenant of Eco-Communitarianism' in Peter Burdon, Klaus Bosselmann and Kirsten Engel (eds.), *The Crisis in Global Ethics and the Future of Global Governance: Fulfilling the Promise of the Earth Charter* (Edward Elgar 2019) 126.

Kahler, Andreas. 'The Significance of Customary Law for Environmental Conservation in Cameroon' in Oliver C. Ruppel and Emmanuel D. Kam Yogo (eds.), *Environmental Law and Policy in Cameroon: Towards Making Africa the Tree of Life* (Nomos 2018) 913.

Kang'ara, Sylvia Wairimu. 'China and Africa: Development, Land, and the Colonial Legacy' in Luis Eslava, Michael Fakhri and Vasuki Nesiah (eds.), *Bandung, Global History and International Law: Critical Pasts and Pending Futures* (Cambridge University Press 2017) 367.

Kaniaru, Donald W. 'The Development of the Concept of Sustainable Development and the Birth of the UNEP' in Tuomas Kuokkanen, Ed Couzens, Tuula Honkonen and Melissa Lewis (eds.), *International Environmental Law-Making and Diplomacy: Insights and Overviews* (Routledge 2017) 127.

Kanwar, Vik. 'Not a Place, But a Project: Bandung, TWAIL, and the Aesthetics of Thirdness' in Luis Eslava, Michael Fakhri and Vasuki Nesiah (eds.), *Bandung, Global History and International Law: Critical Pasts and Pending Futures* (Cambridge University Press, 2017) 140.

Kawall, Jason. 'A History of Environmental Ethics' in Stephen M. Gardiner and Allen Thompson (eds.), *The Oxford Handbook of Environmental Ethics* (Oxford University Press 2017) 13.

Kelbessa, Workineh. 'Indigenous Environmental Philosophy' in Jay L. Garfield and William Edelglass (eds.), *Oxford Handbook of World Philosophy* (Oxford University Press 2010) 574.

Kennedy, Duncan. 'Three Globalisations of Law and Legal Thought: 1850–2000' in David Trubek and Alvaro Santos (eds.), *The New Law and Development: A Critical Appraisal* (Cambridge University Press 2006) 19.

Khoday, Kishan. 'The Mythic Environment: Ecocosmology and Narrative Remakings of Environmental Consciousness' in Usha Natarajan and Julia Dehm (eds.), *Locating Nature: Making and Unmaking International Law* (Cambridge University Press 2022) 284.

Khudori, Darwis. 'Bandung Conference and Its Constellation: An Introduction' in Darwis Khudori (ed.), *Bandung Legacy and Global Future: New Insights and Emerging Forces* (AAKAR Books 2018) 1.

Kolo, Abba. 'Dispute Settlement and Sustainable Development of Natural Resources in Africa' in Francis Botchway (ed.), *Natural Resource Investment and Africa's Development* (Edward Elgar 2011) 49.

Kopfmüller, Jürgen. 'From the Cultural Dimension of Sustainable Development to the Culture of Sustainable Development' in Oliver Parodi, Ignacio Ayestaran and Gerard Banse (eds.), *Sustainable Development: Relationships to Culture, Knowledge and Ethics* (KIT Scientific Publishing 2011) 93.

Koskenniemi, Martti. 'International Law and Religion: No Stable Ground' in Martti Koskenniemi, Mónica García-Salmones Rovira and Paolo Amorosa (eds.), *International Law and Religion: Historical and Contemporary Perspectives* (Oxford University Press 2017) 3.

Kotzé, Louis J. 'Human Rights, the Environment and the Global South' in Shawkat Alam, Sumudu Atapattu, Carmen G. Gonzalez and Jona Razzaque (eds.), *International Environmental Law and the Global South* (Cambridge University Press 2015) 171.

Kotzé, Louis J. and Anél du Plessis. 'The African Charter on Human and Peoples' Rights and Environmental Rights Standards' in Stephen J. Turner, Dinah L. Shelton, Jona Razzaque, Owen McIntyre and James R. May (eds.), *Environmental Rights: The Development of Standards* (Cambridge University Press 2019) 93.

Kumar, Vidya. 'Revolutionaries' in Jean d'Aspremont and Sahib Singh (eds.), *Concepts for International Law: Contributions to Disciplinary Thought* (Edward Elgar 2019) 773.

Kuwali, Dan. 'Decoding Afrocentrism: Decolonising Legal Theory' in Oche Onazi (ed.), *African Legal Theory and Contemporary Problems: Critical Essays* (Springer 2014) 71.

Kwiatkowska, Teresa and Wojciech Szatzschneider. 'Sustainability, Uncertainty and Environmental Ethics' in Oliver Parodi, Ignacio Ayestaran and Gerard Banse (eds.), *Sustainable Development: Relationships to Culture, Knowledge and Ethics* (KIT Scientific Publishing 2011) 201.

Laininen, Erkka. 'Transforming Our Worldview towards a Sustainable Future' in Justin W. Cook (ed.), *Sustainability, Human Well-Being, and the Future of Education* (Palgrave MacMillan 2019) 161.

Landauer, Carl. 'Taslim Olawale Elias: From British Colonial Law to Modern International Law' in Jochen von Bernstorff and Philipp Dann (eds.), *The Battle for International Law: South–North Perspectives on the Decolonisation Era* (Oxford University Press 2019) 318.

Lange, Bettina. 'How to Think about "Nature–Society" Interactions in Environmental Law "in Action"' in Andreas Philippopoulos-Mihalopoulos and Victoria Brooks (eds.), *Research Methods in Environmental Law: A Handbook* (Edward Elgar Publishing 2017) 29.

Lauer, Helen 'Beyond the Labour Market: Reinforcing the Epistemic Advantage of African Universities in the Global Knowledge Society' in Helen Yitah and Helen Lauer (eds.), *Philosophical Foundations of the African Humanities through Postcolonial Perspectives* (Brill 2019) 45.

Lawrence, Peter. 'Justice for Future Generations: Environment Discourses, International Law and Climate Change' in Brad Jessup and Kim Rubenstein (eds.), *Environmental Discourses in Public and International Law* (Cambridge University Press 2012) 23.

Lemons, John and Donald A. Brown. 'The Role of Science in Sustainable Development and Environmental Protection Decision-Making' in John Lemons and Donald A. Brown (eds.), *Sustainable Development: Science, Ethics, and Public Policy* (Springer 1995) 11.

Lim, Michelle. 'Pathways to Equitable Sustainability in the Anthropocene: An Agenda for Legal Research' in Michelle Lim (ed.), *Charting Environmental Law Futures in the Anthropocene* (Springer 2019) 221.

Limon, Marc. 'The Politics of Human Rights, the Environment, and Climate Change at the Human Rights Council' in John H. Knox and Ramin Pejan (eds.), *The Human Right to a Healthy Environment* (Cambridge University Press 2018) 189.

Lohmann, Larry. 'Neoliberalism, Law and Nature' in Philippe Cullet and Sujith Koonan (eds.), *Research Handbook on Law, Environment and the Global South* (Edward Elgar 2019) 32.

Lowe, Vaughan. 'Sustainable Development and Unsustainable Arguments' in Alan Boyle and David Freestone (eds.), *International Law and Sustainable Development: Past Achievements and Future Challenges* (Oxford University Press 1999) 19.

Luis-Hidalgo-Capitán, Antonio and Ana Patricia Cubillo-Guevara. 'Deconstruction and Genealogy of Latin American Good Living (Buen Vivir): The Triune Good Living and its Diverse Intellectual Wellsprings' in Gilles Carbonnier, Humberto Campodónico and Sergio Tezanos Vázquez (eds.), *Alternative Pathways to Sustainable Development: Lessons from Latin America* (Brill 2017) 23.

Luke, Timothy W. 'Sustainable Development as a Power/Knowledge System: The Problem of "Governmentality"' in Frank Fischer and Michael Black (eds.),

Greening Environmental Policy: The Politics of a Sustainable Future (Paul Chapman Publishing 1995) 21.

Lumumba-Kasongo, Tukumbi. 'Land Reforms in the Democratic Republic of Congo (DRC): A Study of the Political Economy of Underdevelopment and Nation-State Building' in Tukumbi Lumumba-Kasongo (ed.), *Land Reforms and Natural Resource Conflicts in Africa: New Paradigms in the Era of Globalisation* (Routledge 2015) 150.

Macekura, Stephen. 'Towards "Sustainable" Development: The UN, NGOs, and the Crafting of the World Conservation Strategy' in Wolfram Kaiser and Jan-Henrik Meyer (eds.), *International Organizations and Environmental Protection: Conservation and Globalisation in the Twentieth Century* (Berghahn Books 2017) 241.

Majekolagbe, Adebayo and Olabisi D. Akinkugbe. 'The African Court of Human and Peoples' Rights Decision in the Ogiek Case: An Appraisal' in Amissi Melchiade Manirabona and Yenny Vega Cárdenas (eds.), *Extractive Industries and Human Rights in an Era of Global Justice: New Ways of Resolving and Preventing Conflicts* (LexisNexis 2019) 163.

Manulak, Michael W. 'Developing World Environmental Cooperation: The Founex Seminar and the Stockholm Conference' in Wolfram Kaiser and Jan-Henrik Meyer (eds.), *International Organisations and Environmental Protection: Conservation and Globalisation in the 21st Century* (Berghahn Books 2017) 103.

Manzini, Nompumelelo Zinhle. 'African Environmental Ethics as Southern Environmental Ethics' in Munamato Chemhuru (ed.), *African Environmental Ethics: A Critical Reader* (Springer 2019).

Mar, Maksymilian Del. 'Beyond the State in and of Legal Theory' in Séan Patrick Donlan and Lukas Heckendorn Urscheler (eds.), *Concepts of Law: Comparative, Jurisprudential and Social Science Perspectives* (Ashgate 2014) 19.

Martin, Paul and Donna Craig. 'Accelerating the Evolution of Environmental Law through Continuous Learning from Applied Experience' in Paul Martin and Amanda Kennedy (eds.), *Implementing Environmental Law* (Edward Elgar 2015) 27.

Maynard, Hélène. 'From Classical Liberalism to Neoliberalism: Explaining the Contradictions in the International Environmental Law' in Usha Natarajan and Julia Dehm (eds.), *Locating Nature: Making and Unmaking International Law* (Cambridge University Press 2022) 45.

Mbengue, Makane Moïse. 'On Sustainable Development: A Conversation with Judge Weeramantry' in Serena Forlati, Makane Moïse Mbengue and Brian McGarry (eds.), *The Gabčíkovo–Nagymros Judgment and Its Contribution to the Development of International Law* (Brill 2020) 166.

McVeigh, Shaun. 'Critical Approaches to Jurisdiction and International Law' in Stephen Allen, Daniel Costelloe, Malgosia Fitzmaurice, Paul Gragl and

Edward Guntrip (eds.), *The Oxford Handbook of Jurisdiction in International Law* (Oxford University Press 2019) 182.

Mégret, Frédéric. 'Where Does the Critique of International Human Rights Stand? An Exploration of 18 Vignettes' in José María Beneyto and David Kennedy (eds.), *New Approaches to International Law: The European and American Experiences* (TMC Asser Press 2012) 3.

Meisch, Simon. 'Fair Distribution in the Anthropocene: Towards a Normative Conception of Sustainable Development' in Philipp Pattberg and Fariborz Zelli (eds.), *Environmental Politics and Governance in the Anthropocene: Institutions and Legitimacy in a Complex World* (Routledge 2016) 62.

Merrills, John G. 'Environmental Rights' in Daniel Bodansky, Jutta Brunnée and Ellen Hey (eds.), *The Oxford Handbook of International Environmental Law* (Oxford University Press 2008) 663.

Merry, Sally E. and Michael C. Canfield. 'Law: Anthropological Aspects' in James D. Wright (ed.), *International Encyclopedia of the Social & Behavioural Sciences* (Elsevier 2015) 535.

Mertz, Elizabeth and Mark Goodale. 'Comparative Anthropology of Law' in David S. Clark (ed.), *Comparative Law and Society* (Edward Elgar 2012) 77.

Michaels, Ralf. 'What Is Non-State Law?' in Michael A. Helfand (ed.), *Negotiating State and Non-State Law: The Challenge of Global and Local Pluralism* (Cambridge University Press 2015) 41.

Mickelson, Karin. 'Critical Approaches' in Daniel Bodansky, Jutta Brunnée and Ellen Hey (eds.), *The Oxford Handbook of International Environmental Law* (Oxford University Press 2008) 262.

'The Stockholm Conference and the Creation of the South–Global North Divide in International Environmental Law and Policy' in Shawkat Alam, Sumudu Atapattu, Carmen G. Gonzalez and Jona Razzaque (eds.), *International Environmental Law and the Global South* (Cambridge University Press 2015) 109.

Mickelson, Karin and Usha Natarajan. 'Reflections on Rhetoric and Rage: Bandung and Environmental Injustice' in Luis Eslava, Michael Fakhri and Vasuki Nesiah (eds.), *Bandung, Global History, and International Law: Critical Pasts and Pending Futures* (Cambridge University Press 2017) 465.

Montini, Massimiliano and Francesca Volpe. 'The Need for an "Integral Ecology" in Connection with the UN Sustainable Development Goals' in Frank Pasquale (ed.), *Care for the World: Laudato Si' and Catholic Social Thought in an Era of Climate Crisis* (Cambridge University Press 2019) 56.

'Sustainable Development: Renaissance or Sunset Boulevard?' in Laura Westra, Janice Gray and Franz-Theo Gottwald (eds.), *The Role of Integrity in the Governance of the Commons: Governance, Ecology, Law, Ethics* (Springer 2017) 169.

Morin, Jean-Frédéric. 'Global Environmental Governance' in Mario Telò (ed.), *Globalisation, Multilateralism, Europe: Towards a Better Global Governance?* (Routledge 2014) 227.

Morrison, Kathleen. 'Provincialising the Anthropocene: Eurocentrism in the Earth System' in Gunnel Cederlöf and Mahesh Ragarajan (eds.), *At Nature's Edge: The Global Present and Long-Term History* (Oxford University Press 2018) 1.

Murray, Rachel. 'The Human Rights Jurisdiction of the African Court of Justice and Human and Peoples' Rights' in Charles C. Jalloh, Kamari M. Clarke and Vincent O. Nmehielle (eds.), *The African Court of Justice and Human and Peoples' Rights in Context: Development and Challenges* (Cambridge University Press 2019) 965.

Natarajan, Usha. 'Environmental Justice in the Global South' in Sumudu A. Atapattu, Carmen G. Gonzalez and Sara L. Seck (eds.), *The Cambridge Handbook of Environmental Justice and Sustainable Development* (Cambridge University Press 2021) 39.

'Third World Approaches to International Law and the Environment' in Andreas Philippopoulos-Mihalopoulos and Victoria Brooks (eds.), *Research Methods in Environmental Law: A Handbook* (Edward Elgar 2017) 207.

Natarajan, Usha and Julia Dehm. 'Introduction: Where Is the Environment?' in Usha Natarajan and Julia Dehm (eds.), *Locating Nature: Making and Unmaking International Law* (Cambridge University Press 2022) 1.

Njenga, Francis. 'The Work and Role of the Asian–African Legal Consultative Committee and its Cooperation with the United Nations' in Najeeb Al-Nauimi and Richard Meese (eds.), *International Legal Issues Arising under the United Nations Decade of International Law* (Martinus Nijhoff 1995) 39.

Obregón, Liliana. 'Martti Koskenniemi's Critique of Eurocentrism in International Law' in Wouter Werner, Marieke de Hoon and Alexi Galán (eds.), *The Law of International Lawyers: Reading Martti Koskenniemi* (Cambridge University Press 2017) 360.

'The Third World Judges: Neutrality, Bias or Activism at the Permanent Court of International Justice and the International Court of Justice' in William A. Schabas and Shannonbrooke Murphy (eds.), *Research Handbook on International Courts and Tribunals* (Edward Elgar 2017) 181.

Odumosu-Ayanu, Ibironke T. 'Local Communities, Environment and Development: The Case of Oil and Gas Investment in Africa' in Kate Miles (ed.), *Research Handbook on Environment and Investment Law* (Edward Elgar 2019) 480.

Okafor, Obiora Chinedu. 'The Bandung Ethic and International Human Rights Praxis: Yesterday, Today and Tomorrow' in Luis Eslava, Michael Fakhri and Vasuki Nesiah (eds.), *Bandung, Global History and International Law: Critical Pasts and Pending Futures* (Cambridge University Press 2017) 515.

'Globalism, Memory and 9/11: A Critical Third World Perspective' in Fleur Johns, Richard Joyce and Sundhya Pahuja (eds.), *Events: The Force of International Law* (Routledge 2011) 234.

Okeja, Uchenna. 'Justification of Moral Norms in African Philosophy' in Eugene Etieyibo (ed.), *Method, Substance and the Future of African Philosophy* (Palgrave MacMillan 2018) 209.

Olupona, Jacob. 'Religion and Ecology in African Culture and Society' in Roger S. Gottlieb (ed.), *The Oxford Handbook of Religion and Ecology* (Oxford University Press 2006) 259.

Onazi, Oche. 'Introduction' in Oche Onazi (ed.), *African Legal Theory and Contemporary Problems: Critical Essays* (Springer 2014) 1.

Ørebech, Peter. 'The Place of Customary Law in Democratic Societies' in Peter Ørebech, Fred Bosselman, Jes Bjarup, David Callies, Martin Chanock and Hanne Petersen (eds.), *The Role of Customary Law in Sustainable Development* (Cambridge University Press 2006) 282.

Ørebech, Peter and Fred Bosselman. 'The Linkage between Sustainable Development and Customary Law' in Peter Ørebech, Fred Bosselman, Jes Bjarup, David Callies, Martin Chanock and Hanne Petersen (eds.), *The Role of Customary Law in Sustainable Development* (Cambridge University Press 2006) 12.

Orford, Anne. 'International Law and the Limits of History' in Wouter Werner, Marieke de Hoon and Alexi Galán (eds.), *The Law of International Lawyers: Reading Martti Koskenniemi* (Cambridge University Press 2017) 297.

Osuji, Peter. 'Laudato Si' and Traditional African Environmental Ethics' in Gerard Magill and Jordan Potter (eds.), *Integral Ecology: Protecting Our Common Home* (Cambridge Scholars Publishing 2018) 184.

Ott, Konrad. 'A Modest Proposal of How to Proceed in Order to Solve the Problem of Inherent Moral Value in Nature' in Laura Westra, Klaus Bosselmann and Richard Westra (eds.), *Reconciling Human Existence with Ecological Integrity: Science, Ethics, Economics and Law* (Earthscan 2008) 39.

Otto, Dianne. 'Subalternity and International Law: The Problems of Global Community and Incommensurability of Difference' in Peter Fitzpatrick and Eve Darian-Smith (eds.), *Laws of the Postcolonial* (University of Michigan Press 1999) 145.

Özsu, Umut. 'Determining New Selves: Mohammed Bedjaoui on Algeria, Western Sahara, and Post-Classical International Law' in Jochen von Bernstorff and Philipp Dann (eds.), *The Battle for International Law: South–North Perspectives on the Decolonisation Era* (Oxford University Press 2019) 341.

'"Let Us First All Have Unity among Us": Bandung, International Law, and the Empty Politics of Solidarity' in Luis Eslava, Michael Fakhri and Vasuki Nesiah (eds.), *Bandung, Global History and International Law: Critical Pasts and Pending Futures* (Cambridge University Press 2017) 293.

'Neo-liberalism and the New International Economic Order: A History of "Contemporary Legal Thought"' in Justin Desautels-Stein and Christopher Tomlins (eds.), *In Search of Contemporary Legal Thought* (Cambridge University Press 2017) 330.

Perelman, Jeremy. 'Human Rights, Investment and the Rights-fication of Development: The Practice of "Human Rights Impact Assessments" in Large Scale Foreign Investment in Natural Resources' in Katharine G. Young (ed.), *The Future of Economic and Social Rights* (Cambridge University Press 2019) 434.

Petitjean, Patrick. 'Science and the "Civilising Mission": France and the Colonial Enterprise' in Benedikt Stuchtey (ed.), *Science across the European Empires 1800–1950* (Oxford University Press 2005) 107.

Petrova, Darina and Tomaso Ferrando, 'Three Enclosures of International Law: Commoning Premises, Processes and Aims' in Usha Natarajan and Julia Dehm (eds.), *Locating Nature: Making and Unmaking International Law* (Cambridge University Press 2022) 255.

Philippopoulos-Mihalopoulos, Andreas. 'Looking for the Space between Law and Ecology' in Andreas Philippopoulos-Mihalopoulos (ed.), *Law and Ecology: New Environmental Foundations* (Routledge 2011) 1.

Picq, Manuela Lavinas. 'Situating the Amazon in World Politics' in Celine Tan and Julio Faundez (eds.), *Natural Resources and Sustainable Development: International Economic Law Perspectives* (Edward Elgar 2017) 165.

Pohkrel, Arun Kumar. 'Eurocentrism' in Deen K. Chatterjee (ed.), *Encyclopedia of Global Justice* (Springer 2011) 321.

Porras, Ileana M. 'Appropriating Nature: Commerce, Property and the Commodification of Nature in the Law of Nations' in Usha Natarajan and Julia Dehm (eds.), *Locating Nature: Making and Unmaking International Law* (Cambridge University Press 2022) 111.

'The Doctrine of the Providential Function of Commerce in International Law: Idealising Trade' in Martti Koskenniemi, Mónica García-Salmones Rovira and Paolo Amorosa (eds.), *International Law and Religion: Historical and Contemporary Perspectives* (Oxford University Press 2017) 313.

Postema, Gerald J. 'Legal Positivism: Early Foundations' in Andrei Marnor (ed.), *The Routledge Companion to Philosophy of Law* (Routledge 2012) 31.

Pottage, Alain. 'Introduction: The Fabrication of Persons and Things' in Alain Pottage and Martha Mundy (eds.), *Law, Anthropology, and the Constitution of the Social: Making Persons and Things* (Cambridge University Press 2004) 1.

Prost, Mario and Yoriko Otomo. 'British Influences on International Environmental Law: The Case of Wildlife Conservation' in Robert McCorquodale and Jean-Pierre Gauci (eds.), *British Influences on International Law, 1915–2015* (Brill 2016) 192.

Rachovista, Adamantia. 'The African Court on Human and Peoples' Rights: A Uniquely Equipped Testbed for (the Limits of) Human Rights Integration' in Emmanuelle Birbosa and Isabelle Rorive (eds.), *Human Rights Tectonics: Global Dynamics of Integration and Fragmentation* (Intersentia 2019) 69.

Radcliffe-Brown, Alfred. 'Primitive Law' in Edwin Robert Anderson Seligman and Alvin Saunders Johnson (ed.), *Encyclopedia of the Social Sciences* (MacMillan 1933) 202.

Rajan, Ravi. 'Imperial Environmentalism or Environmental Imperialism? European Forestry, Colonial Foresters and the Agendas of Forest Management in British India 1800–1900' in Richard Grove, Vinita Damodaran and Satpal Sangwan (eds.), *Nature and the Orient* (Oxford University Press 1998) 324.

Ranjan, Shikhar. 'Asian–African Legal Consultative Organisation (AALCO)' in Petra Minnerop, Rüdiger Wolfrum and Frauke Lanchemann (eds.), *International Development Law* (Oxford University Press 2019) 83.

Rayfuse, Rosemary. 'The Challenge of Sustainable High Seas Fisheries' in Nico Schrijver and Friedl Weiss (eds.), *International Law and Sustainable Development: Principles and Practice* (Oxford University Press 2004) 467.

Richardson, Benjamin J. 'Ties that Bind: Indigenous People and Environmental Governance' in Benjamin J. Richardson, Shin Imai and Kent McNeil (eds.), *Indigenous Peoples and the Law: Comparative and Critical Perspectives* (Hart Publishing 2009) 337.

Richardson, Benjamin J., Ikechi Mgbeoji and Francis Botchway. 'Environmental Law in Postcolonial Societies: Aspirations, Achievements and Limitations' in Benjamin J. Richardson and Stepan Wood (eds.), *Environmental Law for Sustainability: A Reader* (Hart Publishing 2006) 413.

Richardson, Benjamin R. and Stepan Wood. 'Environmental Law for Sustainability' in Benjamin R. Richardson and Stepan Wood (eds.), *Environmental Law for Sustainability: A Reader* (Hart Publishing 2006) 1.

Rittich, Kerry. 'Theorising International Law and Development' in Anne Orford and Florian Hoffmann (eds.), *The Oxford Handbook of the Theory of International Law* (Oxford University Press 2016) 820.

Ruether, Rosemary Radford. 'Religious Eco-Feminism: Healing the Ecological Crisis' in Roger S. Gottlieb (ed.), *The Oxford Handbook of Religion and Ecology* (Oxford University Press 2006) 362.

Ruppel, Oliver C. 'Environmental Law in the African Union' in Oliver C. Ruppel and Emmanuel D. Kam Yogo (eds.), *Environmental Law and Policy in Cameroon: Towards Making Africa the Tree of Life* (Nomos Verlag 2018) 119.

Sachs, Wolfgang. 'Environment' in Wolfgang Sachs (ed.), *The Development Dictionary: A Guide to Knowledge and Power*, 2nd ed. (Zed Books 2010) 24.

Schauer, Frederick. 'Pitfalls in the Interpretation of Customary Law' in Amanda Perreau-Sausine and James B. Murphy (eds.), *The Nature of Customary Law: Legal, Historical and Philosophical Perspectives* (Cambridge University Press 2007) 13.

Scholtz, Werner. 'Human Rights and the Environment in the African Union Context' in Werner Scholtz and Jonathan Verschuuren (eds.), *Regional Environmental Law: Transregional Comparative Lessons in Pursuit of Sustainable Development* (Edward Elgar 2015) 102.

'Trading Rhinoceros Horn for the Sake of Conservation: Dehorning the Dilemma through a Legal Analysis of the Emergence of Animal Welfare' in Werner Scholtz (ed.), *Animal Welfare and International Environmental Law* (Edward Elgar 2019) 235.

Schrijver, Nicolaas. 'Self-Determination of Peoples and Sovereignty over Natural Resources' in United Nations Office of the High Commissioner for Human Rights (ed.), *Realising the Right to Development: Essays in Commemoration of 25 Years of the United Nations Declaration on the Right to Development* (United Nations 2013) 95.

Seck, Sara L. 'Ecological Integrity and Third World Approaches to International Law' in Laura Westra, Klaus Bosselmann and Colin Soskolne (eds.), *Globalisation and Ecological Integrity in Science and International Law* (Cambridge Scholars Publishing 2011) 165.

Segesser, Daniel Marc and Mats Deland. 'The Lawyer as Actor in History and Society' in Mats Deland, Mark Klamberg and Pål Wrange (eds.), *International Humanitarian Law and Justice: Historical and Sociological Perspectives* (Routledge 2019) 175.

Segger, Marie-Claire Cordonnier. 'International Law, Criminal Justice, and Sustainable Development' in Sébastien Jodoin and Marie-Claire Cordonnier Segger (eds.), *Sustainable Development, International Criminal Justice, and Treaty Implementation* (Cambridge University Press 2013) 17.

Shaffer, Gregory and Carlos Coye. 'From International Law to Jessup's Transnational Law, from Transnational Law to Transnational Legal Ordering' in Peer Zumbansen (ed.), *The Many Lives of Transnational Law: Critical Engagements with Jessup's Bold Proposal* (Cambridge University Press 2020) 126.

Shalakany, Amr. 'Sanhuri and the Historical Origins of Comparative Law in the Arab World (or How Sometimes Losing Your Asalah Can Be Good for You)' in Annelise Riles (ed.), *Rethinking Masters of Comparative Law* (Hart Publishing 2001) 152.

Shanguhyia, Martin S. 'Colonialism and the African Environment' in Martin S. Shanguhyia and Toyin Falola (eds.), *The Palgrave Handbook of African Colonial and Postcolonial History* (Palgrave MacMillan 2018) 43.

Shivji, Issa G. 'Whither Africa in the Global South: Lessons of Bandung and Pan-Africanism' in Sam Moyo, Praveen Jha and Paris Yeros (eds.), *Reclaiming Africa: Scramble and Resistance in the 21st Century* (Springer 2019) 257.

Simpson, Gerry. 'The Globalisation of International Law' in Tim Dunne and Christian Reus-Smit (eds.), *The Globalisation of International Society* (Oxford University Press 2017) 265.

Singh, Prabhakar. 'The Private Life of Transnational Law: Reading Jessup from the Post-Colony' in Peer Zumbansen (ed.), *The Many Lives of Transnational Law: Critical Engagements with Jessup's Bold Proposal* (Cambridge University Press 2020) 419.

Smith, Dermot and Miya Isherwood. 'Protecting Sea Country: Indigenous Peoples and Marine Protected Areas in Australia' in James Fitzmons and Geoff Westcott (eds.), *Big, Bold & Blue: Lessons from Australia's Marine Protected Areas* (CSIRO 2016) 307.

Soininen, Niko and Daud Hassan. 'Marine Spatial Planning as an Instrument of Sustainable Ocean Governance' in Daud Hassan, Tuomas Kuokkanen and Niko Soininen (eds.), *Transboundary Marine Spatial Planning and International Law* (Routledge 2015) 3.

Somos, Mark and Anne Peters. 'Christianity, Global Environmental Protection, and Animal Law' in Rafael Domingo and John Witte Jr (eds.), *Christianity and Global Law* (Routledge 2020) 365.

Ssenyonjo, Manisuli. 'The African Commission and Court on Human and Peoples' Rights' in Gerd Oberleitner (ed.), *International Human Rights Institutions, Tribunals, and Courts* (Springer 2018) 479.

Starr, June and Jane F. Collier. 'Introduction: Dialogues in Legal Anthropology' in June Starr and Jane F. Collier (ed.), *History and Power in the Study of Law: New Directions in Legal Anthropology* (Cornell University Press 1989) 1.

Stephens, Tim. 'International Courts and Sustainable Development: Using Old Tools to Shape a New Discourse' in Brad Jessup and Kim Rubenstein (eds.), *Environmental Discourses in Public and International Law* (Cambridge University Press 2012) 195.

Stone, Christopher D. 'Ethics and International Environmental Law' in Daniel Bodansky, Jutta Brunnée and Ellen Hey (eds.), *The Oxford Handbook of International Environmental Law* (Oxford University Press 2007) 291.

Storr, Cait. 'Denaturalising the Concept of Territory in International Law' in Usha Natarajan and Julia Dehm (eds.), *Locating Nature: Making and Unmaking International Law* (Cambridge University Press 2022) 179.

Strong, Maurice. 'Introduction' in *Development and Environment: Report and Working Papers of a Panel of Experts Convened by the Secretary-General of the United Nations Conference on the Human Conference* (Mouton 1972).

Strydom, Hennie. 'Introduction to Regional Environmental Law of the African Union' in Werner Scholtz and Jonathan Verschuuren (eds.), *Regional*

Environmental Law: Transregional Comparative Lessons in Pursuit of Sustainable Development (Edward Elgar 2015) 21.

Sullivan, Sian. 'What's Ontology Got to Do with It? On the Knowledge of Nature and the Nature of Knowledge in Environmental Anthropology' in Helen Kopnina and Eleanor Shoreman-Ouimet (eds.), *Routledge Handbook of Environmental Anthropology* (Routledge 2017) 155.

Sutherland-Addy, Esi. 'The Metaphysics and Politics of Gender in the Arts of Africa' in Helen Lauer and Kofi Anyidoho (eds.), *Reclaiming the Human Sciences and Humanities through African Perspectives* (Sub-Saharan Publishers 2012) 1311.

Taha, Mai. 'Self-Determination, Oil, and Islam in the Face of the League of Nations: The Mosul Dispute and the "Non-European" Legal Terrain' in Duncan French (ed.), *Statehood and Self-Determination: Reconciling Tradition and Modernity in International Law* (Cambridge University Press 2013) 324.

Talshir, Gayil. "The Role of Environmentalism: From the Silent Spring to the Silent Revolution" in Yoram Levy and Marcel Wissenburg (eds.), *Liberal Democracy and Environmentalism: The End of Environmentalism?* (Routledge 2004) 10.

Tangwa, Godfred B. 'Some African Reflections on Biomedical and Environmental Ethics' in Kwasi Wiredu (ed.), *A Companion to African Philosophy* (Blackwell 2004) 387.

Tavares, Antonio. 'Common Features and Trends of Fisheries Legislation in Africa' in Beatrice Chaytor and Kevin R. Gray (eds.), *International Environmental Law and Policy in Africa* (Springer 2003) 181.

Techera, Erika J. 'Legal Foundations for the Recognition of Customary Law in the Post-Colonial South Pacific' in Michael Freeman and David Napier (eds.), *Law and Anthropology* (Oxford University Press 2009) 218.

Terblanché-Greeff, Aïda C. 'Ubuntu and Environmental Ethics: What the West Can Learn from Africa When faced with Climate Change' in Munamato Chemhuru (ed.), *African Environmental Ethics: A Critical Reader* (Springer 2019) 91.

Tieku, Thomas Kwasi and Linnéa Gelot. 'An African Perspective on Global Governance' in Anna Triandafyllidou (ed.), *Global Governance from Regional Perspectives* (Oxford University Press 2017) 119.

Tolentino Jr, Amado S. 'Passage from Natural Resources Law to Environmental Law to Sustainable Development Law' in Rüdiger Wolfrum, Maja Seršic and Trpimir M. Šošić (eds.), *Contemporary Developments in International Law: Essays in Honour of Budislav Vukas* (Brill 2016) 906.

Tuori, Kaarlo 'Transnational Law: On Legal Hybrids and Perspectivism' in Miguel Maduro, Kaarlo Tuori and Tuvi Sankari (eds.), *Transnational Law: Rethinking European Law and Legal Thinking* (Cambridge University Press 2014) 17.

Ugochukwu, Basil. 'When the T(W)AIL Wags Global Environmental Governance' in Frans Viljoen, Humphrey Sipalla and Foluso Adegalu (eds.), *Exploring African Approaches to International Law: Essays in Honour of Kéba Mbaye* (Pretoria University Law Press 2022) 239.

Unuigbe, Ngozi Finette. 'African Eco-Philosophy and Its Implications for Ecological Integrity in Africa' in Laura Westra, Klaus Bosselmann and Matteo Fermeglia (eds.), *Ecological Integrity in Science and Law* (Springer 2020) 99.

'African Eco-Philosophy on Forests: A Path Worth Exploring for the Implementation of Earth Jurisprudence' in Kirsten Anker, Peter D. Burdon, Geoffrey Garver, Michelle Maloney and Carla Sbert (eds.), *From Environmental to Ecological Law* (Routledge 2021) 164.

'The Significance of the Stewardship Ethic of the Indigenous Peoples of Nigeria's Niger Delta Region on Biodiversity Conservation' in Cameron La Follette and Chris Maser (eds.), *Sustainability and the Rights of Nature in Practice* (CRC Press 2020) 167.

VanderZwaag, David L. 'Edging towards Principled Ocean Governance: Law of the Sea and Beyond' in International Ocean Institute: Canada (ed.), *The Future of Governance and Ocean Development: Essays in Honour of Elisabeth Mann Borgese (1918–2002)* (Brill, 2018) 117.

Varbelow, Sonja. 'Curriculum Theory and Ecology of Learning: Understanding Identity and Place' in Bryant Griffith and Douglas J. Loveless (eds.), *The Interdependence of Teaching and Learning* (Information Age Publishing 2013) 67.

Viñuales, Jorge E. 'Sustainable Development in International Law' in Lavanya Rajamani and Jacqueline Peel (eds.), *The Oxford Handbook of International Environment Law*, 2nd ed. (Oxford University Press 2021) 1.

Vogler, John. 'The International Politics of Sustainable Development' in Giles Atkinson, Simon Dietz and Eric Neumayer (eds.), *Handbook of Sustainable Development* (Edward Elgar 2007) 430.

Wagner, Andreas. 'Francisco de Vitoria and the Global Commonwealth' in Rafael Domingo and John Witte Jr. (eds.), *Christianity and Global Law* (Routledge 2020) 72.

Walker, Neil. 'Christianity and the Rule of Global Law' in Rafael Domingo and John Witte Jr. (eds.), *Christianity and Global Law* (Routledge 2020) 197.

Wang, Zhian. 'The Functional Approach in *le Droit International de Développement*: A Theoretical Appraisal' in Shotaro Hamamoto, Hironobu Sakai and Akiho Shibata (eds.), *'L'Être Situé', Effectiveness and Purposes of International Law: Essays in Honour of Professor Ryuichi Ida* (Brill 2015) 37.

Weiss, Edith Brown. 'Intergenerational Equity' in Yann Aguila and Jorge E. Viñuales (eds.), *A Global Pact for the Environment: Legal Foundations* (C-EENRG 2019) 51.

'Rule of Law for Nature in a Kaleidoscopic World' in Christina Voigt (ed.), *Rule of Law for Nature: New Dimensions and Ideas for Environmental Law* (Cambridge University Press 2013) 27.

Wenzel, Volker. 'Sustainable Development: Teleology and Ambiguity' in Hans-Joachim Schellnhuber and Volker Wenzel (eds.), *Earth System Analysis: Integrating Science for Sustainability* (Springer 1998) 210.

Westra, Laura and Klaus Bosselmann. 'Introduction: The Development of the Global Ecological Integrity Group's Research and Its Future Aims' in Laura Westra, Klaus Bosselmann, Janice Gray and Kathryn Gwiazdon (eds.), *Ecological Integrity, Law and Governance* (Routledge 2018) 1.

Whyte, Kyle Powys and Chris J. Cuomo. 'Ethics of Caring in Environmental Ethics: Indigenous and Feminist Philosophies' in Stephen Mark Gardiner and Allen Thompson (eds.), *The Oxford Handbook of Environmental Ethics* (Oxford University Press 2017) 234.

Wilkens, Jan. 'Constructivism' in Anthony F. Lang Jr and Antje Wiener (eds.), *Handbook on Global Constitutionalism* (Edward Elgar 2017) 117.

Williams, Michael. 'The Role of Deforestation in Earth and World-System Integration' in Alf Hornborg, J. R. McNeill and Joan Martinez-Alier (eds.), *Rethinking Environmental History: World-System History and Global Environmental Change* (AltaMira Press 2007) 101.

Zollmann, Jakob. 'German Colonial Law and Comparative Law, 1884–1919' in Thomas Duve (ed.), *Entanglements in Legal History: Conceptual Approaches* (Max Planck Institute for European Legal History 2014) 253.

Zumbansen, Peer. 'Can Transnational Law Be Critical? Reflections on a Contested Idea, Field and Method' in Emilios Christodoulidis, Ruth Dukes and Marco Goldoni (eds.), *Research Handbook on Critical Legal Theory* (Edward Elgar 2019) 473.

'Defining the Stress of Transnational Law: Legal Theory, Global Governance and Legal Pluralism' in Günther Handl (ed.), *Beyond Territoriality: Transnational Legal Authority in an Age of Globalisation* (Brill 2012) 53.

Zurbuchen, Simone. 'Introduction' in Simone Zurbuchen (ed.), *The Law of Nations and Natural Law 1625 to 1800* (Brill 2019) 1.

Journal Articles

Aalberts, Tanja and Ben Golder. 'On the Uses of Foucault for International Law' (2012) 25:3 Leiden JIL 603.

Abel, Richard. 'What Else Is Sociology of Law? Reflections on John Griffiths's *What Is Sociology of Law?*' (2017) 49:3 J Leg Pluralism and Unofficial L 373.

Abelvik-Lawson, Helle. 'Sustainable Development for Whose Benefit? Brazil's Economic Power and Human Rights Violations in the Amazon and Mozambique' (2014) 18:7–8 Int'l JHR 795.

Abi-Saab, Georges. 'The Third World Intellectual in Praxis: Confrontation, Participation, or Operation behind Enemy Lines?' (2016) 37:11 Third World Q 1957.

Abotsi, Ernest Kofi. 'Customary Law and the Rule of Law: Evolving Tensions and Re-engineering' (2020) 37:2 Ariz J Int'l and Comp L 137.

Acharya, Amitav. "Ideas-Shift': How Ideas from the Rest Are Reshaping the Global Order' (2016) 37:7 Third World Q 1156.

'Norm Subsidiarity and Regional Orders: Sovereignty, Regionalism, and Rule-Making in the Third World' (2011) 55:1 Int'l Studies Q 95.

'Studying the Bandung Conference from a Global IR Perspective' (2016) 70:4 Australian J Int'l Affairs 342.

'Who Are the Norm Makers? The Asian-Africa Conference in Bandung and the Evolution of Norms' (2014) 20:3 Global Governance 405.

Adebajo, Adekeye. 'The Revolt against the West: Intervention and Sovereignty' (2016) 37:7 Third World Q 1187.

Affolder, Natasha. 'Contagious Environmental Law-Making' (2019) 31:2 J Envt'l Law 187.

'Looking for Law in Unusual Places: Cross-Border Diffusion of Environmental Norms' (2018) 7:3 Transnat'l Envt'l L 425.

'Transnational Environmental Law's Missing People' (2019) 8:3 Transnat'l Envt'l L 463.

Agbu, Osita. 'NEPAD: Origin, Challenges and Prospects' (2003) 64:1/2 Indian J Political Science 97.

Akami, Tomoko. 'Imperial Polities, Intercolonialism, and the Shaping of Global Governing Norms: Public Health Experts in Asia and the League of Nations Health Organisation' (2017) 12:1 J Global History 4.

Akhtar-Khatari, Afshin. 'Restoration and Cooperation for Flourishing Socio-Ecological Landscapes' (2020) 11:1–2 Transnat'l Leg Theory 62.

Akhtar-Khavari, Afshin and Benjamin R. Richardson. 'Ecological Restoration and Law: Recovering Nature's Past for the Future' (2017) 26:2 Griffith L Rev 147.

Akinkugbe, Olabisi D. 'Africanisation and the Reform of International Investment Law' (2021) 53:1 Case Western Reserve JIL 7.

Akinkugbe, Olabisi D., Ohio Omiunu, Amaka Vanni, Regis Y. Simo and Luwam Dirar. 'Africa's Participation in International Economic Law in the 21st Century: An Introduction' (2020) 17:1 Manchester J Int'l Econ L 1.

Akuffo, Kwame. 'Equity in Colonial West Africa: A Paradigm of Juridical Dislocation' (2006) 50:2 J Afr L 132.

Al Attar, Mohsen. 'Must International Law Pedagogy Remain Eurocentric?' (2021) 11:1 Asian YBIL 176.

'Reframing the "Universality" of International Law in a Globalising World' (2013) 59:1 McGill LJ 95.

'The Peculiar Double-Consciousness of TWAIL' (2022) 19:2 Indonesian JIL 239.

'TWAIL: A Paradox within a Paradox' (2020) 22:2 Int'l Community L Rev 163.

Al Attar, Mohsen and Shaimaa Abdelkarim, 'Decolonising the Curriculum in International Law: Entrapments in Praxis and Critical Thought' (2023) 34:1 L and Critique 41.

Al Attar, Mohsen and Rosalie Miller. 'Towards an Emancipatory International Law: The Bolivarian Reconstruction' (2010) 30:1 Third World Q 347.

Al Attar, Mohsen and Vernon Tava. 'TWAIL Pedagogy: Legal Pedagogy for Emancipation' (2009) 15:1 Palestine YB Int'l L 7.

Alam, Shawkat and Abdullah al Faruque, 'From Sovereignty to Self-Determination: Emergence of Collective Rights of Indigenous Peoples in Natural Resources Movement' (2019) 32:1 Georgetown Envt'l L Rev 59.

Aldeia, João and Fátima Alves. 'Against the Environment: Problems in Society/ Nature Relations' (2019) 4 Frontiers in Sociology 1.

Alexander, LoriKim, Andrews Agyekumhene and Phil Allman. 'The Role of Taboos in the Protection of and Recovery of Sea Turtles' (2017) 4 Frontiers in Marine Science 1.

Allott, AN. 'The Judicial Ascertainment of Customary Law in British Africa' (1957) 20:3 Modern L Rev 244.

'What Is to Be Done with African Customary Law? The Experience of Problems and Reforms in Anglophone Africa from 1950' (1984) 28:1–2 J Afr L 56.

Alter, Karen J., James T. Gathii and Laurence R. Helfer. 'Backlash against International Courts in West, East and Southern Africa: Causes and Consequences' (2016) 27:2 European JIL 293.

Alter, Karen J., Laurence R. Helfer and Jacqueline R. McAllister. 'A New International Human Rights Court for West Africa: The ECOWAS Community Court of Justice' (2013) 107:4 Am JIL 737.

Altwicker, Tilmann. 'Transnationalising Rights: International Human Rights Law in Cross-Border Contexts' (2018) 29:2 European JIL 581.

Amarasinghe, Punsara. 'In Praise of Kaleidoscopic Judge: A Different Reading of Judge C. G. Weeramantry's Jurisprudence before the Power Politics of the ICJ' (2020) 3 Przegląd Politologiczny 109.

Amechi, Emeka Polycarp. 'Linking Environmental Protection to Poverty Reduction in Africa: An Analysis of the Regional Legal Responses to Environmental Protection' (2010) 6:2 L Envt and D 112.

Amin, George Forji. 'A Marxist and TWAIL Reading of the Oxford Handbook of the Sources of International Law' (2020) 19:1 Chinese JIL 182.

'International Law, the Civilising Mission, and the Ambivalence of Development in Africa: Conceptual Underpinnings' (2013) 6:1 J Afr & Int'l L 191.

Anand, Sudhir and Amartya Sen. 'Human Development and Economic Sustainability' (2000) 28:12 World Dev 2029.

Anghie, Antony. 'C. G. Weeramantry at the International Court of Justice' (2001) 14:4 Leiden JIL 829.

'The Evolution of International Law: Colonial and Postcolonial Realities' (2006) 27:5 Third World Q 739.

'Finding the Peripheries: Sovereignty and Colonialism in Nineteenth-Century Law' (1999) 40:1 Harvard J Int'l L 1.

'Francisco de Vitoria and the Colonial Origins of International Law' (1996) 5:3 Soc and Leg Studies 321.

'Legal Aspects of the New International Economic Order' (2015) 6:1 Humanity 145.

'Rethinking International Law: A TWAIL Retrospective' (2023) 34:1 European JIL 7.

'Time Present and Time Past: Globalisation, International Financial Institutions, and the Third World' (2000) 32 NYU JIL and Pol 243.

'TWAIL: Past and Future' (2008) 10:4 Int'l Community L Rev 479.

Anghie, Antony and B. S. Chimni. 'Third World Approaches to International Law and Individual Responsibility in Internal Conflict' (2003) 2:1 Chinese JIL 77.

Anton, Donald K..'The 2012 United Nations Conference on Sustainable Development and the Future of International Environmental Protection' (2012) 7:1 Consilience: J Sust Dev 64.

Appiagyei-Atua, Kwadwo. 'Ethical Dimensions of Third-World Approaches to International Law (TWAIL): A Critical Review' (2015) 8:3–4 Afr J Leg Studies 209.

Arts, Karin. 'Inclusive Sustainable Development: A Human Rights Perspective' (2017) 24 Current Opinion on Envt'l Sustainability 58.

Aseeva, Anna. '(Un)Sustainable Development(s) in International Economic Law: A Quest for Sustainability' (2018) 10 Sustainability 4022.

Asiedu-Akrofi, Derek. 'Judicial Recognition and Adoption of Customary Law in Nigeria' (1989) 37:3 Am J Comp L 571.

Assie-Lumumba, N'Dri Therese. 'Behind and Beyond Bandung: Historical and Forward-Looking Reflections on South-South Cooperation' (2015) 2:11 Bandung: J Global South 1.

Atapattu, Sumudu. 'Climate Change, International Environmental Law Principles, and the North–South Divide' (2017) 26:2 Transnat'l L and Contemp Probs 247.

'Comments on Environmental Justice, Human Rights, and the Global South by Carmen Gonzalez' (2015) 13:1 Santa Clara JIL 197.

'Sustainable Development, Myth or Reality: A Survey of Sustainable Development under International Law and Sri Lankan Law' (2001) 14:2 Georgetown Int'l Envt'l L Rev 265.

Atlani-Dualt, Laëtitia and Jean-Pierre Dozon. 'Colonisation, Development and Humanitarian Aid: Towards a Political Anthropology of International Aid' (2011) 41:3 Ethnologie Française 393.

Attfield, Robin. 'Christian Attitudes towards Nature' (1983) 44 J History Ideas 369.

Atuguba, Raymond A. 'An African Redefinition of Popular Democracy and Development Nomenclature' (2016) 5:10 Int'l J Innov Research and Dev 58.

Auz, Juan. 'The Political Ecology of Earth System Law: Outlining a Lex Capitalocenae' (2023) 40:2 Wisconsin Int'l LJ 216.

Aviles, Luis A. 'Sustainable Development and Environmental Legal Protection' (2014) 6:2 Mexican L Rev 251.

Badaru, Opeoluwa Adetoro. 'Examining the Utility of Third World Approaches in International Law for International Human Rights Law' (2008) 10:4 Int'l Community L Rev 379.

Badejogbin, Rebecca Emiene. 'Judicial Discretion: Problematising the Ascertainment and Application of Customary Law by Formal Courts and Relevant Theories (Nigeria and South Africa)' (2022) 54:2–3 J Leg Pluralism and Crit Soc Anal 252.

Baderin, Mashood A. 'Religion and International Law: Friends or Foes?' (2009) 5 European HRL Rev 637.

Bakari, Mohamed El-Kamel. '"Mapping the Anthropocentric–Ecocentric" Dualism in the History of American Presidency: The Good, the Bad, and the Ambivalent' (2017) 17:1 Consilience: J Sust Dev 1.

Bakulumpagi, Kevin. 'Resolution of the African Commission on Human and Peoples' Rights on the Protection of Sacred Natural Sites and Territories: A Critical Overview' (2021) 5 Afr Human Rights YB 305.

Barral, Virginie. 'Sustainable Development in International Law: Nature and Operation of an Evolutive Legal Norm' (2012) 23:2 European JIL 377.

Banerjee, Subhabrata Bobby. 'Who Sustains Whose Development? Sustainable Development and the Reinvention of Nature' (2003) 24:1 Organisational Studies 143.

Barker, Joshua. 'Beyond Bandung: Developmental Nationalism and (Multi)cultural Nationalism in Indonesia' (2008) 29:3 Third World Q 521.

Barsalou, Olivier and Michael Hennessy Picard. 'International Environmental Law in an Era of Globalised Waste' (2018) 17:3 Chinese JIL 887.

Barzilai, Gad. 'Beyond Relativism: Where Is Political Power in Legal Pluralism?' (2008) 9:2 Theor Inq L 395.

Baxi, Upendra. 'Disasters, Catastrophes and Oblivion: A TWAIL Perspective' (2021) 2:1 YB Disaster L 72.

Beckerman, Wilfred. 'The Chimera of "Sustainable Development"' (2007) 1:1 Electronic J Sust Dev 17.

'Sustainable Development: Is It Still a Useful Concept?' (1994) 3:3 Envt'l Val 191.

Bederman, David J. 'Public Law and Custom' (2012) 61 Emory LJ 949.

Behrens, Kevin. 'African Relational Environmentalism and Considerability' (2014) 36:1 Envt'l Ethics 63.

'Exploring African Holism in Respect of the Environment' (2010) 19:4 Envt'l Val 465.

'Moral Obligations towards Future Generations in African Thought' (2012) 8:2–3 *J Global Ethics* 179.

Bekker, Gina. 'The African Court on Human and Peoples' Rights: Safeguarding the Interests of African States' (2007) 51:1 J Afr L 151.

von Benda-Beckmann, Keebet and Bertram Turner. 'Legal Pluralism, Social Theory, and the State' (2018) 50:3 J Leg Pluralism and Unofficial L 255.

Bennett, Brett M. 'Decolonisation, Environmentalism, and Nationalism in Australia and South Africa' (2017) 41:1 Itinerario 27.

Bens, Jonas and Larissa Vetters. 'Ethnographic Legal Studies: Reconnecting Anthropological and Sociological Traditions' (2018) 50:3 J Leg Pluralism and Unofficial L 239.

Berger, Mark T. 'After the Third World? History, Destiny and the Fate of Third Worldism' (2004) 25:1 Third World Q 9.

'The End of the "Third World"' (1994) 15:2 Third World Q 257.

Berman, Paul Schiff. 'From International Law to Globalisation' (2005) 43:2 Colum J Transnat'l L 485.

'Global Legal Pluralism' (2007) 80 S Cal L Rev 1155.

'The New Legal Pluralism' (2009) 5:1 Annual Rev L and Soc Science 225.

Bernstein, Steven. 'Ideas, Social Structure, and the Compromise of Liberal Environmentalism' (2000) 6:4 European J Int'l Relations 464.

Berros, Maria Valeria. 'Defending Rivers: Vilcabamba in the South Ecuador' (2017) 6 RCC Perspectives 37.

Beyerlin, Ulrich. 'Bridging the North–South Divide in International Environmental Law' (2006) 66 ZaöRV 259.

Bhatia, Amar. 'The South of the North: Building on Critical Approaches to International Law with Lessons from the Fourth World' (2012) 14:1 Oregon Rev IL 131.

Bigler, Gregory H. 'Traditional Jurisprudence and Protection of Our Society: A Jurisgenerative Tail' (2018) 43:1 Am Indian L Rev 1.

Birnie, Patricia. 'The Development of International Environmental Law' (1977) 3:2 Brit J Int'l Studies 169.

Blackmore, Andrew C. 'Public Trust Doctrine, Research and Responsible Wildlife Management in South Africa' (2017) 47:1 Bothalia 1.

Blair, Chase. 'Indigenous Sacred Sites and Lands: Pursuing Preservation through Colonial Constitutional Frameworks' (2020) 25 Appeal: Rev Current L and L Reform 73.

Blanc-Jouvan, Xavier. 'The Encounter between Traditional Law and Modern Law in French-Speaking Africa: A Personal Reflection' (2010) 25 Tul European & Civ LF 197.

Blanco, Elena and Anna Grear. 'Personhood, Jurisdiction and Injustice: Law, Colonialities and the Global Order' (2019) 10:1 J Human Rights and Envt 86.

Blowers, Andrew Jan Boersema and Adrian Martin. 'Is Sustainable Development Sustainable?' (2012) 9:1 J Integrative Envt'l Sciences 1.

Borràs, Susana. 'New Transitions from Human Rights to the Environment to Rights of Nature' (2016) 5:1 Transnat'l Envt'l L 113.

Borrows, John. 'Indigenous Legal Traditions in Canada' (2005) 19 Wash UJL and Pol'y 167.

Boshoff, Elsabé. 'Rethinking the Premises Underlying the Right to Development in African Human Rights Jurisprudence' (2022) 31:1 RECIEL 27.

Bosselmann, Klaus. 'Losing the Forests for the Trees: Environmental Reductionism in Law' (2010) 2 Sustainability 2424.

'In Search of Global Law: The Significance of the Earth Charter' (2004) 8:1 Worldviews 62.

'A Vulnerable Environment: Contextualising Law with Sustainability' (2011) 1:1 J Human Rights and Envt 45.

Bowman, Michael. 'A Tale of Two CITES: Divergent Perspectives upon the Effectiveness of the Wildlife Trade Convention' (2013) 22:3 RECIEL 228.

Boyle, Alan. 'Further Development of the Law of the Sea Convention: Mechanism for Change' (2005) 54:3 ICLQ 563.

'Human Rights and the Environment: Where Next? (2012) 23:3 European JIL 613.

Brass, Paul R. 'Foucault Steals Political Science' (2000) 3:1 Annual Rev Pol Science 305.

Bratspies, Rebecca. 'Do We Need a Human Right to a Healthy Environment?' (2015) 13:1 Santa Clara JIL 31.

'In Countless Ways and On an Unprecedented Scale: Reflections on the Stockholm Declaration at 50' (2022) 50:3 Georgia J of Int'l and Comp L 755.

'Rethinking Decisionmaking in International Environmental Law: A Policy-Oriented Inquiry into Sustainable Development' (2007) 32:2 Yale Int'l LJ 363.

Bratton, Susan Power. 'Eco-Dimensionality as a Religious Foundation for Sustainability' (2018) 10 Sustainability 1021.

Brighton, Claire. 'Unlikely Bedfellows: The Evolution of the Relationship between Environmental Protection and Development' (2017) 66:1 ICLQ 209.

Brown, Trent. 'Sustainability as Empty Signifier: Its Rise, Fall, and Radical Potential' (2016) 48:1 Antipode 115.

Buchan, Bruce. 'The Empire of Political Thought: Civilisation, Savagery and Perceptions of Indigenous Government' (2005) 18:2 History Human Sciences 1.

Buckel, Sonja and Andreas Fischer-Lescano. 'Gramsci Reconsidered: Hegemony in Global Law' (2009) 22:3 Leiden JIL 437.

Buergenthal, Thomas. 'Louis B. Sohn (1914–2006)' (2006) 100:3 Am JIL 623.

Burazin, Luka. 'The Rule of Recognition and the Emergence of a Legal System' (2015) 27 Revus: J Const Theory and Phil L 116.

Burdon, Peter D. 'The Earth Community and Ecological Jurisprudence' (2013) 3:5 Oñati Socio-Legal Series 815.

'Ecological Law in the Anthropocene' (2020) 11:1–2 Transnat'l Legal Theory 33.

'Wild Law: The Philosophy of Earth Jurisprudence' (2010) 35:2 Alternative LJ 62.

Burkett, Maxine. 'Root and Branch: Climate Catastrophe, Racial Crises, and the History and Future of Climate Justice' (2021) 134 Harvard L Rev 326.

Burra, Srinivas. 'TWAIL's Others: A Caste Critique of TWAILers and their Field of Analysis' (2016) 33:3 Windsor YB Access Just 111.

Bwire, Buluma. 'Integration of African Customary Legal Concepts: Restorative Justice: A Kenyan Example' (2019) 9:1 Societies 17.

Byrne, Jeffrey James. 'Reflecting on the Global Turn in International History or: How I Learned to Stop Worrying and Love Being a Historian of Nowhere' (2018) 1 Rivista Italiana di Storia Internazionale 11.

Callicott, J. Baird. 'Elements of an Environmental Ethic: Moral Considerability and the Biotic Community' (1979) 1:1 Envt'l Ethics 71.

Cambou, Dorothée and Stefaan Smis. 'Permanent Sovereignty over Natural Resources from a Human Rights Perspective: Natural Resources Exploitation and Indigenous' Peoples' Rights in the Arctic' (2013) 22:1 Michigan State IL Rev 347.

Capps, Patrick and Richard Collins. 'Doing Law beyond the State: Methodological Questions in International and Transnational Legal Theory' (2015) 6:3–4 Transnat'l Leg Theory 561.

Cardesa-Salzmann, Antonio and Endrius Cocciolo. 'Global Governance, Sustainability and the Earth System: Critical Reflections on the Role of Global Law' (2019) 8:3 Transnat'l Envt'l L 437.

Carlane, Cinnamon. 'Delinking International Environmental Law and Climate Change' (2014) 4:1 Michigan J Envt'l and Admin L 1.

Carlston, Kenneth S. 'Universality of International Law Today: Challenge and Response' (1962) 8:2 How LJ 79.

Castro, Carlos J. 'Sustainable Development: Mainstream and Critical Perspectives' (2004) 17:2 Organisation and Envt 195.

Chalmers, Shane. 'The Mythology of International Rule-of-Law Promotion' (2019) 44:4 L and Soc Inquiry 957.

Chambers, David Wade and Richard Gillespie. 'Locality in the History of Science: Colonial Science, Technoscience and Indigenous Knowledge' (2000) 15 Osiris 221.

Champeil-Desplats, Véronique. 'Law, the Plurality of Modes of Normativity and Their Interactions' (2019) 16 La Revue des Droits de L'homme 1.

Charney, Jonathan I. 'Universal International Law' (1993) 87:4 Am JIL 529.

Chemhuru, Munamato. 'Interpreting Ecofeminist Environmentalism in African Communitarian Philosophy and *Ubuntu*: An Alternative to Anthropocentrism' (2019) 48:2 Phil Papers 241.

Chesterman, Simon. 'Herding Schrödinger's Cats: The Limits of the Social Science Approach to International Law' (2021) 22:1 Chicago JIL 49.

Chilisa, Bagele. 'Decolonising Transdisciplinary Research Approaches: An African Perspective for Enhancing Knowledge Integration in Sustainability Science' (2017) 12 Sustainability Science 813.

Chimni, B. S. 'Customary International Law: A Third World Perspective' (2018) 112 Am JIL 1.

'Is there an Asian Approach to International Law? Questions, Theses, and Reflections' (2008) 14 Asian YBIL 249.

'An Outline of a Marxist Course on Public International Law' (2004) 17:1 Leiden JIL 1.

'The Past, Present, and Future of International Law: A Critical Third World Approach' (2007) 8:2 Melbourne JIL 499.

'The Principle of Permanent Sovereignty over Natural Resources: Towards a Radical Interpretation' (1998) 38:2 Indian JIL 208.

'Prolegomena to a Class Approach to International Law' (2010) 21:1 European JIL 57.

'Third World Approaches to International Law: A Manifesto' (2006) 8:1 Int'l Community L Rev 3.

'The World of TWAIL: Introduction to the Special Issue' (2011) 3 Trade L and Dev 14.

Chouinard, Vera. 'Living on the Global Peripheries of Law: Disability Human Rights Law in Principle and Practice in the Global South' (2018) 7:1 Laws 1.

Chukwuokolo, J Chidozie. 'Afrocentrism or Eurocentrism: The Dilemma of African Development' (2009) 6 OGIRISI: New J Afr Studies 24.

Cisneros, Laura A. 'Environmental Resistance: Defying Capitalism's Structure of False Rebellion' (2015) 8:4 Golden Gate U Envt'l LJ 5.

Claridge, Lucy. 'The Approach to UNDRIP within the African Human Rights System' (2019) 23:1-2 Int'l JHR 267.

'Litigation as a Tool for Community Empowerment: The Case of Kenya's Ogiek' (2018) 11:1 Erasmus L Rev 57.

Cockerill, Kasmira A. and Shannon M. Hagerman. 'Historical Insights for Understanding the Emergence of Community-Based Conservation in Kenya: International Agendas, Colonial Legacies, and Contested Worldviews' (2020) 25:2 Ecol & Soc'y 15.

Coenen, Johanna, Simon Bager, Patrick Meyfroidt, Jens Newig and Edward Challies. 'Environmental Governance of China's Belt and Road Initiative' (2021) 31:1 Env Pol'y and Gov 3.

Cohen, Harlan Grant. 'Finding International Law, Part II: Our Fragmenting Legal Community' (2012) 44:4 NYU JIL and Pol 1049.

Cohen, Julius. 'The Political Element in Legal Theory: A Look at Kelsen's Pure Legal Theory' (1978) 88:1 Yale LJ 1.

Collins, Lynda. 'Environmental Resistance in the Anthropocene' (2020) 10:6 Oñati Socio-Legal Series 1317.

Collins, Richard. 'In Pursuit of Method in Pluralist Jurisprudence: What Exactly Is Wrong with "Non-Pluralist Jurisprudence"?' (2017) 8:4 Transnat'l Leg Theory 407.

Connelly, Steve. 'Mapping Sustainable Development as a Contested Concept' (2007) 12:3 Local Envt 259.

Coomans, Fons. 'The Ogoni Case before the African Commission on Human and Peoples' Rights' (2003) 52:3 ICLQ 749.

Cooper, Frederick. 'Development, Modernisation, and the Social Sciences in the Era of Decolonisation: The Examples of British and French Africa' (2004) 10:1 Revue d'Histoire des Sciences Humaines 9.

Costa, Anthony. 'The Myth of African Customary Law' (1998) 14:4 SAJHR 525.

Cotterell, Roger. 'What Is Transnational Law?' (2012) 37:2 Law and Soc Inquiry 500.

Cotula, Lorenzo. '(Dis)integration in Global Resource Governance: Extractivism, Human Rights, and Investment Treaties' (2020) 23:2 J Int'l Econ L 431.

Cover, Robert M. 'Foreword: Nomos and Narrative' (1983–1984) 97 Harvard L Rev 4.

Craig, Donna and Elizabeth Gachenga. 'The Recognition of Indigenous Customary Law in Water Resource Management' (2010) 20:5–6 Water L 278.

Cullet, Philippe. 'Definition of an Environmental Right in a Human Rights Context' (1995) 13 Nethl QHR 25.

Curran, Deborah. 'Indigenous Processes of Consent: Repoliticising Water Governance through Legal Pluralism' (2019) 11:3 Water 571.

Cutler, A. Claire. 'Gramsci, Law and the Culture of Global Capitalism' (2006) 8:4 Critical Rev Int'l Soc and Pol Philosophy 527.

Daccache, Michel. 'Questioning Biodiversity Governance through Its Articulations' (2013) 18:1 Science Tech and Soc'y 51.

Dados, Nour and Raewyn Connell. 'The Global South' (2012) 11:1 Contexts 13.

Daly, Herman E. 'On Wilfred Beckerman's Critique of Sustainable Development' (1995) 4:1 Envt'l Val 49.

Dancer, Helen. 'Harmony with Nature: Towards a New Deep Legal Pluralism' (2021) 53:1 J Leg Pluralism and Unofficial L 21.

Daniel, R. R. 'The North–South Divide and the Compulsions of the 21st Century' (1999) 77:6 Current Science 770.

Dantong, Rahila Timothy. 'African Union and the Prospect of Sustainable Development in the Twenty First Century' (2015) 8:1 OIDA Int'l J Sust Dev 39.

d'Aspremont, Jean. 'Critical Histories of International Law and the Repression of Disciplinary Imagination' (2019) 7:1 London Rev IL 89.

'International Law, Universality, and the Dream of Disrupting from the Centre' (2018) 7:7 ESIL Reflections 1.

'Turntablism in the History of International Law' (2020) 22:2–3 J History IL 472.

'Wording in International Law' (2012) 25:3 Leiden JIL 5756.

Davies, George Randal. 'Appraising Weak and Strong Sustainability: Searching for a Middle Ground' (2013) 10:1 Consilience: J Sust Dev 111.

Davis, Michael. 'Law, Anthropology, and the Recognition of Indigenous Legal Systems' (2001) 11 Int'l YB Leg Anthro 298.

De Castro, Douglas. 'The Colonial Aspects of International Environmental Law: Treaties as Promoters of Continuous Structural Violence' (2017) 5:2 Groningen JIL 168.

De Lucia, Vito. 'Bare Nature: The Biopolitical Logic of the International Regulation of Invasive and Alien Species' (2019) 31:1 J Envt'l L 108.

'Competing Narratives and Complex Genealogies: The Ecosystem Approach in International Environmental Law' (2015) 27:1 J Envt'l L 91.

'Ocean Commons, Law of the Sea, and Rights of the Sea' (2019) 32:1 Can JL and Jur 45.

Deckha, Maneesha. 'Initiating a Non-Anthropocentric Jurisprudence: The Rule of Law and Animal Vulnerability under a Property Paradigm' (2013) 50:4 Alta L Rev 783.

Dei, George J. S. 'Sustainable Development in the African Context: Revisiting Some Theoretical and Methodological Issues' (1993) 18:2 Afr Dev 97.

Demian, Melissa. 'On the Repugnance of Customary Law' (2014) 56:2 Comp Studies in History and Soc'y 508.

Dernbach, John C. and Federico Cheever. 'Sustainable Development and Its Discontents' (2015) 4:2 Transnat'l Envt'l L 247.

Diala, Anthony C. 'The Concept of Living Customary Law: A Critique' (2017) 49:2 J Leg Pluralism and Unofficial L 143.

Diala, Anthony C. and Bethsheba Kangwa. 'Rethinking the Interface between Customary Law and Constitutionalism in Sub-Saharan Africa' (2019) 52:1 De Jure LJ 189.

Dickson, Julie. 'Who's Afraid of Transnational Legal Theory? Dangers and Desiderata' (2015) 6:3–4 Transnat'l Leg Theory 565.

Dirlik, Arif. 'The Bandung Legacy and the People's Republic of China in the Perspective of Global Modernity' (2015) 16:4 Inter-Asia Cultural Studies 615.

Domínguez, Lara and Colin Luoma. 'Decolonising Conservation Policy: How Colonial Land and Conservation Ideologies Persist and Perpetuate Indigenous Injustices at the Expense of the Environment' (2020) 9:3 Land 65.

Doremus, Holly. 'Environmental Ethics and Environmental Law: Harmony, Dissonance, Cacophony, or Irrelevance?' (2003) 37:1 UC Davis L Rev 1.

Doussis, Emmanuella. 'Does International Environmental Law Matter in Sustainable Development?' (2017) 28:1 YB Int'l Envt'l L 3.

Dowdle, Michael W. 'Do We Really Need a "Pluralist Jurisprudence"?' (2017) 8:4 Transnat'l Leg Theory 381.

D'Souza, Radha. 'Imperial Agendas, Global Solidarity, and Third World Socio-Legal Studies: Methodological Reflections' (2012) 49:3 Osgoode Hall LJ 409.

Du Pisani, Jacobus. 'Sustainable Development: Historical Roots of the Concept' (2006) 3:2 Envt'l Sciences 83.

Du Plessis, Anel A. and C. Rautenbach. 'Legal Perspectives on the Role of Culture in Sustainable Development' (2010) 13:1 Potchefstroom Electronic LJ 27.

Ducarme, Frédéric and Denis Couvet. 'What Does "Nature" Mean?' (2020) 6 Palgrave Communications 1.

Ducarme, Frédéric, Fabrice Filpo and Denis Couvet. 'How the Diversity of Human Concepts of Nature Affects Conservation of Biodiversity' (2021) 35:3 Conservation Biology 1019.

Dupret, Baudouin. 'What is Plural in the Law? A Praxiological Answer' (2005) 1 Égypte/Monde Arabe 1.

Durkee, Melissa J. 'International Environmental Law at Its Semicentennial: The Stockholm Legacy' (2022) 50:3 Georgia J Int'l and Comp L 748.

Dworkin, Ronald. 'Law as Interpretation' (1982) 9:1 Critical Inquiry 179.

Dyzenhaus, David. 'The Genealogy of Legal Positivism' (2004) 24:1 Oxford J Leg Studies 39.

Dzah, Godwin E. K. 'Theorising the Right to Environment: An Africological Typology' (2019) 27:1 Afr J Int'l and Comp L 25.

Dzidzornu, David M. 'Environment Protection in Africa: A Panorama of the Law and Practice' (2004) 22:2 J Energy and Nat Res L 148.

Ebobrah, Solomon T. 'Towards a Positive Application of Complementarity in the African Human Rights System: Issues of Functions and Relations' (2011) 22:3 European JIL 663.

Elias, T. O. 'The Charter of the Organisation of African Unity' (1965) 59:2 Am JIL 243.

Elinoff, Eli. 'Sufficient Citizens: Moderation and the Politics of Sustainable Development in Thailand' (2014) 37:1 Pol and Leg Anthro Rev 89.

Ellison, Kailyn. 'Rio+20: How the Tension Between Developing and Developed Countries Influenced Sustainable Development Efforts' (2014) 27:1 Pac McGeorge Glob Bus and Dev LJ 107.

Emond, D. Paul. 'Co-operation in Nature: A New Foundation for Environmental Law' (1984) 22:2 Osgoode Hall LJ 323.

Enabulele, Amos and Bright Bazuaye. 'Validity and Enforceability of Customary Law in Nigeria: Towards a Correct Delimitation of the Province of the Courts' (2019) 63:1 J Afr L 79.

Eneji, C. V. O. 'Traditional African Religion in Natural Resources in Conservation and Management in Cross River State, Nigeria' (2012) 2:4 Envt and Nat Res Research 45, 47.

Engel, Susan. 'South–South Cooperation in Southeast Asia: From Bandung and Solidarity to Norms and Rivalry' (2009) 38:2 J Current Southeast Asian Aff 281.

Erinosho, Bolanle T. 'The Revised African Convention on the Conservation of Nature and Natural Resources: Prospects for a Comprehensive Treaty for the Management of Africa's Natural Resources' (2013) 21:3 Afr J Int'l and Comp L 378.

Escobar, Arturo. 'Thinking–Feeling with the Earth: Territorial Struggles and the Ontological Dimension of the Epistemologies of the South' (2016) 11:1 Revista de Antropología Iberoamericana 11.

Eslava, Luis. 'Istanbul Vignettes: Observing the Everyday Operation of International Law' (2014) 2:1 London Rev IL 3.

Eslava, Luis and Sundhya Pahuja. 'Between Resistance and Reform: TWAIL and the Universality of International Law' (2011) 3:1 Trade L and Dev 103.

'Beyond the (Post)Colonial: TWAIL and the Everyday Life of International Law' (2012) 45:2 Verfassung und Recht in Übersee 195.

Espinosa, Cristina. 'The Advocacy of the Previously Inconceivable: A Discourse Analysis of the Universal Declaration of the Rights of Mother Earth' (2014) 23:4 Envt and Dev 391.

Etemire, Uzuazo and Nelson Uwoh Sobere. 'Improving Public Compliance with Modern Environmental Laws in Nigeria: Looking to Traditional Norms and Practices' (2020) 38:2 J Energy and Nat Res L 1.

Extabe, Julen. 'Law as Politics: Four Relations' (2020) 16:1 L Culture & Humanities 24

Fagbayibo, Babatunde. 'A Critical Approach to International Legal Education in Africa: Some Pivotal Considerations' (2019) 12 TWAILR: Reflections 1.

'Some Thoughts on Centring Pan-African Epistemic in the Teaching of Public International Law in African Universities' (2019) 21:2 Int'l Community L Rev 170.

Fakhri, Michael. 'Third World Sovereignty, Indigenous Sovereignty, and Food Sovereignty: Living with Sovereignty Despite the Map' (2018) 9:3–4 Transnat'l Leg Theory 218.

Falk, Richard. 'False Universalism and the Geopolitics of Exclusion: The Case of Islam' (1997) 18:1 Third World Q 7.

Fallers, Lloyd. 'Customary Law in the New African States' (1962) 27:4 L and Contemp Probs 605.

Fatouros, Arghyrios A. 'International Law and the Third World' (1964) 50:5 Va L Rev 783.

Favre, Brian. 'Is there a Need for a New, an Ecological, Understanding of Legal Animal Rights?' (2020) 11:2 J Human Rights and Envt 297.

Fayemi, Ademola Kazeem. 'African Environmental Ethics and the Poverty of Eco-Activism in Nigeria: A Hermeneutico–Reconstructionist Appraisal' (2016) 48 Matatu 363.

Feris, Loretta. 'Protecting Traditional Knowledge in Africa: Considering African Approaches' (2004) 4 Afr Human Rights LJ 242.

Fidler, David P. 'To Fight a New Coronavirus: The COVID-19 Pandemic, Political Herd Immunity, and Global Health Jurisprudence' (2020) 19:2 Chinese JIL 207.

'Revolt against or from within the West? TWAIL, the Developing World, and the Future Direction of International Law' (2003) 2:1 Chinese JIL 29.

Fikentscher, Wolfgang. 'United Nations Code of Conduct: New Paths in International Law' (1982) 30:4 Am J Comp L 577.

Fischer, Alison. 'Colonialism, Context and Critical Thinking: First Steps towards Decolonising the Dutch Legal Curriculum' (2022) 18:1 Utrecht L Rev 18.

Fitzmaurice, Andrew. 'Context in the History of International Law' (2018) 20 J History IL 5.

Folkesson, Emelie. 'Human Rights Court Interpreting Sustainable Development: Balancing Individual Rights and Collective Interest' (2013) 6:2 Erasmus L Rev 142.

Fonseca, Manuel Jiménez. 'The Colonisation of American Nature and the Early Development of International Law' (2010) 12:2 J History IL 189.

Foster, Emma A. 'Sustainable Development: Problematising Normative Constructions of Gender within Global Environmentality' (2011) 8:2 Globalisations 135.

Fox, Nick J. and Pam Alldred. 'Sustainability, Feminist Posthumanism and the Unusual Capacities of (Post)humans' (2020) 6:2 Envt'l Sociology 121.

French, Duncan. 'Developing States and International Environmental Law: The Importance of Differentiated Responsibilities' (2000) 49:1 ICLQ 35.

'Revisiting Missed Opportunities: A Self-Reflection on (Not Always) Writing Meaningfully' (2021) 33:3 J Envt'l L 513.

Fukuda-Parr, Sakiko and Desmond McNeill. 'Knowledge and Politics in Setting and Measuring the SDGs: Introduction to Special Issue' (2019) 10:S1 Global Pol'y 5.

Fuller, Chris. 'Legal Anthropology, Legal Pluralism and Legal Thought' (1994) 10:3 Anthro Today 9.

Fuller, Lon L. 'Human Interaction and the Law' (1969) 14:1 Am J Juris 1.

Fulton, Scott C., Lalanath De Silva and Don Anton. 'Twenty Years after the Rio Summit: What Is the Agenda for the 2012 United Nations Conference on Sustainable Development?' (2012) 106 Am SIL: Proc Annual Mtg 91.

Gardner, John. 'Legal Positivism: 5½ Myths' (2001) 46:1 Am J Juris 199.

Garland, Elizabeth. 'The Elephant in the Room: Confronting the Colonial Character of Wildlife Conservation in Africa' (2008) 51:3 Afr Studies Rev 51.

Garver, Geoffrey. 'The Rule of Ecological Law: The Legal Complement to Degrowth Economics' (2013) 5 Sustainability 316.

Gathii, James Thuo. 'Africa and the Radical Origins of the Right to Development' (2020) 1 TWAILR 28.

'Beyond China's Human Rights Exceptionalism in Africa: Leveraging Science, Technology and Engineering for Long-Term Growth' (2013) 51:3 Colum J Transnat'l L 664.

'A Critical Appraisal of the International Legal Tradition of Taslim Olawale Elias' (2008) 21:2 Leiden JIL 317.

'Good Governance as a Counter Insurgency Agenda to Oppositional and Transformative Social Projects in International Law' (1999) 5 Buff HRL Rev 107.

'International Law and Eurocentricity' (1998) 9:1 European JIL 184.

'Mapping African International Law' (2011) 2:3 Transnat'l Leg Theory 429.

'Mission Creep or a Search for Relevance: The East African Court of Justice's Human Rights Strategy' (2013) 24:2 Duke J Comp and Int'l L 249.

'The Promise of International Law: A Third World View' (2020) 114 Am SIL: Proc Annual Mtg 165.

'Saving the Serengeti: Africa's New International Judicial Environmentalism' (2016) 16:2 Chicago JIL 386.

'TWAIL: A Brief History, of Its Origins, Its Decentralised Network, and a Tentative Bibliography' (2011) 3:1 Trade L & Dev 26.

Gearty, Conor. 'Do Human Rights Help or Hinder Environmental Protection?' (2010) 1:1 J Human Rights and Envt 7.

Gebeye, Berihun Adugna. 'Decoding Legal Pluralism in Africa' (2017) 49:2 J Leg Pluralism and Unofficial L 228.

'The Janus Face of Legal Pluralism for the Rule of Law Promotion in Sub-Saharan Africa' (2019) 53: 2 Can J Afr Studies 337.

'Legal Theory in Africa: Between Legal Centralism and Legal Pluralism' (2017) Queen Mary LJ 37.

Geisinger, Alex. 'Sustainable Development and the Domination of Nature: Spreading the Seed of the Western Ideology of Nature' (1999) 27:1 Boston College Envt'l Aff L Rev 43.

Geldart, Carol and Peter Lyon. 'The Group of 77: A Perspective View' (1980-1981) 57:1 Int'l Affairs 79.

Gerstein, Robert S. 'Hart's Positivism' (1985) 10:3 Am Bar Foundation Research J 629.

Gianolla, Cristiano. 'Human Rights and Nature: Intercultural Perspectives and International Aspirations' (2013) 4:1 J Human Rights and Envt 58.

Gibbs, Leah M. '"A Beautiful Soaking Rain": Environmental Value and Water beyond Eurocentrism' (2010) 28:2 Envt and Planning D: Society and Space 363.

Gilbert, Jérémie, Elizabeth Macpherson, Emily Jones and Julia Dehm, 'The Rights of Nature as a Legal Response to the Global Environmental Crisis? A Critical Review of International Law's "Greening" Agenda' (2021) 52 Nethl YBIL 47.

Gilder, Alexander. 'International Law and Human Security in a Kaleidoscopic World' (2020) 59:1–4 Indian JIL 1.

Gilley, Bruce. 'The Case for Colonialism' (2018) 31 Academic Questions 167.

Gjersø, Jonas Fossli. 'The Scramble for East Africa: British Motives Reconsidered, 1884–95' (2015) 43:5 J Imp and Commonwealth History 831.

Glazebrook, Susan. 'Human Rights and the Environment' (2009) 40:1 VUWLR 293.

Go, Julian and Jake Watson. 'Anticolonial Nationalism: From Imagined Communities to Colonial Conflict' (2019) 60:1 Archives Européennes de Sociologie 31.

Goldbach, Toby S. 'Why Legal Transplants?' (2019) 15:1 Annual Rev L and Soc Science 583.

Golder, Ben. 'Beyond Redemption? Problematising the Critique of Human Rights in Contemporary International Legal Thought' (2014) 2:1 London Rev IL 77.

Gönenç, Defne. 'Conceptualising Norm Fusion through Environmental Rights' (2020) 30:3 Envt'l Politics 442.

Gonzalez, Carmen G. 'Bridging the North–South Divide: International Environmental Law in the Anthropocene' (2015) 32 Pace Envt'l L Rev 407.

'China in Latin America: Law, Economics and Sustainable Development' (2010) 40:2 Envt'l L Rep News and Analysis 10171.

'Environmental Justice, Human Rights, and the Global South' (2015) 13 Santa Clara JIL 151.

Gonzalez, Carmen G. and Sumudu Atapattu. 'International Environmental Law, Environmental Justice, and the Global South' (2017) 26:2 Transnat'l L and Contemp Probs 229.

Gordon, Gwendolyn J. 'Environment Personhood' (2018) 43:1 Colum J Envt'l L 49.

Goyal, Yugank. '"Death of a Discipline": Locating Heterodoxy in Law' (2014) 56:4 J Indian L Institute 493.

Gray, Kevin and Barry K. Gills. 'South–South Cooperation and the Rise of the Global South' (2016) 37:4 Third World Q 557.

Grear, Anna. 'Legal Imaginaries and the Anthropocene: "Of" and "For"' (2020) 31:3 L and Critique 1.

'Questioning the Constructs: "The Environment" and "(Human) Rights"' (2016) 7:2 J Human Rights and Envt 165.

Green, Bernard. 'Toward a Definition of the Term Third World' (1980) 1:1 Boston College Third World LJ 13.

Griffiths, Anne. 'Broadening the Legal Academy, the Study of Customary Law: The Case for Social-Scientific and Anthropological Perspectives' (2017) 20:2 Potchefstroom Electronic LJ 1.

Griffiths, John. 'What Is Legal Pluralism?' (1986) 18:24 J Legal Pluralism 1.

'What Is Sociology of Law? (On Law, Rules, Social Control and Sociology)' (2017) 49:2 J Leg Pluralism and Unofficial L 93.

Grovogui, Siba. 'A Revolution Nonetheless: The Global South in International Relations' (2011) 5:1 Global South 175.

Gumede, William. 'The Democracy Deficit of Africa's Liberation Movements Turned Governments' (2017) 44:1 Politikon 27.

Gunderson, Ryan. 'Ideology Critique for the Environmental Social Sciences: What Reproduces the Treadmill of Production?' (2017) 12:3 Nature and Culture 263.

Günther, Klaus. 'Legal Pluralism or Uniform Concept of Law? Globalisation as a Problem of Legal Theory' (2008) 5 No Foundations: Interdisc JL and Just 5.

Gupta, Joyeeta. 'Growth, the Environment, and Development in the Anthropocene' (2015) 114:775 Current History 311.

Gupta, Joyeeta and Nadia Sanchez. 'Global Green Governance: Embedding the Green Economy in a Global Green and Equitable Rule of Law Polity' (2012) 21:1 RECIEL 12.

Hadden, Jennifer and Lucia A. Seybert. 'What's in a Norm? Mapping the Norm Definition Process in the Debate on Sustainable Development' (2016) 22 Global Governance 249.

Hage, Ghassan. 'The Haunting Figure of the Useless Academic: Critical Thinking in Coronavirus Time' (2020) 23:4 European J Cultural Studies 662.

Halme-Tuomisaari, Miia. 'Toward a Lasting Anthropology of International Law/Governance' (2016) 27:1 European JIL 235.

Hammink, Wouter. 'Mother Nature and the Heavenly Father: Christianity and the Environment in a Globalised World' (2012) 30:1 Mac Int'l 63.

Handl, Gunther. 'The Legal Mandate of Multilateral Development Banks as Agents of Change Toward Sustainable Development' (1998) 92:4 Am JIL 642.

Haque, M. Shamsul. 'Environmental Discourse and Sustainable Development: Linkages and Limitations' (2000) 5:1 Ethics and Envt 3.

'The Fate of Sustainable Development under Neo-Liberal Regimes in Developing Countries' (1999) 20:2 Int'l Pol Science Rev 197.

Harden-Davies, Harriet, Fran Humphries, Michelle Maloney, Glen Wright, Kristina Gjerde and Marjo Vierros. 'Rights of Nature: Perspectives for Global Ocean Stewardship' (2020) 122 Marine Pol'y 3.

Harrington, John and Ambreena Manji. 'The Limits of Socio-Legal Radicalism: Social and Legal Studies and Third World Scholarship' (2017) 26:6 Soc and Leg Studies 700.

Hart, H. L. A. 'Positivism and the Separation of Law and Morals' (1958) 71:4 Harvard L Rev 593.

Haskell, John D. 'TRAIL-ing TWAIL: Arguments and Blind Spots in Third World Approaches to International Law' (2014) 27:4 Can JL and Jur 383.

Hassan, Parvez. 'Role of the South in the Development of International Environmental Law' (2017) 1:2 Chinese J Envt'l L 133.

Henderson, James (Sákéj) Youngblood. 'Postcolonial Indigenous Legal Consciousness' (2002) 1 Indigenous LJ 1.

Hens, L. and C. Susanne. 'Environmental Ethics' (1998) 11:1–4 Global Bioethics 97.

Heyvaert, Veerle. 'The Transnationalisation of Law: Rethinking Law through Environmental Regulation' (2017) 6:2 Transnat'l Envt'l L 205.

Heyvaert, Veerle and Thijs Etty, 'Introducing Transnational Environmental Law' (2012) 1:1 Transnat'l Envt'l L 1.

Hitzhusen, Gregory E. and Mary Evelyn Tucker. 'The Potential of Religion for Environmental Stewardship' (2013) 11:7 Frontiers in Ecol and Envt 370.

Hodas, David. 'The Role of Law in Defining Sustainable Development: NEPA Reconsidered' (1998) 3 Widener L Symp J 1.

Home, Robert and Faith Kabata. 'Turning Fish Soup Back into Fish: The Wicked Problem of African Community Law Rights' (2018) 9:12 J Sust Dev and Pol'y 1.

Hongoh, Joseph. 'The Asian–African Conference (Bandung) and Pan-Africanism: The Challenge of Reconciling Continental Solidarity with National Sovereignty' (2016) 70:4 Australian J Int'l Aff 374.

Hope, Aimie L. B. and Christopher R. Jones. 'The Impact of Religious Faith on Attitudes to Environmental Issues and Carbon Capture Storage (CCS) Technologies: A Mixed Method Study' (2014) 38 Tech in Soc'y 48.

Hornborg, Alf. 'Colonialism in the Anthropocene: The Political Ecology of the Money-Energy-Technology Complex' (2019) 10:1 J Human Rights and Envt 7.

Horsthemke, Kai. 'Animals and African Ethics' (2017) 7:2 J Animal Ethics 119.

Hourcade, Jean-Charles. 'The Geopolitical Stakes of Sustainable Development' (2008) 408:2 Études 175.

Hovell, Devika. 'The Elements of International Legal Positivism' (2022) 75:1 Current Leg Probs 71.

Howarth, David and Shona Wilson Stark. 'H. L. A. Hart's Secondary Rules: What Do "Officials" Think?' (2018) 14:1 Int'l JL in Context 61.

Huber, Matt. 'Resource Geographies I: Valuing Nature (or Not)' (2018) 42:1 Progress in Human Geography 148.

Huizenga, Daniel. 'Articulations of Aboriginal Title, Indigenous Rights, and Living Customary Law in Africa' (2018) 27:1 Soc and Leg Studies 1.

Humby, Tracy-Lynn. 'Evaluating the Value of TWAIL, Environmental Justice, and Decolonisation Discourses as Framing Lenses for Environmental Law' (2017) 26:2 Transnat'l L and Contemp Probs 318.

Humphreys, Sally. 'Law as Discourse' (1985) 1:2 History and Anthro 241.

Huneeus, Alexander and Mikael Rask Madsen, 'Between Universalism and Regional Law and Politics: A Comparative History of the American, European, and African Human Rights Systems' (2018) 16:1 Int'l J Con L 136.

Hurrell, Andrew. 'Narratives of Emergence: Rising Powers and the End of the Third World?' (2013) 33:2 Revista de Economia Politica 203.

Huynh, T. Tu and Danson Sylvester Kahyana. 'A General Introduction' (2020) 19:1–2 Afr and Asian Studies 1.

Ikejiaku, Brian-Vincent. 'International Law Is Western Made Global Law: The Perception of Third-World Category' (2013) 6:2-3 Afr J Leg Studies 337.

Ikporukpo, Chris O. 'From Silent Spring to the Sustainable Development Goals: On the Development–Environment Nexus' (2017) 7:2 Afr J Sust Dev 25.

Ipinyomi, Foluke Ifejola. 'The Impact of African Philosophy on the Realisation of the International Community and the Observance of International Law' (2016) 18:1 Int'l Community L Rev 3.

Jabareen, Yosef. 'A New Conceptual Framework for Sustainable Development' (2008) 10:2 Envt Dev and Sustainability 79.

Jackson, Peter. 'A World Charter for Nature' (1983) 12:2 Ambio 133.

Jain, Devaki and Shubha Chacko. 'Walking Together: The Journey of the Non-Aligned Movement and the Women's Movement' (2009) 19:7 Dev in Practice 895.

Jeffery, Michael I. 'Environmental Ethics and Sustainable Development: Ethical and Human Rights Issues in Implementing Indigenous Rights' (2005) 2:1 Macq J Int'l and Comp Envt'l L 105.

Jie, Xu. 'The Asian-African Legal Consultative Organisation and Its Relationship with the People's Republic of China' (2012) 1:1 AALCO JIL 15.

Jodoin, Sébastien. 'International Law and Alterity: The State and the Other' (2008) 21:1 Leiden JIL 1.

Johns, Fleur. 'Disciplinary Privilege and the Promise of Decampment: A Response to James Gathii's "The Promise of International Law: A Third World View"' (2020) 114 Am SIL: Proc Annual Mtg 187.

Jonas, Obonye. 'Neutering the SADC Tribunal by Blocking Individuals' Access to the Tribunal' (2013) 2:2 Int'l Human Rights L Rev 294.

Jones, Henry and Aoife O'Donoghue. 'History and Self-Reflection in the Teaching of International Law' (2022) 10:1 London Rev IL 7.

Jordan, Andrew. 'The Governance of Sustainable Development: Taking Stock and Looking Forwards' (2008) 26:1 Envt and Plan C: Govt and Pol'y 17.

Jouannet, Emmanuelle. 'Universalism and Imperialism: The True–False Paradox of International Law' (2007) 18:3 European JIL 379.

'What is the Use of International Law? International Law as a 21st Century Guardian of Welfare' (2007) 28:4 Michigan JIL 815.

Juma, Laurence. 'From "Repugnancy" to "Bill of Rights": African Customary Law and Human Rights in Lesotho and South Africa' (2007) 21:1 Speculum Juris 88.

Kadir, M. Y. Aiyub and Alexander Murray. 'Resource Nationalism in the Law and Policies of Indonesia: A Contest of State, Foreign Investors, and Indigenous Peoples' (2019) 9:2 Asian JIL 298.

Kameri-Mbote, Annie Patricia and Philippe Cullet. 'Law, Colonialism and Environmental Management in Africa' (1997) 6:1 RECIEL 23.

Kamga, Serges Alain Djoyou. 'The Right to Development in the African Human Rights System: The Endorois Case' (2011) 44:2 De Jure 381.

Kamga, Serges Alain Djoyou and Charles Manga Fombad. 'A Critical Review of the Jurisprudence of the African Commission on Human and Peoples' Rights' (2013) 57:2 J Afr L 196.

Kauffman, Craig M. and Pamela L. Martin. 'Can Rights of Nature Make Development Sustainable? Why Some Ecuadorian Lawsuits Fail and Others Fail' (2017) 92 World Dev 130.

Kawashima, Yasuhide and Ruth Tone. 'Environmental Policy in Early America: A Survey of Colonial Statutes' (1983) 27:4 J Forest History 168.

Keitsch, Martina. 'Structuring Ethical Interpretations of the Sustainable Development Goals: Concepts, Implications and Progress' (2018) 10 Sustainability 829.

Kelbessa, Workineh. 'African Environmental Ethics, Indigenous Knowledge, and Environmental Challenges' (2015) 37:4 Envt'l Ethics 387.

'Environmental Philosophy in African Traditions of Thought' (2018) 40:4 Envt'l Ethics 309.

Kemmerer, Alexandra. 'We Do Not Always Need to Look to Westphalia: A Conversation with Martti Koskenniemi and Anne Orford' (2015) 17:1 J History IL 1.

Kendall, Sara. 'Cartographies of the Present: "Contingent Sovereignty" and Territorial Integrity' (2017) 47 Nethl YB Int'l L 83.

Khan, Irene. 'How Can the Rule of Law Advance Sustainable Development in a Troubled and Turbulent World?' (2017) 13:2 McGill J Sust Dev L and Pol'y 211.

Khoday, Kishan. 'Decolonising the Environment: Third World Approaches to the Planetary Crisis' (2022) 19:2 Indonesia JIL 189.

Khoday, Kishan and Usha Natarajan. 'Fairness and International Environmental Law from Below: Social Movements and Legal Transformation in India' (2012) 25:2 Leiden JIL 415.

Kholsa, Madhav. 'The TWAIL Discourse: The Emergence of a New Phase' (2007) 9:3 Int'l Community L Rev 201.

Khondker, Habibul Haque. 'From the Silent Spring to the Globalisation of the Environmental Movement' (2015) 6:2 J Int'l & Global Studies 25.

Killander, Magnus and Bright Nkrumah. 'Human Rights Development in the African Union During 2012 and 2013' (2014) 14:1 Afr Human Rights LJ 275.

Kim, Rakhyun E. and Klaus Bosselmann. 'Operationalising Sustainable Development: Ecological Integrity as a *Grundnorm* of International Law' (2015) 24:2 RECIEL 194.

Kingah, Stephen Sevidzem. 'The African Union's Capacity in Promoting Good Governance' (2006) 3:2 Int'l Organisations L Rev 317.

Kirchmair, Lando. 'Descriptive vs. Prescriptive Global Legal Pluralism: A Gentle Reminder of David Hume's Is–Ought Divide' (2019) 51:1 J Leg Pluralism and Unofficial L 48.

Kiwanuka, Richard N. 'The Meaning of "People" in the African Charter on Human and Peoples' Rights' (1988) 82:1 Am JIL 80.

Kiye, Mikano Emmanuel. 'Conflict Between Customary Law and Human Rights in Cameroon: The Role of the Courts in Fostering an Equitable Society' (2015) 36:2 Afr Study Monographs 75.

'The Repugnancy and Incompatibility Tests and Anglophone Cameroon' (2015) 15:2 Afr Studies Q 85.

Klabbers, Jan. 'On Epistemic Universalism and the Melancholy of International Law' (2018) 29:4 European JIL 1057.

Klarin, Tomislav. 'The Concept of Sustainable Development: From Its Beginning to the Contemporary Issues' (2018) 21:1 Zagreb Int'l Rev Econ and Bus 67.

Kleinfeld, Joshua. 'The Double Life of International Law: Indigenous Peoples and Extractive Industries' (2016) 129:6 Harvard L Rev 1755.

Kleinhans, Martha-Marie and Roderick A. MacDonald. 'What Is a *Critical* Legal Pluralism?' (1997) 26:2 Can JL and Soc'y 25.

Knox, Robert. 'Civilising Interventions? Race, War and International Law' (2013) 26:1 Cambridge Rev Int'l Aff 111.

Kodiveri, Arpitha. 'The Delicate Task of Including Different Voices in Environmental Law Making in India' (2022) 33:3 J Envt'l L 495.

Koh, Harold Hongju. 'Why Transnational Law Matters' (2006) 24:4 Penn State Int'l L Rev 745.

Kopnina, Helen and Brett Cherniak. 'Neoliberalism and Justice in Education for Sustainable Development: A Call for Inclusive Pluralism' (2016) 22:6 Envt'l Educ Research 827.

Koskenniemi, Martti. 'Histories of International Law: Dealing with Eurocentrism' (2011) 19 Rechtsgeschichte 152.

'Imagining the Rule of Law: Rereading the Grotian 'Tradition'' (2019) 30:1 European JIL 17.

'International Law in Europe: Between Tradition and Renewal' (2005) 16:1 European JIL 113.

'The Politics of International Law: 20 Years Later' (2009) 20:1 European JIL 7.

'What Should International Lawyers Learn from Karl Marx?' (2004) 17:2 Leiden JIL 229.

Kotzé, Louis J. 'The Anthropocene, Earth System Vulnerability, and Socio-Ecological Injustice in the Age of Human Rights' (2019) 10:1 J Human Rights and Envt 62.

Kotzé, Louis J. and Sam Adelman, 'Environmental Law and the Unsustainability of Sustainable Development: A Tale of Disenchantment and Hope' (2023) 34:2 L and Critique 227.

Kotzé, Louis J. and Duncan French. 'A Critique of the Global Pact for the Environment: A Stillborn Initiative or the Foundation for Lex Anthropocene?' (2018) 18:6 Int'l Envt'l Agreements: Pol L and Econ 811.

Kotzé, Louis J. and Rakhyun E. Kim. 'Earth System Law: The Juridical Dimensions of Earth System Governance' (2019) 1 Earth System Governance 1.

'Towards Planetary Nexus Governance in the Anthropocene: An Earth System Perspective' (2022) 13:S3 Global Pol'y 86.

Kotzé, Louis J. and Caiphas B. Soyapi. 'African Courts and Principles of International Environmental Law: A Kenyan and South African Study' (2021) 33:2 J Envt'l L 257.

Kotzé, Louis J., Louise de Toit and Duncan French. 'Friend or Foe? International Environmental Law and its Structural Complicity in the Anthropocene's Climate Injustices' (2021) 11:1 Oñati Socio-Legal Series 180.

Kotzé, Louis J. and Paola Villavicencio Caldazilla, 'Somewhere in Between Rhetoric and Reality: Environmental Constitutionalism and the Rights of Nature in Ecuador' (2017) 6:3 Transnat'l Envt'l L 401.

Kravchenko, Svitlana. 'Environmental Rights in International Law: Explicitly Recognised or Creatively Interpreted?' (2012) 7:2 Florida A and M UL Rev 163.

Kruger, Frans, Adré le Roux and Kevin Teise. 'Ecojustice Education and Communitarianism: Exploring the Possibility for Eco-communitarianism' (2020) 52:2 Educ Phil and Theory 206.

Kuhlmann Katrin and Lisa Akinyi Agutu. 'The African Continental Free Trade Area: Toward a New Legal Model for Trade and Development' (2020) 51:4 Georgetown JIL 753.

Kulamadayil, Lys. '"Petro-States" Shaping of International Law' (2022) 25:2 J History IL 161.

'Placed in Between: The Natural Environment in International Law' (2023) 13:4 Transnat'l Leg Theory 466.

Kütting, Gabriela. 'Globalisation and the Environment: Moving beyond Neo-Liberal Institutionalism' (2004) 9:1 Int'l J Peace Studies 29.

Lamond, Grant. 'Legal Sources, the Rule of Recognition, and Customary Law' (2014) 59:1 Am J Juris 25.

Langford, Malcolm. 'Lost in Transformation? The Politics of Sustainable Development Goals' (2016) 30:2 Ethics and Int'l Aff 167.

Langhelle, Oluf. 'Sustainable Development: Exploring the Ethics of Our Common Future' (1999) 20:2 Int'l Pol Science Rev 129.

Larson, Rhett B. 'Water, Worship, and Wisdom: Indigenous Traditional Ecological Knowledge and the Human Right to Water' (2012) 19:1 ILSA J Int'l and Comp L 43.

Lee, Christopher J. 'At the Rendezvous of Decolonisation: The Final Communiqué of the Asian–African Conference, Bandung, Indonesia, 18–24 April 1955' (2009) 11:1 Interventions 81.

Lee, K.-K. 'Hart's Primary and Secondary Rules' (1968) 77:308 Mind 561.

Leff, Enrique. 'Power–Knowledge Relations in the Field of Political Ecology' (2017) 20:3 Ambiente & Sociedade 225.

Lélé, Sharachchandra M. 'Sustainable Development: A Critical Review' (1991) 19:6 World Dev 607.

Lewis, Liz. 'Exploring the "Ecology" of Laws at the Interface between International Human Rights Law and Subnational Customary Law' (2011) 24:1 Afr J Int'l and Comp L 105.

Lewis, Martin W. 'Is There a Third World?' (1999) 98:631 Current History 355.

Li, Chunlin and Jianqing Chen. 'The Ethical Turn of the Rule of Law in the Global Environment under the Influence of the Concept of a Community of Shared Future for Mankind' (2019) 10:1 Beijing L Rev 98.

Litfin, Karen T. 'Sovereignty in World Ecopolitics' (1997) 41:2 Mershon Int'l Studies Rev 167.

Lima, José Edmilson De Souza and Roberto José Covaia Kosop. 'Decolonial Turn and the Law: Beyond Colonial Restraints' (2019) 10:4 Revisto Direito e Práxis 2596.

Linnér, Björn-Ola and Merle Jacob. 'From Stockholm to Kyoto and beyond: A Review of the Globalisation of Global Warming Policy and North South Relations' (2005) 2:3 Globalisations 403.

Linnér, Björn-Ola and Henrik Selin. 'The United Nations Conference on Sustainable Development: Forty Years in the Making' (2013) 31 Envt and Plan C: Government and Pol'y 971.

Liverman, Diana M. and Silvina Vilas. 'Neoliberalism and the Environment in Latin America' (2006) 31:1 Annual Rev Envt'l Res 325.

Lixinski, Lucas. 'Narratives of the International Legal Order and Why They Matter' (2013) 6:1 Erasmus L Rev 2.

Lizarazo-Rodriguez, Liliana. 'Mapping Law and Development' (2017) 4:4 Indonesian J Int'l and Comp L 761.

Lone, Fozia Nazir. 'Cross-Fertilisation of Westphalian Approaches to International Law: Third World Studies and a New Era of International Law Scholarship' (2020) 34:4 Emory Int'l L Rev 946.

'The "One Country, Two Systems" Model and Political Reform in Hong Kong: A TWAIL Approach' (2018) 21:1 Max Planck YB UN L 404.

Lorentzen, Lois Ann. 'Religion and Violence against Nature' (2006) 19 Scripta Instituti Donneriani Aboensis 242.

Lousley, Cheryl. 'Global Futures Past: Our Common Future, Postcolonial Times, and Worldly Ecologies' (2017) 4:2–3 Resilience 21.

Lumumba-Kasongo, Tukumbi. 'Rethinking the Bandung Conference in an Era of "Unipolar Liberal Globalisation" and Movements Towards a "Multipolar Politics"' (2015) 2:9 Bandung: J Global South 1.

Lyman, Abra and Darren Kew. 'An African Dilemma: Resolving Indigenous Conflicts in Kenya' (2010) Georgetown J Int'l Aff 37.

Lynes, Laura S. 'The Right to Nature and the Duty to Consult in Canada' (2019) 37:3 J Energy and Nat Res L 353.

Lynham, Greg. 'The *Sic Utere* Principle as Customary International Law: A Case of Wishful Thinking?' (1995) 2 James Cook UL Rev 172.

Mabvurira, Vincent, George Alex Muchinako and Elisabeth Ivy Smit, 'Shona Traditional Religion and Sustainable Environmental Management: An Afrocentric Perspective' (2021) 11:3 Afr J Soc Work 111.

Macpherson, Elizabeth, Jill Banwell, Robert Makgill and Adrienne Paul. '*Trans-Tasman Resources Limited v Taranaki-Whanganui Conservation Board and Others* [2021] NZSC [127]; A New High Mark for Seabed Mining' (2021) 25 New Zealand J Envt'l L 277.

Madden, M. Stuart. 'Myth, Folklore, and Ancient Ethics' (2006) 37:1 Cumb L Rev 43.

Mahbub, Nabaat Tasnima. 'Sustainable Development and Its Evolution in the Realm of International Environmental Law' (2016) 7 Nnamdi Azikiwe UJ Int'l L and Jurisprudence 1.

Mahrane, Yannick, Marianna Fenzi, Céline Pessis and Christophe Bonneuil. 'From Nature to Biosphere: The Political Invention of the Global Environment, 1945–1972' (2012) 113:1 Vingtième Siècle: Revue d'Histoire 127.

Makokha, Kibaba. 'The Ethical Foundations of Environmental Conservation and Sustainable Development' (2013) 5:2 Thought and Practice 1.

Makoul, Zoe. 'Environmental Ethics and Environmental Law: A Virtuous Circle' (2022) 47:1 Colum J of Envt'l L 68.

Mälksoo, Lauri. 'Civilisational Diversity as Challenge to the (False) Universality of International Law' (2019) 9:1 Asian JIL 155.

Maluwa, Tiyanjana. 'The OAU/African Union and International Law: Mapping New Boundaries of Revising Old Terrain' (2004) 98 Am SIL: Proc Annual Mtg 232.

'Reassessing Aspects of the Contribution of African States to the Development of International Law through African Regional Multilateral Treaties' (2020) 41:2 Michigan JIL 327.

Mandala, Vijaya Ramadas. 'The Raj and the Paradoxes of Wildlife Conservation: British Attitudes and Expediencies' (2015) 58:1 Hist J 75.

Manley-Casimir, Kirsten. 'Incommensurable Legal Cultures: Indigenous Legal Traditions and the Colonial Narrative' (2012) 30:2 Windsor YB Access Just 137.

Mann, Gregory. 'What was the *Indigénat*? The "Empire of Law" in French West Africa' (2009) 50:3 J Afr History 331.

Mann, Howard. 'The Rio Declaration' (1992) 86 Am SIL: Proc Annual Mtg 405.

Mapaure, Clever. 'Reinvigorating African Values for SADC: The Relevance of Traditional African Philosophy of Law in a Globalising World of Competing Perspectives' (2011) 1 SADC LJ 149.

Marklund, Carl. 'Double Loyalties? Small-State Solidarity and the Debates on the New International Economic Order in Sweden during the Long 1970s' (2020) 45:3 Scandinavian J History 384.

Martineau, Anne-Charlotte. 'Overcoming Eurocentrism? Global History and the Oxford Handbook of the History of International Law' (2014) 25:1 European JIL 329.

Marx, Leo. 'The Idea of Nature in America' (2008) 137:2 Daedalus 8.

Maserumule, Mashupye Herbert and Shadrack B. O. Gutto. 'Critical Understanding of Good Governance and Leadership Concepts Written in the Context of New Partnership for Africa's Development (NEPAD) and the Challenges to the Contextual Discourses on Africa's Development Paradigms' (2008) 3:2 Int'l J Afr Ren Studies 63.

Mason, Michael. 'Transnational Environmental Obligations: Locating New Spaces of Accountability in a Post-Westphalian Global Order' (2001) 26:4 Trans Inst Brit Geographers 407.

Matevia, Marilyn. 'Justice for All: Revisiting the Prospects for a Biocommunitarian Theory of Interspecies Justice' (2016) 19:3 J Int'l Wildlife L & Pol'y 189.

Matheka, R. M. 'The International Dimension of the Politics of Wildlife Conservation in Kenya, 1958–1968' (2008) 2:1 J Eastern Afr Studies 112.

Matson, J. N. 'The Common Law Abroad: English and Indigenous Laws in the British Commonwealth' (1993) 42:4 ICLQ 753.

Maynard, Hélène. 'From Classical Liberalism to Neoliberalism: Explaining the Contradictions in the International Environmental Law Project' (2020) 50:1 Revue Générale de Droit 57.

Mbengue, Makane Moïse and Stéphanie de Moerloose. 'Multilateral Development Banks and Sustainable Development: On Emulations, Fragmentation and a Common Law of Sustainable Development' (2017) 10:2 L and Dev Rev 389.

McInerney-Lankford, Siobhán. 'Human Rights and Development: A Comment on Challenges and Opportunities from a Legal Perspective' (2009) 1:1 J Human Rights Practice 51.

McNeely, Jeffrey A. 'Nature and COVID-19: The Pandemic, the Environment, and the Way Ahead' (2021) 50:4 Ambio 767.

Mebratu, Desta. 'Sustainability and Sustainable Development: Historical and Conceptual Overview' (1998) 18:6 Envt'l Impact Assess Rev 493.

Mensah, Justice. 'Sustainable Development: Meaning, History, Principles, Pillars, and Implications for Human Action: Literature Review' (2019) 5:1 Cogent Social Sciences 1.

Merry, Sally Engle. 'Does Law Matter to Anthropology? A Comment' (2018) 2:2 J Leg Anthro 86.

'From Law and Colonialism to Law and Globalisation' (2003) 28:2 Law & Soc Inquiry 569.

'Legal Pluralism' (1988) 22:5 Law and Soc'y Rev 869.

'New Legal Realism and the Ethnography of Transnational Law' (2006) 31:4 Law and Soc Inquiry 975.

Mertz, Elizabeth. 'Language, Law, and Social Meanings: Linguistic/ Anthropological Contributions to the Study of Law' (1992) 26:2 L and Soc'y Rev 413.

Michaels, Ralf. 'Global Legal Pluralism' (2009) 5:1 Annual Rev L and Soc Science 243.

Mickelson, Karin. 'Beyond a Politics of the Possible? South–North Relations and Climate Justice' (2009) 10:2 Melbourne JIL 411.

'Hope in a TWAIL Register' (2020) 1 TWAILR 14.

'Leading towards a Level Playing Field, Repaying Ecological Debt, or Making Environmental Space: Three Stories about International Environmental Cooperation' (2005) 43:1–2 Osgoode Hall LJ 137.

'The Maps of International Law: Perceptions of Nature in the Classification of Territory' (2014) 27:3 Leiden JIL 621.

'Rhetoric and Rage: Third World Voices in International Legal Discourse' (1998) 16:2 Wis Int'l LJ 353.

'South, North, International Environmental Law, and International Environmental Lawyers' (2001) 11:1 YB Int'l Envt'l L 52.

'Taking Stock of TWAIL Histories' (2008) 10:4 Int'l Community L Rev 355.

Mignolo, Walter D. 'Delinking: The Rhetoric of Modernity, the Logic of Coloniality, and the Grammar of De-Coloniality' (2007) 21:2–3 Cultural Studies 449.

Miller, Robert J. 'The International Law of Colonialism: A Comparative Analysis' (2011) 15:4 Lewis and Clark L Rev 847.

Miranda, Lilian Aponte. 'The Role of International Law in Intrastate Natural Resource Allocation: Sovereignty, Human Rights, and People-Based Development' (2012) 45 Vand J Transnat'l L 785.

Mitcham, Carl. 'Sustainable Development: Its Origins and Ambivalence' (1995) 17:3 Tech in Soc'y 311.

Mkomo, Stella M. 'A Postcolonial and Anti-Colonial Reading of "African" Leadership and Management in Organisation Studies: Tensions, Contradictions' (2011) 18:3 Organisation 365.

Monyamane, Lesetja and Mpho P. Bapela. '*Gongqose v Minister of Agriculture, Forestry & Fisheries*: A Tale of Customary Law Rituals and Practices in Marine Protected Areas' (2019) 22:1 Potchefstroom Electronic LJ 1.

Moore, Frances C. 'Toppling the Tripod: Sustainable Development, Constructive Ambiguity, and the Environmental Challenge' (2011) 5 Consilience: J Sust Dev 141.

Moore, Sally Falk. 'Treating Law as Knowledge: Telling Colonial Officers What to Say to Africans about Running "Their Own" Native Courts' (1992) 26:1 L and Soc'y Rev 11.

Morudu, Ntebo L. and Charles Mailema. 'The Indigenisation of Customary Law: Creating an Indigenous Pluralism within the South African Dispensation: Possible or Not?' (2021) 54:1 De Jure LJ 54.

Motilal, Shashi. 'Sustainable Development Goals and Human Moral Obligations: The Ends and Means Relation' (2015) 11:1 J Global Ethics 24.

Moyn, Samuel. 'Knowledge and Politics of International Law' (2016) 129:8 Harvard L Rev 2164.

'A Powerless Companion: Human Rights in the Age of Neoliberalism' (2014) 77:4 L and Contemp Probs 147.

Mrozowski, Stephen A. 'Colonisation and Commodification of Nature' (1999) 3:3 Int'l J Historical Archaeo 153.

Mulwafu, Wapulumuka O. 'The Interface of Christianity and Conservation in Colonial Malawi, c. 1850–1930' (2004) 34:3 J Religion in Afr 298.

Munarriz, Gerardo J. 'Rhetoric and Reality: The World Bank Development Policies, Mining Corporations, and Indigenous Communities in Latin America' (2008) 10:4 Int'l Community L Rev 431.

Musavengane, Regis and Llewellyn Leonard. 'When Race and Social Equity Matters in Nature Conservation in Post-Apartheid South Africa' (2019) 17:2 Conservation & Soc'y 135.

Mutua, Makau and Antony Anghie. 'What is TWAIL?' (2000) 94 Am SIL: Proc Annual Mtg 31.

Naffine, Ngaire. 'Legal Personality and the Natural World: On the Persistence of the Human Measure of Value' (2012) 3 Special J Human Rights and Envt 68.

Najam, Adil. 'Developing Countries and Global Environmental Governance: From Contestation to Participation to Engagement' (2005) 5:3 Int'l Envt'l Agreements: Pol L and Econ 303.

'Unraveling the Rio Bargain' (2002) 21:2 Pol and Life Sciences 46.

Najam, Adil and Cutler J. Cleveland. 'Energy and Sustainable Development at Global Environmental Summits: An Evolving Agenda' (2003) 5:1 Envt Dev and Sustainability 117.

Napoleon, Val and Hadley Friedland. 'An Inside Job: Engaging with Indigenous Legal Traditions through Stories' (2016) 61:4 McGill LJ 725.

Napoletano, Brian M. and Brett Clark. 'An Ecological-Marxist Response to the Half-Earth Project' (2020) 18:1 Conservation and Soc'y 37.

Natarajan, Usha. 'TWAIL and the Environment: The State of Nature, the Nature of the State, and the Arab Spring' (2012) 14:1 Oregon Rev IL 177.

Natarajan, Usha and Julia Dehm. 'Where Is the Environment? Locating Nature in International Law' (2019) 3 TWAILR: Reflections 1.

Natarajan, Usha and Kishan Khoday. 'Locating Nature: Making and Unmaking International Law' (2014) 27:3 Leiden JIL 573.

Natarajan, Usha, John Reynolds, Amar Bhatia and Sujith Xavier. 'Introduction: TWAIL: On Praxis and the Intellectual' (2016) 37:11 Third World Q 1946.

Natarajan, Usha, Laura Betancur-Restrepo, Amar Bhatia, John Reynolds, Ntina Tzouvala and Sujith Xavier. 'Third World Approaches to International Law Review: A Journal for a Community' (2020) 1 TWAILR 7.

Nayar, K. R. 'Politics of "Sustainable Development"' (1994) 29:22 Econ and Pol Weekly 1327.

Ndima, Dial Dayana. 'Reconceiving African Jurisprudence in a Post-Imperial Society: The Role of Ubuntu in Constitutional Adjudication' (2015) 48:3 Comp & Int'l LJS Afr 359.

Nelson, Robert H. 'Rethinking Church and the State: The Case of Environmental Religion' (2011) 29:1 Pace Envt'l L Rev 121.

Neumann, Roderick P. 'The Post-War Conservation Boom in British Colonial Africa' (2002) 7:1 Envt'l History 22.

Nijar, Gurdial Singh. 'Traditional Knowledge Systems, International Law and National Challenges: Marginalisation or Emancipation' (2013) 24:4 European JIL 1205.

Ntibagirira, Symphorien. 'Ubuntu as a Metaphysical Concept' (2018) 52:1 J Val Inquiry 113.

Nobles, Richard and David Schiff. 'Using Systems Theory to Study Legal Pluralism: What Could Be Gained?' (2012) 46:2 Law and Soc'y Rev 265.

Nursoo, Ida. 'Indigenous Law, Colonial Injustice and the Jurisprudence of Hybridity' (2018) 50:1 J Leg Pluralism and Unofficial L 56.

Nwabueze, Remigius. 'The Dynamics and Genius of Nigeria's Indigenous Legal Order' (2002) 1:1 Indigenous LJ 153.

Nwapi, Chilenye. 'Land Grab, Property Rights and Gender Equality in Pluralistic Legal Orders: A Nigerian Perspective' (2016) 9:2 Afr J Leg Studies 124.

Nwobike, Justice C. 'The African Commission on Human and Peoples' Rights and the Demystification of Second and Third Generation Rights under the African Charter: Social and Economic Rights Action Centre and Centre for Economic and Social Rights v Nigeria' (2005) 2:1 Afr J Leg Studies 129.

O'Donnell, Erin L. 'At the Intersection of the Sacred and Legal: Rights for Nature in Uttarakland' (2018) 30:1 J Envt'l L 135.

O'Donnell, Erin L. and Julia Talbot-James. 'Creating Legal Rights for Rivers: Lessons from Australia, New Zealand and India' (2018) 23:1 Ecol & Soc'y 7.

O'Donnell, Erin, Anne Poelina, Alessandro Pelizzon and Cristy Clark. 'Stop Burying the Lede: The Essential Role of Indigenous Law(s) in Creating Rights of Nature' (2020) 9:3 Transnat'l Envt'l L 403.

O'Gorman, Roderic. 'Environmental Constitutionalism: A Comparative Study' (2017) 6:3 Transnat'l Envt'l L 435.

O'Riordan, Tim and Heather Voisey. 'The Political Economy of Sustainable Development' (1997) 6:1 Envt'l Pol 1.

Ocran, Justice Modibo. 'The Clash of Legal Cultures: The Treatment of Indigenous Law in Colonial and Post-Colonial Africa' (2006) 39:2 Akron L Rev 465.

Odumosu, Ibironke T. 'The Law and Politics of Engaging Resistance in Investment Dispute Settlement' (2007) 26:2 Penn State Int'l L Rev 251.

Ogar, Joseph Nkang and Samuel Akpan Bassey. 'African Environmental Ethics' (2019) 3:1 RAIS J Soc Sciences 71.

Ogundere, Joseph Diekola. 'The Development of International Environmental Law and Policy in Africa' (1972) 12:2 Nat Res J 255.

Ojomo, P. A. 'Environmental Ethics: An African Understanding' (2011) 5:8 Afr J Envt'l Science and Tech 572.

Okafor, F. U. 'Legal Positivism and the African Legal Tradition' (1984) 24:2 Int'l Phil Q 157.

'A Philosophical Reflection on African Native Law' (1988) 22:1 J Val Inquiry 39.

Okafor, Obiora Chinedu. 'Cascading toward "De-Solidarity"? The Unfolding of Global Refugee Protection' (2019) 2 TWAILR: Reflections 1.

'Critical Third World Approaches to International Law (TWAIL): Theory, Methodology, or Both?' (2008) 10:4 Int'l Community L Rev 371.

'Enacting TWAILian Praxis in Non-Academic Habitats: Toward a Conceptual Framework' (2016) 110 AJIL Unbound 20.

'Newness, Imperialism, and International Legal Reform in Our Time: A TWAIL Perspective' (2005) 43:1-2 Osgoode Hall LJ 171.

'Praxis and the International (Human Rights) Law Scholar: Towards the Intensification of TWAILian Dramaturgy' (2016) 33:3 Windsor YB Access Just 1.

'"Righting", Restructuring, and Rejuvenating the Postcolonial African State: The Case for the Establishments of an AU Special Commission on National Minorities' (2005) 13:1 Afr YBIL 43.

Okafor, Obiora Chinedu and Godwin E. K. Dzah. 'The African Human Rights System as "Norm Leader": Three Case Studies' (2021) 21:2 Afr Human Rights LJ 669.

Okere, B. Obinna. 'The Protection of Human Rights in Africa and the African Charter on Human and Peoples' Rights: A Comparative Analysis with European and American Systems' (1984) 6:2 Human Rights Q 141.

Okereke, Chukwumekerije. 'Global Environmental Sustainability: Intragenerational Equity and Conceptions of Justice in Multilateral Environmental Regimes' (2006) 37:5 Geoforum 725.

Okoloise, Chairman. 'Circumventing Obstacles to the Implementation of Recommendations of the African Commission on Human and Peoples' Rights' (2018) 18:1 Afr Human Rights LJ 27.

Olopade, C. O. and N. Kara, 'Sustainable Development in Pre-Colonial, Colonial, and Post-Colonial Africa: Issues and Contexts' (2016) 6:1 Afr J Sust Dev 1.

Oloruntimehin, B. Olatunji. 'Theories and Realities in the Administration of Colonial West Africa from 1890 to the First World War' (1972) 6:3 J Historical Soc'y Nigeria 289.

Onuma, Yasuaki. 'When Was the Law of the International Society Born: An Inquiry of the History of International Law from an Intercivilisational Perspective' (2000) 2:1 J History IL 1.

Onyeaghalaji, Modestus Nnamdi. 'Afrosensitivity in Eurocentric and Afrocentric Narratives for Sustainable Development in Africa' (2015) 17:4 J Sust Dev in Afr 86.

Opoku, Kwame. 'Traditional Law under French Colonial Rule' (1974) 7:2 Verfassung und Recht Übersee 139.

Orford, Anne. 'On International Legal Method' (2013) 1:1 London Rev IL 166.

'Positivism and the Power of International Law' (2000) 24:2 Melbourne UL Rev 502.

Orji, Uchenna Jerome. 'Enhancing Sustainable Development in Nigeria: A Discourse on the Legal Basis and Proposals to Strengthen Legal and Policy Strategies for Its Implementation' (2013) 39:1 Commonwealth L Bull 163.

Ormsby-Gore, William G. A. 'Some Contrasts in Nigeria' (1927) 69:6 Geographical J 497.

Osman, Fatima. 'The Ascertainment of Living Customary Law: An Analysis of the South African Constitutional Court's Jurisprudence' (2019) 51:1 J Leg Pluralism and Unofficial L 98.

Otomo, Yoriko. 'Her Proper Name: A Revisionist Account of International Law' (2014) 2:1 London Rev IL 149.

Owosuyi, Ifeoma Laura. 'The Pursuit of Sustainable Development through Cultural Law and Governance Frameworks: A South African Perspective' (2015) 18:5 Potchefstroom Electronic LJ 2012.

Özkaynak, Begüm, Pat Devine and Dan Rigby. 'Operationalising Strong Sustainability: Definitions, Methodologies, and Outcomes' (2004) 13:3 Envt'l Val 279.

Packer, Corinne A. A. and Donald Rukare. 'The New African Union and Its Constitutive Act' (2002) 96:2 Am JIL 365.

Pahuja, Sundhya. 'The Postcoloniality of International Law' (2005) 46:2 Harvard Int'l LJ 459.

Palmer, Clare, Katie Shane and Ronald Sandler. 'Environmental Ethics' (2014) 39:1 Annual Rev Envt and Res 419.

Palmer, Geoffrey. 'What Went Wrong at Rio?' (1992) 70:4 Wash ULQ 1005.

Panta, Nancy Diana. 'Clashing Perspectives on Sustainable Development' (2019) 14:1 Studies in Bus and Econ 181.

Paradell-Trius, Lluís. 'Principles of International Environmental Law: An Overview' (2000) 9:2 RECIEL 93.

Paterson, Alexander. 'The Interface between Customary Rights and Environmental Legislation: Lessons from *Gongqose & Others vs Minister of Agriculture, Forestry and Fisheries and Others* (SCA) 2018' (2020) 26:1 South Afr J Envt'l L and Pol'y 134.

Pavlovskaia, Evgenia. 'Are We There Yet? A Legal Assessment and Review of the Concept of Sustainable Development under International Law' (2013) 2:1 J Sust Dev L and Pol'y 139.

Paz, Reut Yael. 'Kelsen's *Pure Theory of Law* as a "Hole in Time"' (2015) 7 Monde (s) 75.

Pearson-Patel, Jessica. 'Promoting Health, Protecting Empire: Inter-Colonial Medical Cooperation in Post-War Africa' (2015) 7:1 Monde(s) 213.

Pecharromán, Lidia Cano. 'Rights of Nature: Rivers that Can Stand in Court' (2018) 7:1 Res 13.

Perry, Stephen R. 'The Varieties of Legal Pluralism' (1996) 9 Can JL and Jur 361.

Pesqueux, Yvon. 'Sustainable Development: A Vague and Ambiguous "Theory"' (2009) 4:3 Soc'y and Bus Rev 231.

Petersmann, Marie-Catherine. 'Narcissus' Reflection in the Lake: Untold Narratives in Environmental Law Beyond the Anthropocentric Frame' (2018) 30:2 J Envt'l L 235.

Pezzoli, Keith. 'Sustainable Development: A Transdisciplinary Overview of the Literature' (1997) 40:5 J Envt'l Planning and Mgt 549.

Phelan, Alexandra and Matiangai Sirleaf, 'Decolonisation of Global Health Law: Lessons from International Environmental Law' (2023) 51:2 J L Med Ethics 450.

Polasky, Stephen, Catherine L. Kling, Simon A. Levin, Stephen R. Carpenter, Gretchen C. Daily, Paul R. Ehrlich, Geoffrey M. Heal and Jane Lubchenco. 'Role of Economics in Analysing the Environment and Sustainable Development' (2019) 116:12 Proc Nat Acad Sciences 5233.

Porras, Ileana. 'Appropriating Nature: Commerce, Property and the Commodification of Nature in the Law of Nations' (2014) 27:3 Leiden JIL 641.

'European Origins, The Doctrine of the Providential Function of Commerce, and International Law's Embrace of Economic Growth' (2013) 107 Am SIL: Proc Annual Mtg 374.

'The Rio Declaration: A New Basis for International Cooperation' (1992) 1:3 RECIEL 245.

Posner, Eric A. and Miguel F. P. de Figuieredo. 'Is the International Court of Justice Biased?' (2005) 32:2 J Leg Studies 625.

Powers, Ann. 'One Participant's Diary' (2012) 42:3 Envt'l Pol'y & L 140.

'The Rio+20 Process: Forward Movement for the Environment?' (2012) 1:2 Transnat'l Envt'l L 403.

Přibáň, Jiří. 'A Sociology of Legal Distinctions: Introducing Contemporary Interpretations of Classic Socio-Legal Concepts' (2017) 44:1 JL and Soc'y 1.

Priel, Dan. 'Toward Classical Legal Positivism' (2015) 101:4 Va L Rev 987.

Prost, Mario and Alejandra Torres Camprubí. 'Against Fairness? International Environmental Law, Disciplinary Bias, and Pareto Justice' (2012) 25:2 Leiden JIL 379.

Purcell, Kate. 'On the Uses and Advantages of Genealogy for International Law' (2020) 33:1 Leiden JIL 13.

Purdy, Jedidiah. 'Our Place in the World: A New Relationship for Environmental Ethics and Law' (2013) 62:4 Duke LJ 857.

'The Politics of Nature: Climate Change, Environmental Law, and Democracy' (2010) 119 Yale LJ 1122.

Purvis, Ben, Yong Mao and Darren Robinson. 'Three Pillars of Sustainability: In Search of Conceptual Origins' (2019) 14 Sustainability Science 681.

Putzer, Alex, Tineke Lambooy, Ignace Breemer and Aafje Rietveld. 'The Rights of Nature as a Bridge between Land-Ownership Regimes: The Potential of Institutionalised Interplay in Post-Colonial Societies' (2022) 11:3 Transnat'l Envt'l L 501.

Quijano, Anibal. 'Coloniality of Power, Eurocentrism, and Latin America' (2000) 1:3 Nepantla: Views from South 533.

Quintana, Francisco-José and Justina Uriburu. 'Modest International Law: COVID-19, International Legal Responses, and Depoliticisation' (2020) 114:4 Am JIL 687.

Rajagopal, Balakrishnan. 'Counter-Hegemonic International Law: Rethinking Human Rights and Development as a Third World Strategy' (2006) 27:5 Third World Q 767.

Rajan, S. Ravi. 'Classical Environmentalism and Environmental Human Rights: An Exploration of their Ontological Origins and Differences' (2011) 2:1 J Human Rights and Envt 106.

Rakshit, Santanu. 'Revisiting Environmental Concern: The Role of the United Nations in Development Management' (2015) 22:1 J Pol Ecol 199.

Ramina, Larissa. 'Third World Approaches to International Law and Human Rights: Some Considerations' (2018) 51 Revista de Investigações Constitucionais 261.

Randall, Vicky. 'Using and Abusing the Concept of the Third World: Geopolitics and the Comparative Political Study of Development and Underdevelopment' (2004) 25:1 Third World Q 41.

Rao, Malavika. 'A TWAIL Perspective on Loss and Damage from Climate Change: Reflections from Indira Gandhi's Speech at Stockholm' (2022) 12:1 Asian JIL 63.

Ratner, Steven. 'Ethics and International Law: Integrating the Global Justice Project(s)' (2013) 5:1 Int'l Theory 1.

Ratner, Steven R. and Anne-Marie Slaughter. 'Appraising the Methods of International Law: A Prospectus for Readers' (1999) 93:2 Am JIL 291.

Rawson, Ariel and Becky Mansfield. 'Producing Juridical Knowledge: "Rights of Nature" or the Naturalisation of Rights?' (2018) 1:1–2 Envt & Plan E: Nature and Space 99.

Redclift, Michael R. 'The Multiple Dimensions of Sustainable Development' (1991) 76:1 Geography 36.

'Sustainable Development (1987–2005): An Oxymoron Comes of Age' (2006) 12:25 Horizontes Anthropológicos 65.

Redclift, Michael R. and Graham Woodgate. 'Sustainable Development and Nature: The Social and the Material' (2013) 21 Sust Dev 92.

Rich, Bruce and Michael Hsu. 'Sustainable Development: A Broader Perspective' (1996) 3:2 Brown J World Aff 305.

Riegner, Michael. 'How Universal Are International Law and Development? Engaging with Postcolonial and Third World Scholarship from the Perspective of the Other' (2012) 45:2 Verfassung und Recht Übersee 232.

Robinson, Daniel F. and Nicole Graham. 'Legal Pluralisms, Justice and Spatial Conflicts: New Directions in Legal Geography' (2018) 184:1 Geographic J 3.

Robinson, Nicholas A. 'Caring for the Earth: A Legal Blueprint for Sustainable Development' (1992) 22:1 Envt'l Pol'y and L 22.

Rodrígues-Rivera, Luis E. 'The Human Right to Environment in the 21st Century: A Case for Its Recognition and Comments on the Systemic Barriers It Encounters' (2018) 34:1 Am U Int'l L Rev 143.

Rodriguez, Amardo. 'A Case against Colonialism' (2018) 21:2 Postcolonial Studies 254.

Rolston III, Holmes. 'Justifying Sustainable Development: A Continuing Ethical Search' (2002) 4:1 Global Dialogue 103.

Rose, Justine, Margaretha Wewerinke-Singh and Jessica Miranda. 'Primal Scene to Anthropocene: Narrative and Myth in International Law' (2019) 66 Nethl Int'l L Rev 441.

Rosen, Marc A. 'Issues, Concepts and Applications for Sustainability' (2018) 3 Glocalism: J Cult, Pol and Innov 1.

Ross, Andrea. 'Modern Interpretations of Sustainable Development' (2009) 36:1 JL and Soc'y 32.

'It's Time to Get Serious: Why Legislation Is Needed to Make Sustainable Development a Reality in the UK' (2010) 2 Sustainability 1101.

Rudnev, Viacheslav. 'Indigenous Knowledge: Searching for a Model of Sustainable Development for Humankind' (2015) 26:2 Global Ethics 46.

Rühs, Nathalie and Aled Jones. 'The Implementation of Earth Jurisprudence through Substantive Constitutional Rights to Nature' (2016) 8 Sustainability 174.

Rydin, Yvonne. 'Can We Talk Ourselves into Sustainability? The Role of Discourse in the Environmental Policy Process' (1999) 8:4 Envt'l Val 467.

Sachs, Wolfgang. 'The Sustainable Development Goals and *Laudato Si'*: Varieties of Post-Development?' (2017) 28:12 Third World Q 2573.

Saeed, Raza. 'Law and Coloniality of Empire: Colonial Encounter and Normative Orderings in the Indian Sub-Continent' (2018) 19:1 YB Islamic & Middle Eastern L 103.

Said, Edward W. 'Representing the Colonised: Anthropology's Interlocutors' (1989) 15:2 Critical Inquiry 205.

Salamat, Mohammed Reza. 'Ethics of Sustainable Development: The Moral Imperative for the Effective Implementation of the 2030 Agenda for Sustainable Development' (2016) 40:1–2 Nat Res Forum 3.

Salas-Zapata, Walter Alfredo and Sara Milena Ortiz-Muñoz. 'Analysis of Meanings of the Concept of Sustainability' (2019) 27:1 Sust Dev 153.

Salunkhe, Sarjerao A. 'The Concept of Sustainable Development: Roots, Connotations and Critical Evaluation' (2003) 33:1 Social Change 67.

Samaan, Andrew Watson. 'Enforcement of International Environmental Treaties: An Analysis' (2011) 5:1 Fordham Envt'l LJ 261.

Sand, Peter H. 'International Environmental Law after Rio' (1993) 4:3 European JIL 377.

'International Law on the Agenda of the 1992 "Earth Summit"' (1992) 3:1 Colo J Int'l Envt'l L and Pol'y 343.

'Sustainable Development: Of Forests, Ships, and Law: Some Historical Annotations' (2007) 37:23 Envt'l Pol'y and L 201.

'UNCED and the Development of International Environmental Law' (1992) 8:2 J Nat Res and Envt'l L 209.

'Whither CITES? The Evolution of a Treaty Regime in the Borderland of Trade and Environment' (1997) 8:1 European JIL 28.

Sands, Philippe. 'International Courts and the Application of the "Concept of Sustainable Development"' (1999) 3 Max Planck YB UN L 389.

'International Law in the Field of Sustainable Development' (1994) 65:1 Brit YBIL 303.

Sang, Brian Y. K. 'Tending towards Greater Eco-Protection in Kenya: Public Interest Environmental Litigation and Its Prospects within the New Constitutional Order' (2013) 57:1 J Afr L 29.

Sani, Hanisah Binte Abdullah. 'State Law and Legal Pluralism: An Appraisal' (2020) 52:1 J Leg Pluralism and Unofficial L 82.

Santos, Boaventura de Sousa. 'Public Sphere and Epistemologies of the South' (2012) 37:1 Afr Dev 43.

Sawyer, Cara Victoria. 'The Indigenous Alternative: TEK, IEL and Solutions for the Unsolvable' (2022) 18:1 Loyola U Chicago Int'l L Rev 113.

Schachter, Oscar. 'The Emergence of International Environmental Law' (1991) 44:2 J Int'l Aff 457.

Schauer, Jeff. '"We Hold It in Trust": Global Wildlife Conservation, Africanisation, and the End of Empire' (2018) 57 J Brit Studies 516.

Schmidhauser, John R. 'Legal Imperialism: Its Enduring Impact on Colonial and Post-Colonial Judicial Systems' (1992) 13:3 Int'l Pol Science Rev 321.

Scholtz, Werner. 'Injecting Compassion into International Wildlife Law: From Conservation to Protection?' (2017) 6:3 Transnat'l Envt'l L 463.

Schrijver, Nico. 'A New Convention on the Human Right to Development: Putting the Cart before the Horse?' (2020) 38:2 Nethl QHR 84.

Scoones, Ian. 'The Politics of Sustainability and Development' (2016) 41:1 Annual Rev Envt and Res 293.

Seck, Sara L. 'Transnational Labour Law and the Environment: Beyond the Bounded Autonomous Worker' (2018) 33:2 Can JL and Soc'y 137.

Segger, Marie-Claire Cordonier. 'Inspiration for Integration: Interpreting International Trade and Investment Accords for Sustainable Development' (2017) 3:1 Can J Comp and Contemp L 159.

'Significant Developments in Sustainable Development Law and Governance: A Proposal' (2004) 28:1 Nat Res Forum 61.

Selier, S. A. Jeanetta, Rob Slotow, Andrew Blackmore and Arie Trouwborst. 'The Legal Challenges of Transboundary Wildlife Management at the Population Level: The Case of a Trilateral Elephant Population in Southern Africa' (2016) 19:2 J Int'l Wildlife L and Pol'y 101.

Senaratne, Kalana. 'Judge C. G. Weeramantry: An Alternative Reading' (2016) 56:3–4 Indian JIL 325.

Shaffer, Gregory. 'Theorising Transnational Legal Ordering' (2016) 12 Annual Rev Soc Sciences 231.

Sheehan, Linda. 'Implementing Rights of Nature through Sustainability Bill of Rights' (2015) 13(1) New Zealand J Public and IL 89.

Shelton, Dinah. 'The Benefits and Limitations of a Human Rights Approach to Environmental Protection' (2014) 2 Hungarian YB Int'l L & European L 141.

'Human Rights, Environmental Rights, and the Right to Environment' (1991) 28:1 Stan JIL 103.

Shihata, Ibrahim F. I. 'The World Bank and the Environment: A Legal Perspective' (1992) 16:1 Md JIL 1.

Shrinkhal, Rashwel. 'Evolution of Indigenous Rights under International Law: Analysis from TWAIL Perspective' (2019) 19:1 Oriental Anthropologist 7.

Shumba, Overson. 'Commons Thinking, Ecological Intelligence and the Ethical and Moral Framework of *Ubuntu*: An Imperative for Sustainable Development' (2011) 3:3 J Media and Communication Studies 84.

Sibanda, Sanele. 'When Is the Past not the Past? Reflections on Customary Law under South Africa's Constitutional Dispensation' (2010) 17:3 Human Rights Brief 31.

Silecchia, Lucia A. '"Social Love" as a Vision of Environmental Law: Laudato Si' and the Rule of Law' (2016) 10:3 Liberty U L Rev 371.

Silving, Helen. '"Customary Law": Continuity in Municipal and International Law' (1946) 31:4 Iowa L Rev 614.

Simma, Bruno. 'Universality of International Law from the Perspective of a Practitioner' (2009) 20:2 European JIL 265.

Simons, Penelope. 'International Law's Invisible Hand and the Future of Corporate Accountability for Violation of Human Rights' (2012) 3:1 J Human Rights and Envt 5.

Sinclair, Guy Fiti. 'A "Civilising Task": The International Labour Organisation, Social Reform, and the Genealogy of Development' (2018) 20:2 J History IL 145.

Sirleaf, Matiangai. 'The African Justice Cascade and the Malabo Protocol' (2017) 11:1 Int'l J Transitional Just 71.

Situma, Francis D. P. 'Africa's Potential Contribution to the Implementation of International Environmental Law' (2000) 10:2 Transnat'l L and Contemp Probs 385.

Siyambalapitiya, Janaka, Xu Zhang and Xiabing Liu, 'Is Governmentality the Missing Link for Greening the Economic Growth?' (2018) 10:11 Sustainability 4204.

Sklair, Leslie. 'The Corporate Capture of Sustainable Development and Its Transformation into a "Good Anthropocene" Historical Bloc' (2019) 19:2 Civitas 296.

Skogly, Sigrun I. 'Complexities in Human Resource Protection: Actors and Rights Involved in the Ogoni Conflict in Nigeria' (1997) 15:1 Nethl QHR 47.

Skurnik, W. A. E. 'France and Fragmentation in West Africa' (1967) 8:2 J Afr History 317.

Slattery, Brian. 'Aboriginal Sovereignty and Imperial Claims' (1991) 29:4 Osgoode Hall LJ 681.

Smandych, Russell. 'Colonialism, Settler Colonialism, and Law: Settler Revolutions and the Dispossession of Indigenous Peoples through Law in the Long Nineteenth Century' (2013) 3:1 Settler Colonial Studies 82.

Snyder, Francis G. 'Colonialism and Legal Form: The Creation of "Customary Law" in Senegal' (1981) 13:19 J Leg Pluralism 49.

Soares Jr, Jair and Rogério H. Quintella. 'Development: An Analysis of Concepts, Measurements and Indicators' (2008) 5:2 Brazilian Admin Rev 104.

Sohn, Louis B. 'The Stockholm Declaration on the Human Environment' (1973) 14 Harvard Int'l LJ 423.

Solarz, Marcin. '"Third World": The 60th Anniversary of a Concept that Changed the World' (2012) 33:9 Third World Q 1561.

Sörlin, Sverker and Paul Warde. 'The Problem of the Problem of Environmental History: A Re-Reading of the Field' (2007) 12:1 Envt'l History 107.

Sornarajah, Muthucumaraswamy. 'On Fighting for Global Justice: The Role of a Third World International Lawyer' (2016) 37:11 Third World Q 1972.

'Power and Justice: Third World Resistance in International Law' (2006) 10 Singapore YBIL 19.

Squeff, Tatiana Cardoso. 'Overcoming the "Coloniality of Doing" in International Law: Soft Law as a Decolonial Tool' (2021) 17:2 Revista Direito GV 1.

Sreejith, SG. 'An Auto-Critique of TWAIL's Historical Fallacy: Sketching an Alternative Manifesto' (2017) 38:7 Third World Q 1511.

Ssenyongo, Manisuli. 'Responding to Human Rights Violations in Africa: Assessing the Role of the African Commission and Court on Human and Peoples' Rights (1987–2018)' (2018) 7:1 Int'l Human Rights L Rev 1.

Stalley, Phillip. 'Norms from the Periphery: Tracing the Rise of the Common but Differentiated Principle in International Environmental Politics' (2018) 31:2 Cambridge Rev Int'l Aff 141.

Stark, Barbara. 'Sustainable Development and Postmodern International Law: Greener Globalisation?' (2002–2003) 27:1 William and Mary Envt'l L and Pol'y Rev 137.

Stewart, James G. and Asad Kiyani. 'The Ahistoricism of Legal Pluralism in International Criminal Law' (2017) 65:2 Am J Comp L 393.

Stoddart, Mark C. J. 'The Gramsci-Foucault Nexus and Environmental Sociology' (2005) 21 Alternative Routes 40.

Stone, Christopher. 'Deciphering Sustainable Development' (1994) 69:4 Chicago-Kent L Rev 977.

'Should Trees Have Standing? Towards Legal Rights for Natural Objects' (1972) 45 S Cal L Rev 450.

Storr, Cait. 'Islands and the South: Framing the Relationship between International Law and Environmental Crisis' (2016) 27:2 European JIL 519.

Sunter, Andrew. 'TWAIL as Naturalized Epistemological Inquiry' (2007) 20:2 Canadian JL and Jur 475.

Sveiby, Karl-Erik. 'Aboriginal Principles for Sustainable Development as Told in Traditional Law Stories' (2009) 17:6 Sust Dev 341.

Swenson, Geoffrey. 'Legal Pluralism in Theory and Practice' (2018) 20:3 Int'l Studies Rev 438.

Taiwo, Elijah A. 'Repugnancy Clause and Its Impact on Customary Law: Comparing the South African and Nigerian Positions: Some Lessons for Nigeria' (2009) 34:1 J Jur Science 89.

Takang, J. Manyitabot. 'From Algiers to Maputo: The Role of the African Convention on the Conservation of Nature and Natural Resources in the Harmonization of Conservation Policy in Africa' (2014) 17:4 J Int'l Wildlife L and Pol'y 165.

Tamanaha, Brian Z. 'A Proposal for the Development of a System of Indigenous Jurisprudence in the Federated States of Micronesia' (1989) 31:1 Hastings Int'l and Comp L Rev 71.

'Socio-Legal Positivism and a General Jurisprudence' (2001) 21:1 Oxford J Leg Studies 1.

Tarayia, G. Nasieku. 'The Legal Perspectives of the Maasai Culture, Customs, and Traditions' (2004) 21:1 Ariz J Int'l and Comp L 183.

Taringa, Nisbert. 'How Environmental Is African Traditional Religion?' (2006) 39:2 Exchange 191.

Tatum, Melissa L. 'Customary Law of Indigenous Communities: Making Space on the Global Environmental Stage' (2020) 9 Michigan J Envt'l and Admin L 77.

Tebbe, Nelson. 'Inheritance and Disinheritance: African Customary Law and Constitutional Rights' (2008) 88:4 J Religion 466.

Techera, Erica J. 'Legal Pluralism, Indigenous People, and Small Island Developing States: Achieving Good Environmental Governance in the South Pacific' (2010) 42:61 J Leg Pluralism and Unofficial L 171.

Teclaff, Ludwik A. 'The Impact of Environmental Concern on the Development of International Law' (1973) 13:2 Nat Res J 357.

Thérien, Jean-Phillipe. 'Beyond the North–South Divide: The Two Tales of World Poverty' (1999) 20:4 Third World Q 723.

Thompson, Trevor and Tim Ballard. 'Sustainable Medicine: Good for the Environment, Good for the People' (2011) 61:582 British J Gen Practice 3.

Tortell, Philippe D. 'Earth 2020: Science, Society, and Sustainability in the Anthropocene' (2020) 117:16 Proc Nat Acad Sciences 8683.

Tosam, Mbih Jerome. 'African Environmental Ethics and Sustainable Development' (2019) 9:1 Open J Phil 172.

Toufayan, Mark. 'When British Justice (in African Colonies) Points Two Ways: On Dualism, Hybridity, and the Genealogy of Juridical Negritude in Taslim Olawale Elias' (2008) 21:2 Leiden JIL 377.

Trefzer, Annette, Jeffrey T. Jackson, Kathryn McKee and Kirsten Dellinger. 'The Global South and/in the Global North: Interdisciplinary Investigations' (2014) 8:2 Global South 1.

Tremblay-Huet, Sabrina. 'Should Environmental Law Learn from Animal Law? Compassion as a Guiding Principle for International Environmental Law Instead of Sustainable Development' (2018) 31 Revue Québécoise de Droit International 125.

Tribe, Laurence. 'Ways Not to Think about Plastic Trees: New Foundations for Environmental Law' (1974) 83:7 Yale LJ 1315.

Tsosie, Rebecca. 'Indigenous People and Epistemic Injustice: Science, Ethics and Human Rights' (2012) 87:4 Wash L Rev 1133.

Tulloch, Lynley and David Neilson. 'The Neoliberalisation of Sustainability' (2014) 13:1 Citizenship, Soc and Econ Educ 26.

Twining, William. 'Normative and Legal Pluralism: A Global Perspective' (2010) 20:3 Duke J Comp and Int'l L 473.

Tzouvala, Ntina. 'The Spectre of Eurocentrism in International Legal History' (2021) 13:2 Yale JL and Hum 413.

Udombana, Nsongurua J. 'Towards the African Court on Human and Peoples' Rights: Better Late Than Never' (2000) 3:1 Yale Human Rights and Dev LJ 45.

Ugochukwu, Basil. 'From Reaction to Agency: A "Subaltern" Response to William Twining's Globalisation and Legal Scholarship' (2013) 4:4 Transnat'l Leg Theory 549.

Umar, Ahmad Rizky Mardhatillar. 'Rethinking the Legacies of Bandung Conference: Global Decolonisation and the Making of the Modern International Order' (2019) 11:3 Asian Pol and Pol'y 461.

Uweru, Bethel Chuks. 'Repugnancy Doctrine and Customary Law in Nigeria: A Positive Aspect of British Colonialism' (2008) 2:2 Afr Research Rev 286.

Vadi, Valentina. 'International Law and Its Histories: Methodological Risks and Opportunities' (2017) 58:2 Harvard Int'l LJ 311.

Valera, Luca and Gonzalo Salazar. 'Challenging Sustainability: From Deconstruction to Reconstruction' (2020) 16:1 J Nat and Soc Phil 298.

Van Den Meerssche, Dimitri. 'Performing the Rule of Law in International Organisations: Ibrahim Shihata and the World Bank's Turn to Governance Reform' (2019) 32:1 Leiden JIL 47.

Van der Linde, Morne. 'African Responses to Environmental Protection' (2002) 35:1 Comp and Int'l LJ S Afr 99.

'A Review of the African Convention on Nature and Natural Resources' (2002) 2:1 Afr Human Rights LJ 33.

Van Harten, Gus. 'TWAIL and the Dabhol Arbitration' (2011) 3:1 Trade L and Dev 131.

Vandemoortele, Jan. 'From Simple-Minded MDGs to Muddle-Headed SDGs' (2018) 5:1 Dev Studies Research 83.

Vanhulst, Julien and Adrian E. Beling, 'Buen Vivir: Emergent Discourse or Beyond Sustainable Development?' (2014) 101 Ecol Econ 54.

Vásques Roldán, Julián Santiago and Robert Henao Ng. 'Sustainable Development and Human Development: Evolution or Transition in the Scientific Conception of Sustainability?' (2017) 2:2 Producción + Limipia 103.

Vásquez-Fernández, Andrea M. and Cash Ahenekaw pii tai poo taa. 'Resurgence of Relationality: Reflections on Decolonising and Indigenising "Sustainable Development"' (2020) 43 Current Opinion on Envt'l Sustainability 65.

Vermeylen, Saskia. 'The Nagoya Protocol and Customary Law: The Paradox of Narratives in Law' (2013) 9:2 L Envt and Dev J 185.

'Special Issue: Environmental Justice and Epistemic Violence' (2019) 24:2 Local Envt 89.

Verschurren, Jonathan. 'Sustainable Development and the Nature of Environmental Legal Principles' (2006) 9:1 Potchefstroom Electronic LJ 1.

Vestergaard, Jakob and Robert Wade. 'Protecting Power: How Western States Retain the Dominant Voice in the World Bank's Governance' (2013) 46 World Dev 153.

Viljoen, Frans and Lirette Louw. 'The Status of the Findings of the African Commission: From Moral Persuasion to Legal Obligation' (2004) 48:1 J Afr L 1.

Viñuales, Jorge E. 'A Concise Research Agenda for Environmental Law' (2018) 1 Brill Open L 1.

'The Resource Curse: A Legal Perspective' (2011) 17:2 Global Governance 197.
'The Rise and Fall of Sustainable Development' (2013) 22:1 RECIEL 3.

Viñuales, Jorge E., Suerie Moon, Ginevra Le Moli, Gian-Luca Burci, 'A Global Pandemic Treaty Should Aim for Deep Prevention' (2021) 397:10287 Lancet, 1791.

Von Benda-Beckmann, Keebet. 'Environmental Protection and Human Rights of Indigenous Peoples: A Tricky Alliance' (1997) 9 L and Anthro 302.

Von Bernstorff, Jochen. 'International Legal Scholarship as a Cooling Medium in International Law and Politics' (2014) 25:4 European JIL 977.

Von Bogdandy, Armin, Matthias Goldmann and Ingo Venzke. 'From Public International Law to International Public Law: Translating World Public Opinion into International Public Authority' (2017) 28:1 European JIL 115.

Wade, Robert H. 'Emerging World Order? From Multipolarity to Multilateralism in the G20, the World Bank and the IMF' (2011) 39:3 Pol and Soc'y 347.

Wallman, Diane, E. Christian Wells and Isabel C. Rivera-Collazo. 'The Environmental Legacies of Colonialism in the Northern Neotropics: Introduction to the Special Issue' (2018) 23:1 Envt'l Archaeo 1.

Wanner, Thomas. 'The New Passive Revolution of the Green Economy and Growth Discourse: Maintaining the "Sustainable Development" of Neoliberal Capitalism' (2015) 20:1 New Pol Econ 21.

Wapner, Paul. 'The Changing Nature of Nature: Environmental Politics in the Anthropocene' (2014) 14:4 Global Envt'l Pol 36.
'World Summit on Sustainable Development: Towards a Post-Jo'burg Environmentalism' (2003) 3:1 Global Envt'l Pol 1.

Weber, Heloise and Poppy Winanti. 'The "Bandung Spirit" and Solidarist Internationalism' (2016) 70:4 Australian J Int'l Aff 391.

Webster, Emily and Laura Mai, 'Transnational Environmental Law in the Anthropocene' (2020) 11:1–2 Transnat'l Leg Theory 1.

Weeramantry, Christopher G. 'International Law and the Developing World: A Millennial Analysis' (2000) 41:2 Harvard Int'l LJ 277.

Weeramantry, Christopher G. and Nathaniel Berman. 'The Grotius Lectures Series' (1999) 14:6 Am U Int'l L Rev 1515.

Weiss, Edith Brown. 'The Evolution of International Environmental Law' (2011) 54 Japanese YBIL 1.

Weston, Burns H. 'The Charter of Economic Rights and Duties of States and the Deprivation of Foreign-Owned Wealth' (1981) 75:3 Am JIL 437.

Westra, Laura. 'The Ethics of Integrity and the Law in Global Governance' (2003) 37:1 UC Davis L Rev 127.

Whelan, Daniel J. '"Under the Aegis of Man": The Right to Development and the Origins of the New International Economic Order' (2015) 6:1 Humanity 93.

White, C. M. N. 'African Customary Law: The Problem of Concept and Definition' (1965) 9:2 J Afr L 86.

White Jr, Lynn. 'The Historic Roots of Our Ecologic Crisis' (1967) 155:3767 Science 1203.

Wienhues, Anna. 'Sharing the Earth: A Biocentric Account of Ecological Justice' (2017) 30:3 J Agric and Envt'l Ethics 367.

Wilkins, Hugh. 'The Integration of the Pillars of Sustainable Development: A Work in Progress' (2008) 4:2 McGill J Sust Dev L and Pol'y 163.

Willetts, Peter. 'From Stockholm to Rio and Beyond: The Impact of the Environmental Movement on the United Nations Consultative Arrangements for NGOs' (1996) 22:1 Rev Int'l Studies 57.

William, Idowu. 'Eurocentrism and the Separability–Inseperability Debate: Challenges from African Cultural Jurisprudence' (2009) 2:9 J Pan Afr Studies 123.

Williams, David. 'Managing Sovereignty: The World Bank and Development in Sub-Saharan Africa' (2003) 123:3 Mondes en Développement 5.

Williams, Marc. 'Aid, Sustainable Development and the Environmental Crisis' (1998) 3:2 Int'l J Peace Studies 19.

'Re-Articulating the Third World Coalition: The Role of the Environmental Agenda' (1993) 14:1 Third World Q 7.

'The Third World and Global Environmental Negotiations: Interests, Institutions and Ideas' (2005) 5:3 Global Envt'l Pol 48.

Williams, Mariama and Manuel F. Montes. 'Common but Differentiated Responsibilities: Which Way Forward?' (2016) 59:1–2 Dev 114.

Wilson, David. 'European Colonisation, Law, and Indigenous Marine Dispossession: Historical Perspectives on the Construction and Entrenchment of Unequal Marine Governance' (2021) 20:4 Maritime Studies 387.

Winks, Benjamin Elias. 'A Covenant of Compassion: African Humanism and the Rights of Solidarity in the African Charter on Human and Peoples' Rights' (2011) 11:2 Afr Human Rights LJ 447.

de Witt, Annick, 'Rethinking Sustainable: Considering How Different Worldviews Envision "Development" and "Quality of Life"' (2014) 6 Sustainability 8310.

Wood Jr, Harold W. 'The United Nations World Charter for Nature: The Developing Nations' Initiative to Establish Protections for the Environment' (1985) 12:4 Ecol LQ 977.

Wood, Sally Percival. 'Retrieving the Bandung Conference . . . Moment by Moment' (2012) 43:3 J Southeast Asia Studies 523.

Woodman, Gordon R. 'British Legislation as a Source of Ghanaian Law: From Colonialism to Technical Aid' (1974) 7:1 Verfassung und Recht Übersee 19.

'Customary Land Laws within Legal Pluralism over the Generations' (2014–2015) 1 SADC LJ 189.

Wright, David V. 'Environmental Rule of Law: In Need of Coherence in Contested Terrain' (2020) 15:1 McGill J Sust Dev L and Pol'y 1.

Wyborn, Carina, Amber Datta, Jasper Montana, Melanie Ryan, Peat Leith, Brian Chaffin, Clark Miller and Lorrae van Kerkhoff. 'Co-Producing Sustainability: Re-ordering the Governance of Science, Policy, and Practice' (2019) 44:1 Annual Rev Envt and Res 319.

Wyrtzen, Jonathan. 'Colonial Legitimisation–Legibility Linkages and the Politics of Identity in Algeria and Morocco' (2017) 58:2 European J Sociology 205.

Xavier, Sujith. 'Learning from Below: Theorising Global Governance through Ethnographies and Critical Reflections from the Global South' (2016) 33:3 Windsor YB Access Just 229.

'Top Heavy: Beyond the Global North and the Justification for Global Administrative Law' (2017) 57:3-4 Indian JIL 337.

Xifaras, Mikhaïl. 'The Global Turn in Legal Theory' (2016) 29:1 Canadian JL and Jur 215.

Yang, Tseming. 'The Emergence of Global Environmental Law' (2009) 36 Ecol LQ 615.

Yihdego, Zeray. 'The African Union: Founding Principles, Frameworks and Prospects' (2011) 17:5 European LJ 568.

Youatt, Rafi. 'Interspecies Relations, International Relations: Rethinking Anthropocentric Politics' (2014) 43:1 Millennium: J Int'l Studies 207.

Zoellick, Robert B. 'The End of the Third World: Modernizing Multilateralism for a Multipolar World' (2010) 16:3 L and Bus Rev Americas 317.

Zollmann, Jakob. 'African International Legal Histories–International Law in Africa: Perspectives and Possibilities' (2018) 31:4 Leiden JIL 897.

Zumbansen, Peer. 'Lochner Disembedded: The Anxieties of Law in a Global Context' (2013) 20:1 Ind J Global Leg Studies 29.

'Neither "Public" nor "Private", "National" or "International": Transnational Corporate Governance from a Legal Pluralist Perspective' (2011) 38:1 JL and Soc'y 50.

'Transnational Law as Socio-Legal Theory and Critique: Prospects for "Law and Society" in a Divided World' (2019) 67:3 Buff L Rev 909.

Conference Proceedings

Adedeji, Adebayo. 'From the Lagos Plan of Action to the New Partnership for Africa's Development and from the Final Act of Lagos to the Constitutive Act: Whither Africa?' (Keynote Address delivered at the African Forum for Envisioning Africa held in Nairobi, Kenya, 26–29 April 2002).

News Reports

Black, Richard. 'Rio Revisited: Glass Half-full?', BBC News (24 July 2012), available at: <www.bbc.com/news/science-environment-18967011>.

Howard, Brian Clark. 'Rio+20 Brings Hope and Solutions Despite Weak Talks', National Geographic News (21 June 2012), available at: <www.nationalgeographic.com/news/2012/6/120621-rio-20-hope-solutions-official-talks/>.

Watson, Connie. 'Rio+20 Earth Summit Concludes with Few Commitments', CBC News (22 June 2012), available at: <www.cbc.ca/news/politics/rio-20-earth-summit-concludes-with-few-commitments-1.1270257>.

Web Pages

Environmental Law and Governance Association. 'From Environmental Law to Ecological Law: A Call for Re-Framing Law and Governance' (2016), online (pdf), available at: <www.elga.world/oslo-manifesto>.

Melissaris, Emmanuel and Mariano Croce. 'A Pluralism of Legal Pluralisms' (April 2017), online: Oxford Handbooks Online, available at: <www.oxfordhandbooks.com/view/10.1093/oxfordhb/9780199935352.001.0001/oxfordhb-9780199935352-e-22>.

INDEX

CAMBRIDGE STUDIES IN INTERNATIONAL AND COMPARATIVE LAW

Books in the Series

185 *Sustainable Development, International Law, and a Turn to African Legal Cosmologies* Godwin Eli Kwadzo Dzah
184 *Collective Self-Defence in International Law* James A. Green
183 *Weaponising Evidence: A History of Tobacco Control in International Law* Margherita Melillo
182 *The Justice Factory: Management Practices at the International Criminal Court* Richard Clements
181 *A Communitarian Theory of WTO Law* Chi Carmody
180 *Drones and International Law: A Techno-Legal Machinery* Rebecca Mignot-Mahdavi
179 *The Necessity of Nature: God, Science and Money in 17th Century English Law of Nature* Mónica García-Salmones
178 *Making the World Safe for Investment: The Protection of Foreign Property 1922-1959* Andrea Leiter
177 *National Governance and Investment Treaties* Josef Ostřanský and Facundo Pérez Aznar
176 *Who Owns Outer Space? International Law, Astrophysics, and the Sustainable Development of Space* Michael Byers and Aaron Boley
175 *Intervening in International Justice: Third States before Courts and Tribunals* Brian McGarry
174 *Reciprocity in Public International Law* Arianna Whelan
173 *When Environmental Protection and Human Rights Collide* Marie-Catherine Petersmann
172 *The International Law of Sovereign Debt Dispute Settlement* Kei Nakajima
171 *The Everyday Makers of International Law: From Great Halls to Back Rooms* Tommaso Soave
170 *Virtue in Global Governance: Judgment and Discretion* Jan Klabbers
169 *The Effects of Armed Conflict on Investment Treaties* Tobias Ackermann
168 *Investment Law's Alibis: Colonialism, Imperialism, Debt and Development* David Schneiderman

167 *Negative Comparative Law: A Strong Programme for Weak Thought* Pierre Legrand

166 *Detention by Non-State Armed Groups under International Law* Ezequiel Heffes

165 *Rebellions and Civil Wars: State Responsibility for the Conduct of Insurgents* Patrick Dumberry

164 *The International Law of Energy* Jorge Viñuales

163 *The Three Ages of International Commercial Arbitration* Mikaël Schinazi

162 *Repetition and International Law* Wouter Werner

161 *State Responsibility and Rebels: The History and Legacy of Protecting Investment Against Revolution* Kathryn Greenman

160 *Rewriting Histories of the Use of Force: The Narrative of 'Indifference'* Agatha Verdebout

159 *The League of Nations and the Protection of the Environment* Omer Aloni

158 *International Investment Law and Legal Theory: Expropriation and the Fragmentation of Sources* Jörg Kammerhofer

157 *Legal Barbarians: Identity, Modern Comparative Law and the Global South* Daniel Bonilla Maldonado

156 *International Human Rights Law Beyond State Territorial Control* Antal Berkes

155 *The Crime of Aggression under the Rome Statute of the International Criminal Court* Carrie McDougall

154 *Minorities and the Making of Postcolonial States in International Law* Mohammad Shahabuddin

153 *Preclassical Conflict of Laws* Nikitas E. Hatzimihail

152 *International Law and History: Modern Interfaces* Ignacio de la Rasilla

151 *Marketing Global Justice: The Political Economy of International Criminal Law* Christine Schwöbel-Patel

150 *International Status in the Shadow of Empire* Cait Storr

149 *Treaties in Motion: The Evolution of Treaties from Formation to Termination* Edited by Malgosia Fitzmaurice and Panos Merkouris

148 *Humanitarian Disarmament: An Historical Enquiry* Treasa Dunworth

147 *Complementarity, Catalysts, Compliance: The International Criminal Court in Uganda, Kenya, and the Democratic Republic of Congo* Christian M. De Vos

146 *Cyber Operations and International Law* François Delerue

145 *Comparative Reasoning in International Courts and Tribunals* Daniel Peat

144 *Maritime Delimitation as a Judicial Process* Massimo Lando

143 *Prosecuting Sexual and Gender-Based Crimes at the International Criminal Court: Practice, Progress and Potential* Rosemary Grey

142 *Capitalism As Civilisation: A History of International Law* Ntina Tzouvala

141 *Sovereignty in China: A Genealogy of a Concept Since 1840* Adele Carrai

140 *Narratives of Hunger in International Law: Feeding the World in Times of Climate Change* Anne Saab

139 *Victim Reparation under the Ius Post Bellum: An Historical and Normative Perspective* Shavana Musa
138 *The Analogy between States and International Organizations* Fernando Lusa Bordin
137 *The Process of International Legal Reproduction: Inequality, Historiography, Resistance* Rose Parfitt
136 *State Responsibility for Breaches of Investment Contracts* Jean Ho
135 *Coalitions of the Willing and International Law: The Interplay between Formality and Informality* Alejandro Rodiles
134 *Self-Determination in Disputed Colonial Territories* Jamie Trinidad
133 *International Law as a Belief System* Jean d'Aspremont
132 *Legal Consequences of Peremptory Norms in International Law* Daniel Costelloe
131 *Third-Party Countermeasures in International Law* Martin Dawidowicz
130 *Justification and Excuse in International Law: Concept and Theory of General Defences* Federica Paddeu
129 *Exclusion from Public Space: A Comparative Constitutional Analysis* Daniel Moeckli
128 *Provisional Measures before International Courts and Tribunals* Cameron A. Miles
127 *Humanity at Sea: Maritime Migration and the Foundations of International Law* Itamar Mann
126 *Beyond Human Rights: The Legal Status of the Individual in International Law* Anne Peters
125 *The Doctrine of Odious Debt in International Law: A Restatement* Jeff King
124 *Static and Evolutive Treaty Interpretation: A Functional Reconstruction* Christian Djeffal
123 *Civil Liability in Europe for Terrorism-Related Risk* Lucas Bergkamp, Michael Faure, Monika Hinteregger and Niels Philipsen
122 *Proportionality and Deference in Investor-State Arbitration: Balancing Investment Protection and Regulatory Autonomy* Caroline Henckels
121 *International Law and Governance of Natural Resources in Conflict and Post-Conflict Situations* Daniëlla Dam-de Jong
120 *Proof of Causation in Tort Law* Sandy Steel
119 *The Formation and Identification of Rules of Customary International Law in International Investment Law*
118 *Religious Hatred and International Law: The Prohibition of Incitement to Violence or Discrimination* Jeroen Temperman
117 *Taking Economic, Social and Cultural Rights Seriously in International Criminal Law* Evelyne Schmid
116 *Climate Change Litigation: Regulatory Pathways to Cleaner Energy* Jacqueline Peel and Hari M. Osofsky

115 *Mestizo International Law: A Global Intellectual History 1842–1933* Arnulf Becker Lorca

114 *Sugar and the Making of International Trade Law* Michael Fakhri

113 *Strategically Created Treaty Conflicts and the Politics of International Law* Surabhi Ranganathan

112 *Investment Treaty Arbitration As Public International Law: Procedural Aspects and Implications* Eric De Brabandere

111 *The New Entrants Problem in International Fisheries Law* Andrew Serdy

110 *Substantive Protection under Investment Treaties: A Legal and Economic Analysis* Jonathan Bonnitcha

109 *Popular Governance of Post-Conflict Reconstruction: The Role of International Law* Matthew Saul

108 *Evolution of International Environmental Regimes: The Case of Climate Change* Simone Schiele

107 *Judges, Law and War: The Judicial Development of International Humanitarian Law* Shane Darcy

106 *Religious Offence and Human Rights: The Implications of Defamation of Religions* Lorenz Langer

105 *Forum Shopping in International Adjudication: The Role of Preliminary Objections* Luiz Eduardo Salles

104 *Domestic Politics and International Human Rights Tribunals: The Problem of Compliance* Courtney Hillebrecht

103 *International Law and the Arctic* Michael Byers

102 *Cooperation in the Law of Transboundary Water Resources* Christina Leb

101 *Underwater Cultural Heritage and International Law* Sarah Dromgoole

100 *State Responsibility: The General Part* James Crawford

99 *The Origins of International Investment Law: Empire, Environment and the Safeguarding of Capital* Kate Miles

98 *The Crime of Aggression under the Rome Statute of the International Criminal Court* Carrie McDougall

97 *'Crimes against Peace' and International Law* Kirsten Sellars

96 *Non-Legality in International Law: Unruly Law* Fleur Johns

95 *Armed Conflict and Displacement: The Protection of Refugees and Displaced Persons under International Humanitarian Law* Mélanie Jacques

94 *Foreign Investment and the Environment in International Law* Jorge E. Viñuales

93 *The Human Rights Treaty Obligations of Peacekeepers* Kjetil Mujezinović Larsen

92 *Cyber Warfare and the Laws of War* Heather Harrison Dinniss

91 *The Right to Reparation in International Law for Victims of Armed Conflict* Christine Evans

90 *Global Public Interest in International Investment Law* Andreas Kulick

89 *State Immunity in International Law* Xiaodong Yang
88 *Reparations and Victim Support in the International Criminal Court* Conor McCarthy
87 *Reducing Genocide to Law: Definition, Meaning, and the Ultimate Crime* Payam Akhavan
86 *Decolonising International Law: Development, Economic Growth and the Politics of Universality* Sundhya Pahuja
85 *Complicity and the Law of State Responsibility* Helmut Philipp Aust
84 *State Control over Private Military and Security Companies in Armed Conflict* Hannah Tonkin
83 *'Fair and Equitable Treatment' in International Investment Law* Roland Kläger
82 *The UN and Human Rights: Who Guards the Guardians?* Guglielmo Verdirame
81 *Sovereign Defaults before International Courts and Tribunals* Michael Waibel
80 *Making the Law of the Sea: A Study in the Development of International Law* James Harrison
79 *Science and the Precautionary Principle in International Courts and Tribunals: Expert Evidence, Burden of Proof and Finality* Caroline E. Foster
78 *Transition from Illegal Regimes under International Law* Yaël Ronen
77 *Access to Asylum: International Refugee Law and the Globalisation of Migration Control* Thomas Gammeltoft-Hansen
76 *Trading Fish, Saving Fish: The Interaction between Regimes in International Law* Margaret A. Young
75 *The Individual in the International Legal System: Continuity and Change in International Law* Kate Parlett
74 *'Armed Attack' and Article 51 of the UN Charter: Evolutions in Customary Law and Practice* Tom Ruys
73 *Theatre of the Rule of Law: Transnational Legal Intervention in Theory and Practice* Stephen Humphreys
72 *Science and Risk Regulation in International Law* Jacqueline Peel
71 *The Participation of States in International Organisations: The Role of Human Rights and Democracy* Alison Duxbury
70 *Legal Personality in International Law* Roland Portmann
69 *Vicarious Liability in Tort: A Comparative Perspective* Paula Giliker
68 *The Public International Law Theory of Hans Kelsen: Believing in Universal Law* Jochen von Bernstorff
67 *Legitimacy and Legality in International Law: An Interactional Account* Jutta Brunnée and Stephen J. Toope
66 *The Concept of Non-International Armed Conflict in International Humanitarian Law* Anthony Cullen
65 *The Principle of Legality in International and Comparative Criminal Law* Kenneth S. Gallant
64 *The Challenge of Child Labour in International Law* Franziska Humbert

63 *Shipping Interdiction and the Law of the Sea* Douglas Guilfoyle
62 *International Courts and Environmental Protection* Tim Stephens
61 *Legal Principles in WTO Disputes* Andrew D. Mitchell
60 *War Crimes in Internal Armed Conflicts* Eve La Haye
59 *Humanitarian Occupation* Gregory H. Fox
58 *The International Law of Environmental Impact Assessment: Process, Substance and Integration* Neil Craik
57 *The Law and Practice of International Territorial Administration: Versailles to Iraq and Beyond* Carsten Stahn
56 *United Nations Sanctions and the Rule of Law* Jeremy Matam Farrall
55 *National Law in WTO Law: Effectiveness and Good Governance in the World Trading System* Sharif Bhuiyan
54 *Cultural Products and the World Trade Organization* Tania Voon
53 *The Threat of Force in International Law* Nikolas Stürchler
52 *Indigenous Rights and United Nations Standards: Self-Determination, Culture and Land* Alexandra Xanthaki
51 *International Refugee Law and Socio-Economic Rights: Refuge from Deprivation* Michelle Foster
50 *The Protection of Cultural Property in Armed Conflict* Roger O'Keefe
49 *Interpretation and Revision of International Boundary Decisions* Kaiyan Homi Kaikobad
48 *Multinationals and Corporate Social Responsibility: Limitations and Opportunities in International Law* Jennifer A. Zerk
47 *Judiciaries within Europe: A Comparative Review* John Bell
46 *Law in Times of Crisis: Emergency Powers in Theory and Practice* Oren Gross and Fionnuala Ní Aoláin
45 *Vessel-Source Marine Pollution: The Law and Politics of International Regulation* Alan Khee-Jin Tan
44 Enforcing Obligations *Erga Omnes* in International Law Christian J. Tams
43 *Non-Governmental Organisations in International Law* Anna-Karin Lindblom
42 *Democracy, Minorities and International Law* Steven Wheatley
41 *Prosecuting International Crimes: Selectivity and the International Criminal Law Regime* Robert Cryer
40 *Compensation for Personal Injury in English, German and Italian Law: A Comparative Outline* Basil Markesinis, Michael Coester, Guido Alpa and Augustus Ullstein
39 *Dispute Settlement in the UN Convention on the Law of the Sea* Natalie Klein
38 *The International Protection of Internally Displaced Persons* Catherine Phuong
37 *Imperialism, Sovereignty and the Making of International Law* Antony Anghie
36 *Principles of the Institutional Law of International Organizations* C. F. Amerasinghe
35 *Necessity, Proportionality and the Use of Force by States* Judith Gardam

34 *International Legal Argument in the Permanent Court of International Justice: The Rise of the International Judiciary* Ole Spiermann
33 -
32 *Great Powers and Outlaw States: Unequal Sovereigns in the International Legal Order* Gerry Simpson
31 *Local Remedies in International Law (second edition)* Chittharanjan Felix Amerasinghe
30 *Reading Humanitarian Intervention: Human Rights and the Use of Force in International Law* Anne Orford
29 *Conflict of Norms in Public International Law: How WTO Law Relates to Other Rules of International Law* Joost Pauwelyn
28 -
27 *Transboundary Damage in International Law* Hanqin Xue
26 -
25 *European Criminal Procedures* Edited by Mireille Delmas-Marty and J. R. Spencer
24 *Accountability of Armed Opposition Groups in International Law* Liesbeth Zegveld
23 *Sharing Transboundary Resources: International Law and Optimal Resource Use* Eyal Benvenisti
22 *International Human Rights and Humanitarian Law* René Provost
21 *Remedies against International Organisations* Karel Wellens
20 *Diversity and Self-Determination in International Law* Karen Knop
19 *The Law of Internal Armed Conflict* Lindsay Moir
18 *International Commercial Arbitration and African States: Practice, Participation and Institutional Development* Amazu A. Asouzu
17 *The Enforceability of Promises in European Contract Law* James Gordley
16 *International Law in Antiquity* David J. Bederman
15 *Money Laundering: A New International Law Enforcement Model* Guy Stessens
14 *Good Faith in European Contract Law* Reinhard Zimmermann and Simon Whittaker
13 *On Civil Procedure* J. A. Jolowicz
12 *Trusts: A Comparative Study* Maurizio Lupoi and Simon Dix
11 *The Right to Property in Commonwealth Constitutions* Tom Allen
10 *International Organizations before National Courts* August Reinisch
9 *The Changing International Law of High Seas Fisheries* Francisco Orrego Vicuña
8 *Trade and the Environment: A Comparative Study of EC and US Law* Damien Geradin
7 *Unjust Enrichment: A Study of Private Law and Public Values* Hanoch Dagan
6 *Religious Liberty and International Law in Europe* Malcolm D. Evans
5 *Ethics and Authority in International Law* Alfred P. Rubin

4 *Sovereignty over Natural Resources: Balancing Rights and Duties* Nico Schrijver
3 *The Polar Regions and the Development of International Law* Donald R. Rothwell
2 *Fragmentation and the International Relations of Micro-States: Self-Determination and Statehood* Jorri C. Duursma
1 *Principles of the Institutional Law of International Organizations* C. F. Amerasinghe